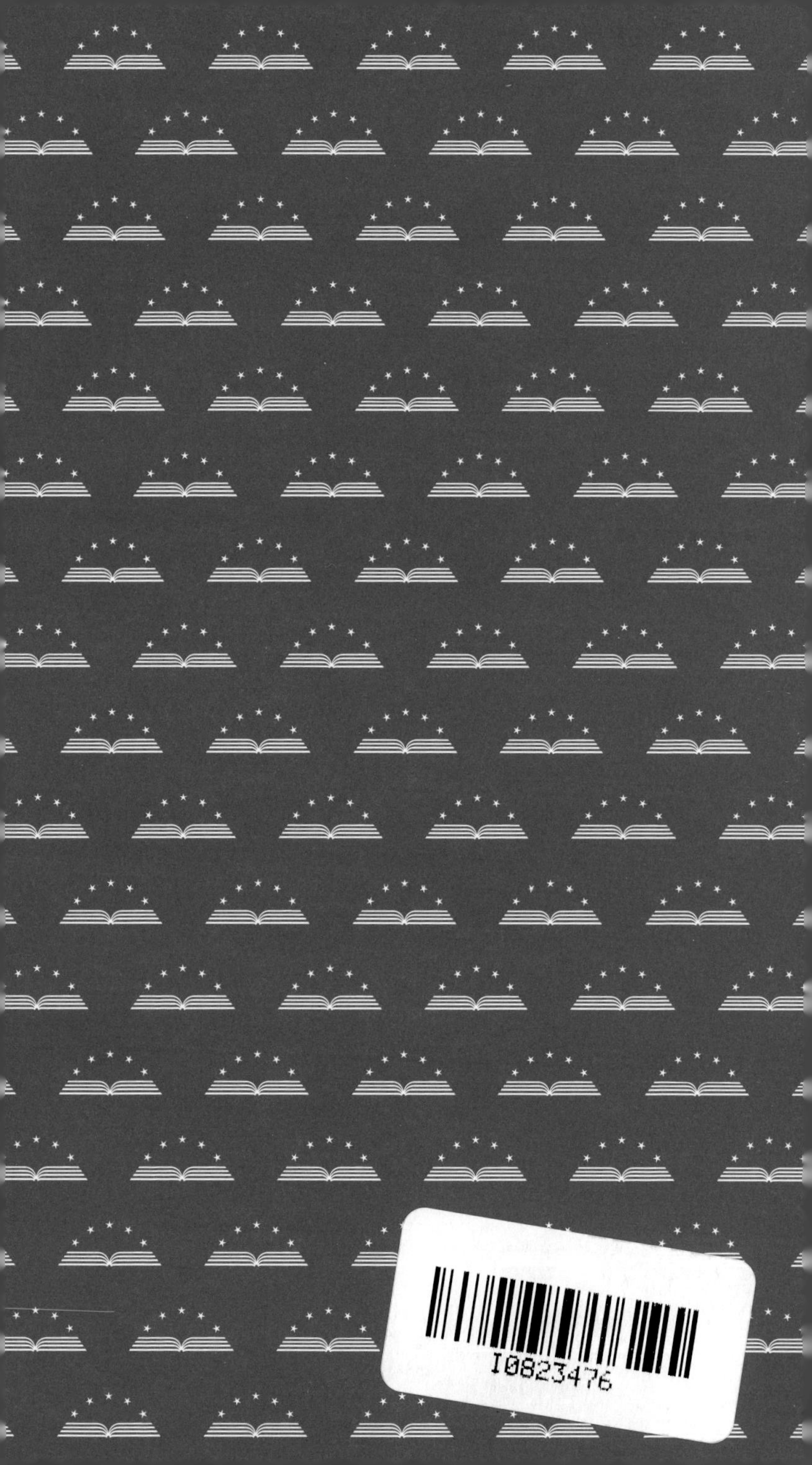
I0823476

Library of America, a nonprofit organization, champions our nation's cultural heritage by publishing America's greatest writing in authoritative new editions and providing resources for readers to explore this rich, living legacy.

GEORGE TEMPLETON STRONG

GEORGE TEMPLETON STRONG

CIVIL WAR DIARIES

Geoff Wisner, *editor*

THE LIBRARY OF AMERICA

GEORGE TEMPLETON STRONG: CIVIL WAR DIARIES

Published in the United States by Library of America,
14 East 60th Street, New York, NY 10022.
Visit our website at www.loa.org.

This paper exceeds the requirements of
ANSI/NISO Z39.48–1992 (Permanence of Paper).

Distributed to the trade in the United States
by Penguin Random House Inc.
and in Canada by Penguin Random House Canada Ltd.

The authorized representative in the EU for product safety and compliance is eucomply OÜ, Pärnu mnt 139b-14, 11317 Tallinn, Estonia.
hello@eucompliancepartner.com

Library of Congress Control Number: 2025933272
ISBN 978-1-59853-825-0

First Printing
The Library of America—396

Manufactured in the United States of America

George Templeton Strong: Civil War Diaries
is published with support from

THE ACHELIS AND BODMAN FOUNDATION

Contents

GEORGE TEMPLETON STRONG

1860

Nov: 2. Friday night. It's so warm that I sit here with the windows opened. Atrocious headache all day. In bed till dinner time. Sent Ellie to Opera in charge of her brother Jem, & sallied out for a debilitated stroll. Found a great Wide-awake demonstration in progress. Inspected them in 14th St. — Seward was making a speech in "Palace Gardens" & the crowd there was dense, the "Gardens" packed full, & impenetrable. The show in the Street was brilliant — Rockets, Roman candles with many colored fire balls, Bengal lights, the "wide-awakes" with their lanterns & torches, & "I wish I was in Dixy's". — I adjourned to Broadway in front of N.Y. Hotel, to see the procession pass. The Southerners of the Hotel groaned & hissed, & the Repubn mob in & about the Lincoln & Hamlin headquarters across the street, cheered & roared, & the din was deafening. But there was no breach of the peace.

N.B. Northerners in a Charleston or Savannah hotel, hissing a Breckinridge demonstration, would have been likely to come to grief.

Nov. 4. Mr R. had a long private talk yesterday with Gen Scott — Some portion whereof he imparted to me — including matters I do'nt care to write here. The General is loyal & Union-loving, intensely & without reservation. He wrote to the War Department Oct. 27 or 28, calling attention to the inadequate garrison of *Fort Moultrie* — only about 100 men instead of the 800 or 1000, required to work it's guns — and to the unprotected state of other Southern forts & arsenals, *but he has received no answer.* — Ingraham, appointed some three months since to command of the *Home Squadron*, is a S. Carolina man.

If old Buchanan be really playing into the hands of Secessionists, and if Disunion come next week — as I think it will — and if his non-feasance enable the fire-eaters to take possession of Fort Moultrie or any other Federal fortalice, then will arise from all the North — (and, I trust, from no small portion of the south) — a reactionary indignant cry for vengeance against traitors in high place, that will make old Buck's neck feel insecure for a season.

Nov. 5. Monday night, & near midnight — the Crisis is close at hand. It has clouded up, after a bright day, & tomorrow is likely to be wet. Do not know which side will lose most votes by fine weather — It's influence is less weighty now than in the old battles of Whig & Democrat, when a rainy election day was sure & easy victory to Locofocoism.

I confidently predict that *Lincoln* will be elected by the People, & that S. Carolina & Texas, & probably Georgia & Mississippi will thereupon be foolish enough to commit themselves to Revolution, which will be a grave calamity. Also that Govr Wise will make several great speeches, & make himself singularly ridiculous. — Also that there will be Northern men enough interested in Southern trade to paralyze our Northern protest agst treason & Disunion, and that their special organ will be the N.Y. Express. Also — that Southern Conservatives will be crushed & silenced, tho' in a majority, and that the Reign of Terror in the Carolinas, Georgia, &c, will be so strengthened that it may become intolerable & be thrown off. I fear the question may have a grim solution in an uprising of the slaves, from Richmond to Galveston, stimulated by their masters' insane talk about the designs of the "Black-Republican" party.

Nov: 6. Tuesday. A memorable day — we do not know yet for what. Perhaps for the disintegration of the Country — perhaps for another proof that the North is timid & mercenary — perhaps for demonstration that Southern bluster is worthless. We cannot tell yet what Historical lesson the event of 6th Nov: 1860 will teach, but the lesson cannot fail to be weighty.

Clear & cool. Vote very large. Probably far beyond that of /56. Tried to vote this morn'g & found people en queue extending a whole block from the polls. Abandoned the effort & went down town. Life & Trust Co meeting. The Magnates of that Board shewed no sign of fluster & seemed to expect no financial crisis. Up town again at two, & got in my vote after only an hour's detention. I voted for *Lincoln*.

After dinner to Trinity School Board — 762 B'way. Thence down town, looking for election returns. Great crowd about the newspaper offices of Fulton & Nassau Sts & Park row. It was cold & I was alone & tired, & came home sooner than I intended. City returns are all one way, but they will hardly foot up a Fusion majority of much above 25000. Brooklyn said to be *Fusion* by 14000. An AntiLincoln majority of 40 000 in N.Y. & Kings, well backed by the River Counties, may possibly outweigh the Repub^{n} majorities in the Western Counties, but that is unlikely. The Repub^{s} have gained in the City since /56 & have no doubt gained still more in the interior.

The only signs of excitement & enthusiasm that I saw were in the crowd about the Bell & Everett headquarters (in B'way below Bond St.) —

There is talk of large AntiLincoln majorities in Niagara Co — wh: I dont believe.

Nov: 7. Wednesday. Lincoln elected. Hooray. Every body seems glad of it. Even Democrats like Isaac Bell say there will be no disturbance, & that this will quiet Slavery agitation at the North. DePeyster Ogden's nerves are a little unstrung — but they are never very steady.

Repub^{s} have carried every state on which they counted, except N. Jersey — and it may be they have carried that too. They have a very fair shew in *Delaware*!!! *Wilmington* gives them a majority.

Kentucky Virginia Maryland & Tennessee are believed to have gone for *Bell* — a sore discouragement to the Extremists.

Telegrams from the South indicate no outbreak there. There is a silly report from Washington that Govr Wise contemplates "a raid" on that City at the head of a ragged regiment of rakehelly debauched Virginians. He has few equals in folly, but this story is incredible. I wish it were true & that he would proceed to do it. Nothing could make Southern ultraism more ridiculous. I would not have him hanged for his treasonable attempt, but publicly *spanked* on the steps of the Capitol.

The next ten days will be a critical time. If no Southern state commit itself to treason within a fortnight or so the urgent danger will be past. Now that election is over, excitement will cool down rapidly, and even S. Carolina will not secede unless under excitement that blinds her to the plain fact that secession is political Suicide.

Nov. 9. Much gasconading from the sunny South, condensed in telegraphic reports fortunately — "Palmetto Flag" raised: great speeches: fuss & fury: messages from Governors: Conventions called: Collector of Charleston resigning: "Secession inevitable" &c &c &c. Its a critical time, but things are not so bad as I expected they would be three days after Lincoln's election.

Nov: 11. Miss Puss at tea to night — afterwards Charley, D'Oremieulx, Dr Carroll, Jem Dwight, Hoffman, Jem Ruggles & G.C.A. Political Crisis thoroughly discussed.

General disposition to concede the right of Secession & to regard it with indifference & contempt — I hold secession unlawful & most calamitous, but the South is less likely to do this wrong & folly & mischief if it find the North acquiescent & good natured. I'm sorry however to find so many Northern men holding the Union so cheap.

These are really most momentous days in the History of the World: they rank with those in which the Reformation was initiated — & the French Revolution, when Charles I. invaded the House of Commons, or that preceded the battle of Lexington. We are just upon a turning point in the progress of all Western Christendom. "What shall the issue be? — God governs all — " —

Nov: 12. No material change in the complexion of Southern news. Unless writers of Telegraph-items lie loudly, secession is inevitable. There is uneasiness here, but mainly as to the possibility of a tight money market from the *financial* crisis Southern folly is bringing upon the South — which must inevitably react on us more or less. People generally treat the *political* peril with what seems to me unaccountable indifference. This financial crisis is already beginning in Charleston & Mobile. Suspension of specie payments there seems close at hand. They have overtraded, & their crops are short, & they would have been hard up, had Lincoln been defeated, & obliged to do their uttermost to get the hog & hominy they need to carry them through the winter. But now that Lincoln is elected, & their Terrorists are raving about confiscating Northern property & repudiating Northern debts, their credit is paralyzed and they are in danger of a general smash. It would injure us, of course: it may bring them to their senses — or it may make them desperate & reckless. They may attribute the disastrous consequences of their own excesses to "le monstre Pitt" [viz: A. Lincoln] as did their analogues in Paris sixty years ago. —

Nov: 13. Stocks have fallen heavily to day, & I think they will fall much lower before this game is played out. One can buy in yet more profitably a fortnight hence. Southern securities are waste paper in Wall St. Not a dollar can be raised on them. Who wants to buy paper that must be collected by suit in the Courts of *S. Carolina* & *Georgia*?

Nov: 15. No material progress in the Political crisis. Stocks have rallied a little here. Perhaps the febrile symptoms & cerebral disturbance of the South seem a shade easier. But the reign of Terror in S. Carolina continues unmitigated. — E.G. Mrs Sally Hampton, now in N.Y., wants to go home — viz: to Columbia S.C. or thereabouts, — and requires an escort, of course. Her husband ca'nt come North without exposing himself to a conviction of "incivisme", & Mr Geo: Baxter, her papa, cannot go South without danger of being tarred & feathered, hanged, or burned at the Stake, as a Northerner & a possible Abolitionist. So Mrs Sally H. & her three pretty babies still abide in Second Avenue. — Willy Alston & Pringle meant to spend another month here, but their neighbors write them that they must come home. Their loyalty to Southern institutions will be suspected if they keep away. So they return, reluctantly.

The real issue in this controversy is whether certain comparatively civilized & law-abiding communities & certain other uncivilized & lawless & barbaric communities can exist together. Every newspaper contains items of news illustrating their barbarism. Wherever popular feeling is tolerably unanimous against persons charged with any criminal offence, *Vigilance Committees seem to have superseded the legal tribunals* — a most significant fact. As the Disunion movement gains strength, & excitement increases, this social disorganization must spread, and I see no prospect for the seceding states but anarchy. They are too poor to support a Military Despotism.

We are generally reconciling ourselves to the prospect of

Secession by S. Carolina Georgia Alabama little Florida & perhaps Mississippi too. We shall be well rid of them. Perhaps the prevalence of this feeling — the cordial consent of the North — will keep them from seceding. I think these porcine communities incline to run out of the Union mainly because they think we want to keep them in. One should never pull a pig in the direction one wants it to travel. — They have long governed us & controlled our votes by the threat of Secession — they naturally think Secession will be a crushing calamity to the North & the severest punishment they can inflict on us for electing Lincoln.

Nov. 19. A most gloomy day in Wall St. Everything at a deadlock — first class paper not negotiable — demand for money greater than in Oct. /57 — stocks falling. It's said the Banks resolved to day to buy three millions of exchange on London. This may probably set the machine going again, for the time at least, and enable the West & South to begin moving their grain & Cotton.

No farther movement in the political game. We talked it over last night — Laurence Williams, Mr S.B.R., Murray Hoffman, Walter Cutting & others, from eight till midnight — and were not much the wiser when we finished.

Very few now deny the probability of Secession by the Cotton States — and S. Carolina is given up as hopeless. Our national mottoes must be changed to "E pluribus *duo*" (at least) & "United we stand, divided we stand easier". It is generally conceded moreover that if Federal coercion be applied to a single seceding state the whole South will range itself against the Government.

Nov: 20. Wall St: was a shade less disconsolate this morning. Stocks rallied at the First Board but began to waver & fall again at the Second. The Banks cannot bring about a decisive reaction: the disease is too deep-seated.

The Revolutionary movement in S. Carolina & the Gulf States seems, on the whole, to be gaining strength & consistency. No signs yet of any "sober second thought". Conservatism & common sense — (if any be left in the Cotton States) are still intimidated & silent.

Probably the Border States, led by Virginia, will try to mediate & pacify. Dissolution of the Union & Re-opening of the Slave trade would be disastrous to them, so they naturally desire to make peace. But their mediation will probably be upon the basis of recognition by the North of the extremest Southern exactions (Slave-trade excepted). The North must consent that Slavery be introduced into the Territories, & Massachusetts Vermont Wisconsin &c must repeal their "Personal Liberty" laws that interfere with the Fugitive Slave law. That plan will not work. Those State laws ought to be repealed but the South has no right to demand their repeal & make their enactment an excuse for treason, because they are utterly unconstitutional & mere nullities, & no one doubts that the U.S. Supreme Court would so adjudge them.

If these traitors succeed in dismembering the country, they will have a front place in the Historical Gallery of Celebrated Criminals. No political crime was ever committed, so disastrous to mankind & with so little to provoke or excuse the wrong, as that which these infamous disunionists are conspiring to perpetrate.

Were the North united — could it be relied on to fight the battle out to the end — I would gladly give up half of what I'm worth in Taxation for a War upon Southern Treason. We could conquer them, I think, & create a rise in the price of Hemp. If we could not, and they should subjugate us & send proconsuls from Charleston & Atlanta to govern N.Y. & Boston & Chicago, even that would be better than *dissolution* & division. We should still be the one great Nation of the Western World. But *coercion* is practically hopeless. It would array every slaveholding state on the side of South Carolina, and after a year or so of War, the North would give up & return to money-making.* Money is the only thing the North really values. The Union, — the U.S.A — is too weak to *coerce* a single county of any state into submission to law, and no government can live long without power to suppress and punish rebellion.

This crisis illustrates the potency of *Words*. The words "*Confederacy*" & "State Sovereignty" — (phrases of Calhoun & his school) are threatening to disintegrate & destroy us.

*Heaven forgive the Slander! 1862.

Nov. 24. Omnibussed down town with M[rs] Sally Hampton. She goes home, to S. Carolina, Wednesday, under her father's escort. Hampton wo'nt come North for her, on principle — (though he's called conservative calm & unimpassioned in S.C.!) — so her father undertakes the perilous emprize & ventures his tarrable & featherable Northern person within the Southern Lion's den. I advised that he accompany her to the *Line* — push her over it — & *run*.

Nov: 25. Charley Peters & little Kate dined here & spent the aft[n] — took tea & spent the ev'g — & had a good time with Johny. Now that change & disaster seem so imminent, I feel that every pleasant day of innocent fun the children have on these premises, is so much *gain* — so much saved. Perhaps these little people will remember 21st St. & the tea table & the library & the big Electrical Machine & their romps in the garret, years hence, when peace prosperity & security are gone.

To night we had at supper, M[rs] Sally Hampton, M[r] S.B.R., Jem R, Geo. F. Allen, Murray Hoffman, Prof: Joy, D[r] Peters & D'Oremieulx. M[rs] Sally goes "to her own place" Wednesday. She talks sensibly & not very hopefully of our prospects — is not carried away by Southern feeling — says that if her clergyman at Columbia omit the prayer "for the President of the U.S. & all others in authority" next Sunday she will walk out of Church. She has the pluck to do it — in the face of a fire-eating congregation. If that were all — but she's a loyal wife & her husband is deeply committed to secessionism.

Nov. 28. No political news of importance. The progress of events has startled & staggered some of our Notables, who were laughing Secession to scorn a fortnight ago. John C Green for one "never dreamed these Southerners would go so far". — I think — from all indications — that the Republican leaders are frightened, and ready to concede everything, — to restore the Missouri Compromise line & ratify the fugitive slave-remedies of the South. A movement that way has certainly begun. But it may be too soon for the North & too late for the South. Suppose it prevail — how will it be received in Massachusetts & Western N.Y.? Will Republicans feel that they have been sold by their leaders, & recalcitrate into more intense Anti-Southern feeling? I think they will & that many *Repub*[s] will enrol themselves as *Abolitionists.* But if this crisis pass over without disruption & ruin, — if our National life endure another year — I think a strong Union party will come into being & control Extremists South & North both.

Nov. 29. No political news to day. Congress meets Monday. M[r] S.B.R.'s friend Senator Dixon is in town on his way to Washington — horribly frightened. Connecticut expects him to do something in the Senate, & he is anxiously enquiring What shall I do to be saved — from the humiliation of admitting that I'm unequal to my high place?

Tom Corwin was in town Tuesday night with the draft of some "Bill of Rights", which he means to propose, affirming the rights which the South pretends to believe endangered.

There's a bad prospect for both sections of the Country. Southern ruffianism & brutality are very bad, but the selfishness baseness & corruption of the North are not good at all. *Universal suffrage* has been acquiesced in for many years. It is no longer debated. But it's at the root of our troubles. What we want is a strong government, instead of a "government of opinion". If there be disunion, a strong government will be demanded & will come into being somehow — both North & South. Democracy & equality & various other phantasms will be dispersed & dissipated & will disappear for ever, when two hostile families of States stand side by side, & a great Civil War becomes inevitable.

To which party will God give a *great general,* when that crisis is upon us?

If Northern leaders, Seward & Corwin &c, decide to make concessions, they may put them on this ground. "We thought our brethren & copartners at the South possessed common sense. We supposed their secession talk to be mere bluster — We find that we were mistaken. Their folly is beyond all we could have expected. They are actually preparing to scuttle the Ship of State, & sink North & South together. We are not strong enough to put down the mutineers & run them up at the yardarm, so we had better concede what they ask, for it is of no practical importance to us or to them."

Dec[r] 1. One hears queer talk in these days of excitement. That whitecravatted conservative old quiet Dutchman Edw: Bancker thinks every man ought to be hanged that voted for Lincoln — & "means to go South & shoulder a musket." So he tells me — but I think fear for the future of his bank stocks & real estate has slightly deranged his mind — for he is said to have experienced some slight aberrations a few years since when he had a fierce quarrel with a neighbor about a right of way on Staten Island. — Willy Cutting talks mysteriously of an *organization* to revolutionize the City immediately upon the secession of the South. N.Y. & Brooklyn are to be a free-port, & with one or two adjoining counties, Westchester & Kings I suppose, to constitute an independent principality. Mayor & Common Council to be kicked out — if not hanged — and suffrage to be confined to owners of $5000. worth of property. A promising project.

Why *do* the people so furiously rage together just now? What has created our present unquestionable irritation against the South? What has created the Repub[n] party?

It's nucleus was the Abolition handful that has been vaporing for thirty years — and which till about 1850 was among the more insignificant of our *Isms.* Our feeling at the North till that time was not hostility to slavery, but indifference to it, & reluctance to discuss it. It was a disagreeable subject with which we had nothing to do. The battles in Congress about the Right of Petition — & the *Giddings* business — made little impression on us. But the clamor of the South about the admission of California ten years ago introduced the question of Slavery to the North as one in which it had an interest adverse to the South. That controversy taught us that the two systems could not co-exist in the same territory. It opened our eyes to the fact that there were two hostile elements in the Country, & that if we allowed slaves to enter any territorial acquisition, our own free labor must be excluded from it. The revelation was unfortunate for our peace. But we might have forgotten it — had not S.A. Douglas undertaken to get Southern votes by repealing the Missouri compromise. That was the fatal blow. Then came the atrocious effort to force slavery on Kansas, by fraud & violence, with the full approval of dirty old Buchanan & his Southern counsellors. — the brutal beating of the eloquent &

erudite Sumner with the cordial approbation & applause of the South — the project to revive the Slave trade — and (a little earlier) a sentimental romance — U. Tom's Cabin — that set all Northern Women crying & sobbing over the Sorrows of Sambo. The Fugitive Slave Law stimulated sectional feeling, by making Slavery visible in our own communities — and, above all, the intolerable brag & bluster & indecent arrogance of the South has driven us into protest against their pretensions, & into a determination to assert our own rights in spite of their swagger.

Decr 2^{d}. At supper Mrs Carson of S.C. — & one *Lowndes* (a very nice fellow) & Laurence Williams, Murray Hoffman & his brother Wickham, Walter Cutting, G.C.A., Mr Ruggles, Dr Peters, Wm Chrystie & one or two more.

Lowndes is quite a young man: seems a specimen of South Carolinian conservatism: is engaged as assistant to Petigru in codifying the laws of his state: but favors Disunion decidedly. His talk is temperate but *unintelligible.* I could make no sense of it, and suggestions that I took to be truisms seemed to strike him as speculative novelties he was unwilling to admit. I fear Northerner & Southerner are *aliens*, not merely in social & political arrangements but in mental & moral constitution. We differ like Celt & Anglo-Saxon, and there is no sufficient force in a "government of opinion" to keep us together against our will.

Dec: 3. These Southern heroics would be inexhaustible mines of fun, were the position a little less grave. E.g. the Govr (Gist) of S. Carolina writing a grand Revolutionary Message & recommending all sorts of measures for "National" Defence & "National" finance &c &c — *and* the enlargement of the State Lunatic Asylum!

"National" indeed! The whole white population of that dirty little spiteful *district* is numerically less than that of Brooklyn — less than the increase of this City & County of N.Y. since 1855.

Decr 4. Presdt's Message appears today — & is gobbled up with avidity by every one. Weak, of course, — but perhaps the "Old Public Functionary"'s positions are on the whole discreet & sensible. The Federal Government is too notoriously weak to menace with effect. Had Buchanan said "Secession is treason — & treason is a capital crime — & we have a Federal judiciary established for the purpose, among others, of punishing crime, and an executive to hang whomsoever the judiciary shall adjudge worthy of hanging", his position would have been more consistent. But I incline to think it's practically the best thing a *commonplace* Presid^{t} could have said at this crisis.

Repub^{s} undoubtedly mean to make overtures to the South in Congress, and I think the prominent men of the party are frightened & ready to give up every principle the party thought established by Lincoln's election. Perhaps the party is no less terrified than it's leaders, & will approve their course: perhaps not. If *not*, concession will be political suicide. But it's a significant fact that a meeting in *Boston* yesterday to commemorate *John Brown's* "martyrdom" was suppressed by a mob. —

No concession will avail now I fear. The Cotton States want to set up for themselves & they will do it.

Decr 5. Presd^{t}'s message finds little favor here, or anywhere.

It's a bad time. This Nation is manifestly "coming in two" — or three — or more. Hopes of a Congressional compromise diminish. I have lost faith in the magic words "Somehow or other" on which I've thus far relied for a solution of the problem.

Dec: 6. Midnight. I'm "sitting up with" the *Union* — the glorious indissoluble Union — now confessedly moribund. Also I'm listening for the ominous clanking of the Fire Bells. For the Croton Aqueduct has *busted*. It's pipes have given out at some weak point in the latitude of 64th St. and for the first time in 16 years, our supply of Water is cut off. Till this mischief is repaired any Fire may be most calamitous.

Very gloomy day down town. "Secession" by Southern madmen felt to be inevitable & Civil War sure to follow it, within the year. Forebodings grow more grave every day. The only man I know who pretends to think we shall get thro' this crisis is Willy Duncan (D. Sherman & Co). He thinks the money pressure in the Cotton states is going to be so severe as to bring the Bobadils & Copper-captains to their senses.

Dec: 7. Stocks fell badly to day — and the difficulty about Exchange has returned — having been merely palliated by the action of the Banks.

A Com: is appointed by House of Representatives to concoct a compromise & save the Union. It will fail. These Cotton States are acting under the influence of spite envy & panic fear all combined. They want no compromise. But the Repub^{n} leaders probably design to put the North right on the record by proposing liberal concessions, knowing that the South will refuse them.

An abstract or summary of the Pres^{dt}'s Message is much quoted. Seward has the credit of it. "No State has the right to secede — unless it wants to. The Executive is bound to coerce a seceding state, unless the Executive be opposed in it's efforts to do so." Do'nt believe Billy Seward ever said so good a thing.

Decr 8. No special progress to day in this our Revolution. Stocks rally a little.

I'm satisfied from my talk with Club-men to night that the North will ratify no compromise about the Territories. Perhaps it may consent to restore the Missouri line — tho' even that concession is doubtful. But it will *not* admit that Slavery exists wherever the Federal Government rules, & that *the Nation* recognizes Slavery among it's institutions.

Dec. 10. Stocks went down to day. But there seem to be gleams of light opening on us — permanent or transitory. To night's Commercial says the tide has turned. The "Seceding states" will merely send Commissioners to Washington to negotiate for dissolution of the Union, & the whole treasonable movement will be procrastinated & postponed & come to naught. Perhaps. Time will tell.

I'm satisfied, too, that Secession of the Cotton States *alone* will do us little harm. If we hold Fort Moultrie &c, the Federal Revenue will not suffer. If S. Carolina & Alabama choose to decline a U.S. postal service & representation in Congress, I do'nt perceive that they will thereby hurt us much. We need not make war on them. Should we find it necessary to do so, they are weak & vulnerable, & powerless for aggressive hostility. It seems questionable whether England & the other Powers of Europe, would feel inclined cordially to recognize a State or Confederacy founded on the one Idea of Slavery & the Extension of Slavery, as entitled to a place in the Family Circle of Christian Nations.

Toombs Rhett Wise Yancey & Co think they can control Christendom because the South produces Cotton. They forget that it is quite as important to Charleston & Mobile that cotton be sold, as it is to Lancashire & Lowell that cotton be bought.

Dec. 12. Yesterday morn'g I submitted my tumefied fauces to Dr *Main*, 32 Bond St. Thanks to *chloroform*, my sinful old Molar seceded without my feeling the wrench of severance. It seems that after I lost consciousness I resisted the dentist — kept my mouth obstinately closed against his pincers — was pugnacious — & talked politics. So he found it necessary to continue the inhalation till everything was completely relaxed, & to give me an unusually heavy dose.

Dec: 13. Thursday. Ellie went to Washington this morn'g under her father's escort — to spend a week there. I hated to let her go, for many reasons, but she was longing to see & hear for herself the incidents of the crisis, and this may be the last opportunity of seeing a Congress of the U.S. in session. Heaven send Mrs E. Soon & safely home again. The house is stupid without it's busy little Mistress.

Col: Henry Scott tells me *Major Anderson* has only forty available men, at most, in Fort Moultrie. The War Department has sent him no orders. If he is repairing the works &c as the newspapers say, he is acting on his own responsibility. In other words, our disgraceful Executive has been & is playing into the hands of traitors. That *Buchanan* might be hanged under Lynch Law almost reconciles me to that Code.

Things look black. But I dont repent of my vote for Lincoln.

It contributed to an experiment that tests our Boiler, and it must have undergone that same test very soon had Lincoln been defeated. The question may as well be settled at once whether we have a National Government that can sustain itself under pressure, or a mere sham government that must perish whenever a set of semi-barbarous Southerners pronounce against it, with or without reason.

Decr 15. This has been *the gloomiest day yet.* Mr Secretary Cass has resigned, following the example of Mr Secy *Cobb* whom no one regrets in the least. Genl Scott has been in council with the Cabinet, giving advice that old Buchanan declines to adopt — viz: that the garrison of Fort Moultrie be strengthened. The necessity for reinforcements there is most urgent & the duty to send them with the least possible delay as clear as the Sun. Is old B. imbecile — or a traitor? Or does he calculate profoundly on uniting the whole North in one flame of indignation agst S. Carolina by tempting the Charleston militiamen & mob to make a rush on the forts & destroy Major Anderson & his little party of less than fifty available men? The folly of his non-feasance, too! With these forts decently manned, the commerce of Charleston is under control — Federal Revenue secured at that port — South Carolinian treason paralyzed. If her chivalry attempt a *Siege*, one month's experience of it's *Cost* would bring that Bedlamite State to it's senses, like a bucket of cold water on the head of a patient in hysteria. The Experiment of War could not be tried under conditions more auspicious for the Union, or more sure to convince the South of it's folly. Yet old Buchanan leaves Anderson & his party unsupported — with orders to defend the fort as best he may. When the calamities that seem at hand are upon us, Buchanan will hardly be able to live at the North. He will have to emigrate below the Potomac & become a "poor white", — a Dirt-Eater of the pine-barrens. Perhaps the South will tolerate the presence of a *Northerner* who has made himself infamous, & become a fugitive & an exile, by truckling to Southern dictation. But perhaps it wont. It may hang Mr B. or tar & feather him & expel him from Southern soil, as being a mere proselyte of the Gate — not a thorough-going Southerner — I dont know where the poor wretch can go with safety after Dissolution is established.

To day's feeling is that Secession is inevitable. That Virginia & Kentucky & the other border states must follow their sisterhood on the Gulf, & that Civil War is at hand. Prospect of conciliation by any Congressional action seems fading away.

Were we only united & unanimous here at the North, I should welcome the prospect of vigorous war on Southern treason. But we are discordant — corrupt — deeply diseased — unable to govern ourselves, & in most unfit condition for a War on others.

Decr 17. Monday. Mild day. Very busy, C.E.S. being under arrest at home with influenza & sore throat. Ellie writes from Wash^{n} — well & comfortably quartered, with her private parlor, at Willard's Hotel. Much exercised about the Union, & that pitiful old Buchanan's traitorous nonfeasance. She *Wont* call at the White House. Very good for my little plucky wife!

Murray Hoffman dined with me. Meant to have seen *Booth* in Hamlet after dinner — but we found ourselves comfortable where we were, procrastinated, & did'nt go. Played two or three games of chess with Johny (odds of a castle). He beat me in one. & then I spent an hour in the library with M.H. vainly hunting thro' the folio Sir Thos More of 1557 for the *Tenterden Steeple* story which I know is there, tho' H. attributes it to Bishop Latimer.

The S. Carolina convention has met & is to adjourn from Columbia to Charleston, being driven away by an Epidemic (qu: is Epizoöty the more accurate expression?) of small pox. *Pickens* is elected Govr of that truculent Commonwealth. He seems committed to Secession & treason now, but when he crossed the Atlantic a few months ago with M^{r} & Mrs Philip Allen, he said his object in coming home was to tell his fellow-citizens that they were making themselves the laughing-stock of Europe. This foul Disunion disease is frightfully contagious however (like other cachectic, asthenic distempers, jail fevers & the like) & Pickens may have caught it. It's making steady & rapid progress in Virginia Kentucky Tennessee & every slaveholding State. Wm Chrystie thinks however that Pickens' movements are those of a Captain whose Company is running away, & that he is trying to get ahead of the runaways that he may *head them back*.

Seward in town yesterday. Report of schism in Republican party of this state. A lot of extreme Free Soilers headed by Horace Greeley & including D.D. Field & Austin Stevens J^{r} pronounce against Seward & Thurlow Weed, & mean to establish an Albany newspaper Organ in opposition to Weed's.

Wade held forth in the Senate to day against Secession, "with much applause from the galleries" according to this ev'g's Commercial. The District of Columbia is Republicanized — a natural result of Lincoln's election. Genl Scott is at Washington urging the Pres^{dt} to reinforce the handful of men that garrisons *Fort Moultrie*, but in vain.

Depression to day deeper than ever. Most people give up all hope of saving the government, & anticipate general bankruptcy revolution mob law chaos & ruin. It is rumored that our miserable Pres^{dt} has gone crazy — and that Genl Scott has resigned. As to Buchanan (our James II), his brain is of little practical worth in it's natural condition, & if he go mad he may be less mischievous. Scott's resignation would be a great calamity.

The defeated Fusionists are holding meetings, & deprecating the wrath of S. Carolina. Their supplications are vain. The only thing they can say to the South with good effect is that they & their organs (Herald & Express) have been lying about the Repub^{n} party all thro' the campaign, for party purposes, & that the Repub^{s} are not abolitionists, & do not seek to raise the Negro to social & political equality with the White man. But this they wo'nt say.

They might refer to the fact that of the 32000 who voted for Lincoln in this City only *1600* voted for the Negro-suffrage amendment to the Constitution & that in the Repub^{n} state of N.Y. that amendment was defeated by 100.000 majority.

Think of O'Conor in his elaborate speech at this last "Union" meeting, maintaining that the great fault of the North is the *organization of a Political Party on a moral question*. He thinks any political organization based on convictions of Right & Wrong dangerous & unjustifiable. Is the man mad? Does the World of Politics & State affairs belong to the Devil de jure?

Dec. 18. Stocks rose this morning — & everybody seemed cheerful & hopeful. There were encouraging indications in the action of Congress yesterday. Gov[r] Fish was oracular, but inclined on the whole to think affairs improving a little. That rather questionable M[r] F.P. James, who voted Fusion & has extensive business affiliations in every Southern State told me his letters satisfied him that Secession would end in a "fizzle" & that if the North did'nt back down the South would have to do it within 30 days — or starve.

But this ev'g's news dont look well. The Secession distemper is spreading fast in the Border States. Ellie mentioned in her letter that Reverdy Johnson had expressed to her great apprehension as to the course of Maryland — and Virginia Kentucky & Missouri are evidently uncertain & wavering now. If the Border States go, they take the National Capital with them!

There is a growing disposition here to offer liberal concessions to the South, and if they be rejected to make WAR on Southern Rebellion with all the resources of the North. And that's the true talk for the times. Suppress the sedition of Massachusetts & the treason of South Carolina with impartial rigor, and so avert our Death as a Nation.

Dec: 19. Nothing new to day about our National Convulsion. Perhaps our prospect may be a shade less blue. Ellie's letter says little of state affairs. She's enjoying the most delightful time at Washington. I see no hopeful symptoms that have any material significance.

Dec 20. Dull wet day. Letter from E. dated yesterday, bewailing the hopelessness of our National disorders which she takes to be past all cure. She is to return Saturday.

Desperate all day with Influenza, & sore bones. Did not even make believe to do any work.

Laurence Williams & G.C.A. dined here. Murray Hoffman came in, & our session lasted till near midnight. Talked of little but North v. South: Secession: Coercion: Buchanan: Fort Moultrie &c. I'm inexpressibly weary of the subject. Could these Algerine states be cut out of our map & transferred to any unoccupied region of the Indian Ocean, it would be a good riddance.

Things certainly a *very* little brighter. Action of the Georgia Legislature conservative as far as it goes, and the Charleston

Convention instead of adopting a Declaration of Independence at once is twaddling with feeble prolixity over twopenny preliminary details, as if it dreaded to approach the main question.

This eruption has certainly spread fearfully through the great Border States within the last fortnight, but there are just the faintest indications that it is beginning to dry up & disappear in the region where it first broke out. Perhaps it's merely a rash that must run it's course, & will leave the Nation healthier & stronger. God grant that so it may be!

Many people look radiant to day, — Moses H. Grinnell, Royal Phelps. Even poor *Bancker* has emerged from the pit of his despair. Laurence Williams, who has great intelligence & sagacity for so young a man, is clear there will be no secession, unless by poor little sulking *S.C.*, and that if she sulk out by herself, she must eat humble pie & come back within six months.

If this movement come to nothing, the Southern Secession brag game will hardly be tried again. The South must either secede & try to set up for itself, or admit that it's predominance & control in our National Councils have departed, never to return. Secession is madness & ruin, so they have but a choice of evils. It's *their* misfortune that they are pledged to a system that's against their own material interests, & of which the Gulf States at least cannot possibly get rid. It compels them to elect between humiliation & suicide, so I dont wonder they are savage & dangerous.

Dec. 21. That termagant little S. Carolina has declared herself out of the Union, & resolved to run away & go to sea. How many of the Southern sisterhood will join the secession jig she thus leads off, remains to be seen.

It strikes me that this proceeding, strictly considered, does not take the soil & the people of S. Carolina out of the Federal Jurisdiction at all, but if it have any legal validity or effect whatever, simply amounts to a resignation of the qualified Sovereignty heretofore enjoyed by that State, & converts what was the *State* of S.C. into the *Territory* of S.C. S.C. belonged & still belongs to the National Government. If it repudiates & resigns the title duties & dignity of a State, what can it be but a Territory? That it's foolish inhabitants want to be called an Empire or a Herzogthum or a Tribe makes no difference.

This proceeding surprises nobody & makes no sensation. It's a grave event, & may well bring tremendous calamity upon the country. It's a grave affair for any family if one of it's members go mad. But as an offset we have the influx of gold from England & the growing hope that Northern Cities will get thro' the winter without the panic & crisis & uprising of hungry Mobs that our Southern friends complacently predict.

The speeches in the Seceding Convention seem amazingly weak muddled & prolix, coming from orators at Treason-heat. No great men appear as yet in the Southern Revolution. I suppose the leaders are of ability not much below the average — but their proceedings (as reported) look puerile. They resolve themselves out of the Union, & then it seems to occur to them for the first time that they have (nominally at least) annihilated all their Postal system & abolished all commercial relations with every port of every Civilized Country on earth — & they begin pottering about keeping up the present system for a time & making arrangements with the Federal Government — in other words (most unfortunately) with Buchanan. (I omit the Adjectives that *should* precede his dirty name — for decency's sake) — O for an hour of ANDREW JACKSON, whom I held (when I was a boy & he was "taking the Responsibility") to be the embodiment of everything bad arrogant and low.

Prospects of compromise in Congress rather diminish. I fervently hope Ample Concessions may be tendered to the South; concessions that will more than satisfy all the complaints of Toombs & Yancey. I could almost say that I hope those concessions may be contemptuously rejected (which is nowise improbable) and that the case may thereupon be brought to a practical issue.

Dec. 22. Sat: Ellie safe home again — thank Heaven, and Vive la Reine! — Arrived at about 9 P.M. with her father — safe & well. Has had the most ecstatic time with Senators Ambassadors Commodores & such cattle, Genl Scott included — mostly men remarkable for want of resemblance to Young America.

To day has been warm & wet. Anxiety about political matters does not diminish but Wall St rejoices in rising stocks an easy money market & returning confidence in our commercial soundness.

Had a couple of hours confabulation with Mr S.B.R. He is exulting over the passage of the Pacific R.R. Bill thro' the House & figures up ten majority in the Senate. It may be Pacific indeed! Louisiana & Texas will pause before they walk out of a Union that wants to spend $36.000.000 on them. The still larger outlay for the Northern Road will ensure the loyalty of Missouri — and at all events the North West & East will be bound up with Oregon & California, whatever the South may do. He is keenly & intensely gratified too, by the introduction of his name into the Bill as a Corporator by general concurrence when it was in it's last stages, & its supporters had resolved to permit no amendment in any one feature.

At about sunset of the day on which Clan Carolina "seceded", the ayes & noes were being called on the question of appropriating Ninety Six Millions for a great National Work! Mr R. says he went out on one of the Capitol terraces or porticos & saw the Sun going down in splendor after a stormy day — and that it was *the* moment of his whole life. He *saw* the Pacific Coast in the glow & glory of the Western Sky, and saw moreover the sign & token that a great Nation was saved. He has been energizing most efficiently in this cause at Washington.

Dec 23. This morn'g's Herald reports that despatches have been rec^d^ at Washington that Fort Moultrie is to be stormed by the young men & braves of the Charleston tribe without delay — and I suppose it's understood that the survivors of the garrison will be roasted and eaten by the victors. I disbelieve the report. S.C. is in no hurry to encounter the logical consequence of her secession brag. But I was glad to hear from Williams that even with a garrison of only 65 the fort is safe against a coup de main, & could hold out a week at least against all the Carolinas. The moment it is known that an attack is contemplated & organizing, even Buchanan must begin doing his official duty, however reluctantly. And volunteer reinforcements would pour down from all the Northern seaboard.

Old B. feels secure against impeachment no doubt. But after 4 March 1861, a Pennsylvania Grand Jury may indict him for treason, and a Pennsylvania U.S. Marshal may have to hang him for treason.

No government enjoys the moral force it should possess, till two or three "respectable" men have been capitally punished for setting themselves up against it.

Dec. 27. Last night, Major Anderson secretly moved his command from Fort Moultrie to Fort Sumter which is isolated in mid channel, commands Fort Moultrie, & is able to resist all the Armies & navies of S. Carolina, even with it's present garrison. He fired Fort M. & some say blew it up — spiked the guns — & doubtless made it innocuous.

An excellent move — no doubt due to *Scott*. It postpones actual collision & saves the lives probably of Anderson & his little handful of men.

"Great indignation" said to prevail in Charleston. I wish I had a penny for every score of drinks drunk & oaths sworn in that town this day.

Also (tho this is comparatively stale) there is a defalcation of nearly a million at Washington — lying at the door of a South Carolina Clerk in the Dep^{t} of the Interior — & that very dubious person Jno B. Floyd. His impeachment freely talked of.

During these four days people have been settling down to the conviction that all the Slave States will go out: — that the South will make an attempt on Washington & that Civil War is certain. All which is not cheering at all.

Dec. 31. Monday night. New Year's Eve. The coming year is like to be among the most momentous I've yet lived to see — but I'm too much debilitated to undertake prosing & prophesying about it.

Kept within doors since my last entry by this pestilent cold. I suspect my *liver* of being at the bottom of all the difficulty. No cold could produce such utter lassitude imbecility & stagnation of every thought & faculty as have characterized the wretched semi-existence of these last few days. I have taken up book after book in vain. Reading has been impossible. Even the newspaper Telegraphic department, morn'g & aft'n, has been too much for me to undertake, and I have relied on Ellie for an abstract or summary of the reports from Charleston & Washington. Have been specially incommoded by sleeplessness. From Wednesday to Sunday I think I did not lose consciousness one moment. D[r] Peters has been very attentive & kind, calling twice a day, but without producing much relief as yet — except that my appetite seems coming up a little.

Rev: Henry Anthon pretty seriously ill with something like enteritis. G.C.A. much alarmed. But it would seem he was better this morn'g. Probably not genuine enteritis, but soreness & distress following a bad attack of bilious Colic.

It seems now that Major Anderson's transfer of his command to the safer position of Fort Sumter was without express orders & on his own responsibility. The Secessionists denounced the movement as a breach of faith on the part of the Administration & demanded his recall — or that he be ordered back into Fort Moultrie. M[r] Sec[y] Floyd — with or without *Buchanan's* concurrence — had promised the Charleston people that there should be no change in the position of this handful of government troops. He had stipulated to give Southern treason every facility in his power. He insisted that Anderson be censured & sent back to Fort M. or that the garrison be withdrawn altogether. But even Buchanan & his Cabinet could not swallow this dose of baseness — so Floyd has resigned, & the Country is well rid of him.

The North is beginning to bristle up at last. There is talk of movements in Penn: Ohio: Mass: & this State for large legislative appropriations to arm & equip such forces as the defence of the National Capitol may require.

Amid such doleful thinkings is A.D. 1860 passing away. Never was night more crystalline & splendid with cloudless sky, & refulgent moonlight, than this — thro' which we enter the momentous year 1861. Let us accept the omen.

1861

Jan: 2[d]. Reports from Washington indicate that our wretched old Chief Magistrate begins to exhibit symptoms of a Backbone at last. He may perhaps be beginning to understand that he has played into the hands of Southern traitors long enough, and that theirs is too hard a service. It is rumored to day that Major Anderson is to be reinforced & that certain Ships of War are under sailing orders for Charleston Harbor. Too late, I fear.

Jan: 11. Friday night. Much to write — too much, for one who was up at 4.30 this morn'g & has travelled a quarter of a thousand miles since daybreak.

Even the most insignificant memoranda of these Revolutionary days may be worth preserving. We are making history just now, fearfully fast.

Thursday — 3[d] — Jersey City ferry & R.R. for Philad[a] at 11 A.M. — Disgusting steady rain: dull headache. An uninteresting monotonous ride at best, but most dreary when all the country looks waterlogged & as if deliquescing into primæval Chaotic Bog; — when the very ducks & geese gaze at the traveller with a mute appeal for pity & warm towels, — when all one's feelings are harrowed up by sympathy for his unhappy fellow creatures condemned to live in the dismal farmhouses & village homes that are visible from the R.R. Cars. Φιλαδελφια 3 P.M. — Girard House. Most lonely & doleful drive thereto from the R.R. depot thro' miles of monotonous dirty streets. Rain held up in the ev'g & I found my way to Horace Binney's in South Sixth St where I was most kindly received by H.B. & M[rs] Eliza & poor Julia Johnson — & urged to take up my quarters with them.

Friday 4th Walked about Philad[a] after breakfast. Snow storm set in. R.R. for Baltimore at Noon. More headache and a black fast. This was the O.P.F's Fast day & I observed it. My sense of it's obligation strengthened by the absence of anything to eat. Except at Havre-de Grace, where something was tendered me called Oysters, but in fact Oyster shells softened by long boiling. Sun came out *hot* at Wilmington. Found W[m] H. Aspinwall on the train at Baltimore — bound for Washington on a Union saving expedition. Shewed me letters from Petigru & others at Charleston indicating an uncomfortable state of affairs in that Metropolis. Washington & Willard's Hotel at 6.15 P.M. Supper — call on Mrs Senator Dixon of Conn: with Mr S.B.R. — also on Genl Scott. Long live the old General! —

Sat: With Mr R. inspecting exterior of Treasury, Patent Office &c &c & to the Capitol. Settled ourselves in Senate Chamber — first calling on Seward at his house in — St. — & calling also on Mr Speaker Pennington in his gorgeously gilt & mirrored Speaker's room. — *Seward* opened the Pacific R.R. question in a dignified statesmanlike speech [which Mr S.B.R. wrote in our little parlor last night] — There was opposition from Missouri — from the extreme factions South of course, & from the N.W. which wants a route yet farther North. *Rice* of Minnesota (?) objected & opposed, with a dirty appeal to Southern prejudice & passion, for which he ought to be burned in effigy from Boston to St Paul's. It went off at last without any decisive vote. I left the Senate in disgust & adjourned to the *Smithsonian*, preferring stuffed penguins & pickled lizards to the dishonest gabble of the Senate Chamber.

Much impressed by the amplitude & grandeur of all the Federal buildings, & by the splendid marbles & frescos of the Capitol. We cannot *spare* these structures quite yet. If a partition of Federal property *is* inevitable, let us give S. Carolina *all* the pictures in the Rotunda, & Clark Mills' Equestrian Statue of Andrew Jackson.

Ev'g. — With Mr R. to Seward's. Sat an hour or two with him & Preston King, talking Crisis & Compromise. Both Senators most jolly genial goodnatured & free from care, laughing at the vagaries of *Toombs* & *Iverson*, talking of conciliation & arrangement as likely to be effected, perhaps — but not worth much effort.

Sunday 6th. To Church. St John's. Sat in Seward's pew by his invitation. The Senator did not appear. Rev: Smith Pyne was emphatic & spasmodic in the Pulpit.

Afterwards called on us Captn Lewis (of the Navy Yard) Thayer (Ev'g Post Correspondent) Stewart — Hon: Edwards of Keene N.H. (a nice sensible old gentleman) and others. Many rumors & reports, mostly lying.

Monday. Patent office, with Prof: Eliot of Hartford & his nice wife. To Senate Chamber. Very earnest & patriotic speech from Crittenden. Labor thrown away. To the House. Nothing of much interest there. —

Heard of the death of *Wm Kent* — and of *Rev: Henry Anthon.* He died Sat: morn'g after severe suffering patiently endured. I hoped he might yet recover, for Fish who arrived Sat: night reported that he was *a little better* Friday aft^n.

Prof: Hackley is gone too. Congestion of the brain. I learned that from this morn'g's papers in the R.R. cars. There are men whose death would have been a heavier loss.

Tuesday 8th. Neither House in session. Dr Peters & Mrs Georgey P. & Mrs Eleanor arrived yesterday. With them & Senator Anthony of R.I. to Navy Yard. Captn Lewis. Dahlgren guns. Maynard Rifles — fuses — percussion caps — &c &c &c. All the processes of the foundry & the laboratory duly expounded. Our four hours scientific session succeeded by a most hospitable lunch. Lewis a decided trump. The ladies adjourned to Hon: Mrs Somebody's Reception — & I revisited the Smithsonian. Ev'g — Party at Hon: Dixon's. Discoursed Fosters & Lorings & Baron Stoeckl the Russian Minister.

Wednesday. Rain. Senate again. Message from Pres^dt. — Bitter acrimonious conversational debate on questions growing out of it between Preston King, Jeff: Davis & others. "Joe Lane" savage & insolent. Wigfall of Texas venomous as one of his Copperhead Congeners. Little hope of any amicable settlement. Pacific R.R. came up & I came off — desponding.

Ev'g. Another alarm of fire. Fires occur every night now. Attributed to incendiaries. Went off to investigate. It was a *schoolhouse* near the Patent office, fortunately isolated. I watched it half an hour at least before a drop of water was thrown on it. Engines & men were on hand but no water was forthcoming. Rumors are rife of an attack on the City by a Virginian mob. People are sending off their families to ϕilad^a & N.Y. — These incendiary fires are supposed to be part of the revolutionary programme. But old Scott has the case under advisement. That may avert any attack. Burglars are apt to postpone their visit when they know the family expects them. Scott tells Senator Foster that he expects 3 companies of light artillery from Fort Leavenworth, & one or two of infantry — also the Sappers & Miners from West Point to arrive in Washington within a week. With this force as a nucleus the militia of the District will be of service. If more men be wanted "I shall write to my friend Genl Sandford of N.Y. who has considerable military capacity, and request him to send me the Seventh Regiment. That regiment, sir, can be relied upon. It will stand being brick-batted without drawing a trigger till it is ordered to fire." — I called on the Fosters to night, in their parlor at the Hotel. Both very agreeable. Mrs F. who was Miss Martha Lyman particularly charming.

Thursday. Great news at the breakfast table. Steamer Star of the West carrying reinforcements to Major Anderson *fired upon* by the savages of S.C. — Rumor No 2 was that she had nevertheless made her way into Charleston harbor & fulfilled her mission. Rumor No 3 — (unfortunately correct) — that being without heavy guns she had turned tail & steamed out of the harbor. — This will produce great excitement — & strengthen the Union feeling all thro' the North. — At Senate. Heard Jefferson Davis talk treason awhile. Thence to *Smithsonian* with Eliot & Judge Huntington of Ct of Claims. Spent four hours there, with Prof: & Mrs Henry — not unprofitably. — Growing cold & windy. Ev'g. Chas Sumner — (the Martyr) — Called to see Mrs Eleanor. *Hawkins*, M.C. from Florida (an unhanged traitor) came to see Mr S.B.R. The two pair sat at opposite corners of our little parlor, discoursing sotto voce. I was introduced to *H.* & had to take his hand, which I dropped with all convenient speed — and then retired to a convenient position where I waited to see whether the gallant Floridian would not rise up suddenly and scalp the Massachusetts man. But there was no breach of the peace. Sumner tells me he has read the notes of Seward's great Conciliation speech soon to be delivered & that it will be effective & conclusive. Much is expected from Seward but I do not believe he can say anything that has not been said before.

This (Friday) morn'g, breakfasted by gas-light — a late supper rather than a breakfast, and off at a little before six, with Mr S.B.R. Dr & Mrs P. & Mrs Eleanor. Lovely cloudless sunrise, clear & cold. But the sky was soon covered with grey frost fog — that became a heavy & uniform cloud, and developed into a snow storm at Philadelphia. Bitter cold ride. Steamboat at Amboy & a hearty supper. Home at 7. All well thank God. Ellie has gone to Musical party at M[me] de Trobriand's.

A visit to Washington gives one no special insight into National affairs. People there are eager for N.Y. papers to tell them what Government did or talked about the day before. But my Prognosis is unfavorable. Virginia & Kentucky & Tennessee will "secede" — (i.e. rebel,) and Maryland will follow Virginia. War seems inevitable. We cannot let the rebels occupy the National Capital without a struggle.

Have been much with Ja[s] W. Beekman. Union saving & Anti-Republican. Wealthy & money loving. But he avows himself ready to spend his last dollar in upholding the territorial integrity of the Union. A significant fact.

Jan: 14. The Star of the West has returned to this port, with a big shot-scar in her timbers, & does not seem likely to revisit the waters of Charleston just at present. The Nation pockets this insult to the National Flag. Calm dishonorable vile submission. But it's wise to postpone actual hemorrhage as long as may be. "Something may turn up."

Seward's long expected speech is a fine Essay, — does him great credit. He's a man of higher faculty than I took him to be. People are disappointed because he proposes no panacea. How could he? The whole subject is talked out. — Gen[l] Dix went to Washington this morn'g to open his portfolio as Sec[y] of Treasury. He had a conference with an informal meeting of bank presidents & Capitalists Sat: & was told that if Government meant to sustain itself & not to acquiesce in it's own disintegration & decomposition, it could have all the money it wanted. Dix's appointment inspires confidence. He is honest, and tho' reluctant to take responsibility, will not decline it when it comes.

Jan: 15. Nothing new from Washington — or from the insurgents of the South, — except that the O.P.F. is rumored to have relapsed into vacillation & imbecility. It seemed a week ago as if he were developing germs of a backbone. Had this old Mollusc become Vertebrate, the theories of Darwin & the "Vestiges of Creation" would have been confirmed.

Rumors multiply & strengthen of an organization *in this City* intended to give aid & comfort to Southern treason by getting up such disturbances here as will paralyze any movement to strengthen Government by men or money. The programme is (as reported) a *nocturnal* insurrection by an armed mob — , taking possession of the *Armories* of the several militia corps — breaking into the banks — & sacking the houses of conspicuous republicans. I know (from T. Bailey Myers) that the editor of the Washington "Constitution" (a renegade Englishman) is privy to this plot — and I have the best moral evidence that Delaplaine, ("Ikey Pig") an M.C. elect from this City, favors it. — Treated myself to a "Maynard Carbine" ($47.50) this aft^{n}.

Jan: 17. Jno Weeks asked me to meet a few gentlemen of the neighbourhood at his house to talk over the expediency of organizing & drilling a special police corps for our own defence in view of possible outbreaks here. Called on Mr Superintend^{t} Kennedy this aft^{n} to take his opinion about it. He discourages the plan. Expects no disturbance — thinks the police able to quell any anarchical demonstration — distrusts all amateur organizations. Regular army always distrusts volunteers.

Jan: 19. The general feeling to day is that political news looks better & brighter. There is evidence that neither Georgia Alabama nor Mississippi is unanimous in rebellion. Even under the present Epidemic of treason & Reign of Terror, there is a Strong Minority (at least) in each of these States, that has thus far been silent — that has not voted or has voted against what they call Secession. Reaction, and the pressure of calamity — (both inevitable) may strengthen this inert & suppressed Anti-Secession party, wake up the whole people to the true state of the case, and bring the conspirators who have raised this storm for their own selfish ends, to a stern reckoning. — Indications from the Border States are encouraging as far as they go — *Crittenden* has taken decided ground in the Senate — and says the Union must be preserved, peaceably or forcibly, according to circumstances.

The suicidal obstructions which the wild men of Charleston have sunk in their harbor seem to be driving trade to Savannah. "Ships filled with stones" sunk in a channel are ugly nuclei for mud deposits & sand bars. Probably the *Teredo* thrives in the semitropical seas of the Southern Coast. Can these ships be raised again six months hence? It may be these maniacs have made their only port inaccessible.

The insecurity of property in all Southern ports seems to be driving all imports & exports away from them & into Northern ports through inland lines of river & railroad. This tendency is like to increase. Rumors (true or false) of Southern legislation repudiating debts & confiscating property will keep capital away from Mobile & New Orleans. And suppose those cities be declared no longer ports of entry??!!???!!!

Jan: 21. Everybody — even Dan[l] B. Fearing — is full of confidence that the National disease has passed it's crisis. I cannot see any reason for thinking so. The Revolution seems to me still in full progress. The conspirators of S. Carolina &c &c have raised a spirit of treason they cannot lay if they would. Many of them intended only a gigantic game of brag, but they have gone a little too far. The ignorant barbarians of their own states, hearing only one side of the question, believe what Toombs & Yancey & Co have been saying, tho' it was said merely to frighten the North.

I fear we are two Peoples, unable to live in peace under one feeble "Federal" government.

Jan: 22. Nothing hopeful in to day's political news. The "Border States" will assuredly drift into rebellion within six weeks. And here we all sit — and prophesy & philosophize & speculate, doing nothing to avert the ruin that impends. But what can we do? What can *I* do? What could I do were I Webster & Clay combined? Concession to these conspirators & the ignorant herd they have stimulated to treason would but postpone the inevitable crisis a year or two longer. The South can be permanently pacified only in one way. The masses of the North must declare Slavery just beneficent & expedient — and allow every Mississippian who chooses to visit N.Y. to bring his niggers with him. Not merely the niggers. His rights over them according to his own slave Code must accompany him, & be recognized & enforced by the Courts & Sheriffs of every Northern State. That's what these madmen demand of us, and Civil War is the alternative.

Their suicidal frenzy tempts me to believe in *Wendell Phillips* & Captn John Brown (hanged a year ago & justly hanged as I've always supposed) — This madness of slaveholders looks as if Slaveholding were doomed.

Jan: 23. No political news to day. The *Border States* will get no concession from Congress. They will secede [i.e. their inhabitants will rebel against the National Government] within 60 days. *Civil War is inevitable.*

Mississippi, or rather her frantic Governor, one Pettus or Pettin, has established a *battery* at *Vicksburgh* & brings to every steamer or flat boat going down the river. This folly must bring on War, if persisted in.

Jan: 25. News to day is that Kentucky Legislature has refused to call a Convention — (but that's too good to be true. It has probably tabled the subject, in hope of action by Congress before March 4th.) Also that the State of Mississippi continues to take indecent liberties with boats going down the river. They are brought to by cannon shot & examined before they can pass Vicksburgh. Fire away, O valiant state of Mississippi! This may bring on the trial of strength (that seems inevitable anyhow) on an issue & in a form that will *not* unite every Southern State, as "coercion" by the Army & Navy of the U.S. probably would. The people of the N.W. will probably take the matter into their own hands — and in that event Louisiana & Mississippi will be wiped out. Kentucky Tennessee & Missouri will not sympathize strongly with the Southern side of that controversy. And it's result may teach all the slave holding states a useful lesson as to their own real weakness.

Jan: 26. Things look a little better to day. Loyalty still asserts itself in Kentucky & Maryland with prospect of success. Virginia seems less promising.

People begin to talk of disruption as likely to make the North richer & more prosperous. Capital will desert these combustible extra-hazardous seceding Communities, they say, — and the trade of New Orleans & Mobile will transfer itself to Northern Ports. Perhaps so. Symptoms of that change have already shewn themselves, unquestionably.

But money cannot pay for our National disgrace. Every citizen of the U.S. is humiliated & lowered in his own estimation and that of the civilized world, by the part his National Government has played in this great crisis. It has not only avowed itself impotent & despicable, but it has been (at least) conniving at the vilest conspiracy since Catiline's, — or rather, all things considered, the vilest conspiracy, with the basest motives, & the largest aim of mischief to mankind, on record anywhere. As much *depravity* may be found in the pages of the Newgate Calendar, but the range of the Conspirators has been far more limited. History may possibly record other political crimes, contemplated or consummated, of equal maleficence & Evil magnitude, but it records none committed on so slight inducement and for ends so base.

Thistlewood is the nearest parallel I can think of for Jeff: Davis & Floyd & Toombs & Co. But the suggestion does Thistlewood wrong. His complaints of an un-reformed Parliament & excessive taxation & starving peasantry sacrificed to sinecure place-holders seem dignified & earnest by the side of the grievances our Southern Conspirators adopt as the pretexts for their Colossal crime.

Floyd's revelations, in his after-dinner speech at Richmond, are appalling to every sane man's moral sense. I rejoice to learn that a Dist: of Columbia Grand Jury has indicted him for malversation in office — as a party to the late frauds on Government. I have long believed him utterly profligate & corrupt — independently of his participation in this treasonable Disunion movement.

In this Richmond speech he calls Jeff: Davis "*the bright Saladin of the South*". Can people who utter such embodiments of concentrated ipecacuanha, — people who talk such heroic doses of tartar emetic — and those who hear & applaud them — live in peace & quietness under the same government with reasonable beings?

Jan: 27. Walter Cutting very lugubrious & despondent this ev'g. Nothing but ruination before us — & all because those

D— Republicans will tender no "compromise" & sit still while the *Border States* are gravitating into Secession.

But is any compromise or pacification desirable until we have ascertained whether we have or have not a Government? Is not our first business now to see that the Law of the Land is executed & Abraham Lincoln Esqr duly inaugurated March 4th? Would not "concession", *now*, be an admission that what we have called the Federal "Government" is & has been all along a mere sham, scarecrow, & practical nullity, unable to assert it's own existence as against a seditious minority?

Jan: 31. Thursday night. Clear & wintry. Nothing very fresh, but we expect to be stirred up, at any moment, by news of hemorrhage at Charleston or Fort Pickens. Meantime we are rather surprisingly inert & apathetic. Opinions make progress nevertheless. Disposition to compromise is far weaker than a month ago — and indignation at the South more general. It is quiet, as yet, and shews itself in no overt acts. This moderation is creditable & promising. When once the sword is drawn, & compromise is no longer possible, we shall act none the less vigorously for having restrained ourselves — in a measure — from brag & bluster.

Am just from French Theatre, with E. Miss Rosalie, & Murray Hoffman. "Les Canotiers de la Seine" — an extravaganza in *five* Acts. (!) Funny — tho' the company is fifth-rate.

Last night at Wm B. Astor's. Great crowd. I spent a pleasant ev'g enough. *Fernando Wood* in a white cravat was remarkable to behold. His invitation was a tribute by his millionaire host to the dangerous democracy — like the distinguished consideration shewn by Isaac of York to Front-de-Bœuf & the Grand Master. Our Fernando has just married a "genteel" wife, to be sure, (N° 4 I believe) and has his Opera-box, & is trying for a "social position". But I do not think I should invite him to this house were I twenty Wm B. Astors, or had he married twenty Miss Drake Mills-es.

People generally talk rather despondently to day. No wonder. All the indications are that this treasonable Inflammation — *Secessionitis* — keeps on making steady progress week by week. A little prophylactic treatment before Nov: 6 (reinforced garrisons & the like) — or even six weeks afterwards would have checked it, or confined it to the insignificant spot of chronic ulceration, where it originated, South Carolina to wit. But there was no such treatment — for the sufficient reason that Gov^{t} was in the hands of the cabal that desired it's destruction, — the doctors were in the interest not of the patient but of the disease. Old Dr Buchanan do'nt certainly know, even yet, whether he wants to see his patient perish — or be cured by remedies alien to his School. So the inflammation is gaining ground every day in the Border States. The chances are against Virginia's continuing loyal to the Union. Farther South it has already produced morbid structural changes that only the knife can remedy. Six States are out of the Union, if legislation can take them out, and their delegates meet next Monday in treasonable convention to organize a new "Confederation."

One's *Opinions* change fast in revolutionary times. Three months ago, I thought with horror & incredulity of the chance that poor little S. Carolina might be mad enough to "secede" alone. Now I am content to let her go, & carry all the Gulf States with her to Chaos & the Devil, if Maryland Virginia Kentucky Tennessee & Missouri will but be true to themselves and to the Union, or rather (it's the better word) to the *Nation*. Let the barbarians of Mississippi & Alabama rebel if they like, & call it "secession." We can get on without them. The National Councils are well rid of their representatives. The North West will take care that it's great outlet into the Gulf is unobstructed. Woe to Natchez & Vicksburgh & N. Orleans if it be blocked. We need not attempt to re-conquer & reclaim the territories of the new Southern Confederacy. It cannot sustain itself long. It must soon decompose into anarchy. The U.S. will gradually establish itself in possession again by a protectorate, & what were once the Gulf States will be the Gulf *Territories*. It is all plain sailing if we can but keep the Border States in line.

Feb: 4th. This is an important day. The seceding states meet in Convention, to form an Algerine Confederacy, and Virginia elects a Convention to decide whether that grand old State shall or shall not abide by the Union. I have little hope of her. This seems the hour of darkness.

Feb: 5th. Political matters look brighter to day. That is to say, the uncertain lying rumors of Feb: 5th happen to be pleasanter than those of Feb: 4th. But Virginia certainly seems to have done better than I hoped. Not merely in the Panhandle & West of the Blue Ridge but even in *Eastern* Va, in the Counties that lie around Richmond & Norfolk, the so-called "Union Party" (i.e. the opponents of *Immediate* Secession, those who want to wait for a "Compromise") has prevailed.

Seward told D.H. Haight last week that he pledged his honor as a man & his capacity as a politician that all this agitation should be ended within 60 days. So Haight tells C.E.S. If Seward said so, he is either the grossest of fools, the most astute of politicians, or the boldest of political liars — perhaps with good intent.

Feb: 6. Everybody in high glee to day. The *immediate Secessionists* of Virginia defeated by some 40.000 majority as estimated. How ready we are to take hold of every little symptom of *recovery* & make more than the most of it! — This result does'nt show that Va decides for the Union, by any means. She merely postpones rebellion for a month, in hope of *concession*. But we have been firing 100 guns in honor of Va, and all Wall St. is confident we are out of trouble now, and that the Border States are all safe. This is premature & absurd. But the Va news is good as far as it goes. It is the first hopeful sign that has been seen since November — the first streak of blue sky since the storm set in. Important not only as indicating the strength of the *quasi*-conservative feeling in that State (or more properly the comparative mildness — the lower grade of malignity — characteristic of the Epidemic as it prevails there) — but also in it's influence on the North. So long as our Southern news was all one way, nothing but fury hatred & malice, overt acts of treason, insolent challenges to Civil War, it was hard for any of us possessing even the rudiments of a back-bone, to tolerate talk about conciliation & concession. But the most important & influential of the Southern Communities now tells us — in substance — that though irritated & affronted & strongly tempted to rebel, it yet prefers on the whole to follow the destinies of the Nation, and that it will uphold & abide by our National Unity if the North will but make some conciliatory move. This alters the aspect of the controversy. To be sure the North is entitled to say it has done no wrong & contemplates none: that it has only exercised the right of a majority to control a Republican Government; that it is not bound to make concessions because a factious & lawless minority threatens treason & rebellion. The North is right, & it's legal position is unassailable. But it may fairly concede something to it's weaker brethren, if in the full tide of their wrath — however groundless & irrational — they avow themselves desirous of peace & compromise. This action of Virginia's changes my view as to the course Repub[s] in Congress should take. I now think they should be diligent in devising measures to satisfy the South, so far as they may without sacrifice of principle. "*Beati pacifici*" is now my motto in the controversy. When pacific offers are finally rejected we will begin enforcing Law & executing Justice. But before that extremity is unavoidable, let us try if we cannot come to some composition with those whose acts shew they desire it, & who are not disposed to rebel from mere love of rebellion & disorganization in the abstract, like S. Carolinians.

Feb: 10. Great news yesterday aft[n]. *Georgia* has seized five N.Y. vessels by way of reprisal for our stoppage of *arms* en route for that rebellious community. This is a calamity. It will strengthen the anti-conciliation party at the North. Tomorrow morn'g's Tribune will make the most of this last manifestation of Southern madness.

The Seceding States (from S. Carolina to Louisiana) seem to have formed a "Confederacy" on the basis of the Constitution of the U.S.

Yesterday, M[r] S.B.R. Murray Hoffman & Henry *Dorr* dined here. Thereafter (11 P.M.) to M[rs] Christine Griffin's for Miss Rosalie, & brought her home. Ellie did not feel well enough to go. Ellie does not seem well or strong since her attack of influenza & fever a fortnight ago.

Northern forbearance is nearly exhausted by successive outrages. War is inevitable. And it will be war in earnest. The savages of the South will give no quarter & ignore the amenities of civilized warfare. We shall have to fight them with their own weapons. We shall be arming & drilling Slave-regiments within a year, and making fortified breaches in the levees of the Mississippi, to drown out New Orleans.

Feb: 13. After dinner E. read Haydn for me — & Ehninger & G.C.A. came in for a few minutes. Jack thinks he & his associates (80 or thereabouts) who have been diligently drilling for six weeks will not be required at Washington on March 4th after all. Probably he's right. Seizing that city by a coup-de-main was certainly on the Conspirators' programme but Scott's preparations to receive them & the unexpected attitude assumed by the Border States have brought that project to naught. The Electoral Votes were counted to day, & as I hear no Extras in the streets, they were probably counted in due form, & the result announced without disturbance. This was the critical day for the peace of the Capitol. A foray of Virginia Gents with Govr Wise at their head & Govr Floyd at their tail could have done infinite mischief by destroying the legal evidence of Lincoln's election — (after they had killed & eaten Genl Scott & his Flying Artillery, that is —) — But preventing Lincoln from taking the Oath of office at the usual place & in the usual way on the 4th of March would be so inconsiderable a result, comparatively, that I do not believe they will try for it. One feature of the Conspiracy seems to have been anticipated & suppressed.

Saw Miss Annie Leavenworth duly married yesterday to R.W. Cameron, by Rev: Edwd Anthon at 222 Tenth St. — It was a damp dingy morn'g, but the sun came out at one, just after the wedding, & shone bright for the rest of the day. I trust the lady's married life may be sunshiny, but it's prospects are not altogether unclouded. — Leavenworth père was not present — confined to his room — & in a critical unpromising state.

Met Henry Fearing this morn'g. He left Washington Monday, & of course brings with him important information from a most reliable source, about which he's not at liberty to go into particulars. Every one just from Washn brings back ware of that sort. It is the chief export of the District of Columbia. F's private & confidential news is that Fort Sumter *has been* reinforced & that the discredited rumors of ten days ago about the Brooklyn & her boats are true. May be they are. Quien sabe? Old Buchanan may have lied in his letter to Tyler or somebody — nothing more likely — it's the dear old creature's way. — F. says all the *Borderers* ask is a concession — no matter what — to enable them to tell their crazy constituents that the North has *given up* something. They do'nt want their States to rebel. Their fire & fury speeches in the House are intended for Buncombe.

This revelation of the gallant Floyd's gigantic larcenies must weaken the cause of Secession — for many Southerners possess a moral sense & must distrust a leader who steals. Certainly Floyd & Co have done more villainy on smaller provocation than any gang on record. The deluded mobs of Charleston & Savannah have some excuse for their criminal outrages. There is none for the Floyds Cobbs Davises & other false prophets who have deliberately stimulated their ignorance to crime by malicious lies, & who have stuck at nothing from theft to Treason & Civil War — that they might hold political power a little longer.

These men want hanging — badly. But they will reap deadly fruit yet from *their own* treason. The Devil they have raised will turn & rend them unless he be laid at once — and that is beyond the magic of Jeff: Davis. The Inflammation has run it's course. It has produced morbid change of structure on the Gulf — Those unhappy states are sphacelated, gangrenous, dead to the Nation. But the Nation itself has passed it's crisis & entered on convalescence. It is sorely shattered though, — convalescence will be slow & precarious: Trifling accident may produce relapse. The peaceable accession of the new Administration, — it's legal control of the National Government, will be sedative & mollifying. Many Virginian Secessionists will be less inclined to rebel when they find that a "Black Republican" regime is not Abolitionism after all. But then comes the ugly question of Peace or War with the Seceded States.

My voice is for War & Gunpowder.

Feb: 18. No political news. Lincoln is making little speeches as he wends his way toward Washington, & has said some things that are sound & creditable & raise him in my esteem. But I should have been better pleased with him had he held his tongue altogether. He enters N.Y. tomorrow aft^{n}. Broadway will be less crowded than it was when the Japanese embassy came, but his advent will make people turn out in great force, if it be a pleasant day.

Feb: 20. Tho' the original Secession epidemic has, I think, exhausted itself, we have yet to see what Virginia, Tennessee &c will do when the contest begins between the Federal Gov^{t} and the rebellious slave states. *Which side will they take*???

Lincoln arrived here yesterday aft^{n} by Hudson R. R.R. from Albany. Walked up town at 3½. Broadway crowded tho' not quite so densely as on the Prince of Wales' *Avatar* last October. The trottoir well filled by pedestrians (vehicles turned off into side streets) and side walks by patient & stationary sight-seers. Above Canal St. they were nearly impassable. At St Thomas' Church I met the illustrious cortège moving slowly down to the Astor House with it's escort of mounted policemen, & a torrent of Tag-rag & bobtail rushing & hooraying behind. The great Rail-splitter's face was visible to me for an instant, and seemed a keen clear honest face, not so ugly as his portraits.

Feb: 23. Extras out at noon to day. How a plot for Lincoln's assassination was revealed at Harrisburgh, late last night. How his R.R. train was to have been thrown down an embankment by obstructions on the rails or undermining the track, between Harrisburgh & Baltimore, and, in case that device failed, how he was to be beset in his carriage between depot & depot in the streets of Baltimore. How Lincoln thereupon left H. privily, disguised "in a Scotch cap & long military cloak" & travelled all night & reached Washington at an early hour this morning. *That* is fact. The conspiracy story sounds a little romantic. But our Southern fanatics are capable of any enormity. I have said, all along, that there was at least an even chance of an attempt to take L's life before 4th March. — It's to be hoped that the *Conspiracy* can be proved beyond cavil. If it cannot be made manifest & indisputable, this surreptitious nocturnal dodging or sneaking of the Pres^{dt} elect into his Capital City, under cloud of night, will be used to damage his moral position & throw ridicule on his Administration.

Other political news indefinite. Schism in Repub^{n} party seems widening. The New England States — Preston King of N.Y. & the N.Y. Tribune are making war on Seward & striving to exclude him from prominent place in Lincoln's cabinet. He is a Compromiser: they are Un-compromisers. — The C.S.A., i.e. "Confederate States of America", are organizing

— on paper. Their leaders crave a Strong government. But how can they get it, without compromising the sacred right of Secession? — Gen[l] Dix is winning honor & applause in his position at Washington. He shews more pluck & vigor than I gave him credit for.

Feb: 26. Political affairs progress — with mingled indications of good & of evil. — There has been an Election in the savage Commonwealth of Arkansaw — result uncertain. That there is any doubt about it, is a strong and comfortable symptom that the Treason-eruption has run it's course & passed it's maximum virulence; for Arkansaw is constitutionally predisposed to whatever things are unlovely lawless & of ill report.

Semble that A. Lincoln sympathizes with Seward & the Repub[n] Right, and not with Greeley & Sumner & the Extreme Left. Glad of it.

Gen[l] *Twiggs* has suddenly become exceedingly infamous. He has surrendered to the Nation of Texas all the military property, moveable & immoveable which the U.S.A. entrusted to his keeping. Faith & honor & common honesty are rare in the Gulf States just now! No Revolution — no great political movement ever combined so much & so various crime — dirty & bold — sneaking & insolent — as this, unless there be a parallel case in the history of France, or that of the Roman Empire in it's days of *rotting*. Southerners have lost all moral sense. Their nerves of moral sensation seem smitten with paralysis. Their "chivalry" exults in treachery, bad faith, oppression of the weak, & everything that distinguishes the Churl from the Knight.

My judgment (wrong very probably) condemns Abolitionism, & sanctions the claims of Slaveholders to use the labor of their slaves according to the settled laws of the communities into which both Master & slave were born — the "state of life in which it has pleased God to place" them both. I censure Slaveholders, of course, for refusing to provide by law, against evils (such as separation of families) which probably occur but seldom, but as to which the Community ought to set itself right by stringent legislation. Thus have I thought of Slavery. But the moral insanity of Slaveholders, & the baseness that men reputed honorable & hightoned commit or applaud because perpetrated in the interest of Slavery, make me distrust my judgment. If Garrison & Wendell Phillips preach the *Truth*, it is natural their adversaries should act as they do. If slave-holding be tyranny & robbery, we can account for our slaveholding states' behaving like a club of thieves, with an inefficient or dishonest Chief of Police. If slaveholding be right & just, their moral position is inexplicable & unaccountable. — Let us keep the comparatively humane & civilized Border States true to their allegiance, if we can, by any compromise or concession, but let us extend no olive-branch to the Algerines of the Gulf. We are well rid of them. Let Government collect it's revenues at their posts, & be thankful that they have renounced, in their fanaticism & folly, the right to be represented in it's Councils by delegations of Traitors & ruffians (like Toombs & Yancey & Davis & the late lamented P.H. Brooks) and the privilege of helping to disgrace & afflict us with such portentous National calamities as Ja^{s} Buchanan, now Pres't of the U.S.A. Old J.B. — the "O.P.F." — stands lowest, I think, in the dirty catalogue of treasonable mischief-makers. For without the excuse of bad Southern blood, without passion, without local prejudices, & in a great degree by mere want of moral force to resist his confessedly treasonable advisers, he has somehow slid into the position of *boss*-traitor & master-devil of the gang. He seems to *me* the basest specimen of the human race ever raised on this Continent.

Feb: 27th. Wednesday. Important news from Washington. The Council of Notables commonly described as "the Peace Congress" has agreed on a Scheme of Compromise at last, and submitted it to Congress. It's main feature seems to be the re-establishment of the Missouri Compromise line — and it restricts future acquisitions of territory. D.D. Field & WC Noyes seem to have opposed it stoutly, so it's evidently distasteful to the Repub^{n} Left. It is not at all clear that it can get such a majority in Congress & in the States as will be needed to make it an Amendment to the Constitution.

Probably there will be a hard battle on the question of it's ratification, and I suppose it will be the duty of conservative & patriotic men to support it. But concession, right or wrong, to the demands of this blustering faction is painful. It may be prudent, for Government is pitifully weak — but the confession of our weakness is humiliating & should make the white marbles of the Capitol blush into red carnelian.

Letter from C.E.S. to day, written Monday ev'g. He's disgusted with the crowd of office-seekers & unfragrant Western men at Willard's. Thinks Lincoln a smart Country politician & Mrs L. a very vulgar old woman — &c &c &c &c. He is assured "on the best authority" that ample provision has been made for reinforcing *Fort Sumter*. Sufficient troops commanded by our old West P^{t} friend Major Porter, are *somewhere*, within hearing of the first shot fired against it. Where can they be? Either in balloons at an exceeding altitude, or in a school of submarine boats astonishing the fish of Charleston Harbor.

March 2. We have relapsed into gloom, & are once more talking despondingly of "what Virginia will do" & which way the Border States will go. The prospect that Congress will do nothing to appease them (& Congress is even now just passing out of legal existence) & the prevailing belief that Ultra Republicanism is to be strongly represented in the new Cabinet, seem to be doing grave mischief. There is "a new hand at the bellows" of sedition in V^{a} & Maryland, and those States are doubtful again. So say newspaper correspondents & telegrams & editors. Perhaps they lie — to frighten the North. I hope so — but these are sad & troublesome times.

The alarm of this morn'g made a ten-strike in the stock-list. Every thing went down. Border State Stocks gave way 5 per cent. No wonder. I would'nt touch them if they fell 50 p: c: lower.

Much depends on the tone of Lincoln's Inaugural next Monday. But I doubt if words will do much good now, however pacific fair & reasonable. *Kennedy* told me this aft^{n} (at the Bank) that he had seen private despatches assuring him it would be a conciliatory & emollient paper. But the general belief is, it will announce Lincoln's intention to uphold the Law — to reinforce Fort Sumter — now actually besieged (& it's garrison likely to get no quarter if it's far outnumbering besiegers prevail) — to retake the other Forts now in the hands of the Rebellion — & to collect Federal Revenue, by blockade or otherwise, at every Southern port. — How can Lincoln say anything else — if he allude to the subject of secession at all — & how can he ignore it without shame? The Logic of the situation is inexorable — and *War* is the only possible deduction from the premises. Civil War is at hand; within a week, if the fire-eaters of Charleston take the initiative, & open their batteries on F^t^ Sumter — which they are like to do at once on reading a virile & honest Inaugural — and within 60 days, any how.

Were we at the North only united — of one mind — loyal to Gov^t^ — I should not fear Civil War. But there are the N.Y. Express & the N.Y. Herald &c &c &c. The *Cuttings* are exposing themselves to remark by wild ultra Southern talk. My old friend Walter C. in the Opera house lobby last night, "hopes for Civil War. Sooner it comes the better. If people *will not compromise*, one party or the other must be *exterminated*. That's all there is about it you know". He for one is ready to go in for a fight, and to give up all he's worth in the world, & his life too, to exterminate those d—d Abolitionists.

March 4. News from Washington awaited impatiently. Everybody longing for the Inaugural. Natural enough. We are on the edge of the Crisis now.

At 12 appeared an Ev'g Post Bulletin. "Great Excitement in Washington. The Pres^dt^ up all night. Great efforts to make him alter his inaugural. The president firm". That is, Weed & perhaps Seward want Lincoln to say nothing about enforcing Law.

Also there was rumor of the rebel batteries opening on Fort Sumter, — but discredited.

March 5. Tuesday. Weather grows cold again. Much wind & dust. — People differ about *Lincoln's* Inaugural — but favorable criticism preponderates, tho' Stocks have gone down. At Trust C^o^ Board this morn'g, Kernochan, & other ultra "Conservative" Southronizers, approved & applauded it as pacific, & likely to prevent collision. May be so, but I think there's a clank of metal in it. — It's unlike any message or state paper of any class that has appeared in my time, to my knowledge. It is characterized by strong *individuality*, & the absence of conventionalism of thought or diction. It does'nt run in the ruts of Pub: Doc: N° 1 to N^o^ ten million & one, but seems to introduce one to *a man* & to dispose one to like him. That is it's effect on Aug[s] Clason — e.g. — a strong Southern Democrat.

The absence of fine writing & Spread-Eagle-ism is a good sign. It's *weak* points, I think, are it's discussion of the *political* authority of the Supreme Court of U.S. and it's admission that *the North* condemns Slaveholding as a moral wrong. That is unfortunate in a paper intended (among other things) to strengthen the hands of Union-men at the South. We Northerners object to slavery on grounds of Political Economy not of Ethics.

March 6. The Inaugural is generally approved, by Democrats as well as Republicans. I think it is doing good, even at the South — tho' Southern politicians denounce it's "coercion" spirit & vapor horribly. Indications in Virginia &c are favorable to day. There is a story this ev'g that *Crittenden* has been nominated to vacancy in Supreme C[t] of U.S. — Too good to be true. It would be a wise statesmanlike measure, hardly to be expected from a party Cabinet.

March 7. Thursday. Exceeding cold & windy. C.E.S. returns from Washington full of news & incidents of the momentous ten days now last past. Of course he has talked to everybody — seen everything — found his way into every place. No time to record details. His report of the aspect of things, as seen from Willard's & Pennsylvania Avenue is decidedly favorable. The Inaugural has done good. Army & Navy men from Virginia & even from the rebel States say they will abide by the flag of the U.S. & the doctrine of the Inaugural, whatever their states have done or may do. — E.g. Capt[n] Lewis of the Navy Yard, whose allegiance was very shaky two months ago. Men of the Border States are encouraged & sanguine.

Wigfall of Texas said in C's hearing, on Monday, that he was disgusted with his Southern friends. They had sworn that Lincoln should be *killed*, & now he was peaceably inaugurated after all. He was tempted to say he'd have nothing more to do with such a d— set of humbugs.

Crittenden is hopeful, even confident. If we can drag thro' the next 30 days without bloodshed at Fort Sumter, or elsewhere, all may be well. Seward's policy has been to procrastinate

— to gain time — to wait, & that will be the policy of this Administration. He urged it daily on Cha[s] F. Adams while the House Committee of 33 was sitting, & he was quite right. Government is weak, & must postpone a Trial of strength, in hope that something may turn up.

March 9. Foster has moved the expulsion of the Chivalric Wigfall, Senator from Texas. Wrote E. this morn'g to give Foster my thanks as for a personal favor. Wigfall's presence in the Senate Chamber after his audacious insolent utterances of treason, in his official place, is an affront to every citizen of the U.S.

The Border States seem convalescing. Even N. Carolina refuses to call a Convention.

March 11. Monday. Fine day with a superfluity of chilliness. Letter from Ellie at W. She tried to attend Lincoln's Reception Friday night, but the fearful crowd of adoring office seekers & wild Western women was impenetrable.

Was active in Wall St. — We are plainly to have trouble with the purchasers of our Trinity School lots & may as well begin a course of "coercion" at once. Then comes a long unpleasant costly litigation. Amen. Law School Committee met at M[r] S.B.R's office (6 Wall St.) at 2 & sat a couple of hours. Trinity Ch: Vestry to night. Rev: Morgan Dix in the chair. After adjourning, I walked down B'way with Gouv: Ogden to look at a fire. It was on E. side of B'way below Rector St. — nearly extinguished, after doing considerable damage.

Yesterday I dined at M[rs] Peters' with M[rs] Lily Clymer & Cha[s] Day. An hour at the Club thereafter.

Gen[l] Dix tells me they have advices at Washington that the U.S. flag is flying on every tavern in N. Alabama. Also that the control of *West Point* was on the programme of Buchanan's traitorous cabinet, & that they came very near getting it into the hands of men pledged to Secessionism & prepared to use it's men & materiel in aid of an expected revolutionary Anti-Lincoln demonstration in this State!

To day's great news is that Gov[t] contemplates withdrawing Major Anderson & his command from Fort Sumter! It is said they cannot maintain themselves there without supplies more than 20 or 30 days longer — & that the batteries in

Charleston Harbor are *now* (thanks to old Buchanan's imbecility or treason) so strong that supplies & reinforcements cannot be thrown in without some 10.000 men & a strong Naval force. We have not got the men or the ships, and they cannot be got, for months. What is to be done? — Withdrawal — surrender — "calm dishonorable vile submission" seems the only course we have left. But it will be a sore occasion for S. Carolinian bullies to bluster & blaspheme. They will laugh consumedly over their whiskey.

If newspaper reports be true, the surrender of F^{t} Sumter is inevitable. The surrender may do good at the South, possibly. Some say it will break the neck of "Secession" in S. Carolina itself, & ruin every Secessionist leader. But it will stir up corresponding exasperation at the North, strengthen the *Greeley* wing of Republicanism, and weaken the Conservatives whom Seward leads.

The proposition is generally received with favor, here. It will be otherwise received in New England & the West I think! — I recognize it as a stern necessity, but as a deep humiliation withal — as an unavoidable submission to gross personal insult from Jeff: Davis & Gov: Pickens & their crew of "chivalric" bullies & braggarts.

The political entity known as the United States of America is found out at last, after imposing on the Community of Nations for three quarters of a century. The Bird of our Country is a debilitated chicken disguised in Eagle feathers. We have never been a nation, we are only an aggregate of communities, ready to fall apart at the first serious shock & without a centre of vigorous National life to keep us together.

March 12. Every citizen of what has heretofore been called the Great Republic of America, every man woman & child from Maine to Texas — from Massachusetts to California — stands lower among the inhabitants of this earth to night than in March 1860. We are a weak divided disgraced people, unable to maintain our National existence. We are impotent even to *assert* our National life. The Country of Geo: Washington & Andrew Jackson [!!!] is decomposing, and it's elements reforming into new & strange combinations. I shall never go abroad. That question is settled. I should be ashamed to shew my nose in the meanest corner of Europe. Naples & Florence & Milan, now triumphantly asserting their *National* life & unity, are entitled to look down on Boston & New York. All my right title & interest in the 4th of July & the American Eagle & the Model Republic can be bought at a "low figure".

I'm tempted to emigrate, to become a naturalized British subject & spend the rest of my days in some pleasant sea-side village in the Southern Counties of Old Mother England. It's a pity we ever renounced our allegiance to the British Crown.

March 14. The talk at the Club is that *Bankhead* says the steamer *Crusader* cleared for Charleston to day, to take off *Anderson* & the garrison of Fort Sumter. — Be it so. There seems no choice.

Newspaper despatches say that this surrender will be promptly followed up by blockade of every Southern port, and that thereupon Jeff: Davis will instantly march on Washington, at the head of a few hundred thousand fire-eaters.

March 19. Tuesday. Home again after my tour to Washington — *once Capital de facto* of our Nation.

At Jersey City ferry 6.30 A.M. Saturday. A bleak grey morning. Streets shrouded in snow that fell Friday night. Into the R.R. cars & away. Sun broke out & clouds vanished. Philad[a], Wilmington, Baltimore, were successively passed without the minutest material for a Journal paragraph, & our locomotive screeched over it's advent at Washington at six o'clock P.M. Proceeded to Willard's, where I found Ellie & M[rs] D.C. Murray & Jem Ruggles in full go. There was a "Reception" at National Hotel that ev'g, in honor of M[rs] J.J. Crittenden's departure. M[rs] Murray assisted. E. staid at home. The Reception seems to have been a specimen of the vilest American Spread-Eagle taste — justifying Dickens in Martin Chuzzlewit.

Hotel lobbies crawling with office seekers. *Germans* from the N.W. in great force. Anthony Bleecker is struggling for the U.S. Marshalship of this district, but will struggle in vain. N.Y. politicians give him little countenance. If that prize fail him, he will jump at any crumb or bone of patronage from the Executive Table, poor A.J.B.! Oscanyan, our Col: Coll: Law

School Janitor wants a diplomatic position in Mesopotamia, or that neighbourhood, I know not precisely where [Probably the Consul-Generalship at Alexandria, salary $3500. which Thayer of the Ev'g Post seems to have secured.] — Gave him the benefit of my Political Influence, for so inefficient a Janitor may make a brilliant Diplomat, and I cheerfully contributed my mite to relieve the Law School of a sweeper & maker of fires, who knows so little of his profession.

Sunday was cloudy & cold. To St John's Ch: with Ellie. Rev: Smith Pyne, whom his parishioners call "Pitch Pine", preached in his usual key. His sermon was spasmodic, but of more than average depth. I rate the Rev: S.P. rather high among preachers. — Long walk thereafter with Jem in the grey ev'g, inspecting Mills' bronze Equestrian Washington in a gale of wind. Afterwards discoursed Senator Foster — M[r] & M[rs] Bigelow Lawrence — Fry of the N.Y. Tribune staff (very clever — & I think consumptive. He's after some diplomatic post & relies much on his terrible cough, the result of speech making over much all thro' N. York & Ohio in the last Campaign).

Monday. Walked alone to that hideous unfinished Washington Monument. Then with the ladies to Senate, at 1 P.M. Very cold & beginning to spit snow. Routine business ended, J.C. Breckinridge opened with an insidious mischievous speech, asking information as to Lincoln's policy, deprecating "Coercion", as sure to drive every "Border" State out of the Union, & deploring the obstinate refusal of the North to make concession. — *Hale* replied in slang-whanging stump-orator style. He is more effective than J.C.B. & made several telling points. — He had a small passage of arms with the irrepressible *Wigfall* of Texas.

Senate went into Executive Session at ½ past three; galleries were cleared, & we emerged from the Capitol into a snow storm. Secured a hack for the ladies, and went at 5 to a little dinner at Sandford's (the Ex-Attaché). There were Ellie & I, Truman Smith, Mr Secretary Cameron, Senators Anthony (R.I.) & Baker (Oregon). Sandford is to be Minister to Belgium. — Pleasant session, but these great men had no light to throw on the mysterious situation of affairs. Even Cameron professed to know nothing about Lincoln's plans & policy — an official white lie, of course, which nobody was expected to believe. They all predict that the Border States will slough off, Virginia first of all. Those States merely weaken & paralyze us. I begin to think they had better go — & make no long tarrying, — that Free States cannot dwell together in unity with Slaveholding States.

The talk about a strong & growing Union Party in Virginia & Kentucky is delusive. This so-called Union Party says, in substance, "If Gov^{t} will sit quite still while it's territory is sundered, it's flag insulted — if it will give up it's Forts, and let it's property be stolen & its revenues cut off by traitors & rebels, without resistance — *then* we will stay in the Union, at least until we change our minds. Otherwise hurra for Secession & the Confederate States of Slave-ownia!" On these terms, the Union is not worth saving.

March 21. We were blue in Wall St. Something must be done about our most injudicious tariff, lest the South get the better of us and absorb the commerce & imports of N.Y. & Boston.

I see no indications thus far of vigor or sagacity in the new Administration. There are vague rumors of a Proclamation that is to be issued within a few days, and that will produce a great effect. We shall see.

March 22. We generally predict to day that there will be no War after all.

Captn Lewis sends me a pamphlet by some man of Cincinnati, whose remedy for the National trouble is that the Constitution be just amended so as to legalize & protect Slaveholding in all the Free States. Of course that little improvement would settle everything comfortably. If not, why not?

April 5. No material change in public affairs, or if any for the worse. Secession fever certainly gaining in Virginia. Rumors of a projected out-break, or Revolutionary coup d'état at Richmond. A dash at Washington is again talked of, as likely to be tried. Then of course comes War — at once — and on what seems a tolerably plain case: bloodshed in an open rebellion against both State & Federal Authority. But would even this aggression stiffen up the spiritless money-worshipping North?

Strange the South ca'nt kick us into manliness & a little moderate wrath. Southerners rule us through our White Slaves of 5th Avenue & Wall St.

There are symptoms of a decisive move by the Administration. Great stir in Army & Navy. Governor's Island, Fort Hamilton & Brooklyn Navy Yard full of business. Troops moving — no one knows whither. Ships getting ready for Sea in hot haste & sailing with sealed orders — some say for Fort Pickens (Pensacola) others, for Fort Sumter. Abandonment of Fort Sumter is *not* determined on, according to present reports — & Pensacola is to be reinforced anyhow. Bellicose rumors abound to day. Col Keese & Col: Henry Scott were off early this morning, I hear. C. tells me they were very doleful & despondent half an hour or so at Dr Van Buren's "Thursday ev'g party". Forsyth, one of the "C.S.A." Commissioners, was expected, but was summoned to Washington by his colleagues yesterday aftn. — All this looks as if things were coming to a crisis.

Virginia will secede within three months. Amen. We cannot live together. Her dictatorial arrogance is unbearable. Let her go in peace, *if that be possible.*

April 6. Sat: — Ev'g Post 2d Edition says advices have been recd at Washington that Major Anderson has been notified by the circumambient traitors of Charleston to vacate Fort Sumter within 48 hours, or in default thereof to take the consequences. — 3d Edition says that *Firing has commenced.* May be so: may be not. Any newspaper rumor is probably a lie; the general presumption is agst it. But the S. Carolinians are doubtless advised of the stir & preparation here — and this may have precipitated the crisis. We shall not be long in suspense. The prevailing opinion to day has been, however, that the troops we are sending off from Governor's Island & Fort Hamilton are destined neither for *Sumter* nor *Pickens*, but for Texas — to strengthen the hands of Gov: Sam: Houston.

April 7. Sunday. Last ev'g's gunpowder news *not* confirmed. There are no despatches from below Va. *Wires are not working.* What may *that* mean?

April 8. Monday. Sunshiny but chill. With C.E.S. at Brooklyn Navy Yard this aft^{n}. A large force sailed on Saturday for parts unknown, but there is still great bustle & activity there, getting the Wabash &c ready for sea. Went on board the old North Carolina (receiving ship) & came off after an interesting two hours, convinced that *something* is about to be done or earnestly attempted at last.

The received rumor is that troops are to be concentrated in Texas, to cooperate with the deposed Govr Sam: Houston.

Another story is that this movement is agreed on by the Administration & the "Commissioners" from the insurgent States. Both dread collision & war. The U.S. forces are to repress the Comanches & Navajos that are already ravaging the Texas borders — and the other Savages that are yearning to assault Fort Pickens & Fort Sumter are to be kept cool by the great moral spectacle of Lincoln's army used not to crush rebellion but to protect the rebels. A very politic programme, in which I do not believe.

A third theory assumes that Anderson has offered to evacuate Fort Sumter, and that Pickens Beauregard & Jeff: Davis refuse to allow him to do so, without going thro' the forms of a surrender. These ships are to wait outside Charleston Harbor, send in a flag and ask to take off the garrison. If leave be refused they are to land their field artillery to take the rebel batteries in reverse, & proceed to extremities.

April 10. Wednesday. This morn'g's Tribune & Times announce positively, & as if by authority, that the fleet has gone to Charleston, & that *Fort Sumter is to be reinforced*. Then shall we soon hear stirring news. But is this force strong enough? It is only about 2000 men, & the talk has been that 20.000 were needed. Perhaps the Administration counts on a repulse as a tonic & stimulant to the North, but I trust there will be no repulse. God forbid that this effort — forced on the Country after long forbearance — to maintain the sanctity of law & the authority of Government, should be defeated.

April 11. Nothing from the Seat of War, (wherever that is) except a rumor that Jeff: Davis orders Charleston to make no opposition to the introduction of provisions into Sumter. A politic move, for everything depends on being *strictly right* on the particular issue in which the first blood is drawn, and many democrats & Border State men would say the South was wrong in refusing to allow the status in quo to be maintained by a supply of food to Anderson & his little force.

At Washington the militia of the district is being mustered & sworn in for active service, so Trouble is evidently anticipated in that quarter.

April 12. Friday. *War* has begun — unless my Extra Herald lies — & it's Charleston despatch is bogus. —

Busy down town. Motion for attachment agst Richardson came up before Clerke (fortunately not Sutherland) — Lord moving — & Bidwell for the purchaser. From appearances, the motion will be denied — perhaps on condition of our giving security till the Court of Appeals has disposed of the other branch of the case. Even that condition seems oppressive in a case so outrageous as this.

Walked up town with Gouv: Ogden & that wooden headed Dunscomb. The streets were vocal with newsboys — "Extry-a-Herald! Got the Bombardment of *Fort Sumter*!!" We concluded it was probably a *sell* and that we would not be sold, & declined all invitations to purchase for about four blocks. But we could not stand it longer — I sacrificed sixpence & read the news to Ogden — & that galvanized pumpkin Mr D. by the light of a corner gas lamp. The despatch is a column long — from Charleston. In substance to this effect. The Rebel batteries opened on Sumter "Twenty seven minutes after four" this morn'g. Major Anderson replied only at long intervals till 7 or 8 o'clock when he began firing vigorously. At 3 P.M. (date of telegram) he had produced no serious effect. "No men hurt" in the Rebel Batteries. No impression made on the "Floating Battery". Fort Sumter suffering much — "Breaches, to all appearance, are being made". The "Harriet Lane" in the offing — but no other government ships on hand. "Troops are pouring in" and "within an area of fifty miles, where the thunder of the Artillery can be heard, the scene is *Magnificently Terrible*". That magnificent & terrible sentence sounds as if it belonged to a genuine despatch from the South. Yet I doubt it's genuineness vehemently. I can hardly *hope* that the Rebels have been so foolish & thoughtless as to take the initiative in Civil War & bring matters to a Crisis. If so, they have put themselves in a horribly false position. The most frantic Virginian can hardly assert that this War is brought on by any attempt at "Coercion". —

April 13. Sat. Here begins a new chapter of my journal, entitled —

"WAR".

Exsurgat Deus et dissipentere inimici ejus, et
fugerunt qui oderunt eum a facie ejus. Amen!

This morning's papers confirmed last night's news — viz: that the Rebels opened fire at Sumter yesterday morning. During the day came successive despatches — *all one way.* Of course — for the Charleston telegraphs are wholly under Charleston control, & in addition to the local taste for brag & lying, there is an obvious motive for a high colored picture of damage done the Fort. It tends to prevent reinforcement by any supplementary expedition that might be extemporized if the parties appeared to be at all equally matched.

In substance the despatches say that firing ceased at 6 P.M. yesterday but shells continued to be thrown into the fort all night at intervals of twenty minutes. Cannonade resumed this morn'g with brilliant success. The fort on fire. "Flames bursting from the embrazures" — Raft outside & men passing up water. Great havoc among them. Two Explosions in the fort. Major A. "believed to be *gradually* (!) blowing it up". Nobody hurt in the rebel batteries. No impression made on that formidable battle-scow "the Floating Battery." "Major A has ceased firing." Then came a 4th Ed: of Ev'g Post, with a despatch that he has surrendered. This was while I was at N.Y. Club. On coming home I find E. in possession of a still later Herald Extra. The Ships are engaged with the batteries. (this we had earlier). Two are sunk. The rest are *shelling the City, which is on fire.* I take this last item to be invented, for the sake of stimulating wrath & fury in the Border States. To shell Charleston, the ships must have worked their way into the Harbor & passed Sumter. If so they must have silenced the batteries & been able to throw supplies into the Fort, which is hardly to be hoped. Had they done so, the object of the expedition would have been accomplished. And I doubt whether they would have fired on the City under any circumstances.

But that damnable little hornets' nest of Treason deserves to be shelled — It's a *political* Sodom.

G.A. dined here with Miss Rosalie. Hoffman came in thereafter. G. & I went off to N.Y. Club — where were a lot of men. The Charleston news generally discredited, except as to the single point that the siege has been opened. L[t] *Bankhead* says that the distance of the nearest battery is 1150 yards — (beyond breaching distance:) that the fort can stand a week's fire before it need reply: that the story of *fire* is absurd, there being little or no woodwork to burn, and that the whole narrative is absurd on it's face.

But people talk dubiously of the success of any attempt to land field artillery & take the rebel batteries in reverse.

Nothing much beside this for to day's journal. Till about 3 P.M. there was a furious S.E. storm of wind & rain. At about ½ past ten tonight a thundershower set in with most vivid lightning & heavy thunder, but no very heavy rain. Headache this morn'g — wh: made me late down town.

A despatch from Baltimore in to night's *Commercial* says that Charleston has telegraphed a heavy order for *Chloroform.* That looks as if there had been a few casualties among the traitors.

So Civil War is inaugurated at last. *God defend the Right.*

The Northern backbone is much stiffened already. Many who have stood up for "Southern rights" & complained of wrongs done the South now say that since the South has *fired the first gun*, they are ready to go all lengths in supporting Government. N.Y. Herald is non-committal this morn'g. It may well be upholding the Administration & denouncing the democratic party within a week. It takes naturally to eating dirt & it's own words (the same thing) — — — Would I were in *Sumter* to night, even with the chance of being forced to surrender (*70* men agst *7000*) & of being lynched thereafter by the Chivalry of Charleston. — The *seventy* will be as memorable as the "four hundred" of the Light Brigade at Balaklava, whatever be their fate.

April 14. Sunday. Fine day. Morning Herald announces *Surrender of Fort Sumter* & great jubilation in Charleston. To Tr: Ch: with E. Miss Rosalie & Johny. On our way back I made a detour to Tribune office. The whole story discredited there. Lots of private despatches quoted, inconsistent with surrender, & tending to shew there had been no serious fight. Mr S.B.R. dined with us. This evening Dr Rae & his pretty wife were here by appointment, with their two young friends from England. *Chaplin* seems a nice young fellow; the baronet rather slow & hard to entertain. There were also Mrs Peters & the D^r. M^r & Mrs Murray, M^r & Mrs Cameron, Hoffman, Miss Josephine Strong, Mrs Clymer, W. Graham, Jno Sherwood, Allen, Dr Lieber &c &c.

There is no doubt *Fort Sumter* has surrendered. Despatches rec^d by Mrs Anderson, Cottenet, & others, settle that point. But no reliable details of the transaction have reached us. If it be true, as Charleston telegrams assert, that after forty hours' firing "no one is hurt", *Punch* & the *Charivari* have an inviting topic for jokes at our expense.

People talk dubiously about Anderson, & ask whether he should have surrendered so soon. I *suppose* his orders were to make a fair show of resistance, and surrender at last to the overwhelming force arrayed against him. The Administration probably holds that his *eviction* will exasperate the North. His fort is of little or no value in a military point of view, for the harbor can be easily blockaded. It is especially difficult to reinforce & hold. It's abandonment sets free a large force that can be made far more available elsewhere.

From all I can learn, the effect of this on democrats, heretofore Southern & quasi-treasonable in their talk, has fully justified the sacrifice. I hear of Fra^s B. Cutting, & Walter C. — Hewitt, Lewis Rutherfurd, Judge Vanderpoel, & others of that type, denouncing rebellion & declaring themselves ready to go all lengths in upholding Government. If this class of men has been secured & converted to loyalty, the gain to the Country is worth ten Sumters. — *CAM.* heretofore strongly Southern in his talk, was declaring his readiness, this ev'g, to shoulder a musket in defence of *Washington*. *That* is the next point to be thought of. "He is true *Pope* who lives in the Vatican". It must be defended at any cost.

April 15. Monday. Events multiply. Pres[dt] is out with a proclamation calling for 75000 volunteers, & an Extra Session of Congress July 4th. It is said 200.000 men will be called out within a few days. Every man of them will be wanted before this game is lost & won. Change in public feeling marked & a thing to thank God for. We begin to look like a United North. Willy Duncan (!) says it may be necessary to hang Lincoln & Seward & Greeley hereafter, but our present duty is to sustain Government & Law, & give the South a lesson. The N.Y. Herald is in equilibrio to day, — just at the turning point. Tomorrow it will denounce Jeff: Davis as it denounced Lincoln a week ago. The Express is half traitorous & half in favor of energetic action agst traitors. The Journal of Commerce & the little Day-Book shew no signs of reformation yet, but though they are contemptible & without material influence for evil, the growing excitement against their treasonable talk, will soon make them more cautious in it's utterance. The Herald office has already been threatened with an attack.

Mayor Wood out with a "proclamation". He must still be talking. It is brief & commonplace, but winds up with a recommendation to everybody to obey the laws of the land. This is significant. The cunning scoundrel sees which way the Cat is jumping, & puts himself right on the record in a vague general way, giving the least possible offence to his allies of the Southern Democracy.

Courier of this morning devotes it's leading article to a ferocious assault on Major Anderson — as a *traitor* beyond Twiggs — & declares that he has been in collusion with the Charleston people all the time. This is wrong & bad. It is premature at least. There are suspicious features in our *reports* about his conduct, certainly. But these reports come from Charleston & are utterly unreliable. No man, reputed brave & honorable, should be thus publicly denounced on mere suspicion, or until facts are fully disclosed.

Expedition to Governor's Island this morning. Ellie & I. C.E.S. & wife, Dan: Messenger, Chrystie, Miss Kate Fearing, Tom Meyer & one or two more. Officer of the day was L[t] Webb (of Maine) whose guests we were. He treated us most hospitably, & had out the Band — playing an hour or two for our delectation. It's programme included that jolliest of tunes

"Dixies Land" & Hail Columbia. We took off our hats while the latter was played. Everybody's patriotism is rampant & demonstrative now. About 300 recruits on the island, mostly quite raw. I discoursed one of them, an honest-looking simple minded boy from somewhere near Rochester, probably some small farmer's son. "He had voted for Abe Lincoln & as there was going to be trouble, he thought he might as well *fight* for Abe Lincoln" so he enlisted two weeks ago. — "Guessed they were going to get some hard knocks when they went down South — but then he had always kind o' wanted to see the world, — that was one reason why he listed." — Great activity on the Island. Guns & all manner of warlike munitions & apparatus are being shipped — generally for Pensacola, consigned to my old acquaintance Capt[n] Vogdes.

We did not leave the Island till near four o'clock.

April 16. Tuesday. A fine storm of wind & rain all day. The Conversion of the N.Y. Herald is complete. It rejoices that Rebellion is to be put down, and is delighted with Civil War because it will so stimulate the business of N.Y. and all this is what "we" (the Herald to wit) have been vainly preaching for months. This impudence of old J.G. Bennett's is too vast to be appreciated at once. You must look at it & meditate over it for some time (as at Niagara & S[t] Peters) before you can take in it's immensity. His capitulation is a set off against the loss of *Sumter*. He's a discreditable ally for the North — but when you see a rat leaving the enemy's ship for your own, you overlook the offensiveness of the vermin for the sake of what its movement indicates. This brazen old scoundrel was hooted up Fulton St: yesterday aft[n] by a mob — and the police interfered to prevent it from sacking his printing office. Though converted, one can hardly call him penitent. S[t] Paul did not call himself the Chief of the Apostles, & brag of having been a Christian from the first.

Thence to *N.Y. Club*. Our talk was of War. Subscribed to a fund for equipment of 12th Regiment, & put down my name for a projected Rifle corps — but I fear my nearsightedness is a grave objection to my adopting that arm. — I hear that Major

Burnside has surrendered his Treasurership of Illinois Central R.R. & posted down to R.I. to assume command of volunteers from that state. — Telegram that 2500 Mass: volunteers are quartered in Faneuil Hall, awaiting orders.

GOD SAVE THE UNION, AND
CONFOUND IT'S ENEMIES. AMEN.

April 17. There was a slight out-break here to day. I was sitting in my office at three o'clock, when I heard unwonted sounds in Wall Street, & looking out, saw a straggling column of men running toward the East River. My first notion was that they were chasing a runaway horse, but they soon became too numerous to be engaged in that. They halted in front of the *Journal of Commerce office*, and filled the street densely for about a block. There were outcries, which I could not distinctly hear, for a minute, and then the American Flag was hung out from a window, and the crowd sent up a cheer that stirred one's blood a little, & the surface of the black mass was suddenly all in motion with waving hats. Then a line of policemen came down the street on a dog-trot, and the Crowd thereupon moved promptly up Wall St. again, cheering lustily.

They were mostly decently dressed people but with a sprinkling of laboring men. — I understand they paid a like domiciliary visit to the Express — the Day-book — & the Daily News — requiring each to put up the Flag. They intended to call on the N.Y. Hotel, it is said, but Cranston was forewarned, & the American flag was flying from it's roof as I came up town. I hear of no violence to persons or property, not even a broken window. It's a most mild form of mob-law. But such demonstrations are to be discouraged — & closely watched.

This looks unlike the threatened "hanging of Republican leaders".

With Geo. F. Allen & Prof^r Lieber to night, at Allen's — (Com: on College Course) — Afterwards for an hour at N.Y. Club — Chas Clark, Jem Ruggles, Pendleton, J.J. Townsend, G.C.A. & others. Military ardor continues unabated. The 7th Reg^t is under orders to be prepared for a summons to Washington at any moment. It expects the order on Friday or Saturday. — There is reason that the sympathizers of Virginia contemplate a dash at the Capital. I predict that a battle will be fought for it's possession — & also that Government will have 300.000 men under arms, within ninety days. — Drums in the 4th Av:. Qu: from Mass:?

April 18. Thursday. Fine day — drizzly ev'g. Journalizing is a serious job just now. We are living a month of common life every day. One general proposition to begin with. My habit is to despond & find fault — but the attitude of N.Y. & the whole North at this time is magnificent. Perfect unanimity, earnestness, & readiness to make every sacrifice for the support of Law & National life. Especially impressive after our long forbearance & vain efforts to conciliate — our readiness to humble ourselves for the sake of peace. — Still, I expect to hear only of *disaster* for a long while yet.

The morn'g papers give us Jeff: Davis' proclamation of Reprisals on Northern Commerce — letters of marque are to be issued to any piratical Spaniard who will accept them. Very well. Then we shall have no scruples about retaliating on "Southern property" — which is peculiar in possessing a capacity for being invited to go away — and legs to take itself off, and arms wherewith to use such implements as may aid it in so doing — if opposed. Davis' proposed privateers can take their prizes into no civilized port. They will have to sink burn & destroy. Every maritime power in Christendom will make common cause against them & his Algerine Confederacy.

With Bidwell on reference in Carter v. Taylor. Little progress. Went to the Hall. The Massachusetts $Regim^t$ (wh: arrived here last night) was marching down — on it's way to Washington. Immense crowd — immense cheering. My eyes filled with tears & I was half choked — in sympathy with the contagious excitement. God be praised for the unity of feeling here! It is beyond — very far beyond — anything I hoped for. If it only *last, we are safe.*

The National Flag flying everywhere. Every cart-horse decorated. It occurred to me that it would be a good thing to hoist it on the tower of Trinity — (an *unprecedented* demonstration, but these are unprecedented times.) Not only good in itself, as a symbol of the Sympathy of the Church Catholic with all movements to suppress privy conspiracy & sedition — but a politic move for Trinity Church at this memorable hour of excitement. Somewhat to my surprise, Gen[l] Dix, Cisco, Skidmore, Swift, & *Gouv: Ogden* cordially concurred with me & signed a note to D[r] Berrian asking his permission to hoist it.—Posted up to the Rector's in Varick St but he was out. Again at four — but he was not very well & could not see me. So I left the note & announced that I should call tomorrow morning for an answer. I expected a negative answer, supported by platitudes of fogyism, easily to be imagined. But while I was at dinner came a note from the Rector, who "very cheerfully" complies with our request. Hurra for D[r] Berrian! *His* consent to this is the strongest indication yet of the intensity of our National feeling just now. May we dare to hope *it will last*?

Ellie dined at her father's. I dined here with Miss Rosalie & the children. Jem Ruggles — (Corporal or Sergeant in the 7th Regiment) received an appointment on "Gen[l]" Hall's staff a week ago, & had intended to resign out of the regiment & be henceforth Judge Advocate with the rank of Major. But the *Seventh* is ordered to Washington, & he has wisely & rightly got leave of absence as staff-officer & decided to go South, in the ranks. I am proud of my brick of a brother-in-law.

After dinner — at 8 o'clock — to Fifth Avenue Hotel. It's halls crowded. Excited individual mounts a pile of trunks & says "Gentlemen, some of us are going to the Brevoort House to call on *Major Anderson*. Who'll go with us?" — General yell & rush. — Excited individual proceeds — "I saw Major A. this aft[n]. He stands by the National Flag, while it floats, & will go to it's funeral when it's buried." Universal roar. Then a tramp down 5th Av: to Brevoort House, (cor: 5th Av. & 8th St.) Cheers for Anderson & groans for Ja[s] Watson Webb of the Courier & Enquirer — Anderson was not there — was dining at W[m] H. Aspinwall's in University Place. Tramp thither thro' the drizzle — but he had gone away a few minutes before & was at Dr Metcalf's in Fourteenth St. Another trot (with an attempt to sing "the Star Spangled Banner", but the musical training of this community is imperfect.) — I fear the advent of this roaring mob frightened the ladies of D[r] Metcalf's household, a little. I saw them peering through the parlor windows. But Major Anderson was not there — & I abandoned his pursuit & betook myself to N.Y. Club.

He & his command arrived here to day in the *Baltic.* I saw her come up the bay from the battlements of Trinity Ch: tower, where were Rev: Ogilby, Cutler the organist, & several others. Strong feeling for Anderson & against Col: Webb for his scandalous attack on A. in the Courier. The Mob that cheered for Anderson to night groaned savagely against the Courier. It's said that if Webb shew himself on the platform of next Saturday's Union meeting as one of it's Vice Presidents, he will be dragged off.

At N.Y. Club much talk & many rumors. Virginia Convention has passed a Secession ordinance, NOT to be submitted to Popular Vote. If so, it has transcended it's powers, & Government can interfere & sustain the strong Union party that exists in that state, without any offence to the sensitive nerves of State Sovereignty. It will be upholding at once the laws of Virginia & of the Union. I hope this report may be true. — Rumors that the Secession party has seized the Harper's Ferry Arsenal — that bridges are destroyed & rails torn up South of Philadelphia — that the Mass: regiment will be unable to pass thro' Baltimore — &c &c — seem authentic but I doubt them.

April 19. Friday. Busy this morn'g in pursuit of a Flag for Trinity Ch: steeple. Hunted thro' the city with Vinton in vain — went off on my own account & secured one at last (20 by 40) from *Rob*[t] *B. Minturn*, who was most kind & obliging. He went to one of his ships with me, & insisted on sending up riggers to help Secor's people hoist it. — At half past two it went up — the Chimes saluting it with Hail Columbia Yankee Doodle & Old Hundred, & a crowd in Wall St. & Broadway cheering. Higbee Vinton & Ogilby led the cheers. The hoisting out of the flag — the clank of the bells — and the enthusiastic cheering, gave me a new sensation. I am amazed by the strong feeling — of gratification strengthened by *surprise* — that this little flourish called out. The solution is, probably, that the ideas of Church & State — Religion & Politics — have been practically separated so long that people are specially delighted with any manifestation of the Church's sympathy with the State & recognition of our National life, on any fitting occasion. This flag was a symbol of the truth that the Church is no esoteric organization — no private Soul-Saving Society — that it has a position to take in every great public National Crisis, and that it's position is important. Some sense of this truth must have been at the bottom of the many emphatic expressions I heard this aft^{n} (from strangers) of approval of the flag raising on Trinity Spire. E.g. "Are they really going to hoist the flag on the Steeple, Sir? — Well, now, *I* tell *you*, that's the *biggest thing* that's been done in N.Y. in my time!"

Thereafter up town with G.C.A. — Broadway crowded. Established ourselves in an upper loft of a Carpet store near Spring St. — After long waiting & watching, the *7th Regt* appeared, far up B'way, a bluish steel gray light on the blackness of the dense mob that filled the Street — like the livid ashiness of the clouds near the horizon just before the thundershower breaks. As they came nearer & passed by, the roar of the crowd was grand & terrible. It drowned the brass of the regimental band.

G.A. dined here — Ev'ng spent in listening to Scharfenberg & a dozen "professional" people rehearsing Haydn's lovely Mass N° 2 for our next "*Concert*."

Thereafter to N.Y. Club. There has been serious disturbance in Baltimore. Regiments from Penn: or Massachusetts assailed by a mob — that was repulsed by shot & steel.

Reports to night indicate that the riot is quelled, and that Gov^{t} troops can pass safely thro' Maryland: that rails are not taken up between Baltimore & Washington.

Rumor that Virginia has imprisoned *Clemens* & hanged *Botts.* (A Secessionist joker might say that the Mère of Presidents is cured of her Botts at last.) Also that *Harper's Ferry Arsenal* has been evacuated & burnt. (Forgot to credit the *Botts* joke to G.C.A.) — Every indication that Virginia has gone utterly frantic — her Union men quenched, & nothing to be hoped in that quarter, unless possibly in the Western Counties.

It's a notable coincidence that the first blood in this great struggle is drawn by Massachusetts men on the anniversary of Lexington. This is a continuation of the war that Lexington opened — a war of democracy against Oligarchy — God defend the Right, and confound all traitors — Amen and Amen.

Mr S.B.R. here to night, just after an interview with Major Anderson, whose quiet dignity & unassuming manner impress him much. Anderson attends the great Union meeting tomorrow, when the flags of Moultrie & Sumter will be displayed.

April 20. Sat: — Another intense day. Morning news — blockade of Southern ports proclaimed. Gloomy reports from the South. R.R. bridges & telegraph wires *down* from Philad[a] to Washington. The 7th Reg[t] & other troops at Philad[a] unable to move — Baltimore mob furious — & determined that troops shall not go through. No despatches from Washington. People talked darkly of it's being attacked before our reinforcements come to the rescue, and every one said we must not be surprised by news that Lincoln & Seward & all the Administration are prisoners. We feel a little better tonight, but without any very definite reason.

Could do nothing in Wall St. — though many things there require attention. Walked up town at two. Broadway crowded & more crowded as one approached U. Square. — Large companies of recruits in citizen's dress parading up & down, cheered & cheering. Small mobs round the headquarters of the regiments that are going to Washington, staring at the sentinel on duty. Every other man woman & child bearing a flag or decorated with a cockade. Flags from almost every building. The City seems to have gone suddenly wild & crazy.

The Union Mass-meeting was *an Event*. Few assemblages have equalled it in numbers & unanimity. To night's Extra says there were 250.000 present. That must be an exaggeration. But the multitude was enormous. All the area bounded by 14th & 17th Sts, Broadway & 4th Av: was *filled*. In many places it was densely packed, & nowhere could one push his way without difficulty. This great *Amœba* (to speak microscopically) sent off its *pseudopods* far down Broadway & 14th St., & in every cross street. There were several stands for orators, & scores of little speechifying ganglia besides — from carts windows & front stoops. Anderson appeared & was greeted with roars that were tremendous to hear. The crowd — or some of them — & the ladies & gentlemen who occupied the windows & lined the housetops all round U. Square sang "the Star Spangled Banner" — & the people generally hurraed a voluntary after each verse. — Mayor Wood — the sagacious scoundrel — committed himself by a straight forward speech. Rev: old Gardner Spring, who opened one of the many *centres* of the meeting, "with prayer", came out soundly & manfully in a little introductory allocution. In substance, "Many of you know my opinion about issues heretofore existing between the North & South. That opinion is unchanged. But the controversy is now between Government & Anarchy, Law & Rebellion". —

Major Anderson spent an hour at Mr Ruggles' before I got there. Ellie & Miss Rosalie are enthusiastic about him.

After dinner I went to *Sharpe's* (cor: 8th St. & Broadway) to attend a meeting, got up by young Nat: Prime & other N.Y. Club men to organize a volunteer Corps for instant training in drill & discipline, & for such further action as the case may require. — About 70 enrolled themselves, & many more will come in. The feeling shewn was earnest & healthy.

April 21. Sunday. Fine spring day. With Ellie Miss Rosalie & Johny to Trinity Church. Drove down Bowery, B'way being packed full of people. E. was suffering from headache & had to leave Ch: during service, taking Miss Rosalie with her.

Major Anderson was there — with his quiet self possessed intelligent look — & penetrating eyes. People crowded about him after service; & tho' *I* should have been glad to be presented, I was disinclined to bore a brave man & increase the pains & penalties of heroism.

The Epistle for the Day was a coincidence. The Lesson (beginning with 9th verse of 3d Chap: of Joel) yet more appropriate. It was electrifying. — "Prepare War: Wake up the Mighty Men: let all the Men of War draw near . . . . . let the "*weak say, I am strong* . . . . Beat your plowshares into swords . . . Multitudes, multitudes in the Valley of Decision for the Day of the Lord is near in the Valley of Decision . . . . Egypt shall be a desolation & Edom shall be a desolate Wilderness . . . . *because they have shed innocent blood in their land.*" The Lesson would have been yet more germain to the present distress, had it commenced a verse or two earlier. "And they have cast lots for my people, and *sold a girl for wine, that they might drink.*"

Walked up town with Johny, thro' the crowd. At Leonard St. or thereabouts, we met *one* of our regiments marching down Broadway, to take steamship for Washington. At Canal St. we were told two others had turned off there from Broadway. I had taken it for granted the men we saw were the *3* regiments that set off to day. If not, we have sent off some four thousand men. Of those I saw perhaps a third were unarmed & in citizen's dress, perfectly raw recruits. But it's believed they can be equipped & armed when they reach Washington. Arms have been withdrawn from Harper's Ferry during the last month, & transferred to Carlisle Barracks. Another Massachusetts regiment is said to have passed thro' the City early this morn'g, & yet another to have arrived here at 7 P.M. — Hurra for the Old Bay State! She is first in the field in 1861 as she was in 1776. *Boston* is reported in white heat over the murder of Massachusetts soldiers by Baltimore *Plug-Uglies.* Gov[r] Andrews' despatch to the Mayor of Baltimore, "praying" that their bodies may be laid out — packed in ice — and "tenderly" sent to Boston, is a model specimen of condensed Telegraphic composition. Nothing could be better.

It seems settled to night that our Seventh Regiment has got to Annapolis, by steamboat from Philad[a] or Havre de Grace. — It must then march some 30 miles across Country before it can report at Washington. I discredit the rumor of a telegram this ev'g that they are at Bladensburg — almost within rifle-cannon range of Washington.

April 22. Monday. Nothing tangible to day, except the report that a special Messenger from the Pres[dt] has reached Philad[a] with instructions to the Gov: of Penn[a], & with the statement that the Capital is considered secure at least agst a coup-de-main, until the Northern reinforcements arrive. This agent got thro' Maryland with difficulty, disguised as a Methodist preacher. All telegraph wires are cut & railroad bridges broken between Philad[a] & Washington. The North & it's millions are cut off from their capital by the mob of Baltimore. That city seems in absolute anarchy. It should receive a severe lesson. When the first indispensable point of reinforcing Washington is attained — the *next* will be to secure our line of communications. I trust the R.R. line will be then promptly repaired, & held — and that Baltimore will be told that so many thousand Northern troops will march through her streets on such a day — and that if they are molested, they will withdraw until Fort McHenry shall have wiped out the City — & then resume their march.

The position of the 7th Reg[t] not yet ascertained. It is probably in Washington before this.

Hard at work this morn'g over organization of our proposed *Corps*. Meeting of the Bar at 3 wh: I could not attend — for there was a special meeting of Sav'gs Bank Trustees. Something a little like a *run*, and authority wanted to sell stocks. I hear the Bar meeting was large & enthusiastic, and subscribed $25.000 to uphold Gov^{t}. — To night an adjourned meeting at *Thorpe's* of the proposed Volunteers association. Great Crowd, unfortunately — & every thing going wrong. A day lost at least. Every thing deferred to an adjourned meeting tomorrow night, when the question of *fusion* with another organization — got up by Lloyd Aspinwall — is to be considered. — Aug^{s} Craven makes a wretched chairman. Everybody has motions — & amendments — & questions of order — & a few remarks to make in support of his views. *Organization* by a mob of 300 is impossible — consistently with Liberty of Speech. — To the N.Y. Club thereafter, where Prime & I did an hour's work in *the* Cause — thence to Vth Av: Hotel — & home. No news.

Barlow married Miss Arabella Griffith at St Paul's Chapel Sat: ev'g, left her at the church door, & went to Washington yesterday.

I have done this People injustice in my thoughts. We are *not* utterly corrupt & mercenary.

April 23. Tuesday. Hot day. Still without reliable accounts of the 7th Regiment. The latest report is that they are in Annapolis — & unable to move, but protected by the guns of the Constitution & the Naval School. This seems authentic. It is said there has been "some fighting" there. The destruction of the Norfolk Navy Yard confirmed — & two or more fine ships have been scuttled or burned. Unavoidable, I suppose.

Broadway packed full as I walked down town & up again. The 79th & 8th Regiments marched down at about four. — The former is the Irish Regiment, Col: Corcoran's — & there was a large infusion of Biddies in the crowd — "sobbing & sighing." Both regiments looked as well as one has a right to expect of levies raised on such short notice. A large portion in citizens dress & without arms — but seemingly respectable material. The uniformed companies looked & marched well. At cor: of Rector St. & Broadway I saw part of another Reg^{t} (I forget it's N^{o}) raised by that notable Aldermanic bully, Bill Wilson. They did'nt clearly know what regiment they belonged to, but said they were "Billy Wilson's crowd". — A desperate looking set. It's said that when they were told they were to have not only the regulation arms but revolvers & bowie knives too, they danced & yelled with delight. "We can fix that Baltimore crowd! Let 'em bring along their pavin' stones — we boys is *sociable* with pavin' stones!" —

After breakfast to J. Cooper Lord's, across the Square, where the joint Com: — of Lloyd Aspinwall's cavalry & Artillery project — & our infantry project — met to confer — on the proposed Constitution. Beside our Com: there were L.A., Dan D. Lord, Potter, & others of that party. We were harmonious enough. They stuck me in the chair — & our constitution was approved with a trifling alteration — for the better.

The rest of the morn'g spent in the same business — conferring with Prime, Ellery Anderson, Talmage & others. — After dinner to adjourned meeting at Delmonico's. Well attended — & it's action business-like & without speechifications or much parliamentary red-tapism. We declined a fusion with L. Aspinwall's horse & heavy guns — on the ground that time will be gained if each perfect it's own organization separately, & then come together on terms of equality — instead of spending time on debates about matters of detail. Reasonable enough — but A. went off in a slight huff. I know him little, but he seems rather weak vain & dictatorial. — We also ordered 400 Enfield rifles — the order to go out by tomorrow's steamer, for they cannot be got here — & adjourned to tomorrow night for business & (thank God) for DRILL — at last — if drill masters can be secured in time. — Adjourned at half past ten, & hurried up to Gen: Dix's (20th St.) where was a small masculine gathering "to meet Major Anderson". They were at supper, & beginning to thin out, but the Major had not gone, and I had the great pleasure of being presented — & of saying to him, in a bungling way what every loyal man that meets him wants to say. Discoursed also, D.D. Field, M.H. Grinnell, R.B. Minturn, Judge Roosevelt (now a renegade proselyte from secessionism & treason) Dr Higbee — Dr Ogilby — &c.

Thence to N.Y. Club. G.C.A. — Chrystie — Tom Meyer — Walter Cutting — Thouron — &c &c —

One's frightfully tempted to hint to men like Walter C. that but for the talk of their party five months ago about Northern sympathy with Southern treason, this would never have come to pass. But it would be ungenerous. They are loyal now. Thank God for it & that the North is united. Let the past be forgotten.

Everyone's future has changed in these six months last past. This is to be a terrible ruinous War — and a War in which *the Nation cannot succeed.* It can never subjugate these savage millions of the South. It must make peace at last with the barbarous communities off it's Southern frontier. I was prosperous & well off last Novr. I believe my assets to be reduced fifty per cent, at least. But I hope I can still provide wholesome training for my three boys. With that patrimony they can fight out the battle of Life for themselves. Their mother is plucky & can stand self denial. I clearly see that this is a most severe personal calamity to me — but I welcome it cordially — for it has shewn that I belong to a community that is brave & generous — & that the City of New York is not sordid & selfish.

"Hear *THIS*, ye old men, and give ear all ye inhabitants of the land. Hath *this* been in your days, or even in the days of your Fathers?" — New York lavishly tendering life & money to sustain a Righteous cause — & without one dissenting voice from 49th St. to the Battery! —

In the Park (the City Hall Park) a line of light wooden *barracks* is being rapidly run up — from its lower apex, opposite Astor House, to Murray St. — A *camp* was being laid out this morn'g on the Battery. This is for the 5th Reg^{t} (I believe) to which Henry Fearing belongs.

April 24. Wednesday. Anxious day. There were early reports, most authentic & indisputable, that our 7th Reg^{t} had reached Washington. But by two o'clock they were distrusted, and the afternoon papers announced the 7th — with a Mass: Reg^{t} — "cooped up" in Annapolis, short of provisions & contemplating a march across country to Washington. It was horrible to think of those young gentlemen exposed to the guerilla (qu: Gorilla?) fire of Marylanders & their Virginian allies along a line of 30 miles, and to remember that all wounded men & prisoners would be in the hands of men like Comanches or revolted Sepoys. Walked up town with misgivings that a terrible calamity might be at hand.

Mr Derby — Mr S.B.R. & G.C.A. dined here, & letter came in from *Jem* R. dated at Annapolis, yesterday, 5½ P.M. The 7th in good spirits & eager for a brush with the Rebels. Their voyage was a bore, but not so bad as it might have been. Provisions not first rate. People of Annapolis not positively hostile. Men have not taken off their clothes since they left N.Y. Reports of hostile parties outside Annapolis prepared to dispute the road to Washington. Nobody knows whether they are to go ahead, or wait for reinforcements. The Regt wants to march at once. The *Baltic* said to be just coming up with reinforcements. That's the substance of the letter.

To night there is a telegram to Sim: Draper that the 7th *is in Washington*, & all well. But in these days I am sceptical about telegrams.

After dinner to the *old* N.Y. Club House (cor: Astor Pl: & B'dway) where we began drill at last. Got on well — & the meeting was satisfactory. Our association has grown to near 200. I've found out what "*Eyes Right*" means. I've long wanted to know the purport of that familiar but mystic phrase.

April 25. The policy of Govt seems defining & developing itself hopefully.

At 3½ attended a meeting of our professional brethren called to organize a school or club for drill & discipline. Met at an office 10 Wall St. *Augs W. Clason* (!) chairman. I came by invitation, to expound the nature of our association — in order that the meeting might consider the question of an alliance therewith. I did so — & replied to sundry interpellations & the matter was referred to a Com: to confer with us & report.

Our "N.Y. Rifles" met — 7½ — at rooms hired for the ev'g — a loft in 814 B'way. It was crowded, so two squads adjourned to the old club house cor: Astor Place where we were drilled more than two hours. Everybody awkward, but earnest & diligent. Then we marched back. I was solemnly elected Presdt of the Association till our Military Commandant shall be chosen, & got thro' my Duties decently well, I believe; keeping the mob of men in tolerable order, though all were on their feet, having nothing but the floor to sit down on.

April 26. Friday. No authentic official reliable statement even yet that our 7th Reg[t] & other reinforcements have reached Washington, but it is generally believed they have got there safely.

N.Y. Rifles from 7½ to 10½. Met at our new rooms, hired for a month, in the new building (Henry Mason's) cor: Broadway & 4th St. My squad of 100 or thereabouts, was marched to Washington Parade Ground, where we were drilled & marched by "Capt[n] Levy", a very efficient & authoritative drill officer, for an hour & a half. I confess myself tired & footsore.

After drill to N.Y. Club awhile & then home — 11½ P.M.

No special news to day. There are people who say there will be no fighting after all — & that the South will collapse when it discovers that we are united & in earnest. I think otherwise.

April 27. Sat: — Fine day. Slightly tired, after another hard ev'g's drill. "N.Y. Rifles" met again at 7½. An hour spent in business — chiefly in organizing *squads* (7 in all). Each chose its squadmaster, & then drew for *letters*. My squad drew letter D. I nominated it's master, a son of Rev: D[r] Ogilby's & a very nice spirited young fellow — who seems much gratified by this promotion. Other business done — I was in the Chair — or rather standing *on* it — and bellowed myself hoarse. When we got through with this we took to drill again. Capt[n] Levy marched us into Washington Square once more — & we faced right & left & marked time & executed sundry strategic evolutions with more or less coherency.

The *Seventh* has undoubtedly reached Washington in safety. That seems settled at last.

Saw H. Binney J[r] this morn'g — convalescing from a low typhoid fever of 40 days, & on his way to Providence & farther North for a restorative holiday. He reports the National spirit in Philad[a] no less earnest than in N.Y.

Here the flag is on every public building — every store — every private house almost. The roof of N[o] 74 East 21st St. is to be honored by a flagstaff & a big flag next Monday. The supply of bunting has been far short of the demand — and the *stars & stripes* multiply slowly but steadily. The example set by Trinity

Church on 19th inst. has been followed. The steeple, tower, or pediment, of every church building, almost, displays the National colors and symbolizes the sympathy of the Church Catholic (& of the Church dissenting & schismatic —) with Law & Order & National Life.

After drill, to N.Y. Club for half an hour, & walked home with G.C.A. & C.E.S.

Army & Navy officers (Virginians mostly) who are resigning their commissions just now, most indignantly censured, & even by men like Walter Cutting. Their resignations should not be accepted: they should be put under arrest & tried for their lives by Courts-martial as spies & traitors.

April 28. Sunday. Doubtful showery weather. At Trinity Church Vinton preached a very virile sermon: the best of his that I have heard. Special prayers were read, set forth by Bp Potter. Have not seen them in print, but they sounded well — especially the second — for the troops who have left the State, modelled on the prayer for persons gone to sea. My nerves must be weak — for my eyes filled so full that I was glad my face was hid. The Ladies' Committee of the Parish (on lint & bandages) was announced, and the three members from Trinity Church proclaimed from the pulpit viz: Mrs Dr Ogilby Ellie & Mrs John Astor.

Into Vestry room after service. Vinton tells me poor old Bp Onderdonk is near his end — dropsy of the pericardium having set in: — and that application had been made to Bishop Brownell, (the senior Bishop,) to remove his suspension, which was refused. Perhaps on the ground that the authority of the senior Bishop to remove it is not clear. At another time poor Onderdonk's death would create a little sensation, but it will attract no notice just now. It's a bad time for notabilities to die. D.D. Barnard's departure a day or two since is forgotten already.

While I was with Vinton an old fellow came in dressed in a shabby half-naval uniform. He was an American of near 50, who might have been a mechanic or a common sailor. He introduced himself as one of "the Naval Brigade" — (got up by Ex Lieut: W.A. Bartlett — of "diamond wedding" notoriety) — & said he was off in a day or two, & "could'nt go without coming in to the old Church to say his prayers." — Thought a great deal "of the Old Church, because it had always been neutral & had kept out of the muss till the time came to speak out — & then it had spoken out on the right side & hysted the flag the first of any on 'em". — Then came in a young fellow belonging to the Firemen's "Zouave" regiment I believe, who had sat near us & whom I had remarked for the accuracy & seeming earnestness with which he united in the choral responses. He looked at first like a Soaplock — only quite *clean* — & his attire was most plebeian. But on closer inspection, his mouth forehead & eye were good, & he was a sturdy lump of bone & sinew with whom one would rather avoid a tussle. Vinton recognized him as a parishioner & they bade each other good bye very kindly — Vinton bestowing a solemn benediction on each of these men, which they received reverently.

To night M[r] Derby here — Charley Day — M. Hoffman — and for a season G.C.A.

Not much news. Reaction in Maryland strengthening itself rapidly. The leaders in that State want to rebel & to have Jeff: Davis to rule over them, but are terrified by the great unanimous rising of the North, & by the certainty that Baltimore will be *razed* if necessary. No wonder they are scared. I look with awe on the National movement here in N.Y. & through all the Free States. After our late discords, it seems supernatural. "The Earth was without form & void & Darkness was upon the face of the deep. And the Spirit of God moved upon the face of the Waters" [N.B. I cannot write those words without thinking of Haydn's music in "the Creation"] — and God "has *visited* & redeemed his people" from utter servitude to money making, from fatal partizan division, and is creating I believe & trust a great Nation out of a sordid Mud-Chaos.

I hear of no exceptions to the general fervor of loyalty in this State. But G.C.A. brings from M[rs] Christine Griffin reports of individual instances of dissent at Newport R.I., & how they were received. — E.g. Rev: L.P.W. Balch undertook to improve the service last Sunday by praying "for the *Presidents of the United States*", and then proceeded to preach a sermon in favor of rebellion. His congregation rose up — & people said "Stop that" — "No", & the like. He went on however, whereupon certain of his vestry walked up the aisle, lugged him out of the pulpit,

& marched him out of church. — "Poke" Wright called at M[rs] Lawrence's, (the widow of Do'nt Give Up the Ship Lawrence) & found that elderly lady scraping lint with a carving knife, & her sweet little grand-daughter, Miss Mary Griffin, making up an American flag. Wright said some flippant irreverence about the flag, whereupon the grand-mamma told him no one should speak with disrespect in *her* house of the banner under which her husband had fought & died — charged on him with her carving knife, & drove him out with directions not to call again. Whereupon, being in the street, he was seized by certain chance passengers who had witnessed his expulsion, & was required to go down on his knees, & hurra for the Flag, waved by pretty little Miss Mary from the front window. This incident may be funny — but it signifies nothing — for *Wright* is notoriously a donkey, & habitually affects a silly dissent from every prevailing sentiment. — Also W[m] Beach Lawrence has had his nose pulled by one Kinsley for talking sympathy with S. Carolina. That is satisfactory, if true. His respectable & wealthy nose has been saving up for that experience, these 20 years.

A portion of the 5th Reg[t] that has been encamped on the Battery sailed on the Kedar this morn'g. Henry Fearing goes with them, as quartermaster I believe.

With the 7th went one *Bostwick*, a kinsman of G.C.A.'s. His wife has just been prematurely confined — of a first child — (her confinement brought on by distress & anxiety about her husband —) & is raving in puerperal mania about war & battle & the Country & the Flag. This is a little specimen of the first instalment of the tragedies of Civil War. On which party rests it's fearful responsibility? Which is guilty of *this* household sorrow & distress? If it be the North, let us repent in sackcloth & concession. But if it be the South, let us treat Southerners as traitors & destroyers of domestic peace deserve, & talk no more about "high-toned gentlemen" & honest differences of opinion.

April 29. Monday. Fine day. Busy in Wall St. Saw a letter from Jem Ruggles written in the Senate Chamber on the desk of a seceded Georgian Senator. He writes in the best spirits. Indited a letter to him, & sent him on a couple of cases of claret. Some 30 ladies, M[rs] Peters, M[rs] Alfred Schermerhorn, Miss Lizzy

Clark, M[rs] Parkyn (who was Miss Fanny Rogers) & I know not who all beside, met here to make what they call "Havelock caps" for the Seventh. — i.e. white coverings for the military cap & for the back of the neck — as a protection against heat. To night E. & Miss Rosalie at work on the same business in the front parlor, while the Keltic handmaidens of the house plied their needles in the Blue room.

On my way up town saw the "Fire Brigade of Zouaves" on their march to the steamer, escorted by the whole Fire Department. This is Col: Ellsworth's regiment, about 1100 strong, armed with Sharpe's Rifles & revolvers. They are a rugged set, a little above Billy Wilson's corps in social status, generally men & boys who belong to Target Companies & are great in a plug-muss. They were coming down Chatham St. & turning up Broadway. At the Astor House they halted & received a Flag. M[rs] J.J. Astor had presented them with another. I got on top of an omnibus & inspected them. The crowd was immense & the cheering uproarious. These young fellows march badly, but they will fight hard if judiciously handled. As a regiment of the line they will be weak, but they are the very men to deal with the mob of Baltimore.

After dinner, drilled severely for two hours & more — perspiring & blundering, but making some little progress. The "N.Y. Rifles" prosper & receive large & steady accessions.

Laurence Williams is in town, & has been here twice to day, but I have failed to see him. He is on his way to Columbus, with secret orders. Ellie & Miss Rosalie tell me I have great influence over him, & want me to talk to him about the question of resigning. He tells them tonight "he has no intention of resigning". Perhaps not — but let us wait sixty days & see where he stands then. It's a severe test of his fidelity. Col: Lee gone — all his relatives at Arlington & elsewhere looking coldly on him as a traitor to Virginia while he holds his U.S. Commission. If I see him before he leaves town tomorrow, I must refer him to Schiller's *Max Piccolomini* as a leading case in support of loyalty.

April 30. Laurence Williams here at breakfast time, and dined with us. He is very unhappy, but declares he has no intention of resigning. Growls & carps at the Administration (but all army & navy men do that always) and is plainly dissatisfied uncertain & unsettled. Naturally enough, poor fellow, with his unconscious education in Southern notions about State Sovereignty, & all his kinsfolk & old associates urging him to join them in rebellion, disguised as an assertion of State Rights. He deserves credit for standing firm thus far — but I confidently predict that sixty days hence he will be in arms against the national flag he has sworn to follow. So malignant & mortal is the moral atmosphere breathed by every officer who comes from a Slave State. — He tells me Captn Lewis is hard at work in the Navy Department of the Rebels — and that his kinsman Col: Lee did not throw up his commission without severe struggle & distress. Lee refused even to invite Williams to follow him — told him to follow the dictates of his own conscience.

N.Y. Rifles to night — cor: 4th St. & Broadway. Did not drill, being engaged on Committee business. Recruits come in quite fast enough. We enlisted Will: Astor, Danl Huntington (the artist) & Tom Cooper among others.

No material news to day, except that Baltimore & Maryland seem to have reacted into loyalty & submission to law, under pressure of our vigorous demonstrations of National life on their Northern borders. This fact is significant. It shews what the last Administration might have done five months ago by a little self-assertion, and how much of our present distress is due to the collusion or inertia of old Buchanan & his cabinet of traitors.

May 1. Wednesday. Showery day. To night is clear but windy & cold. Just returned from two hours of drill under Capt: Levy — tired & discouraged, for I bungle sadly. Never mind — there are others as awkward, and I am sure I can master the problem if I try. But I must be avenged on Southern rebels somehow, for subjecting me to this bore. Among tonight's recruits are Charley Dix (the "marine" artist, Gen: D's son) Ja^{s} Thomson & Joseph Choate.

May 2. Very diligent day. Clear but cold. Murray Hoffman & G.C.A. dined here. Then two hours with "N.Y. Rifles". Did not drill, but worked hard at Com: business, on organization & on admissions. Watched the drill a few minutes, & saw with great satisfaction that others blunder even as I. — Then to N.Y. Club for half an hour with C.E.S. & G.A. —

No material news. Rumors of any amount of "Confederate" troops assembling at *Richmond* or elsewhere for a march on Washington, but all confused contradictory and contradicted. But we should act as if these rumors were true. Beauregard & Bragg & other traitors are brave intelligent & enterprising. The unanimous uprising of the North against their treason makes them desperate. They must make some bold & vigorous move at once, or perish.

Many people detect signs to day of a collapse at the South. Except in *Maryland*, I see no sign of any such thing — unless it be in the intensified Billingsgate of Southern newspapers. The fiercer virulence of their scolding *may* indicate fright. It certainly shews amazement at the attitude taken by New York & by other commercial centres heretofore abjectly submissive to Southern dictation. The Richmond Enquirer expatiates on "Execrable N.Y." — that Sodom — ungrateful for the Southern Custom that has built it up. Thinks the 7th Regiment viler & baser than all the Regiments of Massachusetts because it once visited Richmond & was hospitably received there & nevertheless sets out "to cut the throats" of Virginians — whereas the Massachusetts people cannot help being born on Cape Cod. — Talks of Scott the Arch Traitor and Lincoln the Beast &c &c &c. "The N.Y. Seventh Reg[t] is said to contain men who are decent & respectable *for Lincolnites* but they are quite unworthy to be slaughtered by the *Gentlemen* we send out against them" Etc. — This Southern Dragon certainly emits a large amount of foul stercoraceous matter just now. Perhaps in the mere nervous agitation of surprise & alarm: *possibly* — because the filthy brute is in articulo mortis, like the Dragon of Wantley in Percy's Reliques. But I fear there is much fight in him yet.

May 3. Friday. Dull cold day, deliquescing at last into cold drizzling rain. Very diligent in Wall St. Drilled in an upper loft of 31 Broad St. an hour & a half under *Ashley*, an efficient drill master & a gentlemanlike man. Dined at John Astor's, with Vice President Hamlin, Gen[l] Wool, Major Arnold (one of Wool's aids), Sim: Draper, Moses H. Grinnell, Bancroft Davis, Geo:

Schuyler, Geo: Bancroft, Wm M. Evarts, Wm B. Astor, Chas King, Isaac Bell. *Bell* was a rank traitor sixty days ago. He is very loyal now, but lets drop an occasional sneaking phrase of covert depreciation of our National reaction. I do not trust him in the smallest degree. Our dinner table talk was all of the War & it's prospects. We generally agreed that it is to be a sharp struggle, in which we must use all our energies, but that the South is paralyzed when it's ports are blockaded, and that it has not the resources to keep up an efficient military organization very long: that it will have to concentrate itself for one aggressive movement on the North, — at Washington or some other point — and collapse utterly if it fail. I hope that Time may verify our predictions.

Hamlin impresses me favorably, though he pronounces *NOW*, "Ne-a-ow". He seems a vigorous specimen of the pure Yankee type. His complexion so swarthy that I cannot wonder at the demented South for believing him a mulatto. Genl Wool is quiet dignified & courteous. Arnold, on whose right I sat, a very earnest hightoned young man of about thirty — a handsome fellow, too. He's a West Pointer of 1850.

No news to day, except that troops are concentrating at Washington, and that preparations to blockade every Southern port from the Chesapeake to the Rio Grande, are nearly completed.

May 4. Sat: Cold damp morning, the afternoon clear. Industrious day. Spent the morn'g partly in receiving Government rents for Atlantic Dock Stores, (in arrear this quarter, owing to our disturbed communications with Washington) & paying them out among Mr S.B.R.'s mortgagees, & partly in organizing the measures to be proposed at our N.Y.R. meeting tonight, and in completing the draft of the proposed system of revised and amended by-laws to be reported to the meeting.

This was at Hope Chapel, 8 P.M. I was in the chair. It was a spirited business-like earnest meeting of 150 & upwards — and did a very creditable amount of work, with less speech-making & less "parliamentary" formalism than I expected. Of course however there were amendments & substitutes & points of order in abundance. These last I generally decided in a summary way & so as to promote the prosecution of our work. We carried through the by-laws section by section without material change — & adopted uniform, after discussion of a score of details. For a mob of 150, including a lot of lawyers & others who itch to make motions & observations & suggestions, this was very well. Then we proceeded to election of regimental officers. Our programme was promptly & unanimously carried out. Captn *Alden* (whilome commandant of Cadets at West Point) Colonel — John Astor Lt Col: — Ashley Major — all excellent appointments — & I have reason to believe that all will accept. The meeting was very amiable — passed a vote of thanks to me as Chairman, with three cheers & a tiger — & was remarkably goodnatured in keeping order & minding the raps of my big key.

Three cheers for the *3 As* — Alden Astor Ashley! Not merely A1, but AAA — signifying A in its superlative degree or highest power, like triple R in a numismatological catalogue. I begin to think we may organize this into something respectable & valuable.

No National news of much importance to day. There are signs, more or less reliable, of collapse & intimidation in Virginia & Maryland. A strong party in Kentucky & Western Virginia seems certainly arming for the Nation & against State secession. The *twenty days* within which the Presdt's proclamation called upon all rebels to disperse, expire *tomorrow* — & there are vague rumors of decisive steps thereupon to be taken. We shall see. We are generally hopeful & in high spirits to day. But our levies are very raw — the rebel commanders have the energy & freshness that belong to revolutionary leaders. I have a foreboding that the campaign will begin with defeat & disaster. Never mind. It will brace us up still more strongly. Worse than the loss of three pitched battles would be *overtures of compromise & negotiation* from the swindling chivalry — "the felon Knights" of Jeff: Davis's Round Table. That would divide & weaken us again. I fear the subtle knavish desperate leaders of the South have some such move in reserve.

May 5. Sunday. Pleasant day. Trin: church with E & Johny. A few people here this ev'g: — among them Bigelow Lawrence who thinks of throwing up his diplomatic appointment at Florence, & organizing a light battery of rifled cannon at Boston.

Very plucky of him, for the poor fellow is as deaf as a post, and though he may hear his cannon (by possibility) can never hear an Order, unless pronounced thro' a speaking trumpet.

Jeff: Davis' Message to his "Congress" of Conspirators at *Montgomery* appears to day. It is clever, & disingenuous, and does not indicate the existence of great resources either of men or money.

May 6. Met the Com: (appointed Sat: night to wait on Alden & the others) at U. Place Hotel, at 12. There were Wm Astor, Wm H. Sidell, Danl Smith & myself. We called on Alden in 14th St. & were graciously received. He accepted the appointment kindly, & professed himself gratified by the compliment. Tho' it has no great value when viewed from the *Standpunkt* of a professional soldier, it is nevertheless something to be pleased with, coming from a body of men like ours. Then omnibussed down to the "Union Defence Committee" headquarters in Pine St. where we got John Astor out — & tendered him the Lt Colonelcy which he accepted. Then I rushed uptown again to a meeting of College trustees at Law School. Nothing important done there.

Drilled a couple of hours tonight under Capt. Levy. We improve a little.

May 7. Dined with M. Hoffman, & without Ellie who had gone to M^{rs} DC Murray's (to meet Mme de Vaugrigneuse, who was Miss Sarah Stout — "little Aquila G.") & spent the ev'g at our Military Headquarters. It devolved on me to present to the Corps Col: Alden, Lt Col. Astor & Major Ashley, which I did in the fewest possible words. They were received with enthusiastic cheers. [The brevity of my formula of introduction reminded me of the old story of a presentation of plate by some English regimental mess to it's retiring Colonel — when the Mayor's speech on behalf of the regiment was "There's the Mug" — to which the Colonel responded as follows "Is that the jug?"] — The three thereupon retired to consult on organization, & meanwhile there was drilling of the squads whose night this was. Alden professed himself well satisfied with the material on which he is to work.

Thereafter to N.Y. Club, where I signed a call for a general meeting to consider the case of it's Southern members. Thus much is plain. Either those of our number who have left the City in the Seventh & other regiments for the purpose of killing all they find in arms against Government, *or* those who are arrayed against Gov^{t} & ready to kill the former, are guilty of a crime — viz: unlawful homicidal intent, and ought to be summarily expelled. But the question of *fact* remains & is embarrassing. E.g. Willy Alston's acceptance of a Commission in that nasty little rebellious army of S. Carolina rests wholly on rumor.

Ellie presided to day over a meeting of the ladies of Trinity Parish on supplies (of lint — bandages — clothing &c) for the army — held at St John's Chapel. She was elected "chairwoman" a week ago & has been looking forward to to day with fearful misgivings & sinking of heart, & calling on me to drill her in the duties of a presiding officer. But she seems to have got through smoothly & comfortably, as I told her she would.

May 8. Drilled to night — we were marched into Washington Square, & worked hard. I find myself improving slowly.

E. has letters from Jem & from Weston — Chaplain of the 7th — both in the best spirit & temper.

Weston bears a sword & revolver, which he is ready to use. He would be an ugly opponent in a melée.

News to day is of decided "Secession" in Arkansas & Tennessee. In the latter state there will be an earnest & numerous minority — at least — recalcitrating against treason — with Andrew Johnson at their head. I care little about this. Tho' Kentucky & Tennessee are grand states, & each can send into the field an army far more formidable than can be raised among the poor whites of the Carolinas & the Gulf States, I would rather both should be openly arrayed against us, than that they should continue to paralyze us by standing undecided. Fear of affronting the Border States has kept us hesitating far too long already. When every Slave State has cast it's lot with the Woman-flogging Sepoys of the South, the Nation will breathe more freely & act more decisively.

Arkansas amounts to little or nothing. In Kentucky, Major Anderson's prestige & his appointment to the command of the volunteers assembling in that State, will have great effect.

Strange we should still be ignorant whether the fire of Fort Sumter did or did not prove fatal to some 200 or 300 of it's besiegers. It is a conflict of improbabilities. It seems incredible that no one should have been killed — & equally incredible that the military despotism of Charleston should have kept the fact quiet — if these stories of slaughter be true. They come from independent sources. I incline to disbelieve them.

May 9. At Tr: Church Stand'g Com: meeting I brought forward informally, for discussion, my plan for an appropriation by the Vestry in aid of the Ladies Association of the Parish for the manufacture of clothing & hospital furniture — to which I'm instigated by M[rs] John Astor. I shall carry it through I think. Gouv. Ogden supports it. Verplanck (who is growing senile I regret to say,) demurs on some incomprehensible ground — Skidmore hesitates — Dunscomb — that chief of noodles — objects because relieving the wounded is "humanity" & the Church holds its property in trust for Christianity! — Also because "Secessionists" may set the Church & Chapels on fire in revenge. In fact since the flag was hoisted on Trinity Steeple he has ordered Meurer the sexton to admit no more visitors there — lest they should surreptitiously set said steeple (which is built of red sandstone) *on fire*. I think D. is the most perfect specimen of an absolute dolt I ever knew. —

To night at drill room. Committee business &c — Col: Alden speaks highly of our proficiency, considering the little time we have spent in drill. Then to N.Y. Club. Rumors there of 6000 secessionists occupying Arlington Heights, which story I doubt omnipotently. — But a collision is drawing near, beyond all question — and I greatly fear the result of the first exposure of our new levies to fire. For they have been mostly men of peace — unlike the Southern Sepoy (whether of "gentleman" caste, or dirt-eater) who habitually carries his knife or revolver. Our many reports of Southern movements are discordant, & *severally* unreliable — but they indicate, on the whole, & pretty certainly a convergence of rebels from the Carolinas & the Gulf States to Virginia. If there be means to feed them, they must be assembling there in formidable masses. — Davis cannot afford to wait. With his ports blockaded, he must strike a decisive blow at once — or suffocate. To us every day without actual battle is great gain. We are organizing & drilling & converting our recruits into soldiers, & we can go on for six months without feeling the cost.

May 10. Friday. Fine day. Aft[n] & ev'g rainy. Just home from two hours drill. Fatiguing from the strain on one's attention — in spite whereof many blunders. But I certainly grow a little more familiar with the orders. Only practice can enable one to execute them promptly, & without time to consider. I must change to another squad. Alfred Schermerhorn, who is always in my *quaternion*, is not a pleasant neighbour.

May 11. Ev'g Post contains a first-rate puff of the N.Y. Rifles. To their drill room after dinner, spectator of drill & attending to business. Then to N.Y. Club. The proposed expulsion of traitors, like Major Deas, (who was in treaty, by his own admission, for an appointment in Jeff: Davis' Army before resigning from that of the U.S.) creates much talk. Many of our members are sadly gelatinous emasculate & feeble — morally invertebrate — unable to call things by their right names. E.g. Charley Hoffman. He admits that treason & treachery are criminal & foul, & that this man Deas is a traitor & a criminal & when you ask for a deduction from these premises, or assume that it should be his expulsion from any association of loyal & honest men, comes a sort of wailing protest against straightforward action — "O well, but then you know he's really a very nice fellow" — or "Well but of course you know anybody might say that this is'nt a *political* organization", and so forth.

How many of us could be instantly converted into traitors, were treason once more prosperous & popular in New York! — We may thence draw a consolatory inference as to the course of suppressed & silenced Union men even in Charleston or Montgomery, whenever the National Government shall make itself felt at the South.

The Great Eastern has arrived or is in the lower bay, waiting for a tide to cross the bar. It's said she will be chartered by Government. It may be a capital move. The fact that a steamer carrying 6000 to 10.000 men was somewhere off the Southern

Coast — anywhere between the Chesapeake & Rio Grande — ready to land her troops by help of vessels of lighter draft under the guns of the blockading squadrons — at any point — would at once tie up 30 000 of the rebel army. Troops marching on Washington from e.g. Charleston & N. Orleans would need to be recalled at once for Home defence.

To days news is encouraging. Gov:[t] troops captured a "steam-gun" sent out of Baltimore to Harpers Ferry by the *Winans* concern. The machine is probably of little practical worth — but it's capture looks like vigilance and energy. || There has been collision at St Louis between the National volunteers & some corps of Missouri secessionists — who surrendered to superior numbers. The former were fired on by a mob — & returned the fire with wholesome fatal effect. Good. It's a great honor for St Louis that it's Union men have been the first, in the history of this revolution, to take the initiative with vigor. || The road through Baltimore seems re-opened, & will not soon be closed again. || There is grumbling about delay & red-tapism at Albany in organizing & mustering into service & sending of the regiments of this State that are anxiously awaiting orders to march. Some say the delays are intentional & that the old Fernando Wood spirit is felt in the Military board of the State. — Gen[l] Dix went to Albany, to day, to hurry things up. I devoutly hope & trust we have no traitors in high places.

May 12. News by the morning papers looks well (Tribune & Times appear every morning in the week, now) tho' there is not much of it. The independent movement of Western Virginia in protest against the proslavery mania of the tidewater counties seems extensive & distinctly pronounced. Some seventy counties to meet in convention. Loyalty & Nationality decidedly predominant, West of the mountains. This movement seems most important & I trust the Administration will foster & strengthen it judiciously & vigorously. They talk, it seems, of Secession from the State & of forming a new State — "New Virginia", or "West Virginia". That wont do at all. They are entitled to call themselves *Virginia* without prefix — for the fanatics of Richmond are in rebellion against their own State laws. Eastern V[a] is in revolution, with no color of legal right. Wise & Letcher & C[o] stand where Gov[r] *Dorr* of R.I.

stood 20 years ago. — This decided action in Western V^{a} has its weight too, as indicating the probable disposition of that broad strip of nominally slave holding but practically free territory that slopes southward through E. Kentucky & Tennessee into N. Georgia & Alabama. Should the people of that tract declare for the Nation, or even stand divided & undecided, the phalanx of rebellion is pierced & broken.

May 13. On the Star of the West, wh: the Rebels caught by trick & false colors a week ago, were two or three Northern niggers — steward, cooks, waiters or the like. They have been *sold into Slavery*!!! — That's a little dose of tonic & stimulant for our Abolitionists worth half a million to the North — worth say $3000 at the outside to Jeff: Davis's Confederacy. They must be without sagacity or common sense, these Southern fanatics —, but I dare say they are ready to fight with blind desperation, like cornered rats. — Another street fight in St Louis — it's mob fired on by the U.S. volunteers in a passionate undisciplined way. Not only the mob, but the volunteers, suffered from the firing. — The *German* element seems conspicuous among the Missouri loyalists. This will appeal strongly to Germans not only North, but in Southern States, e.g. Texas, where are large & prosperous free soil German settlements. It will probably be felt along the Rhine & the Danube — and bring us experienced volunteer officers who have seen service. This War will soon be universally recognized as waged by an effete corrupt aristocracy of slave-breeders against the cause of Progress Democracy Free Thought & Equality [for which by the by I have no great respect — tho' I certainly prefer them to the semi-barbarous system of Mississippi & South Carolina] — and the sympathies of Christendom will begin to array themselves against Southern treason.

Raining very hard now. Lightning gleams more frequently thro' the Library windows — & thunder begins to grumble in the distance.

At T.C. Vestry tonight, I moved a resolution giving $1000. in aid of the Ladies' Association of the Parish, organized to supply flannel shirts & other garments, and hospital furniture (not included in the regular Army supplies) to the volunteers from N.Y. — I thought it best to reduce the am^{t} appropriated

— tho' a grant of $5000 or $10.000 would have been more becoming. The motion raised a breeze. Bradford & Cisco supported it vigorously. Ja^{s} G. King — who is always wrongheaded & unaccountable — opposed because the Congregations *ought to* raise the money without calling on the Vestry — Verplanck & Hyslop for some unknown reason — Dunscomb, because clothing the naked & tending the sick is "*Humanity*" not *Religion* — and Tr: Church is a *Religious* Corporation. Heaven help Dunscomb's wits! He is (as Bradford observed to me sotto voce while D. was prosing about misapplication of trust funds & so forth) at the zero point of absolute stolidity.

May 14. Tuesday. Unsettled weather, the early afternoon clear & hot. Spent the morning with Bidwell in Robinson's office. Arg^{t} on the objections to Burrowes' deposition in the Carter case. Shall not be surprised if we have to send the Commission back for re-execution — Burrowes having made defective answer to one or two interrogatories. — Thereafter Maunsell Field seized on me to say I had been appointed (qu: by whom?) on a Committee to issue proposals by advertisement & award a prize for a National Hymn or Popular & Patriotic Song appealing to the National Heart. Was such a thing ever heard of before????!!!!!

Went to meeting — Chamber of Commerce building. Field was there, Arthur Leary, Brodhead, Geo: Wm Curtis the Howadji, & R. Grant White. Talked it over & adjourned to Thursday night. Genl Dix, Cisco, Chas King, Ham: Fish, & others, are of the Committee, so I shall be ridiculous in decent company.

"Wanted by the American Nation — a Marseillaise. Any poet having one to dispose of will please apply to &c &c at &c &c on or before &c &c." — Or. "$250.00 Reward. A Tyrtæus is urgently required by the People. If he be about, any where, he will please call on &c &c by whom a reasonable compensation for his services, not exceeding the am^{t} above named will be promptly paid". — Or in the Herald advertising column of Wants. "$250. worth of Genius & Inspiration embodied in patriotic Music & Words. Apply to &c." This is among the funniest things ever undertaken by mortal man. Never mind. There is possibly one chance in ten million that it may bring out something good.

May 15. Drill to night — an hour in drill room — & an hour & a half (battalion) in Washington Square. Sundry new & strange evolutions. I bungled my way through somehow, in blind desperation, mentally avowing that I would give this up — drill no more — & accept the position of Deputy Assistant Quartermaster's Clerk to the N.Y. Rifles: that I would serve in any ignoble capacity rather than submit longer to this most intolerable bore. But better feelings returned with the Order "Break Ranks". I will try to master this new difficulty & if I fail at last, it shall be after an earnest effort. One difficulty (with my squad) is in Levy's omitting all explanation of the object to be attained by any *new* evolution. It's A.B.C. to him — & he naturally assumes that we see our way at once when he gives the order, & tells us of "files" & "guides" & so forth. He forgets that these are to us obscure words of Art, that convey no meaning (unless after study & consideration) — & that we cannot act on them promptly.

May 17. Friday. Clear & cool. Laurence Williams here at breakfast, & again for a few minutes this ev'g. Returns to Ohio tomorrow. He is on McClellan's staff with the rank of Major, & his heart seems enlisted in the service. He talks largely of McClellan's ability & energy, & of the forces mustering under his command. I think *L.W.* is safe now — and I suspect that Ellie & Miss Rosalie are entitled to a large share in the credit of saving a fine young fellow from the sin of disloyalty.

Law School examination ended today. It has been most creditable to Prof[r] Dwight & his students. I never knew an examination so uniformly good. The sole exception, a son of Judge W—'s, who seemed doubtful on Wednesday, did very well indeed yesterday & today.

Wickham Hoffman dined here. Reports the Seventh Regiment dissatisfied with it's Colonel (Lefferts) — somewhat demoralized & likely to decompose. Many of it's men think of volunteering into some other corps, or of forming a battalion under *Shaler*, their Major. Lefferts said to be fussy & undecided.

May 18. No events in to day's papers, & people begin to grumble about *inaction*. They are impatient for a new excitement — which will come soon enough. May it not come in the form of consternation at calamity! I am well satisfied with the conduct of affairs. Gov^{t} is moving & working "ohne Hast, ohne Rast". Of course both parties gain strength by time — but we gain two per cent while the rebels gain one. Every day a battle is postponed seems worth 1000 men to the Nation.

Gen: Dix, with whom I talked this aft^{n}, seems sanguine.

The fright & fury of the rebels shews clearly in the Billingsgate of Southern papers. Bad language has never been uttered on so grand a scale. Lincoln is a "Beast" & a "Baboon". Scott a "miscreant" & an "arch-traitor". All Northern soldiers "hireling cutthroats" — "ruffians" & scoundrels. A late Charleston newspaper says that all members of our 7th Regiment are "pimps." — that regiment being especially criminal in offering to support Gov^{t}, because it once made an excursion to Richmond & was civilly received there. As I fully believe that Southern rebels will fight bravely, I cannot understand their scolding & bragging so horribly. The sublime swagger of their talk cannot be matched in history, except by the State papers of China.

Meanwhile, the blockade has reached Charleston harbor — Baltimore is coerced into loyalty — & Gen: Harney is vigorously upholding the authority of Government in Missouri. Deus salvam fac Rempublicam!

May 19. Mr Ruggles dined with us. Much exercised about the 7th Reg^{t} generally & Jem in particular — Should it return to N.Y. when it's thirty days of service end? *Can* it do so if battle be then imminent? Should Jem apply for a Commission, & if so in what corps. Many of the 7th are obtaining Commissions, for which they are better qualified than most civilians. — Acknowledgments arrived from the 7th addressed to Mrs Ellie & her colleagues the makers of Havelock caps — Letter from Col: Lefferts — another subscribed by the non-commissioned staff — others from several companies.

After dinner Laurence Williams came to say good bye. Off for Cincinnati at 6 this ev'g.

May 20. Monday. A cold storm all day: now just clearing off. Visit in Wall St. from Alden, discoursing on business of the N.Y. Rifles. Then to a meeting of Col: Coll: Trustees at Law

School, after which I talked with King, who like Alden has just returned from Washington, where they have been in conference with Gen: Scott, Seward, Lincoln & other magnates.

They agree in the impression they received as to the probable course of the campaign — viz: Norfolk to be attacked within a day or so — the movement to commence tomorrow, probably. Then the summer to be devoted to the assemblage & organization of great masses of men at suitable points from Cairo to Washington — the defensive line being possibly pushed a little farther in front of Washington. With the first black frost of autumn that restores salubrity to the sunny South, two great Columns to be set in motion — down the Mississippi valley, & along the Atlantic seaboard. The programme looks sensible and promising. Both King & Alden report Scott clearheaded & sanguine, tho' somewhat shakey on his legs. How he must wish himself twenty years younger! Seward told K. he thought there would be no serious fighting after all — the South would collapse & everything be serenely adjusted. Seward pushes consistency to fanaticism.

The 7th Reg[t] is in fact much dissatisfied with Col. Lefferts & thinks him wanting in energy & in personal pluck.

May 21. Tuesday. Woke with a sharp assault of sick headache, but went down town not much behind my usual time & did a little Wall St. work. Meeting tonight of "Squad D", N.Y. Rifles, organizing as a Company. I am Pres[dt] of the *civil* organization. Rich[d] Grant White V.P. & Theodore Gentil Secretary. He (T.G.) is very efficient & useful. — We got on well & harmoniously. Nominations made for officers, & an adjournment to Friday night after drill. — To day's weather chill, with April showers. — Gov[t] did a good job yesterday in seizing all the bundles of despatches for the past year filed away in every important telegraph office at the North. The descent was simultaneous on all — & the result may be important in identifying & gibbeting (morally if not physically) sundry secret sympathizers with treason.

May 22. Wednesday. Fine day. Accomplished a little in Wall St. On my way up town saw the Troy Regiment (I think) march down Broadway toward the South. Uniformed — not thoroughly drilled — but mostly rugged young farmers — with a few rough loutish Germans & Kelts. Home. G.C.A. dined here. Then to drill room. Discoursed Alden — attended to business — & I'm sorry to say, rather shirked drill. Then to Rich[d] Grant White's with Gentil — we three are Executive Committee of our Company. Then to N.Y. Club, where I waited till late for adjournment of Council — wishing to learn their decision on the proposal that they present charges agst Major *Deas.* They sat long — tried to dodge the question by various devices — and the motion to present was lost *on ayes & noes* 8 to 6. The affirmative vote was, I'm told, Henry Cram, C.E.S. G.C.A. Jn° Sherwood, Russell, & Charley Hoffman. On the result being announced, duplicates of the charge & specifications were handed in, signed by Henry Cram, C.E.S. & myself as members of the Club — which very politic move checkmated the majority, and compelled the Council to call a general meeting of the Club to pass on the question whether Deas shall be expelled as a traitor or no.

Chief talk of to day the attitude of England, as displayed by the utterances of the Times & of Lord John Russell. The rebels "to be recognized as belligerents." Disappointment & exasperation are universal & deep. The feeling of cordiality toward England — of brotherhood — almost of loyalty, which grew out of the Prince's visit last fall [how long ago that seems] is utterly extinguished. England, the ally of free institutions throughout the world — the great Exemplar of a law-abiding Nation — England that has been twitting us with our toleration of slavery for fifty years past — *England* turning agst us in this great uprising of democracy against the treachery of politicians & oligarchs — in the struggle between Law & Anarchy — in the rebellion of a cruel merciless semi-barbarous mob of slave-owners against our National life! It is monstrous & incredible. We are too fast — we are judging England prematurely. When these utterances of English sentiment appeared it was still uncertain whether the Nation had vigor enough to assert its own existence. Washington was still in most imminent danger. Harper's Ferry & the Norfolk Navy Yard had just been successfully abandoned, & that was all we had to shew. The unexpected National uprising at the North was not yet distinctly pronounced. London saw only a united vigorous South, & a North paralyzed by discord. Let us hope the great English people will be true to its traditions & it's better instincts, when it sees more clearly the attitude of both sections of our country.

May 23. I notified Appleton's people this morn'g to import one copy less of such nice English books as they thought me likely to want. I'll buy reprints & pay no more tribute to the shops of England.

Here's an important suggestion — from G.F. Allen, this ev'g. Of course England must buy cotton, as she has done. She has paid for it in goods, ¾ of which at least are consumed north of the Potomac. Should she go to war with us that consumption is stopped — & has she in that case specie enough to move *one half* our cotton crop? Will she not be compelled, as a choice of evils, & as a purely selfish measure, to throw herself heart & soul into alliance with us, so as to stop this disturbance & reopen trade at the earliest possible moment? — We shall see.

Conference with Gen: Dix this morn'g. Wants me to go to Washington next week on a mission from the "Union Defence Committee". Shall be glad to go — if I can find the time.

May 24. Friday. Extras out at 12 o'clock, with important news, of wh: additional details appear this ev'g.

A large force marched from Washington last night, secured Arlington heights & pushed on to Alexandria which was occupied without serious resistance. Col: Ellsworth's Reg[t] of Firemen Zouaves headed the column. Ellsworth entered the principal hotel of the place (the "Marshall House") & himself hauled down the Rebel flag flying over it — and was thereupon or soon thereafter shot by a concealed assassin — said to have been one Jackson the hotel keeper. That flower of Sepoy chivalry was promptly knocked on the head. — Col: Ellsworth was a valuable man, but he could hardly have done such service as his assassin has rendered the country. His murder will stir the fire in every Western State, and shews all Christendom with what kind of enemy we are contending.

I am glad that farther summary vengeance was not taken, though military usage would have justified it. Forbearance has been our rule, and should be, for a season yet. But treachery poisonings & assassinations will make forbearance a crime before many months are gone.

It seems that Corcoran's Irish Regiment is entrenching itself on Arlington Heights. The Seventh, near "Columbia Springs" on the line of the W. & A. Rail Road. From five to eight thousand men in or about Alexandria, throwing up fieldworks, & expecting an attack from a rebel force supposed to be moving from Culpepper County. I rejoice in the field works. In a contest between raw levies, the party that fights under protection of ditches & embankments must prevail.

Rumors that a squadron of rebel Cavalry was taken in Alexandria — & that 300 rebels surrendered to Corcoran's command. This may or may not be true. All prisoners should be sent North at once, & held as hostages, to secure any of our people who may fall into the hands of Jeff: Davis's savages, from the worst treatment.

May 25. Bulletins of an advance by Gen: Butler from Old Point Comfort — a reconnoissance in force — how true I know not. — Found a letter in Wall St. from Horace Binney, in great perturbation about deficiency of arms in Penn[a]. Made enquiry at the shops, & found as I expected, that they can furnish none, for thirty days at least. The best offer I got was 100 Sharpe's Rifles at $45. (!) & 2000 very untrustworthy altered U.S. muskets which one would not like to fire till he had received plenary absolution & the last sacraments. Called on Union Defence Committee. It thinks Philadelphia should have been more provident, & looked out for itself more promptly. So it should — but "tua res agitur cum proximus ardet Ucalegon" — Philadelphia is between us & the rebellion, & the arming of Philad[a] is emphatically our affair.

Reports this aft'[n] of battle at Alexandria — & attack on the Seventh Regiment — wh: sent Ellie to bed after a crying-spell that ended in a bad fit of sick headache. There has been no battle & no attack.

May 26. To day's event was Col: Ellsworth's funeral — attended, I hear by a vast grim silent crowd. Beside the driver of the hearse sat private Brownell of Ellsworth's regiment, (who shot down & bayonetted his Commandant's assassin) bearing his rifle with fixed bayonet & the Rebel flag wh: Ellsworth had hauled down. This close juxtaposition of the murdered Colonel with the bayonet that was red with his murderer's life blood forty eight hours ago, was hardly appropriate to the solemn decencies of a funeral but certainly picturesque & significant — a stern symbol of the feeling that begins to prevail from Maine to Minnesota.

Warm day — heavy thundershower tonight (12 P.M.) with steady growl of thunder & rattle of rain.

Col: Alden called after dinner & spent an hour discussing our proposed military organization. — Tells me he talked over this movement on Alexandria with Gen: Scott a week ago. Scott was then doubtful whether he had force enough, & decided not to move forward till he was so strong as to make success certain. He is a cautious general, & most economical of men — expends lives as reluctantly as a miser parts with dollars. The object of this demonstration is to secure the "Manassas Gap Junction" and cut off the communications of the rebel advance at Harper's Ferry.

May 27. No War news of any importance to day. Our Seventh Regiment has re-crossed the Potomac to Washington — & will be ordered home in a day or two. It is in a painful position. Some five weeks ago it volunteered to march to Washington — then in most imminent peril, & to protect the National Capital till the Nation could bring it's regular levies into the field. We all crowded into Broadway & watched their march with eyes moistened by sympathy & gratitude & with hearts too full to hurra. — They have fulfilled their mission — Washington is safe, at least for the present. Genl Scott says — what common sense plainly confirms — that to use the rank & file of the Seventh as common soldiers & expose men to the casualties of a campaign, every one of whom is qualified to hold a lieutenant's commission at least, would be criminal waste of military material. They cannot be expected to enlist, as common soldiers, for three years or for the War. — But their return to N.Y. will be criticized & censured. Friends of men in the more democratic regiments will sneer at the 7th for coming home when battle seems close at hand. The 7th has been so petted & praised as to create a natural jealousy — — and Republics are ungrateful.

May 28. I'm off for Washington tomorrow 7 A.M. with Wickham Hoffman for fellow traveller — nominally on an errand for Union Defence Committee — but in fact to gratify my own curiosity & see some real soldiers — men, that is, who expect to be shot at, & who are ready to shoot other people, if they can hit them.

At Drill Room tonight. Attendance smaller. Many are offended by what they consider the intemperance of Barnes' & Barnard's speeches at our meeting Saturday night — think there is a plan to entrap them into militia service — & resign. — This is unfortunate, but on the other hand a tangible militia organization will bring us many recruits.

Col: Baker's California Regiment — (several hundred of it's rank & file at least) — quartered in a lower story of our building, is most mephitic. I never knew before what rankness of stench can be emitted by unwashed Humanity. Some foul infectious disease might well break out among the wretches who spend their days & nights in this deadly atmosphere. It poisons the whole building & of course prevails in a concentrated form, in the story they occupy — where it is absolutely *stercoraceous* & of ammoniacal intensity, — nauseous & choking. It half strangles me as I go upstairs.

June 5. Now for the record of these last seven days — wh: is worth preserving. Some of them were interesting beyond any I ever spent in the observation of public affairs.

Wednesday 29th May. Off by early train, after very early breakfast. Fine day. Wickham Hoffman joined me at Jersey City depot. No incidents of travel. Baltimore — that nest of traitors & assassins, was traversed in peace. There were crowds at the corners of the streets watching the trains. They were looking out for the troops that were in a train we passed on a turn off at Havre-de-Grace. But the crowd was silent & innocuous, for Fort McHenry is now strongly reinforced — and Federal Hill is white with the tents of Govt troops. — At Washington in due season, & to Willard's Hotel. Densely crowded. We had to put up with *one* room — a very good one however, on the second floor. The corridors down stairs are *packed* with a mob of civilians, army officers, motley militia men, & loafers of every class. The little reception parlor on the side street is the head-quarters of Col: Somebody (D'Utassy I believe) of the "Garibaldi Guard" — a very promising corps, — & that end of the first floor passage way is permanently occupied by a guard of swarthy Italians & Hungarians.

Called on sundry people with letters & cards, & lodged our pasteboards successfully with all but M[r] Sec[ry] Blair, who was on his own front "stoop" & could not be escaped. We bored him about 20 minutes — not more. He tends a little to prose, but is courteous & intelligent. His talk is encouraging. He thinks there is little fight, if any, in the blustering fire-eating element of the South. It's bar-room swash-bucklers will collapse whenever they are resolutely met. And this element constitutes, he thinks, two thirds of the secession force. — We were presented to *M[rs] Blair* — a lady-like person from New England.

Met Dick Smith, whilom of West Point, who marched me into Gen: Sandford's parlor, where I had some talk with that chieftain & with Clarence Brown & Aleck Hamilton (not Jas A's Aleck, but John C's) who are on his staff. Heard all about the Alexandria movement, for the execution of which Sandford takes much credit to himself. I hear Scott ranks him high — for a "trainband" General, experienced only in marches down Broadway. — I called with Hoffman at Scott's quarters. Saw Schuyler Hamilton, one of his aids, but did not disturb the meditations of the wily old Lieutenant General — who lies there like a great spider in the centre of his net, throwing out cords that will entangle his buzzing bluebottle of an antagonist — if all go well.

Many New Yorkers at Willard's. Clarence Cram, Sam Neill, Willy Cutting & others are begging for Commissions. Hon. F.B. Cutting is diligently backing his son's petition. He has already secured a lieutenancy for Hayward C. his youngest son. The Cuttings begging office from Lincoln — & these offices of all others — are a goodly spectacle to those who remember their extravagant treasonable talk of 60 days ago, & ever since last Nov[r]. Many Republicans are soured by seeing a share of public patronage given to late converted ultra-Southern Democrats. But the Administration is right. All party lines are wiped out now.

Dan Messenger — Judge Cowles — &c &c &c are after jobs in the civil service. Rev: D[r] Bellows concerned with the proposed Sanitary Commission. Pres[dt] Felton — Peirce — & Emory Washburn of Harvard — & Leutze — are lookers on.

Thursday morn'g. Warm walk with Hoffman up Fourteenth St. to Camp of our Seventh Regiment. Camp is on a pleasant hill that overlooks Washington. Col: Leffert's headquarters in a fine old countryhouse surrounded by shrubberies & flowery paths & beautiful trees — an aristocratic mansion a little out at elbows. Talked with M[r] Chaplain Weston — Jem Ruggles — Peyton Jaudon — Capt[n] Nevers — & others. Inspected battalion drill. — Jem dined with us at two.

Afternoon: parade & review of newly arrived regiments: Garibaldi Guard: Col: Blenker's Germans: (very promising corps both) the N.Y. 9th in their effective black & red uniform — & a fourth that I've forgotten. ["Brooklyn Zouaves"]

Friday. Drove with Hoffman, Dan Messenger, & his friend Charley Smith of Boston, to *Long Bridge.* Our *pass* was inspected & we went on. We invaded & (I suppose) "polluted" the Sacred Soil of Virginia. But it is so lacerated & insulted already by entrenchments, that our intrusion was a trifle. A very formidable tete du pont is in progress at the Virginia end of the bridge, & swarming with working parties. It is not yet armed — nor near completion, & it will need 2000 men & upwards to occupy it when completed. Thence drove Southwards passing camps of N. Jersey, Mass:, & other regiments, challenged every half mile at least by sentries & required to shew our *passes.* Michiganders just outside Alexandria (fine looking fellows) & Pennsylvanians in the town. They do not seem to me very promising material. We drove to the famous Marshall House where Col: Ellsworth was assassinated. It's a second-class hotel. Admitted with difficulty & formality; passes countersigned by the "provost Marshal". Explored the house, which is being carried off by relic hunters, in little bits. Flag-staff is nearly cut through — stair-banisters all gone — pieces of floor & stairs gouged out. Ordered dinner at Mansion House & drove a mile & a half N.W. to Shooter's, (or Sutler's) *Hill* where Ellsworth's Regiment (N.Y. Firemen Zouaves) is encamped & working at entrenchments, covering the extreme right of our line. Unfavorably impressed by the Zouaves. The men "*sassed*" the officers and the officers seemed loose in their notions of military subordination. One of them, a Captain, & a rather scrubby specimen of a fire company foreman in regimentals, said "I guess we'll have the Colonel we want" (Ellsworth's successor) "if we dont, we'll let them fellows know we're *about* — we're firemen, we are". Probably a few of the Zouaves will have to be court-martialled & shot before the regiment can be relied on. With or near them are some Mass: soldiers & one of Sherman's light batteries.

Their position is beautiful. Woody hills all around, on one of which stands the Low Church Theological Seminary.

Was introduced to L[t] Col: Farnham, who was diligently superintending the working parties.

Returned to a sumptuous dinner at Alexandria. According to my little experience, the South certainly beats us in good feeding. Looked thro' the town. Two houses out of three closed & abandoned. Only one or two stores open. The men were visible sitting in groups on the steps, or lounging on the corners, talking sulkily, & becoming silent as one approached them. No trace of loyalty to be seen. Our hotel officials professed themselves *anti secession*, but seemed depressed & humiliated & unhappy like members of a *conquered* community. This is a bad sign. Unless there be a loyal Union loving element at the South repressed by mob-law & terrorism but ready to declare itself when it can do so with safety, we have undertaken what we cannot hope to accomplish.

Returned from Alex[a] by a back road, visiting camp of N.Y. 12th, in a secluded picturesque place surrounded by woods & enlivened by a rattling stream. The reg[t] is quartered partly in bush huts, partly in an old tumble-down Cotton factory, built 40 years ago & never worked from that day to this. Glorious old State is old Virginia. One end has settled bodily down about two feet, & sentries in each story keep the men from that end, for fear of accident. Talked with Thurston, the surgeon. Looked for Butterfield the Colonel, & Ward (W[m] G. — pretty M[rs] W's husband) the L[t] Col. — Both sound asleep in a kind of den dug out of the bowels of a haystack. We did not disturb them — but B. tumbled up & joined us before we came away.

We then visited all the lines S. of Long Bridge. Spirit & temper of the men clearly good. Equipment imperfect in many particulars, but I heard no grumbling. One fact is apparent & unmistakeable — viz: that discipline & actual service produce good manners. We were challenged & called on to produce our passes a score of times at least — & the sentinels (except perhaps certain of the Mass: boys) were common men enough — Country laborers or City roughs. But experienced no incivility, even of manner. They scrutinized our passes — asked questions sometimes — but were always respectful & courteous — & generally dismissed us with a sort of apology for our detention, & some reference to their orders as leaving them no discretion.

We recrossed the Long Bridge & drove to Col: Burnside's Rhode Island Camp, far away on the outskirts of the City of Distances — somewhere N.W. of the Capitol. It's a model of neatness & order — with every provision for health & comfort — by far the most sensibly arranged camp I've seen. The huts are well built, & ventilated, with convenient bunks, & a covered *porch* for the mess-table. Talked with Goddards & other Prov: millionaires who are serving in the ranks, and saw their evening parade, wh: was creditable & closed with an ev'g service by Chaplain — Chapter in the bible & extrumpery prayer. It suggested a fieldpreaching in the days of Lauderdale & Clavers, & tho' Puritanism is unlovely, the R.I. boys will fight none the worse for this daily inculcation of the truth that they are fighting for the laws of God & not merely for those of Congress. — Thence to Burnside's quarters. He seems one of the strongest men I've seen in command.

Sat: Morning at War office on business. Visited Capitol, Smithsonian &c with Hoffman. Capitol has suffered no damage from it's occupation by the Northern Hordes. It's beautiful frescos are unscathed by the mudsills who were quartered there. Dined with Wise of the Navy. Mrs W. is daughter of Edw: Everett. W. is extravagantly funny. He is now in prominent & responsible position in the Department. After dinner, walked with the lady & her nice children, & N.P. Willis, in the grounds back of the White House, listening to Marine Band. Loungers numerous & the crowd bright with uniforms. Firing heard in direction of Alexandria — excitement — rumors of battle — & rapid dispersion of the audience. It was probably a salute. Returned to Wise's, & escorted Mrs W. to Reception at Sec: Blair's. Pleasant enough. Seward — Gen: Mansfield — Hamiltons — Trowbridge &c.

Called on *Bache* this morn'g & on Trowbridge. Coast Survey office full of business. Surveys of S. ports, not yet published, are so far advanced that they can be made useful to the blockading squadrons, & copies are being got up and issued with all possible despatch.

At two, I happened to see the prisoners brought in who were taken at the Fairfax C.H. skirmish Thursday night. They were in a covered waggon escorted by dragoons revolver in hand, on their way to Mansfield's headquarters.

This was a dashing little affair — tho' Gen: McDowell tells me it was injudicious & might have turned out very badly. Fifty U.S. dragoons, with Fearing & Cary (Quartermaster & Commissary of the N.Y. 5th) as volunteers, were making a reconnoissance, when they were fired on by a rebel guard of two men. They shot one & captured the other, who was interrogated, & said there were about 100 men in the village. Relying on this, the dragoons rode in, & found themselves in presence of from 1000 to 1500 men. Their treacherous informant was *shot down* at once, & very properly. This I heard in confidence. They charged & dispersed the rebels — rode thro' the village street more than once under fire from windows & from behind fences & came off at last with trifling loss & several prisoners. The rebels fired quite wildly. The prisoners begged & cried & knelt & seemed to expect instant military execution. One of them, (a son of Col: Washington who was lost on the San Francisco) was seized by the hair of his head & dragged across the pummel of a saddle & carried thro' the village with the charging dragoons. He took the oath of allegiance very promptly when it was tendered him, declaring he was a Union man, *coerced* into the rebel service, & was liberated by Mansfield & provided with some cloak or overcoat to cover his rebel uniform.

Fearing (Henry) came off with a contusion on the leg from the blow of a musket butt. He tells me he settled the man who delivered the blow by a revolver — shot in the head. Poor Cary got a musket ball in the foot, that made an ugly *groove* just below the instep & may lame him for life. Dan Messenger sat up with him last night & he was conveyed home today.

Sunday. Very sultry muggy day. Difficulty about getting passes to the Virginia end of the Long Bridge. Called on Gen: Mansfield with letter from Schuyler Hamilton & after waiting awhile obtained what I wanted. — Wh: was beyond my expectations, for passes heretofore issued are now revoked, for some good reason no doubt, & new ones issued very sparingly.

Drove with H. to *Arlington House*, the hereditary mansion of that fine old fellow Col: Lee, now unhappily a traitor. — A splendid place amid beautiful grounds — thro' wh: we strolled awhile. The Sentinels refused us admission to the house & we were walking back to our carriage, when Gen: McDowell came riding up the road with his tail on — staff & orderlies. He hailed me — dismounted — took us through the house — & was very kind & obliging. It's a queer place — an odd mixture of magnificence & meanness, like the castle of some illustrious shabby semi-insolvent old Irish family. E.g. a grand costly portico with half rotten wooden steps. Hall decorated with pictures — battle pieces — by some illustrious Custis or other — (fearful to behold) — also with abundant stags' sculls & antlers.

Thence to camp of 69th — Col: Corcoran's regiment. Inspected their battalion drill. Rather rough. And then visited the N.Y. 28th & 5th Regiments —, a little in advance, supported by the U.S. Dragoons who charged through the streets of Fairfax Court House. Trained soldiers are easily distinguished from even the best volunteers. There was a little bugler of 15 perhaps, a Brooklyn boy, whose narrative of the fray was spirited & modest — wish I had got his name for he's a promising & plucky fellow. "H. was pretty sure he killed two of 'em with his revolver". A dragoon told me afterwards that the boy rode by his side, gay & excited, through the skirmish — & used his revolver effectively. — They all said the affair lasted three quarters of an hour, but that must be a mistake — probably very natural. — Here I saw two or three wounded horses that had been brought off — A sad sight — but they are out of their pain before this, no doubt.

The officers of the 28th would not let us drive to Georgetown by the Chain Bridge. It was too hazardous — rebel pickets were within a mile or two of the road. So we returned by the *rope ferry.* — Orders were issued to night — by telegraph

— for a general *advance*. This I had from Wise. But they were countermanded.

Monday morn'g Hoffman returned to N.Y. — At two I railroaded to Baltimore, with Dan Messenger, Smith, & one Lamson of Boston, who is applying for a commission — a very good fellow he seems to be. — We had agreed to visit Old Point Comfort, — & pay our respects to Gen: Butler & Col: Duryée. From depot to wharf — where we embarked in the "Adelaide", heavily laden with stores for Fort Monroe, but built for first class summer passengers to the fashionable hotel at the Point — "Hygeia Hotel" — a Baltimorean Newport in former days. — Only half a dozen passengers with us. One a Virginian, who wanted to get to Norfolk to look after some property there — & professed himself, in talk with us Union men, to be a sort of Union lover — of a cold-blooded anti-coercion type. A very fat & funny old fellow he was — Jenison by name. He was just from Harpers Ferry, where he had friends to see him through. Reports the rebel force at H. Ferry undisciplined & insubordinate — officers & men "all mixed up together". Says he saw a *Capt*^{n} enter a bar-room in great excitement & address himself to his Commandant — "Colonel, what in H— shall I do with the boys? They say they wo'nt drill this morn'g." — Col. replies — "O, well, get two or three of them to turn out, & then I guess the others will come in by degrees."

Voyage down the Chesapeake is monotonous. North Point, & the steeples of Annapolis, the only objects of interest. Shores are flatter than those of L.I. Sound.

Tuesday. Out of my state room early enough to see the sun rise, red & angry. Landed at Old Point & went into the moated fort — an extensive & formidable stronghold. The runaway niggers who have sought refuge there & have been received by Butler as contraband of War — were bricklaying a structure that is to be a *bakery*, and toiling at piles of sandbags. Most of the officers to whom we had letters were absent on scouting parties. Introduced to Col: Dimmock & to Gen: Butler. *Lamson* had a mission to Butler — of complaint & remonstrance — from Gov: Andrews of Mass: — about the Commissariat & a ship load of provisions sent on by the market-men of Boston (fresh meat & ice) that has been lying off the fort for ten days, & nobody the better for it. Butler met the complaint with clearness & decision. He's a rough clear headed energetic man, I think. — Gave us a Pass, that carried us across the causeway & bridge that connect Fort Monroe with the Mainland of V^{a} & into the camps of Allen's Regiment (Troy) & of Col: Duryée's Zouaves, the "red-legged devils" of whom even Virginia secessionists stand in awe. — They are among the best regiments I have seen.

Talked with Col: Duryée — Hamlin (the Adjutant & a six footer) — Captn DuMont & others. Several companies off on scouting expeditions, to "Fox Hill" & elsewhere, & many rumors of battle. "25 of our men killed" — "200 secessioners made prisoners — " &c &c — In this camp were five contraband niggers, with whom we held converse & exchanged views. "Why Sar" said Julius Cæsar, "I did'nt run away from my Massa, sar. He run away from *me*, sar". — "I heard the Northern gen'l'men were favorable to the Colored population sar — so I thought I'd come over here, sar" — "My friends whar I come from, sar, are all right sar. They've been expecting the Northern Gentlemen down here ever since Massa Lincoln was elected, sar." — "They wanted us to go to York (i.e. Yorktown) to make the batteries — but I said I'd never had no *arms* all my life & I thought I should'nt be exactly *handy* with 'em, sar — " — We started with Hamlin & Lt *Boyd* for a walk to *Hampton* through the woods. Met a detachment of *Duryée's* marching in, footsore after a long nocturnal march in quest of fugitive rebels. Woods & meadows glowing & fragrant with honeysuckle & wild roses & all manner of wild flowers. — Called at Ex Pres^{dt} Tyler's country house & entered it through a cellar window. He was out. He & all his family fled with precipitation some ten days ago. Signs of hasty terrified flight abounded in the house. Bureau drawers pulled out & left on the floor — unimportant papers scattered over the floor. I secured two or three scraps of the Tylerian correspondence.

Mallory's house was abandoned too, but apparently in less haste. All the up-stairs rooms were left locked *& continue inviolate.* There were stories in camp of Vandalism at Tyler's — fine statuary destroyed & furniture cut up. They proved unfounded. The furniture was uninjured. The "statuary" was certain cheap plaster casts. Those in the parlors were intact & still covered by their gauze drapery. Two, in niches on the narrow stairway had been knocked down & smashed, probably by Tyler's people lugging down the Tyler trunks & boxes.

We went from Tyler's to Hampton Creek. The bridge was burned by the rebels, & we paddled across. The town of Hampton is beyond our pickets & I thought our visit imprudent, but we got off unscathed & uncaptured. The town is deserted by all but it's niggers. Houses & stores are all closed & abandoned. Only two white men left. One a very jolly Irishman, & the other probably a rebel spy. All the rest have fled from the anticipated "furor Normannorum". They had begun to loop-hole the brick wall round the churchyard of their ancient church, for musketry, but left the work unfinished. This ch: is a queer old interesting structure of particolored brick at least a century and a half old. We inspected it, & I pencilled a memorandum of "God preserve this one Nation from all treason privy conspiracy & sedition" in the 4to prayer book on the Altar. —

Hampton niggers generally a jolly set of fellows. Discoursed one or two families that reminded me of Eastman Johnson's "old Kentucky Home" picture.

Great vigilance against depredation & violence by our men. *Hamlin* hauled up one of Allen's lieutenants for breaking into a store to get a barrel of nails for the woodwork of a battery, tho' under his Colonels orders, and made him deliver a written acknowledgment of the seizure to the long lantern jawed Virginian above mentioned as probably a spy.

Back to camp thro' a thundershower that wet us through. Dined with DuMont, Hamlin &c, very pleasantly. We contributed the drink — a basket of champagne &c brought with us from Washington.

Got on board the *Adelaide* again at 5. I was in a state of sick headache — went to my state room at once — & after two or three hours of nervous irritation & dyspepsia slept profoundly till

Wednesday morning. Baltimore at 7. Strolled thro' the City with Lamson. Market very fine. Train at about ten. Comfortable day's ride & home at half past eight.

June 9. Wickham Hoffman has been appointed to a nominal position on Gov: Morgan's staff, as a Volunteer aid, with the duty of looking after the material wants of our N.Y. Regiments at Washington & Old Point Comfort. Gibbs is on the "Sanitary Commission" that undertakes a like office as to all the volunteer force. I suggested to them both that they should appoint certain men here (& in Boston & other cities) a Com: to raise funds in aid of their mission. The "Union Defence Committee" wo'nt do. — R.M. Blatchford — Sim: Draper — Prosper M. Wetmore — & others, are distrusted. They are believed to be not above using their place for partizan ends, & perhaps capable of a corrupt interest in contracts for clothing & other supplies. — They are in fact notorious old used up political hacks, all three, & of doubtful repute in private business relations. Should a Com: be appointed, such as we talked of to night, it may supersede them & do good service.

June 11. We are blue to day. Disgusting news from Old P^t^ Comfort, & Genl Butler's command, that strengthens our distrust of Militia Generals. Some three or four thousand men marched between Sunday night & Monday morn'g to break up a rebel congregation at a place called Bethel. They were commanded by a Mass: *Brigadier Genl Peirce* & crossed Hampton Creek in boats. Soon after they resumed their march, two regiments began firing on each other by mistake & two or three men were killed. After this little mistake was corrected, they continued their advance, & found themselves in front of an entrenched position with heavy guns. They had no artillery but a few howitzers. But they were pushed on till they came to a ditch they could not cross — and so they fell back — with a loss of from 20 to 100, killed & wounded.

This looks like murderous bungling.

DuMont, (the L^t^), with whom I dined a week ago, has a bayonet wound in the leg. *Theodore Winthrop* — (Mrs Wm Templeton Johnson's brother, author of the article in last *Atlantic Monthly* on "the March of the 7th Regiment from Annapolis to Washington") reported *missing*. He was one of Butler's aids.

Attacking a fortified position with *militia* was a mistake. Without thorough reconnoissance & knowledge of the ground it was criminal recklessness, for which somebody should be courtmartialled. Our men seem to have been advanced under heavy fire till they were stopped by an impracticable trench, on which their Militia Generals had not counted.

June 12. This ev'g Mr Ruggles, Rev: Dr Weston, Geo: Allen, & half a dozen others, met here to consider about organizing an association or Committee to help Government provide for the material wants of N.Y. regiments at Old Point Comfort & elsewhere. We organized ourselves, and with some little prospect of doing good service. There is much money here that is impatient to burst out of private pockets into the hands of any honest body of trustees for the public good. But Draper & Co have made the *Union Defence Com*: to stink in the nostrils of all good citizens.

June 13. Thursday. Lovely weather. No material news. Washington reported in great agitation about a threatened advance of *Beauregard* with 60 000 men. Has he got them? Nobody can tell. According to the authentic newspaper statements of the last 30 days there must be not less than two millions of rebel soldiery in Virginia by this time. I fear there is no doubt that poor Theodore Winthrop fell in that miserably managed skirmish at *Bethel*. Very sad for his sister, Mrs Laura Johnson. He was a plucky enterprising fellow, who might have made himself a name.

Billy Wilson's Regiment went forth to war to day, with sealed orders. Ellie, who has taken strong womanly interest in these *pariahs*, had provided a flag for them, which she presented at *Schmidt's* (5th Av:) this morn'g, Rev: Weston acting as her spokesman. Wilson, tho' rowdy & soaplock & Alderman, responded with a simplicity of manner & apparent earnestness of feeling that took everybody by surprise. He impressed the ladies favorably — but they say his men march badly & look like a scurvy set, tho' they've had a month of camp life & drill on Staten Island.

G.C.A. suggests that it was injudicious to march them down Broadway after the flag-presentation, with the usual escort, an advanced guard, of *Policemen*. It must have reminded them of disagreeable incidents in their past experience, & tended to damp their enthusiasm.

June 14. Friday. Last ev'g's supper gave poor Ellie a sick headache — so she did not dine with us. Geo. Anthon & George Derby (one of my Boston nephews) assisted. Went thereafter with G.A. to special meeting of N.Y. Club, called to pass on the charges agst Major Deas, late of U.S.A. — *No quorum.* The opponents of the movement, one or two excepted, staid away, & shirked the question. After roll was called, there was discussion whether the Pres[dt] of the Club (Harry Ward) could adjourn the meeting — or whether charges & all fell to the ground, & must be brought forward *de novo. Cram* supported an adjournment with spirit & force, & without violation of good taste. M[r] S.L.M. Barlow pettifogged on the other side & embodied his natural sympathy for deserters & traitors in divers profound Constitutional doubts. An adjournment to next Friday night prevailed.

Talked with Capt: Foster of Fort Sumter — Army officers are justly aggrieved by the appointment of civilians over their heads. — Bankhead of the Navy, who talks the usual platitudes about the ethics of rebellion. The rebels "think they are right" &c &c. But he is a fair-minded manly fellow — not of the same brand with the sneaks who stayed away to night.

I do not believe we can carry our charges against *Deas.* Probably we shall fail of a quorum again. If we get one, Jem: Strong & others avow they will debate points of order till sunrise next day. — The only course is to resign, which I shall certainly do on Saturday morn'g. I'm amazed at the want of moral sense — & of moral courage — and at the positive sympathy with treason, shewn to night. The Club is a rotten concern.

Rev: Tho[s] M. Strong died yesterday. For many years past, clergyman at Flatbush. My first cousin — son of my father's sister & a certain old Joseph Strong — (a lawyer, & according to my recollections, not of the highest standing). He was 64 years old, and reputed a good & useful man.

Templeton Johnson shewed me this morn'g despatches just rec[d] about poor T. Winthrop. He fell while leading a party to take that accursed redoubt in reverse, shot by a Louisiana rifleman. A Vermont volunteer staid with him awhile after he fell & until he died & then rejoined his retreating comrades with difficulty, bringing away Winthrop's hat & spurs.

This afternoon's papers report the rebel Army at *Harper's*

Ferry blowing up bridges & abandoning the position. It looks authentic, & perhaps it is, but philosophic scepticism as to all *news* is the proper temper now. This is important *if* true. The retreating rebels will doubtless fall back on the entrenched camp at Manassas Junction — and the force there may then feel strong enough for a dash at Washington. Who can tell?

But the demonstrations of loyalty in Western Virginia are most encouraging. We are raising regiments there, which, with McClellan's command, threaten the flank of any aggressive move by the rebels.

Visit from Ashley this morn'g. I'm appointed "paymaster" of the N.Y. Rifles. Till we are duly enrolled in the State Militia we are only playing soldier, so my appointment & office have little worth.

This mornings *World* has a telegram about the *Sanitary Commission* & it's appointment by the President — Prof: Bache, Wolcott Gibbs, Rev: Bellows, D[r] Van Buren, D[r] Howe of Boston, & others, & *Geo. T. Strong* of New York. I have heard nothing of my appointment from any other quarter, & never dreamed of such a thing, so I can hardly believe this. So many scores of men are better qualified & more conspicuous — fitter for the place & more likely to be thought of. — Vides, mi fili, quam parvâ sapientiâ &c &c. It is no doubt a newspaper blunder. If not, the appointing Power at Washington is weaker than I thought.

June 16. I learn from W. Gibbs that I am actually on this Government "Sanitary Commission", nominated by himself & Bellows & Prof: Bache, and that I'm expected to act as *Treasurer.*

C.E.S. told us of his last night's talk with Mansfield Davies (Judge D's son) Major in Duryée's regiment — & just arrived here from Fort Monroe. He confirms the general impression that the result of the *Bethel* affair was due to the utter imbecility ignorance & recklessness of Gen: Peirce or Gen: Butler or both. — Theodore Winthrop was shot through the lungs from a rifle pit in front of the redoubt as he was looking for a passage across the creek. He lived but a few minutes.

A flag of truce was sent in to the rebels, Thursday (I think). Magruder admitted his force 2200 men. He spoke highly of *Winthrop's* gallantry — having watched his movements — &

spoke also of his own membership in N.Y. Club. Was annoyed that he could not send on his semi-annual dues — & feared he might lose his membership. When this was mentioned, H.H. Ward or some one of the Council, said "that was all right — that had been attended to". I shall certainly resign from this Club. It's position — so far as it can take any — in this great crisis, is that of an organization for the social aid & comfort of traitors.

June 21. The *Sanitary Commission* has sat in permanence. Morning & ev'g sessions to day lasted eight hours. Yesterday's nearly as long — & we dined at Rev: Dr Bellows' in 20th St. He's our pres^{dt} — Prof: Bache V. Pres^{dt}. We have elected Olmsted (superinten^{dt} of Central Park, & author of certain valuable books of Southern travel) secretary & general agent to reside at Washington — & a member of the Commission. He goes heartily into the work & sets off for the Seat of War next week. I like him much. There are also Dr Agnew, Bache, Dr Newberry of Cleveland, W. Gibbs, Dr Van Buren of this city & one or two more. We have planned much work & done a little.

Wednesday night, a dozen men met here — Vinton — Weston — Mr Ruggles — & others — to talk over our proposed organization in aid of volunteers at Fort Monroe. The feeling seemed to be that the ground was already occupied by existing societies, & that setting up another would rather weaken the public energies. I do'nt quite see it — but this Conundrum clearly prevents my going actively into other work of the sort. I have since had earnest letters from W. Hoffman detailing the wants of several regiments, which need instant attention. Sent them to Mr Ruggles, to bring them before these other organizations.

Poor Theodore Winthrop's remains passed thro' the City to day on their way to New Haven.

In Missouri, Gen: Lyon seems to have gained decided success — routing a large rebel force, at a place called Booneville. The traitorous Governor of that state has fled to parts unknown. Nearer home, there has been another blunder by a militia commander, at Vienna (near Fairfax) losing us a dozen men & upwards. They were in a R.R. train, wh: was fired on by a battery in ambuscade, according to the favorite tactics of southern chivalry. Beauregard seems to be making some kind of forward movement from Fairfax & Manassas Junction — and the newspapers predict a great battle very shortly.

Much apprehension about some manœuvre in Congress, at the approaching Extra Session, to get up a Compromise or Pacification — "Crittenden resolutions" or some such temporary patchwork of concession. Wont do. The North wont stand it. None will be louder in opposition than a large class of the Democrats of last winter (like Fra[s] B. Cutting & Judge Vanderpoel) who were then so clamorous for "conciliation" & so sure that "no troops would be permitted to pass through New York". These men are now at least half Abolitionists.

June 22. Down town early attending to proofs of my Sanitary Com: circular inviting funds. It reads fairly, in print. Commission met at 12 & sat till 4 P.M. at Bellows' house. Bellows goes off for Camp Denison & Cairo with D[r] Newberry on Monday. We meet again at Washington 10th July.

Dined at Union Club, on D[r] Van Buren's invitation, with the N.Y. Commissioners, & old D[r] Mott. Much pleasant talk with Bellows & Olmsted. Came away at 8 — to attend meeting here of our absurd "National Hymn" Committee. (Four or five huge bales of patriotic hymnology were deposited here this aft[n] by an express wagon.) — There were present Gov: Fish, Luther Bradish, J.R. Brodhead, Maunsell Field, Dick White, &c — C.E.S. happened in & acted as amateur assessor.

We got thro' possibly a third of our job between 8 & 12½. There are 1156 "hymns" — many of them with music. The great majority of those we opened were consigned to the great rubbish-bin (or clothes basket) after reading the first three lines. A few were put aside as meritorious & worth looking at & a few others as brilliantly absurd & therefore worth saving. We came across no production to which we could think of awarding a prize.

June 23. Sunday. Hot day. Spent it at home — except for a walk to Rev: Bellows', thro' the baking sunshine a half an hour after noon, to suggest a little addition to his Life Insurance C[o] appeal in aid of the Sanitary Commission. My great original idea was this — that an army thoroughly infected with dysentery or camp fever becomes a centre of poison to the whole community, creates general pestilence, or at least makes every ordinary ailment malignant & unmanageable & then raises the ratio of mortality. I believe this statement generally true. My influence is that all Life Ins: Companies should help the Sanitary Commission, whether they have War-risks outstanding or not.

Ellie improves — took a little drive from 7 to 8 P.M. — was in the parlor awhile this ev'g.

Katy was here, in high vociferous romp with Johny & Temple. Also C.E.S. — Geo: Anthon & Geo: F. Allen & Dr Peters. —

Read to day "Observations on *Diseases of the Army*, by Sir John Pringle, Bar^{t}" — 7th Ed: — London 1774. It was lent me by Dr Peters — & seems a sound sagacious book, though it's details of medical treatment are doubtless obsolete.

June 24. Monday. Fine weather. A busy day. On duty for Sanitary Com: — except a couple of hours at special meeting of College Board. Agreed to cut down all salaries 10 per cent & upwards. How Prof: Lieber will grunt & agonize & parade his poverty!

Monday mostly spent with Dr Bellows & Wolcott Gibbs, trying to organize a Finance Com: to raise funds by begging & hand them over to the *Commission* to disburse. He called on Benjn H. Field, Cisco, & others — but found it (naturally) up-hill work. At last Gibbs took the responsibility of making a change in the Committee appointed by the *Commission* on Saturday, wh: will I think make it work. — Consulted with Olmsted this aft^{n}. He goes to Washington Thursday.

To night with Dr Van Buren Dr Agnew & Gibbs — in the Library — framing queries to be addressed to sundry functionaries, state authorities & regimental officers — on various points connected with the sanitary regulations & precautions they should have attended to. They will no doubt decline answering & d— our impudence in asking them whether they have or have not done their duty.

June 26. Wednesday. Sultry day, with showers. Ellie continues better. Last ev'g she spent with us (Dick White & Geo Curtis & others of the National Hymn Com:) & had a good time. We disposed of bushels of rubbish. This Com: is responsible for the production of an enormous bulk of commonplace watery versification. Fortunately two thirds of the trash is already consumed with fire. But there remains an immense pile of poetry with *music* to match still to be inspected.

It's clear, I think, that we get no *National Hymn*. Perhaps we may secure a dozen bits of second rate lyric that charitable people may justify us for publishing.

To day spent in diligent service of Sanitary Commission. Writing letters & mailing documents all the morn'g. Our outside Finance Committee of "associate" members was summoned to meet here this ev'g. Cyrus Field responded, & Cisco, & Rob[t] H. McCurdy & C.E.S. — no more. But we got on very well — "added to our numbers" very liberally, & adjourned to Chamber of Commerce Friday aft[n]. C.E.S. undertakes to get out notices. This is the real stress of our case. If the merchants & capitalists of N.Y. are prudent enough to sustain the Commission, it will work, & will save the Nation thousands of men & millions of money within the next three months. If they do not sustain it, the loss is theirs, & will be felt in the depression of N.Y. property for ten years to come. An epidemic of camp-fever or dysentery or cholera among our Volunteer Regiments is inevitable within 60 days, unless their sanitary system be reorganized, or rather unless a sanitary system be created for them. The highest medical & military authorities at Washington prophesy a loss of 50 per cent by Oct. 1. When this army is destroyed by disease, we shall have to raise another & at fearful cost. We cannot afford to waste life.

After this financial meeting, Gibbs D[r] Van Buren D[r] Agnew & I adjourned to the library, & worked till after midnight on matters referred to us as a Sub-Committee of the Commission.

Nothing special from the seat of War. — There is great excitement & irritation about alleged offers of compromise by Jeff: Davis & fear lest Government play us false & begin negotiating with armed traitors.

Met a Volunteer Reg[t] marching down Broadway this aft[n] — from Clinton & St. Laurence Counties. Fine stalwart fellows, true Norsemen, tho' inland — & among the best specimens I've seen of our N.Y. levies. God defend them from the perils of camp-disease & of privy assassination by the skulking dog-chivalry of Virginia — (whose valor is manifested in picking off a sentinel from behind a tree & then running away) — In a fair fight they can probably do something (with God's help) to defend themselves — Gen: Dix at Arlington, ranking McDowell, & disgusting all "regular" officers, with some apparent reason. Bade him goodbye on Monday at Cisco's office. He looked careworn & *old.* But he has my entire respect & confidence. I think he will undertake nothing that he has not ability to do, and that he will make no important movements except in consultation with officers whose practical knowledge is more recent than his own.

June 28. Friday. Working diligently these two days, mostly on Sanitary "Commission business".

Last night at Wolcott Gibbs' with Dr Agnew & Dr Van Buren, settling form of printed questions to be addressed to Colonels & regimental surgeons, as to the condition of camps & quarters, & as to precautions against disease, that will I think be unpleasant to answer: that will probably remain unanswered in sæcula sæculorum.

There are indications that the Commission will be sustained by the community. Everybody talks cordial approval, and I have $795. on deposit to day, though not a dollar has yet been solicited. People have sent in contributions to that amount, unasked, except by our newspaper appeal.

This morn'g spent wholly in work for the Commission (sending out papers &c) properly belonging to the Correspond'g Secretary, Harris. He is at Washington & we cannot afford to lose a day.

Informal meeting at Chamber of Commerce rooms, 2 P.M., to organize an auxiliary "Associate" finance Committee, & operate on the great commercial & financial interests of the City. It was not a large meeting, but strong. John A. Stevens presided (head of Bank of Commerce) & there were Morris Ketchum, McCurdy, W[m] F. Cary, & others. Adjourned to Tuesday, appointing a Committee, then to report a plan for permanent organization.

The meeting was harmonious, except that *Prosper M. Wetmore* was troubled by the fact that the Sanitary Commission expects to serve gratuitously. That anybody should work for

Government without making a good thing of it, seems to strike him as something incredible, self contradictory & revolting — a sin against Nature. He wanted an application made to Congress to appropriate money to pay members of the Commission against their will. Old Stevens snubbed & suppressed him. —

Those present seemed fully to recognize the immense practical importance of this movement, & disposed to exert themselves in it's support.

To night "*Com: on National Anthem*" met here. Was there ever before a Com: appointed to carry out a design so irrational & impossible? There were Geo: Wm Curtis, Richd Grant White, J.R. Brodhead & myself. Also as outside assessors, Mrs Ellie, Miss Rosalie, Mrs D.C. Murray, G.C.A. Willy Graham, C.E.S. & Scharfenberg. Scharfenberg came by invitation to help us pass on the vast amount of musical work (380 & upwards) sent in by competitors. We got through with about one half — Generally rubbish. A score or two reserved for further examination. Ev'g was pleasant however, & supper table jolly.

June 29. The War makes little progress. There is nothing to record but insignificant collisions. A steady stream of regiments pours down from the North.

Long talk with Wickham Hoffman this morning — just from Fort Monroe. His report is discouraging. Butler is no General, & his Brigadier, Peirce, utterly ignorant of his duties & unfit for his place. The men feel no confidence in either & are disposed to mutiny agst the latter. Several regiments are demoralized & (H. thinks) ought to be disbanded. Much disorder & plundering by the men. The few Unionists of the district disheartened or alienated thereby. — Col: Allen an especially bad case. This confirmed by the report in ev'g papers that the Col: has been put *under arrest*.

July 1. Last ev'g sundry people here: among them M^r^ & Mrs Jno Sherwood — Geo. Allen — & a very nice young fellow, a son of Dr Ogilby's (of Trin: Ch:) whom I have known these two or three months as an efficient member of the "N.Y. Rifles". He has just got a Commission & is assigned to the 15th Infantry, of which Fitz-John Porter, my old West Point friend, is Colonel.

He reports himself at Wheeling forthwith. I gave him a letter of introduction to Porter this morning. He is a remarkably attractive boy, quiet modest & well bred, full of earnestness & resolution, with a fine frank manly face & manner. Mrs Ellie, Geo. F. Allen, & G.C.A. were enthusiastic about him. He has the making of a valuable officer. I trust he may not be picked off from behind a tree by some of the sneaking Dog-Chivalry.

July 2^{d}. After dinner to Richd Grant White's (186 Tenth St.) where were old Verplanck, Geo Wm Curtis & Maunsell Field of the "National Anthem Com:" — We examined a score or two of efforts that had been laid aside as not manifestly rubbish, on our former inspection. Of these we condemned only about one half. A very tender & merciful judgment. It is conceded that no one of our 1275 contributions answers the conditions of our advertisement & deserves the prize, but it is thought we may publish the best of them. *Not one* seems to me worth preserving, but there may be a dozen or so that the public would buy.

Soon after our session began G.C.A. brought down Ellie & Miss Rosalie to join us. He did not come in, but called me out to witness a *portent* — to wit a great *Comet with at least 20° of tail & a brilliant nucleus*, a formidable apparition, nearly as impressive as it's great predecessor of /58. I had heard nothing of this distinguished stranger, but Curtis tells me he was seen at Staten Island Saturday night.

Walked home with Miss Rosalie, Maunsell Field escorting Mrs Ellie.

No news to day, but confident predictions of an advance from Washington on Manassas Junction & Fairfax — in which predictions I put no faith. *Dr Clymer* "*knows*" that Scott is only waiting for Congress to legalize & adopt the volunteers assembled under Lincoln's April proclamation. Then he will at once make a forward move. Ja^{s} W. Beekman "*knows*" that the unfortunate clamor of the Tribune & other newspapers about inaction & indecision has compelled Scott to order an advance — tho' against his own deliberate judgment — that six days' rations were to be issued today &c &c &c — all which I respectfully disbelieve. Scott is not the man to wait for legal formalities at a crisis like this, or to be driven into premature action by newspaper editorials & "public opinion".

July 4. Thursday. Loveliest weather. Have devoted the day to patriotic pyrotechny. Fired crackers all the morning with Johny & Temple, & little Valentine Black or Blacque or some such thing (his father is a Constantinopolitan Turk or Armenian & his mother was a daughter of our neighbor Dr Mott). Walter Cutting & G.C.A. dined here — & Miss Josephine Strong — on roast pig. An hour of this morning was very pleasant.

Fire works after dinner — Roman candles — mines — flower pots — triangles — & a few larger pieces — all of which went off brilliantly, especially a Roman Candle that fizzed out at the wrong end when just expiring. It's bottom came out, & it spirted it's fire into the palm of my hand & raised a blister there.

July 7. Sunday. A scorching day. Did not go to Church — stayed at home & wrote Instructions to Sanitary agents in camp. A most *ultra-crepidal* job for me. But the Commissioners in town approved my rough draft which I had prepared mainly to systematize my own ideas, & wished it put more fully into shape. It may do at least for a basis on which additions & changes can be made.

If it be lawful to pull an ox or an ass out of the pit on the Sabbath, it must be lawful to do a little something toward pulling a Volunteer out of a pit full of carbonic acid & maleficent morbific emanations, or toward preventing him from tumbling into it, on *Sunday*.

July 8. Monday. Another oppressively hot day. Not encouraging for the expedition of our Commission to the too sunny South tomorrow. — Busy day. Saw Dr Bellows, just returned from Cairo & the western camps, giving encouraging reports of the cordial way in which both officers & men received him — the absence of jealousy, & the desire for advice & help. But sanitary interests in that quarter need prompt action.

July 15th. Monday. Home again. Thank Heaven, for of all detestable places, Washington is the first — in July & with Congress sitting. Crowd — heat — bad quarters — bad fare — bad smells — musquitoes — and a plague of *flies* transcending everything within my experience. They blackened the tablecloths,

& absolutely flew into one's mouth at dinner — Beelzebub surely reigns there, & Willard's Hotel is his Temple.

Went off with W. Gibbs Tuesday morn'g, and got quarters at Willard's by special favor. Saw Olmsted — visited our very grand official room in Treasury building, with its long official green covered table & chairs ranged in official order around it, & official stationary in front of each chair. One could not sit there a moment without official sensations of dignity & red-tapery.

Wednesday Thursday & Friday spent in work. We sat from 10 A.M. till about 4, daily, & then from 7 or 8 till eleven & later. Dr Van Buren & Dr Agnew & Rev: Bellows joined us Wednesday morning. Prof: Bache, Dr Wood & Major Shiras also sat with us — all three interested & useful. Shiras & Wood especially useful as supplying information about the present practical working of our military system, of which none of us (except Dr Van Buren) know anything at all. We did a good deal of business. Extricated ourselves from an entanglement with that philanthropic lunatic Miss Dix — appointed four Agents, or Inspectors — adopted Dr Van Buren's Code of sanitary rules that is to be distributed among the volunteers, and my (!) draft of Instructions to Agents [without material alteration, strange to say] — and sundry recommendations to Congress & the War Department — &c &c &c &c. We attended the Military Com: of the Senate, Thursday & Friday at 9 A.M. — Bellows was chief speaker on our behalf. Wilson, fat Preston King, Lane, & that nasty fellow *Rice*, constitute the Com:. They heard us kindly & with interest. We submitted the draft of a bill endorsing our appointment by the Secretary of War — giving our Agents rations while in Camp — & requiring all *officers* either to comply with the recommendations of our agents or to assign reasons in writing for declining to do so — and giving our President & Secy power to frank documents addressed to officers & soldiers. I opposed asking this last privilege & predict it will kill the Bill. But the *Com*: was fully & strongly with us. Preston King & Wilson actually wanted to give us power to *suspend* any officer who may decline obeying our Sanitary Counsel. That would be most odious & dangerous. We protested against being vested with such prerogative of mischief-making.

The Bill has passed two stages in the Senate unanimously — but I do not expect it will succeed.

Thursday ev'g I had a pleasant drive for an hour or so with Dr Wood. Friday aft^{n} we dined on *desiccated* (qu: desecrated?) meats & vegetables, prepared by *Sanderson*, & then crossed the Long Bridge & drove about a little — visiting Col: Corcoran's Camp.

I shifted my quarters by a forced march, Wednesday, at midnight. Willard's functionaries took the liberty of putting a suspicious-looking stranger in my room. There I found him ensconced in a cot & breathing stertorously when I went up stairs for the night. As they would do nothing about it & declined even giving me a sofa to pass the rest of the night on, I magnanimously paid my bill & packed my trunk, ordered a carriage & fared forth into the night. Visited every hotel in the City without finding a shelter. Made up my mind I must either sleep under the Treasury portico, enlist, commit a breach of the peace & get lodging in the watchhouse, or engage my coachman to spend the night driving up & down Pennsylvania Avenue. But I did worse. Got in at the National — & was assigned a cot in a large omnibus garret room — one of eight or ten. Worse than my room at Willard's but there I had no feeling of being imposed upon. Did'nt take off my clothes & did'nt sleep a wink. My roommates snored — One of them ordered & swallowed three several drinks between daylight & breakfast time — viz: a sherry cobbler — a whiskey julep — & a brandy-smash. His voice & manner were as of one belonging to the better class — a gentleman.

I shifted again that night to *Wormeley's*, a quiet little place in "I street" where Van Buren Agnew Bellows Gibbs & I messed together & fared well.

Sat: aft^{n} to Baltimore (2.30 train) — thence by steamer to Old Point. Of the Commission there were those above named & Olmsted. We took with us also Giraud Foster, Charles L. Brace (ὁ φιλανθρωπος) Taylor (partner of Bancroft Davis) & the distinguished Russell of the London Times. Dr Peters & Dr Alex^{r} Mott also on board. Very pleasant run down the beautiful Chesapeake. Talked much with Russell. Clever & well informed. Only drawback a quiet unconscious Anglican depreciation of everything outside England. So I heard him in discourse with others. I studiously avoided paying him the homage of a single query as to his opinion of anything here or at the South, & talked of India & the Crimea.

Sunday A.M. at Fort Monroe. Walked about the works with Russell, who explained the true significance of sundry ravelins & gorges & so on very learnedly. Saw parade. Regulars & one Company of volunteers from Lowell, who appear on parade nearly as well as regulars. McChesney's Regiment encamped on the paradeground seem a scurvy set. Called on Gen: Butler & on Dr Cuyler. Butler's friend Dr Kimball took us through the Hospital (Hygeia Hotel) — Many wounded there from the Bethel blunder, & others who had been picked off while on guard by the Chivalry of V[a]. One poor boy of 18 who ran away from the sophomore class of Harvard to join Duryée's regiment & got a bullet in the leg at Bethel. All were cheerful plucky & grateful for every kind look or word. None seemed to begrudge his lost leg or arm. Sickness loss of blood & low diet gave them all a look of *refinement*: their eyes were large & bright & their complexions clear, & they spoke slowly & low. There were two or three ugly typhoid cases moreover. Kimball said one of them "might slip thro' his fingers" — "he had been overlooked a little, & they ought to have begun stimulating 12 hours ago". Our medical associates do'nt think much of D[r] Kimball. There is a large staff of nurses, seemingly good & attentive, generally from Massachusetts.

Gen Butler got out a steamboat for us & we went to Newport News. — (N.B. Why do we occupy that point? It's land communication with Hampton is not kept up — the two positions are practically insulated, & what do we gain by two *weak* bases of operation?) — Walked thro' camps there. Lt Col: Geo Betts — Regimental Hospitals crowded & bad — Camp police generally good. Butler exhibited one of his Sawyer guns (42 pounder) & fired a few conical shells at the rebel batteries opposite & about 4½ miles distant. Elevation of gun from 22° to 30°. I think the shells generally fell ½ a mile short — but they said one or two went into or over the batteries. Steamed back to the Fort. Drove with Gibbs & Brace to Hampton. Bridge nearly restored, only a few planks to be replaced. Visited Col: Max Weber who was civil & brought out some Rhein-wein. His soldiers in high feather. They have planted a battery of two guns on this side that rakes the bridge. Crossed it on foot. Hampton still deserted by it's people — a fact that looks badly for our final success, unless by a war of *extirpation* — but crowded with soldiers — mostly Naval Brigade (commonly called *Naval Brigands*) — Just beyond the old Church a stockade & trench in progress, & guns in position. Left the Point by steamer, which waited for us a couple of hours, at 8 P.M. & reached Baltimore at half past eight this morn'g. Home at 9 tonight — having dined in Philad[a] with Van Buren Gibbs &c.

Ellie went to *Savin Rock* with the babies Friday aft. — so I return to a lonely home.

We are in great spirits over McClellan's successes in Western V[a].

July 17. McClellan seems to have crushed secession in Western V[a]. — And all McDowell's column is in advance on Fairfax & Manassas Junction at last. I fear this move is premature — forced on Gen: Scott by the newspapers. A serious check on this line would be a great disaster.

July 19. Dined with C.E.S. & G.A. at the "Maison Dorée" a new & very nice restaurant established in Penniman's house on Union Square. Called on Dr Peters, as a private Sanitary agent on my own account — also at Mr Ruggles'. We are all waiting breathlessly for news from the Army of Virginia. Batteries were encountered by the advance yesterday at "Bull's Run" three miles this side of Manassas Junction, & there was a sharp skirmish, our advance falling back on it's supports at last, with a loss of some sixty men. To day there have been diverse stories of additional fight, stories both good & bad — but the last report is that all are fictions, and that things are in statu quo. This lack of authentic official reports is no sign of success. We seem on the eve of a general action — but perhaps the enemy is holding "Bull's Run" to secure a comfortable retreat toward Richmond. He certainly ran away from Fairfax with great precipitation — but I suppose the Chivalry will fight pretty well behind entrenchments.

July 22. Monday. 10.30 A.M. Just arrived from Savin Rock, which I left at 7 — by N.H.R.R. At Stamford I left the cars &, with a score or two of other anxious enquirers, made a concentric attack on the Newspaper youth as he debouched from the Up-train — nearly rending him limb from limb.

Rewarded for my exertions by *Good News* — certainly good, tho' it may not prove sufficient to justify the crowing & the capitals of the Tribune.

It's rather sketchy & vague, & no doubt exaggerated — but there has been fighting on a large scale at Bull's Run — our men have been steady under fire — & the enemy has fallen back on Manassas. This last important fact seems beyond question.

Gen: Johnston seems to have joined Beauregard, giving him numerical preponderance. Patterson does not seem to have followed Johnston up. We attacked yesterday morn'g, & there was hard fighting till about half past five. Our right, under Hunter, turned the rebel entrenchments, & seems to have repulsed the enemy, where they came out of their cover, & tried to use the bayonet. Hunter is killed or severely wounded. Ellsworth's Fire Zouaves & Corcoran's Irishmen are said to have fought specially well, & to have suffered much. It is rumored that an advance was shelling the batteries at Manassas last night — Not likely.

Thank God for this good news.

We shall probably receive a coldwater douche however before night in the shape of less comfortable intelligence.

7 P.M. My prediction about the *douche* verified indeed! To day will be known as

BLACK MONDAY.

We are utterly & disgracefully routed — beaten — whipped — by Secessionists. Perhaps not disgracefully — for they say Beauregard had *90.000* men in the field, & if so we were outnumbered two to one. But our men are disorganized & demoralized & have fled to the shelter of their trenches at Arlington & Alexandria — as rabbits to their burrows. All our field artillery is lost (25 guns out of 49!) — & if the Secessionists have any dash in them they will drive McDowell into the Potomac.

How it happened is still uncertain. It don't appear whether

the stampede came of a sudden unaccountable panic, or from the advent of *Gen: Johnston* on our flank. In this latter case it was a revival of the legitimate Napoleonic Drama. *Blücher*, Gen Johnston — *Grouchy*, Gen: Patterson. But our reports are all a muddle. Only one great fact stands out unmistakeably — viz: total defeat & National disaster on the largest scale.

Only one thing remains to make the situation worse — & I shall not be surprised if tomorrow's papers announce it. That is, the surrender of our army across the Potomac & the occupation of Washington by the rebels. We could never retreat across the Long Bridge if successfully assailed — even were our men not cut up & crestfallen & disheartened.

July 23. We feel a little better today. The Army is by no means annihilated. Only a small part of it seems to have been stricken with panic. A gallant fight has been made against enormous odds & at every disadvantage. An attack failed & we fell back — Voilà tout. Only there is the lamentable loss of *guns* — some say 18, others nearly 100. That cannot be explained away. It's said to night that Tyler is at Centreville entrenching himself, so *all* the ground occupied by our advance is not abandoned. The rebels shew no disposition to follow up their advantage or venture outside their woods & masked batteries. The first reports of our loss in killed & wounded said to be greatly exaggerated.

Why we delivered battle is a mystery. I suppose the Tribune & other newspapers teazed & scolded Gen: Scott into premature action. I thought him too strong & self sustained to be forced to do anything against his own judgment by outside pressure & popular clamor.

Among those reported killed is Thos F. Meagher of Corcoran's Regiment. —

Busy this morn'g. Visit from Prof: Horsford of Cambridge about a new process for Army bread — mixing an acid phosphate & some carbonate with the flour, thereby supplying the elements lost in the bran, & at the same time cellulating the bread by the liberated carbonic acid.

Dined at the Chamber St. Delmonico's, & home. RG White called. He has a military appointment — is Major of Berdan's reg^{t} of sharp shooters (!) & wants to establish relations with the San: Commission: — then came Bellows, in hot haste from Walpole N.H. —

With him & Mr S.B.R. at his house this ev'g. He goes to Wash^{n} tomorrow. I must follow — tho' it's a bore, & I see little prospect of my being useful there. — Dr Van Buren came in at ten o'clock with important suggestions.

Tomorrow aft^{n} I go to Savin Rock — returning next morn'g. Then I must go at once to *W.* (if I can possibly get ready) & try to uncoil the folds of Medical Department Red Tape that are like to strangle the life out of many a wounded volunteer.

July 25. Very active day in Wall St. Dined at Delmonico's. Regret to record certain premonitions of a headache tomorrow. Possibly due in part to the indulgence, during an ev'g stroll down Broadway, of certain feelings of wrath, acrimony, cantankerous wolfishness, grim dogged rankling rage, atrabilious & sanguinary (but impotent) fury — over which I brooded & ruminated. I'm an embodiment of all the Eumenides this minute.

These southern scoundrels! How they will brag over the repulse at Bull's Run — tho', to be sure, it's not nearly so bad as our first reports. And is there not good reason to fear that their omission to follow up their advantage by a march on Washington indicates a movement in overwhelming force on the column of Gen: Banks (late Patterson's) or Rosencrantz, (late McClellan's)? May we not have another disaster to lament within the next 48 hours?

How the inherent barbarism of the Chivalry crops out whenever it can safely kill or torture a defenceless enemy! Scrape the "Southern gentleman's" skin & you will find a secondrate Comanche underneath it. These felons solaced themselves by murdering our wounded men in cold blood when they found us retiring from the field last Sunday afternoon — and did so with an elaboration of artistic fertility in forms of homicide — (setting them up against trees to be fired at — cutting their throats, &c &c) that proves them of higher grade in ruffianism & cowardly atrocity than anything our Five Points can show.

We *must* soon begin treating the Enemy with the hempen penalties of treason. We have tried the emollient system of rosewater & conciliation long enough. It's insufficiency begins to be recognized. Let us henceforth dismiss no more rebel prisoners "on taking the oath of allegiance" which they laugh at the instant they are set free, but send them North, to work at coast fortifications & the like, under stern taskmasters. Let all rebels of Northern birth — or deserters from the National Army or Navy — be summarily hanged, after a fair trial. Let all slaves belonging to men in arms against Government be declared free by Act of Congress & Proclamation. If this cannot be done under Constitutional forms let it be done outside them — only let it be done somehow.

These men shewed the *National Flag* that they might lure our regiments unsuspectingly up to be fired upon. Such caitiffs are surely entitled to none of the courtesies & amenities of humane civilized warfare — they should be extirpated, like rats, or venomous snakes, or other vermin.

July 26. The 8th & 71 Regiments (3 month volunteers) returned to day — welcomed by crowds that blocked Broadway. — They will be missed at Washington.

We feel rather blue to day — tho' without special reason. — It seems clear that the loss of the rebels last Sunday was fully as severe as our own. — Russell (London Times) writes Sam. Ward that the Union Army "ran away just as it's Victory had been secured by the superior cowardice of the South" — Pleasant. — But Russell headed the race.

Aug: 2. Friday night. Exceeding sultry. Up before 3 this morn'g, for the early train. But as the ticket office of that wretchedly managed Baltimore & Washington R.R. was not opened till long after the hour for starting, our train got off near half an hour behind time, & missed it's connection at Balt: — so we were detained there till ten o'clock, & might just as well have postponed our arising till six. A most sultry ride. There were Dr Bellows Van Buren Geo: Gibbs, Wolcott G. & myself. Breakfasted at the Gilmor House & dined at the Continental (Philada) — Saw H. Binney Jr at his house a moment. We have elected him & Bishop Clark of R.I. full members of the Commission — & I think both will serve. — Home at half past nine.

Washington hotter & more detestable than ever. Plague of flies & musquitoes unabated.

Went on by night train Saturday. — Spent the night filed away like a bundle of papers in one of the "Sleeping" (!)-Car pigeon holes, where I perspired freely all night —

Sunday at the Hospitals — two at Georgetown ("Seminary" & "Union Hotel") & one at Alexandria. Much to write about both — were there time. Condition of the wounded thus far most satisfactory. Every thing tends to heal kindly. But our professional colleagues say this is deceptive — the time for trouble has not yet come — & hospital disease is inevitable within 60 days. The medical men in charge are doing what they can, but radical changes are needed. The buildings are defective in many points. As at Fort Monroe, the cheerfulness & pluck of the men are most touching. I saw several hideous cases of laceration by Minie balls & fragments of shell — too hideous to describe. But all doing well. One poor fellow (a Glasgow man of the 79th — "*Rutherfurd*") was in articulo mortis with dysentery & consequent peritonitis — Another died while we were there — after undergoing amputation an hour or two before. One or two typhoid cases looked unpromising. — Visited "Fort Ellsworth" in front of Alexandria. It is finished now & very formidable — easier to defend than to assault. But it seems to me (in my ignorance) insufficiently *armed* — & commanded moreover by the neighbouring hills. The Chivalry will never try to storm it but I dont see why they should not shell it's defenders out. — This seems true also of the most important works at the head of the Long Bridge.

Our session adjourned late last night — having sat, as before, morn'g & ev'g. It engrossed all my time except that we took two or three drives in what should have been the "*cool*" of the evening to visit certain regiments that are specially demoralized by the disaster of the 21st. — the 79th & others.

We did a deal of work. Among other things we recommended the Sec: of War to remove Dr *Kimball* (Gen: Butler's amateur interloper) from Fort Monroe — a step which at once put us on intimate cordial & endearing relations with all the Medical Bureau, Dr Finley included. — But we receive no sincere cooperation from our pretended Congressional allies. Senator Wilson seems to have played a double game with us. The President, with whom Prof: Bache & Dr Bellows had a conference Thursday night, is our friend. So is Meigs the

Quarter Master General — with whom I had an interview. He is an exceptional & refreshing specimen of sense & promptitude, unlike most of our high military officials. There's not a fibre of red-tape in his constitution. — *Miss Dix* has plagued us a little. She is energetic — benevolent — unselfish — & a mild case of monomania. Working *on her own hook*, she does good, but no one can cooperate with her — for she belongs to the class of Comets, & can be subdued into relations with no *System* whatever. —

Long talk with Gen: McDowell. He is sadly depressed & mortified, most unlike what he was a fortnight ago. Says he has nothing to reproach himself with, & that he did his best. He took 31000 men into the field, & of these the reserve of 1.000 was not under fire at all. The enemy were twice his strength. — Col: Cullum tells me we lost 25 guns, just one more than half those that went into action. — Though at the head of Scott's staff he cannot ascertain & does not know what produced this ruinous panic & stampede, or what regiment began it. Nor does he know whether the rebel force in V[a] is *70 000*, or *over 200 000*. History is worth little.

From conversations with eye-witnesses, I am satisfied that the Rebels treated our wounded men with characteristic barbarity. D[r] *Barnes* found 30 wounded officers & men whom he had collected in a shady place & left for a few moments (while he went for some surgical implement or assistance to the Church that was used as a temporary Hospital) bayonetted, on his return. Two very intelligent privates of a Michigan Regiment now in one of the Georgetown Hospitals tell me with all minute detail of time place & circumstance how they saw rebel soldiers deliberately cut the throats of wounded men.

I return from Washington depressed & despondent. Our Volunteer system with it's elected Colonels — & it's political Major Generals, is very bad. We are fighting at sore disadvantage. The men have lost faith in their officers, & no wonder, when so many officers set the example of running away. Of the first 300 fugitives that crossed the Long Bridge, 200 had commissions. Two Colonels were seen fleeing on the same horse. Several Regiments were left without field officers — & without a company officer that knew anything beyond company-drill. The splendid material of the *Scotch 79th* & the Fire Zouaves has been wasted. Both regiments are disheartened & demoralized. Neither would stand fire for five minutes — they are almost in a state of mutiny: their men deserting, & the sick list enlarging itself daily. — Why the Rebels did not walk into Washington July 22^d or 23^d is a great mystery. They could have done so with trifling loss.

Aug: 6. Tuesday night. Still cruelly hot. Very diligent in Wall Street. Dined at home, 6 P.M., on a cup of coffee & a slice of cold ham. On my way up town I called on a rather handsome & very clever "Mrs Weaver" who boards in Bond St. (N° 32) & represents herself as compelled to make her living by her pen, as Newspaper Report*ress.* Gave her sundry facts about the Army & the Hospitals of Washington to be worked up into a newspaper article.

Augt 8. Diligent in town to day. Stopped at Mr S.B.R.'s this ev'g where I met George F. Allen. We discussed the new process for the dressing of flax (& other vegetable fibre) by blowing it out of a kind of steam gun. Allen is interested in the patent. If half Allen tells me be verified in practice his steam gun will hit King Cotton & his Sepoy subjects harder than any artillery yet brought into the field. But these splendid inventions come to naught generally.

Our last news is of a successful affair in Missouri. We have poor McDowell's official report of the Bull Run battle (Stone Bridge they begin to call it) — & what is more consolatory, the Sepoy version of that same. It admits that they were fairly broken & beaten ("by immense odds" of course) when Johnston came up to reinforce them — unchecked by that imbecile or traitorous Patterson. Maledictions on the memory of the Accoucheur who brought Patterson's maternal grandfather into the world!

Aug: 12. Monday night. The three Medici, viz: Van Buren Agnew & Harris, have spent the ev'g here in high discourse de Re Sanitariâ. V.B. is a little sluggish & red-tape-y. We cannot get him to see the importance of putting on record our objections (or rather the objections raised by himself & his medical colleagues) to the Hospitals of Washington Georgetown &

Alexandria. We ought to do so, if only because defective ventilation & other grave defects will very shortly convert them into pest-houses, & because the public will then enquire why the Sanitary Commission did nothing in the matter.

———

The only material War news is our withdrawal from *Hampton* & the burning of that town by the rebels. I hope the queer quaint old Church survived the conflagration, but our newspapers report it as having shared the fate of the secular structures around it.

Aug: 13. Monday. Violent storm all day, with most copious rain. Bidwell has gone out of town — ditto C.E.S. — so I worked all day in solitude — chiefly on San: Com: affairs.

Rumor in ev'g papers, by telegraph from St Louis, that Gen: Lyon's command in S.W. Missouri is routed — & the General killed. Wonder when the tide of disaster will turn. But the misfortune may be exaggerated.

Aug: 15. To town this morning, & very busy all day over San: Com: letters & papers to the exclusion of everything else. *$3000.* came in from the Mutual Life Ins: C°, of which F.S. Winston is President. I trust we may do some good service to justify the confidence the community reposes in us. *$894.00* came in yesterday from Providence, collected by Dr Snow, of that ilk.

Long walk down Broadway & up the Bowery tonight.

We claim the Missouri battle as a Victory: Gen Sigel having retreated in good order after Gen: Lyon fell, and left only a *very* few guns on the field. If these be victories, may we soon enjoy a few defeats! — Lyon is killed undoubtedly — some say the rebel Genl Price, too, & that notable land-loafing partizan *knight* of the knife & the revolver, *Ben McCulloch*. I'm sure I hope both are in heaven — but I do'nt feel confident about it. — Nothing new at Washington or from Fort Monroe. Except that "Willy Alston" is named as one of "Gen." Magruder's Aids. Can this be our amiable bulbous little friend? [1862. Even so]

I think the rebels contemplate an aggressive move on the line of the Potomac. Not merely because "well-informed people" state facts that look that way, for the statements of the best-informed people are very worthless — but because it seems — (on the whole, after weighing the multifarious lies that are in circulation —) as if the rebel Pay Master & Commissaries were hard up for money & provender — & as if an offensive move was essential, to prevent utter disorganization. I'm sure I hope so. Three to two against the *attacking* party in all battles between raw levies, and *five* to two if the party attacked fight behind fieldworks.

We are not yet fighting in earnest. *Not even yet.* Our sluggish goodnatured pachydermatous Northern People requires a deal of kicking to heat it's blood. Not a traitor is hanged after four months of rampant belligerent rebellion. We must change all this. The Southern Oligarchy is making war with hysterical unscrupulous energy, like France in her unblessed First Revolution.

Augt 19. Olmsted here (from Washington for a day or two, looking after Central Park) also Drs Van Buren & Agnew: a Sanitary Council. We heard & discussed the Hospital Report of the two Medici. It's voice of warning seems to me not nearly strong enough, but Van Buren is anxious to keep on good terms with the U.S. Medical Bureau, and I have great respect for his practical good sense & judgment. We had a little supper — & much to talk over — & sat late over our modest cold chicken & Beaune.

Olmsted thinks ill of affairs at Washington. Demoralization — discouragement — desire to get home again — have shewn themselves in many regiments. There are mutinous tendencies. We have not yet sounded all the depths of disaster & disgrace. Government seems limp & nerveless & unequal to the crisis. A dozen mutineers — or a score of dozen if necessary — should be summarily shot at once. Government stocks would instantly rise three per cent, on the strength of that or any other like decided action. For the People feel that Gov^t is not making War with all it's heart & soul & mind. I almost suspect that it is trying to keep a door open for some compromise or Convention. If so the error is chargeable to Seward. He & Cameron can be spared from the Cabinet. — The People themselves are far less fully aroused & in earnest than their Southern enemies. The two surgeons, Winston & Swift, just released from their captivity at Richmond, report to Dr Agnew that N. York & Washington seem to them indifferent & careless in comparison with the fever heat of V^{a}. — Mrs Ogden Hoffman, who was on the train this morning, says that Miss Linton, the lovely heiress of Natchez, who has been spending her winters here & her summers at Newport, receiving kindness & attention from everybody, writes among other things, that she wants no prettier ornament for her bed-room than the Scalps of a few members of the Seventh Regiment. The vindictive darling!

Aug 22. Glad to hear that Dr Higbee, at meeting of Trustees of Theolog: Seminary, turned a cold shoulder on his quondam friend Judge Chambers of Maryland, & being interrogated by the latter told him distinctly that he did so because of his disloyal course in that state. Very good for Dr H. with his Southern connexions & antecedents. This is a little like the temper that ought to prevail here and that must prevail, if we expect to fight this battle out to any result but National disgrace. The first duty of Government at this time is to hang some highly respectable gentlemanlike wealthy & well connected person, after due trial & condemnation, for Treason — There are plenty of cases within it's reach. One such proceeding would do more to consolidate the Nation & invigorate its Life, than all this Cabinet has done since the 4th of March.

Not much War News. Genl Wool has superseded Butler at Fort Monroe. An important change, that (rather than the Potomac) being the true base of operations for an advance on Richmond. Excitement about a Rebel move on Washington has in some degree subsided. "The late rains have made the Potomac unfordable" & so protected the Armies & the Capital of the poor little North. How does it happen that notwithstanding our immense natural advantages over the rebels, in numbers, in money, in all the arts by which the material of War is made & moved, we have yet been inferior to them in strength & in armament at every contested point? Distrust of *Cameron* & *Wells* grows stronger daily — and people no longer hold *Gen: Scott's* name sacred! We begin to talk of him as an honest well intentioned superannuated old gentleman. The hope of the People is in McClellan. Perhaps popular judgment may be right, but it looks ungrateful. — We begin to receive the rebound from England & France of the first news of the Bull Run battle. It is bitterly galling. The Nation is disgraced, for a time at least, in the eyes of Christendom. Later reports — from Southern newspapers, shewing that the Rebels were absolutely beaten when the arrival of reinforcements turned the tide of battle in their favor, & that their loss exceeded ours on their own shewing, may restore our credit a little. But this more accurate statement of the case may come too late to prevent France & England from recognizing the rebellious confederation of our Southern states & introducing new & serious complications into our National trouble.

Who could have dreamed, a year ago, that England would hesitate one moment as to the side of this controversy entitled to her sympathy & moral support?

Aug 23. To night, Olmsted, Dr Van Buren & Dr Agnew here, in the library, & afterwards at supper down stairs, in desperate consultation over the short-comings of Government. We decided on extreme measures, & open warfare with the War Department & the Medical Bureau. The non-feasance of the Administration is abominable & intolerable. We must come to an issue with our imbecile Cabinet sooner or later — & the sooner the better.

Dr Peters has at last announced in one of our Medical Journals, his independence of all Medical-*isms* — or, in other words, has publicly renounced *homœopathy*.

No War news — except that Govt (to do it justice) begins to shew some little energy apropos of Northern Treason — It is arresting spies at Washington — Philada — & in this City — without much warrant from statute & consigning them to Fort Lafayette at the Narrows. It is dismissing a few of it's many disloyal employees — & even beginning to take liberties with the Press, interfering with the circulation of such traitorous newspapers as the Daily News & the Journal of Commerce.

Aug: 26. No important news from the Southern Seat of War. Govt continues to shew increased activity in suppressing domestic treason. It is vigorously seconded by lawless & dangerous outbreaks in the Eastern states, suppressing secession newspapers. The patriotic populace of Bridgeport Conn: enjoyed the lark of gutting a Bridgeport newspaper office Saturday night.

This ev'g Gibbs here — D[r] Agnew — & one of our Sanitary Inspectors, D[r] Douglas. He has been with Gen: Banks' Column, now retrograding from Harper's Ferry toward Baltimore — (nobody knows why,) & gives an encouraging report of it's morale & it's Sanitary Condition. — Gibbs read me a letter from D[r] *Suckley* however — at Alexandria — giving the most deplorable account of our volunteer regiments about Washington. Disorganized, demoralized, without spirit or discipline or confidence in their officers. He predicts another grand defeat — "Was ne'er prophetic sound so full of Wo" — Suckley is partial to a grey tone of color — & minor keys — but I fear his prophesying is a genuine article. Our volunteer system, with it's Elective officers, is radically weak.

McClellan sent in his resignation last week, *Lincoln* having given him a list of subordinates whose appointment was a political necessity. After 24 hours consideration *Lincoln* concluded it would not do to let McClellan resign, & withdrew his list of appointees.

Aug: 27. Dined at Delmonico's; walked up town thro' by-ways on the West side of the town; occupied the evening with a stroll as far as Canal St. Found G.C.A. here on my return, fresh from Newport where he has been spending three weeks in Geo. F. Jones' cottage. — He is savage & nearly despondent. But I am satisfied the Administration means right & is timidly & tentatively asserting it's existence as it finds the People prepared to uphold it in decided measures. That it is a weak cowardly Administration, however, & unequal to the crisis, is a fact that nobody can deny. We could afford to lose Washington if the Sepoys would rid us of Lincoln, Cameron, Seward, & Wells.

It is almost time for another great disaster. It will occur in Western Virginia probably. Can any disaster & disgrace arouse us fully? Perhaps we are destined to defeat & fit only for subjugation. Perhaps the oligarchs of the South are our born rulers.

Northern communities may be too weak corrupt gelatinous & unwarlike to resist Jeff: Davis & his confederates. It is possible New York & New England & the Free West may be unable to cope with the South. If so, let the fact be ascertained & established as soon as possible, & let us begin to recognize our masters. But I should like a chance to peril my life in battle before that question is decided.

Aug 30. Cup of coffee — then called on Agnew & with him on Van Buren. We must go *to Washington* next week — probably Tuesday.

Things look as if we might be just in time for a great battle. The rebels are certainly moving up toward the Potomac. Skirmishing between pickets has become lively. We seem threatened by preponderance of hostile force all the way from Fort Monroe to Missouri. Loyalists in East Tennessee are vainly calling for help to save them from subjugation. Kentucky is slipping thro' our fingers, I fear. Everything is somehow all wrong, & nobody is to blame.

Sept: 2^{d}. John Kernochan takes no pains to conceal his seceshism. I wo'nt talk with him on public affairs — but he allows himself full freedom of speech, for which he got insulted by an irritable Yankee on the piazza last night, who overheard some quasi-treasonable utterance of his & told him he ought to be tarred & feathered. K. seems a good fellow enough (barring these stercoraceous political notions) — but I think he would be none the worse for treatment by external terebinthinate applications so popular with his Southern friends. His handsome wife is as true as steel, however.

Rumors came at dinner time of some success gained by the Naval expedition from Fort Monroe, under Com: Stringham & Genl Butler. Then they were contradicted & disbelieved, & our spirits collapsed again. But at eight o'clock a despatch began coming over the wires of our little Hotel telegraph. Everybody crowded into the office listening eagerly to the news as it was read off slowly & staccato. Everybody looked more & more radiant as the words dribbled out — (except Kernochan) & we made up a purse on the spot for Jemmy the Operator σωτηριων πραγματων ευαγγελος.

It's certainly good news. We all look brighter in Wall St. to day than we have looked for five weeks at least. Tho' these forts at Hatteras inlet were no doubt attacked in overwhelming force, & we are probably entitled to no prestige or credit, we have struck a blow none the less damaging. We have materially strengthened our blockading arrangements — put a ne exeat on shoals of sharking privateers — gained access to all the shores of Pamlico & Albemarle Sounds, where vessels of light draft can carry War to the doors of N. Carolina & S.E. Virginia seceshers for many a mile — made a diversion by threatening Beauregard's flank & rear, & gained a new base of operations to be used whenever we feel strong enough. Also we have got about 700 prisoners, including several High-Caste Sepoys, & 25 heavy guns to offset our losses at Bull Run. The Minnesota arrived here this morn'g with the prisoners.

With a little care this new position can be held against all Secesh-dom. But I fear an onslaught upon Fort Monroe & Newport News, weakened by withdrawal of troops (Col: Weber's *Turner* Regiment & *Hawkins' Zouaves*) to garrison Forts Hatteras & Clark.

Olmsted writes me from Washington, Saturday, that *Russell*, & English officers sojourning there, interpret Beauregard's late movements to mean an attack in force. I doubt whether he can attack our field works successfully, or cross the Potomac at Leesburgh or anywhere else, without strong odds against him. People say he must make a forward move at any risk for want of provisions, & to prevent discord & disintegration within his command but I do not believe people know much about it — We hear to day of a move by *Gen: Frémont* that looks like *War in earnest* at last — a proclamation of Martial Law in Missouri — confiscation of all rebel property — and *Freedom* to all *Slaves* owned by *Rebels*, in that State. A most significant step, & in the right direction, tho' it may weaken the National cause in Kentucky.

Home by RR as usual this morn'g. Attended to Wall St. matters as usual, dined at Delmonico's, walked up town, & this ev'g had Dr Bellows Dr Van Buren & Dr Agnew here — & a modest Sanitary supper. G.C.A. came in at ten o'clock. Talked over sundry matters that are to be acted upon at Washington this week. — Sorry to hear from G.A. that poor young Julius

Ellis — son of D[r] Ellis in 2[d] Av: — affianced to a Miss *Willett* (a descendant of old Marinus Willett's & one of our neighbours) is dying. He was in the Bull Run fight — (Captain in the 71st Reg[t] I believe) — behaved well — & got a bad blow from a fragment of shell below the ancle. The case was obscure, but he was on the whole doing well till yesterday morning when chills & nausea set in, & he became a hopeless case of *pyæmia*. Insensible to day, & I dare say dead by this time.

Sept. 3[d]. No material war news to day. Firing has been heard at *W*. from some point below Alexandria, an affair of outposts probably. Why does *McClellan* let the rebels go on entrenching themselves closer & closer, without interference. Their plan is no doubt to attack, & to prepare strong positions to fall back on, if repulsed.

Who knows but the whole San: Com: may be carried away captive to Richmond!

M[r] S.B.R. & Jem here awhile this ev'g. M[r] R. in exaltation over Geo: Allen's Flax Cotton. I am going in as director of the Company & shall immolate myself in the cause to the extent of two or three hundred. Of course there will be found a weak point somewhere in the demonstration by facts & figures that Flax Cotton is a "big thing". It's always so — But I will sacrifice a moderate amount for the chance of dealing a blow at King Cotton, tho' the chance is small.

Young Ellis died early this morn'g. — Among the pleasant talk brought out by M[rs] —'s precipitancy in parturition is the current story that KHAM vows the premature baby is *not* of his begetting, & means to abandon it & it's mother. Also — (& this may well be true) — that poor *M[rs] L.* is left penniless & that her youngest son (Johny) is degenerating into a mere street loafer & drunkard. Edward L. has sailed for *Sydney*, & the Antipodes. Nothing is heard of poor Fred: L. since he failed of his Commission. Clarence Cram, by the by, whose appointment the Senate also refused to confirm, has been reinstated. — The 700 prisoners from Fort Hatteras are to be housed in a prison ship at the Navy Yard. — I suppose their chief, the traitor Barron, will be made an exception & will receive the elegant attentions & hospitalities of dinner giving Seceshers in 5th Avenue — Sam: Barlow, e.g., & Royal Phelps.

Sept: 16. Last night I spent in R.R. cars between Baltimore & N.Y., reaching the place a little after day light. Night before I was given over as a sweet morsel to a large room full of secessionist Baltimore Gallinippers at the Eutaw House, & slept none. Night before that, at Washington, I retired at 2 A.M. & arose at 4.30, & slept as little, being quartered near the gathering place of a select circle of roystering volunteer officers who destroyed my natural rest. So I have a right to feel shakey — and an excuse for being unequal to the duty of chronicling the details of this last Washington expedition.

Went thither by the usual day-train Wednesday the 4th. Dr Bellows & Gibbs my fellow-travellers. Found B^{p} Clark there. He is a brick. The Medici, Van Buren & Agnew, arrived next morn'g & we duly inaugurated our session in Treasury Building. It adjourned last Thursday night, but Rev: B. & I staid one day longer, hoping to consummate certain material reforms (in the Medical Bureau) that seemed all but accomplished. They are only inchoate however to this day. Put not your faith in princes, nor in the confidential pledges of Secretaries & Heads of Departments.

I experienced little beyond our ordinary routine of a morn'g session at 10 — & an ev'g session at 8. "The battle" was always coming off tomorrow morn'g — but it did not come off at all.

Saturday (7th) we all dined at Prof: Bache's. Sunday morning I went to the camp of R.I. 2^{d} Reg^{t} (at "Brightwood"). Bishop Clark preached — from the top of a military chest or box of pinewood with the R. Islanders & a Mass: Reg^{t} for audience. A very vigorous honest unconventional sermon it was. It was like one of Chas Kingsley's sermons, & it was not thrown away. I saw many a rather dirty handkerchief pulled out. — Monday aft^{n} we revisited that camp by invitation. It's Colonel, *Wheaton* of the Regulars, seems a fine young fellow. Ev'g parade & Ev'g service with an address from Dr Bellows. He told the men, in substance, that there were several ways of serving God, varying according to one's position & surroundings, & that their way, at this particular crisis, was to obey orders, & to fight like the D——.

Wednesday aft^{n}. Gen: *Keyes* invited us to review his brigade at the Race Course, just across the Long Bridge. It was a fine sight, the movement of some 4000 men, with bands playing

& field & staff officers galloping about. Found an acquaintance in one of the Genl's aids, young Chetwood, a Col: Coll: Law School graduate of last year. We were saluted & took off our hats in due military form, & it was all very high & mighty & grand. — There were one or two other pleasant drives on the other side of the Potomac. It is a lovely region, richer brighter more exuberant & better (barring malaria) than Gt Barrington. Poor Virginia ought to be Queen State of the Union, but she is crushed by nigger-dom. If this War rid her of that incubus, she will be the centre of Western civilization A.D. 1875. — McDowell dined with us. He is very sore about the Bull Run battle, & insists on talking about it & explaining his defeat. — Genl Tyler went beyond his orders on the 18th, & Butler & Patterson were severally to have moved forward on the fatal 21st — wh: thing they did not. — I like McDowell. A civilian always like Major Generals who as it were appeal to him for sympathy & a candid judgment. Shameful that our venomous critics of defeat should say he was *drunk* at B.R. — The man is an ultra Total-Abstainer. — He invited me to go up in the Army balloon with him & I hope to do so yet. Gen: Burnside tendered the like hospitality to Bishop Clark — & the Bp made an aeronautic assignation with him which he was prevented from keeping. So the unprecedented conjunction of a balloon & a bishop is still in fieri — among the unconsummated concatenations of Future Time. Burnside is a brick (he & the bp roomed together & they seem old friends). He says our men were steadier & fired better than the enemy, on the 21st July, & all was going well & the victory substantially won when officers & men went suddenly to the rear in the wildest stampede. He remarks farther that it was "the worst planned battle he ever saw or heard of". When his brigade was deployed pursuant to orders, he found it at right angles to the line of battle. Curious story of *Col. Slocum* who had been with B. in Mexico — a man of peculiarly sanguine temperament & light heartedness. He told B. on that Sunday morn'g as they were leaving the Council of War that he was sure he should be hit — & *hit twice* — he knew he should not come out alive. His prediction was accurate. He was shot twice — in the leg & in the head — & died at Richmond two or three days after the battle. — My former friend E.K. Smith (of West P^t in /52) is not killed — but only "kilt" — by a ball in the shoulder. He is the "Gen: Kirby Smith", it seems, who led up the rebel reinforcement that turned the tide of battle against us.

Debates at this session were livelier than heretofore. We had the question constantly before us, in one form & another, whether we should go on in alliance with the War Department & Medical Bureau, or denounce their inefficiency. Our Gov^{t} members — Prof: Bache, Dr Wood, Major Shiras, & Col: Cullum, — stood up vigorously for the Officials of course. There was much discussion about a queer clever report by Olmsted as to the causes of the volunteer demoralization that culminated in the race to Washington after Bull Run. An able paper certainly — but it's publication would have done mischief — would have retarded recruiting. —

I do'nt know about Cameron & the War Department, but the inefficiency of the Medical Bureau is criminal and scandalous. It's superannuated officials are paralyzed by the routine habits acquired in long dealing with an army of ten or 15 thousand, & utterly unequal to their present work. Ten days ago there were not in or about Washington medicines beds or hospital provision of any kind for 300 additional patients — though the head of the bureau admitted that any hour might bring on a great battle & 5000 or 20000 cases to be provided for. "They could send to N.Y. for medicine" — &c &c &c. The fogies of that department manage it in the spirit of a village apothecary. But the day after the skirmish at Lewinsville (last week) some half dozen wounded men were brought in, & the Medical Purveyor (Dr Lamb) wrote us that the Medical Department was "out of Bandages" & begged for a supply from our storehouse.

Old Finley — the head of that office — is utterly ossified & useless. The next available man on the list is our excellent warm hearted colleague, Dr Wood. His main defect is blind fanatical loyalty to his chief — Finley to wit. If the Commission oust Finley, I doubt whether Wood could be prevailed on to take his place. Dr Tripler, Gen: McClellan's Medical Director, is an energetic spasmodic positive crotchety genial old gentleman — (he would make an admirable Sir Anthony Absolute if he would consent to go on the stage) — He might be made to do, as head of the Bureau. He would certainly do better than it's present Wooden head. But McClellan, in conference with Bellows & Bishop Clark, hinted a doubt of his capacity. He was with McC. after the little Lewinsville skirmish, & sat on his horse ten minutes in full view of a wounded man who lay on the ground with a shattered tibia or femur or some such thing, & never even offered to dismount. This little omission seems to have settled Tripler in McClellan's estimation.

"We the Commission" think well of McClellan. His activity & industry & attention to details may not be equivalent to military genius but are of great practical value nevertheless. He has a talent for Silence. Nobody knows whether he has 100 000 or 250 000 men in camp around Washington. I discovered for myself that there were great field works going up on the E. side of the City — the Maryland side. They were unknown to the gossipers of *Willards'*.

I left W. early Sat: morning by R.R. — Stopped at *Baltimore* — Eutaw House. (Barnum's & the Gilmor House are *Secesh*) — breakfasted — took carriage — visited the new field work on *Federal Hill* & *Duryée's* redlegged Zouaves (now *Warren's*, Duryée being a Brigadier General) — & drove to Fort McHenry, where I found Genl Dix in a most jolly frame of mind over his wholesale arrest of Seceshers. The Maryland Legislature is seized & locked up. Not a particularly Constitutional or habeas-corpus-sy proceeding, but one ca'nt stand on forms & ceremonies when the house is on fire. — I saw the "French Lady" so-called — at the door of her or his casemate, in a dirty red dressing gown, apparently engaged in washing out certain undergarments.

Sept. 23. Friday aft^{n} to Savin Rock, taking Murray Hoffman with me. All well there. Ellie & her babies & her handmaidens sole remnants of the departed summer's housefull. Spent Saturday morning mostly in Maynard Rifle practice (rather wild) on the shore. Neither H. nor I is qualified for Berdan's Sharp-shooter Regiment. — Drove in the aft^{n} to Fair Haven. — Sunday was a grey cold N.E. day, but I enjoyed it. Loafed & waded a good deal & bade farewell to those fascinating rocks & shallows & tide pools. — Off this morn'g — for the season — by 9.45 A.M. train bringing Ellie babies baggage & all home to winter quarters. Dined at home at two o'clock & proceeded down town, to find among other pleasant things that I had overdrawn my bank a/c.

I'm resigned to speedy & total insolvency. War-taxes & cessation of business will have done their work before long. Poverty will soon drive me to enlist if patriotism do not, & then, if I survive the war, I will set up a street microscope exhibition — I recur for consolation to the remembrance of my microscopic experiences at S.R. — I never bottled so rich a tablespoonful of mud & water as I got from a certain salt-water ditch in the meadow behind the hotel. It produced, *inter alia*, a profusion of that marvellous self-acting carpenter's rule, Bacillaria paradoxa, sliding about in the liveliest way.

To night Bellows, Gibbs, Van Buren, & Agnew here in the library in Council. Slight supper thereafter, with Ellie presiding & very happy. Our reformation of the Medical Bureau does not make headway but rather drifts to leeward. McClellan is so busy & Mr Secy Cameron so slippery that it is hard to get decided action from either. So the M. Bureau continues to be an invertebrate organism with Finley for it's head. Gen: Frémont seems to have set up a local Sanitary Commission of his own at St Louis — "to act under the direction of Miss Dix". Success to it's action, regular or irregular. There is plenty of work to do. This has doubtless been got up by that indefatigable woman. She is disgusted with us, because we do not leave everything else & rush off the instant she tells us of something that needs attention. The last time we were in Washington she came upon us in breathless excitement to say that a cow in the Smithsonian grounds was dying of sunstroke, & she took it very ill that we did not adjourn instanter to look after the case.

Bad news from Missouri. Hard fighting at Lexington & Col: Mulligan compelled to surrender to a much superior force. There is room for doubt, but it is safe to believe reports of disaster. Frémont must look sharp or he will be superseded.

Kentucky seems to pronounce distinctly for the Nation. That is well — better than I hoped. But this is a doleful time, & I am intensely blue.

Sept. 25. Visit from Jack Ehninger. He gives up hope of appointment on anybody's staff & proposes to study Hardee and qualify himself for the next vacancy in Warren's (late Duryée's)

Zouaves, now at Baltimore, & probably the very best of all our volunteer regiments. — The bad news from Missouri confirmed of course. Lexington is lost. People lay this to Frémont & hold him responsible for Gen: Lyon's death & for all that has gone wrong in the West since he took command of that department. We pass quick judgment on our military leaders. Two months ago we reposed implicit faith in *Scott* & *McDowell.* Both are condemned now as worthless & we all swear by *McClellan*. I do not think we are yet quite prepared to supersede & shelve Frémont, but appearances are against his efficiency & fitness for his place.

The Navy Dep[t] shews signs of an awakening perception that capacity is more important than seniority, & is shelving centenarian commodores.

Sept. 26. Weather infelicitous for a National Fast Day, being singularly festal & sunshiny. To Trin: Church with Ellie & Johny. Vinton preached voluminously — confuted all who do vainly talk about State Rights, and fired heavily into Slaveholders. He maintains that slavery demoralizes the Master. Right enough. Absolute arbitrary power is a dangerous possession — and V. in his pulpit with a congregation at his mercy illustrates that truth.

Rev. V's conclusions were sound enough, though he got at some of them irregularly. Most sensible people begin to see that there can be no enduring peace in our borders till this baneful Slavery system is *reformed*, or put under a course of gradual extirpatory treatment. We are not in a condition to talk about dictating terms, just yet, to be sure. I fear the end will be postponed beyond my day. But the longer it is put off the more searching will be the reformation. Opinions are moving. We are fast drifting into Abolition notions that would have horrified us a year ago. The people who "want to see Jeff: Davis hanged, & Greeley & Beecher hanged with him" are thinning out. The extreme Wendell Phillips abolition party has no doubt quadrupled since Bull Run & is daily gaining converts.

Sept 27. Friday. Day overcast — tonight a lively S.E. storm. Not a jolly day. People do not like the way things are going in Missouri, & every one abuses *Frémont* except a St Louis editor who says the loss of Lexington is part of a Grand Strategic Plan. No doubt the Emperor had firm friends in Paris who took that view of Waterloo and maintained that *now* he had got the Allies at last just where he wanted to have them. Moreover reports keep obstinately multiplying & coming up again when contradicted, that the Rebels have closed the lower Potomac with batteries. Surely this could have been prevented. I am much exercised by omissions that seem unaccountable.

Some talk of great news to be hourly expected from an apocryphal Expedition that sailed from no place in particular nobody knows when — this is bosh — but another blow will soon be struck on the southern coast — & probably at Pensacola. Clitz says we must have the Navy Yard there before the fall gales set in, so as to give the blockading ships safe anchorage. Gen: Burnside is or has been here very active about something — & a R.I. regiment sent back from Wash^{n} is now in camp at Fort Hamilton.

Sept. 28. Sat: Visit from Bellows before breakfast. Knapp is in town & reports everything at Wash^{n} rose colored — everybody in the best spirits & troops steadily improving in spirit & discipline. The Commission doing good service & in high favor with all military authorities.

Olmsted telegraphs that McClellan is going on at once with Hospital accommodation for 15000 men. I think our plan (for *pavilion* hospitals) which was sent off this week has been adopted by the War Department.

Ellie spent the day at Staten Island, with Mrs Annie Cameron.

Mr S.B.R. here awhile this ev'g — i.e. till 12.½ — discussing a measure to be brought forward in next Diocesan Convention, viz: some declaration or protest against secession of southern Dioceses, or proclamation of the Church's loyalty to Government. He objects to any action — influenced by feelings of personal kindliness toward misguided deluded or possibly coerced Southern Churchmen & by that unhappy popular notion that "Religion has nothing to do with politics" — which seems to me practical Atheism. Bishop Potter prefers that all action be postponed till next General Convent^{n} and so it will be, I suppose.

We are not thoroughly in earnest even yet. When all Missouri is abandoned to the Seceshers — when Washington has fallen, & we are hurrying our new levies to the line of the Susquehanna, our blood may be warmed up to the true point. We need a stimulus even stronger than Bull Run.

Sept: 29. To day's papers strengthen the impression that the Potomac *is* closed by rebel batteries — Disgraceful to Government, if it be so, & discouraging to the People. It may force McClellan into premature offer of battle. — Nothing new from Missouri. Gen: Frémont has not left St Louis. He seems clearly unequal to his duties. They demand a great man, & his conduct of affairs, thus far, has been that of a small man.

Was ever so grand an issue of National life or National death fought with such little men for leaders!

Sept. 30. Monday night. To day's news is that the Rebels have suddenly abandoned Munson's Hill, which is occupied by our men. Probably intended to tempt McClellan into a forward movement in force. The enemy is now reported to be concentrated between Manassas Junction & Acquia Creek, contemplating the passage of the lower Potomac into Maryland — a most improbable movement. — There has been a brush at Pensacola, a privateer burned by a boat party from Fort Pickens, under the nose of the rebel batteries. No improvement in Missouri.

Called on Mrs Dr Mott (Senior) after breakfast. She wants me to be one of a Committee in aid of a grand "Mammoth" Fair to be got up in December for the relief of the poor, & especially for families of volunteers. I have misgivings about our lavish Charities. They are creating a dangerous pauper class. Volunteers fed & clothed by Gov^{t} ought to send their pay home to their families.

Business meeting tonight at Dr Van Buren's, with Bellows Agnew & Gibbs.

Olmsted's letters indicate that excitement & hard work acting on a sensitive nervous temperament are making his views morbid. He sees only present imbecility & future inevitable disaster. Seems to think the army a mere mob — war department paralyzed by corruption — Navy department ditto — &c &c &c.

We do not meet the revolutionary energy of the South with a corresponding intensity & unanimity — but I think Gov[t] seems trying to do it's work honestly & diligently —

Oct: 1. Hoadly, to whom I mentioned D[r] Van Buren's paper on quinine as a *prophylactic* agst Southern malaria (read last night) fully appreciated the importance of bringing that subject to the immediate attention of the War Department & gave me many instructive facts about the experience of the Panama R.R. C[o] in protecting it's employees from fever by the enforced systematic use of quinine. All this he promises to put on paper. It will make a valuable appendix to D[r] V.B.'s report.

Standing Com: of Tr: Ch: met this ev'g & sat till near eleven. The Vestry has much work before it. On the 25th March the "*Lispenard lease*", of some 80 lots, expires, & there are many grave questions about the disposition to be made of the property — rights of tenants in improvements — arrearages of taxes & assessments, etc: — Pity that lease should fall in when the times are so out of joint.

Our Washington news to day looks a little as if the rebels were falling back & McC. following them up, step by step. We have re-occupied our old position at Falls' Church, & some say there is but a curtain of Beauregard's army left before Washington & that it's masses have been moved off to the upper Potomac or Eastern Tennessee or elsewhere. McC. has moved his outposts forward a little but no Advance of the Army is as yet clearly pronounced, and (from what Col: Cullum told me) I think McClellan will make no decided advance till he is stronger in *field artillery*.

In Western Missouri everything seems still going *badly*.

Oct. 2[d]. Wednesday. Having been reminded last ev'g that I was a Delegate to the Diocesan Convention from Tr: Church — which fact had somehow slipped out of my remembrance, I took my seat awhile this morn'g at S[t] John's. My colleagues are Dunscomb & Gouv: Ogden. Nothing important had been done or seemed like to happen when I came away, as I was obliged to, before adjournment.

The proposed division of the diocese will no doubt be brought up, but it will not get beyond reference to a Committee at this session. Some declaratory resolution has been talked of by Judge Murray Hoffman & others recognizing & affirming the duty of loyalty & the guilt of treason, but the subject will probably not be stirred. The Bishop's *Address* discouraged it's introduction & recommended that it be left for the Gen: Convent^{n} to deal with next year. John Jay proposes to move that Queen Elizabeth's Homily against Rebellion be referred to a Committee to rewrite & disseminate. Not at all a bad notion. That Homily is a strong paper. But can it be purged of it's formalism & 16th century scholasticism — translated into a style now popular — without losing it's identity? J.J. means to omit his annual motion for a denunciation of the *Slave Trade*. It will be missed, having become by usage part of the Convention's regular business & entitled to a place in it's permanent Order of Business. Do not know why he should make an exception to his uniform practice for so many years. Perhaps because his party threatens to grow inconveniently large. He seems to have a natural instinctive taste for being in the minority — an oppressed protesting minority. He is a minoriti-colous animal, & can work heartily only with a whole public clamorous against him. Unless on that theory his exceeding moderation for the last six months is inexplicable.

Long talk with Dr Higbee. Were half our Northern population as earnest masculine & consistent in their hate of rebellion & of rebels, (many of his old friends are among them) this war would soon be ended. He told me about his interview with *Judge Chambers* of Maryland at the last meeting of Theolog: Seminary trustees, & how he cut his old friend, for disloyalty.

Miss Rosalie — returned from Delhi — dined here, & I escorted her to 24 Union Square.

Higbee — an old friend of Frémont's — is inclined to think him unequal to his great place. I fear Higbee is right. Frémont's recently published letters are weak. His great published catalogue of his staff, with an "*Adlatus*" & a "*Musical Director*" is characteristic of a vain ostentatious weak man, intoxicated with the importance of his high position. It is unfortunately very high & important. If we lose Missouri we lose all that lies West of it, even to the Pacific, & are no longer a Continental Nation. It looks just now as if we were fast losing *Missouri* & *Kentucky* too.

Oct. 3. Thursday. Summer weather. Wasted two or three hours at Convention this morn'g: heard much feeble wandering debate. Only notable feature was that somehow or other, every body managed to take a pot-shot at John Jay for his attempt to lug the Slave trade question into the Convention last year. Even Luther Bradish talked about "indecencies which had been committed" &c. J.J. was constantly jumping up to defend himself, which he did with little tact or force. — This ev'g I went to St John's but the edifice was closed. Convention probably adjourned finally at close of this morn'g's session — a sensible proceeding.

Mrs Ruggles the elder dined with us. This is her eighty second birth-day.

It's generally believed to day that Frémont is superseded by Wool and that Mansfield succeeds Wool at Fort Monroe — Bad business, but the Cabinet has only a choice of evils. —

Oct. 4. Friday. Still unseasonably warm. Woke headachy & got late down town. Did some little work there. Meeting at Dr Bellows' this ev'g (Sanitary Commission) — Bellows, Van Buren Agnew Gibbs & that invaluable Knapp, of Walpole N.H., one of our Inspectors. He's of a type rarely met among us — energetic intelligent self-sacrificing, but shy & timid when not in his work, & deficient in social self-assertion. Not unlike *Tom Pinch* in Dickens' "Martin Chuzzlewit." — Letters indicate that our business at Washington is going on favorably. Our plans for pavilion hospitals seem to have been referred to Tripler by the War Department & approved by him. They will provide for 15000 men. Tripler tells Olmsted that "for their hospital clothing he must rely on the stores of the Commission" — a pretty confession indeed!

It is time now for another money-grabbing movement. The influx of cash has become feeble of late, & we must stimulate the current with a few circulars & advertisements.

Frémont is not superseded in the least, nor is he ordered to Washington. That is certain. I think Gov[t] is right in this. A change of commanders just at this crisis would be prima facie wrong. When the storm is at a maximum it is a bad time to change one's umbrella. And it would seem (from newspapers) that Frémont's personal popularity in the West is an important feature of the case. Reports of his removal were ill received at St Louis. Wool is to leave Fort Monroe however, & Mansfield succeeds him. I *guess* Wool is to join Frémont as Military Duenna & keep the erratic "Pathfinder" in order. Such binary commands come seldom to good, but this may be the best disposition of this difficult case.

Oct. 7. At 2 P.M. to meeting of Col: Coll: trustees. No quorum. Pres[dt] King just from Washington — where he has been consorting with Gen: Scott, McClellan, Seward, & other notabilities, with whom he says the Sanitary Commission is in the highest favor. He returns sanguine of our success in the *next* battle, & gratified by the progress of the troops in organization & discipline — Vestry meet'g of Trinity Church tonight. Nothing material. Cisco tells me that Chase tells him that when Frémont came last to this country he travelled with a lady who was not his wife & that this was what kept F. out of Lincoln's Cabinet. The impression that F. is a bad man & without special talent gains ground. But it would not do to supersede him just now — so the National cause makes no headway in Missouri.

Oct. 8. Very energetic in Wall St, but chiefly in Sanitary Commission work. The Law and it's Profits are in the background. Sent off a cord of Knapp's Reports to the Commission to about 200 people. That Report should bring us many contributions of money. To night at D[r] Van Buren's till 12 o'clock with Gibbs & Agnew, incubating over proof sheets of his paper on Quinine as a prophylactic agst the Malaria of the Potomac — & of positions farther South — if we ever reach them. —

Ellie spent this morn'g as *Presidentess* of meeting of ladies of Trinity Parish, at S[t] John's Chapel, about supply of Hospital clothing & other feminine wares for the Army. She had awful misgivings & forebodings about it, but got through with her duties very comfortably, as I told her she would —

Olmsted came to town Sat: night, but I have not yet seen him. *Dr E. Harris* seems to be doing harm by his private communications with the Medical Bureau & Dr Tripler, about Hospital Buildings.

Oct. 9. Today's news is of another loss in Missouri — not very serious in itself, but these repeated failures & disasters must dishearten the loyalty of that region. Also there has been fighting near Hatteras (where the Devil helped the rebels to capture the *Fanny*, one of our gunboats, a few days ago.) It seems from the blind obscure report in the ev'g papers (via Fort Monroe & Baltimore) that one of our outlying positions was attacked & driven in, and that the Navy Department thereupon intervened, & the Monticello shelled the rebel assailants on the narrow strip of sand beach with most satisfactory results. — With all it's *material* advantages, with it's superior command of men & money & mechanical intelligence & skill, the North is still fighting at disadvantage agst Southern revolutionary desperation.

Oct. 12. Goddard (just from Wash^n) thinks less progress has been made there, in completing & arming fieldworks & in other respects than we suppose. Eleanor still in bed, but rather improving.

Last ev'g a *Sanitary* dinner here — viz: Gibbs, Olmsted, Bellows, Van Buren, Agnew. Session seemed agreeable — lasted into this morn'g, though only a little way. We were discussing the work we have got to do at Wash^n next week. — We must reinvigorate the movement to turn out Surgeon General *Finley* — & we must devise means & employ Special Agents to make the Allotment system more fruitful of results. The health of the Army will be improved if pay be more generally sent home, to wives or mothers of the soldiers or to Savings Banks, instead of being expended in the purchase of bad pies & rot-gut whiskey — and the health of the Community will gain in like measure if these remittances can be made more general for they will go far to avert the disease of pauperism with which we are threatened.

Oct. 13. Gen: Burnside is in town — missed tonight's train to Wash^n. Says there is to be another reconnaissance in force tomorrow — an offer of battle — which the rebels will not accept. Gunboats & transports have been leaving the harbor yesterday & today, to rendezvous at Annapolis & Fort Monroe. 20 000 men are said to be ready for embarkation on the Chesapeake. Destination of this great expedition unknown. Opinions divided between Brunswick — the neighbourhood of Charleston — & N. Orleans. N.O. is contra-indicated by the large supply of surf-boats. Perhaps that is only a blind. Great stores of *brick* have been embarked. That looks like lodgment of some sparsely settled point. *We* can only guess, but I dare say the rebel ringleaders *know* for the loyal North is infested by rebel spies & traitors, whose hemp is not yet grown, I fear.

Dr Hammond U.S.A. of Baltimore is in town. Only an Assist: Surgeon but has had intimations from the War Department that the last may be first & that he *may* take Dr Finley's place. It would be a curious coincidence after my expedition to Baltimore last month expressly to guage his calibre. Dr Bellows thinks well of him.

Oct. 23. Wednesday night. Rather fagged after a day's railroading thro' foul & chilly weather. Left Wash^n^ at 6 A.M. Took steamboat at Amboy 4.25 P.M. just as the sun was beginning to break through the decomposing clouds & shed its yellow sunset rays on the landscape of the Kills. Home by 7 P.M. & find all well here, & a telegram that poor Eloise who has been most seriously ill with inflammation of the lungs (acute bronchitis) is better.

I must record my memorabilia of this visit to the seat of War.

W. Gibbs — Bellows — Dr Frank Vinton — Walter Cutting, John Astor — K. Armstrong — & others — went on with me Monday morn'g (14th) — Journey was as usual — we reached Willard's tired famished and dyspeptic. From Wilmington to Wash^n^ there was the usual tossing of newspapers out of the car windows to expectant picket guards & sentries. I bought 50 cents worth of Tribunes in Baltimore & experienced great delectation in dribbling that pestilent sheet all through the state of Maryland.

The field work on Federal Hill is armed now — & another fort this side of Baltimore (on Murray's Hill) is nearly finished. Rather a bitter pill for the genteel chivalry of that Homicidal little town.

Willard's jammed full. I was quartered in 7th story & away back on the F Street end, so I had plenty of healthy exercise daily. There was a suggestion of fine bracing mountain air in this apartment and it commanded a magnificent view of everywhere.

The Commission no longer occupies it's room in the Treasury — having outgrown it. Government has hired for us — in addition to our *store* house — the old rambling 3 story "Adams House" for our offices & council room. It is now being repaired, polished up, & papered, and will make commodious headquarters.

We met there. Dr Wood (excellent loyal old gentleman —) Bishop Clark — Dr Howe — Dr Newberry attended, beside our N.Y. members. Col: Cullum was out of town, & we saw little of that inveterate red-tapist Major Shiras.

The business before us was to kick out the Surgeon General — to get our Hospital plans approved & the work of erecting them begun — to get increased efficiency put into the Allotment system, & so encourage volunteers to send their pay home to their families, & check the growth of pauperism, instead of spending it in the sutler's tent, to the detriment of their own condition, moral & sanitary. We worked efficiently toward these several ends & made good progress though without absolutely attaining either.

As to our groups of one story pavilion Hospitals — we overcame the protest against their cost, by demonstrating that it did not very much exceed the aggregate of exorbitant rents paid for old buildings (unfit for Hospital purposes & sure to become pesthouses when it shall become necessary to close their windows) & the expense of alterations & ventilating arrangements, that would be defective & insufficient at best. Gen: Meigs (the ablest man I have seen in Washington) spent a morning with us discussing this & other subjects. N.B. He is very uneasy about the iron-plated rebel steamer *Merrimac*: thinks we have only two guns that can make any impression on her, viz: the "Union Gun" at Monroe & another that is not yet mounted: expects her to sally forth "on the Rampage" in a few days, shell the camp at Newport News, pass Fort Monroe, and play the devil. If he is right & she is invulnerable, there is no reason why she should not steam up the Narrows & lay this city under contribution. D[r] Tripler was an early convert to the Hospital scheme & brought over *McClellan*. They united in endorsing it to the extent of 5000 beds, but ask for two groups of buildings instead of five. Tripler says they have not Medical Officers enough to take charge of more than two. We left the plan approved in writing by Gen: Meigs, Gen McClellan, D[r] Tripler, & Cameron, & only waiting for Lincoln's endorsement — which Cameron insisted upon because of the large outlay involved. Cameron is sadly wanting in moral courage, & the first question he asks about any measure is "What will the newspapers say?"

The Surgeon-General question is still undecided. Scott, the Assistant Sec: of War, is earnest for Finley's removal & Hammond's appointment. After the Com: adjourned (Sat: ev'g) D[r] Bellows & I staid behind for an interview with Cameron Tuesday night. Cameron talked about the newspapers, demurred & hesitated about removing Finley tho' admitting his utter imbecility to be most deleterious just now — & pronounced against *H.* most emphatically the moment he was named. "Whatever he did, he should not appoint *that* man". Some official pique or personal grievance was evidently in his mind. — Then I brought up the *Allotment* matter, & suggested that the *Pension Agents* be charged with the duty of receiving & distributing monies sent home — but Cameron — tho' admitting the propriety of employing them & the immense importance of the work to be done — was afraid of the newspapers. "There would be a howl" about increasing the patronage of the department — he did'nt think he could safely take any action about it. I do'nt know whether Cameron is corrupt or not, but he is certainly a most cowardly caitiff.

We had an audience of Lincoln from 9 to 11 A.M. Thursday — (I think it was Thursday). He is lank and hardfeatured — among the ugliest whitemen I have seen. Decidedly plebeian. *Superficially* vulgar & a Snob. But not *essentially*. He seems to me clear headed & soundhearted — tho' his laugh is the laugh of a Yahoo, with a wrinkling of the nose that suggests affinity with the Tapir & other pachyderms, and his grammar is weak. — After we had presented our views about the Surgeon General, & after Lincoln had charged us with "wanting to run the machine" & had been confuted — Bishop Clark introduced the subject of *exchange of prisoners.* Of course L. replied that such Exchange implied recognition of the Rebel Government as a legitimate belligerent power — & spoke of the flag of truce sent out to recover Col: Cameron's body after the battle of Bull Run, & of Gen: Scott's reluctance to send it. The Genl said he had always held that if *he* fell in battle he should be quite satisfied with his place of sepulture & with his company — that he should be quite satisfied to rest on the battlefield with his soldiers. — Poor old Scott, by the way, is sinking — grows lethargic — sleeps half the day — & entertains certain jealousies of McClellan. His career is finished.

Had a talk with poor *McDowell.* Still sore & morbid about Bull Run.

Sunday morn'g I spent with that admirable *Knapp* (a combination of *Tom Pinch* & *Mark Tapley* — vide Dickens' Martin Chuzzlewit) at the "*Soldiers' Home*" which is under his special charge. Discoursed sundry convalescent wounded prisoners from Richmond, & the women & children of Col: Cooke's regular regiment just returned from Camp Floyd & Salt Lake City, travelworn & weary, & most thankful for their temporary shelter in this charitable Hospice.

Monday I had a long ride, from breakfast time to 5 P.M., with Dr Bellows & Knapp. We crossed the Potomac at the Georgetown rope ferry, & went to Munson's Hill, & Falls' Church, through beautiful byeways & wood-roads. The landscapes of Virginia are lovely. "Where's the coward that would not dare to fight for such a land!" — Our steeds were cavalry horses put at disposal of the Commission by Uncle Sam. We spent a little time in camps of the Mass: 18th (Col: Barnes) & 22^{d} (Col: Wilson — the Senator). Returning home, very tired, I was gladdened by a telegram from Mr Derby, announcing that Eloise is decidedly better. His last letter, rec^{d} that morn'g, indicated that she was hopelessly ill, & given over by her physicians.

Another matter was the schismatic St Louis Sanitary Commission appointed by Gen: Frémont on his own authority with plenary powers, ignoring our authority derived from the War Department. It's an excellent board, of five or six prominent St Louis men. The Sec^{y} of War — being only too happy to snub Frémont sent him orders to revoke this appointment or to instruct his local Commission to report to us — neither of which he has yet done. Of course all we want is to keep the peace & secure concert & unity of action, so I telegraphed them to send us one of their number with power to treat & adjust all matters in controversy. They sent us their chief, Rev: Dr Eliot of St Louis, a Unitarian philosophe & a great man in his own City. He is fluent & plausible, fond of power, & with a mental apparatus constructed on a curiously illogical feminine plan. He appeared to us Wednesday ev'g in high wrath at our interference. His dignity was cruelly abraded, & he talked of appeasing it by the sacrifice of the sanitary interests of the Western Division. He & his colleagues would probably feel it due to themselves to abandon their work, & leave the field to us. To be sure we should probably be able to do very little with all the local feeling of St Louis against us &c &c. We represented that we had no notion of interfering with them: that we only wanted to do what the War Department had entrusted to us: that we only asked them to work under authority from headquarters instead of working without it & so forth — And above all, that no appearance of wrong ought to be done just now to the principles of National Unity. He was fractious & petulant, & we spent one ev'g in a very jolly little discussion. Bellows our chief speaker. Bellows & Eliot are in some sense professional rivals, & clawed each other in an urbane velvety brotherly Christian way. Dr Vinton (whom we invited to the honors of our sitting as an Associate) put in his oar once or twice more efficiently than I expected. Ja^{s} W. Beekman & Dr Hartshorne of Philad^{a} were also present as associate members, but said little. I gave Eliot one or two touches on the jaw, that seemed to tell. He hauled off a little after midnight much shattered & in an ill humor. But he was in a better frame next day, & I guess our proposition will be well received — viz: to make one of the St Louis men a full member of the Commission, & to let them retain their organization as a local auxiliary Board.

There was sharp fighting near *Leesburgh* Monday. (Ball's Bluff.) We crossed the Potomac & encountered the rebels in superior force. Poor Col: Baker was killed, & Cogswell of the Regulars, who married Miss Susan Lane a year ago was wounded & made prisoner. — Gen: Burnside told me last ev'g that it was a substantial success; that we have crossed the Upper Potomac & are entrenching ourselves on that side, but have lost 3 guns — a rifled cannon & two mountain howitzers & have suffered a good deal, generally. It is an obscure story as yet. Knapp & D[r] Douglas left Wash[n] at 4 this A.M. on horseback, with a wagon load of hospital stores, & I came rather near going with them.

I had a pleasant aft[n] drive with Walter Cutting to Arlington House — and a morning ride with J.W. Beekman to Munson's Hill, where we dined with Major Wainwright.

The lower Potomac is now closed by rebel batteries. This may precipitate a general action. But our attention is concentrated on the Naval expedition that has sailed from Annapolis for some point on the Southern coast — a fleet of 400 guns with near 20 000 men in it's transports. Some say for Charleston — others, for Norfolk — for Pensacola — New Orleans &c &c &c. Great Armadas are risky things. This may well produce nothing for us but another disaster & disgrace. — Be it so, if God so will it. Defeat & disgrace may do us good. If Missouri & Kentucky were wholly lost, Washington & Cincinnati sacked, our line of defence on the Susquehanna instead of the Potomac, & England in arms against us, we should be stronger than we are now.

Oct. 24. Thursday night. Cold autumnal day. Dyspeptic, but diligent. Letter from M[r] Derby indicating that Eloise is through the worst of her severe illness. Murray Hoffman dined here. Afterwards there were G.C.A. M[r] Ruggles, D[r] Bellows & D[r] Peters. Bellows had an interview of an hour or more with *Cameron* yesterday — moved the *Hospital* plans a step forwards & made some progress in the matter of the Surgeon General.

News to day is important. The rebel demonstration agst the blockading squadron at the mouth of the Mississippi — about which we have heard such depressing reports — seems to have been a failure. — So with the attack on Fort Pickens & Billy Wilson's regiment. It was repulsed, though after sharp fighting & loss on both sides. Major Vogdes is a prisoner. He can give the rebels much valuable information on points of Military History — Monday's affair at "Edwards' Ferry" seems to have been a bad business — a blunder & a repulse — Ellie calls it a "microscopic Bulls' Run" — To day's reports are of repulse & defeat with loss of 1000 men. — Col: Baker is killed,

Cogswell, who married Miss Susan Lane a year ago, wounded & a prisoner.

I think it will turn out that Baker transgressed his orders, & converted a mere reconnoissance into an attack on a superior force. We are not in Leesburgh, but I believe we hold our position on the Virginia side of the Potomac at "Edwards' Ferry".

Oct. 26. Sat: night. Dull weather. The "Edwards' Ferry" affair was a decided emphatic *defeat* with serious loss, & we have retired across the river. The rebels are fortifying themselves unmolested this side of Leesburgh. I'm tempted to apply for a commission as Brigadier General at least, for I am sure I should not have made this blunder. I should not have attempted to move a column across a river with *one scow*, & without artillery to protect the passage. What can Gen: Banks & Gen: Stone be doing?

Oct. 27. Sunday. Legitimate autumnal cold. I fear it will tell on our camps, & make itself felt in a crop of pneumonias, rheumatisms & dysenteries.

This next week will be an anxious time. Much depends on the success of our Armada, with it's 400 guns & 20 000 men, now fairly under way for parts unknown. Naval expeditions are full of hazard. If we succeed in making a lodgment on the rebel coast, the question will be fairly tested whether there is or is not a strong latent suppressed Union feeling in Secesh-dom. I do not believe it exists.

Oct. 28. Monday. Cool weather. Busy day. Mrs Wise (Edwd Everett's daughter & wife of Lt Wise of the Navy) dined here — also Capt Thatcher of the 14th Infantry — (regulars) who rose from the ranks, a rare instance — also Jem. Thatcher is a wellbred gentlemanlike young fellow enough, & has his heart in the cause — would there more *regular* officers like him! The despised "*seculars*" have the advantage of them generally on that point.

We went to the Opera. Full house, & two little operas given; "Les Noces de Jeannette" which was utter drivel, & Donizetti's "Betly" which seemed high art by contrast. On the whole a very feeble performance. Lasted from 8 till near 12. If there were 2000 people in the house, some 8000 hours of human life — equivalent to nearly a year, (more than a year if sleeping time be allowed for) were absolutely wasted on this imbecility.

Rumor prevalent in the House that our great Naval expedition is checkmated by somebody's treachery who has conveyed the rebels intelligence of it's destination. Do'nt believe it.

To day's news generally encouraging. Success at Romney, V^{a}. Frémont doing well in Missouri. Loyal feeling crops out in N. Carolina — & the planters throughout Secesh-dom begin to grumble about unsalable cotton. They are probably drawing Plutarchian parallels between King U.S. Log & King C.S. Stork to the disadvantage of the latter.

Oct. 29. Tuesday. No events. — N.B. I predict there will be no great battle on the Potomac line before next spring — if then.

The Grand Armada was still in Hampton Roads Saturday. This pause does not seem strong proof of high military capacity in Com: Du Pont & Genl Sherman, but perhaps it is all right. The report that these commanders have been "sowld" by a treacherous official, who ran away with the sealed orders in his pocket that shew their destination, is still current.

It's our great misfortune that the North is not yet thoroughly purged of spies & traitors. I could name a dozen people in this City, whom I believe fully capable of conveying intelligence to the rebels. There are commissioned officers of high grade in Army & Navy whom many distrust — among them, I'm sorry to say is *L.W.* He is most unjustly suspected no doubt — but we have Colonels & Navy Capt^{ns} now in active service, who would have no serious objection to seeing the rebels triumphant. — — — — Charles Davis died this morn'g after a long illness. Dropsy. Drink. — He was a brother-in-law of Dr Bellows. — A telegraph operator called on Wolcott Gibbs Saturday with a singular story. He was lounging about the streets of Alexandria on the 21st or 22^{d} when he heard the familiar tapping of a telegraph, & being a *Sound-Reader*, stopped to listen. It was the Army telegraph & he heard it tell the story of the Leesburgh defeat, & heard moreover one or two important orders from headquarters. Most experienced Telegraph operators are *Sound Readers* & this gross want of precaution may account for the rebels having been forewarned of certain intended movements — e.g. that on Munson's Hill. The Secretary of War has been duly notified of this.

Oct. 30. Wednesday. Diligent in Wall St. on San: Com: business. This ev'g to meeting of Trin: Church Stand'g Com: from 8 to 11.

According to the aft^{n} papers our great Naval Expedition sailed from Hampton Roads this A.M. at daylight. Nobody knows it's destination. It may have sailed for Pensacola, New Orleans, *Brunswick*, Hatteras Inlet, Charleston Harbor, Beaufort, or Norfolk. God prosper it! — But that *iron-plated steamer Merrimac* is an ugly complication. If what I hear about her be true, she can lay New York under Contribution, whenever she please to come this way. But I do'nt quite believe all I hear. Anyhow, Merrimac or no Merrimac, this is a depressing time. We have made little progress during these six months toward crushing this Colossal Rebellion. The more conspicuous events of the war have rather disgraced us thus far. They have been ignominious blunders failures & defeats. McClellan has accomplished nothing. Frémont is distrusted & with good reason. This grand Naval Expedition is a most hazardous move, that may well terminate in fearful disaster & loss. The times seem out of joint generally. Were I "born to set them right", I should take one or two vigorous steps not contemplated by Lincoln & Seward.

Nov. 2^{d}. Sat: A most violent storm. Barometer still falling: blowing a gale all day. It's an ill wind — a secession-sympathizing disgrace to our loyal Northern winds, & I fear it has blown disaster on the Country. Our fleet may well be dispersed, or worse, and it is hardly possible but that great mischief has been done on board the horse carrying transports. Prof: Bache, at the Century Club to night, is very anxious. He says we shall hear from the expedition by Wednesday. I predict we shall hear grievous tidings.

Last night a San: Com: meeting at Dr Bellows'. Van Buren Agnew Gibbs Olmsted Prof: Bache & myself.

Dr Tripler has presented charges against the Surgeon General for conduct unbecoming an officer & a gentleman —

I believe the S.G. kicked the Medical Director out of his office or something of the sort. Very likely Tripler deserved it. — Gen: Scott *retires* & McClellan is Commander in Chief. Saw a letter from Wash[n] tonight stating that Col. Baker had a Major General's Commission in his pocket when he fell, that he knew Scott was to retire, that he advanced in disobedience of his orders hoping to gain a brilliant success, & to be appointed to Scott's place over McClellan's head. It would be incredible, but for the fact that he was intimate with Lincoln & is believed to have possessed great influence with him. Quam parvâ sapientiâ &c! Baker was undoubtedly eaten up by inordinate personal ambition.

Nov. 3. Sunday. A fine clear cool day. Morning papers say that yesterday's terrible storm did not probably prevail south of Hatteras. Perhaps. I think we shall hear of national loss & damage on a large scale, and of Bishop-General Polk quoting "Afflavit Deus et dissipantur" & issuing a form of thanksgiving for this fatal Northeaster. It was a gale of most unusual severity, but it is possible our fleet was outside it's range.

Nov. 4. This aft[n] dined here D[r] Van Buren — Agnew — Gibbs — Prof: Bache & wife — D[r] Bellows — Olmsted — a sanitary symposium from 6 to 12. (M[r] Ruggles & Col: Cullum joined us.) We decided on a Newspaper War. Sec[y] Cameron & Sec[y] Seward keep no faith with us. The Washington Hospitals are not yet commenced & Finley is still Surgeon General notwithstanding their assurances.

Cullum says Scott actually means to go abroad — for the sake of some ailment that he wants treated by Parisian Surgery — & which Van Buren says can be as well treated here.

This will be an ugly blot at the end of Scott's bright record. Cullum regrets it & has remonstrated in vain. He says Charles King has more influence with the Gen: than any other man. M[r] S.B.R. will enlist C.K. in the service. — His flight will do us harm abroad. He goes with his daughter & son-in-law Col: Henry Scott, who is just put on the retired list because of certain apocryphal *piles*. Both sympathize with secession. — *Punch* will picture the General as a Rat leaving a sinking ship.

Nov[r] 5. Tuesday. Election Day. Vote apparently light. Rumors this A.M. of great success in Western V[a] — at or near "Gauley Bridge". Floyd is "wiped out by Rosecrans". Also that the Naval expedition is not materially tempest-tossed, was approaching Bull's Bay near Charleston, Sat: ev'g. Bull's Bay is an ill-sounding name. I hope it is not the destination of an Armada. B. is an unlucky letter, teste *B*ig *B*ethel, *B*ulls' Run, & *B*all's *B*luff.

Tonight with Ellie & M[rs] D.C. Murray to one of Mason & Thomas' Classical Soirees. A quartette of Mozart's ("in G. major N[o] 1") was very lovely. The rest of the programme not impressive.

Cha[s] King has seen Gen: Scott, who says "You distress me Sir" & adheres to his fatal determination.

Nov: 6. Wednesday. Cloudy day, to night wet & windy. Meeting at Chamber of Commerce this A.M. of an Executive Auxiliary Committee in aid of the Sanitary. Our finances begin to wane.

Election yesterday has gone ill. Lynch has run for Sheriff as successfully as he ran with Varian's Battery in July. Murray Hoffman & LB Woodruff are ousted from the bench of the Superior Court by a couple of scurvy fellows of whom no one knows any good.

Nothing special from the seat of War, & no definite news from the Naval Expedition. I see no assurance yet that it was unscathed by Saturday's storm.

Gen: *Frémont* is superseded & notifies his army of the fact in a becoming & dignified General Order, that is exactly what it should be. I suppose his removal was a necessity — even at this moment, in the face of the enemy & with mutiny imminent as it's consequence. Frémont has undoubtedly shown lack of discretion & foresight. He is in the hands of California gamblers & speculators, many of whom are his creditors. But it was a most lamentable necessity, and will probably be followed by the retreat or defeat of his disgusted Army. He seems to possess a personal magnetic influence over his subordinates, if he have no other qualification for command.

The criticisms on his memorable Proclamation are absurd. I wonder if Gov[t] has sent out a real estate agent with the Naval

Expedition to arrange for a temporary hiring of the land on which 15000 men are to be encamped, & has instructed Gen: Sherman not to disembark his troops till a proper ground for their occupation is secured with all respect for the legal & Constitutional rights of the proprietor. — If not — why should it treat rebel slave property with more delicate consideration than other property of rebels?

Nov. 8. Friday. Went to Philad^{a} yesterday 2 P.M. Steamboat to Amboy — with Prof: Bache, Dr Bellows, Olmsted Agnew & Van Buren. Detained near Burlington — reached Continental (admirably appointed hotel) at 7 P.M. & after gulping down a cup of tea proceeded to H. Binney's, who had convened some 30 or 40 solid men of Philad^{a} professional & financial — to meet us, & consult as to organizing our Associates in that City for action in aid of the San: Commission. I knew few of them. There were Caleb Cope, Henry Carey, Judge Hare, Dr John McClellan (the Genl's brother) — Dr Meigs — Dr Gurney Smith, Sam: Powel, Dr Ducachet, Dr Furniss & others. Bishop Alonzo Potter took the chair, & we of the Commission made statements & explanations. Dr Bellows, Dr Van Buren & Prof: Bache delivered themselves very effectively. The result was the appointment of Committees &c. It may or may not lead to something substantial. Binney is not well enough to do much work, & Dr Hartshorne, tho' very willing, does not look like an efficient man.

Off with Olmsted at 9½ A.M. today & was in Wall St. before two o'clock.

The first hint or germ of important news from two several points arrived this aft^{n}. 1. In S.E. Missouri, a severe engagement, which does not look like a victory. We attacked Belmont & defeated the enemy with immense loss, but somehow or other found it convenient to retire, with loss of guns & men — as usual. — Secondly Reports rec^{d} at Fort Monroe, thro' Norfolk, of the fate of the Great Naval Expedition, are that two transports, with horses, were lost in last week's gale on the N.C. coast, & that seventy odd shipwrecked prisoners had been carried to Raleigh — that the fleet had commenced operations at *Port Royal*, where "it was meeting with a warm reception" — one of our vessels disabled. That's all. As this comes thro' rebel reporters, it seems reliable evidence that we had experienced no serious disaster or repulse up to it's date.

But *Beaufort* is at the head of this inlet — & it begins with the fatal B. — as do *Belmont* & Buchanan & Breckinridge & Blunder — Botch — Bungle — Behind-hand — & other words that Military Historians will use in commenting on our strategy.

Leaving the Jersey ferry boat this aft^{n} we met the distinguished Charles Sumner. He says he knows the instructions given to Gen: Sherman as to his relations with the Contrabands of the district he is to occupy, & all the secret history of their discussion & settlement in the Cabinet, & that they are equivalent to *Emancipation*. We shall see. I put no great faith in Sumner — & we may as well effect our landing & secure our foothold before we consider that question. — I observe that the word "Contraband" has established itself in a new sense, as designating a class of biped mammalia. This we owe to Gen. Butler. "Secesh" is another novelty that may become classical English. Some one suggests "Shecesh" as a legitimate derivative, applicable to the disloyal womankind who give us so much trouble at Baltimore & all along the border. The Maryland election, by the by, results in a great majority for the "Union" ticket. Of course the rebels will swear that state is overawed by an armed force.

Nov. 9. Sat: Feel comparatively jolly today, notwithstanding dismal wet weather, grievous dyspepsia, & grave anxiety about the fate of our Naval Expedition, which is still unknown. The jollifying agent is potent: Beethoven's C minor Symphony, which I have heard twice to day, namely at morn'g Rehearsal & at the ϕil: concert (with Ellie) tonight. What a glorious — perfect — inspired — & inspiring work it is! Clearly, I think, the first of Orchestral compositions. New points shew themselves at every performance. I never appreciated the 3^{d} movement till to day.

Our reports about the *Belmont* battle of the 7th look better, but are still loose & indefinite. Nothing farther from the Naval

Expedition, now generally believed to have descended on Port Royal & Beaufort.

Little Lewis begins to utter certain articulate sounds & can almost walk alone.

Gen: Scott sailed for Europe this morn'g, in spite of remonstrances. I doubt his return. He is very shaky.

$900.00 for the Sanitary Commission to day from the little City of Troy, & more coming.

Nov. 11. No despatches from Commodore Du Pont or Gen: Sherman even yet. But reports have been received, through rebel channels, at Old Point & Hatteras which agree in substance — viz: that the batteries at the mouth of Port Royal Harbor were silenced or stormed, & that we have occupied *Beaufort*, & advanced toward the line of the Charleston & Savannah R.R. May the news be true! I do not venture to believe it yet.

Nov. 13. Wednesday. Gloria in Excelsis Deo! Thank God it is established at last that loyal seamen & soldiers can win battles. "Rebellion has bad luck" just now. Port Royal forts shelled out & their defenders cut & run after five hours firing. Serious damage to our Armada. *Beaufort* abandoned by the Chivalry. Only one white man left in the town, & he was *vino gravatus*, or more probably comatose from excessive whiskey — In Eastern Kentucky, at *Piketon*, what looks like an important victory on a considerable scale — 1000 prisoners taken, it is said, & after a fight that lasted two days. — Signs of loyalty reasserting itself in N. Carolina & in Eastern Tennessee — & lastly a report (which I do not believe) that the famous privateer Sumter is nabbed at last.

Nothing of importance for the Journal of private life. Long session this morn'g with our Auxiliary Committee men of the San: Commission, who agree to memorialize the Pres^{dt} for reform in the Medical Bureau.

Novr 16. Sat: Today's chilly wind was an anachronism & belonged to March. Walked up town this aft^{n} with G.C.A, on the East side of the City, & he dined here. Ellie not quite well & could not join us. Great news. Captn Wilkes of the San Jacinto has reported himself in Hampton roads, with Hon: Mason & Hon: Slidell, prisoners. He overhauled a British steamer — near the Bahamas — to which they had been transferred from their vessel that ran the blockade, boarded her, and brought off the Rebel Emissaries. Perhaps he brought us into a War with England at the same time. We shall see.

Executive Com: of Sanitary Commission met last night at Wolcott Gibbs' — 29th St. Dr Bellows — Dr Agnew Dr Van Buren, Gibbs & I. — Dr Godfrey Aigner present — our Cairo Inspector.

Night before (Thursday) Standing Com: of Tr: Ch: Vestry met at the Vestry office. After the meeting I visited & inspected a big fire in Water St. near Market.

We are very jolly over the bombardment of Port Royal. May our exultation not prove premature! —

Novr 19. Tuesday. A most crystalline night, perfect December ten nights too soon. The streets white with moonlight as with snow, & the sky above dusky sapphire specked with diamond dust. It is 12.30 & I'm just from a Sanitary Commission session at Dr Bellows' — with Gibbs, Van Buren & Agnew — Dr Jenkins & Dr Aigner — Inspector — also present, and a Dr Pollak of St Louis. [a gas-bag?]

No special news these last few days. It would seem that our seizure of Mason & Slidell is within the rules of International law as laid down by British authorities & supported by British precedent. But I fear John Bull will shew his horns & that we shall have increased ill feeling on both sides. Foreign war would be an ugly complication of our internal disease. — I have no respect for John Bull any more. He ought to be called John B. Pecksniff.

Dr Jenkins, just from Washington, tells me McClellan is steadily moving ambulance trains to the front. Arrival from Port Royal to day. We have not yet occupied Beaufort. — Dan Messenger is appointed Quarter Master on *Foster's* staff — Foster was one of Anderson's officers in Sumter — & goes South with Burnside on our next Naval expedition. Willy Cutting & George Fearing are on Burnside's staff — both likely to make useful officers.

Nov[r] 20. We talk very stiffly about the capture of Mason & Slidell — but I greatly fear that it will give our mean cousin across the water an excuse for quarrelling with us. I am ashamed of England — if the Saturday Review the Times & Blackwood be exponents of English feeling.

Dear little fair haired Templekin began school — i.e. entered on the cares & troubles of life — to day. At a little baby establishment in 15th St. with one M[me] Aubert for head nurse.

Letter to day inviting members of the "*Senatorial Commission*" to inspect a "*Portiable Oven*" in 3[d] Avenue.

Nov. 24. Experimented on a "Russian bath" in 27th St. Thursday aft[n]. Very severe experience — alternation of steaming & cold water douche. But I mean to try it again. *Sanitary* meeting at Van Buren's Friday night. An important movement comes off in Boston on Tuesday & Wednesday in aid of the Com:. Bellows & Gibbs are to attend & cooperate. I cannot accompany them, having my hands full of work for the Com: here, in anticipation of it's Wash[n] session next Friday. Our Philad[a] organization of Associates seems to be moving energetically.

Miss Mattie Ward engaged to Winthrop Chanler. Sorry for the young lady. W.C. is a copperhead.

Nov. 27. Wednesday. Wet night. Very diligent on San: Com: affairs. Meeting of N.Y. Commissioners here Monday ev'g — with M[r] Ruggles as "Adlatus" — Have corrected & re-corrected proofs of a "begging letter" — a mendicatory whine some 20 pages long. Unless we the Commission be soon reinforced with money, we must begin to wind up — dismiss inspectors — & go into liquidation. — Battle with the Surgeon General is upon us at last. The "*World*" of a week ago published an attack on his inefficiency. The "*Times*" — (instigated of course by old D[r] Satterlee, U.S.A.) — defends him by assuming that the attack came from the Commission — (which it did'nt — it was D[r] Agnew's own private dab at red-tape & mismanagement) & charges the Commission with presumption & ambition in assailing Gov[t] Officials & trying to supersede them. The "World" responded this morning — in a damaging way. Other shots will follow, and from heavy ordnance.

Nov. 28. Weather tonight looks unpropitious for tomorrow's Wash^{n} journey. The Commission meets Saturday, & I take with me this time Ellen & Miss Rosalie & several trunks that look like model huts for Army winter quarters. I fear the ladies will not have so good a time as they expect. They will be without any reliable escort, for my time will be wholly occupied. I feel uncomfortable, too, about deserting the children, though they will have abundant & vigilant supervision from N° 24 & from next door. God grant no sickness or accident occur while we are away!

We dined at Mr S.B.R's. Johny & Temple convives — also Geo. F. Allen.

Tho' I have not entered a Church today, I am none the less devoutly thankful for many things that belong to the history of the past year — above all, for the resolution patriotism & unselfishness the North has shewn, as a whole — and the value this has added to the life of every one of us.

We are waiting anxiously for news from Fort Pickens. We know that the long-deferred game was opened there some 10 days ago. The intelligence comes via Norfolk & includes breaches in Fort Pickens & two of our frigates obliged to haul off. But this current of information has run dry these last two days. Thence I infer the probability of a decided success. — Had they actually damaged the masonry of Pickens or repulsed the Colorado & the Niagara, they would have reported ships & fort annihilated. But one looks uneasily for authentic reports, nevertheless.

Burnside seems on the eve of going forth from Annapolis, in command of another Naval expedition some 15000 strong — destination unknown but much guessed at. Foster (of Fort Sumter) is one of his Brigadier Generals. Willy Cutting — Dan. Messenger — Tip Hoffman — & Geo. Fearing go with the expedition in various staff-capacities — assistant quartermaster and the like.

Were I Dictator at this time, my military policy would be — 1. To defend & hold Washington Western V^{a}, Kentucky, Missouri. 2. To make a vigorous demonstration in support of the oppressed loyalty that survives in North Carolina & in Eastern Tennessee. 3. To recover & hold, (or destroy with sunken ships,) every port and inlet from Hatteras to Galveston. The inland forests of Georgia & Arkansas cannot be overrun & occupied, but the rebels of the South can be locked up & left to suffer & starve till they repent & beg pardon. That is our true policy.

Dec. 14. England seems wrathful about the seizure of Mason & Slidell, but disposed to admit that we were technically right. Soreness & irritation are increasing & may well lead to War somehow. England's last War was to uphold Mahometanism — her next may be in aid of slavery. It's a mean people.

Signs multiply of an *Opposition party* — founded on Anti-slavery feeling stronger than that of the Administration. I am content to leave that very delicate & difficult question in the hands of Gov^{t} — tho' my instincts seem to tell me that it's present policy is weak vacillating & timid.

Memorabilia of Washington.

Off early on Friday the 29th — with Ellie, Miss Rosalie, & *Annie*, Mrs Ellie's Chief of Staff. John Astor was with us — en route for Wash^{n} to enter on his novel duties as a volunteer aid to McClellan. He is a very fine fellow, were he tenfold a millionaire. Reach Wash^{n} comfortably & find excellent rooms including a nice private parlor, secured us by Mr Knapp.

Find also that the meeting of San: Com: is adjourned to the following Tuesday. Thus I had a spare day or two to devote to the ladies. Took them to Alexandria & through Fort Ellsworth, on Saturday. Next morn'g we went to St John's church & I dined in the ev'g with Gen. Keyes, & Astor, who lives with him for the present. — There are officers of high position who do not hesitate to denounce *Gen. Scott* as of lukewarm loyalty & more Southern than National. They say his intimate associates of last winter & spring, up to the very outbreak of the War, were all traitors — men like Mason of V^{a}. Keyes was dismissed from his staff for advising about the reinforcement of Pickens at the Presdt's request without Scott's privity. It is even said that Col. Henry Scott disclosed to the rebels an intended move of McClellan's agst Munson's Hill, thus enabling them to withdraw without loss — and that McClellan demanded the retirement of both the Gen: & his son in law

— under threat of exposure. Hence the retreat of both to Europe. All this may be true or not — probably not. I do not believe Col. Henry Scott knew anything about McClellan's plans & though it is certain his heart has never been in the war, he has always seemed to me a man of the highest honor & principle. I'm almost ashamed to have recorded the existence of so shameful a story.

The next (Monday) morn'g with the ladies to Camp of 6th Cavalry (Regulars) to see parade & drill. Col. Emory (Bache's brother in law) late suspected of secessionism, in command. Laurence Williams Major. One of the Captains, *Lowell* of Boston, a notably promising officer — admired & commended by his Regular brethren as the best appointment ever made from civil life. Clarence Cram is in the same Regiment & working hard to fill a position for which his physique & all his former habits rather tend to disqualify him.

Last Sunday morn'g, we drove across the river — heard service at a Mass: camp (Fort Albany) & a thoughtful appropriate Kingsley-esque sermon from it's chaplain. It's Colonel (Green) is reported erratic eccentric & half-cracked. Thence to Arlington House where we had a long talk with Gen. McDowell & Mrs McD. whom I knew a little at West Point ten years ago. She has not gained in personal beauty. Poor McD. is still sore about *Bull's Run*, and insisted on shewing me his military maps, & how he had ordered one division to advance on this road & another on that, & how they would certainly have cut off or destroyed one of the enemy's advanced brigades of S. Carolina soldiers, only they were dilatory in advancing. This was a specially pleasant drive, in the loveliest & warm hazy Indian summer weather. Such weather has prevailed during this visit. It has been a December worthy of Naples. It changed two or three days ago & became much cooler, but still clear & genial.

Last Wednesday I went with the ladies directly after dinner to camp of Brooklyn 14th at Upton's Hill, returning at midnight — a fine frosty moonlight drive, passing great camp fires & groups of ghostly white tents. There was a "performance" by soldiers of the 14th: songs, pathetic & comic — recitations — nigger minstrelsy — &c. Very creditable. Afterwards a jolly supper at headquarters.

The Commission met Tuesday & sat till Sat: night. I remained to help Olmsted with his Report to the Secretary of War, & worked harder than I've done for years — writing steadily from Sunday aft^{n} till Thursday night every day till midnight — Wednesday ev'g alone excepted. I traced out most of the ground & left a great pile of crude MS matter for Olmsted to polish into shape & comeliness. It will be an interesting & valuable paper, I think.

The old Surgeon General has been making war on us through the *Times.* Raymond is his personal friend. The attack has done us little harm. "Wo unto you when *all* men speak well of you". If one's attack on a hornet's nest be really vigorous & useful, one must expect to be buzzed about at least, if not severely stung.

Ground for our Model Hospitals was duly staked out a week ago last Tuesday — but they are not yet begun. Some red tape tangle interferes.

Health of the Army continues tolerably good. But the practice of closing tents tight against cold, is producing some little show of pure typhus, & the murderous folly of sending cases of measles &c into the Smallpox Hospital at Kalorama has naturally infected several regiments with variolous disease. The wretched inefficient ill provided Medical Bureau issued it's "last crust" (of vaccine virus, to wit), last Saturday.

Dec. 16. This has been a day of perturbation. The rumor of last night's supper table was confirmed by the morning papers. John Bull is rampant about the capture of Messrs Mason & Slidell & demands their restoration with an apology. — Some think war *inevitable*. I do not. But I think it *probable* that within thirty days our chief solicitude will be not the Army of the Potomac but the harbor of New York, & the question whether we can stop iron plated steamers from coming up the Narrows & throwing shells into Union Square.

It would be an immeasurable calamity — & I fear England is bent on War & Cotton, & is merely availing herself of this pitiful technical pretext. If so the calamity cannot be averted & we must prepare to meet it as grimly as we may. But the bitterness of the blow is in it's coming from *England* — & in it's shattering so many traditions of loyalty & respect.

Dec. 19. Wasted two hours tonight with Dr Peters in the Tribune office, waiting to see Dana — in vain. I want to enlist the *Tribune* against the *Times*, which continues to defend the imbecile Medical Bureau by the dirtiest little suggestions of hostility to the Sanitary Commission. Raymond of the Times tells Dr Agnew frankly & unblushingly that he is obliged to take this position because Dr Finley is a friend of his. So it seems the Medical Bureau will neither do it's official duty & protect our soldiers, nor allow a volunteer organization to make up for it's shortcomings.

"Russian bath" this aft^{n} & Tuesday. It seems a good thing. The alternation of steaming & shower bath is severe, but one feels better for it.

Temple not very well — nor Ellie.

War news. We seem to be pushing a column toward Winchester, V^{a}. — They say it is not strong enough for serious work. We have occupied Beaufort S.C. & there are whispers of operations in progress against Charleston or Savannah or both. We hold Ship Island, in the Gulf, & thus threaten both New Orleans & Mobile. A battle is hourly expected in Kentucky.

But for the threatened interference of England in aid of the slavebreeding & womanflogging interests, I should think the National prospects brightening. As it is, they look dark. I fear England wants a pretext for breaking up our blockade of Southern ports & supplying her manufacturers with Cotton — . So much for British philanthropy & humanity. This generation must pass away before we forget the baseness of England toward her own children in this hour of their trial & distress.

I have always been Anglophile & Anglomaniac, but I am disillusionated now. I feel like repudiating the Archbishop of Canterbury & transferring my allegiance to the Patriarch of Constantinople. I sympathize with old G.C. Verplanck's Democratic father, who doubted in 1812 whether the American people ought to speak English. "Why should they not speak *French* or *Dutch* instead of that d—d anti-democratic language?"

Dec. 23. Monday. Vile weather, cold, wet, blowy, rainy, sleety. Walked up town through it this aft^{n} in a cantankerous frame of mind though I was buying Xmas presents. Very busy day—but among my duties was the receipt acknowledgment & deposit in Bank of $11700 & upwards for the Sanitary Commission. ($10.000 from Boston — $1500 from the Pacific Mail Steamship Co — $200. from the generous little City of Troy.) — The Washington "Republican" publishes a long dirty attack on us & our operations, evidently under the inspiration of the Medical Bureau. It is so dirty & so manifestly malignant & spiteful that I think we ought not to make any reply. It is evidently from the same person who contributed a couple of articles to the N.Y. Times over the signature of "Truth". — *Miss Powell* is reputed to be their Authoress. She is said to have ingratiated herself with the Medical Bureau. Pity that Bureau will neither do it's official duty nor permit volunteers to help it without throwing filth at them. But I care little about this attack except so far as it may diminish the influx of funds into our treasury, and we are now strong in money. If we can only secure decent attention by Gov[t] to the health of our volunteers, my character & repute may take care of themselves. Damage to them is a very trifling matter in comparison, & I do not expect they will suffer very seriously.

Down town after dinner to Trinity Ch: Standing Com: meeting. No quorum.

War news not material, but good as far as it goes. We gain ground in Missouri, and have fought a good fight at or near Drainesville, visiting Rebellion with a decided repulse.

Dec. 25. Xmas. Winter set in yesterday morning with a sharp cold, after a night of noisy wind, & with a little snow on the streets. It was a bleak sharp day. I spent it busily, partly in work appropriate to the season — and last night we had our usual Xmas Eve roast oysters, with Charley & his wife & D[r] Peters & M[rs] P. to partake. There was the usual busy time unpacking & grouping presents for the delectation of the children.

Dec. 29. *News.* We surrender *Mason & Slidell* on the demand of our mean Transatlantic Cousin. The act will be generally approved, & will raise little or no protest or clamor here, notwithstanding Russell's prophecy that the administration could not stand against the wrath of the mob, if it conceded what

England so ungraciously demands. We are generally satisfied that the form of their capture was technically wrong — and that we cannot afford a controversy with England just now. The general acquiescence in this concession is a good sign. It looks like willingness to pass over affronts that touch the Democracy in it's tenderest point, for the sake of concentrating all our National energies on the trampling out of domestic treason.

At a Bank Council last night, *it was resolved to suspend specie payments tomorrow morn'g.* — a grave fact.

Dec. 31. Poor old 1861 just going. It has been a gloomy year of trouble & disaster. I should be glad of it's departure, were it not that 1862 is likely to be no better. But we must take what is coming. Only "through much tribulation" can a young People attain healthy vigorous National life. The results of many years spent in selfish devotion to prosperous easy money-making must be purged out of our system before we are well, and a drastic dose of European War may be the prescription Providence is going to administer.

1862

Jan: 2^{d}. It was a pleasant day, but in these times one can not get rid of the presence of National peril. Even when one gives up a whole day to mere amusement he is haunted by a phantom of possible calamity & disgrace. Yesterday specially clouded by rumors that McClellan was seriously ill with typhoid fever. They are contradicted to day — but who knows?

Jack Ehninger was to have sailed for Port Royal S.C. this morning. He goes to paint studies of Contrabands, & to get a position on Viele's staff, if he can.

Russell (*London Times*) dined at N.Y. Club last ev'g on invitation of Sam: Ward & others. His presence stirred up a little row outside the dining room. Fred: Gibert & G.C.A. denounced his entertainers' bad taste in extending the hospitalities of the Club to a man who was writing slanders against us & our cause to the most important newspaper in Christendom. The difference was assuaged, I hear, by drinks all round. But we are beginning to hate England & Englishmen — not without reason. The course of the English press has been flagitious — but perhaps the newspapers of England misrepresent the feelings & sympathies of England. Let us hope so.

Jan: 9th. This evening a meeting of Associate Members of San: Com: at Century Club — about 60 present — a highly respectable lot — including such men as Minturn McCurdy Jonathan Sturges, & a large delegation of Doctors. Opdyke, our new Mayor, presided. There was good discourse from Bellows, Van Buren, Ordronnaux, Mr Ruggles, Dr Osgood & others & we passed, with great unanimity, a series of strong resolutions urging reformation in the Medical Bureau. Adjourned at 11 to a slight refection down stairs.

Jan. 15. Had myself *revaccinated* by Peters this aft^{n}. Do not expect that it will take, but I may go to Washington next week, and smallpox prevails there extensively — (the city being infected by the Army thanks to D[r] Finley) — and it seemed a reasonable precaution.

At W. Gibbs' tonight with Ellie. M[rs] G. & M[rs] S. played four handed music while Gibbs & I talked Sanitary. — Last ev'g spent in conference with Van Buren Agnew & Bellows: over the prospects of the Bill before the Senate for reformation of the Medical Bureau. Senator Wilson has become slack & inert. This is the second time he has failed us. I fear he is of a low type, essentially a "Natick cobbler" still. We contemplated a meeting of the Commission, but it's expediency seems doubtful. Perhaps we may go to Washington "individdly".

The Burnside expedition seems to have set forth from it's rendezvous at Fortress Monroe, and against general expectation to have passed outside the Capes of Virginia. Probably it has reached it's unknown destination. God prosper it! The general belief is that it has sailed for Albemarle & Pamlico Sound, to destroy the rebel "musquito fleet" harbored in those waters, to attack the works on Roanoke Island & to take *Norfolk* in the rear. May be so, but W.G. & I, studying the map to night agreed that it could strike most effectively at *Wilmington — N.C.* — There are forts at the mouth of the Cape Fear River, that can be treated like the forts of Hilton Head. Or perhaps the expedition can land it's forces a little north of the embouchure, under cover of a line of detached sandbank islands, & march five or ten miles across country to Wilmington, leaving these forts to be reduced at leisure. If it can occupy Wilmington it stops a most important line of R.R. communication — ties one of the three great arteries that supply life to the rebel army in Virginia. Another is already embarrassed by the loyal "bridge burners" of Eastern Tennessee. — We shall know in a few days what this Armada has sought to do & what it has done.

Many of my friends are in it. Willy Cutting Dan Messenger Geo. Fearing Tip Hoffman Edw[d] Strong as volunteer aids — Jem Strong & Fred: Sheldon as amateur spectators by Burnside's permission.

Jan. 17. No news from Burnside. It is taken for granted his destination is Albemarle Sound. Bob Messenger (in 4th Av: car to night) had had a note from Dan: M. (Quartermaster) who knew all about the programme but of course was not at liberty to divulge it. Quite characteristic of Dan — whose vocation is omniscience.

Mason & Slidell are probably safe. There has been apprehension that the *Rinaldo* had gone down in the heavy gale to which she was exposed just after leaving Boston Harbor with her two restored traitors. But they are destined to no watery death, & the Rinaldo has reached Bermuda. We may be able, some day, to repay England for the treatment she has given us in our hour of National Agony.

Sometimes comes a dismal doubt — (wh: I always suppress, with a *Vade retro Sathanas*) — whether we are not engaged in an undertaking beyond our powers. Can we — even with good generals & good luck & resolute perseverance, conquer this vast semi-barbarous region, with its millions of virulent rebels, and no Union feeling left that ventures to assert itself? We shall see.

Strange no one takes the ground that the "Seceding States" have estopped themselves from claiming any right under the Constitution, committed *State-suicide*, and lapsed into the condition of Territories of the U.S. — to be readmitted as states whenever the General Government shall see fit, & on such terms as it may prescribe.

We are very slow in learning to use the Slave population. Paralyzed I suppose by fear of offending Kentucky. I should enlist and drill all black volunteers at Port Royal & elsewhere, were I Commander in Chief.

From reports by Geo: Schuyler, Judge Daly, & others who have lately talked with Generals at Wash^{n}, I think it probable there will be an advance and hard fighting before March 1st. May God uphold the Right! — McClellan has a plan unquestionably. Perhaps he is waiting till Burnside, or the Port Royal division, shall have cut one of the Rebel lines of R.R. transportation on the seaboard, & Buell shall have intercepted another in Eastern Tennessee, and the rebels are compelled by want of supplies to abandon their lines at Centreville. The chances are against them if they move forward — they can hardly hope to carry the field works in front of Washington. If they fall back they will speedily become demoralized & a pursuing army will convert their retreat into a rout. This may be the programme — But suppose we fail to cut these lines of R.R.? — Suppose the rebel army of the Potomac be still supplied after they are out? Suppose Beauregard's main body to retreat leaving the Centreville forts garrisoned by a rear-guard? Could all McClellan's army storm them? — It's consolatory to observe that Richmond & Charleston newspapers are generally disgusted & desponding.

Jan: 20. Tomorrow morning early — (or rather, late to night) I'm off for Washington. We expect to organize a strong lobby there in favor of reforming the Medical Bureau. Delegations from N.Y. & ϕiladelphia are to meet us there. Nobody has ever heard of the Medical B. but it ought to be an important & respected & well known B. & *we* hope to make it so. "*We*" hope — but as an Individual I despond. I have no faith in Senators & Secretaries, & Chairmen of Military Committees.

Ev'g papers announce a *Victory* in E. Kentucky. Gen: Schoepf encountered the rebel Gen: Zollicoffer & there was a fight from the rising of the Sun to the going down thereof. Rebels "effectively defeated" — Z. killed — "Heavy loss on both sides". A hopeful bulletin, but tomorrow's news may convert our alleged victory into a defeat. This despatch says nothing about prisoners, or guns taken, and it's "heavy loss on *both* sides" is a suspicious statement. But if it be substantially true, we have gained ground where gain is most valuable just now, and are like to pierce & break the rebel line of defence at it's central & vital point —

Jan: 29. Wednesday night. A period of pestilent weather. The sun has shone but one day since I went to Wash^{n} — viz: Sunday last. With that exception the reign of fog & drizzle & sleet & chilly wind has been unbroken. Roads across the Potomac impracticable by sight seeing visitors except on horseback — & every camp-site reported an area of abysmal mud. An advance impossible just now. Mud of Wash^{n} streets in it's highest perfection.

Up & dressed at ½ past 4 this A.M. — Very dreary R.R. ride. With me Fred Sheldon, bearer of despatches from Burnside — whose expedition he accompanied by invitation as an outside civilian spectator. He reached Wash[n] yesterday. The expedition is safe inside Hatteras Inlet after some considerable loss by perils of the sea, but not materially weakened. Valuable time for preparation has been gained by the rebels however.

Jem Strong has become a volunteer aid to Foster.

We took steamboat at Amboy at 5 o'clock this aft[n] & came to in dense fog near New Brighton at 6. There we lay till ½ past nine, & there we expected to pass the night — & there was much vituperation of the New Jersey Rail Road monopoly among the passengers. My own frame of mind was unChristian — ferocious — vindictive — & viperous. But we steamed up again at last & I got home at eleven. Ellie & the babies well, thank God. Miss Josephine Strong is staying here. — Have not yet got over my three hours paroxysm of blue rage on board the Amboy boat.

This has not been a session of the Commission. Bellows — V. Buren — Agnew & I went on to grease the wheels of the N.Y. & Philad[a] Delegations & help them urge Reform in the Medical Bureau. The muster was beyond my expectation. From this City we had Wm H. Aspinwall Robt B. Minturn Stewart Brown, F.S. Winston, J.W. Beekman & others. Our Philad[a] associates sent Judge Hare (Binney's brother in law & a notably attractive person) Wm Welsh, & a platoon of high caste M.Ds, including John McClellan, Gurney Smith, Stillé, LeConte & others. We spent two days mostly in council over the details of sundry bills now before the Senate or the House, or got up by some of the Medical Bureau, and settled at last the form of a highly concentrated bill, embodying the minimum of Revolution. Thursday, the new Sec: of War — *Stanton*, — and Gen: McClellan spent a couple of hours with us. The General seems entirely convalescent but looks careworn. Stanton impresses me, & everybody else most favorably. Not handsome but on the contrary rather pig-faced. At lowest estimate worth a wagon load of Camerons. Intelligent, prompt, clear headed, fluent without wordiness, & above all, earnest warm hearted & large-hearted, — he is the reverse in all things of his cunning cold-blooded selfish old predecessor. Cameron looked like a hybrid between Reineke Fuchs & some large chilly batrachian reptile — but *this* is a live man, and of a genial robust Lutheroid type. He is most fully committed in favor of Reform, but doubts whether he can accomplish anything till Congress acts.

He is the most popular man in Washington now — but will it last? The Δημος begins to carp at McClellan, it's idol six months ago.

Senator Wilson was with us a good deal — professes to be the special friend & Senatorial organ of the Commission, & as Chairman of the Military Com: is an important personage. But I distrust him. He is full of little politic stratagems, lacks straightforwardness & sincerity & reliability — seems a mere manœuvring politician & no true man. I believe nothing he says about his own views & purposes. He is playing some kind of game with us, which I do not comprehend.

We had a hearing before the House Com: Monday — & before the Senate Com: Tuesday. Bellows chief speaker of course. Presented the case forcibly & well. Both Military Committees seemed impressed, if not convinced. But for my experience of the vanity of all assurances from politicians, I should feel sure satisfactory measures would be speedily carried. As it is, I expect nothing.

It does seem not improbable, though, that old *Finley* the Surgeon General will be retired, or somehow eliminated. He has no friends that I can discover (except "Miss Powell") and even the Medical Staff begin to admit he must be thrown overboard. Who would succeed him? Probably old Dr Wood. This would be great gain — but Wood is far too old & too far gone in the ossification of routine to be fully fitted for the place.

Bellows & I called on the President yesterday, to make the modest proposition that if any bill passed giving him power to *appoint* (doing away with the fatal principle of seniority) he would hear us before making any appointments. It was a cool thing. Lincoln looked rather puzzled & confounded by our impudence but finally said "Well, gentlemen, I guess there's nothing wrong in promising that anybody shall be *heered* before anything's done". We had the unusual good fortune to catch our Chief Magistrate disengaged, just after a Cabinet Council, & enjoyed an hour's free & easy talk with him. We were not boring him, for we made several demonstrations toward our exit, which he retarded, severally, by a little incident he remembered, or a little anecdote he had *heered* in Illinois. He is a barbarian — Scythian — Yahoo — or Gorilla, in respect of outside polish (e.g. uses "*Humans*" as English for *Homines*) but a most sensible straightforward honest old codger. The best President we have had since old Jackson's time at least, as I believe — for Zach: Taylor's few days of official life can hardly be counted as a presidential term. His evident integrity & simplicity of purpose would compensate for worse grammar than his, & for even more intense provincialism & rusticity.

He told us a lot of stories. Something was said about the pressure of the extreme Anti-slavery party in Congress & in the newspapers for legislation about the status of all Slaves. "Wa-al" says A.L. "that reminds me of a party of Methodist parsons that was travelling in Illinois when I was a boy thar, and had a branch to cross that was pretty bad — ugly to cross ye know — because the waters was up. And they got considerin' & discussin' how they should git across it — and they talked about it for two hours & one on 'em thought they had ought to cross one way when they got there, & another another way, & they got quarrellin' about it — till at last an old brother put in, & he says, says he, Brethren this here talk aint no use. I never cross a river *until I come to it.*"

I had a private "siffication" to present — on behalf of one *George Dower* the husband of little Lewis' excellent devoted nurse, *Ellen.* He was convicted a year & a half ago of manslaughter — in causing the death of a seaman — he being mate of a merchant vessel & sent to Sing-Sing for a term of years. The case is hard & doubtful & I wanted to get his pardon. The papers were referred to the Att^y^ General. — "It must be referred to the Att^y^ Genl" said A.L. "but I guess it will be all right, for me & the Atty Genl's *very* chicken hearted."

Feb: 1st. No progress in the War, except that Sherman seems feeling his way toward Savannah. Tone of English & French papers bad, notwithstanding the surrender of Mason & Slidell. "Recognition" will soon come, & then armed "intervention" in aid of our slave breeding traitors. Civilized Christendom has no principles that can withstand a commercial pressure. I shall become a Timon, hostis humani generis, repudiate my species, file a protest somewhere against my Human nature as a disgrace imposed on me without my consent, if the highest types of civilized humanity perpetrate so infamous an outrage on all human instincts. — These are dark blue days. Discouragement about the war is silently spreading, I fear. — We still have Emancipation in reserve, but I doubt whether a proclamation would be felt in the enemy's country except immediately around the points we occupy.

Feb: 4. *Fish* has gone to Fortress Monroe on his way to Richmond as Commissioner to look after our prisoners there. A certain Western Methodist Bishop — one *Ames* — is his colleague. Do not believe the rulers of Secessia will give him access — but there are those who think there is something under this mission.

There is evidence that the Rebels are more depressed & discouraged than we are. A "Proclamation to the People of Georgia" by certain very valiant rebels of that State has just appeared. In a Minor Key. It says little about Southern valor & Southern steel (qu: *steal*?) but strongly recommends all Georgians to burn their cities villages & homesteads and flee before the "Federal" invader. It is not an inspiring trumpet blast. I guess this period, of foul weather & miry roads, that bars our advance, is a blessing in disguise. People grumble about our "inaction" on the Potomac, but the rebel army is equally inactive, & we can afford to wait for decisive results longer than the enemy. — May God give us good news from Burnside's expedition! It has doubtless come into contact with rebel batteries before this.

Fifty years hence *John Brown* will be recognized as the *Hero* or Representative Man of this struggle — up to 1862. He will be the Wycliffe of the Anti-Slavery Reformation.

A queer rude song about him seems growing popular.

"John Brown's body lies a-mouldering in
the grave — [repeat]
But his soul's a marching on.
Glory Hally Hallelujah —
Glory Hally Hallelujah —
But his soul's a marching on."

Feb: 8. Excellent tidings from Tennessee. "Fort Henry" a rebel earthwork on the T. river bombarded & taken. One of our gunboats disabled by a ball thro' her high pressure boiler: the escaping steam scalded some of her crew — & others jumped overboard. But for this our loss would have been trifling. The point thus gained is manifestly of the first importance. — From Hatteras we have indications of a move on Roanoke Island, & from Port Royal less distinct premonition of an attack on Savannah.

The War news is decidedly encouraging, but we are very blue indeed. Signs of speedy intervention — (probably by France with Pharisaical England looking doucely & cannily on) increase & multiply. — The Treasury of the U.S. is vacuous, & the House has passed the "*Legal Tender*" bill. The Senate will not dare to dissent & thereby delay the supply of means. So we are in immediate prospect 1st of National humiliation & permanent dissolution, for we cannot wage war with the Rebellion & a foreign Power at the same time — and, 2d, of general private ruin. C.E.S., returned last night from Washington, croaks dismally. Somebody says that Mr Secretary Chase says it is quite possible we may be negotiating with the rebels within 30 days. Disbelieve it.

Bidwell croaks chronically & offensively: finds fault with every thing Govern't does or leaves undone, & considers every official either imbecile or corrupt. His talk is exasperating & depressing.

If the Virginia roads would but dry up for one week, & enable McClellan to advance! The chances would be at least three to two in favor of his defeating the rebel hosts, & that would not only check interference from abroad, but break the backbone of all Secession-dom. But as it is, American Nationality is perishing ingloriously, smothers in Virginia Mud. The "sacred soil" of that state is serving Treason well, and earning it's Canonization by the Church Diabolical.

Feb: 12. Wednesday. Laus Deo! — The best day we have seen since War began. The *Norfolk* papers announce Burnside's occupation of Roanoke Island — the whole rebel force prisoners — the gunboats captured — Elizabeth City abandoned & burned — Alleged severe loss on our side, but that is doubtless magnified by Rebel report. — Burnside is pushing on — up

Albemarle Sound it would seem. Hurra for Burnside! — Even better than this is the news from the West. Our gunboats have made their way up the Tennessee River & into Northern Alabama as far as *Florence*, on an unopposed reconnoissance, & find *strong Union feeling* manifested at many points on the river. This seems reliable & is most important. I did not expect it. — Fighting is now probably going on at "Fort Donelson" on the Cumberland River — which will probably be a tougher job than its neighbour "*Fort Henry*". We have had an unwonted run of luck this fortnight — or rather since Schoepf's victory three weeks ago. It is time for luck to turn, & for news of a disaster somewhere.

Monday aft^{n} everybody was astounded by the news that Genl *Stone* had been arrested. He is now in Fort Lafayette, charged, it is said, with treasonable correspondence. Very marvellous. That there has been treason somewhere in high quarters is certain — & if Stone be guilty, I hope he may be speedily hanged. He has had certain strong Southern affinities — vehement Anti-Abolition tendencies, undoubtedly. Having been under a cloud ever since the Ball's Bluff disaster, for which he was generally held responsible, rightly or wrongly, & sharply censured & abused by the press & perhaps by his military superiors, — it *may* be, it is at least conceivable — that he has become disgusted with the cause of the Country, & has listened to overtures from old friends in the Rebel Army. He was certainly not reputed a rebel when I saw him last June: people then gave him credit for having saved Washington from an irruption of wild Virginians when the City was at their mercy & the Railroad torn up, by his presence of mind & forethought in taking military possession of certain steamboats running on the Potomac.

Feb: 15. Authentic intelligence from Roanoke Island at last. Among the killed is Lt Col: Vignier, Johny's French teacher of last year. Hawkins' Zouaves seem to have behaved splendidly. Troops that can advance on an entrenched work along half a mile of narrow causeway raked by heavy guns & drive out the enemy can do anything. Our whole loss less than 50. Loss on both sides in every battle thus far has been remarkably small — carrying out the bloodless precedent of the bombardment of Sumter. It must seem strange in Europe, where the returns with which people are most familiar are those of Leipsic & Eylau & Borodino & Waterloo. But Jack Ehninger suggests that we can make up for these National short-comings by our returns of R.R. accidents. — Burnside seems pushing forward energetically — striking at *Weldon*, an important point. I wish he had 40 000 men instead of 15000. — Everything looks well in that quarter. We hear tonight that Bowling Green K^y^ is abandoned by the rebels. They are in full retreat. — But we are panting for news from "Fort Donelson" on the Cumberland River, an important point which we are beleaguering by land & water. There was sharp fighting there all day, 13th inst: without decisive result. Our reports are all rose-colored of course, but not quite satisfactory. I trust we may not meet a severe check at that important point. If we succeed fully we shall bag some 15000 rebels & half a dozen very valiant rebel Generals (including A.S. Johnston, the larcenous Floyd, Beauregard & Buckner, if our reports be reliable) & open the way for our gunboats straight to Nashville.

Feb: 16. Hoppin brought in an Extra Herald. Telegram from Louisville or St Louis that news had been rec^d^ there of *Victory at Fort Donelson* — after hard fighting & with great loss. Dare not believe it — but God grant it may prove true! This has been a battle on a larger scale than Bull Run & harder fought. News of a National Triumph is too good to be credible.

Coupling what Fitz-John Porter told me in Washington, with the advertisement of the War Department for light river steamboats & other like craft, I expect a speedy movement of the Army around Washington on the lower Potomac, crossing that river & flanking the line of rebel batteries. I suppose such movement to have been contemplated in connexion or combination with an attack by Burnside on the rebel railroad lines of communication at Weldon or some other point in N. Carolina.

Feb: 17. Laus Deo again! We are victorious at Fort Donelson. It was doubted by a few till 1 P.M. when the Commercial bulletin board confirmed the tidings (rec^d^ via Norfolk — Fort Monroe

— & Baltimore) by despatches from the West. The fort is taken. We have 15000 prisoners. Perhaps an exaggeration. Rebel loss in killed & wounded = 10.000: doubtless vast exaggeration. Our loss heavy. Gen[s] Albert Sidney Johnston — Buckner — & Pillow among the prisoners. Floyd said to have *stole* away — more suo. But Judge Daly tells me tonight that *Floyd* is reported *caught*. If so, what shall we do with him? Commit him to Barnum's custody as a special deputy U.S. Marshal pro tem: for a consideration? He could be most profitably exhibited along with "Commodore Nutt" & the "What-is-it?" The point of the Exhibition would be intensified by employing a genteel Virginia contraband as Exhibitor. "Ladies & Gemmen. Dis here remarkable specimen is Massa Floyd who" &c &c &c.

Feb: 18. Warmer — liquefaction all-pervading. No reliable news to day. There are fresh reports that Savannah has been taken, and they say now "without firing a gun". I wholly disbelieve the story. Rumors also that Burnside is moving on *Suffolk*, the centre of a plexus of Railroads not far from Norfolk. To venture so far inland with so small a force seems rash, but I suspect Rebeldom is just now in a state of what doctors call "prostration — with excitement" & not unlikely to be awed by signs of audacity & vigor.

Meeting of Executive Committee of San: Com: at D[r] Bellows' 2 P.M. Olmsted with us. We propose now to prepare at least to put our house in order, wind up our affairs, & resign. Government keeps no faith with us. From last July till this time there has been a series of promises unperformed. We got our Hospitals erected, to be sure. Gen: Meigs kept his word with us. But that is the single exception. M[r] Sec[y] Cameron promised & re-promised reforms, but nothing was done. McClellan has promised us *general orders* "this afternoon or tomorrow" begging us always to tell him what we thought necessary at once — but he has issued *nary order* on our suggestion. So with Lincoln. So with Stanton. It is nearly a month since he pledged himself — with apparent warmth — to decisive steps, that have not been taken to this day. We cannot go on asking the Community to sustain us with money as an advisory Government organ, after six months experience like this. I heartily approve of the proposition to resign. We have been shielding the Medical Bureau all this time from the hurricane of public wrath it's imbecility would have raised, by our volunteer work. Active operations are beginning now. The Bureau is still imbecile, notwithstanding all our remonstrances. For our own sake we had better retire — & leave the responsibility where it lawfully belongs.

Feb: 20. No news, except that Gen: Grant has bagged another batch of 1000 Rebels innocently marching to reinforce *Fort Donelson*. But the captured Gen: Johnston is not the genuine A.S.J. He is a bogus Johnston, "Bushrod Johnston" that nobody ever heard of. We have also caught a *Genl Price* in Missouri, but the real original *Price*, (who is predisposed to diarrhæa) continues to outrun us. We have chased him out of Missouri into Arkansas. There is a singular concurrence just now of reports & rumors — severally untrustworthy & probably unfounded — of things that indicate Rebel collapse. Stories for instance that Gov: Harris of Tennessee orders all Tennesseans to lay down their arms — that several hundred Virginia rebels are marching to join the Army of the Potomac — that Faulkner of V[a] has been making speeches agst secession — that there are Union demonstrations in New Orleans — & at Richmond. These are doubtless fictions, but they are novel fictions, & the appearance of so large a crop of fictions — all pointing one way — is remarkable.

M[r] Secretary Stanton's *letter to the Tribune* this morning is admirable. No high Official in my day has written a dozen lines half as weighty & telling. If he is not careful, he will be our next President! — I think the Army of the Potomac is about moving, or trying to move, non obstante Virginia mud. The newspapers are goading McClellan, as they goaded Scott & McDowell last July. Heaven defend us from another premature advance — & *another* Bull — or Bull Calf — run back again!

Feb: 22. Sat: — Parade, jubilation, universal efflorescence of Flags. Little business done in Wall St. It was deserted by 2 P.M. & I walked up town with G.A. struggling through the crowd that obstructed Bdway. To night there was a quasi-illumination. In all the houses around Gramercy Park, the front window blinds & shutters were thrown open & the gas lit in every story — Effect quite brilliant. — M[r] & M[rs] Peck of S. Francisco (the lady was Miss *Anna Ruggles*) & Colden Murray & his wife, & Jem R. dined here.

Only news to day is a repetition of the *Norfolk* rumor that we have occupied Savannah.

Last ev'g at Dr Van Buren's — : meeting of Executive Committee of S. Com.

Yesterday at noon was *hanged* Gordon, convicted of piracy as a Slave-trader. "Veré dignum et justum est, æquum et salutare". Served him right, & our unprecedented execution of justice on a criminal of this particular class & at this particular time, will do us good abroad — perhaps with the Pharisaical shop-keepers & bag-men of England itself. Immense efforts were made to get the man pardoned, or his punishment commuted. Lincoln told me of them last Jan[y]. He deserves credit for his firmness. The Executive has no harder duty, ordinarily, than the denial of mercy & grace, asked by wives & friends & philanthropes. Gordon, poor wretch, made a very pitiful exit. He went to the gibbet half dead with a dose of Strychnine privily swallowed with suicidal intent, and more than half drunk with brandy. The Doctors drenched him with stimulants and thus kept life in his body for the Law to extinguish in due form.

Feb: 27. Thursday. Snowstorm XII lasted till noon. The *dejecta* are now thawing fast. At W. Gibbs' to night. Executive Com: of San: Com: — Van Buren detained by illness. We go to Wash[n] Monday. Sanitary Legislation is marching on — but slowly. Letters — from Geo: Gibbs & others. Stanton tells G.G. that his relations with McClellan are as cordial as ever, but that the War Department has not time to contradict every newspaper lie.

Death of Edmund H. Pendleton, æt: 74. Miss Lizzy Clark married to her Britisher, Lt Col: Pakenham. Miss Lucy Johnson to Dr Carroll. — We are suffocating from suppression of War News, Government having taken possession of all telegraph lines. Highly unconstitutional of course, & certainly very aggravating, for the step indicates that critical movements are in process or at hand — but a wise step nevertheless. — We do not certainly know whether Nashville & Cumberland Gap are occupied.

Two significant advertisements in last night's papers from two steamboat lines. They discontinue their trips for the present because Gov[t] has *engaged all their vessels*. For the Potomac? — or perhaps for James & York Rivers. It's *said* that heavy reinforcements have been sent to Fortress Monroe. The "*Mortar fleet*" has mostly sailed for some port unknown. So has the Ericsson Battery. M[rs] Foster writes to E. "you know the right wing has commenced moving". — E. comes in, with Jem, from a reception at M[rs] Thayer's & reports two rumors, viz: that Fitz-John Porter's command *has taken the Potomac batteries* at Aquia Creek, and that Gen: Banks has moved on Winchester. Maybe so, may be not — but these are critical days in our national sickness. — Deus salvam fac Rempublicam!

Feb: 28. I have been working here in the Library over Sanitary Com: correspondence, with unsatisfactory results. — Eheu! — No definite news to day from any quarter. Newspapers, 1st ed[n], 2[d] ed[n], & all, are silenced. Amen: but it's a sore trial of one's patience. Called at the Sub-Treasury in desperation. Cisco has news of an advance, & of no disaster up to last ev'g — but of nothing more.

March 2. We have *undoubtedly* occupied Nashville. Seceshdom has *probably* evacuated Columbus. *Banks* has crossed the Potomac at Harpers Ferry & advanced to *Charlestown* without opposition.

March 16. To Wash[n] Tuesday 4th inst. 11 P.M. with Agnew, who watched over my health & comfort kindly & assiduously. — Bellows — B[p]. Clark, Gibbs, Harris & others of the Commission were already in Wash[n]. Van Buren did not report himself till Saturday. Our sessions during that week were diligent. We had reports from Inspectors, — discussion of relations with Gov[t], & of our financial prospects &c. —

Sat: night at M[rs] Sedgwick's (wife of an "abolition" M.C. from Western N.Y.) where were Senator Foster & his wife — M[rs] Kemble & her most charming daughter M[rs] Wister &c. The last named lady I discoursed agreeably to myself, but "her awful mother I had in dread & likewise my power (of conversation) was limited", so I exchanged no shots with the

Tragedienne. — This was my only "social" experience. *Sunday* came the news that Banks had occupied Leesburgh —, & a few minutes later the disastrous tidings that the *Merrimac* was on the rampage among our frigates in Hampton roads, smiting them down like a mailed robber-baron among naked peasants. — General dismay. What next? Why should not this invulnerable marine demon breach the walls of Fortress Monroe — raise the blockade — & destroy N.Y. & Boston? — [and qu: are we yet quite sure she cannot?] — Nonfeasance of Navy Dep^t & of Congress in leaving us unprotected by ships of the same class, after ample time & abundant warning denounced by every one. — Tea at Prof. Bache's where were *Stevens* of the Hoboken Battery, & Prof: Henry of the Smithsonian. Our talk was of floating batteries & mail clad steamers — & of the minimum time needed to finish the Stevens battery. Henry approves its design. He was the minority of the Commission that reported agst it. The majority consisted of old bureaucratic fogies unable to receive a new idea unless trepanned for it's introduction. Returning from Bache's, Eliot & Dr Jenkins met me with news of the advent of the *Ericsson*, sicut deus ex machina, & that the *Merrimac* (new baptized the "Virginia") is beat back to her den, more or less damaged. — We sent Judge Skinner of Chicago (one of our new Western colleagues, & a decided acquisition) to the White House, being an old friend of Lincoln's, to make a casual call, & fish for authentic news. He brought back intelligence of Victory in Missouri, or in N.W. Arkansas. The Pres^dt. produced his telegram from Halleck & read it with this preface. — "Here's the despatch. Now, as the showman says — 'Ladies & Gentlemen, this remarkable specimen is the celebrated Wild He-Goat of the *Mountings*, & he makes the following noise, to wit.'" — || Monday morn'g we had a hearing before the House Military Com: on the bill to reform the Medical Bureau. Bellows blew an effective blast. Blair & his colleagues seem heartily with us. Bill is special order for next Tuesday. It has passed the Senate, but with paralyzing amendments we must get stricken out. Thence to Bache's. On our way home, we find a *crisis at hand*, Army of the Potomac moving at last. All the reserves on this side the river moving toward the Long Bridge. Artillery from near the Capitol down the Avenue & 14th St. — a long line of rifled guns & caissons. Cavalry from the opposite direction. Regiment after regiment of infantry pouring down 14th St. These three lines converged at Willard's corner. There was a crowd of lookers on assembled at that point, but none of the jollity & jubilation that cheered the premature & disastrous advance of *July*. People looked anxious — soldiers looked as if they felt there was serious work before them, though rumors were already rife of general flight along the whole line of the rebellion. This was no bad sign. Perhaps the weather helped repress any unseemly manifestations of anticipated triumph, such as tempt the Destinies. It was chill & overcast & gusty, with a wan sun struggling through cold watery clouds. We watched the sky anxiously that night. There were indications of heavy rain early in the evening, that suggested soaking bivouacs & roads yet more miry. But the clouds vanished at last, and the stars shone bright, and a drying North West Wind worked diligently on our side. The old English proverb "*a bushel of March Dust is worth a King's ransom*" which I met somewhere when I was a child & which fixed itself in my memory the more firmly perhaps because incomprehensible, is understood & appreciated now, when we see a Nation's life depending on practicable roads, & the disappearance of mud.

Agnew & Gibbs departed Sat:. On Wednesday we set forth for Centreville & Manassas & Bull Run. The rebels had abandoned the line they held so long. They seem to have begun retreating before we advanced. The wicked flee when no man pursueth — . "Afflatus Deus". Warned by the winds of Heaven that were making the roads of Virginia passable, the rebel host had broken up it's cantonments & retired across the Rappahannock. — Our party was Bellows, Van Buren, Olmsted, Rogers (of Boston — a wealthy stolid citizen who has left his home & taken up his abode in Wash^{n} to work for the Commission without pay) Dr Chamberlain (one of our Inspectors) & myself. The expedition took a carriage (driver *Uncle Ned*, whose services entitle him to the highest commendation) three saddle horses — forage for man & beast — blankets buffalo robes & one revolver. — We alternated between the Carriage & the Saddle. Left 244 F. St. at 8 A.M. Wednesday. Crossed at Aqueduct Bridge. Roads miry & abominable till we struck the Alexandria & Fairfax Turnpike. It was a bland sunny day.

Dined at Fairfax Court House al fresco. Great accumulation of troops there. It was far the largest exhibition of war I have yet seen. Camp after camp — ("tents d'abri" introduced at last) — long lines of brigade drill — & great columns moving over the dreary hill sides. Thence to Centreville over miry roads. Halted there & set off for Manassas. We got separated by mistake. Olmsted, Chamberlain & Rogers, the equestrians, took the road to *Blackburn's Ford*. The rest of us, in the carriage, made for the *Stone Bridge*, plunging thro' perilous quagmires & vainly looking for our companions. At *Cub Run* we found the bridge burned & the ford dangerous in the uncertain evening light. No civilians on horseback had passed that way, as we were assured by certain contrabands marching Northwards with bundles on their backs. So we reluctantly & anxiously retraced our steps to Centreville, meeting ghostly looking cavalry pickets going off to their posts over the black plains. — All this region of V^{a} is detestable, the meanest & most repulsive portion of this earth I have yet seen. Independently of damage from military occupation it is nothing but mud, worn-out fields, mangy with broomsedge & sprinkled with ugly "loblolly pines", roads worthy of Chinese Tartary, & squalid houses. Centreville is the ne plus ultra of all this & has at present "neither horse meat nor man's meat nor a place to sit down." The one decent house is that of a Mr Grigsby, an alleged Union-man, carried off prisoner by the retreating rebel Genl Stuart, & of this we took possession. The rebels had cleared out most of it's furniture & our men had been taking liberties with the remnant. His contrabands wanted to have some Northern gen'l'men on the premises as a sort of protection. A couple of Reporters were there & one Alvord, a Tract Soc^{y} agent. The head of the colored family "Aunt Polly" did her best for us & eked out our stock of provisions with cornpone bacon & eggs. She is a most favorable specimen of the Institution. "Hoped Mas' Grigsby & the family would soon come back. Always been like father & mudder to me, sir — never had a hard word from nary one of 'em sir". We slept in our shawls & overcoats on the floor. Van Buren snored in a steady severe classical style — Bellows in a vehement — spasmodic — passionate — Sturm und Drang — Byronic way characteristic of the Romantic school. — Up early Thursday morning & drove to Blackburn's Ford. Overcast &

chilly. Walked whenever we came to a dry spot. Country covered with dead horses & deserted cantonments. Rebel huts well & substantially built. Stopped at one William Weir's — an abandoned brick house that had been Beauregard's headquarters. He's another "Union man" & has run away to Culpepper. Rummaged the premises & found quantities of military papers wh: we confided to certain stray soldiers with directions to take them to Gen. McDowell. — Reach Manassas Junction at last. Olmsted met us, bristling with bowie knives & shooting irons picked up on the ground, & looking like Robinson Crusoe. They had found shelter provisions & blankets in the rebel huts & got comfortably thro' the night.

What a scene! Acres & acres of huts — some of them burned — the ground literally covered with abandoned baggage & arms, wh: contrabands were diligently collecting & bundling up in abandoned portmanteaus & chests. Most of the swords & knives had been collected in heaps apparently & burned with other more combustible articles, so as to destroy their temper, but many were still intact & we brought off a supply of trophies. Letters abounded. I could have collected a bushel. Their spelling generally bad. Some of them more obscene & filthy than anything I ever read. One (in vilest spelling) very plucky & manly. All indicate severe distress in Secessiondom — want of money & of whatever money can buy.

From Manassas we drove over what these benighted Virginians call a road — (in fact a mere miry wagon track through dismal miry fields) & over the battlefield of Bull Run to the Run itself which we forded just below Stone Bridge. The Bridge had been blown up. We bivouacked: made a fire, & dined, on this side, just below the Warrenton turnpike & the ruined bridge, & returned to Centreville & Aunt Polly at dusk.

Next morn'g we drove into Wash^{n} — crossing the Long Bridge before 4 P.M.

We have been humbugged by the Rebels. Their position at Centreville is strong — (reminds one of descriptions of *Borodino*) — but their works on the crest of the hill were flimsy & armed with logs painted black instead of heavy guns. The Manassas redoubts are no better. They seemed to have been armed but that position has no special strength. We could have carried it last December with ease. McClellan is suffering sorely.

He is denounced for inaction — for letting the rebels escape. Mr Sec^{y} Chase denounces him freely — & wants McDowell to supersede him. People talk of this retreat as a great disaster. I think not, unless they lure us into direct pursuit thro' an exhausted beggarly country. It certainly lowers their prestige.

What next? Clarence Brown told us his Chief, McDowell, was relieved from command of his division. Yesterday aft^{n} it was said he was to embark 5000 regulars (besides Artillery) in certain transports & that McClellan in person was to follow. Whither? Either Old Point or Fredericsburgh I guess. — We distinctly established the truth of stories that have prevailed about rebel atrocities committed on the bodies of those who fell at Bull Run. We enquired at the house of one Peirce Butler, a farmer just this side of Blackburn's Ford. He is a "plain man" with a good face & simple hospitable courteous ways — his wife a pretty little emphatic woman innocent of crinoline. They told us they had seen the Mississippi, S. Carolina & Louisiana men prying up the buried bodies with rails, boiling down bones, sawing the larger bones into *rings* & stringing the small ones — for necklaces I suppose. "No Virginians did any thing of the kind" — on the contrary the Virginia men had called the others "cannibals" & declared they were ashamed of serving with them. A dozen lank, sallow, straighthaired natives with whom we talked at Manassas confirmed the statement. Van Buren found a Caucasian skull kicking about the camp of an Alabama regiment there. It had been carefully cleaned & was not near the Surgeon's quarters. Alvord exhibited another, which he had picked up in the Camp at Centreville. On the Bull Run field near the Warrenton turnpike lay many unburied bodies — not quite reduced to skeletons — mostly *minus* head & feet. Parties of our soldiers loafing about there professed to identify them by the faded rags of uniform as belonging to the 14th N.Y. the Fire Zouaves & Col: Cameron's regiment. — Scratch the Chivalric Southern gentleman & you come to the Feejee.

March 19. Good news from Gen: Burnside at Newbern. Sharp engagement & complete success. Our N.Y. boys — Potter, Jem Pendleton, Phil Lydig, Ned Strong &c mentioned by newspaper reporters as cool & active under fire. Little George Fearing is specially commended. Honor to the jeunesse dorée of the Clubs & the 5th Av: and thank God that the National cause triumphed in this severely contested battle. — But there is no news to day from "Island N° 10" on the Mississippi —. We know it was attacked yesterday by our gunboats, & that the day was spent in fighting — at long range — without decisive result. I expect to hear of a check or repulse. This run of luck must end before long. — Among the killed at Newbern is one O.N. Benton — a very nice intelligent *Chaplain* with whom I have had interviews & correspondence about supplies for the Hospital of his Regiment. — Murray Hoffman is convalescent. Called on him (37th St.) Monday aftn, — News of the Fort Donelson battle has been received in England, & American securities are rising in the stock-market of London. But I am more & more disgusted & exasperated by English views of our National crisis & struggle.

March 23. There seems no doubt that a large portion of the Army of the Potomac has gone down that dishonored & traitorous river in transports — destined either for Fredericsburgh or Old Point. Or possibly to join Burnside, move on Norfolk, & then cross to Fortress Monroe & strike at Richmond, threatening the new rebel line on the Rappahannock in the rear? 80.000 men said to constitute the corps thus shifted. Gen: Keyes told Van Buren that his division, 40.000 strong, was of the party. At "Island N° 10" much powder has been burned without decisive result. — Many *rumors* prevail: e.g. that the attack on that Island is a mere feint, covering a demonstration agst Memphis. — that Com: Foote is killed. — that we have taken New Orleans. — that McDowell is intriguing to supplant McClellan (incredible) — that we are to hear in a day or two that Savannah is taken — that Yancey has been captured in disguise on a schooner trying to run the blockade, & is in close custody at Key West. — that the *Vanderbilt*, duly strengthened & iron beaked sailed yesterday to sacrifice herself by running down the *Merrimac* under full steam. May this be true. Tho' the tide of victory keeps steadily setting in, this iron clad Ganoid sea-monster is a dangerous enemy, far more serious than any rebel army. News of action by Parliament on the blockade question most satisfactory. — N.B. Gustave Doré ought to produce a picture of the battle at Pea Ridge Arkansas, where some two thousand Indians, enlisted by the rebels, &

dosed with whiskey in advance, went utterly wild, & shot & scalped both sides indiscriminately.

On the whole, we seem to make decided progress in crushing out rebellion & barbarism — thank God.

March 24. Good news. Burnside has taken the N.C. Beaufort. Fort Macon blown up & the pirate ship Nashville burned by the fugacious chivalry. — Action at or near Winchester yesterday. Rebels pushed back with loss of guns. Thank God for this steady advance of the National cause.

Sorry to learn the death of Abel T. Anderson (T.C. Vestry) a rubicund peppery irascible indolent old gentleman. He had excellent points, but has lately been a little under a cloud, from alleged mismanagement as Treasurer of the Theological Seminary.

To night at Dr Bellows'. Exec: Com: of San: Commission. Chief question discussed the propriety of our resigning & telling the Public that Government is so shamefully negligent of the lives of our soldiers & so apathetic & slow about reform in the Medical Bureau, that we decline any farther responsibility for the work we consented to assume nine months ago as extemporized provisional agents to aid Government at a moment of extreme sudden pressure — that Government has had ample time to look about & to organize this business — that it has taken no step in that direction — & that we respectfully leave the matter in it's hands. Van Buren & I approve this course. Olmsted & Agnew incline that way. Bellows & Gibbs are undecided. We must soon wind up for lack of money, anyhow, & I think we make our withdrawal beneficial to the Army by putting it on the ground of nonfeasance & stupidity on the part of Government. That is in fact abundant reason for it, & has been since last August. Though Lincoln & Stanton are true men, our National Government is a failure. The People conduct this war. Congress is a national calamity. The Pres^dt & the Sec: of War mean well but are paralyzed by the traditional inviolability of Departments & Bureaux.

From Olmsted's report of Washington rumors (he left W. Thursday last) I suppose the large force detached from the Army of the Potomac has gone to Old Point. From that base they are to strike either at *Norfolk* or *Richmond*.

March 28. That fatal *Merrimac* is ready for sea again. With a little luck to help her she may do infinite mischief. Is Congress or the Navy Department accountable for our want of preparation? Somebody ought to be hanged because we have not six *Merrimacs* now in Commission. The N.D. is certainly responsible for the escape of the Nashville, which has run the blockade at Beaufort N.C. — At Island N° 10 we are still hammering away. That expedition seems a failure, but as we have not come to close quarters, we have sustained no loss. Then there is no doubt that the great expedition to N. Orleans has come to blows with the rebel batteries on the Mississippi before this, & that is a risky unpromising enterprise — periculosum plenum opus aleâ — with *Butler* in command. So there are excuses for my feeling blue & anxious.

Van Buren Bellows Agnew Gibbs Olmsted & Bishop Clark here last night & well into this morning in debate over the question of resigning our Commission & publicly protesting agst the non-feasance of Government. Resolved not to resign — but to define our position & try to shield ourselves from blame, stimulate Government, & wake up the people, by an able Manifesto or proclamation. This is unwise — for our own sakes, because we shall be held accountable in some degree (however unjustly) for the sickness & suffering with which the Army will soon be visited, — and for the Army itself, because we have ascertained after six months work that we cannot force into official heads the urgent importance of reforming the Medical Bureau. Our resignation might call public attention to the subject & a clamor might be thereby raised to which Government could not close it's ears. But an elaborate statement will effect nothing — except that it may slightly aggravate the uncharitable feeling of the Medical Bureau toward the Sanitary Commission.

April 3. People offer bets that McClellan will dine in Richmond next Sunday. Safe bets to take. He is believed to be at Old Point, with 100.000 men. Maybe so, may be not. The rebels certainly seem abandoning Virginia & concentrating their force in the South West.

April 5. It is generally supposed that something important is going on at Old Point or elsewhere, & that important news good or bad is in the city, but suppressed for some politic purpose — Heaven knows what.

Thus much we know — that old Finley is relieved from duty at Washington & D[r] Wood is acting Surgeon General!!! D[r] Bellows brought the news from Olmsted by telegraph last night, & to day's papers confirm it. A most hopeful sign — a good change, though not the best, & full of promise. We have been striving to effect it ever since last summer but in vain. Very possibly Finley himself has done our work by a display of his own arrogance & insolent pride of place. While we were in Wash[n] three weeks ago, he forbade our actuary Elliot access to the records in his office on the ground that he was an agent of the Commission — admitting that these were accessible to citizens generally. D[r] Bellows reported this fact to the War Department very briefly & drily — using neither adjectives nor adverbs, referred to the Order of the Department under which we act, & left the subject for the Department to act upon according to it's own judgment. This letter was referred to Finley & he returned an Answer to Sec[y] Stanton of which I have a copy. It is an amazing production to come from a high public officer — not merely spiteful & undignified but weak & silly. [I wrote a Replication in D[r] B's name which was sent to Washington yesterday. It was forcible feeble — but certainly a thousand degrees above the Surgeon General in temper & in relevancy to the question at issue.] Possibly this rabid communication of Finley's was the final exhibition of his unfitness for his place that decided Stanton to oust him.

April 7. Monday. How slowly this grand Tragedy develops itself to us the impatient audience! No news to day. Yesterday's "most reliable" reports are without confirmation. We do not appear to have taken Yorktown, & McClellan probably dined to day outside the City limits of Richmond. Fitz-James O'Brien, who was on Lander's staff, has died of lockjaw, from a wound received in battle. — I forgive him his bad poetry.

April 8. Weather detestable — streets white with *snow* that has been falling since noon. Through this unseasonable infliction I went at 1.30 as usual to Com: Adv: bulletin, seeking news, in a black rage with the weather & with things in general. Found an announcement there that raised my inward barometer. "Island N° 10" surrendered, with all it's chivalry & chattels guns transports & munitions of war. So it is stated — but some of the chivalry *must* have run away. These wholesale surrenders are remarkable in the history of War. The rebels do not behave as if they really felt that raging thirst for close quarters & carnage under which they have professed to be laboring. Fort Henry Fort Donelson Roanoke Island & this numerically indicated mud flat of the Mississippi must be classed in history with Ulm & Baylen — not with Saragossa. The Chivalry seems fastidious & critical about the last ditch it means to die in.

McClellan was cannonading "Jack Magruder" (well known to habitués of Newport) at *Yorktown*, Saturday — the renegade replying from behind "well constructed earthworks", probably with guns stolen at Norfolk. No result yet known. It seems extravagant to expect two such prizes at once. — From the S.W. ("Corinth") we have rebel rumors of a grand success by Beauregard — "eight batteries taken" — which give me little concern, for of the many species & varieties of Lie known in History the Mendacium Chivalricum is biggest & most impudent. — To night at Van Buren's. Sanitary Com: meeting. Mrs V.B. countenanced us at supper.

April 9. Morning spent mostly over letters (San: Com:) & like work. Money comes in to our Treasury more freely. Deposited $1470.00, a good day's work.

There has been a great battle indeed in the S.W. — a conflict of two days, closely fought & with varying fortune, & by great armies. It seems entitled to a place among the first class battles of history, & quite above any passage of arms that this campaign had produced. "Pittsburgh Landing", on the Tennessee River, was the field. According to the reports now received we were outnumbered two to one the first day — pushed back — in imminent danger of defeat. On the second day *Grant* was reinforced & after a hard struggle recovered his lost ground, repulsed the rebels, took guns & prisoners, & pursued the retreating enemy: *Sidney Johnston* killed & *Beauregard* minus an arm. — So says rumor. Also that the rebels carried off prisoners, Gen: Prentiss among them: that our casualties are 20.000 & the enemy's 40.000!!! Exaggerated figures no doubt, but there has certainly been a big fight & "a murder grim & great". It will probably turn out an important National Victory with heavy loss. For which *Gratias agimus Tibi.*

McClellan does not seem to get on very fast at Yorktown. But our weak spot just now is Norfolk — where the *Merrimac*, with her iron carapace, may do us infinite damage.

April 10th. We are without much farther detail of events at "N° 10" & Pittsburgh Landing. At the former our operations seem to have been masterly — but at the latter we deserved to be beaten. It was another *Ball's Bluff* blunder, on a larger scale, but our supports came up in time to save us from ruin. What little we hear to day seems to shew that our loss was not more than a quarter of that reported yesterday. There must probably be a corresponding reduction of the rebel loss. The death of Albert Sidney Johnston is confirmed, more or less reliably. His body is said to have been left in the field. I hope the story is true, & unless this our war on Southern rebellion & barbarism be a colossal crime, I need not be ashamed to say so. Johnston's course was not founded on any mistaken sense of duty. He talked to Ham: Fish, just before he went over, about his attachment to the National Flag & his duty to support the National cause whatever happened.

No intelligence from McClellan, before Yorktown — or McDowell on the Rappahannock. But I should begin to hope that Rebellion had got it's death blow — were it not for *Norfolk* & the *Merrimac*. There lies our great danger just now. It is a very great danger, which we are not fully prepared to meet. The North with all it's resources & mechanical ingenuity & skilled labor is unequal to the semi-barbaric but intense & earnest Rebellion in it's command of iron clad War steamers. Government knew what the rebels were doing months ago. Gen: Meigs told me last fall about the Merrimac & the terrible mischief she could do. We could & should have had a dozen Merrimacs afloat today. Congress & the Secʸ of the Navy must settle between them why we have them not, & who is responsible for the disasters we may yet suffer for want of them.

April 12. Sat: Spring weather at last. Busy day. This ev'g spent with our sanitary brethren at Van Buren's: last ev'g on same business with Agnew. Our affairs prosper beyond those of the public generally. We are qualmish & forlorn to day. In the first place, *Pittsburgh* Landing was no such crushing victory as we thought. We regained our ground the second day & held it, but did not pursue the rebels — nor occupy Corinth. Non cuivis hominum &c. The traitor A.S. Johnston is certainly killed however, & Gen: Mitchell has occupied Huntsville Alabama thus cutting the important Memphis & Charleston R.R. line. — Secondly, that pernicious Merrimac is out again at last — has insulted us safely & carried off two or three of our small craft. May this Goliath soon find her David. — Should the rebels get control of the water communication, what could McClellan do but surrender? He would be cut off from all supplies.

There is no progress at Yorktown. We are in great ferment & fever, nervously looking for news from that place. B'way is full of people this beautiful moonlight night, collecting in knots at corners, from which one is sure to hear in passing the words *Merrimac* or *Monitor* or *Fortress Monroe*. I am tired of this state of tension, wh: has now lasted a year.

But we have gained something already. Emancipation in the District of Columbia has passed both Houses by more than two to one, & (unless Lincoln *veto* the measure, which is unlikely) the Nation has washed it's hands of slavery. Only the d—dest of "d—d Abolitionists" dreamed of such a thing a year ago. Perhaps the name of Abolitionist will be less disgraceful a year hence. John Brown's "Soul's a marching on", with the People after it.

April 13. At Trin: Church this morn'g. Thanksgiving sermon by Ogilby. Music a shade better — or less bad & unmeaning — than usual. With E. & Miss Rosalie & Johny in the robing room after service. Major (now Genl) Anderson there, with J.R. Livingston. *Johny* introduced; & shook hands with the Commandant of Fort Sumter — a fact Johny will do well to remember. Anderson's manners are generally good, but to children he is singularly kind & genial. I suppose him to be among the truest and most reliable of mankind. But he is disabled for active service, & cannot even look after his own private affairs. I understand his brain is diseased, & that the terrible anxiety of his beleaguerment in Sumter is supposed to be the cause.

April 15. Last ev'g to T.C. Vestry meeting, Morgan Dix in the chair. Thence to *Agnew's*, where we sat till midnight or a little later — the Executive Com: of the S. Com: with Bache as assessor. *Stanton* has telegraphed Van Buren & *Dr Hammond* to come to Washington at once. Van Buren & Bellows were to depart this ev'g, & Hammond is doubtless also *en route.*

Congress has smashed the Medical Corps. Thanks to old Finley's mulishness. Had he been a reasonable creature & united with the Commission in urging improvements & resisting mischievous innovation, "the Corps" would have been saved. As it was, he insisted on directing the official influence of the Bureau agst any change whatever.

To day's news is the shelling & reduction of *Fort Pulaski.* The unconditional surrender of it's garrison, commanded by a certain chivalrous Col: Olmstead, opens our way to the cottoniferous city of *Savannah.*

Nothing material from Yorktown. Our items of vague intelligence from Pittsburgh Landing look more & more like victory. Rev: Ogilby's son telegraphs to his father "Great battle — great victory" &c. But it is strange that authentic reports are so tardy. This official reticence is of bad omen.

April 16. We have Grant's Report of Pittsburgh Landing. Substantially as I supposed — an attack repulsed after a narrow escape. Nothing said about guns taken by either party. It seems a victory if holding the field of battle be the test. It's moral effect on the rebels must be disheartening & *de*composing. They are not made of the stuff that bears failure well. Gen: Mitchell is the hero of the hour. His successful cutting of these main R.R. arteries through which flows the life blood of the Rebellion is a great stroke. He has won a Major Generalship. — To day has been warm & very busy. Money comes into the Treasury of the Commission so fast now that my office is no Sinecure. "Pour on, I will endure." — Acad: of Design open: looked thro' the rooms this aft^n. Noticed two striking pictures — by *Bierstadt* & by one Wüst, of whom I never heard. Haseltine has two decidedly good landscapes. He is steadily improving & already ranks high.

Strolled out this ev'g — in quest of news. That's my normal condition now. Learn that Foote was engaging the batteries at Fort *Pillow* (just above Memphis) last ev'g. Should he take them, the last barrier of the Mississippi, so far as we know, will be broken.

Lincoln has signed the Emancipation Bill. Has any President, since this country came into being, done so weighty an act? The Federal Gov^{t} is now clear of all connexion with slaveholding. — We are uneasy about *McClellan*. He is in a tight place — possibly in a trap — and the cabal against him at Washington may embarrass & weaken him. I am sorry to believe that McDowell is privy to it. He knows better, I am sure — but ambition tempts men fearfully.

April 19. I have been most diligent & "eident" over S. Com. business. Letters without end — conferences with newspaper people — documents to be distributed all over the country &c.

The War has made no notable progress. We have details of the Pulaski business. That fort was breached & ruined by our *new* artillery at the distance of one & two miles. This War seems likely to change our received notions about fighting on land as well as at sea. The most remarkable event of these last three days is an article in the Norfolk Day-Book, copied into the N.Y. Herald, in substance thus "The South has now established it's prowess by a series of splendid victories" [over the left, as Johny would say] "It is therefore able to take high ground & be magnanimous. It can afford to propose a parley & make the first move toward peace. This destroying of our *brothers & fellow countrymen* is really unpleasant, tho' chivalric." This may or may not be an important symptom. It is the first of the kind that has appeared. This article is probably a *feeler*.

Am just from Van Buren's where I met W. Gibbs by appointment at half past nine. The D^{r} & Dr Bellows left Wash^{n} this morning with tidings of weight. The Commission seems to have achieved at last the work it has been prosecuting for at least seven weary months of hope deferred, of official promises sliding away under it's feet like the slopes of a steep sand-hill, of repulses, snubbings, & misrepresentation, & of late (in my own case at least) of disgust & despair — the work, to wit, of reforming the Medical Department of the Army. A Bill to increase the efficiency of that rheumatic lethargic paralytic ossified old Institution passed a few days ago — under pressure brought to bear on Congress by US and by the public opinion we have been educating. It is our bill — except that it impairs the integrity of "the Corps" by making *volunteer* Brigade Surgeons eligible to the newly created offices of Sanitary Inspector &c & in a few minor particulars. We resisted these revolutionary measures before the Military Committees of both Houses. Had the Bureau united with us we could have saved it from what it considers to be disorganization & destruction. But the bureau was inspired by that blind arrogant old Finley, who ruled it as the last Bourbon ruled France. It fought for it's own Divine right of imbecile misgovernment & for nothing else. It learned nothing from the fact that it had become guardian of half a million of men instead of 15000, & refused to concur in any enlargement of it's resources or change in it's venerable routine. So the Bill passed, & "the Corps is ruined" according to Dr Satterlee & Dr Wood & every Army Surgeon of twenty years standing.

This is all by way of prologue to Dr Van Buren's narrative. The Sec^{y} of War telegraphed for him to come to Wash^{n}. (He did not send for Hammond) — Bellows went with him. V.B. reported at the War Department & the Sec: asked frankly what shall I do with the Medical Bureau? "I have called you in to a bad case." "What are the symptoms, Mr Secretary?" — "General imbecility". They had more than one free discussion, & V.B. submitted a list of names for the new offices with Dr Hammond at their head, & Vollum & Edwards of the Regular Corps & Dr Lyman & Dr Clymer of the volunteers &c &c wh: the Sec: approved. Then it appeared that Lincoln had been subjected to political pressure, & was moreover influenced by personal regard for our excellent old colleague Dr Wood, who hates Hammond. The Medical Staff judges of it's members by their "military record" rather than by scientific or professional rank. Bellows tackled Lincoln while he was being shaven next (Thursday) morning, & seems to have talked to him most energetically & successfully. He was with the President again last night, & was informed that Hammond was appointed. "Should'nt wonder if he was Surgeon General already" said the Pres^{dt} & they shook hands upon it. I believe this, coming from Lincoln — but would'nt believe it if it came from any other Wash[n] official. "I haint been caught lying yet & I do'nt mean to be" said A.L. during their discussion, & such is probably the fact.

Another *Lincoln.* D[r] B. apropos of something he said advised him to take his meals at regular hours — His health was so important to the Country. A.L. loquitur "Well I can*not* take my vittles regular. I kind o' just browze round". — He says "Stanton's one of my team & they must pull together. I cant have any one on 'em a kicking out". — San: Com: is treated with profound respect by all Wash[n] officials. Our relations with Gov[t] are now more intimate than they ever have been. We have carte blanche from the War Dep[t] as to Hospitals at Yorktown.

April 22. Tuesday night. Showery weather. Hard at work on S. Com: matters, tho' I was so clawed with sickheadache yesterday that I could work effectively at nothing. Exec: Com: met last night at Father Bellows'. Acknowledging contributions gives me the Treasurer much to do. $2200. deposited to day! $7500. more collected in Boston! What a sordid money loving race we are to be sure. I wish it could be ascertained how many millions have been freely given for the benefit of the army during the last year of diminished incomes & anticipated ruin.

Walked up town with *Agnew* this aft[n]. Telegram from Olmsted that Gov[t] has put the *Commodore* at our disposal as a floating Hospital or Sanitary Transport. She is at Fort Monroe or Ship Point & it is thought necessary that Agnew inspect her equipment. He will go if I go with him, & not otherwise — tho' I shall be the merest cypher of utter uselessness — so I may probably undertake another Southern pilgrimage at 6 P.M. tomorrow. — Walked about Town tonight making arrangements therefor. Knapp is at Old Point. This journey is a dismal prospect. If we go to "Ship Point" we shall doubtless see much that is interesting & exciting — but there is the painful mean feeling that one is so far below the men who are perilling life & limb for the country.

April 30. Wednesday night. Tired exceedingly — having returned from "Cheeseman's Creek" & the lines before Yorktown at 7 this P.M., after several days of hard work & several nights of sleeping in my clothes. I have not disintegumented myself since Saturday & yearn for the warm bath I hope presently to enjoy.

Ellie & the children well thank God. E. has just come in. She was dining with M[rs] Murray & attending a Gottschalk concert when I got home. After a beef-steak & cup of coffee I posted up the 5th Av: to report to M[rs] Agnew & to Mrs Astor the latest news of their respective husbands, & then called at Gibbs', Van Buren's & Bellows'. They are all out of town. — — — The last event of the campaign is the occupation of New Orleans, after a hard fight. Our details of the transaction are obscure & come thro' a rebel medium, viâ Norfolk. But they indicate a staggering blow at a vital centre of the Rebellion. In Virginia, McDowell is still at Fredericsburgh; Banks' column within a few miles of Stanton — : Frémont a-marching on. "Glory Hally-Hallelujah — The Country's marching on!"

Wednesday last I dined early — called for Dr Agnew — & proceeded to Wash[n] by the ev'g train. Walter Cutting was with us. Sleeping car at Philad[a] — Wash[n], & Willard's piggish hotel, early Thursday — & after a hasty breakfast reported at S.C. headquarters 244 F. St. [Forgot to record that on Wedn: morning came news of *M[rs] Bidwell's* death. She has been in most feeble health for twenty years & more, with bronchial & pulmonary trouble, hemorrhages &c & died away Tuesday night without special warning. Poor M.S.B. will be sadly cut up. She was carried to Stockbridge Mass: to lie with his ancestors & kinsfolk.]

Thursday & Friday occupied mainly with D[r] Hammond's affairs. Medical Bureau opposed his confirmation of course. D[r] Wood had sent in formal objections — founded on alleged malingering & ill health. Rice & Preston King of the Senate Com: were understood to be hostile. We telegraphed for W[m] Welsh of Philad[a] & R.B. Minturn — & consulted with Hammond about the course he should take before the Committee of the Senate, wh: he had been invited to attend. We boiled down his defence to the production of a single document, viz: the testimonials to his fitness given by his present assailants when he was re-appointed Assistant Surgeon last June. Result was a triumph unhoped for. Unanimous recommendation by the Committee & unanimous confirmation by the Senate, without delay or discussion. So that long battle is won, & the

Commission has met & beaten the Medical Bureau. The Bureau is doleful, & says 'that d—d Commission has ruined the Corps'. Our answer is "We invited you to help us in reform but you would'nt do it, & revolution is the natural consequence." I think the revolution great gain — far beyond any reformation we could have expected the Corps to approve.

Hammond may be our Laney. He is certainly full of life & energy, honest & earnest but perhaps over-sanguine. He may need our service as a *drag* for he seems inclined to plunge at once into sweeping changes. Within an hour after his confirmation he asked me to help him draft a bill to facilitate the discharge of disabled soldiers, which Sen: Wilson has since introduced & which will save Government hundreds of thousands within a month & end a vast amount of most useless & unnecessary suffering.

Gov[t] changed the arrangements for our floating Hospital. The Steamship Daniel Webster, Capt[n] Bletham — lying at Alexandria was turned over to us Friday at 6 A.M. She had been used as a *transport*, & was full of filth & fœtor, — had to be thoroughly disinfected & purified & gutted — berths torn down & new ones put up. Gangs of carpenters were sent down, to work night & day — & a dozen contrabands, supplied by Gen: Wadsworth. They attended to the scrubbing & scraping & whitewashing. Spent Sat: morning on board, & went down by steam-tug Sunday morn'g. We were delayed many hours by failure of supplies. Messengers were sent off to ransack Alexandria for fresh meat. They returned at last after an expedition into the back country, & we steamed down the Potomac at 4 P.M., past *Mount Vernon* & Fort Washington & the Stone Fleet (waiting to be sunk whenever the *Merrimac* shall appear) & anchor off Aquia Creek when daylight fails.

We have on board Olmsted, Agnew, Knapp, Dr Hartshorne of Philad[a] — Lewis Rutherfurd & his son "Stuyvy" (guests of the Com: as is also that florid & gassy gent Caleb Lyon "of Lyonsdale") Stillé of Philad[a] — Mrs Christine Griffin Mrs David Lane Mrs Howland & Miss Woolsey — a dozen he-nurses from Philad: — & six or eight nice young medical students from N.Y. who rank as "dressers". Haight, Woodruff, & Conolly seem very fine intelligent young fellows. Also Dr Grymes of Wash[n] — a few officers & some 50 soldiers. These were

Govern[l] passengers. The soldiers were well behaved & orderly. One of the officers, a chaplain from Western N.Y., Cleveland by name, gave us a "service" Sunday night, by invitation, the like of which I do not care to hear again.

Rutherfurd his son & I occupied a state room. Monday spent steaming down the Potomac & Chesapeake Bay, under a cloudy sky, watching the low shores, & the loons & ducks we scared up, & the unsuccessful revolver shots fired at them. Carpenters & contrabands hard at work all the time.

Toward four o'clock we open York River & the gunboats that guard it — & then turn off into "Poquossin" bay — I am not sure I have got it's chivalric name right — & enter "Cheeseman's Creek" after grounding once or twice.

It was a goodly spectacle. A narrow estuary, with low wooded shores, studded with tents, & alive with moving masses. Some hundred transports congregated on it's still waters — sailing vessels & steamers big & little, of every degree, some of them black with men of Franklin's division, wh: has now been afloat & waiting, for a fortnight. As night came on all these vessels were lit up, and great campfires glared out on either shore, & there were conflagrations (of brush wood & obstructive timber probably) that reddened the sky. Men were singing on board the transports — bugle calls & drumbeats were all around, & through these noises came every few minutes the boom of a heavy gun from the lines. These sights & sounds were suggestive. — Tuesday morn'g. Up by daylight — boat up the Creek with D[r] Chamberlain, Agnew, Olmsted & D[r] Hartshorne of ϕilad[a] — landed after a long row thro' the congregation of transports with little tugs steaming about in all directions in high pressure hurry & feaze — got horses from Col: Ingalls, & pushed into the luxuriant leafy woods, full of swamp malaria, lovely *holly trees* — *misletoe* & other novelties. Too much occupied in picking our way to notice these things closely. An interesting little tree lizard prevails there & moves about like a flash. Came upon a regiment of Mainote lumbermen marching in line upon the forest, tree after tree crashing down before them to be made useful as corduroy road. Took to the road at last — an alternation of deep quagmire & perilous corduroy — & after frequent detours through bush & briar to avoid the immense army trains, came out where we looked down on about a square mile of tents & found ourselves at McClellan's headquarters. Conference with D[r] Tripler, utterly & disgracefully unprovided for the work before him. Men are lying on bare hospital floors & perishing of typhoid fever who could be saved if they had a blanket or a bed, appropriate food & sufficient stimulants, & proper hospital clothing instead of their mud-encrusted uniforms. The region is pestiferous. As I returned, under a broiling sun that *blistered my face*, the whole country was sending up a *steam* that rose some four feet from the ground. By five o'clock there was a cold wind coming from a black cloud that rose behind Fort Monroe, and an icy deadly penetrating rain — through which I saw typhoid patients carried ashore to D[r] Cuyler's Hospital.

After our interview with Tripler I saw John Astor & others. Campaigning agrees with him. His abdominal equator has been enlarged six inches at least. Ascended a high tree by a very dubious ladder & had a view of Yorktown & rebel batteries about a mile off. They were throwing shell every three minutes or thereabouts, but their practice was bad. The shells burst in the air generally, about 45° up. Only one did well, & that burst in a wood on our left, where it no doubt damaged the forest-growth of Virginia but accomplished nothing more. McClellan's staff in the best spirits, confident of success. They say that our batteries when they open will be heavier than those arrayed against Sebastopol, & that one of them, N° 1, on York River, on our extreme right, will be the heaviest ever mounted. — The best rebel sharp shooters are niggers. One of them seems to bear a charmed life & has been very successful. — he is known as the "irrepressible nigger" and Berdan's best operators have thus far failed to touch him. — Rode back to the landing alone, the rest of the party proposing to visit "battery N° 1" & I being compelled to return in time for the one o'clock boat to Old Point, so as to be here tomorrow. It was a perilous ride over roads blocked by army wagons & mortars & siege guns going to the front, & with abysses of mud on either side. I was thankful to get back without being ingloriously suffocated by a slip of my steed off the narrow margin of shaky corduroy into the profound syrupy bog just below. Steamboat took me to Old Point, & then with D[r] Packard of Philad. (a nice person) I transferred myself to the Adelaide — reached Baltimore in good season this morn'g, and after a day's railroading here I am. E. & the children well thank God.

May 3[d]. Saturday. Warm after two days of cold rain that must have put McClellan back. Have been full of work, mostly Sanitary. Telegram from Olmsted that the "Ocean Queen" is put in our charge for Hospital service, & urgent call for Surgeons nurses dressers supplies &c. At D[r] Bellows' to night with Van Buren &c arranging to send off a force by tomorrow ev'g's train. This may indicate battle close at hand, but I think not. These two days of heavy rain must have put our trenching preliminaries back two days, or more probably four. The impression at headquarters last Tuesday was that we should open fire to day or Monday, but even without this retarding spell of foul weather we should not be ready quite so soon as we expected.

The nation has been making progress. We have occupied New Orleans & thus tied a main artery of treason. *Fort Macon* has been shelled into surrender. We have taken Baton Rouge. Also there are reports (too good to be true) of Burnside's threatening Norfolk from the rear. The traitor Beauregard is said to be evacuating Corinth.

May 4th. At dinner, while E. & I were debating about her project of going down to Cheeseman's Landing as a quasi-nurse on the S.C. floating Hospitals, in came our neighbour Col. Howe with a telegram from McClellan. "Yorktown abandoned last night. Heavy guns and stores left behind" — !!!! This does not materially affect our operations. There will be fewer casualties to provide for, but McClellan will doubtless advance at once, & empty his regimental hospitals. Their 3500 patients will more than fill the Dan[l] Webster & the Ocean Queen. — The movement is puzzling. Will the rebels abandon Richmond & Virginia & concentrate in the Gulf States, or do they intend to throw themselves in overwhelming force on Banks or McDowell or Burnside?

Van Buren Bellows & Agnew came in after dinner, & I went down town with A. to see about getting off our thirty nurses, & half-dozen doctors &c &c by this ev'g's train.

May 5. Monday. Sultry & showery. Busy day. Part of the morn'g spent with Gibbs buying Hospital stores. — This ev'g awhile at

Charley's. Went down to the depot with E. & her faithful Annie & saw them off. About a dozen women go, ladies & their servants, with Bellows as Chief Pastor. There are M[rs] B. Miss Harriet Whetten & a daughter of Cha[s] E. Butler's.

I send E. off with sore misgivings & at her own earnest request — relying mainly on Van Buren's excellent judgment. He thinks there is no exposure & no risk of typhoid or malarial fever. I have armed the little woman with prophylactic quinine. May she get safely home again & may this crusade plant no seeds of disease in her impressible system. — The rebels are in full flight & our last advices are that McC's advance was engaging their rearguard two miles this side Williamsburgh. —

May 6. Tuesday. Anxious days — & blue withal. Busy morning, bored by many things & worried about Ellie. What a born fool I must be to have let her go off on this expedition! — Walked up town with Agnew: stopped awhile at N.Y. Hospital, and then at Col. Bliss's, where we learned that the Daniel Webster had been telegraphed below. Omnibussed at once to Whitehall — found she was lying off Castle Garden, & took boat. Made a hurried inspection. She came away yesterday morn'g with 187 sick — of whom 4 have died. Two more are moribund, if appearances be reliable. Some 30 or 40 are convalescent. They were on deck enjoying the tonic N.W. wind & bright sunshine & doubtless appreciating the visible signs of Home & civilization all around them. In the wards below we found excellent ventilation — no smells — attentive & vigilant officers — comfort & order. But with all this the bunks of the forward cabin were tragic. Gaunt wan wild faces — restless tossing forms — arms that were ready to strike hard for the Country against the Country's enemy strapped relentlessly to the fevered body. Great big eyes looking at us without intelligence. One poor fellow had just died, & lay with unclosed eyes glaring upwards, as if appealing to the God of Justice for Vengeance on those who have brought this murderous war upon us.

I was much gratified by the talk of the soldiers. "Nothing at all to complain of sir" — "Have you been treated as well as you were in your Shore Hospitals?" — "O there aint no comparison sir. We've been treated like gentlemen *here* — but in them holes there was'nt nobody to look after us." — This is satisfactory, — a tangible result that justifies our appeal to the public for aid & support, & the time we have spent in work for the Sanitary Commission.

May 7. Letter from Ellie at Baltimore, in good spirits. God send her safely home.

McClellan has driven the rebels from Williamsburgh, & is "marching on". We have news of the fight below New Orleans. It seems to have been resolute & bitter, ending in complete triumph.

May 9. Friday. These two days desperately busy & hurried. Yesterday occupied mainly in buying supplies for the *D. Webster* & seeing that they were got on board, & in providing for her thorough cleansing & disinfection — the airing of her bedding &c. We need an efficient head there. Dr Grymes (of Washington) has no physical stamina — & is in the early stages of consumption I fear. Peverly is afraid to do anything till he is ordered — But Agnew Gibbs & I have succeeded in getting affairs into something like proper shape.

Last ev'g at Standing Com: meeting of Trinity Ch: — The Com: "stood" from 8 to 10, & there was earnest discussion on our future policy as to applications for aid from other parishes. Skidmore & I propose to button up the parochial pocket, and the others acquiesced at last. This question comes up in an application from All Saints Church in the 7th Ward.

Today busily engaged about the Danl Webster. Telegram from Olmsted at noon that another of our Hospital ships, the Ocean Queen, would be here this afternoon with more than 1000 sick & wounded. Went to Col: Howe's New England Hospital (cor: John St. & B'way —) & to Park Barracks to give warning. Col: Bliss tells me of certain new regulations to be enforced here that will prevent our getting the men out of this crowded ship without endless formalities & murderous delay. Active telegraphing thereupon to Bellows & Van Buren at Wash^n^ — responses indicating that Hammond has interfered with effect. — With Gibbs to the D.W. at foot of Canal St. at 4 P.M. She was just putting off. Mrs Christine Griffin on board

— Mrs Blatchford, Miss Wormeley of Newport & Mrs Raymond, (wife of the N.Y. Times!) & a staff of doctors dressers & nurses.

Thence we took a carriage to the Battery. Ocean Queen not arrived. Boated to Governor's Island & had an interview with the Commandant (Col: Loomis I believe), & left word for Dr Sloan U.S.A. about the expected cargo of moribund typhoid patients. Home to dinner with Gibbs at half past six — & omnibussed down town again with him. O.Q. has arrived. We take boat & board here, & go through her crowded wards with her Captn (Terry) & certain of her Medical Corps. Everything looks well. The doctors have had stores enough, the men find no fault & are grateful.

Saw but one man who was believed sick unto death & past cure.

Agnew has just called (a little after midnight) with Dr G.A. Peters, to discuss the situation.

This Hospital-ship business throws on me an amount of work simply impracticable. We must employ an Agent here to purchase supplies & see to details.

Nothing from Ellie — except that I learn to night she was established on board the *Knickerbocker* yesterday & in good health & spirits. What a fool I was to let her go off on this cruise!

McClellan seems to press hard & vigorously on the rear of the fugacious Chivalry. There has been a fight in Hampton Roads — Monitor vs. Merrimac. No decisive result. We are probably about undertaking a move agst Norfolk at last. On the Virginian Peninsula we have advanced beyond Williamsburgh. Report of severe fighting at or near *West Point* on York River, facing the rebel hordes across the Chickahominy, a tributary of James River.

May 10. Agnew here tonight, with Dr Gurdon Buck, who returned on the O.Q. We cannot keep her, I am sorry to say, for Government must send her to New Orleans. B. seems a solid sensible old practitioner, with tendencies to prose. Our transport system needs revision by his account — or rather we have yet to devise a commissariat department &c &c for these ships. Olmsted is great on details in certain matters, but has no faculty for organizing that particular thing — in other words "keeping a Hotel".

Letter from E. to day written in the saloon of the Old Point steamer. All well so far. Glad to know that the Knickerbocker is probably to be a *surgical* hospital.

The more we learn about the New Orleans fight the better it looks. It seems likely to be remembered as among the more notable battles of history — being full of picturesque incidents, such as fire ships — mortar-boats clothed in leafy branches or with long canes from the swamp — & belching out 13 inch shells from the recesses of a green bower — iron rains — etcetera. There are fine displays of individual pluck, too. We have contributed a sensation chapter to the world's history.

Dr Buck who went over Yorktown & the parts adjacent tells me of a rebel trick almost too savage for belief. One of our sharp-shooters was killed in his rifle pit. Under cover of night the chivalric Southerners planted torpedoes around the spot where he lay & then withdrew to watch the explosion when our men stole out to bring away the body of their comrade. I begin to think that the venomous barbaric malignity & ruffianism of the South is beyond cure & beyond palliatives. We must proceed to exterminate them I fear.

No news at all to day. No Old Point boat reached Baltimore this morning. This may mean mischief. It is conceivable that our naval force in Hampton Roads has been knocked into smithereens by the Merrimac — tho' I ca'nt think it probable. In which case poor E. would be cut off.

May 11th. Did not go out this morning — sent Johny to St Paul's with his grandmamma, & dawdled over books in the library, & snuffling snorting sneezing & choking with this pestilent cold. Soon after dinner the streets were full of noises — the cry of panting newsboys with their *Extrees.* I posted myself at the front door — & discoursed a patriotic old gentleman who recognized me as enquirer & imparted the news. I do'nt know who he was, & it made no difference. We waved our hats to passers by & they waved theirs. The City was jubilant. At last a youthful ευαγγελος came along & I invested in an extra Tribune, declining to receive change for my quarter — read the news, which I had not dared fully to believe till I saw it in print, & executed a war dance round the Hall, to Temple's astonishment.

Gen: Wool landed at Willoughby's Point yesterday morning & marched on Norfolk. *Lincoln* seems to have been with him in person. There was some little fighting & firing & bridge burning, & Norfolk & the Navy Yard were surrendered. Viele is Military Governor, & at five this morning the Merrimac was *blown up*. Her destruction & the occupation of Norfolk are two great facts. It is also reported that the *Galena* has advanced up James river, sunk the *Yorktown* & captured the *Jamestown*, but this looks less reliable.

Took tea with the children, Kate & Charley Peters included — strolled out on the West side of the City — returned & at 10 P.M. rejoiced in another Extra, & more good news. Eight rebel gunboats attacked six of Foote's flotilla near Fort Pillow. Three of the eight were destroyed, the rest fled, — McClellan seems to be pressing the braggart fugacious Dog-Chivalry of Secessia with vigor & success. They are in full flight on Richmond & Petersburgh, with the National Army close on their heels.

May 12. C.E.S. returned this morn'g after a week's absence at Yorktown & brings full reports of E. She was drudging among sick & wounded men in a plucky noble womanly way & doing severe prosaic work. God bless her. This will be a precious memory to her & her children, *if only she escape fever*. Telegrams to day that the *D. Webster* left Yorktown 10 A.M. & will be here tomorrow. Had hoped E. would return with her — but she does not. Next *15th May* must be spent without her.

May 13. Tuesday. No material news to day. Busy bothered & blue. This ev'g came a letter from *Ellie* brought by Mrs Dr Bellows. The D. Webster arrived this aftn, at 4 — several hours earlier than we expected. E. enjoys her Bohemian life — works hard — sleeps profoundly — finds coarse fare appetizing — & has a good time generally. I have brilliant reports of her energy & efficiency in "arrangement" — of her cordial acquiescence in drudgery. God bless her for her vigorous devotion to this work. May she only get safe home unpoisoned by Southern typhoid.

With Van Buren to night to Danl Webster, lying off Castle Garden. About 240 on board, generally doing well. Evening wet.

May 14. Wedn. Hurrying day, tho' young Winston has kindly undertaken to serve as volunteer aid in getting supplies for the Webster on her return trip. He was among the volunteer Medici whom the rebels nabbed at Bull Run & has experience of Richmond prisons. Law School Exam: from half past two till near six. Best exam: yet. No one this time whom we can hesitate about passing, and there are some most promising young fellows in the class. — After dinner to Van Buren's with Gibbs. (His wife & a pretty little Miss Eustis asked leave to spend the ev'g here by themselves practising 4 handed music on the organ) Agnew & the venerable *Harris* were with us. The quartermaster gives us leave to send hospital stores to N. Orleans by the Ocean Queen & we settled details of an invoice amounting to about $1500.00.

May 15. Thursday. Too bad that Ellie should be away on this anniversary — even on so good a work as hers, & laboring so nobly & cheerfully as I hear she is. Telegram from D[r] Jenkins, just rec[d], that she came to Wash[n] on the Elm City this A.M. with a cargo of pathology for the Wash[n] hospitals — & was quite well. I suppose she means to return to Yorktown but dont know. We get the Webster off *tomorrow*, & I have written & telegraphed her to return with that steamer.

After dinner came in Bellows fresh from a row with the Sec: of War about appointments under the Medical Reform Bill, in which Stanton was petulant & insolent & then emollient & apologetic. Bellows thinks he has some cerebral disease. — Took a stroll & on my return found Agnew here & we accomplished a little work. Much gratified by a letter from Raymond of the Times apologizing for the attacks that paper made on us last fall & winter, & sending us $100.00 as evidence of his conversion. Miss Powell (alias "Justitia") is found out at last & Raymond has thrown her over. Truth is apt to prevail, if one wait patiently. I wish it might prevail *soon* with C.E.S. & G.C.A. I confess to feeling profoundly embittered by having to fight this battle with my two most intimate friends dead against me, readily absorbing & reissuing every lie that Official spite sets in motion agst us. I fear it will be long before this feeling wears out. Of course they are entitled to form their own opinions — & so are the people of England, but it will be a weary while before England can be to us what she was a year ago.

To day's news is that Gen: Hunter at Port Royal proclaims a *general Emancipation* in S. Carolina Georgia & Florida!!!! Very strange & startling — John Brown IS a-marching on, & with seven league boots.

May 18. Sunshiny day, with chilly news. Our four gunboats, Monitor, Galena, Naugatuck & Aroostook, that went up James River repulsed by batteries 7 miles below Richmond, & it would seem with serious loss & damage. — Very bad, & discouraging but we must try again. The brief despatch that announces this gives no particulars — and conveys the impression that we have not heard the worst. — Telegram from Dr Jenkins. E. "has resumed command of the Elm City" — was quite well at half past nine last night — off Alexandria — was to go down the Potomac at day-light this morning. — Vive la Reine! I hear (from Bellows & others) delightful reports of her zeal & self-denial & administrative power — & am on the whole rather proud of her.

Only God grant this may not cost her a fit of illness!

Lay a-bed this morn'g late, with sick headache. Van Buren came in with a story of two steamers just arrived with 1000 patients. Dressed took a carriage drove to Agnew's — out of town — then to Gibbs' where I took a mouthful of dinner & then with him to the battery. Bellows & Van Buren had preceded us. The Arago was at the foot of Beach St. but had brought no sick. Back to the barge office at foot of State S^t^ & to various other points making enquiries, which resulted in this — that the transport Gen: Burnside arrived at 6 A.M. with a few sick & wounded from Newbern & that they were all safe ashore & in hospital. —

Stroll this ev'g — very blue. Things in general look badly. Bellows came in afterwards, & we discoursed our Sanitary affairs & the State of the Nation till eleven o'clock. The nation is in a bad state — and the prognosis of the case rather unfavorable. Lincoln ought to "exhibit" a call for 200.000 additional volunteers at once. They can be had for the asking.

May 20. Sad reports about Laurence Williams, now commanding 6th Cavalry. He is *under arrest* on the charge of treacherously communicating with the enemy. People believe the story, and it certainly looks very black, but it must be slanderous. — L.W. is a Southern Gentleman, like Floyd & Twiggs, & Southern Gentlemen are a peculiar race, with ethics, and notions about honor & good faith, unlike those of Northern E. or W. gentlemen, or any gentlemen I ever heard of, outside the Newgate Calendar — but I will not believe him a caitiff on mere newspaper report. — Letters from Ellie. She is in brave spirits & I hear of her, with pride & thankfulness as working efficiently, & stepping naturally into command of our volunteer Corps of Nurses &c on the Elm City.

May 22. With Bellows & Van Buren at 498 B'way this aftn. We have hired a loft by the month for our central business agency for N.Y. T.H. Faile Jr, a very nice fellow, volunteers to serve as superintendent. It has become indispensable. Since May 6 I have had to disburse some $20.000 for the Commission, on small bills for stores & supplies — besides attending to advertisements, writing no end of letters, acknowledging donations, & wasting hours daily in answering questions. Agnew & Van Buren have been run down with applications from doctors & dressers & nurses. This office, when systematized & in operation will be a grateful relief to all of us. While we were there, in came a despatch from the Operator at Sandy Hook that the *Daniel Webster* was below. She was to have gone to *Boston*, & Gibbs was sent thither this morn'g, to see to her discharge & equipment. It seemed dubious, but E. might be on board, so I went down town, sent a messenger home to account for my default at dinner-time, fed at Delmonico's, encountered Jem Ruggles & took him with me, & boated out to the D.W. Boarded her five minutes after her Anchor dropped & spent an hour on deck & in the wards with Capt. Bletham, Dr Grymes, Peverly &c. 250 sick on board. One had died. Men generally doing well, satisfied, grateful & jolly.

Learned that E. was *not* on board. She stays for the *next* transport: Is away up the "Pamunkey" river — at "White House" only 18 miles from Richmond: on the *Elm City* or

Spaulding (uncertain on which) — with Miss Whetten &c: well & energetic. *Laus Deo.*

Boated ashore again through a lovely sunset — & spent the ev'g at Stand'g Com: meeting of Trinity Church.

Last night at Law School Commencement. Very satisfactory, but too long. Left it prematurely & went to S.C. meet'g at Agnew's. — To day's news is Evacuation of Fort Pillow, & probable renewal of efforts by our gunboats to force their way up James River to Richmond. From "*Pillow*" the rebels probably fall back to another stronghold "Fort Randolph" still N. of Memphis. But our gunboats are pushing northwards from New Orleans & seem to have reached Vicksburgh. Rebellion on the Mississippi will soon be between two fires.

May 23. Nothing from Ellie — mail facilities being scant on the "Pamunkey". But I had a visit from D[r] Hinton, who reports her quite well last Tuesday. His report confirms that of the D.W. people as to her energy efficiency & administrative talent. She seems to have been tacitly elected Dux or Duchess of her party of ladies — and she has got into the N.Y. Times of this morn'g. If she only do'nt get into a nervous fever or typhoid malarious trouble of some sort within the next 30 days!

Olmsted telegraphs that Tripler is getting up hospital tents for 4000 men at "White House", in hot haste — so McClellan's staff expect a fight before Richmond. Our advance said to be within five miles of that Chivalric centre of treachery land-piracy, & assassination. Many predict that the chivalry will "skedaddle" [a new verb with which Rebellion has enriched our vocabulary] but I think they must stand & fight — or confess that Secessiondom is "done gone".

There are hopeful germs of Union-ism budding in New Orleans & N. Carolina. Arkansas seems uncertain about loyalty to a "Confederacy" that leaves its pals without protection.

May 24. Sat. To day's news obscure & particolored. Nothing from McClellan except stronger rumors that Secesh is retiring beyond Richmond. From Gen. Banks' column comes a bulletin of "repulse" & "with heavy loss" at *Front Royal*, & from Lewisburgh (somewhere in W. V[a]) another of a successful "affair" & the capture of cannons & stores. *Sitch is War.* That Richmond is in frenzy & fury & desperation, even as a nest of hornets invaded by unfriendly fumes of brimstone, seems certain. But hornets have stings, & the Southern gentlemen have shooting irons wherewith to assassinate picket guards, & defend earthworks, & make ambuscades deadly. They are wild with rage & fright but they are not conquered quite yet. Perhaps it is best so. Complete victory *now* would be recognition of the Constitutional rights claimed for Southern institutions, restoration of Southern influence at Washington, magnanimous amnesty to traitors of every degree, from Jeff: Davis down. Complete victory six months hence will be something remarkably unlike that, unless I mistake the way public opinion is developing. — [Here comes a great clamor of newsboys — "Extry-a-got the great battle in Virginia — defeat of General Free-mont!" — Rush down stairs, & cool my stockinged feet on the front stoop while I watch for one of these κακαγγελοι. Their cry dies out, & a circumambient policeman being interrogated responds, "I guess it's Bogus, sir". So I come up to the library again, & resume this Journal.] Two letters from Ellie to day — dated 19th & 20th — on the Elm City at "White House". Full of energy & enthusiasm, humble reverent thankfulness for capacity to do service in organizing or "arranging", earnest desire to stay & work just a little longer. I cannot say nay — but my misgivings & forebodings are very grave.

May 25. A lonesome Sunday spent at home in sanitary work, or rather Sanitary *waiting* for telegrams about steamers. Mr S.B.R. came in this aftn — late from Washington: has been taking counsel with Father Abraham, & rates him high, even as I do — afterwards Gibbs with a cord of letters & despatches — & Miss Rosalie to see Ellie's last reports, & little Kate — (the adjective is fast becoming unsuitable) — later C.E.S. — Wandered out at 9 seeking news, but found none later than what the 4 P.M. extra gave me.

These are critical hours. The rebels are pressing Banks in great force, & he has fallen back from Winchester on Harper's Ferry. We have no details, but it is generally believed that the rebels are doing what an inferior army in a central position ought to undertake against a larger force distributed around the circumference — viz: strike at some one point before it can be strengthened. Their object is probably to annihilate Banks, & then make a rush for *Baltimore*. There are already signs of out-break & disturbance in that guilty town — but secessia will not have exclusive control of it's ruffianism this time. Unionist Plug-Uglies seem to have something to say *now* — they have been mobbing people, & trying to hang them, for demonstrations of rejoicing over this rebel advance. A Baltimore regiment (Col. *Kenly's*) seems to have suffered severely in the affair at Front Royal reported yesterday, & the friends of these Baltimore soldiers have been infuriated by the exultation of genteel sympathizers with rebellion. That city has long been justly held in low repute, as practically governed by the vilest of it's people. But God makes the wickedness of men to serve Him. If the blackguardism of Baltimore has been ranged on the side of Law & Order & civilization, let the Country accept it's new ally. Glad to hear from Mr S.B.R. that Gen: Dix is ready to deal with the genteel traitors of that town in a virile way whenever it shall become necessary.

But is Washington safe? I doubt if there be 15000 men left to man it's defensive fieldworks! — McDowell at Fredericsburgh seems to have his hands full. Our N.Y. Militia regiments have orders to be ready to march. The City is in great excitement, & the lobbies of the 5th Av. Hotel nearly as full tonight as they were a year ago — (it seems more like ten years) — when we were gasping for news from Fort Sumter & Annapolis & the 7th Reg^{t} — knots of people are gathering on corners, talking of Harper's Ferry & Wash^{n} & Richm^{d}. — I *guess* that Jeff: Davis has left a mere curtain of men before Richm^{d} — barely enough to make McClellan advance with his usual cautious deliberation — & has sent half his force to crush Banks & the other half to reinforce the S.W. rebellion or to overwhelm Burnside, possibly.

May 26. Monday. Fine day, but to night is cloudy. I hope Ellie may not have a stormy sea-sick voyage on the steamer Spaulding from Old Point home. Olmsted telegraphs that she was to leave *White House* on that steamer, with Miss Whetten & 325 sick & wounded this morn'g. So we may expect her tomorrow. God grant her hard work & experience of the last 3 weeks may have done her no harm. Olmsted gives great praise to her energy intelligence & willingness in P.S. to a letter recd to day. — It is a very satisfactory character from her "last place" — viz: (as she writes) that of housekeeper, nurse, chambermaid & undertaker combined. God bless her. I thought I rated her rather high, but I have never done her half justice in all these years, & have never known till now the resolute pluck & capacity for usefulness that are in her pretty little delicate fragile person. — To day has been very busy, as usual. With Bellows, Van Buren & Agnew at 498 B'way this aft. — After dinner, strolled down town to see the *Seventh Regt* march off once more. Disgusting crowd. It came along when I was at cor: Canal St & Broadway, & was accompanied by much rush & cheering. But it's advent was less imposing than a year ago, being in darkness (9 P.M.) & the regt not moving by company front, but four abreast, a mere rivulet of bayonets through the mob. — No news to day — or none that Govt Censorship of the press lets us hear. We have abandoned the valley of the Shenandoah. Our Union converts in that region will have short shrift from the rebels. This wo'nt help us in N. Carolina & New Orleans. — Dont like this general Order seizing all Rail Roads for Govt transportation. It looks like panic.

May 27. No *Spaulding* yet. She was not telegraphed below at 9.30 to night; so *John* reports. I hope she encountered the storm before leaving Hampton Roads last ev'g, & prudently anchored to avoid a rough passage. But I have been worried all day by visions of poor Ellie prostrate with seasickness. It has been a dark blue day generally, of the lowest grade. There is another matter — about *B. & C.* — that worries me. Never mind saying more about it. If it come to anything, it will appear in my journal soon enough. If I saw my way clear, it should appear instanter.

Dined at Dr Van Buren's with Bellows, Agnew, Gibbs, Routh, & Dr Hammond. Old Dr V. Mott came in afterwards. Much talk about the appointments under the Medical Bill. We are disposed to protest agst the nominations of Dr Wood & Dr Tripler as Assist: Surgeon General & Chief Inspector. Neither is qualified for high responsible office in these times. Much said about Mr Secy Stanton, who is no longer a popular idol.

The bulletins disclose nothing weighty. Banks seems to have withdrawn his handful of men successfully & creditably. Instead of pressing him, Jackson's rebel column is falling back on Winchester. *McDowell*, reinforced by *Shields* (whose transfer compelled Banks to abandon the valley of the Shenandoah) is advancing from Fredericsburgh, as if about to move on Richmond, & seems unopposed.

May 28. Dr Newberry drummed me up at 8 A.M. with news that the Spaulding had arrived. He came with her. Drove down at once — took boat at the Battery & boarded her. Found E. well jolly & energizing in a pantry, over milk punch & beef tea — without crinoline & decorated with a white apron. She suffered much yesterday from seasickness. Brought her & *Annie*, who has been an invaluable aid-de-camp, home by noon. Newberry Bellows & Gibbs dined here — & we adj^{d} to D^{r} B's for a session — reinforced by Dr Hammond, Van Buren Agnew & Faile, our new Superintendant.

We incline to an open rupture with the Sec: of War — in which we should find many backers. Unless the strange movements of the last five days lead to a decisive victory in V^{a}, he can hardly keep his place. There is a good deal of evidence that his brain is diseased. His delay in appointing officers under the Medical Bill is paralyzing Hammond, & costs the country scores of lives every day. It is a great crime. It is still uncertain whether *any* nominations have been sent to the Senate. His relations with us convict him of the utmost unsteadiness & capriciousness, if not of bad faith & downright lying. I believe that he means well — but is impulsive flighty & excitable, & so forgets to day what he said yesterday — that he errs in endeavoring to attend personally to details he should leave to his subordinates, & that overwork, & a sensitive temperament, & perhaps disease, account for his erratic performances. People talk agst him almost as freely as they did agst Cameron, but unjustly. They overrated him absurdly at first, & now condemn him as knave & fool.

June 1. Sunday. E. continues well & jolly. No sign of malaria yet, thank God. — I hear from many quarters of her usefulness & administrative faculty on the Elm City. Willis puts an editorial about her into the Home Journal — most snobbish & disgusting of course. Olmsted writes to D[r] Jenkins that she has done great service & "can keep a Hotel".

News. Corinth evacuated. Does this indicate collapse of rebellion in the S.W. — or transfer of reinforcements to the rebel hordes that defend Richmond? People mostly adopt the former theory — but it is doubtful. Beauregard's retreat shews symptoms of flight & demoralization. — *Little Rock*, Arkansas, said to be occupied & the Rebel Legislature to have "skedaddled". Gen: Banks, or some other Gen[l], has recovered Front Royal. Burnside is now in direct communication with McClellan through Norfolk.

To night M[r] Derby here, D[r] Peters & Walter Cutting — *Temple* is in breeches. *Ludoviculus* growing garrulous. Johny doing well, but for that confounded thoughtlessness & carelessness, that compel me to be harsh & savage with him much oftener than is pleasant. Poor little innocent boys, their financial future looks dark. They will have to trust in God & fight their own way without much patrimonial help, I fear.

Feeling very grim & black these last few days, not without reason.

June 2. Sultry & cloudy. Just as I was putting out the library gas burners last night, (or rather at half past one this morn'g) came a cry of newsboys — "Extry-a-& great battle at Richmond". Waited half an hour on the front stoop, listening to the clamor that rose & fell on Third & Fourth Avenues, but in vain. No newsboy came within hailing distance, & as everybody in the house had gone to bed, I could not venture on an expedition outside. This morn'g we have the news — of a hard fight. The rebels before Richmond made a sortie Saturday, successful at first. *Casey's* division behaved badly, broke, & lost guns. Reinforcements came up, & the rebels were repulsed. (the guns are *not* said to have been re-taken) — Attack renewed & again repulsed yesterday. Such is our report of this affair. We are uncertain whether it is to tell for or against us.

June 3. Tuesday. Not much for the Journal. Sultry weather: hot sunshine masked by a hazy muddy sky. — The battle before Richmond looks better, the more we learn about it. Rebel attack in force on a weak point handsomely repulsed & severely punished. —

Dined at 5 & drove with E. & Temple in Central Park thereafter. Meeting at Bellows' tonight. Satterlee with us.

June 4. Wednesday. Rainy day: an Easterly storm with the habits of a thundershower. These twelve hours since 11 A.M. of roaring rain & umbrella-cidal wind are out of place in June, & seem prestigious — ominous of disaster. Thinking all day of the 250 wounded men who left *West Point* V[a] last night for *Boston* in the *D. Webster* & the 450 who are voyaging up the Chesapeake to Wash[n] in the *Elm City*, according to our telegram of last ev'g — & of the Webster especially in this severe storm, pitching & rolling, — every movement inflicting agony on her cargo of brave men. Perhaps she will put for Philad[a] or for this port. I trust she may.

Busy & sulky down town. After dinner to Van Buren's to meet Bellows & Gibbs. There is a little fissure in Olmsted's relations with the new Surgeon General, that may widen into a mischievous breach unless *puttied up* at once. D[r] B. was to have gone to Wash[n] at 11 tonight, but this furious storm keeps him back till tomorrow. Perhaps Agnew & I may go with him. We could spend a day at Wash[n] & three at *White House* just now [W.H. V[a] meaning, & *not* the Presidential Chateau) with prospect of advantage.

The voice of the Newsboy audible thro' the storm at eleven. After waiting awhile in my stocking feet on the wet front door steps I secure an Extra. It's essence is a despatch from Gen: Halleck to the War Department dated this morning, that seems to indicate the disorganization & dispersion of the S.W. Rebel army — Gen: Pope "with 40.000 men is 30 miles S. of Corinth, pushing the enemy hard: 10.000 prisoners & deserters captured & 15.000 stand of arms" — beside no end of locomotives & R.R. running stock. Hurra for Halleck. A sanguine man would pronounce this the death-blow of Rebellion in the S.W. — Hope so, but time will tell.

Absolutely nothing from McClellan's army to day.

June 5. Cloudy cool & blustering. Fervent in Wall St. Miss Mary King Ja[s] Ruggles & Walter Cutting dined here, & went to theatre with E. — Met Bellows & V.B. at 498 B'way before dinner. — B. off for Washington to night. Stroll, westward this ev'g, & met Agnew here by appointment afterwards. He takes a gloomy view of our Floating Hospital arrangements, & is doubtless right. Want of organization — an insubordinate lazy staff of nurses & dressers — inefficient surgeons — undefined relations with Tripler & other medico-military authorities seem to have driven poor Olmsted nearly wild. The volunteer system has failed & we must engage paid officials.

Nothing from the Army before Richmond later than Sat: & Sunday last, when the battle of "*The Seven Pines*" was lost & won — except rumors that our position was unchanged Monday the 2[d]. That was a grim fight. We *held our own* & did no more. Doubtful if we can claim to have done so much, for tho' we occupied the field, we lost guns.

We are not at all jolly to day. People complain of McClellan's slow progress — wonder if he is not overmatched — guess that Beauregard's army has left Corinth only to turn up in overwhelming force on James River. It's so easy to transport say 60 000 men with all their supplies over 1300 miles of R.R. in a single week! — The contest in V[a] will be close enough without counting in the S.W. Rebellion. — Croakers & grumblers abound, & cite facts & rumored facts more than enough to justify their chilling talk. — But one of them, my excellent old friend of 24 years — M.S.B. to wit — drives me daily to the verge of dementia & fits. He has always been finding fault, justly enough, with the administration of public affairs, & yet declining for some wholly incomprehensible reason to vote & thereby do his share toward mending them. Recent domestic calamity makes his view of our future darker than ever. — Tho' all his feelings are with the National Cause, his way of helping the Country is to carp at everything that is done — to growl because everything else is'nt done — to disbelieve in everybody's honesty & capacity — to predict every conceivable misfortune — & to refuse to raise a finger in aid of any movement for the public service or to give his sympathy to those who do so. — He has notions in his head about the legal aspects of this slavery problem — emancipation bills

— & all that — new & valuable. I tell him he should divert his own mind — gain reputation — & do the country service by putting them into form & publishing them. — & that I'll be responsible for the printer's bill. But his only answer is "Oh dear no! Why should *I* undertake any such thing?" — He suggests the following points. 1. The Slave is bound by law to render aid & comfort to the Master in every way & at all times. The slave exists in the eye of the law for that purpose & no other. That is his sole function in the social system. He can no more exist *as slave* without this allpervading legal duty than a radius without a circle. 2. But by Common Law every one who gives aid & comfort to a rebel or traitor is guilty of rebellion & treason, & that not as accessory but as principal. The law obliges every one to arrest the rebel if he can & hand him over to justice. To fail in this duty — to harbor or assist the rebel is the highest crime known to the law. 3. Therefore this legal obligation to render aid & comfort to another must be terminated by operation of law whenever that other commits an overt act of treason. For the Law cannot recognize or enforce an obligation to do what is unlawful. It liberates the slave. He is freed by his master's act in attending one day's drill of the Mud-Creek Tigers — or contributing a shinplaster to defence of Memphis or Charleston. And being then & thereafter a free man — sui juris — Mas'r's subsequent penitence & allegiance-swearing cannot re-enslave him. If this view be sound, nine tenths of Cuffeedom are free men tonight whatever Congress may think about it. — There is an obvious objection to this reasoning. The relation of husband & wife is not *annulled* by the husband's treason — nor the obligation of a contract by treason of a party to it. The equally obvious answer is that the wife, & the contracting party, are presumed able to elect between treason & loyalty. They are responsible for their own acts, being able to know good & evil. But the slave is, according to Southern decisions, *ex vi termini*, his master's irresponsible instrument, incapable of deciding for himself on any point — not even whether he will be free or slave. His sole duty is to do his master's bidding. And from that duty he must be discharged by his master's treason. Having no power to choose between loyalty & crime, the law must choose for him.

June 7. Sat. Affairs advance but slowly. The only novelty of to day is an energetic thundershower, setting in at 8 P.M. — thro' which I went down town to get some printing done, & returned in a damp state, re infectâ. Meeting this aft^{n} at 498 Bdway — as usual. We are in permanent session every aft^{n} at 3½.

The only reliable war news is that another point on the Mississippi is given up. — (Fort "Pillow", or "Wright", to wit) & that Foote's flotilla has taken another stride toward Memphis. Another piratical stronghold exists (or existed) N. of that town — Fort "Randolph" by name. There are untrustworthy reports that it is abandoned & that Memphis has fallen. — Also, that our gunboats have worked their way thro' Stono Creek to within four miles of Charleston (may they soon be within comfortable shelling range of that snakes' nest) — Also that the Monitor &c have cleared away the barricades of James River. — Also that Gen: Joe Johnston was more or less mortally wounded in the battle of Seven Pines or Fair Oaks or the Chickahominy (whichever title History may adopt) last Sat: & Sunday — and also that Gen: Magruder has lost heart & is going to resign. Also &c &c &c.

These are a few of the current rumors. Every day produces its crop of phantasms & fictions, each detailed as fact by somebody [— Is not that the chant of a Newsboy rising above the patter of rain?] — From McClellan we have *nothing* — a negative fact of some importance. Nor from McDowell. Banks seems to be re-occupying the valley of Virginia & driving Jackson's raid back again. But we feel uncomfortable about the army before Richmond — there are forebodings of another Bull Run. If we escape disaster there, & drive Joe Johnston & G.W. Smith out of their capital, the whole Rebellion is broken. Otherwise it may maintain its maleficent life nobody knows how long.

June 9. Yesterday (a bleak sour day) spent mostly on the St Mark, our new Hospital Ship, now nearly equipped & ready. Arrangements seem admirable: credit mainly due to W. Gibbs, who took charge of that business. Aft^{n} came an important extra — (Sunday is the regular day for important news.) Naval fight off Memphis: some eight gunboats & rams on each side.

Rebel fleet came to grief. Only one gunboat got away down the river, the rest taken or sunk. This settles the control of the Mississippi & the Nation's intestinal canal is obstructed & constricted no longer. Rebel fleet being thus smashed under the eyes of the Memphian chivalry, who watched the fray from their leveé & housetops, their fire-eating city — the most pyrophagous, hyperbolical & high-sniffing of all Chivalric communities — (Charleston hardly excepted) — gently surrendered. It's pledges of suicide by fire, after the pattern of Moscow, were not redeemed, & it's said there was even a display of National feeling when the American flag was raised. May be so — maybe not.

Sunday people here in the ev'g: among them C.E.S. & G.C.A.

To day clear & cool & busy. — Meeting this afternoon at N° 498. Captⁿ Stimson of the Q.M. depᵗ with us: also Elwell one of the owners of the Sᵗ Mark — & long discussion with the latter about questions arising under the charter party. A most sordid fellow he is — without an impulse above that of bargain driving. Do'nt know but we shall have to give up this fire ship after all the care & labor bestowed on her equipment. That would be bad — but we cannot consent to be swindled beyond a certain point. M. Hoffman dined here — & then Carpenter came in, & Collins the purser of the Sᵗ Mark — & I took a stroll in the moonlight afterwards, E. having gone, with Jem, to the theatre —

News to night from Charleston papers of a vigorous demonstration Charleston-ward, by way of *Stono Creek*, getting behind Fort Sumter. The Charleston editor talks of a "repulse" & 20 prisoners & then of another advance under cover of gunboats. As he does not report the utter destruction of the invaders, we have reason to hope that we are getting on decently well down there, and that the chivalry — or Mule-ry rather — of S.C. will soon be taught a lesson. That wild scrubby animal, the lowest species of the Equine family, analogous to the worst conditioned Zebras & Onagras, needs a *Rarey* to train it's faculties such as they are into subordination to Law & capacity of usefulness to mankind. I trust Gen: Hunter has made some progress before now in rubbing in the first rudiments of this teaching.

But *Richmond* & *McClellan*!!!??? There is the critical position. Success there kills the Rebellion, or leaves it only a feeble life, like that of a decapitated hornet, able to sting careless fingers but sure soon to perish innocuously if let alone. Can we hope for the "crowning mercy" of victory there? People are not sanguine about it — they think McClellan too slow, and fear Joe Johnston (or G.W. Smith, for they say J.J. was badly wounded at the battle of 7 Pines, or "Fair-Oaks") has been largely reinforced by fugitives from Corinth. Time will tell. — But why does not McDowell move down from Fredericsburgh with his "40.000 men" more or less? — & why does he visit Washington so often, to collogue with Stanton & Chase?

June 12. Thursday. Summer, after two days of chill weather. Eleven P.M. Shirt sleeves & opened Library windows. — Chief labor of these days has been the equipment of the *St. Mark.* Her owners have collapsed. They are penitent now & amiably cooperative. We shall get her off Saturday — not sooner. *Ellie* is to be on her staff. That seems settled. Her capacity of usefulness & intense desire to employ it constitute a "Call" to this humane & patriotic womanly work, — & a loud call, of 200 trombone power — wh: I cannot but hear, tho' unwillingly. She takes with her Annie, her invaluable handmaiden. M[rs] D[r] Draper is to go, & perhaps M[rs] D[r] Noyes. Both seem nice women.

This aft[n] on board the *S[t] Mark*, & then on the *Euterpe*. Telegraphed Bellows this morn'g to ask Gen: Meigs to charter this ship which is well adapted for our work. — Miss Rosalie & D[rs] Agnew Draper & Noyes dined here.

Little news except of obscure fighting in Western V[a]. Many rumors good & bad.

June 13. Friday night. Sultry. Thundershower this P.M. — Nothing new. Letter from Olmsted this aft[n] at N[o] 498, ten pages long giving a fearful, sickening account of the weakness & inefficiency & imbecility of D[r] Tripler & his subordinates on the Peninsula — of car-loads of wounded men dumped on swampy river shores without food medicine or attendance — of men with fractured thighs lying neglected & forgotten forty eight hours in two inches of water, struggling to raise themselves so as to pick the maggots from their rotting wounds & fainting after the effort — & yet keeping a good heart through it all. — God prosper E. in her mission! The S[t] *Mark* sails tomorrow, & she is to report on board at 10 A.M.

June 15. Sunday night. Weather has changed this ev'g, and there is a cool bracing drying wind from the North West.

Yesterday was sultry. With E. & Annie to the foot of Rutgers St — Johny with us & I took him on board. Ellen (the nuse) brought little Lewis & Temple down to the wharf to see Mamma off on the big ship, but I thought the tall narrow plank by which alone one could gain the deck unsafe for these very little people. Everything on board looks well — but 6 of our 20 nurses failed to report. With E. are associated M[rs] D[r] Noyes, & M[rs] Draper, a very sweet youthful gentle mannered little woman, hardly twenty, I should think. — Came off at eleven & worked in Wall St. — Had a plain talk with C.E.S. that somewhat cleared up the oppressive moral atmosphere from wh: I have suffered of late. He is candid & kind & to me personally perfectly true, but he is strangely prejudiced against the Commission. Thinks that though it does great good, it also does harm by inducing Gov[t] to rely on volunteer aid. Yet Government & volunteer aid together dont meet one tenth part of the work that ought to be done. Thinks that V.B. & Agnew &c &c are using the Com: to make capital for themselves!!!! — Thinks that *I* do nearly all the work of the Commission & am being used by my colleagues, whereas I have long felt inclined to resign my place from mere shame that I do so little compared with them.

As the S[t] Mark had not got off at 5 P.M. & was still anchored in the bay, I took boat with C.E.S. from the Battery & boarded her once more, to leave letters & papers for Olmsted. E. is delighted with her quarters & her company, & everything is promising *so far*. Then home. Miss Rosalie dined here. Went to Van Buren's — where were Bellows & Gibbs. Agnew was missing. He has just been enlisting a new recruit — a little girl-baby. M[rs] A. doing well I hear. — Bellows brings back *Knapp* seriously prostrated by malarious fever. — He saw *Burnside* in Wash[n], who reports that he was four hours in driving eight miles to McClellan's headquarters in a light wagon with four horses — that he saw two mules perish by drowning in the fluid mire of the road — & that three days of dry weather will bring a crisis & enable McClellan to deliver a battle. It is believed in Wash^{n} that McDowell's division has joined McClellan. Telegram from Dr Hammond: "*15000* men to be provided for in five days — 5000 in N.Y." This looks like serious work at hand.

But there is no news in this morn'g's papers, & no extra this aft^{n}. Stroll to night. Called on Mrs Georgey Peters & Mrs Eleanor Strong. Both these ladies are rendering priceless aid & comfort to sick & wounded men in our N.Y. Hospitals, the former in 51st St. & the latter at the City Hospital.

June 17. Tuesday night. Fine weather; clear & cool. Telegram from Dr Draper that the St Mark reached Hampton Roads yesterday aft^{n}, all well.

But we are generally cast down to day; there's villainous news abroad, & worse tidings may come at any moment. Rebel Army in the valley of Virginia largely reinforced (qu: from the disintegrated army late at Corinth?) — Banks & Frémont in danger once more. — Clever raid in McClellan's rear by a party of rebel Cavalry, that threatened his communications, got up to the *Pamunkey* River & destroyed transport schooners & a wagon train before it was beat off. This dashing successful audacity is a bad sign. — McC. seems to make no progress. We feel as if he were paralyzed by Washington intrigue, denying him reinforcements. God forbid. If so, & if a great disaster come of it, Stanton or somebody will be held to a stern account. The disaster seems likely enough, but I have a lively faith in the honesty and singlemindedness of old A. Lincoln. There will be no personal intrigue in his Cabinet — "not if he knows it".

June 20. Friday night. Weather clear & cool of late. Letter from E. dated Monday aft^{n} just this side Old Point. Excellent spirits, & no seasickness. Subsequent telegrams say the St Mark is off Yorktown, en permanence, as receiving ship. No military news except our occupation of Cumberland Gap, an important point. Hard worked these last few days. To night at Gibbs' with Van Buren Bellows & Dr Douglas.

Poor honest irascible feeble old Tripler's nomination as Inspector Gen[l] unanimously rejected by the Senate. Not surprising, for Senators have been visiting White House & seeing for themselves what he can accomplish. Letterman & Vollum are to report to McClellan as Medical Director & Inspector. Tripler is relieved & McClellan's army still more so.

Perhaps we are a shade less blue than three days ago, but still very blue indeed. We think McClellan has been reinforced but that the desperate Rebel Army before Richmond may make a dash on Washington, & develop the latent sympathies of Maryland.

June 22. Sunday night. Rec[d] telegram from Olmsted at White House (thro' Bloor) that the D. Webster & the Spaulding sail for N.Y. to day with cargoes of sick & wounded, & must be sent back at once — "should not remain over night". This has kept me employed all day, conferring with Bellows & Van Buren. The Elm City is also here, having discharged her freight of damaged humanity at Albany, so we have three transports to equip — besides the Euterpe. — Agnew is at White House doing "exsections" & the like. T.H. Faile J[r] our volunteer Superintendant for N.Y. went off with him, deserting his post. Bellows goes to Ohio to night, to look after "Antioch College", now in financial extremity. I suppose it to be a Humbug in collapse, but D[r] B. says he must go & look after it, so the duties of the Executive Committee devolve on Van Buren Gibbs & myself.

No news from Ellie since last Monday aft[n]. — One of our nurses (*Janes*) has died of fever contracted in our service. Knapp continues very ill. He's at D[r] Bellows'. — Am very blue to-night, after a long lonely stroll. Troubled about E. — Anxious about affairs before Richmond. — Wounded by private & personal silence & unkindness I had no reason to expect. Signs of weakness in a friendship of near 30 years are unpleasant.

June 23. Monday. Fine day & drizzly night. Letters from E. bring her biography down to Thursday. She is enjoying the sea-breezes & *high thermometers* of York River (she was meant to reside in a house bisected by the equator —) but has had no work yet.

Busy day down town, & from 3 to 5 at 498 Bdway examining & enrolling nurses. — Spaulding & D Webster arrived early this morn'g and we hope to send them back Wednesday.

Sent poor Johny dinnerless to bed, for grave misdemeanors. Heaven deal more mercifully with our elder & deeper sins! The true line of discipline is hard to find. I dread falling into either extreme, harshness or over-indulgence.

To night to concert at Acad: of Music. It was got up, spontaneously, by the young men of Mercantile Soc^{y} Library for benefit of San: Commission. Tolerable house — guess we shall net $1000. & upwards. The wonderful Seventh Symphony was on it's programme, & of course covered a multitude of sins — solos vocal & instrumental — fiorituri & bosh. The overtures to Tannhauser & Euryanthe also are not to be heard every night. The symphony was well enough rendered. It's second movement certainly stands alone — unrivalled in it's way — as an expression of hopeless supplication in sorrow — of a despairing cry from the Depths & from a horror of great darkness. One might write about it for pages, but what he wrote would be nonsense to everyone but himself, so intangible & incommunicable is the message addressed by the highest musical art to each individual that feels it. Then that grand mournful march that comes "sweeping by", like Tragedy, "with sceptered pall", Silencing the festal phrases of the scherzo — the few massive awful chords that connect these two parts of the 3^{d} movement, & lead the orchestra back from D. Major to F — the roaring triumphant chaos & anarchy of the 4th movement — what do they all mean? There must be — or must have been once, in Beethoven's heart — a key to this wonderful symphony.

Dr Grymes & Dr Chamberlain, both just from White House are prophets of evil. They say McClellan is in sorest need of reinforcement — that McDowell is *not* with him, after all we have heard! I feel very blue tonight, & as if heavy disaster might be at our doors.

June 24. Rainy day. We continue forlorn & fearful, expecting from minute to minute to hear the howl of newsboys announcing their Extry of fatal tidings from Richmond. — McClellan is far too weak already, & the Rebels are doubtless receiving daily reinforcement from their disintegrated S.W. Army. — — — We were premature in rejoicing over the reopening of the Mississippi. *Vicksburgh* still holds out, & commands the river. — From Charleston papers we learn there was severe fighting on James Island, only four miles from that pestilent city, a week ago. They claim a victory but their reports look, on the whole, as if we were making substantial progress there.

Letter from E. at Yorktown. Very jolly, but no work yet. — To Col. Coll. meeting at 2 P.M. We gave an A.B. "*honoris causa*" to certain of our undergraduates who have left their coll: course unfinished to take Commissions in the Army. This inspired my patriotic colleague, Martin Zabriskie Esq. to move that we give that degree to all Second Lieutenants in all N.Y. Volunteer Regiments. — Fish duly announced the motion — & that it was *not* seconded. I wish I had seconded it, and said a few words of & concerning the spirit that prompted the mover. "*Esprit de l'escalier*!"

Thence to 498 Bdway. Chaos & confusion. Fifty people waiting — engaged or to be engaged in this that & the other steamer — wanting to know when she will sail — when & where they shall report — & nobody able to tell them. Unless we get this office decently organized I will resign from the Sanitary Commission, for I cannot carry on my work as Treasurer in this way any longer.

June 25. Faintheartedness still prevails. The Presdt's visit to Gen. Scott at West Point has stimulated the production of most authentic reports & reliable statements, mostly "asthenic" & unfavorable. To day's crop has been enormous. E.g. "McClellan is dead". "He is not dead yet, but dying of dysentery with typhoid symptoms". "A.B. was told by C.D. that he has a letter from his cousin Major X.Y. on Gen. *fx*'s staff stating that McClellan has lost his mind & gone crazy with anxiety & excitement" — "Lincoln wants Scott's advice about McClellan's successor". — "Scott is to resume Chief Command of the Army." — "Scott's confidential relations with the Rebel Leaders can be legally proved at last, & Lincoln went to West Point to tell him so in person". — "Gen Buell has arrived at Baltimore with 30.000 men from the S.W. to reinforce McClellan"

[Would that were true!] — "Banks is Sec^{y} of War — vice Stanton sent home". — "Lincoln has concluded to resign" — "Gen. Halleck has been totally routed — but it has been kept out of the newspapers". Lies swarm & buzz in the streets, thick as the musquitos of a Rockaway salt meadow in August.

June 26. News this morning of a successful move before Richmond that advances our left wing & is important or is to lead to important results. Took place yesterday aft^{n} — & with trifling loss — as reported. [Very well — but at this moment (10.40 P.M.) there are newsboys rampaging up the 4th Av: shrieking "Extry something — Great battle at Richmond — & defeat of McClellan" or what sounds dismally like it. — I lie in wait for the first of the κακαγγελοι that shall make a detour through 21st St. — Guess it is bogus. But it may be disastrously true.]

Note from Van Buren. Agnew has returned from V^{a}. Reports Yorktown Hospitals broken up — the S. Mark taking on board the worst typhoid cases. V.B. warned me that he thought E. might be endangered by the presence of a concentrated crowd of fever patients. This disconcerted & alarmed me seriously. Telegraphed her at once directly & also thro' Bloor at Wash^{n}. Wrote her by mail & also by the Spaulding which returned this aft^{n}, entreating conjuring & commanding her to quit the S.M. — & if there be no vacancy on any less febrile ship to come straight home. — This af^{tn} at 498 Bdway. Agnew was there. Encouraging report from him of the condition of the Army, in all but Sanitary respects. Discipline, equipment, *morale*, excellent. But Hospitals are in a horrible state. Malarious fever & diarrhœa prevalent. Scurvy has appeared unmistakeably.

E's account of her interview with the Medical officer in charge of the Yorktown Hospital Monday or Tuesday is worth noting. Two thousand patients, *typhoid mostly*, on the hands of this official gentleman & his staff of *one* "Contract Surgeon". — "How are you off for hospital diet, sir?" — "Well I dont think we have any — the men draw their rations" [salt pork & the like] "Indeed! Why we have quantities of condensed milk, beef stock" &c &c &c "on the S. Mark, & the Commission will no doubt be glad to supply you". — "O, thank you, it's of no consequence. They generally die in two or three days

— & it is'nt worth while". — "You have stimulants enough, I suppose?" — "O, yes — that is, we *have not got any now*. We had so many gallons of brandy &c &c but I thought they were used up very fast, & I'm glad they are gone. I sha'nt make requisition for any more". — Is not this murderous & horrible? I believe the new Inspector *Vollum* has removed this imbecile wretch, whose name was, I think, *Wheaton*.

June 27. Friday. Letters from Ellie in high health & spirits, complaining only of idle hours & light work. Also a telegram from D[r] Draper, who thinks there is no danger from fever on the S. Mark. — Work as usual today. After 3 P.M. at N[o] 498. Man is born to *boredom*.

Big dinner at old D[r] Mott's from 6 to 11.30. Heavy work in this hot weather. To day has been summer full-blown. There were the Surgeon-General — & D[rs] Satterlee, Van Buren, Flint, Marcou, Watts, Judge Hilton, &c: — about a dozen. Sat next to Hammond. Like him better & better. Full of original thought & plans of vigorous action & organization. Some already carried out. There is a curious blending of coarse & fine grain in his composition. — He is considering the qu: of an Act to give the Med: Department it's own independent transportation, the want of which seems to me to lie at the bottom of a large portion of it's short-comings. I have been trying to shew Bellows & V.B. that this should be reformed & the M. Bureau no longer depend on the Quarter Master Gen[l] for conveyance of stores & of sick men, but in vain. As H. is disposed to agree with me, I consider him, of course, a man of great practical good sense.

Bad news from Charleston. A decided repulse on James Island, after hard fighting & with heavy loss. It looks like the affair of *Big Bethel* in many respects, may it be the precursor of no *Bull Run*! Gen: Benham has come to N.Y. under arrest, (or perhaps *not* under arrest, for no one can be sure about anything) having made this attack in violation of Gen: Hunter's orders.

June 30. Monday. 5 P.M. The darkest day we have seen since *Bull Run*. We have rallied a little & picked up a certain am[t] of hope since noon, but the general feeling is of dismay.

An extra late last night intimated that something of firstrate importance was in progress — disclosure not yet allowed — magnificent results at hand.

This morn'g comes another, stating — (let us see how much we can consider established.) very hard fighting from Thursday to Sat: & probably yesterday. McClellan's right wing has fallen back. White House is abandoned. Transports &c going down the *Pamunkey* — & a certain amount of stores abandoned & burned. This is called a *strategic movement.* Polite language, I suppose for a retreat. The fighting has been desperate. My gallant friend Clitz *is mortally wounded* — his reg^{t} (the 12th U.S.A.) cut to pieces — Duryée's Zouaves have lost their Col. (Warren) & many more. Churchill Cambreleng, one of their Capt^{ns}, is wounded (I got his father a pass from Hammond this aft^{n}) — The Rebels no doubt terribly punished by our artillery.

That is about all. The War Department is "without farther information", a fearfully bad symptom. It is all obscure. We cannot make out exactly what's coming — but it has the *walk* of a defeat & a very bad one. I would compromise for a drawn battle.

Possibly *McC.* may have moved so as to make the James River his base — & put himself in *rapport* with the gunboats. This would explain the abandonment of W.H. & transfer of stores & transports to James River. There is a story that Burnside is on the *other* bank of that river, 20 miles from Richmond — but I do not believe it. — Rumored that that very valiant rebel *Jackson* has reinforced the main rebel army. Like enough, but why are not McDowell & Banks on his heels? — Seward is in town (colloguing with Thurlow Weed & certain Governors, at the Astor House) & says it's all right & very jolly: his usual parrot formula. He has no reliable intelligence. The indications taken all together — the "totality of the symptoms" — are of disaster & ruin.

11 P.M. The black cloud may have lifted & lightened up a very little, perhaps, but it is still dangerous & impenetrably dense. Telegram came from Olmsted (at F. Monroe *yesterday*) about the movements of our Hospital Steamers. It says nothing about any battle, but concludes with the words "All well *& in the best spirits*". O. knows the value of words, & these were not written without consideration. — Went after dinner to C.E.S. with this intelligence. Found him in his dining room with Mrs Eleanor & G.C.A. I supposed G.C.A. had gone to Saratoga. He has been detained by sore throat. Was formal stately sulky and grim. Poor fellow, what a fool that temper of his makes of him sometimes! — A storm of Extras came howling thro' 22nd St. — "Got the Bombardment of Richmond". (Mrs Eleanor in tearful spasmodic excitement.) The Extra on the whole consolatory. Withdrawal from W.H. effected without loss — that seems reliable. McClellan's left within short range of Richmond — Burnside taking "Fort Darling" in reverse — these are unreliable. This great battle has been lost or won. We shall know by tomorrow night.

July 1. We *do'nt* know: we are no wiser than last night: not an atom of news has arrived. But we are comparatively jolly & comfortable to day — perhaps because of the bright sunshine & bracing air. McClellan's dubious movements are strategy — "high old strategy". Our new base on James River is doubtless established, & it's all right. So we talk to day.

Letters from Ellie. She seems to have left the St Mark at Yorktown Thursday & gone up the Pamunkey to the Knickerbocker at White House, just in time to assist at the general movement to the rear. She writes in the best spirits, undisturbed by all the rumpus & hurry about her, & thinking mainly of her work. She is a very *great* little woman! Heaven send her safe home!

Visit from Prof. Lieber. One of his three sons lost an arm at Fort Donelson. Another, Oscar, of S. Carolina, was badly hit at Williamsburgh, fighting in the ranks of the rebellion, & when last heard from was lying at Richmond, attacked by erysipelas, which disease is ravaging the hospitals of that town. His 3^d^ son is in the 11th or 12th Regulars, reported much cut up in this last battle, & Lieber called to enquire about passes to Yorktown &c &c. — His visit a specimen of the practical effects of Civil War. Who is guilty of this Civil War, & what punishment do those on whom it's guilt rests deserve?

July 2. Wednesday. Roaring rain all the aft^{n}, & its now roaring & clattering louder than ever. If this irrigation extend to Virginia, & the James River & the now classic Chickahominy rise "a feet" or so? It would seem a good thing for them to do, if I understand the situation aright, which I probably *dont.* No news to day. Everything absolutely impenetrable. McClellan & the Fiend Secessia are having it out behind the scenes, we do not know yet who is to come up to the footlights presently as Victorious Hero. This strange unaccountable obscurity reminds one of the great battle between Cosmos & Chaos in the last canto of *Kehama.*

"Then too the Lord of Hell put forth his might.
Thick darkness, blacker than the blackest night
Rose from their wrath, & veiled
The unutterable fight."

— The "Lord of Hell", by the way, was champion of Law & Order in that combat and came out all right at last, though badly punished in the first round. It is very important to Secessia that there should be an active "Lord of Hell", wide awake & up to his work, to take care of her case. "Under the constitution" his appointment devolves on the General Government. — I said "no news", but there was an Extra Tribune at 7 P.M. reporting a despatch from Memphis to Louisville that we have taken Richmond. Bogus unquestionably. It gives me no comfort whatever. But if it had reported our army in retreat from Richmond, I should doubtless have been disconsolate — even more disconsolate than I am. This *suspense* — this hanging by the *neck* & wondering whether the halter will hold or break — is a trying process. — The silence of the War Department is a bad symptom. I have a vague presentiment — a dim instinctive sense — of something all wrong down there & very bad. Thank Heaven the President has called for a few hundred thousand volunteers to reinforce the Army, at last. Would he had invoked them three months ago! — We retire, repulsed & beaten, from James Island, & the capture of Charleston is put off to a more convenient season. — Things look ill in the West — Our European news is bad. France & England are itching to "intervene", and sustain the slavebreeding woman-floggers of Charleston & New Orleans & Richmond in their rebellion. I never expected much from *France*, but the political immorality of *England*, as revealed by her press, confounds me. I cannot understand or explain it. If her sense of National right & wrong be so utterly perverted as it seems, she will surely be punished before many generations have passed away.

Letter from Ellie, at *West Point* Sunday, full of interesting details of the "strategic" abandonment of White House. What a plucky little thing she is, & how she enjoys this philanthropic gipseying & drudgery — & her uncertain Bohemian life on steamboats & transports — & her work in relieving & comforting sick & wounded soldiers. God send her safe home!

July 3. Thursday. Very bad. What news will come to night no man can tell — but just now (*5 P.M.*) things look disastrously. Fighting continued Sunday & Monday — when our gunboats seem to have done good service once more. McClellan seems now jammed up against the James River, with his left 15 miles below Richmond, having abandoned siege guns & left his wounded in the field. Worse is behind no doubt, or the War Department would speak out. That fellow Stanton probably fears the storm a full report will raise about his ears. — Has McClellan ammunition & supplies? Can he maintain himself where he is? Has he transportation if he find it necessary to retreat? Is'nt it very possible that his whole army may have to surrender?

It's an immense disaster, as it stands, & of course we do not know the worst yet. Intervention now of course — & another war on our shoulders, & disgrace & ruin for the two alternatives to choose between.

Significant that the two French Princes have left McClellan's staff "with despatches".

Bitterly worried about Ellie — she has no doubt gone up James River on the Webster — & God knows what risks she may run — for the Sepoy Chivalry are not particular about firing on Hospital ships.

It has been a dismal day. I have worked hard, in desperation, to keep my thoughts off our great calamity. — G.C.A. & C.E.S. as blue as myself. — *It is said* however that McClellan has taken guns, & 2000 prisoners, including Gen: Magruder, who is hardly worth the cost of his keep. He will take captivity with much resignation (if he is captured) for the price of decent whiskey in Secessia puts it beyond the reach of all but the wealthiest class. —

10.30 P.M. G.A. dined with me, & we had a talk afterwards. His cantankerous ways when out of temper with a friend are certainly compensated by unusual frankness & fullness of kind apologetic selfcondemning talk when the fit is over. — I helped the children ignite certain crackers &c. It seemed indecent at this period of disaster & anxiety — but I decided in it's favor as a patriotic avowal of "Never say die" & "Do'nt give up the ship" embodied in pyrotechny. — During this performance there came an Extra.

In substance, McC. at Harrison's Bar (qu: H's *point*? — vide maps) on James River, yesterday 5.30 P.M. Has lost but one gun which broke down. Only one wagon abandoned. Severe battle yesterday — enemy repulsed — "men fought even better than before — Army in good spirits. Reinforcements from Washington have arrived". — This looks better than I hoped. No doubt all the rebel hordes, Beauregard's army included, have been precipitated on McClellan, & hoping to crush him by six days fighting with immense preponderance of force — near two to one probably. If so, & if he has saved his army, tho' with heavy loss, & inflicted still heavier loss on the Rebels, & can maintain himself till he is reinforced, — things do not look so desperate as they did this morn'g.

Took a stroll — beautiful night it is — & then took out the Journal — & while I write, comes an *Extra World*. "Our special correspondent" left "the field of battle before Richmond" (rather vague) "Tuesday ev'g 9 P.M." "McClellan's advance (!) then within 15 miles of Richmond". — Rebels terribly repulsed Monday. Heintzelman captured 8 guns & 1600 prisoners including 3 colonels. Gen[s] McCall & Reynolds supposed to have been taken by the enemy. "Stonewall Jackson undoubtedly killed". As he is (or looks like) a first rate man, & is on the wrong side, I hope this is true. It cannot be uncharitable to hope that he has gone to Heaven, his great crime of treason being committed under invincible prejudice & error of judgment, and that no notion of primary allegiance to his state will tempt him to set up a secession movement against the Unity of the Eternal Kingdom. — Alas for the peaceful quiet days that are gone! — These reports are comforting, but why are official despatches withheld? — On the whole, my construction of the result is this. We are beat back by a superior force but not destroyed. The enemy was superior because we have been outgeneralled. The blame rests, probably, on the War Department. The remedy is speedy reinforcement. This call for 300.000 volunteers would have provided the remedy had it been issued two months ago. But it comes too late to meet this crisis. Whether we can spare men from before Washington, or get them up from the S.W. in time, is a question. — Ev'g Post announces that the *Webster* arrived at Baltimore this morning with wounded men. God grant E. was on board of her. If so, she will be here tomorrow.

July 4. It has been a lovely day & quite as noisy as usual. This household has contributed it's share to the general racket. The morn'g spent mostly with Bellows & Van Buren at the house of Dr B. — in council. Saw Knapp, convalescent from a sharp attack of typhoid malarious fever & "Pamunkey-ness" as Agnew calls it. He leaves town this ev'g for Walpole & a week's holiday which he needs before returning to active duty. — Mr Rogers came in. He is a slow solid old-fogyish philanthropic wealthy & admirable person — of Boston (or Brookline rather) who worked all winter as a volunteer aid in connexion with the "Home" at Wash^n & has been working for two months on the Peninsula as an aid to Olmsted. He left McClellan's headquarters Tuesday aft^n. — Reports in substance — Left his Hospital Depot, at Savage's Station, Sat. aft^n. Of the 2500 sick & wounded then there, all who could not march were abandoned. Our change of base, however "strategic", was compulsory, for we could not rely on our communications with White House. It's necessity appeared last Monday week, when a reconnoissance was made which shewed that a certain coveted position quite near Richmond (probably "Tavern Hill") was too strong for us. Our line is now parallel to the general course of James River. We have not 70.000 effective men. Few of these are thoroughly effective, all are suffering more or less from diarrhœa &c. — Present position secure. Everybody has faith in McClellan, & is in good spirits. The army must be *doubled*, to take Richmond. *Stanton* generally denounced for not sending on reinforcements. McClellan is, in R's judgment, a hard-working intelligent efficient officer, but over-cautious, & incapable of seizing opportunities.

Fire works after dinner for the childrens' delectation. G.C.A. Walter Cutting & D[r] Peters came in afterwards & we talked till late over whiskey & soda water & affairs of state. Complexion of our talk, *dark-blue*.

July 5. Sat: — Uncommonly sultry & lazy day. Aft[n] at N[o] 498: to night Bellows, V.B., Agnew, & Gibbs here in council, over claret & cold chicken. — We decide that next meeting of Com: be in Cincinnati — August.

We have revived a good deal to day, & feel much better. McClellan's despatch of yesterday allows us to believe the army safe & full of fight — & the Rebel attacks of Monday & Tuesday seem to have been beat back with terrible execution. Also there are rumors of very large reinforcements at hand from Halleck & from N.W. V[a]. These stories seem authentic, & unless Gov[t] is reinforcing McC. largely & promptly, at every cost, we may as well give in at once, & save blood-shedding. We have a despatch that "*Vicksburgh* is ours", — no details. Cutting that last ligature on the great Artery of the Nation is a great fact, but all our hopes & fears are concentrated on the Peninsula now.

No news from Ellie. I am worried about her. She is exposed not only to disease, but to rifle shots from the bluffs of James River, for the dwellers on it's banks are just as vindictive barbarous & base as the savages their ancestors found there in the days of Capt[n] John Smith. These churls, who call themselves "chivalry", can murder a wounded enemy & shell their enemy's hospitals, & I believe them quite capable of firing on Hospital Ships & picking off any "Yankee" woman they may see within rifle range.

July 6th. Sunday. A cruel hot day. At home & in shirt sleeves getting up a circular or statement asking contributions for the Army. No church I regret to say. M[r] Ruggles came in this ev'g, just from Washington where he has been fighting for enlargement of canals as a highway for *gunboats*, & is defeated or rather *put off* by a majority small beyond all expectation — so small that the result is a triumph. He came on with sundry officers wounded during the last week of continuous battle before Richmond. They are amazed at the feeling of depression they find here. "We never supposed we were retreating" they say — "We thought we were gaining a victory every day". — He reports Seward full of secret policy & mysterious hints & charlatanism. L. Napoleon tempted to *intervene*, according to Seward, because he wants his son recognized as his successor by European powers, & thinks he will secure recognition of his dynasty by active hostility to Free Institutions. It seems an unreasonable impractical motive, not at all in the style of that most wily & wary potentate. But I see the danger, tho' unable to detect the motive, unless we gain decisive results within 30 days.

With C. & Mrs C. in 22^{d} St. at supper this ev'g. Very kind & cordial.

Not a word from poor Ellie. Were she only safe at home again! — Mr S.B.R. is in exaltation over what he considers our grand perilous movement toward James River, achieved by resolute dogged fight for a week against overwhelming odds — & much exasperated by the omission of the prayer for the Army from the services of Calvary Church today. No wonder.

July 7. After dinner to Dr Van Buren's to consult over proof-sheets. Summoned into the dining room where I find the D^{r} & Madame, Miss Addie, a quiet young lady of mature years — to wit eighteen or so — (& they say a remarkably nice thoughtful little personage) & rampagious Miss Sally of 10 or 12, domestically known as "Bird o' freedom" with whom I may claim to be on terms of intimacy. — After a little talk, & an adjournment for a while to the Dr's office, I loafed up town with Agnew.

Spaulding, St Mark, & Webster arrived, full of wounded men. Letter from E. this A.M. dated Friday night. Then leaving the Webster for the Knickerbocker, at Harrison's Point, so as to avoid an outside passage & seasickness. The K. being destined for Washington. To night another hurried pencil note, brought by private hand, dated yesterday on board the K. off F^{t} Monroe. (I am thankful she has escaped assassination on her way down James River) — Very tired, but quite well (I hope so) & to be at home again tomorrow night at latest.

She writes "Our dear old friend, & as gallant an officer as ever laid down his life for his country, *Henry Clitz* lies dead on the field." Too true I fear. The report is that he was struck by a cannon ball in the leg, & when last seen was dying of hemorrhage. A nobler fellow I never knew. He was the embodiment of all that is frank generous genial kind manly & good. Shall we talk Conciliation to the traitors who murdered him in his duty? — We feel more comfortable about McClellan to day. Newspaper reports tho' meagre are encouraging as far as they go. Our agents who return on these transports say that the enthusiastic loyalty of the rank & file toward their Genl is something very notable. Men lying in the mud with an arm shot off raise the surviving member & cheer feebly as he rides past them. — Poor Clitz — so bright & full of life — cannot we yet hope that he may have been saved? — Dr. V.B. reports the Prince de Joinville full of admiration of McClellan & of the Army, and satisfied we should have occupied Richmond before this but for the politico-military caballings of Stanton & (I'm sorry to add) McDowell. McDowell is falling fast in popular favor. McClellan's want of reinforcements is laid to him, — unjustly I hope.

N.B. I don't think *Vicksburgh* is finally our own even yet, tho' we have undoubtedly shelled it with vigor & effect. We are digging a canal round the root of it's peninsula that is to make an inland town of it anyhow, which is of course equivalent to it's annihilation.

July 11. E. returned by R.R. Wednesday aft^{n} in best spirit, & good health, except for a slight symptom of "Pamunkeyness" that will not prove lasting or serious I hope. Has had a jolly time of hard work & useful work amid the tragedies of visible War. No time to write her story. Wish there were, for it's worth recording. — She came to Wash^{n} from Harrison's Landing on the Knickerbocker, a *government* transport, with Miss Gilson of Chelsea Mass: and a staff of dressers. It was an experiment of her devising. Government & San: Commission had not worked together on the same ship before. The combination succeeded triumphantly. E's tact sense goodnature & energy conquered the U.S.A. Surgeon in charge, Dr Page, at once, & coerced all his official dignity into loyal submission — or rather into hearty grateful cooperation in the care of his cargo of 500 "cases" mostly bad ones. She had the great satisfaction of producing from the little stock of Commission stores she brought on board, hastily got together at half an hour's notice, from the Danl Webster — & of producing while *amputations were going on — the bandages* & the *stimulants*, of which the surgeon really believed he had not any on board. The little woman has come out amazingly strong during these two months. Have never given her credit for a tithe of the enterprise pluck discretion & force of character she has shewn — God bless her.

She went to *Newport* this aft^{n} with D^{r} & Mrs Peters on a reconnoissance after summer quarters at Bateman's or elsewhere — Dont think the outlook that way remarkably pleasant or promising. I sent *Johny* thither yesterday aft^{n} with C.E.S. who kindly solicited the charge of that cub for two or three days. He wants country air. C.E.S. & Dr P. have taken a joint cottage at Newport for the summer.

There seems a gleam of hope that poor Clitz is living — a wounded prisoner — but I hardly see it. — Tom McCarty, a very fine fellow, Captn in one of our Volunteer Reg^{ts}, is missing. Trobriand's 55th Reg^{t} is gone — only a score or two left. Cambreleng is safe, so is Hayward Cutting — so is Chetwood. John Astor is in town. How he swears when one names the Sec^{y} of War. He for one believes that Stanton wilfully withheld reinforcements from McClellan lest he should make himself too important, politically, by a signal victory. Many, the majority of people, I think, share his belief. Stanton is being awfully rasped & punished: he's the target for a concentric newspaper fire. My faith in the man failed some time ago: it was a lively faith when his career began: but I dont feel quite justified by the evidence in bringing him in guilty of a crime so base & so tremendous in it's consequences. — I have got positions as *Nurses* on the Spaulding, which sailed to day, for *Chas Kuhn*, who wants to look after his brother Hamilton K. reported killed (truly reported I think, but C.K. clings to a straw of uncertainty) & for a young Costar who is on a similar errand for one of his house now lying badly wounded at Harrison's Landing. We are run down with like applications. Granting these made a bad precedent & opens a door we shall find it hard to close, but we could not resist the appeal.

Nothing notable to day. No news. From eight to 10.30 at Bellows' with Agnew. Settling sundry matters of importance particularly as to the organization of our office at 498 Bdway, & the framing of rules to prevent abuses on our transports. —

We have been & are in a depressed dismal asthenic state of "anxiety" & "irritability" — The cause of the country does not happen to be thriving just now. McClellan's army is "safe", but how soon will James River be closed by Rebel batteries & supplies cut off? May he not be compelled to capitulate within ten days? Are not the Rebels now moving a column on Washington? Stonewall Jackson is not killed.

Letters from Olmsted tonight. Not cheering. He writes 4th inst. on his way to Washn (on the Wilson Small) to make report to Surgeon Genl of sanitary condition of the Army & to plead for reinforcements. Army fatigued & worn, but of good heart: men are confident they can do whatever McC. tells them to do, & that he knows his business & can save them. Full of faith in McClellan. But sorely exhausted, anxiously looking over their shoulders for reinforcements — for Burnside or somebody — & for 50.000 more men. [Where can we find them on demand? — Why was recruiting stopped?] Letterman — Surgeon U.S.A. — says our loss is 30.000 — residue 60.000. Sanitary aspect of the Army very bad — no camp police — no time for it. — On the 7th — after his visit to Washn, wh: seems to have made no impression — he writes in still darker mood. Seems to think McClellan's whole Army may be cut off from it's supplies & destroyed. Rebels may close up James River with batteries suddenly opened. (That is certainly our most pressing peril) — Reaction after terrible tension & excitement appears in the Army. Officers sneak, or bully their way, on board Hospital transports under flimsy pretexts of sick-leave. They long to get away on any terms.

July 14. We are in the depths just now, permeated by disgust, saturated with gloomy thinking. I find it hard to maintain my lively faith in the triumph of the Nation & the Law. I fear to-morrow's War-Meeting in Union square will be unlike that of April 20 /61 — (a time never to be forgotten. It was among the most intense & memorable hours of my life) — People without virile loyalty are bolder in their talk. Recruiting is dull.

I have certain notions on that subject by the way about which I wrote to Bellows at Walpole N.H. this morn'g — he's rusticating there — happy man — It seems to me the great point is to use the new levies to fill gaps in our existing experienced regiments, before forming new ones. 300 new regiments with their officers & men all equally raw will be a mere mob of Bull-Runagates for six months after they are mustered into service. — News this morn'g that the Rebels have re-taken Murfreesboro', Tennessee, & threaten Nashville. Rumor to night that Van Dorn has retaken *Baton Rouge*. Very bad.

On the other hand Gov[t] seems waking up to the duty of dealing more vigorously with Rebellion, by acts of Emancipation & Confiscation. — And Clitz is reported a prisoner, wounded, at Richmond. May that be true!

July 15. Tuesday. To day's heat has been overwhelming. We have not known so broiling a time since the hot spell of June /58. But each of these still blistering days adds millions to our National Wealth in bread-stuffs. Let us sweat therefore in silence & with thanksgiving. E. & Johny returned from Newport this morn'g by nightboat, tired but jolly. Rooms engaged there, at one Vose's. My expectations are at or below zero, but I can be there so little, probably, that they are of no importance. E. likes the prospect, and Johny & Temple will find safe waters to sail their boats & wade in. So we may do very well.

At 498 Bdway as usual. Thence walked languidly up town with Agnew to assist at the great Union meeting or War Meeting on Union Square, watching certain lowering but indolent masses of thundercloud in the West that threatened to disperse the assemblage prematurely. But their rain was withheld till after 6 P.M. The Meeting was well enough — better than I expected, but not what it should have been & what this crisis demands. Mere hack-politicians, like Delafield Smith & Manierre &c &c were it's prominent actors. Tho' the gathering was very large it will not help us much — it was apathetic & dead. And we need now the muscular energy of mania, such as the Rebels exhibit.

Agnew dined here. Our talk was not exhilarating. McClellan's Army must lose 15000 men by disease within 30 days. It is *certain* that within that time strong rebel field works &

batteries will be unmasked on the right or S.W. bank of James River, closing it as the Potomac was closed last winter. What then? Will McClellan be able to retreat on Yorktown or will he be forced to surrender? Everything looks black & blue.

July 17. Thursday. Less severely hot — a little. Affairs make no great progress, recruiting included. Laurence Williams, just from V[a] on sick leave (touch of typhoid) dined here yesterday with Murray Hoffman. Olmsted arrived this morning from Harrison's bar, on the D. Webster, sunburnt & worn but in better health & less doleful in his prophesyings than I expected. When O. is blue, the logic of his despondency is crushing & terrible. L.W. on McClellan's staff during the week of battle. Perfect confidence in McC. — Admirable coolness & equanimity throughout. Fighting earnest & desperate on both sides. We can hold our present position & may do well yet if reinforcements come fast enough & if McC be not bothered by interference from Wash[n]. Burnside at Newport News with 10 to 15.000 men (W.) 7000 (O) — Health of the army decidedly improved during last week (O) — Only a few points on the river where serious mischief could be done by masked batteries, & these could be made secure by felling the trees. — *Clitz certainly at Richmond.* I trust that is true. L.W. denounces the Administration, Stanton especially, with plainness of speech that does not altogether become a Major in the U.S.A. He shudders at Abolitionism, as hydrophobic patients at the sound of falling water. But it is remarkable that his estimate of Lincoln has changed. He don't call L. a "Gorilla Ape" as he did last winter, but relies on him as the only honest & patriotic man in the Administration. Perhaps he is not so far wrong. — He introduced the subject of his own arrest last Spring: has not even a suspicion of the reason for it. McC. discharged him as soon as he knew of it. "As to his communicating with the enemy, why, if he were to go over, his own family would be the first to kick him out of Richmond". I do not dream that W. could be guilty of treason, & I know little of his distinguished F.F.V. relatives. But I think it doubtful whether there are many Southerners who would kick him very hard for any baseness whatever, committed in the interest of the South. The cases of Brooks & Floyd are in point. Long walk this ev'g while E. was at N° 24. No incidents save a false alarm of fire on Broadway & Eighth St. & a roaring tearing concurrence of fire companies, that looked for a time like a "muss." Why do not these sturdy ruffians *enlist*?

I'm sole representative in town of Exec: Committee of San. Commission. Bellows is frisking at Walpole N.H. and Gibbs at some place in R.I. — Van Buren circumambulating New England — Agnew at Newport, professionally. Olmsted went straight to Staten Island this morn'g.

Geo. F. Allen has returned safe from his visit to Jamaica unharmed by Yellow Jack, centipedes or Scorpions. Met him this morn'g at the barber's. (Potter's). He's in best spirits, not cast down a bit. Glad of it, for discouragement is the evil most to be dreaded now. The rebels are fighting us with the fury of a frantic ram-cat driven into a corner, & unless we can meet them with calm undismayed resolution, we are lost.

July 19. Sat. Much cooler. Fervent in business (San: Com:) all day. Our affairs are prosperous. R.G. White dined & spent the ev'g. No events to record except the occupation of Gordonsville by Gen: Pope's advance, under Hatch, and Halleck's appointment to chief command as head of the Army. I profess no legal evidence of Halleck's military genius, but one bad general is worth *two* good ones. A "Commander of the Forces", no matter who, if not below the average in energy & commonsense, will accomplish more than a dozen clever generals of detached divisions working independently & at cross purposes & thwarted by an antic Council in the War-office. — G.C.A. returned prematurely from his vacation tour to Saratoga & Oswego, ill, & much run down. He caught a severe cold two months ago, which has not left him. He has congestion of one lung, is nervous & anxious, & looks badly. He dined here yesterday, & staid till late. C.E.S. came in, & Otis Swan to inspect our big parlor organ. He contemplates building something of the sort. Brought with him an artiste, one Conolly, to try the instrument.

July 23ᵈ. No material events. The Nation still in a state of languor & malaise "with great anxiety" (I am acquiring doctors' dialect). Abundant ground for it. The quiescence of the

Rebel host may be due to the punishing McClellan gave them during the Battle Week, but it is mysterious & looks menacing. Perhaps a great disaster & the invasion of Penn: or Ohio would be a healthy tonic & stimulant. Recruiting gets on decently well. Agnew & I (our colleagues all out of town) have been stewing over a Letter to the President, asking more thorough Medical Inspection of recruits, & that regiments now in the field be filled up by the men to be levied under the new call, instead of making up raw regiments of raw recruits — as they are doing now. The "Sniperfidgets Brigade" & the "Alderman Boole Battery" & the "Swindle-city Dragoons" will be worth little for six months to come, but their men might do great service if distributed among our quasi-veterans, many of whose regiments are reduced to skeletons by casualty & disease.

E. has not been quite well, suffering slightly from Pamunkeyness I think. This family goes to Newport tomorrow morn'g — by "Shore Line". *Escort* John the Waiter. I must stay, for a meeting of Exec: Com: of S.C. Friday. Bellows Gibbs & Van Buren are coming to town for it, & Olmsted has important suggestions. He proposes a general review of our position & a fresh start.

There is one piece of good news. *Clitz* arrived here yesterday on the *Euterpe*, & has gone to his mother's or brother's at Fort Hamilton. He was a prisoner at Richmond & sent down on parole under flag of truce. Dr Merritt, the Euterpe's Med: Director tells me has two bad gunshot wounds in the leg — that may compromise the knee joint but probably will not, & that he is doing well. Thank God for *that*.

July 26. Busy day. Sanitarian work of course. — Emigration of the Strongidæ yesterday by shore line (R.R.) at 8 A.M. Heavy rain forbade their departure Thursday morning. C.E.S. & Dr Peters went to see *Clitz* at F^t^ Hamilton. On his back, but doing well. His prophesyings woful. He says we shall be the worst-whipped people in history unless we wake up & begin working in earnest: Rebels full of pluck & audacity & faith in their cause: Say they mean to take Washington within 30 days. & Philad^a^ & N.Y. next fall or winter. Clitz saw Willy Alston who is still on Magruder's staff, (or gang of personal attendants).

The rebels suffered fearful loss at the battle of *Malvern Hill.* Richmond is a charnel-house. Corpses lie unburied for days.

Clitz's talk has made me blue-black. I greatly fear that we are on the eve of some vast calamity. *Why* in the name of — Anarchy & ruin, do'nt the Pres^{dt} order the draft of *one million fighting men at once*, and the liberation & *arming* of every able-bodied Sambo in Southronia? We shall perish unless Gov^{t} begin singing in that very key (of *all* the sharps.) War on Rebels *as criminals* has not begun. We have dealt with these traitors as a Police Officer deals with a little crowd that threatens a breach of the Peace. He wheedles & persuades & administers his club-taps mildly & seldom —

Old Matty Van Buren. His name was last in close contact with the people, twenty two years ago. We were all singing then "Tippecanoe & Tyler too —

"And with them we'll beat little *Van*,
Van, Van Van Van is a used up man.
And with them we'll beat little Van!"
— From 1836 to 1840

M.V.B.'s name was a word of power. He has just died, after a long period of withdrawal from public life. To his honor be it said that he lost a Democratic re-nomination afterwards because he would not bind himself to Southern service as a white slave of the Chivalry, and that in the weakness of extreme old age all his aspirations were National & loyal. His genus, the Democracy, is of low type, but he belonged to a sub-genus that must not be confounded with wretches like Toucey of Connecticut & that pitiable old Buchanan, now hiding from universal execration & contempt on his farm in Penn: — Miserable old creature! It would do great good if the U.S. Att^{y} Gen[1] would dig out the proofs of his sympathy with treason in 1860 — have him duly indicted & tried, &, if convicted, solemnly splendidly & conspicuously *hanged* on a high gallows in front of the Capitol at Washington.

Everything looks dismal. But the events of 1861–2 are hardly a single scene in the Great Tragedy, now opened, that may need half a century to develop itself. It's title will be Downfall of a barbaric social system.

July 29. With Agnew & V.B. at 498 this P.M. — We are getting off a propeller-load of *antiscorbutics* for the Army of the Potomac. Urgently needed. —

Miss Rosalie came in at 7 to ask me to get some little Savings Bank deposit for her — made long ago. I escorted her — quite ill, poor thing, to 24 Union Square & then walked down town to Canal St. — Driven prematurely home by lowering thunder clouds lightning & patter of rain, but the shower proved an abortion. Agnew came in & we took counsel about "garden-sass" & the Cargo of our Anti-scorbutic bark.

July 31. Thursday night. We still stew. If I have shed no blood in the Country's service, I have been liberal with another secretion — viz: sweat, with which I have bedewed the streets & sprinkled my papers, so that I was obliged to protect them with umbrelloid blotting paper. Do'nt wonder that the National Cause so prosperous in Feb^y^ & March, goes "all ajee" in this weather, or rather in that intensified form of summer that now reigns & roasts alive below the Potomac. How can honest Northern men fight when the very marrow of their bones is oozing out at every pore of their bodies?

Astounded by Ellie's sudden appearance at my bedside this morn'g early. From Newport with Annie, her faithful aide, by last night's boat, for a day's necessary shopping. Delighted with Newport — & well, except for a disturbance which I suppose due to the *Pamunkey*. It's not severe & will pass off under the influence of sea air, I hope. — Down town early. Energetic day at 68 Wall & 498 Bway. — *Bannister* promises to make an efficient supercargo for our Antiscorbutic Propeller, the Delaware.

C.E.S. dined here. Strolled out with him, & called for E. at N° 24, where she spent the rest of the ev'g. Long talk with Mr S.B.R. just returned from a journey West even to the Falls of St Anthony. He was full of what he had seen — of the thousands of miles of *wheat-harvest* through wh: his iron road had carried him — of the enormous resources of the N.W. — of our National Wealth & ability to feed the World — of King Cotton dethroned & King Breadstuff crowned as his successor. He has a wonderful way of giving life & poetry & power to the driest statistics.

From what C.E.S. tells me, I fear poor Bob Le Roy is going down hill again. After two years of sober & righteous life, he has once more begun to be reckless & to drink too freely. Another turn of "*D.T.*" will probably dispose of him. His plucky little beautiful wife stands by him. She was in Wall St. to day, poor thing, consulting C.E.S. about Bob's vague efforts to get a *Commission*. Would he be safer if he got one? Her relatives urge her to go back to her father, which she stoutly refuses to do. I think she's as noble as she's handsome & I should take my hat off, if I had it on, while I write of her.

No war news that's reliable. But Gov^t is said to be engaging transports to day & hurrying them down to James River. If so McClellan's Army is about to move, & it's movement will be to the rear.

Aug. 4. Monday night. I remember no summer so inveterately hot since that of /53. Hard-worked to day — S.C. of course. Everything is S.C. It's in my pocket & in my bed & in my boots. I'm crawling with sanitary considerations. The more work I put off on N° 498 Bdway, the more crops out for me to do. — Visit from G.C.A. this morn'g, just from *Cornwall* — jolly — & quite convalescent. At home this ev'g. Mr S.B.R. looked in awhile.

Extra to night. Advance of a column of Pope's Army to Orange C.H. — & a reconnoissance & little affair of Cavalry 14 miles from Petersburgh. — Recruiting goes on better than was expected, & there is a little tentative move toward drafting at last. Inaction of the Rebels surprises me. Are they weaker than we think, or are they gathering themselves together for some decisive blow where we do'nt expect them? McClellan's great name is growing very obscure, I regret to say & we generally doubt whether he is a genuine congener of Napoleon after all. As we deified him without reason, I suppose we are free to reduce his rank whenever we like. Prevailing color of people's talk is Blue. What's very bad, we begin to lose faith in Uncle Abe. "Most honest & true, thoroughly sensible, but without the decision & the energy the Country wants. Government does not lead the People — the People has to keep up a toilsome *vis a tergo*, & shove Gov^t forward to every vigorous step." Such is the talk I hear wherever I go. There seems some element of truth in it: but who can tell, that is not behind the scenes? — Our Letter to the Pres^{dt} about filling up old regiments before forming new ones, is much approved — & the policy it recommends *adopted*. A most important result, but the good sense of the people had expressed itself so strongly through many channels in favor of that policy, that we cannot claim the credit of having persuaded Gov^{t} to adopt it. — Siege of Vicksburgh ingloriously given up & the Mississippi not *open* after all!

Ellie returned to Newport Friday aft^{n}. Sat: morn'g on my way down town I experienced sundry strange gripings in my innards, recurring every five minutes or so, as if some vindictive secessionist had a handful of my bowels in his grasp & was giving them an occasional wringing squeeze. When I got to Wall St. I was in such pain that I could only stay long enough to open a few score letters & then omnibus back again, stopping at a drug store for a dose of morphine, & at *498* to give directions & sign checks in blank. Home & sent for Peters, who gave me more morphine & a heroic dose of jalap, & spent most of the aft^{n} & ev'g with me. Not a very jolly time. My vomiting was oceanic. I never realized my own cubic contents before. Knowledge of my capacity gives me quite a sense of self respect. Yesterday (Sunday) was hot flaccid & dismal. But I picked up my energies so far as to go to Union Club at half past four & assist (as spectator rather than convive) at a little dinner of Van Buren's. There were the Surgeon Genl, Agnew, Gibbs, Bellows, Olmsted, & myself. Many important questions talked over. This was another "bilious colic", a disorder against wh: I am prejudiced. It's recurrence may do great & irreparable mischief to my intestinal canal. The enemy keeps up some slight guerilla warfare to night with transient twinges.

Aug: 6. Wednesday. Last night's severe thundershower made this morn'g a little cooler, but the City swelters & stews again to night. — Usual routine down town. Dined with C.E.S. & G.C.A. at Maison Dorée.

There are little indications (more or less reliable) that McClellan is *resuming offensive operations*!!!!!!!!

Aug. 7. Broiling hot. Has the South prevailed on the Sun to intervene? Busy day, but nothing special. Dined at Maison Dorée as yesterday. Martinez, the proprietor, discovering that I was the individual who had paid him some thousand dollars for beef-stock during the last two months, became warmly interested in us, & insisted on getting up a little artistic recherché dinner for us of his own devising. Very pretty little dinner it was — full of elegant but surprising effects — & the bill was unquestionably reasonable. G.C.A. here afterwards. — Bad news to day. California steamer Golden Gate burned at sea, 180 passengers lost & more than a million of treasure. Nothing from the Army. McClellan seems about making an important move. Some say a withdrawal from before Richmond to the Potomac — others the transfer of his whole Army to the S. side of James River. Nobody *knows*, & people's speculations are not worth a damaged Delmonico shinplaster. — I hope to go to Newport tomorrow aft^{n}. — Van Buren is to operate on poor Clitz's damaged leg tomorrow, & extract the ball. — We gradually come round to a better opinion of McClellan's movements during the memorable Battle week — , incline to believe his march on James River a most delicate & critical operation successfully executed under most disadvantageous conditions, winding up with demoralizing repulse & slaughter of the rebels at Malvern Hill. As to that, Clitz's report of what his former friends (now in the service of Rebellion & the Devil) told him seems conclusive. *Magruder* was drunk or reckless & pushed column after column into the overwhelming fire of our artillery which destroyed or disorganized whole brigades.

Aug: 11. Pope has had a battle with Jackson. "Cedar Mountain." No decisive result apparently.

Aug: 16. Sat. Weather continues more bearable, but still hot. Busy days. San: Com: work of course. Everything else is thrown overboard — to my loss & damage. But I believe we are doing a considerable amount of service to the Country, & that we have saved more men than have been lost in any two days fighting since the War began. Thank God that a miserable nearsighted cockney like myself can take part in any work that strengthens & helps on the National Cause. Should have gone to Newport this aft[n] but that my semi-annual turn of duty at Bleecker St. Bank comes next week, & I must be in town Monday morning. I shirked it last time — turned it off on Bidwell — & it would be indecent to trespass on his good-nature again so soon. After all, two days at Newport are no great loss (leaving E. & the children out of view) — Newport is'nt "the Country" at all, but something singularly unlike it. — *War News.* Important movements of McClellan's Army probably in progress. His present position said to be untenable. Gen: Scott tells Cha[s] King (who tells M[r] S.B.R.) that no army can exist on James River after Aug. 15th. It must advance, retreat, or perish — poisoned by malaria. Some say the Army is transferred to the *right* bank of the river — others that it is falling back on Williamsburg & F. Monroe — others, that it is to be carried to Aquia Creek & Fredericsburgh, & take a fresh start. Certainly nothing can be more vicious than the present position of our forces in V[a] — Our two armies, McClellan's & Pope's, are unable to support each other, while the enemy tho' inferior in force, is concentrated between them, & can make a dash at either with fair prospect of success. That campaign on the Peninsula seems to have been a great strategic blunder. An enterprising General, willing to risk something on prompt vigorous offensive movements, might have carried it successfully through & taken Richmond — or he might not. But that is not McC's style of work. He means to be safe & is therefore obliged to be slow. His theory of an invasion is to entrench himself, advance five miles & then spend three weeks in getting up another line of fieldworks. This would be good practice, were not *Time* so important an element. Perhaps no one whose specialité is *military engineering can be* a great Captain, & handle men in the field with decision & promptitude. Todleben of Sebastopol & Marshal Blücher cannot be combined in the same General. The Expert in siege operations is most valuable in his proper place, but he cannot be a Marshal "*Vorwärts*", and is very likely to become a Marshal *Rückwärts* if his opponent be enterprising & vigilant.

I fear Lincoln is what Wendell Phillips calls him, — "a first rate *second-rate man*". Stanton is certainly three parts lunatic. His preposterous order about drafting & persons seeking to evade the draft is decisive as to his fitness for his great place. Under that order, I being "absent from my state", at Newport, last Sunday was liable to be arrested, carried to Fort Adams, & kept on Military duty for nine months, the expense of my arrest being deducted from my pay. If arrested, I had no opportunity to shew that my visit to R.I. was in good faith & without design to evade military service. The letter of Stanton's order made my presence in R.I. cause for nine months' imprisonment at hard labor. If I am obliged to go to Brooklyn tomorrow to inspect books &c in the Co: Clk's office, I shall be "absent from my County" & liable to the same treatment. Stanton's folly & our generous acquiescence in it are great phenomena.

Aug. 19. Tuesday. Pleasant weather. Days spent in S.C. work as usual. The mere correspondence is a serious business. One or two distasteful unthinkable professional complications loom up threatening & grim. — V. Buren Agnew & Olmsted in council here last night. Fell asleep in the library chair, over the Pension Laws, after our session broke up, & woke at half past four A.M. — Olmsted returns to Wash[n] this P.M. — He is wanted there, for the personnel of the office is demoralized. Knapp is absent, ditto Bloor who has taken leave of absence, ditto ditto D[r] Douglas, & D[r] Jenkins has the jaundice — a malarious gift from the nymph or Undine of the River Pamunkey — & Elliot & the document distributing C.C. Bellows are no one knows where.

Agnew & Van Buren are hard at work every aft[n] from 2 to near 6 on physical inspection of candidates for enlistment as Nurses. The Surgeon Gen[l] orders enlistment of 500. They reject about ⅓, for hernia, syphilis, cardiac disease &c. — It's funny. The men are peeled — the doctors inspect their alimentary canals at both ends — poke at their teeth with pen holders — peer down their throats — listen sagaciously for flaws in their respiration & the working of their hearts — make them assume Acrobatic attitudes &c.

Dined at Maison Dorée with Agnew & Hoffman.

McClellan has gloriously evacuated Harrison's Landing, & got safe back to where he was months ago. Magnificent Strategy. Pity it has cost so many thousand men & millions of dollars. Our repulse of Breckinridge's attack on *Baton Rouge* seems to have been creditable — a superior force beat back after hard fighting. We lost Gen: Williams, a good officer. He was Major Williams (on Scott's staff) at Rockaway & West Point years ago. The rebel ironclad Ram Arkansas, wh: has given us some uneasiness, blew herself up — (or else was blown up by our incendiary shells, — uncertain which —) & sleeps with her elder sister the Merrimac. — McClellan stock is falling fearfully. He is held accountable for the thousands of lives expended without result in digging trenches in the Chickahominy Swamp & on James River. Unjustly perhaps. Stanton may have withheld reinforcements. But Generals are judged by the results of their generalship.

Aug. 21. Thursday. A sombre splenetic atrabilious saturnine day, of annoyance & evil forebodings — to which was added the irritation of excessive heat. In the first place I have been tingling with rage at a malignant mis-spelt anonymous letter, apparently from some one of the servant gal sisterhood. It is false enough to be worthy of the Grand-mother of lies, i.e. the dam of their father. I'm quite sure of that, & free from even a misgiving on the subject. But that this dirty drab, whoever she may be, should have dared so to insult the person she presumes to mention, makes me furious. — Then we are most anxious about affairs in V^{a}. The streets are filled with rumors of a great disaster to Gen: Pope's command. They cannot be traced and are disbelieved, but these shadows are too often the forerunners of some calamitous fact. Such disaster is but too plainly probable, thanks to the refined strategy that has thus far directed the campaign. McClellan's withdrawal to the lower end of the Peninsula makes the whole rebel Army available for a dash in any direction it's leaders may select. It is set free — disengaged — for offensive operations. We are not quite sure that their transportation is so deficient as people think it. If they possess common sense they will surely move agst Pope with their whole available force, wh: certainly far outnumbers his, hoping to crush him & move on Washington before McClellan can join him. This is their hour. The new levies that are daily pouring Southward from N.Y. N. England & the West, will soon make offensive movements impossible. They must strike *now*. Within a week the sediment of McClellan's grand Army will be in a position to support *Pope*, I trust, & to meet the rebels on terms of equality. I have been listening all day for a screech of newsboys proclaiming "*Extry: Got the great battle & the defeat of Gen: Pope*". Every hour decisive battle is postponed is great gain, for at least a week to come.

We want a strong man — a great General — very badly. Such a man would be dangerous, but we want him.

Aug. 22. Friday. Muggy day. No news yet of any disaster. I trust nothing is suppressed by Government censorship. Long talk this morn'g with Walter Cutting. We exchanged lamentations & forebodings, & succeeded I think in making each other appreciably more miserable, — in screwing each others' spirits several degrees farther down. To day's event was Col: Corcoran's arrival in town. (Tomorrow's papers will call it an "Ovation".) Great crowds awaited him. Broadway was filled with expectants, as I came up town, & looked as it did two years ago, when people were waiting & watching for the *Prince of Wales*. Times have changed since Oct. 1860! Dined with Dr Peters at Maison Dorée, & after dinner watched the procession escorting the valiant Corcoran as it wound around Union Sq: — It was a pretty sight, & will stimulate recruiting.

Aug. 27. Wednesday night. Returned from Newport by "Shore line" at 8 P.M. — But I must begin with the State of the Nation. It has undergone no material change. We seem to be falling back successfully & maintaining our defensive line on the North Fork of the Rappahannock. There has been sharp fighting at several points. An enterprising rebel foray seems to have beat up Gen Pope's headquarters, destroyed supply trains, & carried off important papers & letters. Scandalous & disgraceful, if we have the whole truth. Some considerable portion of McC's Army has got back to Alexandria or Aquia Creek, & it is probable that the whole Army of V^a^ will be concentrated within ten days or a fortnight. We have a special *canard* to day — viz: that Gen: Sigel has personally pistolled Gen: McDowell as a secret traitor. Strange to say, there are people who accept the story as credible, & only wanting confirmation. Such a goose is the Enlightened Public.

Went off last Sat: aft^{n} (a cruel muggy day) in the *Metropolis* for Newport. Voyage was a little less cruelly afflictive than I expected. We had a most beautiful — solemn — gorgeous — polychromatic & poly*morphic* sunset to watch, & it's wonderful series of splendid effects of color & form occupied my attention for at least an hour.

Aug: 28. Thursday night. This should have been a very busy day, but it has been nothing of the kind. Woke dyspeptic after a perturbed night, slugged a-bed as late as I decently could, then rose & dressed & took a little breakfast & was going down town, when I found myself nauseated. Reposed awhile in the Library chair, but in vain. Emesis triumphed & for a couple of hours I *puked*, like a Croton Hydrant discharging dilute aqua fortis. Situation was complicated by a lively little diarrhœa.

Aug. 29. Friday. All right again. Very active day. Report from C.E.S. of experiences at Point Judith. At 3½ to N° 498 Bway, where I was surprised to meet *Dr Bellows*, called to *town* from the woods of Walpole N.H. by some clerical duty, & *Olmsted* on sick leave from Washington. Jaundiced — yellow as butter. The poison of Pamunkey & James River malaria is in his very bones.

Olmsted reports Stanton hostile to the Commission, & refusing to let the Gov^{t} printers work for us any more. We need their services just now to reprint large editions of certain of our documents for the benefit of the new levies. If the Sec^{y} make up his mind to take this position, we can go before the People with very fair prospect of success. He will hardly venture on a collision with us. — Dr Hammond working vigorously, but in danger of collision with Meigs, which would be a pity. — Dined with G.C.A. at Maison Dorée. & thence at 9 P.M. to Dr Bellows', settling the draft of his Report from the Executive Com: to the Commission at its contemplated meeting Sept. 16th.

Still these brilliant dashing successful raids or forays of Rebel Cavalry within our lines. They have penetrated to Manassas, destroying supply-trains, capturing guns, taking us *by surprise*. Are our Generals traitors or imbecile? Why does the Rebellion enjoy the monopoly of audacity & enterprise? Were I a General — even I — poor little feeble myopic flaccid effeminate G.T.S.

— I think I could do better than this. Thank God that Johny & Templekin are getting the Physical Education that was denied me in my boyhood — the accomplishments I despised 20 years ago because I thought Coleridge's philosophy & the Old English Drama the only things worth living for, & riding & shooting & all physical culture disagreeable & of the nature of Evil. So I am now a mere Cockney, a M[r] Pickwick or a Punch's M[r] Briggs. Full of valiant impulses but incapable & imbecile. I would give ten years of life this minute to be able to go into service as a private.

Aug. 30. Sat. A noteworthy day, for good or evil. We do not certainly know which. The morning papers were not cheerful. We were outgeneralled — out-flanked — Washington in danger again — everything bungled & botched. It was clear that both armies had got into each other's rear & were so mixed up that they could'nt be disentangled without breaking something. The Rebels were supposed to be making a bold move on the Upper Potomac, said to be fordable now, with designs on Maryland & the back door of the Capitol. There was an epidemic of indigo. At 3 came a despatch from Pope to Halleck. "Terrific battle" that lasted all yesterday. On the field of Bull Run. We took the initiative. Drove the enemy. Occupy their position. Fitz-John Porter coming up this morn'g when we mean to go in again, but we are too tired just now. Our loss say 8000. Rebel loss twice that. Grand Victory. God grant this may be true & the whole truth. But I am not prepared to crow quite yet. Pope is an imaginative chieftain & ranks next to Cooper as a Writer of Fiction. Good news from Bull Run is suspicious *per se* moreover. I cannot forget the exhilarating intelligence from that locality that reached us on a — in point of fact on what may be called a former occasion, about 13 months & 9 days ago. I expect to be informed by tomorrow morn'g's papers that strategic considerations lead Gen. Pope to follow up his Victory by skedaddling toward the Potomac at full speed, leaving guns & prisoners in the hands of the Enemy. It is a bad sign that we have no extra to night. If the rebels were beaten yesterday, they ought to be crushed & annihilated to day. Their line of retreat is toward the difficult gorges of the Bull Run range of hills.

Aug. 31. Sunday 11.30 A.M. Waiting for news. The suspense is trying. Anticipations not brilliant. No further particulars that are at all reliable in morn'g papers — an ominous stillness. McDowell telegraphs that it's "*decidedly*" a Victory. The adverb produces a negative impression on my mind. It seems fighting was resumed yesterday — and the firing ceased to be heard at Wash^{n} about noon. Whence it is inferred that the Rebels then capitulated. Unlikely enough. I look for bad news this aft^{n}. The Department would have been prompt to publish any decisive success. — Pope's despatch looks well enough — but "if P. ever writes a Work of Romantic Fiction, it will sell". It is to be remembered however that the Rebels are in a tight place generally, & can't get on with anything less than complete Victory. At the same time, our supply of complete victories is not quite up to the demand.

10 P.M. This citizen does not despair of the Republic. Most of his friends do. But tho' things look badly, & there is reason enough for anxiety & apprehension, people are making up their minds to the worst much too fast. — I can find no tangible evidence of serious disaster, *yet*.

At about one o'clock in came Dr Harris with a telegram from Stanton to the Mayor, calling for Surgeons to be sent on at once. Dated yesterday 3.45 P.M. but was not received till nine this morn'g. The Sec'y says Friday's battle was a hard one but the enemy was beaten at all points. It was resumed this (Sat.) morn'g & was still going on at date of the despatch. No suggestion of misfortune. — Harris had been working hard & had already secured some 30 Surgeons who were to go South by this ev'g's train. He has considerable capacity for usefulness, in spite of his faults. — After conferring with him I went by appointment to G.C.A.'s in E. 35th St. & dined with him — his mamma — Miss Emily & young Mrs Reginald A. who evidently contemplates furnishing the Nation with a raw recruit before long, & we went after dinner to the upper end of Central Park & walked down. Great progress made since my last visit. The long lines of carriages & the crowds of Gents & giggling girls suggested peace & prosperity. There was nothing from which one could have guessed that we are in a most critical period of a great Civil War, in the very focus & vortex of a momentous crisis & in imminent peril of grave National disaster. Being caught in a lively little shower, we walked homeward rapidly, & looked out for an *Extra* as we got into the City. But there was none. Took a cup of coffee in the dining room, & received G.C.A. at about 8 P.M. He was a messenger of Evil. *Pope has fallen back on Centreville*, if the reports that prevail be reliable. That does not look like decided Victory! But the situation is utterly obscure & we can form no opinion about it. Walked out with him to 5th Av: Hotel & elsewhere seeking information, but in vain. I fear tomorrow morning's papers will tell a disheartening story.

Sept. 1. Monday 10 A.M. Overcast. Morning papers leave the aspect of affairs unchanged, & confirm report that Pope fell back to Centreville Saturday. Nothing said of fighting yesterday. — I dont know why I take the trouble to note — these insignificant matters — unless it is from a morbid impulse to record the successive steps by which the memorable calamity I anticipate draws nearer & nearer. But Spero Meliora.

11 P.M. Raining hard all the ev'g, wh: has prevented me from going forth to seek news. I thought I heard the shriek of an Extra half an hour ago, & sent out John in pursuit, but he could find nary Extry. The shriek of a Newsboy in these days is about as exhilarating as the Wail of the Banshee — a presage of something disastrous.

Down town to day, I find the office topsy-turvy. Painting & cleaning. All the ancient dust heaps sacrilegiously invaded & a mortal stench of benzine (a new vehicle for paints) that made the premises almost uninhabitable. C.E.S. is at Newport. I wrote a few letters & cleared out early. — There was an Extra at one o'clock. It's statements unofficial & contradictory, but on the whole *bad*. Story of a general stampede & rout of part of the Army across Bull Run, Saturday; & another of the destruction of McDowell's command by a grand charge of 5000 rebel cavalry. Where could 5000 cavalry find ground to manœuvre or charge within ten miles of Manassas? But the tide is setting strong against us just now: everything is all wrong: Government bungling & blundering.

At Sanitary Com: rooms this aftn. Bellows there, Agnew & Van Buren.

Sept. 2. Tuesday. Octobral weather. No reliable news. Apparently no change in the position. I think it will be found that we were heavily punished in the battle of Saturday. But as the rebels have the affirmative on this particular issue, & have put themselves in a tight place, the fact that there has been no serious fighting since Saturday is favorable. Is it a fact though? We cannot say, for Censorship of the Press is fully established by the War Department. This is no time to oppose any act of Government, but if this war ever end we must deal with Stanton for his lawless interference with the press and for his arbitrary arrests without color of lawful right. — *McClellan* has finally collapsed I fear. Reports to his disadvantage multiply & pass uncontradicted. Nobody stands up for him any more.

Wall St as usual. 498 Bdway as usual & then dined with Dr Van Buren & Jem Ruggles at Maison Dorée. Sat till near eleven, in high discourse. I had ordered $1000. worth of *beef-stock* from Martinez, so he insisted on making me a present of our nice little dinner, & our two bottles of champagne. A very corrupt transaction, but I could not make the man take his money.

Sept. 3. The morning papers & an Extra at mid-day turned us livid & blue. Fighting Monday aft^{n} at "Chantilly", the enemy beat back (more or less) — Pope retreating on Alexandria & Washington to our venerable fieldwork fortalices of a year ago. "Stonewall Jackson", (our National Bugaboo) about to invade Maryland, 40.000 strong. General advance of the Rebel line, threatening our hold on Missouri & Kentucky. *Cincinnati* in danger. A rebel army within forty miles of the Queen City of the West. Martial Law proclaimed in her pork-shops. — On the other hand, we hear that Gen: *Stahel* & Gen: *Kearny* have come to life again, or were only "*kilt*", not *killed*, after all. — Everybody talks down McClellan & McDowell. McDowell *is said* to have lost us the battle of Sat: aft^{n} by a premature movement to the rear, tho' his supports were being hurried up. He is an unlucky General.

Sept. 4. It is certain now that the Army has fallen back to it's old burrows around Wash^{n}. It will probably hybernate there. So after all this waste of life & money & material we are at best where we were a year ago. McClellan is Chief, under Halleck.

Many grumble at this, but whom can we find that is proved his superior? He is certainly as respectable as any of the Mediocrities that make up our long muster roll of Generals. The Army believes in him undoubtingly — that is a material fact. And I suppose him very eminently fitted for a campaign of redoubts & redans, though incapable of vigorous offensive operations. — There seems reason to hope Stanton is trembling to his fall. May he fall soon, for he is a public calamity. McDowell & Pope are "universally despised" — so writes Bellows. Poor Gen: Kearny is dead & no mistake & will be buried in Trinity Churchyard next Saturday — so says Meurer the sexton. He's a great loss. I dont know whether he understood strategy, but he was a dashing fearless *sabreur* — had fought in Mexico Algeria and Lombardy, and loved war from his youth up. I remember my father talking thirty years ago about young Kearny who was studying law in his office, & about his strange foolish passion for a military life. He was under a very dark cloud six years ago, & was cut by many of his friends. But, — bad as it was — the lady's family were horribly to blame, most imprudent, and K. made all the reparation he could — married her and treated her with all possible affection & loyalty. Whatever his faults we shall miss him.

Our San: Com: stores were first on the field after the battle of Saturday, & did great service, for all the forty two wagon loads of the Medical Department were bagged by the Rebels at Manassas. D[r] Chamberlain, our Inspector in charge, was taken prisoner, but the rebels let him go. Stanton is reported rancorously hostile to the Commission — Probably because Bellows has talked to him once or twice like a Dutch uncle, with a plainness of speech that was certainly imprudent though quite justifiable.

Sept. 5. Friday. Fine weather. I do not hear since yesterday of any new disgrace. All is quiet on the Potomac, & the Army is "safe". My unfortunate friend McDowell is the subject of much damaging talk. They say regiments refuse to fight under him. He has mistaken his vocation if half one hears be true. But it probably *is'nt*. There are gleams of uncertain light from the S.W. — legends of an alleged victory in the Chattanooga country. Do'nt believe them, for National victories are out of season.

Sept. 7. The Country is turning out raw material for History very fast — but it's an inferior article. Rebellion is on its legs again, East & West, rampant & aggressive at every point. Our lines are either receding, or turned, from the Atlantic to the Mississippi. The great event now prominently before us is that the South has crossed the Potomac, in force, above Washington, & invaded Maryland, occupied *Frederic*, proclaimed a Provisional Governor, and seems advancing on the Penn[a] line. No one knows the strength of this invading column. Some say 30.000 & others five times that. A very strong force doubtless pushed up the Potomac to cut off the rebel communications. If it succeed, the rebellion will be ruined, but if it suffer a disorganizing defeat, the North will be at Jeff: Davis' mercy. I dare not let my mind dwell on the tremendous contingencies of the present hour. It seems to me not quite certain that our next S. Com: meeting will be held at Washington punctually on the 16th!

The Nation is rapidly sinking just now, as it has been sinking rapidly for two months & more, because it wants two things: viz: Generals that know how to handle their men — and strict military discipline applied to men & officers. God alone can give us good Generals, but a stern & rigorous discipline visiting every grave military offence with Death can be given us by our dear old great-uncle Abe, if he only *would* do it. With our superiority in numbers & in resources, Discipline would make us strong enough to conquer without first rate Generals, unless an Alexander or Napoleon should be born unto Rebeldom.

Sept. 11. Letters from Agnew, full of interest. He has been all over our last battle fields under flag of truce. 36 hours in the saddle, & feels "as if he had a chronic horse between his lower limbs". Our wounded left in the field without shelter food or water from Sat: night till Wednesday morn'g because "that Scoundrel, Pope" was too busy cooking up his Report to think of sending out a flag of truce. Very many perished from starvation & exposure. Our Commission wagons were first on the ground & did good service, thank God — and the relations of our Inspectors & Agents with the Medical staff seem perfectly harmonious. All, from the Surgeon Gen[l] down, recognize the value of what we are doing, or rather of what the People is doing through us as it's Almoner.

Our public interests continue in a state of prostration approaching Collapse. We do not know what force the Rebels have thrown into Maryland. It is probably large. What a blessing a heavy rain would be, that should raise the Potomac above fordable depth! There are clouds in tonight's sky, anxiously watched but probably barren. Newspapers tell us little or nothing about the situation in Maryland. From a letter rec[d] by D.B. Fearing from his son, spunky little Geo. F. on Burnside's staff — & from Agnew's letters, and from Burnside's telegram to F.B. Cutting to day, the following facts are clearly established. 1. McClellan's headquarters were at *Rockville*, Tuesday. Burnside was then at *Leesboro'*. He was at *Brookville* this morning. He commands our right (40.000 strong?) Sigel the centre, McClellan the left, which I *suppose*, rests on the Potomac. No collision as yet. The rebels have *not* occupied Hagerstown.

I suppose we shall soon hear that McClellan has commenced a series of masterly field works, & is engaged on an irrefragable first parallel from the Potomac to the Susquehanna, with a series of dashing & brilliant zig-zags toward the enemy. But it is idle to criticize his practice, until we can name some stronger & better man to put in his place. It's a controlling fact that the Army confides in him, & may mutiny if he be superseded. — Gen: Pope's Report bears hardly on Fitz-John Porter & others — charges them with declining to support him with their commands, at critical moments, & seeks to make them responsible for our latest disasters. It's a plausible paper & (were Pope's veracity unquestioned) would be damaging. As it is, the Report has generated a swarm of rumors about one General & another committed to Fort Lafayette for treason. Nobody who knows Fitz-John Porter, Franklin, or McDowell (this last affected by rumors for which Pope's Report is not responsible) can believe either guilty of positive disloyalty — of conscious deliberate treason. But may not their partizanship for McClellan have made them unconsciously backward in supporting his rival? Quien sabe. Weiss nix. Jealousies exist among our Generals beyond doubt — tho' one would think them impossible in a time like this. Their existence is a fearful source of weakness & paralysis. — Among to day's rumors is this, that Gen: Halleck has ascertained *M[rs] A. Lincoln* to be the mysterious channel thro' which so many state secrets have reached the rebels & enabled them to anticipate our action, — that he has formally demanded her exportation from the Seat of Government; & that her Durchlauchtigkeit has been sent off West under military guard. Highly probable to be sure! But I suppose she may be a very tattling woman. Underbred, weak, & vain she certainly is, by all accounts. She may have talked too freely. — Hurra! There comes a sound of rain. Sabrina fair — nymph of the Potomac — please listen where thou art sitting & never mind the loose folds of thy amber-dropping hair, but hurry up the floods of thy river & make it impracticable for Rebel Artillery — if you will have the goodness, marm.

Sept. 13. Agnew returned to day & was with us this afternoon. Has been several days on the battlefields around Manassas, rendering surgical aid, and with McClellan's advance in Maryland organizing our S. Com. supply trains. His report not encouraging. Many Regiments are "asthenic" or worn out. Line of march traceable by the deposit of dysenteric stools the Army leaves behind it. Discipline slack & nerveless. Swarms of stragglers, marauding, or making up select card-parties by the road-side. From other sources I hear of alarming demoralization. McDowell's people are said to have fought badly & to have run with great alacrity a fortnight ago. I fear our Army is in no condition to cope with Lee's barefooted ragged lousy disciplined desperate ruffians. They may get to Philadelphia, or N.Y., or Boston, for Fortune is apt to smile on audacity & resolution. What would happen then? A new & most alarming kind of talk is coming up, emitted by old Breckinridge democrats (like W.L.C.) mostly, and in substance to this effect. "Stonewall Jackson, Lee, & Joe Johnston were all anti-secessionists till the War broke out. No doubt they still want to see the Union restored. They are personally friends, allies, & political congeners of Halleck, McClellan, F. J. Porter &c &c. Perhaps they will all come together & agree on some compromise or adjustment, turn out Lincoln & his "Black Republicans" and use their respective Armies to enforce their decision North & South & re-establish the Union & the Constitution". A charming conclusion that would be of our uprising to maintain the law of the land & uphold Republican Institutions! But we have among us plenty of rotten old Democrats like Judge Roosevelt, capitalists like Joe Kernochan, traders & money dealers like Belmont, & political schemers like James & Rat Brooks, who would sing a *Te Deum* over any pacification however infamous, & would rejoice to see Jeff. Davis our next President. Perhaps he may be. If he is magnanimous & forgiving he may be prevailed on to come & reign over us. I would rather see the North subjugated than a separation. Disgust with our present Government is certainly universal. Even Lincoln himself has gone down at last, like all our popular idols of the last eighteen months. This honest old codger was the last to fall, but he has fallen. Nobody believes in him any more. I do not, tho' I still maintain him. I cannot bear to admit the Country has no one man to believe in, & that honest A.L. is not the style of goods we want just now. But it is impossible to resist the conviction that he is unequal to his place. His only special gift is fertility of smutty stories. Quam parvâ sapientiâ mundus regitur. What must be the calibre of our rulers whose rule is so disgraceful a failure? — If McClellan gain no signal decisive Victory within ten days, I shall collapse — and we have no reason to expect anything of that sort from him.

Rebel ravages in S. P[a] may stir up a general arming & enrolment, but even that would give us only an undisciplined mob for months to come. O Abraham, O mon Roi!

Sept. 24. A cloudy sour autumnal day, succeeded by an almost frosty ev'g, with a stern Northerly wind. Bad for those wretched halfnaked & sorely wounded rebel prisoners who are still lying, no doubt, as they lay night before last, on a thin stratum of straw without blankets or shelter, at French's Division Hospital! This keen Northern air will probably put some of them out of their pain before morning. I should be glad to help several of them through it — especially one, an honest looking fresh blonde boy of 17 from Georgia (Whitman was his name I think) who had enlisted "because all the young people about were enlisting" & he had tried to do "his duty" and was glad he had lost his leg and had got through with it & could not fight any more now, & could go home & take up his Latin again. His sisters would be so glad to have him back & attending to his studies. — Another poor fellow, also from Georgia with a ball in his lungs had no clothing but a pair of pantaloons & a calico jacket split up the back. Both were of the "gentleman" caste. — I come back from this expedition with clearer perception of the horrors of War and of the tremendous guilt of those who have brought it on us.

Home tonight at half past six. Spent an hour or two at D[r] Bellows' in council with our Sanitary Commission Colleagues. Our affairs are prospering. Agnew's report of personal experience in Maryland confirms mine — or rather vice versa, his being so many times larger. Medical Department utterly destitute & shiftless as usual, and now confessedly leaning on the Commission for supplies, looking to it for help to get forward it's own stores, waiving all it's official dignity under the pressure of work for which it has made no adequate provision & in an attitude of general supplication & imbecile self-abasement. *Times is changed* & scornful dogs have to eat dirty puddings. The fossil old Bureau is not yet galvanized into life, with all D[r] Hammond's energy. Want of *independent Transportation* seems it's main difficulty. Hammond is paralyzed by dependence on the Q.M. Department. We must try to mend this — even at the risk of alienating Gen: Meigs.

Memorabilia of this Sanitary Anabasis. To Wash[n] by the accustomed R.R. Monday morn'g the 15th. Found Wolcott Gibbs & Bishop Clark on the train — also Binney & Judge Hare. At Baltimore we came in contact with Extras. Battle in Maryland on the 14th. Rebels routed. Grand Victory. The politic City of Baltimore was in a confluent eruption of National flags. We bought fifty cents worth of "*Baltimore Clippers*" & hurled them out of the car-windows at the lonely picket guards all along the B.&W. Road. But as we drew nearer Washington the glorious news began to dwarf & dwindle. The Rebel Army was not absolutely disorganized & still shewed fight. There were unpleasant rumors — unreliable of course — that Col: Miles had surrendered Harpers Ferry. — Reached Wash[n] & received excellent quarters from the Magnates of Willard's Hotel. Binney & Hare & McMichael & a lot of others, committee of Philadelphians to wait on the Sec[y] of War & Gen: Halleck & secure a Military Chieftain to assume the defence of Pennsylvania returned despondent. *Halleck* was very blue. *Stanton* could not be seen but was heard cussing frightfully in an adjoining apartment. — Our Session began Tuesday morning & lasted till Friday night. Agnew & Harris were sent off Wednesday, I think, in charge of Medical stores for the battlefield. We did a good deal of work. Had an interview by appointment with Gen: Halleck, & a conference of an hour's duration. We walked away from Halleck's quarters in dismal silence & consternation. Van Buren broke it with the words "God help us!" That aspiration was never more appropriate. Halleck is not the man for his place. He is certainly — clearly — weak — shallow — commonplace — vulgar. He is a strong friend of the Commission & ready to do whatever it asks, so I am not prejudiced against him. — His silly talk was conclusive as to his incapacity unless he was a little flustered with wine, an inadmissible apology for a Commander-in-chief at a crisis like this. He seemed to think it facetious to keep calling Dr Bellows "Bishop" — maundered about certain defects of discipline which he said prevented McClellan from moving more than 6 miles a day, & Buell more than 3, "when he moves at all, that is". Some one suggested an order from Headquarters as the appropriate remedy (he might have referred to the Army Regulations now in force) whereupon Halleck became stately & said he was'nt a *writer for the newspapers.* "No *sir.* No I thank you sir. That is not my line. I cannot do *that*" — & so on, in the silliest style. His revelations were most imprudent. "People expect me to send a column to Gordonsville or somewhere & cut off the rebel communications. Where are the men? Only 42 000 left for the defence of Wash^{n} to day. Government has paid bounties to 350 000 men under the new levy. Less than 75 000 have reached Wash^{n} — none at all these last two days. So many at Cincinnati — at St Louis" &c &c "less than 50.000 all told. Governors keep them back till each man has his tin cup & his carpet bag, and then a week longer, to enable some politician to make a speech to the Regiment, & shake hands with every recruit individually". — And so forth &c &c. We adjourned formally Sat: morning, after an efficient session. Bishop Clark was as genial & enlivening as of old. He reports a rebel prisoner received in R.I. who was scrubbed for two hours with soap & water before they got down to the shirt he wore in 1860. — Some one said that blatant gassy Geo. Francis Train (now blowing at Willard's) abstains from all stimulants & narcotics — from coffee tobacco & alcoholic drinks. The Bishop replied it would be a pity to *dilute* G.F.T.

with whiskey. — From all accounts, A.L. is far from easy in his mind. Judge Skinner, who knows him intimately says he wanders about wringing his hands, & wondering whom he can trust — & what he'd better do. What's very bad, he has been heard to utter the words "*War for boundaries*" — to speak which words should be Death.

Heaven help our rulers. Never was so great a cause in the keeping of much smaller men. But I still have faith in A.L.

Left W. 5 P.M. Saturday. Baltimore cars densely packed. I rode on the platform & took a dessert spoonful of cinders out of each ear on reaching that town. Took car for Harrisburgh at half past nine, and arrived there at 2 or 3 A.M. Met Binney there & got decent quarters at the *Jones House.*

Sunday morn'g proceeded with B. to the State House. The Town swarming with Penn: militia, & all the paraphernalia of War. Men were drilling in all the streets. The great battle of Wednesday & the withdrawal of the rebels from M^d^ were not yet fully understood & people looked grave enough. The militia however were in good fighting humor & would have done all that utterly green undisciplined men could do. We found Scott, Cameron's former Assist: Sec^y^ on duty as representative of Gov: Curtin & he ordered out a special train for us. Inspected the surrounding country from the State House Cupola — lovely landscape, broad pure peaceful river, (most fordable, unhappily, as it might have proved) flowing down thro' a gap in the N.W. line of wooded hills, & all flooded with the misty sunlight of an Indian summerish morning. Off at about ten o'clock thro' a fertile rich thriving region, full of nice farmhouses big barns & comfortable villages a most tempting prey for Lee's hungry battalions. At Carlisle & the other places we passed through the whole population seemed to have turned out with anxious faces — many of the women crying, & no wonder. They were yet uncertain whether the pressing danger of devastation was passed. At Chambersburg we were delayed a couple of hours to await a special train from Hagerstown with Gov. Curtin. It is a pretty village enough. Found Dr Cuyler there. Traversed every street a dozen times in quest of Dr Crane, our Inspector, without success. Here we met a telegram announcing a sort of Ball's Bluff blunder on Saturday. A brigade sent across the Potomac by Porter to feel the enemy had got caught in an ambuscade & was driven back. The 118th Penn: regiment much cut up. As young Horace Binney is a Lieut: in this reg^{t} the news gave his father some cause of perturbation — but he bore up bravely. We got to Hagerstown at 9 o'clock. Rooms at the hotels not to be thought of. It was not easy to get inside their doors. Soldiers & officers were bivouacking in the streets. By good luck we found Dr Hartshorne who put us in rapport with Dr Dorsey — one of the F.F.s, & a thorough going loyalist, & in his comfortable house we were received at once, with a frank cordiality & kindness beyond all my experience. They only knew we were Union men & engaged in some kind of work for the Army. I never appreciated the meaning of the word Hospitality before. The lady of the house a most thoroughbred kind of person, with the most charming genial manner. They have a son in the Rebel Army! But one must go into the Debateable Land to see fullblooded genuine Union feeling. Ours at the North is a second-rate article. Mrs D. told me much of the rebel forces that occupied the town some four days — how dirty & wretched they were — how they scampered at midnight on the news of McClellan's approach & what a smell they left behind them. Stuart, a chaplain from Alexandria told her they meant to take Philadelphia. "Philad^{a} or death" —

Next morning — Monday — I made arrangements to put the Med: Director, Surgeon A.K. Smith, in funds for the immediate equipment of his Hospital, & then took ambulance & drove off over the Sharpsboro Turnpike with Binney & Hartshorne & a certain indefatigable Mrs Harris, rival of Miss Dix & agent of some Philad^{a} Relief Association. We soon entered an atmosphere pervaded by the scent of the battle field — the bloody & memorable field of Antietam ["An tée tum"] Creek. Long lines of trench marked the burial places — Scores of dead horses — swollen, with their limbs protruding stiffly at strange angles, & the ground at their noses blackened with hemorrhage, lay all around. Sharpsboro, a commonplace little village was scarified with shot. In one little brickhouse I counted more than a dozen shot holes, cleanly made probably by rifle projectiles. Here & there was seen the more extensive ravage made by an exploding shell. The country is most lovely — like Berkshire C^{o} Mass: — only more luxuriant & exuberant. At Sharpsboro' we found the little Church used as a Hospital for the 118th Penn. — Some 50 wounded lay there on straw. The Regt had suffered badly. Young Binney was safe & off on picket duty. His men spoke of his conduct enthusiastically & said he was the last man to leave the ground. His father fairly broke down under this — & no wonder. — In the crowd of ambulances army wagons beef cattle, staff officers, recruits, kicking mules &c &c &c who should suddenly turn up but Mrs Arabella Barlow née Griffith, unattended, but serene & self possessed as if walking down Broadway. She is nursing the Col: her husband, (badly wounded,) & never appeared so well — talked like a sensible practical earnest warm-hearted woman, without a phrase of hyperflutination. We went to McClellan's headquarters, & to Fitz-John Porter's. McClellan has 20 regimental standards & more — & guns — substantial trophies. But for the miserable misconduct that lost us Harper's Ferry, had that unhappy Col. Miles held out eight hours longer, the rebel retreat would have been a rout. — Miles has gone to his account, and whether he was a deliberate traitor or only fainthearted & incapable will never be known. Left Binney at Sharpsboro & proceeded in the direction of Keedysville & French's Division Hospital — where we staid two or three hours. Horrible congregations of wounded men there & at Porter's — our men & rebel prisoners both — on straw, in their bloody stiffened clothes mostly — some in barns & cowhouses some in the open air. It was fearful to see — Gustave Doré's pictures embodied in shivering agonizing suppurating flesh & blood.

Walked with Hartshorne over another section of the battle field — strewn with fragments of shell & conical bullets — here & there a round shot or a live shell, dangerous to handle. We traced the position in which a rebel brigade had stood, or bivouacked in line of battle, for half a mile, by the thickly strewn belt of green-corn husks & cobs, & also, sit venia loquendi, by a ribbon of dysenteric *stools* just behind.

It grew dark — & we watched the light signals from a woody hill in the direction of Harper's Ferry — supped on Bologna sausage — drove off at last like mad & got back to our hospitable home at Dr Dorsey's very late but not too late for a generous & most acceptable tea.

Off next morning. Hot day: Crowded train: Waited for it to

start from six till ten. Then we advanced 20 minutes & stopped an hour, & so on all day. It would have been intolerable, but I had for neighbours a nice little simple minded warmhearted loyal Baltimore woman, with six little well-mannered children, whom I cultivated. She was a lady, tho' she did say "*seen*" when she might better have said "*saw*", but she & her little brood were a great comfort. I established sentimental relations with Miss Emma of seven or thereabouts — who wo'nt play with any little girls that are Secessionists. — Slept at Harrisburgh that night — very soundly, after an exploring stroll all about the town. Our progress thither was triumphal. All the population of the Country assembled again along the R.R. line, but jubilant & exultant now — cheering their returning militia men. Left H. at 8 this morn'g. Road runs thro' a very lovely country.

Sept. 27. Saturday. Fine weather. Nothing very noteworthy in these few days. Position on the Potomac unchanged. Lee said to be entrenching at Winchester. Sigel & Heintzelman's corps operating in V^{a} to bother his lines of communication. Perhaps so. By the by how hard it is to get at ultimate reliable facts about men & things. We all suppose *Sigel* to be a first rate officer — but *Cullum*, who represents Halleck's opinions no doubt, says Sigel is a coward & a humbug — that he did not distinguish himself at all at the battle of Pea Ridge, but ran away & *hid in a cellar* till the battle was over! What's History worth & what are we entitled to say we *know* about the battles or the generals of e.g. the League or the Thirty Years War?

Dined with C.E.S. this aft^{n}. Mrs Eleanor is resuming her Hospital Campaign with vigor. Very disgusting transaction at N.Y. Club the other night. Row between Dr P. & Major L.W. Mars pulled the nose of Esculapius. Both were in the wrong, & I think the D^{r} deepest. Major L. says the reason he does'nt return to his regiment is that he has a bad rupture, & cannot sit his horse.

President's Emancipation Manifesto much discussed — & generally approved, tho' a few old Democrats (who ought to be dead & buried but persist in manifesting themselves like Vampyres) scold & grumble. It will do us good abroad, but will have no other effect.

Oct. 3^{d}. My first experience of the New Era of Taxation was to day — paying out checks with a kind of *postage stamp* stuck on. Welcome Taxation in any form — with short-commons in it's train. It looks a little as if we were beginning to *suffer* in the cause of War against the Chivalric woman-flogging baby-selling Enemies of the Nation. — — Our Army is in statu quo. No advance yet. Sigel seems in trouble. According to Olmsted's letter this aft^{n}, Heintzelman has now 80.000 men in front of Wash^{n}, & means to do something important as soon as the new levy adds 20.000 to his force. — Judge Skinner has had certain long confidential talks with his old friend A. Lincoln, revealing the unknown thread that one hopes may have run thro' the policy of Government, seemingly so incoherent, for the last 18 months, & Bellows, who has discoursed Skinner, feels better for the information. — Dear old Granny Lincoln, I do want to think him not utterly unfit for his post.

Poor Mrs Sally Hampton, who was Miss Sally Baxter, is dead — according to a telegram sent Gen. Dix & by him transmitted to Rev. Morgan Dix. — Poor girl — married to a semi-barbaric South Carolina Rajah, & dying by inches of pulmonary disease, cut off from her own family & from the help of civilized medical science, & knowing all the time that her adopted Countrymen were guilty of this savage war that condemned her so to perish. — Hard to find now so beautiful & wilful a brunette as was my *cousin Sally B.* some seven years ago.

Oct. 8. Canvass for Fall Elections fairly begun. Wadsworth & Seymour candidates for Governor. I hope Wadsworth & the so-called Radicals may sweep the State, & kick our wretched sympathizers with Southern treason back into the holes that have sheltered them for the past year, & from which they are beginning to peep out timidly & tentatively, to see whether they can venture to resume their dirty work. The result will be an important indication of the way popular feeling tends to flow. I *think* it will shew important progress the right way — but we must not be over-confident. Seymour's Election would be an encouragement to Jeff: Davis worth 100.000 men.

Thus ends this volume of my Journal — in days that are chilly and grey, but not without gleams of light that promise the return of sunshine. So let us hope — & in that hope let us *Work*. If we work faithfully, & do our duty in freely putting forth all our resources we can hardly fail — with God's blessing — to crush the Rebellion & vindicate our existence as a Nation. — God enable us so to do our duty — Amen.

Oct. 12. Weather cloudy raw & sour, with occasional rain. Trinity Church this morning, with E. & Johny. To night C.E.S. here & Miss Kate, Geo. F. Allen, Major Laurence Williams &c. No special news to day. There were two considerable engagements last week, at Corinth, & at Perryville Kentucky. We seem to have been successful, on the whole, in each, tho' with heavy loss. Another rebel foray into Pennsylvania. They have occupied Chambersburgh, & will no doubt get safely back across the border, after destroying a few hundred thousand dollars worth of property. But it may do a few millions' worth of good in its influence on the Pennsylvania State Elections now just at hand. — Debates in the General Convention at St John's Chapel on the Resolution agst Schism & rebellion still in progress. Bishop Clark tells me that the temper of both Houses improves & the prospect of a decided expression of healthy opinion brightens every day. I regret to say that the position of my venerated Father in law is severely censured. The newspapers are giving him pepper. His old friends came to me enquiring what this seeming tenderness for traitors *can* mean — whether he is under the influence of poor invertebrate Hon: Wash^n^ Hunt, or of that plausible rancorous abettor of Treason, Rev. F.L. Hawks. He is influenced by neither. He suffers from a morbid appetite for Conciliation & fraternization, & also, I fear (it's a grave thing to write of so good a man) from want of clear perception of the infinite unspeakable difference between Right & Wrong. He is too kindly & charitable fully to appreciate the enormous guilt incurred by any man who takes part in a great Political Crime like this Rebellion. His impulses are to temporize with Rebels & persuade them back to their allegiance, & to invent excuses for Churchmen who have violated their obligations as such, in the interest of Secession.

Oct. 15. News to day of our *second* hundred thousand from S. Francisco. I deposited the first yesterday. — O pleasing task! We are to send $50.000 to our Secessionizing off-shoot at S^t^

Louis which is a less agreeable duty. M. Hoffman dined here & we went to Wallack's old theatre, now a German Opera House & heard the Entführung aus dem Serail, for the first time, & under disadvantage, our seats being within whispering range of the Big Drum. But many lovely things were perceptible, as in a glass, darkly. I hope to hear it again. There are an exquisite tenor solo — a delicious cosy drinking song — & a lovely finale, for the soli & chorus — antiphonal as Rev. Vinton & his Choir-boys at Trinity Church. These came out clearly & well defined; every thing else somewhat blurred.

Bishop Clark dined here Monday, with Vinton Bellows Van Buren Agnew & Gibbs, & we had a jolly symposium & much good talk though gold is nearly at 140 premium, & McClellan's army immovable as the Pyramids. That General has sent for his wife his mother-in-law & his baby, & is going to housekeeping, it seems, somewhere near Sharpsburg. He may move next first of May but I fear he is settled till then. Heaven help us! It is good however that the Elections yesterday in Penn: & other States seem to shew that the spirit of the Nation is unbroken. May the voice of New York next month be in accord with theirs — and Horatio Seymour, John Van Buren, Fernando Wood, Richard O'Gor-r-r-man & Hon. Wash^{n} Hunt (whom as Mr S.B.R.'s friend I regret to see in such dirty company) experience the snubbing a loyal people ought to give them!

Oct. 17. Election news from Penn: & the West looks cold, but I hope the Opposition men elected are "War Democrats". — Nothing material from the Seat of War, except that McClellan shews signs of life. He has wiggled a little, & made a reconnoissance in force as far as Charlestown (the City of John Brown,) with loss of one man killed & six missing. Some say this is the beginning of a general advance, forced on him prematurely by the Cabinet & by popular clamor. — Last night our Sanitary Brethren of the Ex: Com: met here, according to rule of rotation, & with the usual slight supper & good talk. Our Rev. Pres^{dt} has been making a gander of himself, I regret to say, in the course of an Address on the War before his Unitarian Convention or Heretical Assenagemote & Convocation of philosophical wiseacres now or lately in session here or at Brooklyn or somewhere else. He said much that was good valuable & new (to the public at least) but went out of his way to eulogize the Southern race, & is much assaulted & belabored for having done so. He maintained last night, & very plausibly, that he did *not* go out of his way, & that what he said about the generosity & gentility of Southern traitors & the nobleness of Southern blood was intended to enforce & did enforce his practical conclusion — viz: the necessity for concentrating all our National energies to crush Southern Treason. Perhaps. But he certainly went too far — as reported — & depicted the good points of the South in colors too glowing. He described the Southern gentry of 50 years ago. What he said was true of a past generation, but most untrue of the existing Southern People that honors Brooks the bully & Floyd the thief. That people has been undergoing a process of moral degradation & gravitating toward Barbarism, ever since it adopted & began to act on the theory that Slavery was the το καλον of Social Science. My hope of our triumph in this War rests not on the strength or the merits of the North, but on the guilt of the South, for which God must have ordained some instrument of Vengeance. North is very bad, but South is much worse.

Oct. 19. Sunday. In bed all day. Sick headache. Am still cephalalgic & cantankerous. "Sinfully dogged & snappish". No news. No forward movement. No progress in the War. McClellan must confound his proper office with that of a milestone or the land-mark of a boundary. To night little Kate here — growing into a great ponderous lump of girlhood — Murray Hoffman — Dr Bache, U.S. Vol., a relative of the Professor's — G.C.A. — Geo. F. Allen, little Gerry, & others. Mrs Eleanor included. — Last night with E. G.C.A. & Johny to Niblo's, where we saw Hackett as *Rip Van Winkle* & as *D^r O'Callaghan* in "His Last Legs". He was funny in both, & the ev'g was most satisfactory, tho' it kept Johny out of his nest till eleven o'clock. — He (Johny) enjoyed it all most keenly. — C.E.S. is off at Point Judith on a fishing expedition with Peleg Hall. — This War is injuring my moral nature. I have done more *hating & detesting* during the last 18 months, against the Rebels & against Englishmen, than in all my life before.

Oct. 23. Meeting of Exec: Com: of Sanitary Com. & slight supper thereafter. Olmsted present, also an intelligent well-mannered Dr Fowler, a refugee from Montgomery Alabama. That town cast him out, because he was thought over-zealous in caring for a Hospital full of Union prisoners, of which he was in charge. San. Com. is waxing fat. It's California remittances will foot up not much below a *quarter of a million*, and may exceed that sum.

Our War on Rebellion languishes. We make no onward movements & gain no victories. McClellan's repose is doubtless majestic, but if the couchant lion postpone his spring too long, people will begin wondering whether he is not a stuffed specimen after all. Fat Col: Sackett tells Aug: King that there will certainly be a grand movement & great results within a week, but I am tired of such talk. One thing is clear — viz — that unless we gain decisive success before the Nov: Election, this State will range itself against the Administration. If it does, a dishonorable peace & permanent disunion are not unlikely. The whole community is honey-combed by secret sympathizers with treason, who will poke out their heads & flaunt their "red white & red" tentacles, the moment avowed division of Northern sentiment enables them to do so safely. Here have my cousins the *Bs* just been disclosing a new species of the great *Snob* family for the next edition of Thackeray's monograph, & caressing the Rebellion at the same time. The usual notice of Mrs Sally H's death describes her as "wife of Frank Hampton, of so and so, South Carolina, Colonel of the — regiment *C.S.A.*" Until their daughter married this Southern Pacha, they were bitter Abolitionists.

Poor Mrs H. died it seems 10th Sept. Old B. & Miss Lucy penetrated to Columbia S.C. and have been allowed to bring back with them two of the four children.

Oct. 29. Wednesday. Not an indefatigable day: have been in fact about as industrious as a woodchuck in winter-time. My abominable lethargy due, in some degree, to Dyspepsia. At our new San: Com: rooms this aft^{n} — 823 Broadway. Bellows Gibbs & Olmsted there. Certain delicate questions are before us as to our relations to the branches at Cincinnati & elsewhere. They want a slice of California's fat contribution to our Treasury, &

I suppose they must have it on some terms or other. S. Francisco has sent us more than $200.000 & promises to carry it's munificence up to a quarter of a million!! — Mr S.B.R. here to night. Also Agnew. N.B. I predict the "Orpheus C. Kerr papers" will live, as a first rate specimen of genuine humor, not of the most refined grade, but intense after it's kind.

———

War news not very important & rather mixed in quality. McClellan's Army seems to be advancing across the Potomac, after a fashion, against Lee's & Jackson's swiftmoving spitfire battalions, — as a gelatinous inorganic sluggish *Amœba* protrudes it's pseudopods in quest of prey. — We seem to have occupied Galveston & Sabine Pass without serious opposition. I suppose somebody at Washington can tell why they were not occupied a year ago. — In S. Carolina, we (Gen: Mitchell to wit) have made a dash at the Charleston & Savannah R.R. by an expedition up "Broad River" to "Pocotaligo" & "Coosawatchie". The nomenclature of Southern geography is barbaric. Beauregard telegraphed a Rebel victory to Richmond, but later reports indicate that the expedition did it's work, broke up the R.R. track & telegraph wires, & then fell back to it's gunboats & transports. Sunday skrimmages at the West seem to have turned out well. Kentucky & Missouri seem safe for the present. — But New York is far from safe, & I fear the coming State Election will consign the State to the guidance of H. Seymour as Governor, with F. Wood & B. Wood & Barlow & LaRocque & Belmont & Isaiah Rynders & J.G. Bennett to back him.

Oct. 30. Thursday. Just from a protracted S.C. meeting at Agnew's. Matters discussed were of first importance & affect all the future course of the Commission. Olmsted's iron logic has compelled me to change my views a little. Dr Bellows will probably go to Cincinnati next week, & looks not altogether unkindly on the suggestion of a Missionary tour to California! There is a nomadic element in the D^{r}'s constitution.

Wm Henry Anthon wants me to be a Commissioner for the draft. I could give him no definite answer till tomorrow — and have reason to hope that he has sent for C.E.S. instead.

Private advices from the War Department that the Virginia rebels are greatly reinforced & that McClellan is to wait a little longer. Alas for next Tuesday's election! There is danger — great & pressing danger — of a disaster more telling than all our Bull Run battles & Peninsular Strategy — the resurrection to political life & power of the Woods, Barlows, LaRocques & Belmonts, who have been dead & buried & working only underground if at all for eighteen months, & every one of whom well deserves hanging as an ally of the Rebellion. It would be a fearful National Calamity. If it come, it will be due not so much to the Emancipation manifesto, as to the irregular *arrests* Gov^{t} has been making. They have been used against the Administration with most damaging effect, & no wonder. They have been utterly arbitrary, and could be excused only because demanded by the pressure of an unprecedented National crisis — because necessary in a case of National Life or Death that justified any measure however extreme. But not one of the many hundred thus illegally arrested & locked up for months has been publicly charged with any crime, or brought to the notice of a Grand Jury. They have all been capriciously arrested, so far as we can see, and some have been capriciously discharged — locked up for months without legal authority & let out without legal acquittal. All this is very bad — imbecile — dangerous — unjustifiable. It gives traitors & Seymourites an apology for opposing Government & helping South Carolina, that is hard to answer. I know it is claimed that these arrests are legal & perhaps they are, but their legality is a subtle question that Government should not have raised as to a point about which people are so justly sensitive. — There go drums thro' the street. It's a Democratic procession (Democratic!) with torches, parading dirty James Brooks' name on a dirty banner. I met this, or it's brother, marching down 5th Av: on my way to Agnew's, & felt as if a Southern Army had got into New York.

Oct. 31. Feeling about next Tuesday's election more hopeful to day — do not know why. I can see only a most gloomy unpromising prospect. War news is *Nil.* McClellan stands like some huge rock. Which is very creditable. But no firmly fixed rock can crush a Rebellion.

Nov. 1st. God deliver us from the calamity next Tuesday's election may bring! If the vote of New York Nov. /62 be applauded by the Richmond Enquirer & the London Times, we are lost.

Nov. 3^{d}. About $26000 *more* from California! Telegrams announce still farther contributions coming. — At Soc^{y} Library an hour to night, looking at reviews & papers. Found G.C.A. here on my return. Miss Rosalie is staying here, suffering from very severe cold & generally out of order. She sent for Dr Van Buren this morn'g. — Poor Mrs C.E.S. has to undergo a second supplementary operation tomorrow. The first left some of these "fungoid" growths uneradicated, & the hemorrhage not wholly suppressed. Richd K. Haight's death announced to night. From all reports, he had quite survived his usefulness & was permanently very drunk during the last three years. — War news is that McClellan has occupied "Snicker's Gap" west of Leesburgh & is advancing with method & deliberation — also that a piratical Rebel Steamer, the "Alabama" alias the "290" is cruising effectively a couple of hundred miles off Sandy Hook. Can we stop her if she undertake to steam up the Narrows & throw a few shell into New York? I hope so, but without any definite ground for my hope. Her alias is "290" because 290 Liverpool traders subscribed to the fund that set her afloat, to sink burn & destroy Northern ships. What would England have said if 290 American merchants had subscribed to fit out a privateer against British Commerce in the interest of Russia or of Nana Sahib?

Tomorrow's prospects bad. Seymour-ites are sanguine. Vote will certainly be close. A row in the City is predicted by those who desire one, but it is unlikely, tho people are certainly far more personally bitter & savage than at any election for many years past. A Northern vote against the Administration may be treated by Honest Old Abe as a vote of want of confidence. He may dismiss his Cabinet & say to the "Democrats", "Gentlemen, you think you can do this job better & quicker than Seward & Chase. Bring up your men, & I'll set them to work." It would be like him. And there is little to choose between the two gangs, after all. Seymour & his tail want the offices — public pay & public patronage. As Governor, Seymour will probably try to outbrag the Republicans in energetic conduct of the War. He cares more for his own little finger than for all the Body Politic, and will be as "radical" as Horace Greeley himself whenever he can gain by it — i.e. whenever popular feeling calls for "Radical" Leaders. As yet the People are sound. They see that stopping the war now would be like leaving the dentist's shop with a tooth half extracted. There are traitors of course, now beginning cautiously to tamper with the great torrent of National feeling that burst out April /61 — and there is also a great mass of selfishness frivolity, invincible prejudice, personal Southern attachment, indifference to National Life &c &c quite ready to be used as a mud-bank to dam the flood that broke out so gloriously a year & a half ago.

Have we the People, or have we not, resolution & steadiness enough to fight on thro' five years of taxation corruption & discouragement? All depends on the answer to that question.

Nov. 4. Tuesday. A beautiful bright day, but destined to be memorable, I fear, for a National Calamity. Voted this morning, & did not much beside. Indications at the several polling places I visited in the course of enquiry for my own proper civic locality (which I found at last in E. 19th St.) were of a rather light vote — no excitement or disturbance — & a fair prospect for the Wadsworth ticket. — Came up town at 4, stopping at No 823 Bdway. G.C.A. & M.H. Jr dined here [Roast Pig] — I spent an hour at Bellows' in session with Executive Committee returned here & with M.H. & G.A. took a 4th Av: R.R. car down to the Park, to look for Election news. Horace Greeley was in our car — and not jubilant at all. We found excited crowds around all the Newspaper offices of that region —Times, Herald, Tribune, World — everybody craning over everybody's head to get a glimpse of the bulletins. These assemblages rather unusually clamorous & demonstrative, & all the feeling displayed was on the Seymour side. "Where's Greeley's 900.000 men?" — "Gen: Wadsworth ca'nt run for Governor but he *can* run sometimes" — "Bully for F'nandy Wood" &c &c &c. Down-town returns indicate overwhelming defeat, the election of Seymour, & a vote of Censure on the Administration by the People of this State. The Seymour majority in the City is claimed to be 31000. The Democrats carry *every Ward*. F. Wood & B. Wood & Winthrop Chanler are sent to Congress — Walbridge & Conkling defeated. Brooklyn goes the same way. The Western counties may save the State yet, but it's improbable. I think the battle is lost & Seymour is Governor. — God help us. I believe He will, if we be not utterly untrue to our Cause.

Nov. 5. As anticipated, total rout in this state. Seymour is Governor. Elsewhere defeat, or nominal success by a greatly reduced vote. It looks like a great sweeping revolution of public sentiment — like general abandonment of the loyal generous spirit of patriotism that broke out so nobly & unexpectedly in April /61. Was that after all nothing but a temporary hysteric spasm? I think not. We the People are impatient dissatisfied disgusted disappointed — we are in a state of dyspepsia & general indefinite *malaise*, suffering from the necessary evils of War & from irritation at our slow progress. We take advantage of the first opportunity of change, for it's own sake, just as a feverish patient shifts his position in bed tho' he knows he'll be none the easier for it. Neither the blind masses — the swinish multitude — that rule us under our accursed system of Universal Suffrage — nor the case of Typhoid — can be expected to exercise self-control & remember that tossing & turning weakens & does harm. Probably two thirds of those who voted for Seymour meant to say by their votes "Messrs Lincoln Seward Stanton & Co, you have done your work badly, so far. You are humbugs. My business is stopped, I have got taxes to pay, my wife's third cousin was killed on the Chickahominy, & the War is no nearer an end than it was a year ago. I am disgusted with you & your Party & shall vote for the Govr or the Congressman you disapprove, just to spite you".

If I am mistaken, & if this vote *does* endorse the policy of Fernando Wood & John Van Buren, it is a vote of National Suicide. All is up. We are a lost people. U.S. securities, "greenbacks" & all, are worth about a dollar a cord. The Historical Soc^y^ should secure an American Flag at once, for its Museum of Antiquities. I will forge certificates shewing that I was not born in America, but in *Hingland* — expatriate myself — & become naturalized as a citizen of Venezuela, Hayti, or the Papal States. But I will not *yet* believe that this People is capable of so shameful & despicable an act of self destruction as to disembowel itself in the face of the Civilized world for fear Jeff: Davis should hurt it.

Nov. 9. Sunday. *Great news. McClellan relieved & Burnside in chief command*!!! It may breed a row, but I rather think it will not. This unseasonable storm was prolonged till tonight. Snow-flakes were falling fast at dinner time. It is splendidly clear now, and cold. Have not been out of the house, except to go next door & bid Eloise goodby. She returns to *Boston* tomorrow. Have been embargoed by *swelled face.* My visage is absurdly unsymmetrical. We had a very merry party of noisy little people here this aft^{n}, & at the tea-table. There were Johny & Temple & Lewis & Miss Pussy Strong & my little niece Miss *Lucy Derby* & Charley Peters. They had a glorious time, God bless 'em. I want the children to remember *Sunday* as a *holiday*, & the pleasantest day in the week, and to enjoy all they can *now*, before the advent of the dark & troublesome days of discord & disaster in which I fear they are destined to live when they become men & women.

Nov. 13. Thursday. Detained in bed till late by some forty roasted oysters, by me devoured & gulped down at a Sanitary (!) Commission symposium on these premises last night. The slaughtered bivalves avenged themselves upon me by a sharp sick headache, which my disordinate piggishness well deserved. Also my tumefied jowl continues to disturb my peace. Peters shall lance it tomorrow. Nothing important down town. Walked up with G.C.A. stopping at 823. After dinner to a T.C. Vestry meeting. Talked much with our new Rector, & like him particularly. Failed of a quorum by one. An unusually large proportion of our members is cut off from our sessions on pathological grounds. Robt Hyslop has disease of the heart with dropsical complications — probably final — Nelson Jarvis d^{o} of the kidneys, probably d^{o}. McDonald has something else, & hopeless infirmity of age beside & Swift is just setting off for Europe with a sick son. Gen: Dix is not to be had, of course. So we are very short handed just now. — — — Last night's Sanitary session devoted mainly to our relations with the Western "branches". There are signs of War. The Cincinnati branch recalcitrates against Olmsted's proposed system of centralization & absolute subordination, & Judge Hoadly goes with Cincinnati. We shall have a row — that branch will lop itself off after the manner of St Louis — & we shall have to consider whether we have money enough to enable us to occupy that field without it's support & with it's quasi-hostility. I rather guess we can for a few months at least — thanks to California.

California sends $30.000 more to the S.C.!!!

The War languishes. We are slowly invading Virginia, but there is nothing decisive or vigorous done there, or elsewhere. I've a dim foreboding of a coming time when we shall think of the War not as "languishing" & too slow to satisfy our appetite for excitement, but as a terrible crushing personal calamity to every one of us, when there shall be no more long trains of carriages all along the Fifth Av: bound for Central Park, when the wives & daughters of Contractors shall cease to crowd Stewart's & Tiffany's, & when I shall put no Burgundy on my supper-table. Much of the moral guilt of this terrible murderous convulsion lies at our doors. South Carolina would never have dared to secede but for our toadyism — our disposition to uphold & justify the wickedness of Southern institutions. The logic of History requires that we suffer for our sins far more than we yet have suffered. "Without the shedding of blood there is no remission of sins". It is impossible this great struggle can pass without our feeling it more than we have yet felt it. It is inevitable, but in what particular way we shall be visited I cannot foresee. Perhaps a Rebel Ironclad steaming up the Narrows & throwing shell into Union Square & Gramercy Park. Time will tell.

Nov. 23. Went to Wash'n last Monday morn'g by 7 A.M. train. Bellows Van Buren Gibbs Prof: Bache, Binney, C.J. Stillé fellow travellers. Dreary dingy wet day. No incidents. Got an ill ventilated dark unwholesome room at Willard's Hotel, & then went to work, & kept at it till Friday night when we adjourned. A satisfactory & diligent session. I spent all my time between the Hotel & the San: Com: office 244 F. St. except one ev'g, Thursday, at the Surgeon General's, where was a little gathering — gentlemen of the Medical Staff & Sanitary Commissioners. Talked with Abbot, Vollum, Gouley, &c, & had a pleasant time enough. Our meetings from 10 to 2 & 7 to 11 were most interesting. The Reports of Inspectors &c, submitted & in part read, would make three or four octavo volumes of most valuable information about the progress of the War. — Bishop Clark & Judge Skinner of Chicago were absent. Binney present — a most loyal & useful addition to our number. There were also Mr C.J. Stillé of Phila & Mr J. Huntington Wolcott of Boston, representing our Associates.

Cincinnati sent us two Associates — Mr S.J. *Broadwell* & Judge or Genl *Bates*, to represent the quasi-secession claims of the Cincinnati Branch. They favored us with much vehement talk about the relations of East & West & of the Commission & it's branches, as regarded from an *Attorney's* point of view — but we voted them down unanimously, & *resolved* that the Commission is Central, Federal, National, & must & will control the action of State organizations calling themselves branches of the Commission. These gentlemen were fluent in talk. They had supposed themselves our equals, but find that they are expected to be mere "hewers of wood" &c &c &c — i.e. expected to conform to a general system in the distribution of Hospital & other supplies. Had much talk with them, & found them fair but false — governed, perhaps unconsciously by jealousy of the East. Their principal pretext is the theory that "Associate Members" of the Commission are full members of the Commission — not ὁμοιουσιου but ὁμοουσιου — which mistake may lead to a disastrous schism of the Sanitary Church, into East & West. — We sent a Committee to confer with Halleck on the two important points of an Ambulance Train, & independent Medical Transportation. They had an hour's talk with him, that confirmed the impression we received last Septr, viz: that he is second-rate & commonplace. Probably Meigs is the strongest man in the service. Would that he — or *F.L. Olmsted* — (!) were Secy of War. I believe that O's sense energy & organizing faculty, earnestness, & honesty would give new life to the Administration were he in it.

Nov. 27. Died the other day, old Geo: C. Morgan — one of my colleagues in vestry of Trinity Church. Dr Carnochan operated on him about a month ago & removed a *fungus in the antrum*, by a tedious & terrible process of surgery which the patient endured without help from anæsthetics. He was doing well till some Inflammation stepped in & took him off. — Died also Wm Platt J[r] of Philad[a], superintend[t] of our San: Com: Agency there. *Typhus* from exposure & hard work in field hospitals after *Antietam*. All the delirium of his fatal disease took him back to Sharpsboro' & Keedysville. He was constantly refusing medicines & stimulants because those poor fellows over there on the other side of the room wanted attention — or that wounded soldier ought to have a blanket at once. He is enrolled now in the Noble Army of Martyrs, beyond all harm from a typhus-poisoned circulation, free from all delusions engendered by a ruined brain. — Dr Hasket Derby, my nephew, in town: dined here Tuesday with Dr Agnew. Agnew rates him high in their ophthalmological specialité. — Burnside still hanging around Fredericsburgh, without results. — Genl Banks' expedition generally supposed to be moving for James River. But the stores he is shipping look like Texas. We send with him an Inspector, Dr Crane, with two aids, & some $10.000 worth of extra supplies. I wish he might be destined for some line on which he would cooperate with Burnside directly. The feeling of the general Public is bad — a dull hopeless resignation to inevitable failure & disaster — distrust of Government — discouragement & apathy. Sorry that McClellan, now in N.Y. should consort mainly with such cattle as John Van Buren, Barlow, & Belmont, & so strengthen the hands of his enemies.

Nov. 29. Dined here, Walter Cutting & Cap[n] Tom McCarty of the 101st N.Y.V. — brother of pretty Miss Rosa. He is a specimen of the compensating good that *War* sets off against it's evils. He *was* a young man "of Society", rich, well regulated, & good, but working in no sphere much above the German Cotillon. He *is* an experienced efficient Company officer who has gone creditably through the hard fighting of *Fair Oaks* & the terrible *Seven Days*, & Pope's disastrous campaign, & who tells the story of things he has seen done & suffered with Modesty & manliness. This disastrous War has made a man of him & of thousands like him.

Dec. 2^{d}. At San: Com: Rooms this aft^{n}. We are entering on a new period of our existence — viz: of abuse & reviling — I fear, for collision with our Cinnci*nasty* colleagues seems inevitable, and they will be unscrupulous & unsparing in the use of all weapons at their command, & though their guns are of small calibre they will be venomously worked. I anticipate much serious unhappiness from this, tho' it will be, in fact, a most insignificant annoyance.

Gen: Banks has not yet got off. The secret of his destination is well kept. Some say there are to be *two* Expeditions, that Banks goes to *Texas* & some other General to some other point — North Carolina, or Charleston or James River. I am sure I dont know anything about it. Nor do I know why Burnside is stationary so long on the wrong side of the Rappahannock. "Expectat dum defluat amnis." He may be pausing for Banks' cooperation ("The Earl of Chatham, with sword drawn, Stood waiting for Sir Richard Strachan" &c &c). Charter Election to day was apathetic private & select. I put in my poor little vote for *Haws* as Comptroller, but the whole opposition ticket, of dirty political hacks & professional suckers, will doubtless prevail by 10.000 majority at least. Our system of Government, at least in our great Cities, is simply *Kakistocratic*. As a general rule, a man's chance of filling high office is inversely as his moral fitness for it.

Dec. 7. My letter to the N.Y. Club, thro' G.C.A., withdrawing the letter I wrote in June /61 stating reasons for my resignation, seems to have been most kindly received. It looked like a charge of disloyalty against members of the Club — tho' it was not so, in fact, but a mere statement that unfavorable inferences might be drawn from their action. Very many of them have volunteered since then, & one at least, poor Jem Pendleton, has lost his life in the service of the Country. I did not want to have any letter of mine on record anywhere that could be construed as a slur on the loyalty & patriotism of men who have done so much more for the Country than I have.

Dec. 11. Thursday. The crisis seems to have come at last. Burnside commenced throwing his pontoons across the *Rappahannock* at day light, & being met by a fusillade from the houses of Fredericsburgh, opened on that unhappy town with 143 guns from our side of the river. Fredericsburgh *fuit*. Meantime Franklin was effecting a passage some 3 miles farther down, & gunboats were shelling the Rebel right still lower. There the newspaper telegrams of this aft^{n} stop. We have no news later than noon or thereabouts. This indicates that we have gained no splendid or decisive success. It is consistent with our repulse, with a fall-back by the rebels to a new line, or with the completion of arrangements preliminary to a great battle. We shall see. God help us. I have little faith in the men to whom our destinies seem confided.

No other news in Wall St. Laurence Williams dined with us. He appeared well, as he has done of late. — After dinner, took Ellie & Miss Rosalie to Acad: of Music. Grand meeting got up by our faithful auxiliaries of the "Womens Central Relief Association" to stimulate the contribution of material supplies from this City. Mayor Opdyke presided. Our $25.000 worth of *pig silver* from Storey C^{o} Nevada (!) was duly displayed — a great row of ponderous massive 250 lb. chunks of pure metal. Not quite pure however, for they contain a considerable percentage of gold. It was a splendid symbol of the National feeling that reigns in S. Francisco — Stockton — Yuba-ville — Copperopolis — Volcano — & other places, new to Geographical science. Would that Cincinnati were half as loyal! — I was on the platform, with all the Nobs, from Minturn & Aspinwall & Dr Mott & Gen. Anderson, down to — well, no matter — down to myself. Bellows made the main speech of the ev'g, expounding the purposes & methods of the Commission, it's relations to Gov^{t} on one side & the popular effort to aid the army, on the other. He was clear compact & forcible — kept the large audience wide awake for about an hour & a quarter, & was briefly followed by Dr Adams, Dr Vinton, & Dr Hitchcock, who were severally more ambitious & less effective. Dr B. has a most remarkable faculty of lucid fluent easy colloquial speech, & sympathetic manner, with an intensely telling *point* every now & then, made without apparent effort. A most enviable gift!

Dec. 13. Sat. — *Burnside* having established himself on the right bank of the Rappahannock, seems to have engaged the rebels at 9 this morn'g, advancing his left under Gen. Reynolds. The rebels meanwhile have been throwing cavalry round his right, threatening Aquia Creek, & the vital umbilical cord of Railway on his rear. I knew & predicted they would do it, & I would bet that there is not a gun or a regiment in position to block that old dodge of theirs, so often successful. — We know nothing of the progress of the fight. I anticipate only disaster — an addition to the catalogue of Bull Runs, Big Bethels &c, already so large. Defeat at this point, with a broad river in our rear, is destruction. But Burnside may be only feeling the enemy. — I have been out exploring for news — there was a bogus extra — but I can get no later intelligence, & dread it's arrival. Want of discipline in the Army is our great danger, & that is due to want of virility in those who should enforce it — the ultimate cause being the weakness of the Pres'dt himself. At all our battles nearly one man out of three has shirked & straggled, & not one man has been shot down by his commanding officer.

Olmsted tells me he called on the Pres^{dt} the other ev'g to introduce some ladies (members of his recent "Hen-Convention" from Relief Societies all over the Country) & A.L. expatiated on this terrible evil. "Order the Army to march to any place!" said A.L. "Why it's jess' like *shovellin' fleas.* Hee-yah, ya-hah!" Whereupon one of the ladies timidly asked, "Why do'nt you order stragglers to be *shot*, sir?" & the query not being immediately answered, was repeated. — O. says the Presidential guffaw died away & the Pres^{dt} collapsed & wilted down into an embodiment of everything weak irresolute perplexed & annoyed, & he said "Oh, I ca-ant do *that* you know". — It's an army of Lions we have, with a sheep for Commander in Chief.

Dec. 14. Sunday aft^{n}. I think the fate of the Nation will be decided before night. The morning papers report a general engagement that lasted all yesterday, with no result but a little advance by part of our line, & heavy loss apparently on both sides. Taken together, the little scraps of fact & incident, & humor that have come over the wires, look unpromising, but they might be much worse.

Night. We had at supper, D[r] Peters & his wife & Laurence Williams, G.C.A. & Walter Cutting, & *Robinson* (Cram's law-partner of Virginian descent, & ½ Secesh) Gerry — &c — a collocation of elements that might have combined into a fulminating compound. But we got through the ev'g without manslaughter. — No news from the Rappahannock even yet — *except* that Burnside telegraphed to M[rs] B. at Providence about noon to day "all right & all well", which despatch the lady transmitted to Dan. Fearing.

Dec. 15. *Sultry* weather. Nothing definite from the Rappahannock. There was only skirmishing yesterday. Saturday's business seems to have been on a large scale & not successful. Peace Democrats & McClellanites call it a Repulse, & say that our *main body* was engaged. We have reports to day that *Banks*, after shewing his fleet south of Hatteras, turned short round & has disembarked at Norfolk or somewhere else & is to cooperate with our forces at *Suffolk*. May this be true! If so, certain cotton-speculators who have embarked their persons on Banks' ships & their aspirations on going to Texas, have been cruelly deluded. — But it may be so, notwithstanding the many indications the other way, for old Cullum told Olmsted there were only six men in the Country that knew where Banks was going, & that the President was not one of the six. — This aft[n], San: Com: session at N° 823. Beside members of Exec: Com: there were Binney, Prof: Bache, Newberry, & our admirable ϕilad[a] associate Judge Clark Hare. We adjourned at 5, met again at 8 & sat till 11½. Olmsted occupied most of our time with a long close reasoning paper in reply to the allegations of our pettifogging Cincinnati associates. — Dined here to day, sweet little Miss Mary Griffin, one of the loveliest little creatures that lives, & possibly conscious of it, just a little, also Jem Ruggles, & Jemmy Otis. They went to the Opera with Ellie who has just returned.

Poor Bayard, killed last Saturday, was to have been married next Wednesday to a pretty girl of seventeen daughter of the Commandant at West Point. Her trousseau was all ready, & Miss Bessy Fish was to have gone up the river on special service as Bridesmaid. Such details help one to appreciate the depth of meaning embodied in the words *Battle — War — Rebellion*.

Ought we to tolerate among us men who sympathize with those who have brought these tragedies into our peaceful homes? Can we rightfully — or without *crime* — greet in social intercourse people whose influence, so far as it goes, strengthens & encourages the authors of this War, & weakens & discourages every effort the Nation is making to execute just vengeance on their wickedness & scourge them back to their duty? — There is poor Joe Curtis too, Geo. & Burrill Curtis' brother, who rose by merit, step after step, from the ranks of the 1st R.I. to it's Lt Colonelcy.

Dec. 17. Wednesday. Burnside *recrossed* the Rappahannock, unmolested, Monday night. The operation seems to have been skilfully performed. It was ticklish work. Secesh might have smitten us fearfully during it's progress. But it is a *cognovit.* Burnside pleads guilty to failure & repulse. This news, arriving yesterday afternoon, has produced serious depression & discouragement. The Battle of Fredericsburgh was a defeat with heavy loss, damaging to the National cause. And Banks has not landed anywhere in N.C. — We are now sure his force is diverted from the vital centre of contest & destined for the extremities — for Florida, Mobile, or Texas. This looks like bad economy of our strength.

Sanitary Commission sat yesterday morning at No 823. Bellows, Prof: Bache, Olmsted, Agnew, Gibbs, Van Buren, Binney, Judge Hare, Stillé, dined here yesterday, & Dr Howe came in *pendente Symposis.* It was a satisfactory evening. — This morn'g we resumed our session & adjourned at three P.M.

Our special business has been the Cincinnati imbroglio. We settled this by a reference with power to a Committee of Heads of Western Branches. Perhaps our best course, but it will cost our Treasury just $50.000 & will not stop the mouths of Hon: Geo. Hoadly & Co. — We had much debate also about the relative authority of the Commission [or Executive Committee when the Commission is not sitting] & our Executive Officer — F.L. Olmsted, to wit. Were he not among the truest purest & best of men, we should be in irreconcilable conflict. His convictions as to the power an Executive officer ought to wield & his faculty of logical demonstration that the Commission ought to confide everything to it's General Secy on general principles, would make a crushing rupture inevitable, were we not all working in a common cause & without personal considerations.

Dec. 18. Thursday. Wintry. Busy day. At Exec: Com: this aft^{n}, & again at Agnew's till midnight. Gen. Crawford joined us there — Wounded at Antietam, but convalescent & ready for duty. Our loss at Fredericsburgh is crawling up to 17000. It is generally held that Stanton forced Burnside to this movement against his earnest remonstrance & protest. Perhaps Stanton did'nt. Who knows? But there is universal bitter wrath agst him throughout this community — a deeper feeling more intensely uttered than any I ever saw prevailing here. Lincoln comes in for a share of it. Unless Stanton be speedily shelved, something will burst somewhere. The general indignation is fast growing revolutionary. The most thorough Republicans, the most loyal Administration men express it most fiercely, & seem to share the personal vindictiveness of the men & women whose sons or brothers or friends have been uselessly sacrificed to the vanity of the political schemes of this meddling murderous quack. His name is likely to be a hissing, till it is forgotten, & the Honest Old Abe must take care lest his own fare no better. A year ago we laughed at the H.O.A.'s grotesque genial Western jocosities — but they nauseate us now. If these things go on, we shall have pressure on him to resign & make way for *Hamlin*, as for one about whom nobody knows anything, & who *may* therefore be a change for the better, none for the worse being conceivable. "O Abraham, O mon Roi!"

Dec. 21. Seward has tendered his resignation! Whether it will be accepted & if so who will succeed him — & whether other changes in the Cabinet are to follow, we do'nt yet know. Edwd Everett & Chas Sumner are named as candidates for the succession. I do not think Seward a loss to Government. He is an adroit shifty clever politician, in whose career I have never detected the least indication of principle. He believes in *majorities*, and it would seem, in nothing else. He has used Anti-Masonry, Law Reform, the Common School system, & Antislavery as means to secure votes, without possessing an honest *conviction* in regard to any of them.

We have a decided success in N. Carolina, but it attracts little notice. We are a strange people. Suppose Burnside had been attacked at Fredericsburgh, had repulsed the attack, & then allowed Gen. Lee to recross the Rappahannock unmolested & without loss. — What a howl we should have raised against him, & how we should exalt & magnify the Southern Generalship! But "mutato nomine" we talk only of Burnside's inefficiency & incapacity, & of the immense ability displayed by Lee & Longstreet & "Stonewall Jackson".

Dec. 24. Xmas Eve. Lewis much better, but still languid drowsy feverish & forlorn. He is cantankerous tonight, & roars howls & screeches like a demon whenever any one comes near him — which is a favorable indication. He came very close to Death yesterday morning. Thank God this Xmas eve is so different from what it narrowly escaped being.

Affairs in the West seem going backward. In N. Carolina Gen: Foster has achieved decided success. If Banks' regiments were supporting him instead of being wasted at remote points, we might hope everything from his vigorous movements. But as it is they are mere raids, & I fear Lee can afford to detach thirty or forty thousand men from the Rebel Army of Virginia, & compel Foster to fall back to the cover of his gunboats. — The little tempest in the Cabinet has cleared up. Nobody resigns after all. — Burnside comes out with a frank honest manly Report, taking on himself whatever blame attaches to the repulse before Fredericsburgh. I regret one passage, in which he says he was unwilling to be entrusted with the command of the Army, when McClellan was relieved, because he felt himself unequal to the place. But the paper, as a whole is honorable to him & of good omen for the Country. We are sure now of *one* fact, & we are sure of very few. We have one man in high place who is single minded & unselfish & sincere. His identification is great gain, even admitting his ability to be third rate.

Dec. 27. Xmas went off comfortably. Johny & Temple revelled in their presents. Poor little Lewis, up stairs, refused to be entertained by the most resplendent of harlequins. Trinity Church was artistically decorated under the Supervision of young Egleston, who is equally strong in Ecclesiology & Palæontology. The Christmas service was long. Its music was dismal in quality, & its execution produced acute suffering. Vinton's sermon was swaggering commonplace. All N° 24 dined here, also Mrs Herman Ruggles & Miss Julia. || Last night at Dr Bellows' — Exec: Com: meeting. || Public affairs unchanged. || Will Uncle A.L. stand firm & issue his promised Proclamation 1st Jan. 1863? Nobody knows, but I think he will. || Chas J. Stillé of ϕiladelϕia has published a clever pamphlet, comparing our general condition as to blunders, imbecility, failures, popular discontent, financial embarrassment &c with that of shabby old England during the first years of her *Peninsular War*. He makes out a strong case in our favor. It is a valuable paper, & we must have it reprinted here, for there are many feeble knees in this Community that want to be confirmed & corroborated. It had an excellent effect on Bidwell — a bad case of typhoid Despondency in a state of chronic collapse & utter prostration. He rallied a little after reading it, & was heard to remark that "we might possibly come out all right after all". — Jeff Davis' ferocious Proclamation!! Butler & all Butler's commissioned officers to be hanged, whenever caught. Ditto all armed negroes, and all white officers commanding them. This is the first great blunder Jeff. has committed since the War began. It's evidence not only of barbarism but of weakness, & will disgust his foreign admirers (if anything can) and strengthen the backbone of the North at the same time. If he attempts to carry it out, retaliation becomes a duty, and we can play at Extermination quite as well as Jeff. Davis.

Dec. 30. After dinner went to D[r] Bellows' & spent the ev'g. Exec: Com: meeting. At our aft[n] session one Hyslop was present with certain working models illustrating a Theory of *Ventilation*. Most interesting & satisfactory. We appropriated $300.00 tonight to apply his principles to *S[t] Joseph's Hospital* (Central Park) where foul air is breeding *hospital gangrene* at a terrible rate. It looks like an important invention.

We know Banks' destination now. He has relieved Butler at N.O. — Is this wise? Perhaps they expect to take Charleston or Mobile & want Butler to do the same organizing work there which he has done so successfully at N.O. — But to day's story is that Sec^{y} Stanton goes out & Butler succeeds him. That would be gain, I think. Also that *Frémont* is to supersede *Burnside* — God forbid. I do not believe Government can do anything so preposterous, but there are sundry signs that make this not absolutely beyond belief. — It's said that "*Port Hudson*" a rebel ligature lately put on the Mississippi just above *Baton Rouge* is untied & given up, & that another effort agst *Vicksburgh* is to be made forthwith. It's a very grave drawback & misfortune that the Cumberland & the Tennessee & other Western Rivers are unseasonably late in rising this year, & that our Trusty gunboats are still unable to circulate within the vital arteries of Rebeldom. There is a Report of 19 colored chattels *hanged* in Charleston. If true, the presumption is that this large amount of property was thus sacrificed because it exhibited symptoms of contumacy & insubordination, produced by the expected Proclamation of Jan: 1st — *Day after Tomorrow*!!! A critical day that will be. Will Lincoln's backbone carry him thro' the work he is pledged then to do? It is generally supposed that he intends to redeem his pledge, but nobody knows, & I am not sanguine on the subject. If he come out fair & square, he will do the "biggest thing" an Illinois jury-lawyer has ever had a chance of doing, and take high place among the men who have controlled the destinies of Nations. If he postpone or dilute his action, his name will be a bye word & a hissing till the annals of the 19th Century are forgotten.

Dec. 31. Wednesday night & New Years Eve. A busy day, without achieving much. Usual Committee this aft^{n}. We have many details to arrange, in the comparatively small matter of relief to the local hospitals of N.Y. & to regiments passing thro' the City, and I believe that in this quiet unnoticed way we do a good deal, daily to diminish suffering & save life. I am thankful that there's any way in which I'm instrumental in doing substantial good, anywhere — even tho' my agency in the matter is merely that of drawing the checks that pay for labor & stores.

1863

Jan 3. Anxious looking out for news from *Murfreesboro'* where was terrible fighting all thro' the 31st and 1st — probably renewed yesterday, but we dont know. A very bloody business, & I fear, a black one for the Country. It's *Rosecrans* v. *Joe Johnston*. We have also Rebel reports of a repulse at Vicksburgh, but they are unreliable of course. — Exec: Com: from 4 to near 6. Telegrams from Olmsted & various unimportant matters. We conclude to send off D[r] Douglas who's fortunately in town on a week's leave, to the West at once, with a credit for $15000 to be used in Cincinnati, & with two or three thousand dollars worth of stores beside purchased here. — We adjourned to Gibbs' at 8, from which session I have just returned. Douglas was with us & we settled details. But Douglas brought in with him an "authentic" rumor, that Rosecrans is badly beaten — & another that he & all his host have surrendered. Should this story prove true we are saved the cost of the proposed expedition, & also the necessity of troubling ourselves about the fate of Kentucky & Tennessee. Our Western War ends in hopeless disaster. Cincinnati must fall within thirty days, & the National cause is past hope. But I do not yet believe it. — The President has signed the bill admitting "West Virginia" as a State of the Union. And be it remembered, with gratitude to the Author of all Good, that on Jan. 1st the *Emancipation Proclamation* was duly issued. The Nation may be sick unto speedy death & past help from this or any other remedy, but if so, it's last great Act is one of Repentance & Restitution. — But this is too large a matter to write about at 11.45 P.M. I have been fidgetting about E's not coming home from M[rs] Tighe's & she has just returned, — under convoy of John the Waiter.

Jan. 4. Sunday. At home all day. News from Murfreesboro' still indecisive. Conflicting indications of Victory & of defeat, but the struggle & conflict there have been fearful, & the carnage on the scale of Eylau & Borodino. — It looks *at present* like a drawn battle with a preponderance in our favor. News from Vicksburgh looks well — though is vague. But the illustrious *Monitor* has foundered off Cape Hatteras! She should have survived the war, to be mounted on a great pedestal of monumental masonry somewhere, with a statue of *Lt Worden*, in cast iron, on the top of her Turret.

Jan. 5. Monday night. Indian summer still prevails. Diligent in Wall St. & at Surrogate's office. People are generally anxious & blue. Col: Coll: Trustees met at 2 P.M. I assisted. Nothing done, except a little progress made in that ancient job of revising our Statutes. Left the meeting before adjournment & proceeded to 823 Broadway. Twenty one thousand dollars & upwards from California awaited me there. Home in time to bid E. goodbye. She set forth at five for a visit to *Washington*, in charge of her father, leaving Miss Rosalie to look after the children.

Worked at home this ev'g. — A whirlwind of *Extras* came roaring through the street. Invested fivepence, tho' with hesitation, & find despatch of this date from *Louisville*. "*Murfreesboro' advices represent the Union Victory Complete. The entire Rebel Army is fleeing toward Tullahoma in great disorder*." May be so. God grant it! Also a despatch from Gen. U.S. Grant, dated Holly Springs, 4th inst. "*From Rebel sources I learn that the Grenada Appeal of the 31st says the Yankees have got possession of Vicksburgh*." Much too good to be true.

Jan: 7. *Rosecrans* has certainly gained a victory, if holding the field be the test of victory. The Rebels have cut & run. Perhaps, as on former occasions, they have fought as long as they thought expedient, & then retired to some new position, carrying off captured guns to reinforce their Ordnance Department. However that may be, *Murfreesboro'* was a very earnest struggle while it lasted & involved great consumption of men & of materiel. It may have been indecisive, but our resources will stand the wear & tear of indecisive conflict longer than those of Slave-dom, and can be sooner repaired. The stronger party at Chequers must win if he can effect a series of exchanges. — Whether we have got *Vicksburgh* is still uncertain — But it is certain we have made a brilliant raid into Eastern Tennessee, equal to any dash by the glorified Rebel Stuart & with results beyond anything his audacity has achieved, viz: his destruction of a most important line of R.R. communication.

Jan. 8th. Letter from E. Safe at Washington — an excellent private parlor at Willard's — Everything bathed in serene sunshine. — Agnew & Gibbs at N° 823 — 4 P.M. — Long session. Gibbs went away & then A. & I had a talk with one of our maimed Volunteers, whom we support, in consideration of their doing a little office work, until they can find something better. This was the one-*legged* man, Corporal *Echelan*. He called at our office a month or so back to make some enquiry about back-pay or some such matter. We found, without his volunteering the statement, that he was literally penniless & shelterless, so we took him into temporary service. His handwriting & his language were clerkly, and he turned out to be an alumnus of Col: Coll: tho' not a graduate — a shipwrecked gentleman. The cause of his decline soon became patent. Drink, to wit. We have treated him forbearingly, & A. & I had a kind serious talk with him this afternoon. It was very sad & touching. The poor fellow's conscience is sensitive, & his feeling of humiliation profound, but I fear the case is hopeless. Still, we must try to save him. He is not the only man in N.Y. who does habitually wrong, while he clearly sees the right — *to my certain knowledge*. Perhaps there are several, and "highly respectable" men, too.

Jan: 10. Last night at Dr Van Buren's. Meeting of Exec: Com: — Letters from E. at Wash^{n}. She is having a grand time with all sorts of delightful people. — She writes that Fitz-John Porter looks jaded disgusted blasé & incapable of enthusiasm in the National or any other cause. He is doubtless sore about his Court martial, & Genl Pope, tho' he can hardly fail of honorable acquittal. McClellan's letter urging him to support Gen: Pope cordially was a very damaging piece of moral evidence against him, but McClellan testifies that it was written at the *Pres'dt's* earnest request — by the Pres'^{dt}'s order, in fact, & thereby neutralizes all unfavorable inferences. —

I am clear as to F.J.P.'s honesty & loyalty, but public affairs generally are awfully obscure & muddled — Can it be possible — as people say — that Gov^{t} is preventing our Generals from gaining decisive victory, for fear of inconvenient Anti-administration candidates for the Presidency? — God forbid!

Jan. 12. More bad news. Naval force off Galveston surprised by rebel steamboats armored with cotton bales. The Harriet Lane captured: her commander, poor Mayhew Wainwright (Bishop W's son), killed: the Westfield blown up & her Commander, Renshaw, with her: a small land force captured: the survivors of our flotilla dispersed. Disaster & disgrace, & strong indications of negligence or misconduct somewhere. — Thoroughly disgusted all day: never so tempted & beset by that Evil Spirit *Despondency*, before. No ray of light peeps through at any point. We are gaining no ground, and here are enlistments about to expire, and the reptiles of the pro-slavery & peace-at-any-price Democracy, growing bolder every hour!!!! What help or hope can we look to?

Jan. 13. Our general conviction is that the National cause is fast going to Destruction — that we are without Leaders & on the verge of bankruptcy, and that Vallandigham & Cox & F. Wood & Ja[s] Brooks & other Dirt Eaters of the North will soon have all the game in their own hands. Heaven help us!

Jan. 16. There is talk in the Cabinet of an *Emancipation Bureau*, which will soon be needed, if not needed already. Horace Binney was proposed as it's chief, but conceded to be past active service, an octogenarian retired from public life. Then they talked of Stillé — "C.J.S. of ϕilad[a] who has written that admirable pamphlet" &c. I do'nt know whether they agreed at last about anything or anybody — but that Stillé was brought forward & discussed is certain. It's a hopeful sign. It shews that Government is feeling about for strong & honest men wholly outside of party lines. Stillé is a quiet reading man, wholly unfit for the difficult & most delicate duties such position would throw on him, — probably of insufficient mental & moral calibre for the great social problem it would require him to solve. Nevertheless, the fact that he has been talked about for high public office because he has published a valuable paper on a national subject, & for no other reason whatever, is a most weighty fact & full of encouragement. We sorely need Encouragement just now.

Jan. 18. The Army of the Rappahannock is moving, or about to move. That seems unquestionable. To day's rumors of fighting at or near Fredericsburgh probably unfounded. Hope so, for it's an unlucky army, likely to be beaten.

C.E.S. had been discoursing Geo. Boker of ϕilad[a]. Bad account of poor Bob Le Roy, who seems sinking into a state of mere bibulous loaferism & degradation. "Democrats" of that City & state reported to be thoroughly treasonous. Party lines far more strongly drawn than here. Boker predicts civil war & revolutionary scenes in northern Cities before next Summer — thinks pro-slavery dis-loyalists will have to be taken in charge & hanged by Vigilance Committees of loyal men — or vice versâ.

The next ten days will bring weighty tidings. The destinies of the Continent may be decided by the events I shall, in my ordinary course, note down on the page & three quarters of Journal now open before me, blank, & awaiting the record to be inscribed on them. I am not sanguine at all — but I have faith in Divine Justice.

Burnside is moving. — Rosecrans is to be attacked from Chattanooga, it's said. — We must resume our movement agst Vicksburgh — an expedition has been sent to Wilmington or to Charleston, we do not know which, — Our victory at Murfreesboro' enables us to attempt, *at last*, the occupation of E. Tennessee. The result of any one of these conflicts — each or any of them perhaps actually in progress while I write — this very minute — may decide all the future of this Country, & determine the Social Status of John R. Strong & his two younger brethren.

Jan: 20. We seem drifting blindly & hopelessly to National destruction, like a boat-load of drunken Indians on the rapids above Niagara. God help us. I fear there is no help in man. Of course I dont *talk* that way, down-town or up. On the contrary, I bray loud about what our armies have achieved, & the unprecedented strength of the National position, & the dreadful straits to which we have reduced J. Davis & Co. — & I think I do it tolerably well. — Very diligent these two days, occupied, *inter alia* with Circulars about the proposed "National Club" — a splendid possibility. Called on Cisco & Cha[s] E. Butler about it this morning. Result satisfactory.

Jan. 22. When I came down to breakfast the morning papers took my breath away with the statement that the Court Martial on Major Gen[l] Fitz-John Porter finds him guilty of disobedience of orders & neglect of duty, & that the President confirms the sentence dismissing him from service, a disgraced & ruined man. It seems incredible. The Court was composed of good men, so far as I know them. *Porter* has been a favorite with the army. *Pope*, his virtual accuser, disliked & despised. This finding is therefore entitled to every presumption in it's favor, though so astounding to all who know the accused, as I have known him for twelve years at least.

Everybody expected his triumphant acquittal. All his antecedents made it most improbable he should have failed in the execution of plain military duty. Tho' I never thought him brilliant or clever, he seemed the embodiment of the ideal of military subordination, discipline, respect for authority. The evidence has been irregularly & imperfectly reported in the papers & has seemed of little weight. McClellan's letter to him, when Pope was put in command, begging him to support Pope cordially was — morally — very damaging. McC. testified, to be sure, that he wrote that letter only because the Pres[dt] asked him to do so. But one of the Ev'g papers asks, very pertinently, whether such a letter would not have been treated as an *insult* by any officer who meant to do his duty & obey the commands of McClellan & Pope with equal alacrity. It is all a muddle as yet. Perhaps the report is not true. Miss Rosalie tells me that Fitz-John's wife was *making calls* to day with her mamma, M[rs] Holbrook, & pooh-poohed the whole story. — If true it is a wholesome indication of vigor. Northern Dirt-eaters will of course represent it as a blow at McClellan through one of his friends.

Jan. 24. Burnside seems to have made demonstrations toward an advance. Wet weather, miry roads, & the inevitable blunders of somebody in the Q.M.G's department, baffled him, & he drew back again.

The Army makes little progress. That's bad. But far worse is the fact that Northern Dirt-eaters grow more insolent & shameless every day, here, in New Jersey, in Illinois, &

everywhere else, & that there is no National virility anywhere sufficient to intimidate them. Their last dodge, in this City, is to sow distrust of Government paper among tradespeople & mechanics. — Ex: gr: C.E.S's oysterman rather demurred to a one dollar greenback this morning because the Alderman of his Ward — who knows what's what — had confidentially advised him that Treasury notes were wastepaper.

Jan. 25. C. says he thinks the report of Bob Le Roy's death premature — but that it cannot long be postponed except by miracle. — Porter's case does not improve, as one learns more about it.

Jan. 26. Aft^{n} papers bring weighty news. Hooker relieves Burnside in command on the Rappahannock. *In*judicious Hooker! Perhaps he is the fated Knight that is to break the spell under which that army has lain enchanted so long. If he fail, a heavy penalty awaits him — the same that has been visited on McDowell, McClellan, Pope & Burnside. He undertakes the emprise at the worst possible moment. I cannot guess what he will try to do. But he is a fighting general, who goes under fire without taking much thought for his own skin, & will be just as active as Virginia mud permits. Pity his reputation is that of an unprincipled California gambler & mauvais sujet. In view of the most grave political or revolutionary complications that are within the range of possibility, the General commanding the Army of the Potomac should be a man of high moral tone. The personal honesty & purity of Burnside, McClellan & Rosecrans, disinterested high-minded patriots, all three, has been an important element in the chances of our National Salvation. — Franklin & Sumner are also relieved. I fear because more than suspected of deserving F.J. Porter's doom.

At 823 Bdway this aft^{n} talked with Agnew, receiving his Report of the sayings & doings of the San: Com: session at Wash^{n}, just adjourned. Olmsted is in an unhappy sick sore mental state. Seems trying to pick a quarrel with the Executive Committee. Perhaps his most insanitary habits of life make him morally morbid. He works like a dog all day & sits up nearly all night — does'nt go home to his family (now established in

W.) for five days & nights together, works with steady feverish intensity till four in the morning, sleeps on a sofa in his clothes, & breakfasts on *strong coffee & pickles*!!!

[Here enter George Gibbs, with certain information about the proposed "National Club" & full of blowing talk about National affairs, *more suo* — imbecility here — corruption there — Seward an ass & Stanton a beast & Lincoln an idiot, Everything going to ruin & so forth. Authentic information of *this* & the best authority for *that*. I discoursed him like a Dutch uncle, on the mischievous tendency of such utterances.] — It will be a terrible blow to the Commission if we have to throw Olmsted over. We could hardly replace him.

This ev'g at W. Gibbs' with Geo. F. Allen discussing & settling programme of "National Club".

E. writes she will be at home tomorrow night. *Perhaps.* — Senator Fessenden tells Dr Van Buren that we need not be uneasy about the regiments to be mustered out of service within a few months on expiration of their enlistments. There will be 300.000 enrolled Ethiops to fill the gap. *Possibly.* — My first emotion when I heard of Fitz-John Porter's condemnation was sorrow for the downfall of an old friend — regret that he should have put himself in a technically false position. But as I look farther into the matter it assumes another aspect, & F.J. Porter's name now seems to me likely to hold the lowest place in our National Gallery but one — that of Benedict Arnold. Holt's review of the evidence for & against him is crushing.

Jan: 28. The out-look over Gramercy Park is white & ghastly, & carriages roll by with a wintry muffled sound. — Dr Bellows got home from our San: Com: session at Wash^{n} this morning, & sent for me. Called at his house on my way down town. Ellie was well & jolly yesterday aft^{n} & is to return, squired by Geo: Bancroft tomorrow. (This is confirmed by my daily bulletin from her, rec^{d} this morn'g.) — Bellows was full (in one sense) of the little dinner this little woman & her father gave Monday to Sec^{y} Seward & Usher & Gen: McDowell, Judge Loring, Bancroft, Bellows, &c, — about a dozen, all told. Seward seems to have selected the occasion for a free statement of his past & present views & policy. Talked from ½ past 5 to 11. Nobody could stand against his talk. Geo. Bancroft & Loring "were like shingles under Niagara". Bellows seemed much impressed by it all, & was writing notes & reminiscences, wh: he means to ask Ellie & Mr R. to revise correct & complete. He thinks Seward's revelations frank & open beyond precedent, & says all their convives agree with him. Seward said he urged *Buchanan* to hold & reinforce Fort Pickens, but *to abandon Sumter*, his object & aim being to postpone the inevitable collision till Lincoln should be in power. He thought he had done the Country substantial service in two things — viz: in retarding actual conflict some 30 days, & in getting Lincoln inaugurated Pres^{dt} of the U.S. without a shadow of question as to the regularity & legality & technical accuracy of his accession to office. The faintest shade of question on that point would have been felt for generations to come. That's very true. He eulogizes L. without limitation. Thinks him the best & wisest man he has ever known. Perhaps. Lincoln's grade & place in history will not be settled, probably, till fifty years hence. — &c &c &c.

At N° 823 this aft^{n}. I generally find Miss *Louisa Schuyler* there now, working for the "Women's Central" Assoc^{n} about the organization of a system of forwarding supplies from all parts of the Country, & carrying on a correspondence with some 1400 affiliated village societies churches clubs & circles. The young lady works there from 10 A.M. till 3 or 4 P.M. daily, & I should designate her as a *Brick & a half*, if it did'nt look irreverent. She is certainly a most intelligent energetic diligent young damsel though not pretty at all. — N.Y. Common Council has passed resolutions eulogizing F.J. Porter & declaring his condemnation unjust. The tender mercies of the wicked are cruel. This will do Porter no good. —— Inter alia, Seward said that during the 100 days before Lincoln's accession he kept 100 hired roughs from N.Y. in the Senate gallery to take care of Northern Senators if necessary (wh: sounds so Munchausenesque that it makes me distrust all the rest.) — that he was personally more cordially intimate with *Davis* than any one else in Washington (which is true) & that Davis never dreamed Secession would bring War.

Jan. 30. Friday 11 P.M. — Will Ellie get home tonight I wonder? Hope so. She is nearly due now, but may have decided to spend the night in Philad^{a} instead of coming straight through.

Cloudy day, squashy under foot, but with some feeble drizzle of snow for an hour. — Very active all the morning. At 823 on my way up town, & at 8 o'clock went to W. Gibbs', a conciliabulum having been called to meet there & consider about the "National Club". Only some 18 invited. No one ignored the invitation. Everyone came promptly & punctually or excused himself on good grounds. There were Prof: Dwight, Agnew, Geo. Gibbs, Rev. S.H. Weston, G.C. Anthon, Judge Murray Hoffman, Wolcott Gibbs of course, Dr Bellows, Geo. F. Allen, Horatio Allen Dr Dalton, Wm Hoppin, & myself, — 13. — Judge H. presided, & I was Sec^y. We appointed a Com: of 3 — viz Gibbs (W.) Dwight & G. F. Allen, to devise & report a scheme of organization & adjourned to next Friday. Temper of the meeting more than satisfactory. — The only point on which there seemed a difference, was whether we should make determination to support Government *through thick & thin* a condition of membership. There was sound & sensible talk on both sides of this question. It is plain that no absolutely decisive test can be devised. No one can be expected to pledge himself to uphold whatever any set of men at Washington or elsewhere may hereafter think proper to do — and on the other hand no one can expect to be admitted to a Club designed to sustain Government who goes about denouncing the d—d idiocy of Sec^y this, & the corruption of Sec^y that, & the infernal ruinous imbecility of "that wretched old blackguard Abe Lincoln". The Committee on organization will have to devise some formula for signature by members that will distinguish the Bianchi & the Neri — the sheep & the goats — with approximation to accuracy. It can do no more, for it has no moral or political *Spectroscope* wherewith to detect the ten millionth part of a grain of Disloyalty that is latent in the composition of Mr A. or Mr B. who is ready to sacrifice all his assets, & his life beside, to the National Cause, but cannot always control his inclination to growl at the War Department. — They (the Committee) must try to formalize — or formularize — the notion or theory that loyal men are bound to treat the shortcomings, errors, & sins of *Government* in the same spirit of forbearance & reticence with which they would deal with the misdeeds or mistakes or follies of a brother or a wife. — I prefer the most severe & stringent rule, but it's application would be plainly impossible.

Feb. 3. Murray Hoffman dined here & I went at 8 to Ex: Com: meeting at D[r] Bellows, where were also Gibbs & Agnew. — Among other little matters that came before us was a draft for some *$1100.00*, the third article of the sort received from *Honolulu*. Agnew says he expects the next big Aerolite that arrives will bring us a contribution from American citizens in the Moon. The success of this San: Com: has been a marvel. Our receipts in cash up to this time nearly $700.000 at the Central office alone, beside what has been received & spent by auxiliaries, & the three or four millions worth of stores of every sort contributed at our depots. It has become a "big thing", has the S.C. — a considerable fact in the history of this People & of this War. — Our work at Wash[n] & at Louisville, our two chief nervous centres, is on a big scale, employs some 200 agents of every sort & costs not much less than $40.000 a month. — — — National affairs seem stagnant, but I suppose we shall very soon hear news of the first importance from Vicksburgh & possibly from Rosecrans. I think the National destiny will be decided in the S.W., not in Virginia. Richmond is an ignis fatuus. We have mired ourselves badly in trying to reach it, twice at least, & can apply our strength more advantageously at other points. I am more & more satisfied as I have been from the first that our true policy is to occupy every Southern port — to open the Mississippi, to keep a couple of armies in strong & comfortable & healthy positions on the Rebel frontier, & then to say to Jeff. Davis "We are not going to advance into your jungle over your muddy roads. If you want a fight you must come to us. If you do'nt want it, stay where you are & let us see which party will first be starved & wearied into submission". We do not need enterprise & dash, near so much as resolution & steadiness — perseverance & pluck; the passive pluck that can suffer a little & wait quietly for the inevitable result. Therein this people seems wanting. Perhaps I do it injustice, but all the symptoms of the last four months indicate a fearful absence of vital power & constitutional stamina to resist disease & pain. The way the Dirt-Eaters & Copperheads & Sympathizers and Compromisers are coming out on the surface of Society, like ugly petechiæ & vibices (?), shews that the Nation is suffering from a most putrescent state of the National blood, & that we are a very typhoid community here at the North.

Thank God for the rancorous vindictive ferocious hysterical utterances that reach us from the South — for the speeches & the Richmond-Enquirer-editorials declaring Compromise & reconstruction impossible, that "Southrons" would not take back "Yankees" even as their *slaves*, that Northern Democrats who talk about restoring the old Union are fools & blind. Were the South only a little less furious savage & spiteful it could in three months so strengthen our "Peace Democracy" as to paralyze the Nation & destroy all hope of ever restoring it's territorial integrity. It is strange Jeff. Davis & Co fail to see their best move. With a few unmeaning insincere professions of desire for reconstruction, additional Constitutional guaranties & so forth, they could bring us grovelling to their feet, & secure an Armistice most profitable to them, most dishonorable & disastrous to us.

Feb. 4. Lt Ash of 5th Cavalry dined here — a very dashing fellow, with near a dozen battle scars on his person — sabre cuts included, which few of our National Soldiers can shew. — The Herald's black tidings of a naval sortie from Charleston Harbor — destruction of our blockading gunboats, & raising of the blockade — generally distrusted. — We may look hourly now for news of an attack on Charleston Wilmington or Savannah by land & sea — periculosae plenum opus aleæ — Charleston especially. We shall not have so good a time there as at Port Royal & Pulaski.

Feb. 5. This has been a sluggish day, utterly wasted. I try to shuffle off the blame on the State of the Nation. It is so hard to apply one's self to trivial duties of business & routine when this Great American Nation is hourly awaiting it's doom. It is because of my ardent & earnest Patriotism that I am the laziest lubber now out of jail. On which Conscience observes sotto voce that she "dont see it". — No Remittances from Wash^{n} to pay Atlantic Dock Rents yet received at the Custom House. Very annoying & very strange. Though gold has risen, Government can still manufacture Greenbacks at a profit. — Wrote to Hon. Isaac C. Delaplaine, otherwise Ikey Pig, about an appointment to the Naval School for Willy Little.

As our little dinner for the Kuhns was countermanded by reason of E's inability to preside, I went to Trin: Ch: Standg Com: meeting at 7½, & we had a long session. Inter alia, we squelched the renewed application of the Theolog: Seminary for pecuniary aid. We could not have given it anyhow — but I took great pleasure in assigning as one of the reasons for my adverse vote, the recent appointment of so disloyal a man as Rev. D[r] Seabury to a professorship in that institution. Verplanck alone favored the application, & he is as disloyal as Sam: Seabury.

These be dark blue days. Of course every man's duty is to keep a stiff upper lip — fortem in arduis rebus servare mentem — "to talk turkey" about the moral certainty of triumph at last. I do so very valiantly. It's fearful & wonderful, the way I blow & brag about our National invincibility, the extent of our conquests during the last twenty months, & our steady progress toward subjugation of the South. It is the right kind of talk for the times, & is more than half true, & has materially relieved the moral & political *adynamia* of at least one man — viz: Bidwell — already. — But (between me & my journal) things do in fact look darker & more dark every day. We are in a fearful scrape, & I see no way out of it. Recognition of the "Confederacy" is impossible. So is vigorous prosecution of the war twelve months longer. This proposition is self-evident "if this Court understand herself, & she think she do". How can these two contradictions be reconciled? *Rabelais* furnishes a case equally difficult. Jupiter created a Fox that was destined never to be caught, & afterwards, by inadvertence, a Dog destined to catch all Foxes, so that the Olympian Ledger of Destiny could not be made to balance. If I rightly remember my learned & pious author, Jupiter got rid of the embarrassment by turning Dog & Fox into two stars, or two constellations, or two stones, which was a mere evasion, & no solution of the great problem he had to deal with. We are in a similar deadlock of contradiction I fear. North cannot be defeated & South cannot be conquered. (Of course this is taking the *worst* view of the case) — What then? I rather think the Supreme Providence that regulates all affairs of this world will settle the question by turning us, N. & S., not into two *Stars*, but into two worthless erratic Comets, condemned for ages to get into each others' orbits & be public or cosmic nuisances till the world's end, or until their own feeble cohesion & the wear & tear of frequent collision reduce both to mere unwholesome Nebulæ & degrade them back to primæval Chaos. — Permanent division is death to North & South alike. New forms of political life will be generated by our National Decomposition I suppose. But it will make a terrible smell. We shall be recorded in history as the great example of Sham Nationality — a People that strutted & bragged out of all reason & beyond all precedent, & then came in two at the first discord, & perished & rotted because it had not vital force enough to assert it's National Life.

Feb. 6. Meeting here to night of people interested in our "National Club" organization. A dozen or fifteen, Judge Hoffman presiding. There were Wm C. Bryant of the Post, Rev. Dr Hitchcock, & Fred: Sheldon — the others were at W. Gibbs' last Friday. We made some progress. "Union League" seems preferred as our title instead of "National Club", & the tendency is toward an *association* or *Society* rather than a *Club* like the Century or the New York.

Feb. 9. At Century Club Saturday night. Went there for the sole purpose of shewing a cold shoulder to two or three of it's habitués who *seceshionize*, or, what amounts to the same thing, throw their influence, whatever it may be, into the scale of opposition to the efforts of Government to repress rebellion at the South & privy conspiracy sedition & disaffection at the North. Succeeded I hope & believe in manifesting to them my desire we may be better strangers. *Ned Bell* is a Jackass, but I am sorry for *Macdonough*, who ought not, for many reasons, to have allowed himself to be misled into alliance with traitors & into writing smart editorials for the "World" newspaper.

Feb. 11th. Our "National League" makes hopeful progress. Only one man to whom I've spoken of it, declines subscribing himself a member — viz: John P. Crosby, who is thoroughly loyal & strongbacked. But he has the example of the Athenæum Club before his eyes, & fears personal liability for debts of the concern. No wonder, for I was stuck for $100.00 there in the most ridiculous way, long after I had resigned, & though I had never entered the Club House more than once or twice, & then for the sole purpose of paying my dues. I paid up promptly to save Pierrepont harmless, he being primarily liable. — Savings Bank Trustees met at 3½ P.M. Thence to 823. — Thence home. Thence to dinner at C.E.S.'s house. Present, M^r & Mrs Fred Sheldon, gorgeous Mrs Ritchie, Miss Georgey Berryman, Genl Burnside, Gen: Parke, Capt Bankhead of the Navy. After the ladies withdrew, there was an hour of good healthy talk on the value of Unconditional Loyalty. Parke was silent & seems insignificant, but Burnside & Bankhead are bricks. The latter is a South Carolinian! — Burnside is most honest noble & love-able, just what he was a year or sixteen months ago, at Willard's Hotel, with Bishop Clark. — N.B. There are signs of reaction in the Anti-administration party. John Van Buren's speech last night confirms them. Old Democratic leaders begin to see the impossibility of compromise & that opposition to the War must be their political ruin. Seymour & his pals are said to have decided that honesty is the best policy. The very *Herald* inculcates the duty of upholding the administration to the end of it's term! "Wonders have never done ceasing". The *World* & *Express* however continue to be coprophagous. — Talking of Bishop Clark — that dry caustic old Sir Mungo Malagrowther, the ingenious H.C. Dorr, says that what the Bishop especially loves & seeks to imitate in the life of our Great Exemplar is this — that "the Son of Man came Eating & drinking". I note this merely as an exquisitely characteristic Dorr-ism. The B^p's geniality, & healthy enjoyment of the good things of this life, are the reverse of ascetic, but they never run into excess, so far as my knowledge & information go. — Burnside said this ev'g that he fought the battle of Fredericsburgh on his own responsibility, & under no orders from Washington. That he considered victory certain, up to the moment when word was brought him that one of our Generals (on the right, I think — probably *Franklin* —) *was doing all he could to make the attack a failure*. That his first impulse was to ride off as fast as possible, confront the delinquent, & *shoot him*. But that considering the demoralization it would have produced, & the critical position of the army with a river in it's rear, he decided that it would not do & withdrew his columns. I fear Franklin & many of his brethren are, like the *late* Gen. F.J. Porter, bad cases of blood poisoning & paralysis from hypertrophied McClellanism. McC. has done the State some service, but is now doing it vast mischief — involuntarily & ignorantly, as I suppose. His popularity is unaccountable to me. It must rest on his unquestionable integrity, & his uncommon faculty of brilliant *Silence*, for his name is connected with no great victory. This Eastern lionizing tour of his, with it's addresses & receptions & presentations will do him no good. It tends to dethrone him.

Feb. 14. Last ev'g, we (i.e. Bellows Van Buren Gibbs & I, Exec: Committee &c) dined at Agnew's with D[r] *Bell* an eminent physician of Louisville & a leading man in his own community. He is here on special Hospital Inspection duty for the San: Com: — & seems a kindly cultivated intelligent person, of white-hot steel-edged loyalty. He says McClellan is decidedly unpopular with soldiers of our Western Army. [This confirms what Burnside said, that tho' McC possessed the highest qualifications for the conduct of the siege of Vicksburgh, he could not be safely sent to the West, because he would not be obeyed.] Bell says *Pope* is to Western soldiers what McClellan is to Eastern soldiers (!). And he thinks highly of Pope, whom he knows well. "You cannot believe a word he says & he would rather lie than tell the truth. But that is a constitutional weakness — a monomania. He is true & reliable in business & money matters, and probably the best General we have". A curious case, if Bell is right.

Feb. 16. To day's news is not from the South, but comes across the Atlantic. L. Napoleon seems steadily & stealthily picking his way toward Recognition or Intervention or both, encouraged by Northern Dirt-Eaters' shameless sympathy with Treason. It's a consolation to know that those scoundrels are most assuredly pickling a rod for their own backs. The game of *Anti-War* politicians is always difficult & dangerous. If Seymour Vallandigham & Co bring *foreign interference* upon us, political d—nation awaits them deeper than that of "Black-Cockade Federalists" & Hartford Convention men. — In England there seems strong reaction in our favor, mainly among the ungenteel classes. Large meetings applaud the Emancipation Proclamation of Jan. 1. The *Saturday Review* sneers at them in it's usual cynical style ignoring Right & Wrong in it's characteristic refined cultivated scholarly nobby godless way. These demonstrations will be duly considered by the Machiavel of the Tuileries, before he commits himself, — and they will have some influence in the action of Parliament which was to meet on the 4th. — but, strange to say, they will rather weaken the Administration with the masses here, as being British sympathy with accursed Abolitionists.

Feb. 17. Visit from G.A. in Wall St. He moves his school May 1st from the "old established stand" cor: 18th St. and Broadway to Dodworth's building on Broadway, 5th Av. & 27th St. This will be an improvement & enlargement. He means to get up drill classes, for which he will now have room, & I suggested the purchase of a light brass 6 pounder & carriage, wherewith to teach the manipulations of Artillery & take the wind out of the sails of all other Institutions of the sort. John Weeks called to talk "Union League". He is a well-to-do man but if he could draw checks as liberally as he draws inferences against the Administration, he could paper the outside of the Universe with $10.00 bills, & have fifties enough left for a deep border all around. That's a quotation from *Orpheus C. Kerr, second series*, just out. Not quite equal to first series, of course, but very smart & fresh.

The Judicious *Hooker* is said to have prohibited the circulation of the N.Y. World, Express, & other disloyal & dirt-eating papers within the lines of the Army of the Rappahannock. Good for Hooker. I dare say it's "*unconstitutional*", but I know of nothing so unconstitutional as Armed Rebellion against the Constitution. If the suppression of that Rebellion will be aided & expedited by the unconstitutional exclusion of Marble of the World & Brooks of the Express from their right to the "pursuit of happiness", & of profit, by the sale of their traitorous demoralizing newspapers in the camps of the National Army, I acquiesce in their suppression & exclusion as the lesser of two "Unconstitutional" alternatives.

Feb. 18. I will divert myself by recording the shindy at Belmont's Ballo in Maschera last night, as narrated to me by C.E.S. an eye-witness thereof. This was one of those stupid diluted masquerades at which all the women are masked & all the men *exposed*, like a fleet of old fashioned line of battle ships encountering a squadron of Iron-clads. His Durchlauchtigkeit the *Marquis of Hartington* was there, a gawky young English swell, of the Dundreary type, as I hear, with a lady in domino on his arm (who proved to be that handsome Secessionizing Mrs Yznaga). They stopped to speak to *Gen: McClellan*, & C.E.S. then observed with amazement that the illustrious μιλορδος was parading a showy little *Secesh flag*, conspicuously stuck in his button hole. After a little polite talk with McClellan, *disturbed by no manifestation of disapproval on his part*, (!) the pair resumed their promenade, & C.E.S. was looking about for *Belmont*, intending to make representations to him of this impropriety on the part of his guest, when little Johny Heckscher came along & gave the Marquis a decided jostle or *butt*, observing at the same time, "It was intentional sir — quite intentional". The peer said "Hee-haw-w-w-what's the matter? — it's really vewy extawawdinawy" & walked on, followed by H. who repeated his aggressive demonstration, with a like protest against it's being supposed an accident, & added "I want to insult you, sir". The man stammered — decided to leave the lady on his arm in charge of some one else, & to go outside the ball-room with Heckscher for an explanation, & H. told him at last, "if you do not instantly take that thing out of your button-hole, I'll pull it out." So Great Britain took it out & put it in it's pocket, & (I'm told) apologized to Heckscher afterwards, very frankly, on the ground of ignorance, & absence of intention to offend. Good for Heckscher, & not very bad for the young Englisher, who had been consorting with W. Duncan & Belmont & naturally thought sympathy with Rebellion *the thing* in N.Y. — — Pity it's wrong & disreputable to put incidents like this into the newspapers. An ingenious operator could use this affair so as to do much good. McClellan's indifference — the ire of the young lieutenant, discharged for disability from wounds received on the peninsula — the Bloated British Aristocrat flaunting a Rebel flag in a gorgeous ball-room crowded with the millionaires of New York — but snubbed & suppressed & driven to apologize! The subject has immense capabilities.

Feb. 19. More piracies by the "Alabama" reported today. Gold up to 162! Even pennies — nickel & copper, at a premium of 18. — Ruination confidently to be expected. Let it come if we can only save the Country. I can make my living as a pauper with any man, & E. would enjoy Bohemia. The three boys can fight the battle of life for themselves, as their betters have done before them.

Feb. 20. No news in Wall St. The little shreds & chips of intelligence that reach us from Vicksburgh are worth little, but their indications are good. Our glimpses into the position & prospect of affairs on the Atlantic Coast are less encouraging. We are about making a grand attack by land & Sea in Charleston or Savannah, probably the former, and either Skunk will require a great deal of killing. Binney telegraphed me that a Committee of the Philad: Union Leaguers was coming here for conference & fraternization, so I telegraphed back, inviting them to meet a few of our N.Y. friends on these premises to night. — Reluctantly — because I feared to disturb poor Ellie with front-door-bell-ringing. But she declared it would do her good to hear "something going on", so I abandoned certain half-formed plans of calling on my next door neighbour, C.P. Kirkland, & asking him to let me turn over my guests to him, and received the delegation here. They were Judge Hare, Welsh, Gerhard, Trott (who tells me poor Bob Le Roy is in an insane asylum) Brown, Ashhurst (grandson of Chancellor Kent), Ellis Yarnall, Harding the patent-lawyer, & two or three more. To meet them were Agnew, Gibbs, Bellows, G.F. Allen, Hoppin, Prof. Dwight, & a few others, including Chas King, whom we made a sort of informal chairman. Satisfactory ev'ng. We are much stimulated & stirred up by the vigorous talk of our Philad^n brethren.

Feb. 24. We had a meeting of some 50 or 60 "Union Leaguers" at 823 Bdway, Sat: night. Besides those heretofore enlisted, were Geo: Griswold, Jona: Sturges, Dr Lieber (a nuisance), Jno Austin Stevens J^r (J^r in the superlative degree), F.H. Delano, Dr Buck, Dr Parker, Otis D. Swan & Albert Mathews, &c &c &c. Meeting was long & earnest, & it's result unsatisfactory to me. Dr Bellows went off at half-cock — a way he has — & proposed to substitute the vague unsubstantial "platform" of the Philad[a] League for ours — wh: was done accordingly. The rest of our work was comparatively unimportant. They offered me the Sec ship — wh: I declined & Otis Swan was elected — a very good man. I tend to become disgusted with the League. James Brooks & F. Wood could sign its test of membership conscientiously, if either had a conscience.

Also a little if not a good deal disgusted with certain movements at our S. Com: Washington office, about which Gibbs & Agnew discoursed me while in bed last ev'g. — Also a great deal disgusted with the general coloring of our reports from Vicksburgh, which is livid bluish & looks very bad. — Henry Derby looked in a few minutes just now — my young Harvard nephew now on a visit next door. He's a fine spirited handsome young fellow, & has just been improving his vacation by a tour all over the West, seeing everything & everybody, & bringing up at the White House for a week's visit — the junior Lincoln being one of his classmates. He saw much of Uncle Abe & seems to have been favorably impressed. Of M[rs] A. he would say nothing but that she was very kindhearted. Henry is a wellbred boy.

Feb. 26. I have spent the day mainly in arranging pamphlets & Circulars, & "mounting" newspaper slips with paste & a hot flat iron, for a 4th volume of San: Commission Documents. Mine is the only complete series of our papers that's extant, & includes a great deal of what Prof: McVickar used to call "additional information" — Circulars — advertisements — exsected paragraphs — &c &c &c. It is worth while to keep it up now. The three volumes already bound up in full russia will be valuable 50 years hence.

March 2. To night at 823. Meeting of Committee of "Union League". We are sticking in the mud, floundering among diverse theories of what we ought to be. Club-house or mere Association with $10. or $25. annual dues? — After we have passed a certain point & settled these & other questions finally, no matter which way, we shall begin to develop fast.

No public news of any moment to day. This *Congress* has little more than 24 hours of life left it, & a vast deal of most weighty work to finish up. If the "Copperheads" undertake to "fillibuster", & retard legislation, they can do fearful mischief before the next midnight — they can paralyze the Administration & kill the Country. But I do not think they will try to do it.

March 5. Last ev'g at meeting of Nominating Committee of Union League. We make progress toward organization, but far too slowly. This ev'g at D[r] Bellows' with Agnew & Gibbs — meeting satisfactory as to work done & supper eaten. We agree fully as to the necessity of a radical change in the relations of the Washington office to the Commission & the Executive Committee. Olmsted is unconsciously working to make himself the Commission. Perhaps he is competent to do all the work of the Commission without advice or assistance. If so, I for one am inclined to withdraw & let him have all the credit of doing it. — Wall St: in great commotion to day. Gold suddenly down to near 150! Jewry is grievously stricken & the tents of Israel are in affliction. The hooked noses that have infested Exchange Pl: & William St. for the last two months were quivering & pale with ill concealed emotion this morning. This fall is an important event, probably. It may however prove to be nothing but a temporary fluctuation. — War news very little, & not good — though people seem generally in a sanguine fit just now — I can't tell why. At or near Vicksburgh the rebels have certainly captured the valuable iron-clad gun-boat *Indianola* — & will doubtless use her against us with damaging effect. There were reports that seemed credible of success at Vicksburgh, but they are not confirmed & must be given up. Letters from D[r] Newberry's Inspectors there received at N[o] 823 give a fearful account of the sickness that prevails in the besieging army. More than 13000 men in hospital with diarrhœa & pneumonia. Hardly one third it's numerical strength free from disease. Great destitution. We telegraphed Newberry to be reckless in expenditure of money & in requisitions for supplies.

March 6. At 823 Broadway this aft[n] on my way up town from a brief excursion to Wall St. Did not dine. Took a cup of tea in the library & enabled myself to totter feebly down to 823 again at eight for a meeting of our nascent *Union League*. Thirty or forty present. Among them R.B. Minturn & Geo: Griswold.

Both seem inclined to take hold very hard. Leading merchants are essential to our success. We made considerable head way to night — raised annual dues from $10. to $25. and gravitated toward the *Club-house* plan, on which alone we can accomplish anything. There was a little *scena* with Jn° Austin Stevens J[r], who has been cantankerous & disputatious & obstructive because it was not taken for granted that *he* was to play first violin part in our organization.

March 10. A dingy day. Returning from Geo. Griswold's (90 5th Av:) an hour ago, I found with disgust that it was snowing again, & the same continues. Griswold, Minturn, Geo. C. Ward & I were together as Committee on building for the Union League Club House. We agreed that Henry Parish's house on Union Square would make the best of possible club houses, & I am to get the refusal of it.

March 11. At 823 this aft[n]. — A curious correspondence sent us by the Surgeon General. Autograph letter from the President to him, asking him to employ in the Hospitals a certain quack named *Forsha*, proprietor of a certain Oil, which acts like magic on all wounds & contusions. Another letter to the same effect signed by Blair, Bates, Welles & others of the Cabinet, & a copy of the S.G's reply, stating that *Forsha* is an ignorant pretender, & that if he wants his panacea used by the Med: Bureau, he must reveal it's ingredients. This does not indicate a profound wisdom in our National Councils.

I fear Olmsted is mismanaging our San: Com: affairs. He is an extraordinary fellow — decidedly the most remarkable specimen of human nature with whom I have ever been brought into close relations. Talent & energy most rare. Absolute purity & disinterestedness. Prominent defects, a monomania for system & organization *on paper* (elaborate, laboriously thought out, & generally impracticable) and appetite for *power*. He is a lay Hildebrand. There will be a battle when the Commission meets — & incredible as it seems to myself, I think without horror of the possibility of our being obliged to appoint somebody else *General Secretary*.

The Cincin*naughty* "Branch" seems to have repented & returned to it's allegiance.

March 13. Conferred with R.J. Dillon about a lease of the Henry Parish house on N. side of Union Square for our "National Club" or "Union League" Headquarters. His views about rent are high-toned but not impracticable. To night some 30 or 40 of us met at the small Chapel of the "University". Cha[s] King in the Chair, received reports of Committees & made a little headway, harmoniously & smoothly. R.L. Kennedy, Delano R.B. Minturn, Geo. Griswold, &c seem resolved that the Club shall be established. They have much influence & much money, & can command much more — but it is always safe to predict the failure of any project that requires $25000 a year, & holds out no promise of profit in return.

Exec: Com: of Sanitary Commission met here last night, worked from 8 to 10, & supped from 10 to 12 or a little later. E. & Miss Rosalie at the supper table, & much good talk there. — It would seem that D[r] Jenkins has resigned his position at Washington. If so, it will be hard to replace him. — Is this another fracture produced by Olmsted's intense strain on our system?

March 15. To night M[r] S.B.R. here, Murray Hoffman, the rather dilute Dixon, Senator from Conn:, Judge Shipman, & George C. Strong, late Adjutant Gen[l] on Butler's staff at New Orleans, & now promoted to a Brigadier Generalcy. We made us out cousins in the nth degree, as descendants of the venerable *Elder John Strong*, & he seems a man worth claiming as one's kin. Seldom so favorably impressed by a new acquaintance. He told us much that was interesting about Butler's rule at N.O. — the outrageous indecencies of the rebel women there, and their instantaneous suppression by Butler's much reviled *order* — the candid admission by leading secessionists that the order was right & necessary, & that they were grateful for it as keeping their wives & daughters from putting themselves in a false & perilous position — the embroilments with foreign Consuls — the black regiments — &c &c &c. It was interesting & instructive, but not encouraging as to the present prospects of the National Cause, with Banks ruling at N.O. instead of Butler. But allowance must of course be made for his official prejudice in Butler's favor.

March 16. Committee to nominate officers of Union League Club met at 823 this P.M. — viz: Griswold, R.B. Minturn, Agnew, Wolcott Gibbs, Franklin S. Delano, R.L. Kennedy & myself. On ballot Minturn nominated for Pres'dt. He protested against it, with entire sincerity & frankness, & urged Ham: Fish. But Fish's place in Ichthyology is with that fine high flavored East River species known as the *Weak Fish.* I do'nt doubt his loyalty, but he croaks & grumbles & desponds & does harm. *Non tali auxilio nec defensoribus istis.* We could'nt take him at any price. We also made up a good list of Vice Presidents. Every one seems hopeful & earnest, but I am not confident of success.

March 17. Caught Ja[s] W. Beekman just off for Albany, & discussed the advantages of an Act of the Legislature incorporating the U.L. Club. He agreed to try to put it through, if possible. It would be of great use, for weak brethren are deserting from dread of personal liability. Fred Sheldon & G.C.A. among the back sliders I regret to say. They should be ashamed of themselves, & will be, some day, I hope. Nominating Com: met 4 P.M. at 823 B'way & made progress. To night Exec: Com: of San: Com: met & supped at D[r] Van Buren's. Talked mostly of the feud between Stanton & the Surgeon Gen[l]. — & of measures to restore harmony between them, or to bring the case before the President or before the People. We came to no decision. Stanton seems trying to undermine D[r] Hammond, refusing to let him send an Inspector to the West, or to go thither in person, & using the general complaint of inefficiency in the Western Department against him. Hammond made a great mistake a year ago, when he generously asked for the appointment of our excellent old friend D[r] Wood — a fogy of the fogiest type — to his high place in the Medical Department. By virtue of that request Wood is presiding at S[t] Louis, & the good old gentleman is about as fit for that work as I am to take charge of A.T. Stewart's wholesale & retail departments.

March 18. This aft[n] at 823. Inspected the Parish House on Union Square with Griswold & Minturn. It is spacious & sumptuous & will suit the *National Club* or *Union League* better than any house in the City, location & all taken into account. But its elaborate profusion of plaster & putty decoration is fearful & wonderful. — Plaster Caryatides, life size, by the dozen, in attitudes of permanent agony, most uncomfortable to behold.

March 20. Friday. Winter not yet dethroned, by any means. It has been a frosty day. Personally plagued with sore throat & "coryza" — but did some little work down town, & got some little farther insight into the financial visitations that threaten us all. No matter. If we can save the Country I will enter the poor-house with resignation. Our War-news continues mixed. We have distinct intimations, thro' Rebel channels, of failure on the Yazoo, & repulse with loss at Port Hudson. But the latest Richmond papers are seeking to console Rebeldom for recent "*reverses*" in the S.W. by the assurance that the judicious *Hooker* is to be catawampously chawed up some of these days, & Washington to be taken. Hooker can probably take care of himself. Everything indicates that he has worked up that Army on the Rappahannock — thus far so unfortunate — to a degree of efficiency beyond the power of McDowell McClellan Pope & Burnside. Extras announced that our gunboats & Monitors have run past Fort Sumter & are bombarding Charleston. I am incredulous. — Meeting at N° 823 Bw. this aft^{n}. Exec: Com: of San: Com: & afterwards Nominating Com: of Union League Club. — At 8 P.M. to general meeting of the latter at the "Small Chapel of the University". It was harmonious & promising. Report of Nominating Com: confirmed nem. con. — Minturn Presdt & a very respectable catalogue of moneyed men V.P.s. — We may make the thing work. Minturn, Geo. Griswold, Delano, & other strong representatives of Capital & Commerce, are interested & active. Our negotiations with Danl Parish & Dillon will result in our hiring the hideous but spacious Parish house for one year, with the privilege of four or five, at $6000. rent — the lessor making all repairs & putting the house into a decent condition as to paint & paper. To furnish & carpet it throughout would cost not less than $20.000, but once in possession, we can make the basement rooms habitable, & with them as our own headquarters, bring in hundreds of new members, whose fees will enable us to fit up the whole house. We may thus associate into an organism some 800 or 1000 influential New-Yorkians who desire to sustain Government against Southern Rebellion & Northern Sectionalism, & strengthen Northern loyalty to the Nation, stimulate property holders & educated men to assert their right to a voice in the conduct of public affairs, National, State, & Municipal, & do a little something toward suppressing the filthy horde of professed politicians that is now living on us & draining our National Life by parasitical suction.

March 21. At two, Minturn, Delano, Geo Cabot Ward & Geo. Griswold came in to consult about the Parish house. The negotiation is in a most hopeful state, and seems virtually concluded on terms more favorable than I hoped for. It looks as if we should effect something. Walked up town with G.C.A. who is a little sore & sulky because he resigned off the proposed Club on certain cowardly crotchety frivolous grounds (dread of personal liability among them) & now begins to suspect he has done a silly thing. His mental constitution is peculiar, but he means right. — At 823 Bw: the Ex: Com: of San: Commission did a large amount of business. *Inter alia*, we despatched a detective to Conn: to look into a reported consignment of tons of lint & bandages to a certain paper mill, with directions to go thence to Baltimore & identify the consignors. — Also we ordered Dr H.G. Clark & one or two Medici beside (of his Hospital Inspection Staff) to *Louisville* to investigate the alleged discovery that *Bromine* is omnipotent against Erysipelas, pyæmia, & Hospital Gangrene.

March 23. The indomitable Farragut has run past the rebel works at Port Hudson, with loss of one steamer, grounded abandoned & burned. The tidings seem trustworthy. — Griswold & Delano came in to report that the Club-house negotiation with Dan'l Parish is happily concluded. — Walked up town with G.C.A. & attended to business at 823, some of which was interesting. After dinner to Com: of Admissions to "National League Club", (at 823) where we passed on near 100 names. That concern seems in a promising condition. — N.B. I am disappointed in my *moustache*, which now dates back to Feb. 22^d^, Washington's birthday, & the beginning of my recent "furuncular" seclusion. It's present aspect is imposing, but it is nevertheless a *failure*. For in the omnibus this morning, my next neighbour, to me unknown, entered into discourse with me on the weather, the state of the Country, & the price of gold, with a degree of freedom & facility for which I could not account, till I pulled the check string & rose to leave the vehicle, when he remarked — with an accent of cordial respect & regard "*Good* Morning, *M*^r *Jay*" — !!! It was a staggering blow, but I controlled myself. Is the establishment of my personal identity hopeless? Must my position before the Community continue incurably equivocal? Am I to walk the world all the residue of the days allotted me, half G.T. Strong & more than half John Jay?

March 24. At 823 as usual this aft^{n} — & on my way up with W. Gibbs, looked in at the Parish house. Workmen are already busy in the basement. The vulgarity & vileness of its costly decoration even *more* apparent on this second inspection. It's plaster caryatides are sufficient to account for it's late owner's cerebral disease. What sum of money would repay me for the necessity of *seeing* these hideous images every time I went up stairs to bed & for the consciousness that they were an integral part of my home & dwelling place? They are scarcely tolerable in a *Club-house* — or a gin-palace.

Long visit from Dr Lyman — Medical Inspector U.S.A. — this morn'g. Eulogizes work of San: Com: — thinks the Louisville discovery that Bromine controls Hospital Gangrene to be a fact — upholds Surgeon Genl Hammond — & tells me that he understands Inspector Genl Perley of Maine (a creature of Stanton's) has resigned.

Laurence Williams dismissed the Service!!! So say this morning's papers. He went to Washington a week ago, & has, I fear, got into some squabble with his superiors. We lose an accomplished officer, & I'm heartily sorry for his disgrace — But his heart was not in his duty, & his reckless imprudent talk has been bad enough to justify even this extreme & summary action against him.

March 26. The ev'g at meeting of Tr: Church Standing Com: at the Vestry office, & thence up town to W. Gibbs' where our Executive Com: brethren were in Session, Prof: Bache being added unto them. The usual symposium, lasting till near 12. — Dined yesterday with E. at C.E. Habicht's, with Osten-Sacken, Count Piper (?) the new Swedish Minister & eight or ten more. Sat between Miss Jenny Field & nice little Mrs Chapman, John Jay's daughter, and enjoyed myself of course. The atmosphere of Habicht's house is wholesome. (West 16th St. — Lewis Jones' house six or seven years ago, & afterwards, poor little Jemmy Pendleton's) — His tastes are refined, & the talk at his table is not confined to horses, wine, & stocks.

Gold down again! — 139 & thereabouts. Deo Gratias. Fears expressed in the street that it may get *below par*, yet. General tone of confidence. Gov^t^ stocks rising. There is ground for this blessed state of feeling — indeed it may be said to justify it's own existence. Our great peril has been diffidence & distrust of our own strength. But we seem a little more sanguine just now than the position & the progress of affairs entitle us to be. Rebellion is not yet squelched by any means, & we are not half thro' our troubles. On the Mississippi, in Tennessee, at Fredericsburgh, & at Charleston, great battles are imminent, and there are abundant chances of disaster at each point. — Moreover, we are (me judice, & between ourselves) nearer a War with England than we have been since the Trent affair. The exasperation of our leading merchants is becoming uncontrollable. If English shipyards send out any more *Alabamas* "to the Emperor of China", they are prepared to insist on *reprisals* & the seizure of every British ship or steamer in Northern ports. All this looks anxious. On the other hand, we learn from Southern newspapers that the Rebels are suffering for want of *food* — and that their Railroads are giving out — rails & rolling stock being used up. Ten miles an hour is their maximum speed, with half a load. Chivalry is powerless against this calamity, & it can get no base "mud-sill" mechanics to help it, even if it would condescend to invoke their aid.

March 29. Story of Senator Dixon calling on the Pres'd^t^, & suggesting a parallel between Secession and that first rebellion of which Milton sang. — Very funny interview. A.L. did'nt know much about *Paradise Lost* & sent out for a copy, looked through it's first books under the Senator's guidance & was struck by the coincidences between the utterances of Satan & those of Jeff: Davis — whom by-the-by he generally designates as "that 'tother fellow." — Dixon mentioned the old joke about the Scotch Prof^{r}, who was asked what his views were about the Fall of the Angels & replied "Aweel, there's much to be said on both sides". "Yes", said Uncle Abraham, "I always thought the Devil was *some* to blame".

March 31. Rumors abound, & seem to come from several & independent sources, that the Rebels are preparing to abandon Richmond. Incredible unless their lack of supplies & the failure of their R.R. transportation be much more serious than we suppose. The surrender of V^{a} would be a *cognovit* & concession, & would be recognized as such by the whole civilized world, & perhaps even by the rank & file of Alabama & Mississippi. I have not the least hope that they are as yet *near* being driven to so desperate a move. — — — But they deserve to be, for they are the Chinamen of Anglo-Saxondom, "fools & blind". They set up their dirty & wicked Rebellion relying on the Royal Supremacy of *Cotton*. *Cotton* was to control & coerce the sympathy and the money of Christendom into alliance with them. They did not count on blockaded ports. But suppose their ports had been left free, & rebel planters had enjoyed every facility for raising cotton & selling it — suppose their own programme had been performed — *how would they have got their bread-stuffs*? Yancey Davis Memminger & Co reply (tho' happily not present in the body) "with the proceeds of, or in Exchange for, our own Imperial Vegetable". They forgot that England & France & all Europe could not supply the plebeian wheat & corn the Confederacy would need, unless they bought the flour of the *Northwest*, and that their own traitorous scheme, if successfully carried out, would merely transfer the value of their Cotton-crops to the pockets of loyal farmers in Western New York Ohio &c.

April 2^{d}. Weather continues gray, chill, & ungenial. We have news to day of successful fighting in the West, tho' not on any large scale, and the Rebel foray into Kentucky seems advancing backward. Report that Burnside is advancing on East Tennessee. I hope he is. Why that important wedge of loyal territory, penetrating into the heart of seceshdom, has been so long neglected, & it's people left to be harried by beastly gangs of merciless rebel marauders, is (to me) *the* one great inscrutable mystery in our conduct of the War. — From Vicksburgh & Port Hudson our tidings are bad, and indicate probable failure. *Fiat Voluntas Tua* — and let us try again. — — Rhode Island Election results in decided triumph of the Administration party. May the Copper-heads and coprophagous vermin of Connecticut expend their venom and their stink to as little purpose as their R.I. congeners have done!

April 3. From Trinity Church to Wall St. Walked up with G.C.A. who dined here. Stopped at N° 823 on the way. Agnew & Bellows there. A new knapsack submitted for our inspection, that seems a material improvement on the Regular Army article. — "Gen[l] Talcott", our State Q.M. Gen[l] called to talk of a proposed "Home" for N.Y. soldiers — for which the State Legislature has appropriated $50.000, & about the organization of which he wants *advice*. Our long conference gave him new ideas, & may prove worth much to our discharged & disabled N.Y. volunteers, now returning in crowds.

Our Club Com: on Admissions entered into possession of the Parish House to night, with all its appurtenances, plaster nymphs & papier maché grotto included. The dining room is now furnished & carpeted, neatly & inexpensively. Griswold, Delano, John Weeks & Hoppin were with us. The Exec: Com:, Griswold Weeks Delano &c seems to be working diligently & discreetly, & the whole house will soon be in order. Not much less than 1000 paying members will be necessary to run the machine. I think we can find them. 250 are now registered & in full communion. 100 more, or thereabouts, have signified their adhesion informally.

April 4th. Sat. As bleak & wintry a day as any last January. Snow set in heavily at one P.M. and its now raining hard, & blowing like mad from all quarters at the same time (11.30 P.M.) & the rain freezes as it falls — at many points. — Nothing notable down town. At N° 823 this aft[n] was D[r] Van Buren & no one else. We discussed & despatched sundry matters. — V.B. is among the best specimens of humanity I have ever known.

His moral weight & worth are immense — but he is utterly unconscious of his own value. I can think of no other living man whom I would class with *my father* as of absolute moral integrity — as governed always by a clear instinctive perception of duty, unclouded by personal or party considerations. — A. (for example) sees things wrongly now & then because of his intense Calvinistic Ultra Protestantism — B. is constantly acting prematurely & repenting it afterwards. X. Y. & Z. are disinterested honorable public spirited men, but considerations of personal interest seem to influence them sometimes. — But V.B. is always right.

We have not yet opened the Mississippi. Our strategic operations for the reduction of *Vicksburgh* & *Port Hudson* have failed, and Farragut now between the two strongholds, with only two armed vessels, may be in a tight place. But he can fight himself out of it, if any one can. This aftn's report is that our batteries are about opening on Vicksburgh across the river, that strategy and circumvention are abandoned, & the place is to be taken by an attack in front. An unpromising enterprise. Our batteries do not out-weigh those of the Rebels, & theirs hold the better position & can deliver a plunging fire from the bluffs on their side of the river.

April 6th. There is reason to believe that the attack on Charleston has commenced. Heaven prosper it. What little Dr Winston told me of the state of affairs at Port Royal, when he returned thence a week ago, was discouraging. The Navy takes 36 or 40 guns into action against 250 in Sumter, Moultrie, "Battery Bee" &c, and the coöperating land force is (by his account) inefficiently commanded by Hunter, in internal discord about the propriety of enlisting black men, & distrustful of their General. — Very bad, but Dr Winston is a talking windy superficial fellow. — Report of the Joint Committee of Congress on the conduct of the War appears this morning. A very important paper, which I have not yet fully digested. It seems to damage Gen: McClellan & Gen: Franklin seriously, & the Presdt somewhat, — and furnishes farther evidence of Burnside's honesty singlemindedness & straightforwardness.

April 8. Wednesday. Another chill cloudy day, with a gleam or two only of sunshine this morning. I long for sunshine, of which we had so little these six weeks, and feel as I were becoming *etiolated* for lack of it. Wall St. as usual: then a meeting of Savings Bank trustees in Bleecker St. — then N° 823 — & after dinner to U.L. Club, where both the front basement rooms are now in order, & then was an irregular quasi-meeting of about 40, including a good many new faces — as John Alsop Griswold, one Schulze, Philetus H. Holt, Pierson, Satterlee, Wm A. Hall, Whitehead &c. — Com: on Admissions met thereafter. The fire was dying out, the rooms were chill, & I felt myself catching a new cold to help this plaguing cough, which is due I suppose to this pestilent weather.

Poor Larry Williams writes from Wash^{n} that he *supposes* his dismissal from the Service to be founded on his alleged "disloyal talk at the N.Y. Club", & especially on that unfortunate supper of 31 Dec. last, & seems to suspect *Cram* of having brought this upon him. I confess I am sorry for his dismissal disgrace & ruin, tho' I fear the justice & expediency of the action of Government are undeniable. Would that like measure could be meted to scores of other officers, whom I *do'nt* personally know. — — The grand meeting of Anti-Conscription Copperheads at Cooper Union last night was large but not lively. Fernando Wood & Co were depressed by the Connecticut elections. Very sad that Chas O'Conor should be found in such company. — — We are looking for weighty news from Charleston. We *must* be repulsed there I think (barring miracles) but many sensible people believe that the mass-meeting called for the 11th in Union Square to commemorate that Anniversary will have news of the recapture of *Sumter* to rejoice over. I trust their judgment may be better than mine, & thank Heaven that I have no rudiment of a Prophetic gift. — May this meeting escape dispersion by a rainy aft^{n}, & may it not have for it's chief office that of trying to stiffen up the backbone of loyalty against the depressing effect of bad news from N. Carolina! Genl Foster & his command seem in a tight place, — entrenched at "Little Washington" (?) but surrounded, & cut off from reinforcements by rebel batteries that command the river & shut off reinforcements from Newbern.

April 9. At 823 awhile with D[r] Bellows. Rec[d] a Report from D[r] Page, Inspector at Port Royal, which gives a favorable account of our affairs there, & of the prospects of this fearfully critical move upon Charleston. Dated, I think, 31st March. — It is good that we have no news of our operations in that quarter. The game must be opened before this, & if we were doing badly we should have heard of it by way of Richmond & Fortress Monroe. Still I hardly dare hope for success — though I try.

After dinner went off by myself to Acad: of Music (a thing I have scarcely ever done before), took a parquette seat & heard *Fidelio*, done by Madame Johannsen & the rest of Karl Anschütz's German Company. House was full, interested, unconversational, & applausive. Performance might have been much better, but it was a most satisfactory evening. The music tho' rather tough & refractory to one not familiar with it, is very noble. And the opera, dramatically considered, is less base & idiotic than most operas. The grave-digging scene & Leonora's *pistol* business are effective. They bring water into the eyes of weak people like myself, which hydraulic power is possessed by no other opera I know, except the Freyschutz & *Sonnambula*.

April 10. Another fine day, so the chances are it will rain tomorrow. Three consecutive days of sunshine would violate the meteorological laws now in force. As tomorrow's *Mass-Meeting* is likely to be saturated with metaphorical cold water, it can the less afford to be literally douched. — We have a glimpse of affairs in Charleston Harbor at last — through Rebel glasses. It is in substance this. Attack commenced 7th & was continued all day. The Ironsides & Keokuk grounded & were cut up, but got off afterwards. Nothing done on the 8th. A few casualties in Sumter. No reports from the other batteries. That is about all. It looks like a repulse. But rebel telegraphs lie fearfully — these despatches are silent as to many positions that must have been involved in the action — and their general tone is not jubilant. We may be doing well there. God grant it. But the odds are fearfully against us. 36 guns afloat are surely no match for *hundreds* on shore — some say 250, others 400. To me the enterprise has seemed insane & hopeless from the first. But it would not have been undertaken unless men who know vastly more about the matter than I do saw reason to expect it would succeed.

April 11. Sat: Fine day, *mirabile dictu.* Did little if anything in Wall St. for I shared the general gasping eagerness for news from Charleston. Nothing as yet that's authentic & trustworthy. The despatch, via Nashville, that reports "the Iron Clads repulsed" & a great battle on shore within sight of Charleston, is worthless. People are very anxious, but on the whole inclined to think favorably of the position, & to expect that the Nursery of Treason will be reduced & subjugated within ten days.

Up town rather early. John the Waiter brought Temple to Irving Hall, & we two heard Beethoven's 7th Symphony. How earnestly that dear little creature's head & hand — his whole little person, indeed — kept marking the time, & moving in response to the rhythm of the 2d & 3d movements! —

For the sake of this fascinating music I cut the earlier stages of the great Union Square meeting, the reception of Philada Delegates at the Astor House, the collation we gave them at Delmonico's, with speech by Judge Murray Hoffman — & the flag raising on the new Clubhouse (flag & fifty five feet of flagstaff presented by Geo: Griswold) & Bellows' *Gratias* on behalf of the Club. My default was wrong, unpatriotic, self-indulgent, but then life is short, & one's opportunities of hearing first-rate specimens of Beethoven's orchestral work are so few! I was not missed at the Collation or the Flag-raising. Both were fully attended.

April 13. Monday. Dingy weather again. We are fairly repulsed at Charleston, and with loss of one vessel, the *Keokuk*, an inferior soft-shelled variety of the Monitor. The odds were too great — & the harbor, with its obstructions, piles, nets & seines to entangle propeller screws, torpedoes, earth works, heavy guns &c &c, does Secesh-dom credit. — A bad business. Moreover Gen: Foster is still surrounded at Little Washington N.C. The attempt to reinforce him failed & he will probably have to surrender. Bad again. Jem & Ned Strong are on his staff & at W. — also Dr Fred Snelling. — Tippy Hoffman &

Messenger are at Newbern, which is also threatened. — How soon shall we crush the Rebellion at this rate? But the bread riots at Richmond Raleigh Petersburgh &c seem to indicate exhaustion & disorganization, or what D[r] V.B. calls "prostration with excitement."

April 14. *Laurence Williams* came in late to dinner, & we talked over his dismissal from the Service. He is full of talent tact and plausibility. Says he demanded a Court of Inquiry, a Court Martial, an investigation in any form, again & again — Does not incline to denounce the Administration for the wrong it has done him, but regrets for the sake of the Country that it should so treat it's officers. — Means to live down all charges of disloyalty — Has sacrificed all ties of family to the National cause & cannot go back without dishonor, however ill he may be treated, &c &c &c.

He announced his engagement to Miss *Law*. May it prosper. She is reported not handsome at all, but kindly & good. A rich wife & a few years in Europe will be best for him. — How to treat him is a doubtful question, but an old friend should have the benefit of every doubt. I w'ont throw him over, especially while he is under this cloud, without clearer evidence against him.

Miss Rosalie left us & returned to her home in Jersey City, yesterday, after a visit of several months!

We drift fast toward war with England, but I think we shall not reach that point. The shop-keepers who own England want to do us all the harm they can, & to give all possible aid & comfort to our slave breeding & woman-flogging adversary, for England has degenerated into a trader manufacturer, & banker, and has lost all the instincts & sympathies that her name still suggests. — She would declare war against us fast enough if she dared follow her sordid impulses, but there are dirty selfish considerations on the other side. She cannot ally herself with slavery, as she inclines to do, without closing a profitable market, exposing her Commerce to privateers, & diminishing the supply of bread-stuffs on which her operatives depend for life. — On the other side however is the consideration that by allowing piratical *Alabamas* to be built armed & manned in her ports to prey on our commerce she is making a great deal of money. — It's fearful to think that the sympathies of England — the England of Shakespeare & Hooker, Cowper, Milton, Somers, Erskine, &c &c &c &c &c — with North or South, Freedom or Slavery, in this great continental battle of her children, are guided by mere considerations of profit & loss. Anglo-maniac Americans, like myself, are thoroughly "disillusionated".

April 21. Tuesday. Fine weather again. Gibbs & Van Buren have returned from Washington. They bring full reports from Olmsted & Knapp of results of their Western explorations, which have been thorough & satisfactory. Olmsted candidly admits that sending him to Louisville Murfreesboro' & Vicksburgh was judicious.

Miss Sue Le Roy married to night, at Calvary Ch: to one L[t] Dresser U.S.A. She was with us at Vose's, Newport, last summer, & is a large generous kindly fine looking young lady, who will make a good wife, & to whom I hereby wish all manner of matrimonial felicity. E. has gone to the Wedding Reception, & I'm awaiting her return.

Yesterday's mass meeting of the *other* Union League (Cha[s] Gould's & Prosper M. Wetmore's) on Madison Square was successful in spite of the cloudy sky & cold wind. It looked more imposing than that of John Austin Stevens Jr's Union League a week ago. They say the former is a machine run by Seward, & that Chase pulls the wires of the latter, — & that each is an organization intended to influence the next Presidential Election. All stuff & nonsense probably, but these stories shew how watchful we must be in our U.L. Club to keep above suspicion of mere political partizanship. — Our Com: on Admissions met last night, & did *not* pass Hiram Barney on this ground alone — tho' I could have given additional reasons for not passing him as fit to associate with hightoned & honorable men.

Death of M[rs] D[r] Metcalfe (Ja[s] Colles' daughter) — She sank after a premature confinement brought on by an attack of "gastritis" or some such thing.

Gen: Hooker seems pushing his left toward Gordonsville. If he can take & hold that point he will reduce Lee's facilities for transportation of supplies by R.R. one half at least, & will compel Lee to elect between an attack at disadvantage or a retreat toward his base of operations. The rebels seem to have given up their attack on Gen. Foster's position at Washington N.C. as a bad job, and there has been fighting on the *Nansemond*, resulting in the capture of prisoners & guns. So says Report.

Dr Marsh, one of our San: Com: Inspectors, just from Port Royal, says the *1st S.C.* is the best Regiment he has ever seen — the best disciplined & drilled, the most subordinate, & the most pugnacious. It's a Regiment of Niggers with an infusion of Florida Seminole blood. One Sunday morn'g he hid behind a tent & heard a sermon addressed to them by an Ethiopian Habakkuk Mucklewrath of ninety & upwards, to whom they listened as to an Apostle & Prophet. He told them they must kill as many rebels as possible, but treat all prisoners kindly — that if killed while on duty they would go straight up to Heaven, and that the more rebels they had knocked over, the faster they would get there. Whereupon the congregation hallooed & Hallelujahed.

April 22. Fine weather. Walking up town with G.C.A. met Lt Col. Kimball's funeral procession, a showy turn-out. He was a good officer. Genl Corcoran shot him in a controversy about the Genl's right to pass somewhere, which Kimball forcibly resisted. One or the other was guilty of flagrant violation of military rule, but it is uncertain which. — At 823, spent some time with Agnew, just from Hooker's headquarters. He dined with H. who says that he intends to destroy Lee's army or his own within a week. Morale of our people good. Sickness rate low, about 7 p:c: — Agnew much dissatisfied with the administration of our supply-depots &c connected with this Army, & thinks all our agents there but Kerlin & Harris incompetent. — There is a set-off in the complimentary & eulogistic resolutions the Ohio Legislature has been passing about the Commission.

At G.F. Allen's to night — 42 E. 24th St. — Com: on College Course. We agreed on a sensible course for Prof. Nairne's department. I wish there were hope that it's adoption would make him resign. No danger of that!

Bull Anthon rather seriously ill. Rheumatic gout. Much reduced, feverish, flighty, & talks Greek all night long.

Public affairs have looked brighter for a day or two. Rebel attacks on Suffolk V[a], & Little Washington N.C. have failed — & we have taken prisoners & guns. Fighting near Corinth — Memphis — & in Louisiana — with advantage on our side, as it seems. The upper Mississippi flotilla has run the batteries of Vicksburgh with inconsiderable loss. "Choctaw County Mississippi" said to have seceded from secession-dom, disgusted by conscription laws & short commons. Georgia Legislature declines endorsing Confederate Bonds. "Bread-riots" in the cities of the South that were to wax so wealthy & prosperous the moment the incubus of Yankee rule was taken off them. — Our iron-clads at Port Royal having repaired damages are as good as new & ready for another shy at Sumter & Charleston. — Strong signs of reaction in England, for her shop-keepers begin at last to perceive that the precedent of neutrality they are setting may be used to their fearful damage the next time they are at War & that if we had allowed *Alabamas* to be built equipped & manned in N.Y. & Boston in /54, England would have lost much monish — the only thing England cares for now. So England is beginning to look a little into her Ship-yards.

April 25. Bellows has returned from Washington & Gen: Hooker's headquarters, & told me part of his experiences this aft[n]. — The War Department has issued an order (N[o] 87 I think) about transportation of medical & sanitary stores, that seriously curtails the privileges Government gives us. I think it was issued inadvertently & in no unfriendly spirit, but D[r] B. declares he will resign & make open War on Stanton unless it is resolved or corrected by an explanatory order. He discussed the matter with the Solicitor of the War Dep[t] (Whiting?) an old College friend of his, & in confidential relations with Stanton, Whiting brought the matter before his chief. Stanton said he had not intended to attack the San: Commission & had not foreseen the injury his order would do the Commission. But that he did not want to revoke or retract anything at it's request or to promote its objects. He was no friend of the Commission — disliked it — & in fact detested it. "But *why*, M[r] Stanton, when it is notoriously doing so much good service, & when the Medical Department & the whole Army confide in it & depend on it as you & I know they do?" — "Well" said the Sec[y] "the fact is the Commission wanted Hammond to be Surgeon Gen[l] & I did not. I did my best with the President & with the Military Com: of the Senate, but the Commission beat me & got Hammond appointed. I'm not used to being beaten, and do'nt like it, and therefore I am hostile to the Commission". This is certainly frank. It does not increase one's respect for Stanton, or indicate that he is specially qualified for his great place by peculiar unselfishness or patriotism. It is in fact a *Cognovit* on which mankind can enter judgment against Stanton as a Caitiff & a Scoundrel. But whatever he may do or say, it is our plain duty to make no assault on him, & to do nothing that can tend to weaken any one man's faith in the National Government. With our money, our affiliated organizations all over the Country, & our good repute with the People, I believe we could unseat the Sec[y] of War, if Agnew & Bellows & Gibbs & I chose to use the resources of the Commission against him, & that within 30 days. We shall make no such attempt however, with my consent, but on the contrary be to his virtues (whatever they are) very kind, & be to his failings very blind indeed, & *stick up for* the National Government, i.e. the present Administration, — Stanton & all — thro' thick or thin.

Stanton must keep his griefs mostly to himself, for Seward told D[r] B. that the President & the Cabinet were strong in approval of the Commission; that they had consented to recognize an outside agency, & give it a semi-official position, very reluctantly, & only because they could not decently say no, & that they had taken it for granted the Commission would collapse & die a natural death within a year after it's appointment, at latest. But "the Commission has made itself a necessity, and it has done it's very difficult & delicate work with so much discretion tact & ability that" — &c &c &c.

"Fine words". I wonder what Seward really knows about the matter.

April 27. Monday. News from Gen[l] Banks most satisfactory. He is doing a good work in Western Louisiana. This will re establish public confidence in his capacity, which has been weakened, justly or unjustly, by bad reports from New Orleans ever since he succeeded to Gen. Butler's place.

April 29. After dinner to U.L. Club house, by appointment, to meet F.H. Delano, Ja^{s} B. Johnston, Dodge, Faile &c. Capital pencil sketches of battle scenes by a drummer boy in David's Island Hospital, who comes from the mountains of Vermont & never saw a *picture* or had an hours' teaching in his 16 years of life. Julian Scott is his name, I think. — — — Last night we had the Exec: Com: of San: Com: here, with Prof: Bache, & at the supper table Dr Gouley U.S.A.

This aftn's papers report Gen: Hooker crossing the Rappahannock.

April 30. No newspapers this aft^{n} and no news to day reliable or unreliable. Hooker is supposed to be making a flank movement & proposing to cross the upper Rappahannock. He will either succeed splendidly or fail disastrously within twenty days. Chances about even. Meantime the South must suffer for lack of food at least six weeks longer, or until their wheat is harvested, and I think their suffering is & will be serious. There may be corn & bacon enough South of the Ohio & the Potomac to feed the people of that region, but it's worn-out R.R. transportation hardly suffices for military purposes & cannot be used to carry a surplus from one point to another where there is deficiency. Hence our contradictory reports of starvation & of abundance — each time at the locality whence it comes. — It is nearly time for the Pestilence which, by Physiological Law & according to History, comes after War & Famine. It's horrid to think coolly & almost complacently of these miseries present & prospective — but if any people ever deserved a desolating visitation of Divine Vengeance, it is this Slaveholding tribe who brought this cruel ruinous War upon the country in sheer wilfulness & personal pique, because an Election resulted in what might be considered a vote of want of confidence in certain peculiar privileges of their own, which it neither affected nor endangered in the smallest degree — these peculiar privileges being the legal right to do the greatest wrong authorized by the laws of any Nation in Civilized Christendom. — — — It is nearly time, too, for this Rebellion to produce it's *B. Arnold* — a commodity the South must be able to manufacture on the largest scale. I predict a "pronunciamento" in favor of the Union from some Southern General within a year — at longest.

May 1. Our only news is that Hooker seems to have crossed *below* Fredericsburgh, taking rebel pickets & outposts by surprise. The movement seems to have commenced on the 27th. All details are kept very close, as they should be. There is rumor that the attack on Charleston is to be repeated forthwith. Improbable.

At Socy Library to night, looking thro' English magazines & papers. Their misrepresentations about us are amazing & many of their blunders must be dishonest & malignant. *Fuit Anglia*, at least for me. The fairminded honest old English people, in which I believed so many years so firmly, has ceased to exist — "subjectively", that is.

May 2d. To day's news is good, tho' somewhat obscure. Hooker's great movement across the Rappahannock seems to prosper. Within a week we shall hear of a great decisive battle between Fredericsburgh & Richmond. God help us! Amen. — There is report of a demonstration agst Richmond by our forces in S.E. Va, at Ft Monroe, Yorktown & Suffolk. What I most fear is that Hooker is dislocating his Army, but the few details given by the newspapers cannot be relied on. Bellows & Agnew estimate him 140.000 strong, & he told them he did not believe he had 80.000 in front of him.

May 4th. Monday. A mild showery day. Morning papers tell us nothing, but at 10 A.M. the boys are shrieking an Extra Tribune with "reliable" intelligence dated yesterday A.M. In substance as follows. Our left across the Rappahannock, occupying Fredericsburgh & the "first line" of works behind it — carried with little loss — and "feeling its way" toward a hypothetical "second line". Our Right (and our centre also I suppose) at a one house Village called *Chancellorsville*, around which there was *battle*. The traitor General, Lee, held the works behind F-burgh with only a rear-guard & had thrown himself in force on Hooker at Chancellorsville or thereabouts. Stoneman is believed to have cut the R.R. lines behind the Rebel Army. If so, Lee's position is most critical. He is likely to be destroyed unless he gain decisive victory over our superior force.

Telegram at N° 823 this P.M. from San. Com. Washington office — *calling for large supplies of Hospital stores.*

After dinner to U.L. Club House. Agnew Faile Gibbs, Swan &c there. Sought news but there is none in town.

We are strangely phlegmatic & philosophical, for hours so awfully critical as these. No sign of special excitement in Wall St. this morning; no crowding around newspaper offices. The common talk was that we are doing well, & that Hooker has executed a splendid bit of strategy, with great promise of decisive success. Many expect the annihilation of Lee's Army, but the majority are more reasonable. McClellanites already laying an anchor to windward as a precaution against the effects of any possible achievement of Hooker's. "Officers & men are so much more experienced now than a year ago" when our Fabius Minimus commanded them — "Hooker is not thwarted by Government as McClellan was" &c &c &c. The tone of feeling is indicated by a *fall* in *Gold*. But Croakers think H. will be cut up — that he has been enticed into a trap & fights with a river behind him — that x + y men have joined Lee from S. Virginia & as many more from Charleston. They dwell moreover on a rumor of disaster & stampede in one of our divisions. We have had about 250 rumors good & bad, all of them "Authentic".

My anticipations are gradually settling downward. I now expect Hooker to *fail*, tho' perhaps after punishing the enemy severely. The obstinate silence of the War Department — the absence of official reports — is uncomfortable, and if the rebels be in the tight place in which we suppose them, they will assuredly fight like cornered Rats.

May 5. Tuesday. N.E. storm. Details in morning papers of fighting on Sat: & part of Sunday. Very severe & deadly, but we seem to have gained ground on the whole, taking guns & prisoners & colors, in spite of the dastardly defection of certain German regiments which broke & ran. The best report is that of the *Times*, but it's writer is too manifestly a *claqueur* of Hooker's. A son of John P. Crosby's, Captn or L^{t} in a U.S. Artillery regiment, & a promising spirited young officer, with whom I had some slight acquaintance, has died in his duty.

This aftn's papers enlighten us but little. The rumors they publish are that Lee attacked again yesterday morn'g & was repulsed — that Stoneman has cut the R.R. bridges on the Mattaponax & the Mattapony, & that part of his command "has taken Gordonsville & 7000 prisoners". The last item I wholly discredit. The rest is not incredible. But the continued reticence of Gov[t] is a bad sign.

May 6. Storm continues uninterrupted all day, with hard rain & ferocious N.E. wind. News *bad*. Sedgwick's division has been pushed off the heights behind Fredericsburgh, after severe fighting, in which it was grievously outnumbered, and seems to have recrossed the river to Falmouth, & then moved up the river to rejoin Hooker. But that can hardly be — for it would leave our vital R.R. artery between Falmouth & Aquia at the Mercy of the Rebel right wing, wh: now holds Fredericsburgh. It has been a "dark & dreary" day. We hear to night that Heintzelman is on his way from Washington with 30.000 men to support Hooker — & also that there are indications that *Aquia is to be abandoned*. Inexplicable, unless Hooker means to change his base to the Orange & Alexandria R.R. & make a dash for Richmond. If Stoneman has broken up the other R.R. line, on which Lee would in that case be obliged to depend, this move would seem promising. But where *is* Stoneman & why have we no information about him? He seems to have vanished into Space with his 12000 horse. This heavy rain makes it impossible to move either Army just now, I suppose, & *may* be bothering Lee more than it bothers Hooker. If Stoneman has done his work & cut that R.R., (this storm swelling the streams & making the country roads impracticable), the traitor Army can get neither reinforcements nor supplies. Much depends on that IF! Stoneman's operations probably decide the result of the campaign.

Lazed in Wall St. finding any kind of work impossible. At N[o] 823 this aft[n]. We have sent off D[rs] Marcou, Gurdon Buck, & Harry Sands, to assist the Medical Staff, & three "dressers" with them. To night at U.L.C. house, where were about a dozen of us. The 2[d] Story rooms are now carpeted & somewhat furnished, & were lit up. — The Exec: Com: has done it's work very well. — We discussed arrangements for the Opening on the 12th, when there is to be a slight soirée with nothing to eat or drink — also a few little speeches.

It is delightful to perceive that "respectable" Copperheads begin to be aware of this Club, and to squirm as if it irritated them somehow. E.g. Willy Duncan at the Opera last night favored Mrs Eleanor Strong with his views about it. He thought it very wrong & bad. "No Club had ever been established before on a political basis. (!!!) It would do great mischief. Great efforts had been made by it's leading members to prevail on him to join it, but he had felt it his duty to decline." Very funny; for in all our talk about organization & tests of admission, the name of W[m] Butler Duncan has been familiarly used as a convenient familiar specimen of the class we would not admit on any terms.

May 7. Thursday. Storm continues, but grows less savage. It is cloudy & cold & Northeasty, but rain has ceased. Moral coloring of the day livid-blue. *Failure* & *Repulse* again! Hooker has retired across the Rappahannock, & is where he was a month ago, but no doubt sorely shattered. It's some consolation however to believe that the Rebel Army has likewise undergone a fearful clawing & suffered more than we have. The worst consequence of this failure is that we lose the faith we felt in Hooker a few days ago, when he seemed likely to be the man we have been so long trying to find. An incomprehensible telegram came to N[o] 823 from D[r] Kerlin at Aquia or D[r] Douglas at Washington, I forget which. "*Col.*" [qu: Columbia?] badly hurt but not mortally. Obliged to retire from active duty for a few days. No operation likely at present." We conclude that it is framed in reference to Telegraph Censorship & means "the army has been unsuccessful but is not defeated. Another battle will not take place immediately."

I fear many of our wounded have been left on the field.

This afternoon's tidings tend to raise our spirits. Hooker largely reinforced (why not a week earlier?) & Stoneman said to have done his work thoroughly, cutting both lines of R.R., destroying no end of bridges, depots, & rolling stock, & penetrating to within 5 miles of Richmond. — If so, & if we are correctly informed as to the mode in which Lee & his men get their dinners, Lee will have to *move* — for these R.R. bridges cannot be rebuilt in a day, even were all these rivers, creeks, & "runs" not in fullest flood by reason of this rain-storm. — Will Hooker be strong enough to follow him up if he fall back toward his base of supply?

May 8. Friday. This weary storm seems to be ended, & a few stars shew themselves to night. Our news from V[a] is scanty, but on the whole favorable — especially so as regards the condition of Hooker's Army. His movement has failed, but he brings back guns, colors, & prisoners. Gen: Banks' success in over-running & occupying nearly all Louisiana, & the Capture of the Rebel Works at "Grand Gulf" (confirmed to day) with prisoners & heavy artillery, more than offset this check, in which, moreover the rebel loss doubtless exceeds our own.

Still, I cannot help feeling fearfully depressed — on many grounds. These are dark days. But I take credit to myself for letting nobody know I think so — for consistent optimism in all my talk, and especially for throwing a stone every day at those two inveterate Croakers C.E.S. & Bidwell. They are not copperheads in the least, but Frogs, or Ravens, whichever you please.

Went into the New Club House with Agnew after we left N° 823 this aft[n], and from it's balcony saw the Return of that Splendid Regiment the N.Y. 5th — "Duryée's Zouaves" — or rather of it's debris — less than 300. A touching sight when I remembered in what force I saw them march down Broadway two years ago — & that they had been twice recruited since then. They looked rugged bronzed & soldierly. The crowd was enthusiastic. Occasionally an officer, or one of the rank & file recognized some one on the sidewalk or at a window. The spectacle was a reality, & somewhat intense. It's sentiment is in the 4th movement of Beethoven's *Eroica*. I always thought that the meaning of the Finale of the Eroica & now I'm sure of it.

May 9th. Sat. — Sunshine once more, and hopeful news with it. Grant has taken "Willard Valley", wherever that is, & *Port Gibson* & is moving rapidly upon the Vicksburgh & Jackson R.R. after a battle in which he drove & disorganized a Rebel corps of 11.000. If he can cut that R.R. Vicksburgh falls without farther trouble. Accounts of Hooker's condition are satisfactory.

More "bread-riots", so called, in Southern towns — i.e. assemblages of viragos breaking into shops & helping themselves to whatever they want, & mostly to dry-goods of superior quality. This looks a little as if society were beginning to decompose down there. There seems to be no attempt at punishment. "Leading Citizens remonstrate", as Jeff Davis did at Richmond, with more or less effect, but I do not hear of any plundered miller or shop keeper being indemnified or getting his wares back.

May 12. Tuesday. Hot, & to night a lively thundershower. Down town late & cephalalgic. At N° 823, I find indications that a squabble with the Sec: of War & Dr Letterman (Hooker's Med: Director) may be at hand. Not an atom of tangible news to day — but "it is believed at" Memphis or some other place that Gen: Grant has taken *Jackson* & thereby made Vicksburgh untenable. We shall see. On the whole, we are hopeful & jolly to day. Van Dorn's death is established. He was shot by some other gentleman for certain liberties with the other gentleman's wife, a fit conclusion to a life of scoundrelism. It is also established that Stonewall Jackson lost an arm at Chancellorsville. Hooker's advance & Lee's retreat are *not* confirmed.

The Union League Club House was thrown open to night — "inaugurated," as the newspapers say. Each of our 350 members had three tickets & there were invited guests beside, Gen: Wool & his staff, Dr Vinton &c &c &c. The house was very fairly filled, & was very appropriately & prettily decorated for the occasion under Richd Hunt's artistic supervision. The assemblage was made up of nice people, & included many very nice & pretty women. Several persons said it was "brilliant", but I do not precisely know what they meant. Ellie enjoyed the ev'g hugely. Our Pres'dt, Minturn, made a little speech & introduced successively Geo: Bancroft & Dr Bellows who made, each, a good & effective 15 minute oration. The performance was decidedly successful. Only two Copperheads got in, to my knowledge, Ned Bell & W.H. Appleton, the bookseller. *Bell* was frightfully out of place. Who could have given him a ticket? Griswold, Delano & Minturn seemed half disposed to wait on him as a Committee & request him to clear out.

May 13. Wednesday. Warm day. Aft^{n} & ev'g showery. To day's only news is a seemingly trustworthy report that that very valiant rebel *Stonewall Jackson* died last Sunday of pneumonia, which attacked him while weakened by a recent amputation. He seems to have been a brave capable earnest man, good & religious according to his Presbyterian formulas, but misguided into treason by that deluding dogma of State Allegiance.

May 15. At U.L. Club awhile to night. I go there whenever I can, on principle, to help make the place seem frequented. Twenty or thirty men there. Prospects good. Griswold, Hoppin, Delano, Swan, Jno Weeks & others are working hard. One element of Club life appeared on our premises for the first time. We had Lager & Cigars.

May 16. Little news, or none, these two days. Our attention is now concentrated on Vicksburgh. If Grant carry that stronghold of Rebellion he opens the Mississippi & cuts Seceshdom in two, as an unfeeling schoolboy bisects a wasp. The (Eastern) tail of the insect may be able to sting cruelly for a certain period thereafter, but it's speedy death & decomposition are inevitable.

June 15. Thank God, I feel a little like myself this morn'g — and seem to see a glimpse of coming Emancipation. Last ev'g I spent two or three hours down stairs. A lot of people came in, & I retreated before ten o'clock, & our usual slight supper, tired out. I have gained strength during these last three days, but am still as weak as warm water in it's 20th homœopathic dilution. No wonder, after four weeks of confinement to library & bedroom, & mostly to bed — thin diet & heroic dosing — two weeks of the four having been, also, a weary period of intense physical pain recurring hourly at least — night & day. This illness began the 19th of last month, when I felt utterly prostrate & limp.

As to the War & Things in General. Much has been going on. I am too flaccid to particularize. This is the first day I've omitted undressing & going formally to bed for four or five hours in the afternoon. There is a dreamy recollection of great news & much jubilation some 3 weeks ago, over Grierson's splendid cavalry raid from the Tennessee frontier all the way to Baton Rouge, & of Gen. Grant's brilliant campaign behind Vicksburgh, fighting five battles, & taking 80 guns & 10.000 prisoners. Vicksburgh had fallen — or was to fall day after tomorrow at latest. But it has'nt fallen, & Grant is laying formal siege to it, an assault having failed. Banks is addressing himself to Port Hudson in like manner. Good prospect of success at both points.

Lee & Hooker both seem moving. Col: Geo: Ruggles, who is in town organizing & inspecting the new Invalid corps, told me last night that Hooker's base of supplies is shifted from Acquia to Alexandria. Lee seems to contemplate either an attack on Wash^n^, or an invasion of Penn: —

Col: Frank Hampton, who married my poor cousin Sally Baxter, seems certainly among the killed at the recent Cavalry fight on the Rappahannock.

Laurence Williams' younger brother, Orton W, & another Rebel officer, caught within our lines, somewhere near Murfreesboro', in U.S. uniform, passing themselves off as belonging to Rosecrans' staff, were duly tried by Court Martial & hanged as spies. I believe all parties concede that their treatment was perfectly regular. L.W. does so fully. "Is'nt it a d—d pleasant thing," said he to Geo. Gibbs, "to take up your newspaper at the breakfast table, & find that your brother had just been hanged?" He is to be married today at Staten Island to Geo: Law's daughter — A note from Mrs G.L. to Ellie, announces that the "reception" is postponed, "*on account of a death in Mr Williams' family*" —

June 16. Lee is invading Penn: & may be in *Harrisburgh* by this time. One hundred thousand militia called out. The 7th & other N.Y. Regiments probably march tomorrow. There is much excitement — rather more than is necessary I think.

June 17. Wednesday. Thundershowers morn'g & ev'g. Suffered cruelly last night & all day from this relapse into *inflammation.* Scarce a moment free from intense local irritation, & visited half hourly by times of grinding pain. I console myself by thinking of the hundreds of better men than myself whom I've seen agonizing, without attendance or comfort, in field hospitals at Antietam & elsewhere, & then of the unlimited appliances of relief & care that I enjoy. — One of these & not the least of them is the hearty good will with wh: all the *servants*, from John the waiter to Lizzy the little half-fledged chambermaid trot about the house on my numerous errands. Their willing eager service is a very pleasant thing.

Just now I'm easier — 10 P.M. — having 20 drops of morphine on board.

June 22^{d}. Monday *morn'g*. A man who takes out his journal for sheer lack of something to do — compelled thereto by necessity, but without anything to record — must be in a bad way. But what can I do? My brains are mere desiccated gelatine, & a mouldy damaged unmarketable article, at that.

June 24. There are indications of strong pressure on Lincoln to restore *McClellan*. It would be a dubious step.

Very considerable & creditable naval successes reported. The vaunted rebel gunboat "Atlanta", alias "Fingal", the iron-clad sea-dragon of Savannah, forced to surrender to one of our Monitors & carried off to Port Royal, little damaged. We are damaging Rebeldom moreover fearfully, of late, by "raids" & expeditions, destroying property, transportation especially, that cannot be replaced. And our Cavalry is becoming a most distinguished & useful Arm of the service. On a fair field it generally drives the enemy's troopers handsomely.

Nigger Regiments seem to stand fire & fight well — an immense point in our favor. It is certainly natural they should exert themselves to avoid being made prisoners! On the whole things look well, if we can but take Vicksburgh & Port Hudson.

June 25. Thursday. Wall St. again this A.M. — This ev'g, after assisting Johny & Temple with a few crackers & torpedoes, I went to the Union League Club, where matters look promising. Over 500 members now. Fifty or sixty present to night. Adjourned to one of the 3^{d} story rooms with Olmsted, Bellows, Griswold, Gould of Cambridge & half a dozen more to discuss the project of a *weekly paper* — independent of mere party politics — & upholding sound principles of loyalty & nationality. What vast good such a paper might do — if honest & able men could be found in sufficient number to form an Editorial staff.

According to this aftn's rumors & despatches, chronicled in 1st Edition, 2d do, & 3d do of the aftn papers, Lee is aiming at Harrisburgh in force. Do not believe he has shewn his hand yet. He is probably watching to strike at any point we may leave uncovered, & helping himself meanwhile to the horses & cattle of Penn: by a series of cautious forays right & left. The unpatriotic well-to-do farmers of that region will doubtless suffer some, & it will do them good. The Harrisburghers are shewing themselves uncommonly base sordid & spiritless. — Penn: is in fact the meanest state in the Union. Even in this crisis, she is doing little to help herself, & depending on militia from this city, Mass: & elsewhere, out of whom the dirty drab-colored men of the invaded district are making all the money they can — much too full of this pleasing task to think of enrolling in defence of their own firesides & pigstyes [perhaps tautologous!]. — Govr of N. Jersey said to have withdrawn his militia regiments in disgust, & no wonder. It would serve these degenerate mongrels right to leave them to themselves & let them be harried by Lee's hungry hordes.

June 26. Friday. Overcast & the aftn drizzly. Ellie Temple & Johny spent the day at Mrs Cameron's, Staten Island, very pleasantly. Went to Wall St. — worked feebly. Visit from Olmsted & Howard Potter, & long talk about our *Dream* of an Honest Weekly paper. Potter, Wm Hoppin & I are to be Trustees of a fund to be raised by subscription, & a strong effort will be made to carry out the design. Griswold puts down $1000. to begin with. — Afterwards at 823 B'way. Bp Clark with us. Long session & much done. I fear a collision with Dr Newberry, our Western Secy, & that he must be thrown over. He is useful & will be hard to replace, but unmanageable & insubordinate — as it seems — but perhaps he is'nt.

June 27. Lounged awhile at U.L. Club to night. Many there. Despatches & letters from Washn posted on one bulletin board, throwing some light on the "situation" in Maryland & Penn: — Dix has reached Balt: with 10.000 men, & Foster is expected. Everything points to a fearfully decisive battle within a few days on or near the field of Antietam. May God avert a great disaster! I fear Joe Hooker, drunk or sober, is no match for Lee, and that his army, tho' in excellent order & condition, is discouraged by it's repeated failures. Should it be badly defeated & disorganized, there is nothing in reserve, & Wash^{n}, Baltimore and Philadelphia will be lost before another army can be raised. — Our frivolous self-indulgent apathy is marvellous.

Rebel pirates are playing the deuce with our commerce. They are now engaged in the Chivalric work of burning fishing smacks off Cape Sable. But their sending boats into Portland Harbor & capturing the Revenue Cutter Caleb Cushing does them credit. She was pursued & blown up & her crew brought back in irons however.

June 29. I am smoking my usual after breakfast cigar, & inundating my interior with Kissingen — [the half hour thus lazily spent being in part a concession to my demi-semi-invalid state, & partly a privilege earned by early rising] and repeating to myself involuntarily over & over again, the hardly credible news that *Hooker* is relieved, & *Gen: Meade* is in command!!! A change of Generals when a great decisive battle seems all but actually begun, & may well be delivered before the new Commander is comfortably settled in his saddle! — God help us!

Ev'g. Tired, having walked up town from Wall St. This ev'g at U.L. Club — Com: on Admissions. Adjourned thence to these premises with Bellows, Olmsted, Agnew & Gibbs for an Exec: Com: meeting of the San: Commission. — E. has gone to spend a day or two at Norwich with Mrs Foster the Senator's wife.

People far better pleased with the change of Commanders than I expected to find them. — Clitz, dining with Henry Fearing at West P^{t} yesterday, & of course knowing nothing of this change, said that Meade was sure to come out "at the top of the pile" before the war was over.

June 30. Tuesday. Is it the very decided heat, or yesterday's walk up-town that's responsible for today's paralyzing sense of weakness & weariness? I was about as useful & active in Wall St. as a Pre-Adamite Toad in an Old Red Sandstone Cavity.

After I came home a lively little sickheadache set in, of the acrid exasperating species, and I fear I was not good-natured with the boys at dinner-time!

Made my way to U.L. Club at 9 nevertheless to keep an appointment for consultation over the proposed *Periodical*, & half a dozen of us adjourned to one of the committee rooms. But it was hot & smelt of fresh paint & I was faint, & *sweaty* & ¾ sick, & the effort to follow Olmsted's clear compact well considered statement of plans & probabilities made me desperate & fidgetty "comme un Diable dans un benitier", so I excused myself, staggered homeward with Dr P. thro' the most splendid sultry moonlight, & deposited myself, for an hour's stagnation, in the Library chair.

July 1. A more diligent day. But after even writing a commonplace letter I feel as if I had just returned from the ascent of Mont Blanc. At U.L. Club to night I found a large assemblage — also sundry telegrams confirming what the newspapers tell us, viz: that Meade is advancing & that Lee has paused & is calling in his scattered columns & concentrating either for battle or for a retreat with his wagon loads of plunder. Harrisburgh breathes more freely, & Pennsylvania militia is mustering in considerable (numerical) force. Much good they would do to be sure, in combat with Lee's desperadoes — cunning sharp-shooters — & stark hard-riding moss-troopers.

July 3^{d}. Friday, ½ past 9 of a muggy morn'g. We can scarcely fail to have most weighty news before night. There was a battle at or near Gettysburgh on the 1st, resulting apparently in our favor. We lost a valuable officer in Gen: Reynolds. Fight probably renewed yesterday, but no information on that point. There are no official reports — an unpleasant indication, but Gov^{t} has maintained the most resolute silence as to all Army movements during this campaign.

July 4th. Saturday. A cloudy muggy sultry *Fourth*. Awake nearly all last night, tormented by headache, and wakened out of each successive cat-nap by pyrotechnic racket. At or soon after daylight Calvary Church bells began clanking, & cannon firing "a National Salute" in Union Square. I arose bilious, head-achy, back achy, sour & savage. Read morning papers. Their news from Meade's army was fragmentary & vague, but hopeful. Spent the morning watching over Johny & Temple, & Johny's friend Master Lewis French, firing off no end of crackers little & big — "Columbiads" included. What an infernal noise they make!

At half past five appeared Walter Cutting with news from the Army up to 8 last night.

There was fighting on the aft^{n} of the 2^{d}, renewed yesterday, when the Rebels attacked Meade's left centre in great force & were twice repulsed with severe loss. Our cavalry was operating on their flank. Both armies seem to have held their original position. *Gratias agimus Tibi.* — This can hardly turn out to have been worse than a *drawn* battle, & that, to an invading aggressive army, is equivalent to Defeat, as we have good reason to know. — Defeat & failure in this desperate undertaking is a serious matter to the Womanfloggers.

Dined here Walter Cutting, M^{r} & Mrs S.B.R. Jem R. — After dinner came in Ellie's grandmamma, and Mrs Binney & her young daughter Miss Maria. We had a grand display of the most gorgeous fireworks in the lot between the two houses, 70 & 74.

It would seem that Gen: Dan: *Sickles* has lost a leg. Wadsworth is wounded. Poor Gen: *Barlow* (Mrs Arabella Barlow née Griffith's husband) severely wounded again & probably a prisoner.

July 5. Sunday. A memorable day, even should it's glorious news prove but half true. — Tidings from Gettysburgh have been arriving in fragmentary instalments, but with a steady crescendo toward complete overwhelming victory. If we can believe what we hear, Lee is smitten hip & thigh, & his invincible "Army of Northern Virginia" shattered & destroyed. But I am sceptical, especially as to news of Victory, and expect to find large deductions from our alleged success in tomorrow morning's newspapers. There has been a great battle in which we are on the whole victorious. The Woman-floggers are badly repulsed and retreating, with more or less loss of prisoners guns & *materiel.* So much seems certain, and that is enough to thank God for most Devoutly — far better than we dared hope a week ago.

This may have been one of the great decisive battles of History.

It has been a day of quiet rain. Ellie went to Trin: Church with the children. I staid at home, read, and lay in wait for Extras. An Extra Herald came at noon, another an hour or two later. Both encouraging. At 6 P.M. appeared D[r] Bellows with a telegram from *Olmsted* at Philadelphia as follows to wit. "Private advices tend to confirm report of capture of over 15000 prisoners & 100 guns. Lee retreating. Pleasanton holds Potomac fords". — Olmsted is wary shrewd & never sanguine. This despatch was not sent without strong evidence to support it. I carried it down at once to Union League Club & saw it posted on our bulletin board to the intense delectation of half a dozen people who were hanging about the premises hungering for news.

M[r] S.B.R. came in to tea. Afterwards appeared one Hill of Davenport Iowa, an ally of M[r] R's in his great Ship-Canal Campaign & a very intelligent cultivated person, with no perceptible Westernisms. Also D[r] Peters & Walter Cutting.

At supper-time, 10 P.M., a Tribune Extra. News of victory confirmed. "Prisoners & guns taken". — x + y prisoners arrived at Baltimore & "acres of cars" laden with prisoners blocked on the R.R. — Lee retreating toward Williamsport. Official despatch from Gen: French to Gen: Halleck announcing capture of pontoon train at Williamsport. Significant. The Potomac fords are full just now. Just suppose *Meade* should bag *Lee* & his horde of traitors, as Burgoyne & Cornwallis were bagged near a century ago. Imagine it! But there is no such luck now.

At half past eleven, in rushed the exuberant Col: Frank Howe with a budget of telegrams. Lee utterly routed & disorganized, with loss of 30.000 prisoners (!) & *all* his artillery. Details of capture of three or four blockade-running Britishers at Mobile & Charleston, I omit as comparatively uninteresting.

Now to bed — and then for the morning papers. We may be fearfully disillusionated even yet.

July 6. Monday. Mugginess continues. Morning papers give us little additional light, if any. Ev'g papers do. — I regret to see no official statement of guns captured. But an Extra Herald despatch dated at noon to day gives us a splendidly colored picture of Lee's retreat, & tells how teamsters & Artillery men are cutting their traces & riding off for life on their draft-mules — how even Couch's militia Regiments are following up the defeated Army & bagging whole brigades — & how there is general panic, rout, & sauve qui peut. All which is pleasant to read, but probably fictitious. So is a Telegram, no doubt, that I find at U. League Club to night: "All Lee's artillery captured & 30.000 prisoners".

I take it Lee is badly whipped, but will get across the Potomac with the bulk of his Army, more or less demoralized.

I think of going to Lynn tomorrow aft[n] to pay Eloise my long deferred visit. I do not get quite well even yet & D[r] Peters strongly advises a day or two of strong sea-breeze & loaferism.

Ellie is busy packing her baggage train for *Cornwall* next Sat: — Her trusty handmaiden & Chief of Staff, Annie, is unhappily laid up with a sprained Ancle.

The results of this victory are priceless. Philad[a], Balt: & Wash[n] are safe. Defeat would have seriously endangered all three. The Rebels are hunted out of the North, their best Army is routed, & the charm of Rob[t] Lee's invincibility broken. The Army of the Potomac has at last found a General that can handle it, and it has stood nobly up to it's terrible work in spite of it's long disheartening list of hard-fought failures, and in spite of the McClellan influence on it's officers.

July 11. Supper & then to U.L. Club. Saw Gibbs & Collins. The Com: has spent near $20.000 this week & received as much. It is doing an immense business around Gettysburgh. Olmsted reports our losses there inside 7000, & Bellows *20 000*!!!

From negative evidence it appears that Lee's retreat was no rout. He shews a firm front at Williamsport & Hagerstown, seeking to recross the Potomac now in high freshet. Meade is at his heels, & another great battle is expected. — O. thinks it will be more severe than the last.

I observe that the Richmond papers are in an orgasm of brag & bluster & bloodthirstiness beyond all historical precedent even in their chivalric columns. That's an encouraging sign. Another is the unusual number of stragglers & deserters from Lee's Army. Rebel generals, even when defeated, have heretofore kept their men well in hand.

July 12. Despatches in morning papers tho' severally worthless give one the impression when taken collectively that Lee is getting safely across the Potomac & back to Old Virginny's shore, bag & baggage guns plunder & all. Whereupon the Able Editors begin to denounce Meade, their last new Napoleon, as incapable & outgeneralled.

At U.L. Club to night I hear that the Herald bulletin reports that Lee has crossed the river without loss. — Doubtful.

People forget that an army of 50.000 & upwards can hardly be bagged bodily unless it's General be a Mack or a Du Pont. — But I shall be disappointed if the rebels get home without a clawing.

Draft has begun here & was in progress in Boston last week. Δημος takes it goodnaturedly thus far, but we shall have trouble before we are through. The critical time will be when defaulting conscripts are haled out of their houses, as many will be. That soul-less politician *Seymour* will make mischief if he dare. So will F'nandy Wud Brooks Marble & other reptiles. May they only bring their traitorous necks within the cincture of a legal halter!

This Draft will be the *Experimentum crucis to decide whether we have a Government among us.*

July 13. Monday. A notable day. Stopped at the San: Com: office on my way down town, to endorse a lot of checks that had accumulated during my absence, and heard there of *rioting* in the upper part of the City. As C.E.S. is at Newport and Bidwell in Berkshire C° I went to Wall St. nevertheless, but the rumors grew more & more unpleasant, so I left it at one & took a 3^d^ Avenue car for up town. At the Park were groups & small crowds in more or less excitement (which found relief afterwards, I hear, in hunting down & maltreating sundry unoffending niggers) but there was nothing to indicate serious trouble. The crowded car went slowly on it's way, with it's perspiring passengers, for the weather was still of this deadly muggy sort, with a muddy sky & lifeless air. At 13th St. the track was blocked by a long line of stationary cars that stretched indefinitely up the Avenue, & I took to the sidewalk. Above 20th St. all shops were closed, & many people standing & staring or strolling up town, not riotously disposed but eager & curious.

Here & there a rough could be heard d—ing the Draft. No policemen to be seen anywhere. — Reached the Seat of War at last, 46th St. & 3^{d} Av: — Three houses on the Av. & two or three on the street burned down: engines playing on the ruins — more energetically I'm told than they did when their efforts would have been useful.

The crowd seemed just what one commonly sees at any fire, but it's nucleus of riot was concealed by an outside layer of ordinary peaceable lookers on. Was told they had beat off a Squad of police & another of "regulars" (probably the 12th Militia) — at last it opened & out streamed a posse of perhaps 500, certainly less than 1000, of the lowest Irish day laborers. The rabble was perfectly homogeneous. Every brute in the drove was *pure Keltic* — hod-carrier or loafer. They were unarmed. A few carried pieces of fence-paling & the like. They turned off West into 45th St. & gradually collected in front of two three story dwelling houses on Lexington Av: just below that street that stand alone together on a nearly vacant block. Nobody could tell why these houses were singled out. Some said a drafting officer lived in one of them, others that a damaged policeman had taken refuge there. The mob was in no hurry: they had no need to be: there was no one to molest them or make them afraid. The beastly ruffians were masters of the situation & of the City. After a while sporadic paving stones began to fly at the windows — ladies & children emerged from the rear & had a rather hard Scramble over a high board fence, & then scudded off across the open, heaven knows whither. Then men & small boys appeared at rear windows & began smashing the sashes & the blinds & shied out light articles, such as books & crockery, & dropped chairs & mirrors into the back yard — the rear fence was demolished & loafers were seen marching off with portable articles of furniture. And at last a light smoke began to float out of the windows & I came away. I could endure the disgraceful sickening sight no longer — and what could I *do*?

The fury of the low Irishwomen in that region was noteworthy. Stalwart young vixens & withered old hags were swarming everywhere — all cursing the "bloody *draft*" & egging on their men to mischief.

Omnibussed down to N° 823 where is news that the Colored

Half Orphan Asylum on 5th Av: just above the Reservoir is burned. "Tribune office to be burned tonight". R.R. rails torn up — telegraph wires cut &c &c &c. If a quarter one hears be true this is an organized insurrection *in the interest of the Rebellion*, & Jeff: Davis rules N.Y. to day.

Attended to business, then with Wolcott Gibbs to dinner at Maison Dorée. During our Symposium, there was an alarm of a coming Mob, & we went to the window to see. The "mob" was moving down 14th St. & consisted of just 34 lousy blackguardly Irishmen, with a tail of small boys. Whither they went I cannot say, nor can I guess what mischief the handful of *canaille* chose to do. A dozen policemen would have been more than a match for the whole crew, but there were no policemen in sight.

Walked up town with W.G. Large fire on B'way & 28th St. Signs of another to the E., said to be on 2^{d} Av: — Stopped awhile at G's in 29th St. where was *Madame*, frightened nearly to death — & then to St Nicholas Hotel, to see the Mayor & Gen: Wool. We found a lot of people with them. There were John Jay & Geo. W. Blunt & Col. Howe & John Austin Stevens Jr — all urging strong measures. But the substantial & weighty & influential men were not represented. Out of town I suppose. Their absence emboldened Gibbs & myself to make pressure for instant action — but it was vain. We begged that Martial Law might be declared. Opdyke said that was Wools business & Wool said it was Opdyke's — & neither would act. "Then Mr Mayor, issue a proclamation calling on all loyal & law-abiding citizens to enrol themselves as a volunteer force for defence of life & property." — "Why" quoth Opdyke "that is *Civil War* at once". — Long talk with Col. Cram Wool's chief of staff who professes to believe that every thing is as it should be & sufficient force on the ground to prevent farther mischief. Dont believe it. Neither Opdyke nor Gen: Wool is nearly equal to this crisis. Came off disgusted. Went to U.L. Club awhile. No comfort there. Much talk but no one ready to do anything whatever, not even to telegraph to Washington.

We telegraphed, two or three of us, from Gen: Wool's rooms, to the Pres'dt — begging that troops be sent on, & stringent measures taken. The great misfortune is that nearly all our militia regiments have been despatched to Pennsylvania.

All the military force I have seen or heard of to day was in 5th Av: at about 7 P.M. There were two or three feeble companies of infantry — a couple of howitzers — & a Squadron or two of unhappy-looking "dragoons".

These wretched rioters have been plundering freely I hear. Their outbreak will either destroy the City or damage the copperhead cause fatally. Could we but catch the scoundrels who have stirred them up, what a blessing it would be! God knows what to night or tomorrow may bring forth. We may be thankful that it is now (quarter past twelve) raining briskly. Mobs have no taste for the affusion of cold water. — I'm thankful moreover that Ellie & the children are out of town. I sent Johny off to Cornwall this aftn in charge of John the waiter.

July 14. Tuesday. 11 P.M. Fire bells clanking, as they have clanked at intervals thro' the ev'g.

Plenty of rumors throughout the day & ev'g, but nothing very precise or authentic. There have been sundry collisions between the rabble and the authorities, civil & military. Mob fired upon. It generally runs — but on one occasion appears to have rallied, charged police & militia & forced them back in disorder. The people are waking up, & by tomorrow there will be adequate organization to protect property & life.

Many details come in of yesterday's brutal cowardly ruffianism & plunder. Shops were cleaned out — & a black man hanged, in Carmine St. for no offence but that of *Nigritude*.

Opdyke's house again attacked this morning, by a roaming handful of Irish blackguards. Two or three gentlemen who chanced to be passing saved it from sack by a vigorous charge & dispersed the *Popular Uprising* (as the Herald, World, & News call it,) with their walking sticks & their fists. Teste R.B. —

Walked up town perforce, for no cars & few omnibi were running. They are suppressed by threats of burning R.R. & omnibus stables, the drivers being wanted — to reinforce the mob. Tiffany's shop — Ball & Blacks — & a few other Broadway establishments are closed.

[Here I am interrupted by report of a fire near at hand, & a great glare on the houses across the Park. Sally forth, & find the 18th Ward station house, 22d St. near 1st Av:, in full blaze.

A splendid blaze it made, but I did not venture below 2^d Av: finding myself in a crowd of Celtic spectators disgorged by the circumjacent tenement houses. They were exulting over the damage to 'them bloody Police' &c &c. I thought discretion the better part of Curiosity. Distance lent enchantment to *that* view.]

At 823 with Bellows 4 to 6: then home. At 8 to U.L. Club. Rumor it's to be attacked to night. Some say there is to be great mischief to night & that the rabble is getting the upper hand. Home at 10 & sent for by Dudley Field J^r to confer about an expected attack on his house & his father's which adjoin each other in this street just below Lexington Av: — He has a party there, with muskets, and talks of fearful trouble before morn'g — but he is always a blower, & a very poor devil.

Fire bells again — 12.15. — No light of conflagration is visible.

Bellows' Report from Gettysburgh & from Meade's headquarters very interesting. Thinks highly of M. Thinks the battle around Williamsport will be tolerably evenly matched, Lee having been decidedly beaten a week ago, but not at all demoralized. — But there's a despatch at U.L.C. to night that Lee has moved his whole army safely across, except his rear-guard which we captured.

A good deal of yelling to the Eastward just now. The Fields & their near neighbour Col. Frank Howe are as likely to be attacked by this traitor-guided mob, as any people I know. — If they *are*, we shall see trouble in this quarter, & Gramercy Park will acquire historical associations.

O how tired I am — but I feel reluctant to go to bed. — I believe I dozed off a minute or two. — There came something like two reports of artillery — perhaps only falling walls. — Then go two jolly Kelts along the street singing a genuine Keltic howl — something about "Tim O'Laggerty" with a refrain of pure Erse. — Long live the Sovereigns of N.Y. — Brian Boroo Redivivus & multiplied. Paddy has left his Egypt — Connaught — & reigns in this promised land of milk & honey & perfect freedom —

Hurra — there goes a strong squad of police marching Eastward down this street — followed by a company of infantry with gleaming bayonets. — 1. A.M.

Fire bells again — S.E.ward — "swinging slow with sullen roar". — Now they are silent — & I shall go to bed, at least for a season. —

July 15. Morning papers report nothing specially grave as occurring since midnight. But there will be much more trouble to day. Rabbledom is not yet dethroned, any more than it's ally & instigator, *Rebeldom*.

News from the South is consolatory. Port Hudson surrendered. Sherman said to have beaten Joseph Johnston somewhere near Vicksburgh. Operations commencing agst Charleston. Bragg seems to be abandoning Chattanooga & retiring on Atlanta.

Per contra — Lee has got safely off. I thought he would.

10 P.M. Here's an illustration of the vanity of Human Labors — A man writing diligently in his journal for the instruction of posterity, & quite uncertain whether his house wo'nt be burned over his head, & journal & all with it before morning. Sebastian Brant might have made a good picture out of it, for his *Navis Stultifera*. There go the firebells, with appropriate music.

C.E.S. in from Newport this morn'g. It was too sultry to walk to Wall St. & our most gracious Δημος, Sathanæ Gratiâ Rex Neo-Eboracensium, has suppressed the Omnibus lines, so we took a carriage. Find Bidwell returned from Berkshire C° & in a nervous twitter of course. Lots of talk & rumors about attacks on the Custom House (ci-devant Merchants' Exch:) & the Treasury Building (late Custom House). Went to see Cisco, & found his establishment in military occupation — sentinels pacing — windows barricaded &c. He was as serene & bland as the loveliest May morning — ("so cool, so calm, so bright,") & shewed me the live shell ready to throw out of the windows & the "battery" to project Assay-Office-oil-of-vitriol &c &c. He's all right. Then called on Collector Barney & had another long talk with him. Find him well prepared with shells, grenades, muskets, & men — but a little timid & anxious — "wanting counsel" — doubtful about his right to fire on the mob, & generally flaccid & tremulous — poor devil!

Walked up town with C.E.S. & Hoppin, & after my cup of coffee went to U.L. Club. A delegation returned from Police headquarters, having vainly asked for a squad of men to garrison the Clubhouse. *None can be spared.* What is worse, we were badly repulsed in an attack on the mob in First Av: near 19th St. at about 6 P.M. — Fired upon from houses, & had to leave 16 wounded men & a *Lt Col: Jardine* in the hands of these brutes & devils. — This is very bad indeed. But to night is quieter than the last — tho' there seems to be a large fire down-town, & we hear occasional gun-shots.

At the club was Geo. Gibbs — full of the loudest & most emphatic jawing. "Gen: Frémont's house, & Craven's to be attacked tonight. — Croton mains to be cut & Gas works destroyed" — &c &c &c &c —

By way of precaution I have had the bathtubs filled, & also all the pots kettles & pails in the house.

Dr Peters has just called to prescribe for some ailment of Bridget the Cook's — fright, I believe. — Thinks the worst over. So do not I. Mayor's Proclamation this morning is *bosh.*

Some say the 7th Reg^{t} arrived at 5 P.M. & is at Astor House. — Uncertain.

12.30. — Light as of a large fire to the South.

July 16. Rather quiet down town. No trustworthy accounts of riot on any large scale during the day. General talk down town is that the trouble is over. We shall see. It will be as it pleases the Scoundrels who are privily engineering the outbreak — agents of Jeff: Davis, permitted to work here in N. York.

Omnibusses & R.R. cars in full career again.

Coming up town to night I find Gramercy Park in military occupation. Strong parties drawn up across 20th & 21st Sts at the East end of the square, by the G. Hotel, each with a flanking squad, forming an L. Occasional shots fired at them from the region of Second or First Av: which were replied to by vollies, that seem to have done little execution. An unlucky cart-horse was knocked over, I hear. This force was relieved at 7 by a company of regulars & a party of the 7th with a couple of howitzers, & there has been but a stray shot or two since dark. The Regulars do not look like steady men. I have just gone over to the Hotel with John Roberton & ordered a pail of strong coffee to put a little life into them.

Never knew exasperation so intense unqualified & general as that which prevails against these rioters & the politic knaves who are supposed to have set them going — Gov: Seymour not excepted. Men who voted for him mention the fact with contrition & self abasement, & the Democratic Party is at a discount with all the people I meet.

[Apropos of discount, Gold fell to *126* to day — with the City in insurrection — a gunboat at the foot of Wall St — Custom House & Treasury full of soldiers & live shell — & two howitzers in position to rake Nassau St. from Wall to Fulton!!!!]

Every impression that's made on our people passes away so soon — almost as if stamped on the sand of the seabeach. Were our moods a little less fleeting I should have great hope of permanent good from the general wrath these outrages have provoked, & should put some faith in people's prophesyings that F. Wood, & McCunn, & the N.Y. Herald, & the Brookses &c &c are doomed henceforth to obscurity & contempt. But we shall forget all about it before next November. Perhaps the lesson of the last four days is to be taught us still more emphatically, & we have got to be worse before we are better. It is not clear that the resources of the conspiracy are yet exhausted. The rioters of yesterday were better armed & organized than those of Monday, & their inaction to day may possibly be meant to throw us off our guard, — or their time may be employed perfecting plans for a campaign of plundering & brutality in yet greater force. They are in full possession of the Western & the Eastern sides of the City from 10th St. upward & of a good many districts beside. I could not walk four blocks Eastward from this house this minute without peril —. The outbreak is spreading by concerted action in many quarters. Albany, Troy, Yonkers, Hartford, Boston, &c have each their Irish, Anti-conscription, Nigger murdering mob, of the same type with ours. It is a grave business — a Jacquerie that must be put down by heroic doses of lead and steel — Dr Peters & C.E.S. called [11 P.M.) They have been exploring & report things quiet except on 1st Av: from 19th to 30th St. where there is said to be trouble. A detachment of the Seventh Reg^{t}, 5 or 600 strong, marched to that quarter from their Armory an hour ago.

July 17. Friday. Hot day & showery ev'g. Dined at Maison Dorée with C.E.S. & Agnew who is just from Gettysburgh & W^{ms}port. Riot seems quelled for the present, or reduced to a system of guerilla assassination & robbery, which is mostly confined to the quarter East of 3^{d} Av: & above 18th St. — Police authorities say however that the Conspiracy may renew it's work at any moment.

[N.B. Is there among the minor miseries of life any much more pungent than the advent of a Bore who drops in to spend an hour with you, & has nothing to say, & says it over & over again, & sits & sits in spite of your brief replies to his prosings & your manifest symptoms of suffering & prostration? I have just gone thro' that trial, and what made it worse was that Ατκληπιος had just left the N.Y. Club, & was stupidly tight — mumbling the dreariest platitudes.]

The Army of Gram: Park has advanced it's headquarters to 3^{d} Av: — leaving only a picket guard in sight. Rain will keep the rabble quiet to night. We are said to have 15000 men under arms, & I incline to hope that this movement in aid of the Rebellion is played out. It was intended, no doubt, to sustain & work in with a successful invasion by Lee. — A lively rumor in Wall St. this morn'g that Charleston is taken. Doubtless false.

July 18. Sat: — Not having seen my household for a long while I made my way to Cornwall this morn'g, on the steamboat Daniel Drew. Landed at Newburgh & drove to Roe's house, where I find Ellie & her trio prosperous. Took a walk with her — saw Master Temple straddle a horse for the first time in his life — dined, came back to N. Crossed & took a tedious way train to N.Y., arriving here at about 8. I did not care to spend a night away from 21st St. while affairs are so unsettled.

But to day seems to have passed off peacefully. Gram: Park still occupied by two or three companies.

July 19. Sunday night. Have been out, seeking information, and getting none that is to be trusted. Col: Frank Howe talks darkly and predicts outbreak on the East side of the town to night, but that's his way. I think this Celtic Beast with many heads is driven back to his hole for the present. When Government begins enforcing the draft we shall have more trouble, but not till then.

Not half the history of this memorable week has been written. I could put down pages of incident that the newspapers have omitted, any one of which would in ordinary times be the town's talk. — Men, & ladies, attacked & plundered by daylight in the streets. Private houses suddenly invaded by gangs of a dozen ruffians, & sacked, while the women & children run off for their lives. — Then there is the unspeakable infamy of the nigger persecution. They are the most peaceable sober & inoffensive of our poor, and the outrages they have suffered during this last week, are less excusable, — are founded on worse pretext & less provocation, than S[t] Bartholomew's & the Jew-hunting of the Middle Ages. — This is a nice town to call itself a centre of civilization! Life & personal property less safe than in Tipperary, & "the People" (as the Herald calls them) burning Orphan Asylums & conducting a massacre. How this infernal Slavery system has corrupted our blood, North as well as South! There should be terrible vengeance for these atrocities, but McCunn Barnard & C[o] are our Judges & the disgrace will rest upon us without atonement.

I am sorry to find that England is right about the lower class of Irish. They are brutal base cruel cowards, and as insolent as base. Choate (at U.L.C.) tells me he heard this proposition put forth by one of their political philosophers in conversation with a knot of his brethren last Monday. "*Sure & if them dam Dutch would jine us we'd drive the dam Yankees out of New York entirely*!" — These caitiffs have a trick, I hear, of posting themselves at the window of a tenement house with a musket, while a woman with a baby in her arms squats at their feet. Paddy fires on the police & instantly squats to reload, while M[rs] Paddy rises & looks out. Of course one ca'nt fire at a window where there is a woman with a child!! But how is one to deal with women who assemble around the lamp-post to which a negro had been hanged, & cut off certain parts of his body to keep as souvenirs? Have they any womanly privilege immunity or sanctity?

No wonder S[t] Patrick drove all the venomous vermin out of Ireland! It's biped mammalia supply that Island it's full average share of creatures that crawl & eat dirt & poison every community they infest. Vipers were superfluous. But my own theory is that St Patrick's campaign against the snakes is a Popish delusion. They perished of biting the Irish people.

July 20th. Monday. Hot. Atmosphere mucilaginous. City quiet. Nothing special to record. Dined with Agnew at Maison Dorée, & spent a little time at the Club. — I see a frequent placard bearing these two words, "SAM, ORGANIZE!" It plainly means that there is a movement to revive the old Native American party with it's Know-Nothing Clubs. A very natural consequence of the atrocities just perpetrated by our Irish canaille. Talking with Americans of the middle & laboring class, even of the lowest social grade, I find they fully appreciate & bitterly resent these Keltic outrages. But the obstacle in the way of a revived Know-Nothingism is that it would be obliged to discriminate between Kelts & Teutons. The Germans have behaved well & kept quiet. Where they acted at all, they volunteered against the rabble, as they did, most effectively, in the 7th Ward. A mere Anti-Hibernian party would have no foundation on principle — would seem merely vindictive & proscriptive — and would lead to no lasting result, I fear. For myself personally, I would like to see war made on Irish *Scum* as in 1688.

July 21th. Quiet continues, tho' the *Express* & that yet more beastly *World* are doing all they can to instigate outbreak.

Morgan's raid across the Ohio has failed very badly. His whole force is captured, artillery & all, & he escapes by slinking off while negotiations for surrender are in progress. Chivalric Morgan!

July 26th. Sunday night. A fearfully fervently hot day. Meant to go to Church, but on protruding my head from the front door I was driven back to the Library by the withering heat reflected from pavements & brick walls. The Army of Gramercy Park has moved at last, leaving a picket guard in an Engine house to our Eastward. G.C.A. came in at 6 P.M. & we went to Maison Dorée & dined together, quite elaborately. Stopped at U.L. Club on our way home. Dr Peters came in, with one Budd, the father-in-law of Gen: *Geo: C. Strong*, & a Captn Harrold of the Gen'l's Staff. The *Arago* arrived to day, bringing home Gen: G.C.S. very severely wounded in the thigh by a fragment of shell. He was hit during our second assault on *Fort Wagner*, one of the out-works of Charleston. We were *repulsed* it seems, with great loss; 1500 hors du combat out of 5000. It looks like a bad business. But this Capt[n] Harrold says our batteries on the salt marsh, to the left of the strip of beach, are within breaching range of Sumter, and that their 200 lb Parrott shells can reach Charleston itself— distance 5¼ miles. Perhaps so. Perhaps not.

July 27. Monday night. White-hot till about three, when a weakly shower tried to cool the air & did'nt much. Worked faithfully down town: thence to 823. D[r] Jenkins there. Edwd Mitchell came in, a son of ex-judge W[m] Mitchell, just from N. Orleans. He has been spending several months there, & in the Têche country with Banks, as San: Com: Agent. His report on the state of affairs in the S.W. agrees with that of his chief, D[r] Crane, who returned with him. Mitchell says he went South conservative & Constitutional & that he comes back Radical & Abolitionist. No wonder, if all his stories of what he has seen be true. Both Crane & Mitchell speak highly of the discipline of our new Black Regiments. They report the Plantation Aristocracy generally inveterate in treason, it's womankind specially virulent — New Orleans absolutely subjugated & submissive however. The liberated negroes, now working for wages, behave like Christians bear no malice & commit no outrages. Southern Cuffee seems of higher social grade than Northern Paddy. The generous & chivalric Sons of Erin are under a cloud just now.

Dined with Murray Hoffman at Maison Dorée. Thence to U.L. Club. Discoursed Barney the Collector of this Port. He thinks that Fernando Wood, nasty little Tucker the Surrogate, Butterworth & McCunn, with others, are at the head of a secret organization, that did not fully shew itself in the late riots, but is held in reserve for a far more serious out-break in aid of the Rebellion — and that F'nandy Wud aims at being Doge or First Consul or something of New York. Barney is feeble & frightened, but we should be prepared for any violent desperate move by Copperheads & Peace Democrats to get control of the City.

Talked over the position with Agnew & G.F. Allen. We must make the Clubhouse defensible, — provide muskets, grenades, & the like. It's windows were darkened & its flag lowered during the riots, & such disgrace must not be incurred again.

Long talk with Cisco this morn'g, from wh: I infer that Dix stands where he should, & is no ally, open or secret, of Seymour's.

July 28. Tuesday. Oppressed all day by this painful news about poor Gen: G.C. Strong. Lockjaw has set in. I saw Van Buren this aft^{n}, who is called in consultation with Peters, & it is clear he thinks his patient doomed. The disease announced itself as long ago as Friday by twitchings in the wounded limb, & there is now constant trismus & rigidity of the abdominal muscles, but as yet no severe paroxysms. I called at his lodgings in 19th St. this aft^{n} & saw a young officer, one of his staff, I suppose, who reported the Gen: "no better". — Thro' the opened door of the parlor into wh: I was shewn, there was a glimpse of the darkened sick room, & a couch, & a *fan* going — in the hands of the poor little wife, no doubt. She nearly broke down even Van Buren's practised professional self-command, by the simplicity of her appeal to him "to save her husband". But I suppose it's a hopeless business, & so passes away one of the bravest officers & manliest men in our service — murdered by certain organized gangs of traitors while in the discharge of his official duty. Shall we ever begin calling things by their true names, & doing our duty as instruments of God's justice upon the masterful law-breakers, whom we now treat with wicked forbearance because they style themselves the First Georgia Regiment, the 2^{d} S. Carolina Artillery, & so forth? — If our policy toward them — our recognition of them as belligerents — our omission to hang their leaders as fast as we catch them — be just, our War on the South is *un*just & wicked. If these scoundrels had the right to "secede", they should enjoy it, but if they had *not*, hanging is too good for them. They have wrongfully & causelessly brought into the homes of the land North & South — into ten thousand households — misery & heart-breaking, waste of life & wreck of hope, such as was in full progress toward it's consummation in that sick-room this evening.

July 31. Gen: Strong *died* 3 A.M. yesterday. Agnew saw him & says it was the worst case of tetanus he ever had to do with. He was spared pain by saturation with opiates. Whenever he was conscious, his cheerfulness patience & worth shone out. Peters' announcement of his doom staggered him only for a moment, & then he said "Well I have always tried to live honestly, & now I must try to *die* honestly". — When his poor little wife made some prayer for his recovery at his bedside, he united in it, but then told her that was not all, & went on to frame a prayer that she, and their child, might be able to give hearty thanks that he had died *for the Country.*

"Uns ist in Alten Mähren wunders viel gezait
Von Helden lobebæren, von grossen Kuonheit."

Few of them much nobler than this fearless and gentle soldier.

People here are much puffed up with recent victory, expect speedy peace, & talk of N. Carolina, Louisiana & even Mississippi, as penitent, & willing to come back to the Union, the moment they are assured that their "Constitutional Rights" will be respected. This is all delusion, and God be praised that it is. Any overture from a Rebel Community should be received with an Apage Satanas. — The disappearance of an acute symptom has tempted many a patient to renounce his treatment & his regimen, & make a "compromise" with some deepseated "constitutional" disease, & has thus caused him to die & decompose. The virtue of this People is far from strong enough to resist an invitation to Peace now at the cost of far worse & deadlier War hereafter. Lasting Peace with Southern Rebels can be attained only by *subjugation* & *abolition*. We see now that victory at Bull Run two years ago would have been a National calamity, & that statues of *McDowell* & *Scott*, Saviors of the Country, should be set up in every loyal village — *McClellan* making a third, perhaps, as a great Public Benefactor in a way he never dreamed of.

Marvellous are the chances of Battle. These chieftains are sleeping at home at ease, while the mangled body of poor Gen: Strong, a fighting General, accustomed to lead columns of assault, lies at 62 E. 19th St. waiting to be carried out tomorrow morn'g to it's last resting place.

Aug: 1. Gen: Thomas goes to Tennessee tomorrow, & expects to organize 50 black Regiments in that region at once. Heaven prosper his work.

This war will result either in dismemberment of the Country, & humiliation of the North, *or* in a standing army of some 50.000 Negroes garrisoning the South for at least ten years to come.

Aug. 3. Monday night. Heat continues intolerable. It drove me up town early, absolutely sickened, & I spent the aft[n] mostly in my bath-tub. After dressing, & a modest repast, I proceeded to U.L. Club, where I perspired awhile. Gen: *B.F. Butler* there among others.

August 4. Twenty or thirty cases of sunstroke yesterday are reported. To day is less oppressive, for there is some movement in the air. But it's cruel weather still. I lard the lean earth — a walking shower — & cool the pavements as I go.

C.E.S. still at Newport. Did my duty in Wall St. — Only news is the death of that notable scoundrel W.L. Yancey, & the severe illness of the larcenous Floyd. The gallows do'nt always get it's due in this world, but the Devil commonly gets *his* in the next — and if men are to be judged by the quantity of mischief they have done and of misery they have caused, these deliberate authors of Civil war deserve a hot corner of Tophet. But I do'nt pretend to judge them. I would of course hang them or any of their tribe were I in authority & they in my power, but I would conclude my sentence with the usual formula of merciful aspiration.

Dined alone at Maison Dorée after a couple of hours at 823. This solitary consumption of terrapin soup and champagne is swinish work. — Reading Tyndall's Lectures on *Heat & Motion* — interesting & weighty book. Talked it over with W. Gibbs this ev'g at U.L. Club (it's balcony the coolest place in town) — Leibnitz's notion that in the act of Creation a certain definite amount of *force*, as well as of *matter*, was put into the Κοσμος. Tyndall's positions seem to confirm it. But I do'nt like the theory that the Universe was wound up & set going 6000 (or 6000 x 6000 x 6000000. . . . . .) years ago, & then left to itself & to the "laws" which matter in some inconceivable way obeys. It's hard enough for reasonable creatures, so called, to obey the law of their being. The obedience of the insensible atom of carbon or oxygen, in the absence of a living Power enforcing obedience to Law is incomprehensible — to me, at least.

Walked home from Club with D[r] Peters. General G.C. Strong, it seems, led the attack on *Wagner*, up the glacis, through three feet of water in the trench & up the scarp of the work — "*led*" literally, on horseback, in the front. They held this position about an hour. Then the failure of supports obliged him to withdraw them, which he did in good order. They were halted & he gave the order to lie down, & was in the act of dismounting, himself, when hit by a fatal fragment of shell from *Sumter*.

He foresaw his doom soon after he was brought here; touched his stiffening face, & said "Doctor Peters, *this* is what is going to *kill* me". — Peters has a notion of using *acetate of lead* in his next case of tetanus — thinks the disease may be neutralized & controlled by *lead-poisoning*. Dubious. I dwell on details of poor (?) Gen: Strong's Exit from this World, because he is the ennobling ornament of his name & family. The distinguished Caleb Strong, our kinsman, Gov[r] of Massachusetts 50 years ago, was, I suppose, distinguished as a States-Rights-man & copperhead. This brave & good young gentleman fought & died for the Country, & for no State, East or West, & if half what I hear be true, of his enterprise & courage & kindness to the unprotected at New Orleans & Ship Island & elsewhere, he was the Bayard of our Armies, & my children should be proud to claim kinship with him, however remote.

Thank God there seems reason to hope that Gillmore's Engineering will smash *Sumter* before long.

Col: Frank Howe (at U.L.C.) says the draft is to begin next Monday, without fail. May be so. He knows everything. May it begin soon, anyhow.

By D[r] Peters' account, his patient's death bed, round the corner there in Nineteenth St., must have manifested such Christian heroism & humility & patience, as one seldom hears about. Medical notification that he must die in a day or two was accompanied by the remark "I hope it's for the best" — to which he responded "If it's so, of course we *know* it's for the best". And in that spirit he went through with his last march toward death, always serene & patient in suffering, cheerful & trying to sustain & brighten those about him, never making himself a martyr, but awaiting death as an accident befalling him in his *duty*, for which he was not responsible, & which with it's results, he left, in full faith, in the hands of his Heavenly Father.

God grant me such a Departure from this world. It's a great fact that altho' we are suffering so much from shoddy contractors & politicians who support Government, & copperheads who oppose it, we have soldiers who can fight as bravely & die as grandly & as humbly as *Gen: George Strong*, whose namesake I am unworthy to be.

Aug: 8. Sat: night. Summer is pushing it's legitimate fervor to fanaticism. The heat is asphyxiating, and the evening sea-breeze, our legal remedy against a hot day, is non inventus.

Woke Thursday morn'g, perspiring as usual, & much afflicted with diarrhæa, colic, and general prostration. Down town late. It was the Day of Thanksgiving for July /63, which many generations will remember, I hope, as the Month of National Victory. But I could not go to Church, tho' I wanted to. The day was well observed. Broadway shops & Wall St. banks & offices all closed, & the general stillness beyond that of Sunday. — It was most oppressively hot, and a roaring thundershower, at one o'clock, cooled the pavements but little.

Newspapers brag far too loudly about our having "broken the backbone" of the Rebellion — and about development of Union feeling in Tennessee, Mississippi, & N. Carolina. The vertebræ of Southern Treason still cohere, as we may yet learn to our terrible cost — especially if Lee reinforce himself with the debris of Rebellion from the S.W. — And I would not give tenpence for all the loyalty that can be extracted from any Slaveholding State except Maryland, Missouri & Kentucky.

Lincoln has sent Gen: G.C. Strong's widow his Commission as *Major General*, dated the day of the battle that cost the Country his life. A very graceful recognition of the General's worth & gallantry.

Aug. 10.

A DEFUNCT DARKEY CANONIZED.

"Among the 'American citizens of African descent' that occupied those 'prominent positions' in the assault upon Port Hudson, May 27, *was a well-known 'bull-nigger' of New-Orleans, named Cailloux*. He was one of those much-praised native guards that had the choice between the batteries of their foes in front and the bayonets of their friends in the rear. CAILLOUX fell. His carcass lay rotting on the ground, exposed to sun and rain for forty-one days, from the date of the assault to the capitulation of Port Hudson. * * * It was well known here [in New-Orleans] that CAILLOUX was killed. For weeks past scarcely a wench in the city has appeared in the streets without a crape rosette in memory of 'Saint CAILLOUX.'"

This is a quotation from the *N.Y. World* — apropos of the parade that attended the burial of a black or mulatto Capt. Cailloux of N. Orleans, who fell while doing his duty at Port Hudson, leading his men, & so far as we can judge from reports, fighting bravely for the country. The N.Y. World's suggestion of "bayonets in the rear" is ingenious, but false & base & mean.

This dirty paragraph about the "defunct darkey" — the "bull-nigger" — whose "carcass lay rotting" — where he fell in battle against Rebellion, is most significant. It shews that the genteel clique of scoundrels & traitors who engineer the N.Y. World is of one mind with the vulgar mob of rag-tag & bobtail who burned & plundered the "Nigger" Orphan Asylum & hanged all the unoffending Black men it could catch — defiling their "carcasses" with every unnamable indignity. — It shews moreover that my squib about changes in the Burial Service & the Liturgy, required to adapt them to Southern institutions (or at least to the taste of Northern Dirteaters, who would lick the boots of a Southern planter for the profit to be got out of him in the way of trade) was no caricature of Slaveholding sentiment, or of the feelings of Northern white slaves.

Aug. 11. Olmsted at 823 this P.M. — Bad news. The "Mariposa Company" wants him for Superintend[t] of its mines & lands (a whole County, producing $100.000 a month —) & offers him a salary of $10. or $15000 with contingent profits beside. Olmsted has not a mercenary nerve in his moral organization, but he has a wife & children to provide for — and he wants the luxury of paying certain debts of the old Putnam's Magazine concern with which he was connected, for which debts he was never legally liable nor morally liable, so far as I can make out. — Then this position would make him the leading man in a colony of some 7000 dependents of the Company, thus far unorganized & uncivilized, without a Church or a schoolhouse, & such position has great attractions for him. I fear he will take it — & that he ought to take it — even tho' the San: Com: suffer, & the contemplated Periodical come to naught.

Dined with C.E.S. & G.A. [M: Dor:] & to U.L. Club thereafter.

Would I knew that E. & the children were well to night.

Symptoms reported of reaction toward loyalty, submission, or pacification, in Mississippi & N. Carolina. Southern newspaper quotations confirm them. Such reaction if strong enough to determine the policy of any one Rebel State would do harm, by strengthening the feeble brethren who would like to settle affairs by patching up any sort of compromise with Rebellion. But if just *short* of that degree of importance, it is a most favorable symptom. Any Rebel State negotiating about Reconstruction at this time would weaken the North, but the more penitence & contrition among individual Rebels, the better — of course. And it would seem that those gracious tempers are becoming manifest in the S.W.

We hardly appreciate, even yet, the magnitude of this War — the issues that depend on it's result — the importance of the chapter in the World's History that we are helping to write. In our hearts we esteem the struggle as the London Times does, or pretends to. — God forgive our blindness! It is the struggle of two hostile & irreconcilable systems of Society for the rule of this Continent. Since Mahometanism & Christendom met in battle this side the Pyrenees, there has been no struggle so momentous for mankind. I think that Grant & Rosecrans, Lee & Stonewall Jackson & Joe Johnston &c &c &c will be more conspicuous, & better known to students of history A.D. 1963, than Wallenstein & Gustavus, Condé, Napoleon, Frederick, Wellington, & the late Lord Raglan. Not as greater Generals, but as fighting on a larger field & in a greater cause than any of them. So will our great great . . . . . grandchildren look back on them a century hence, whatever be the result.

Aug: 12. Wednesday. We still broil. — Meeting of Sav'gs Bank Trustees this P.M. Usual routine. Thence to 823 — thence to dinner with C.E.S. & then to U.L. Club. Night for monthly meeting, but no quorum of course. Gen: Canby there, a tall dark grave silent man. He looks as if we could trust him. Dix & he may have important work to do within a month — for many believe that Gov: Seymour means to assert his state right theories & get up a collision with Government. I do'nt believe he has the pluck to do it, but the insidious editorials of the N.Y. World, growing bolder daily, look as if Seymour & his friends were feeling their way toward a Northern Rebellion — as a diversion in aid of Jeff: Davis. The coprophagous Coleoptera! But I can't do justice to that subject.

Aug. 13. A general attack by land & water on Sumter, Wagner, & Cumming's Point was to have been delivered to day, according to the ev'g papers. Our officers confident that Sumter will be destroyed & the Rebel works generally pulverized in about two hours. I have known an equally rose-colored prognosis to fail, in more cases than one, since the War began. The chances are that the masonry of Sumter will go down before our 200 lb: rifled Parrotts, but the earth works & sand bag batteries will stand much pounding.

Gen: *Grant's* Report of the campaign for the reduction of Vicksburgh is modest businesslike & creditable. His operations seem to have been most brilliant & enterprising. No general on either side has a record so distinguished. Dix tells me that when Adj^{t} Genl Thomas went to the S.W. last spring he had an order in his pocket relieving *Grant* and putting *McClernand* in his place. Personal observation satisfied the A.G. that it was a blunder, so he kept it in his pocket, telegraphed to Washington that the change would do harm, & got the order recalled — most fortunately, it would seem.

Nigger-recruiting prospers. Rumor of a Corps d'Afrique to be raised *here*. Why not? Paddy, the asylum-burner, would swear at the dam Naygurs, but we need bayonets in Negro hands, if Paddy is unwilling to fight for the Country that receives & shelters him in his poverty, & transmutes him into an Alderman & a wealthy citizen. If he back out, let us accept, with contrition & humiliation, the services of this despised &

rejected race, & be thankful that it is willing to enlist in the cause of a nation from which it has received only contumely & persecution.

Experience of a N.Y. "Rough" who visited *Boston* for the purpose of assisting at the attempted Anti-Draft Riot there, which was dispersed by a discharge of grapeshot from the Arsenal or Armory. "I've come away from Boston. Never saw such a dam place. Aint a-goin' back to a place like that, I tell yer. Why, *if a feller picks up a brick, they just heave a peck of Shot at him*". — Bully for Bosting.

Aug. 18. At N° 24 I find Mr S.B.R. full of his mission to Berlin, & coruscating brilliantly with facts & figures & views. He will go, next Saturday, barring accident, & I'm glad of it, for he will do us credit. He is the very best man in the Country, I suppose, for that particular job. The ultimate object he contemplates is to shew Europe that we can supply all the food & all the gold the world requires, and that we can do it better & cheaper than we could if disintegrated. To establish these two propositions will help & strengthen us abroad, not a little. It's a pity & a shame that Seward gave Mr R. so little notice of his appointment & so little time for preparation.

At U.L. Club. Henry Winthrop, Agnew (just escaped from the crowd & discomfort of Saratoga) Delano, Dudley B. Fuller &c — also Col. Howe, whose trumpet is in fine working order to night. "By tomorrow noon there will be 12000 more troops here" — "two regiments of Sykes' corps" — "Gen: Ayres — who is to take charge of the East Side of the City" &c &c &c. Blood & thunder in general. Government displays such force here that there will be no "muss" tomorrow, I think. The Copperheads cannot be strong enough to try that game a second time — nor have they forgotten the damage done their wicked cause by the little experiment they made a month ago. Treason & insurrection are distasteful to the meanest Copperhead, if he have Taxes to pay. It's most fortunate that Gov: Seymour is at least as much Coward as Traitor. Were he both bold & bad he could do fearful mischief; he might perhaps even succeed in degrading the country to his own level, by arraying this state against the Administration. But it's unwholesome to think too much about him, or about the Woods, Brookses, Barlows,

Duncans, & other vermin of his family. They will have their reward. Their names will be infamous & their children will be ashamed of them twenty years hence, or I am no prophet. The poor fellows do'nt see the greatness & importance of this struggle. They do'nt appreciate the times they live in — they underestimate *to-day* — "a Prince in disguise" to every man. They suppose their dirty work sanctioned by Political Party usage, & that they are fighting the Administration just as Opposition partizans have been fighting administrations for the last thirty years, honestly & fairly or dishonestly & unfairly, nobody cares to remember how. But people *will* care to remember the details of the battle now pending between Slavery & Free Labor for the control of this Continent, & the Northern backers of Slavery & Rebellion are making themselves *Historical* scoundrels & earning a place beside Benedict Arnold in the text books of our Common Schools. Whether we succeed or collapse, their future is certain.

Aug: 19. Drafting began to day. We have all felt some secret misgivings that Government might leave the law unexecuted here in N.Y. & so give the rioters of last month a substantial triumph. But we are spared that disgrace & calamity. The draft is in full progress, & thus far without sign of disturbance. I visited the scene of operations (6th Av: near 12th St.) at two, & found a small crowd on the Avenue, looking at the working of the wheel on the 2^{d} story of the building & in full view. They were orderly & in good humor. I heard no snarling. The Vis major is on the side of Law & Order. A battalion of the 14th Regulars, & the 5th Wisconsin, have taken military possession of Madison Square, & little Squads of Hirelings & Myrmidons have been marching up & down all day, looking very busy.

Geo: Anthon's friend *Beaver*, a highly educated Englishman, Fellow of Jesus Coll: Oxford, who went off West & got a position on Sibley's staff, for the sake of a little adventure & Indian shooting I suppose, is reported killed in one of Sibley's Indian fights on the Missouri. G.A. was much attached to Beaver.

Our batteries have been at work in Charleston Harbor, but it's uncertain whether we have made any progress. Rumor that Parrott shells have been tossed from Morris Island into the City itself — about 5 miles — seems incredible — but we have heard marvellous statements as to the range of these 200 & 300 pounders.

Much importance attached to a very elaborate N: Car: newspaper publication, said to be the work of some noted Chivalric & political magnate of that beggarly province. It does credit to it's author's common sense, be he who he may: denounces secession as a crime & a blunder, administers pepper to the "Confederate" Gov[t], expatiates, *not* very ruefully, on the failing fortunes of the Confederacy, & clamors loudly for Peace. People over-estimate it's significance, but it certainly proves that the Chivalry of N. Car. is not a Unit in favor of protracted resistance & death in the Last Ditch, & that there is a Reaction at last among *rational* N. Carolinians. Whether this reasonable minority is large or small does'nt appear.

Governor of Alabama orders a Negro conscription! "Eget mauri jaculis", not being altogether "integer vitæ" probably. Two years of Southern hysterics & an inferior article of whiskey must have brought on softening of his brain. These madmen have made a nice mess of their rebellion for the maintenance & extension of Slavery. Every month weakens that blessed institution more & more fatally. Arming & drilling Cuffee in it's defence seems likely to give it a final blow. Russell was right in calling the Southerners a strange compound of *tigers & children* — see his "Diary". They are not tiger-monkies like Revolutionary Frenchmen, but tiger-donkies, or tiger-goslings.

Aug: 20th. Called at N[o] 24 this ev'g. Saw M[r] S.B.R. & *Baron Gerolt*, the Prussian Minister, who recommends that M[r] R. take with him to Berlin some sets of San: Com: reports & documents, which he thinks will be appreciated. — Thence to U.L. Club. Com: on Admissions had a session. Surgeon Gen: *Hammond* was there with *Van Buren* — also *Gen: Ayres* — &c &c &c.

Olmsted has completed his arrangement with the Mariposa people, & is to busy himself for five years in a mountain gorge of California. We can ill spare him.

Aug. 21. At 823 were important letters. D[r] Marsh, at *Morris Island* reports *Scurvy*, & wants more *curried cabbage*, which he finds a sure anti-scorbutic, when potatoes & onions & lemon juice fail. — Dr Steiner, our Acting Executive Officer at Wash^{n} in Olmsted's absence, has confidential intelligence that there is to be a movement on Texas, led by Gen: *Dan Sickles*, & wants a good Inspector to send with it.

Collision with L. Napoleon not impossible in that quarter! I suppose Sickles, with his one leg, among our best volunteer officers. His recuperative powers are certainly wonderful. Four years ago he was a ruined man in every sense, a *Pariah*, whom to know was discreditable.

Aug. 22. Rebel reports from Charleston are encouraging. Our heavy guns have nearly silenced Sumter, and are demolishing it's masonry. I think we shall hear in a day or two that we have *mashed* that memorable fortalice. It's destruction will not be the conquest of Charleston, but it will be an important step that way, and an intense gratification to all loyal people.

Confound those Dutchmen, outside, — drunk probably — who are trying to keep themselves cool by singing Scraps of Martha, hideously out of tune.

I'm nearly *done through*. The half-moon visible thro' the Library windows is of a sultry dark red.

Troops continue to arrive here from Meade's Army, which must be seriously weakened. We have already more than enough to ensure the execution of the draft in this City, & I suppose these newcomers are to be sent to Texas or possibly to Morris Island. It looks hazardous & imprudent to withdraw so many men from the Potomac, but I suppose that Halleck & Stanton know what they are about.

Carlyle's "*Ilias Americana*" — a summary of the American War, in a London Magazine, is an astounding concentration of blunders about matters of fact into a dozen lines. Carlyle *has* had much influence on my notions about things in general, for twenty years, but I have no more respect for, & no confidence in, the man who wrote this flippant little bit of falsehood & immorality. It's his misfortune to labor under a monomaniacal inclination to abase himself before *Strength* when contending successfully with Law & established System. He worships "the God of Forces", not the God of Justice & Right. Hence his deification of Cromwell, Napoleon, & Frederick. See the 3^{d} vol: of his Life of Frederick for a specimen of the style in which he disposes of the rather important question whether that Hero had or had not a right to seize occupy & hold Silesia — whether his conflict with Austria was just or unjust. Frederick was able to make his Rights, whatever they were, *valid* against "Owleries" & "Enchanted Wiggeries" &c. That's all Mr C. can say or tries to say in defence of his Hero's moral position. Natural enough & quite consistent that Carlyle should love the Rebels, who are fighting against a Constitution — have shewn most creditable pluck, & were seemingly in a fair way toward success when this dirty little squib was written.

Aug. 24. Down to Clinton Place this ev'g to enquire after G.F. Allen, seriously prostrated by dysentery. His brother Horatio says he's better, but there's still room for anxiety about him. We cannot afford to lose men like him in these times — nor men like Olmsted, who is to entomb himself in an auriferous ravine of the California mountains. He goes to Wash^n this ev'g to wind up his Sanitary Com: work. — From Clinton Place to U.L. Club, where were twenty or thirty members & C.A. Dana (whilome of the *Tribune*) who has been spending several months in some official or quasi-official position with Gen: Grant, & went thro' all the splendid campaign that ended with the surrender of Vicksburgh & Port Hudson. Dana was under examination, the object of a concentric fire of queries, which he answered very intelligently & clearly. I do'nt know what his judgment is worth, but he thinks that Rebellion in the S.W. has gone to Eternal Smash, & that we have only to settle details of reconstruction & pick up the pieces. He says that many great Slave-holding princes of Western Mississippi have been & are doing their utmost to further Grant's operations, being satisfied that the cause of the Confederacy is hopeless, & desiring only peace & order on any terms, with Slavery or without it. Expects that *Arkansas* will soon formally secede from Secession & return to her normal condition. Says that Grant *does'nt* drink. Tells an interesting story of characteristic illbreeding snobbishness & arrogance displayed by Gen: Pemberton & his chivalric pals during the negotiations for surrender of Vicksburgh — &c &c &c. *Northern manners* are less showy & splendid than *Southern Chivalry*, but sounder & better nevertheless.

News from the siege of Charleston, up to Wednesday or Thursday last, is promising. Sumter badly pounded: Fort Gregg ("Cummings Point") silenced. *Wagner* seems to hold out.

Burnside is moving on Knoxville in East Tennessee, & Rosecrans on Chattanooga. His advance is in contact with the Rebel forces there, according to the 3^d edition of Post & Commercial.

Aug. 25. Tuesday. Ev'g overcast — no sea-breeze — brutally hot all day. Good tidings from Charleston by Richmond papers. Charleston telegraphs on Sunday that Sumter is "a ruin", it's guns silenced, gorge wall beaten down, one or two faces breached, it's interior swept by shot & shell. Also that Gillmore has notified Beauregard that shells mean to begin making calls in the City "Monday at 11 A.M." & that noncombatants had better move. I dont understand, nor does Prof: Bache (at the Club tonight) how Gillmore is going to get his projectiles into *Charleston* but this warning would not have been given unless Gillmore saw his way reasonably clear. — *Aliunde* there are reports that Sumter has surrendered & that shelling of the City has begun; but they are less trustworthy.

Aug. 26. Wednesday. Weather has changed: to day gloriously cool & clear. From Charleston we have a despatch to the Richmond papers dated Monday, stating that the town began to be infested by Parrott shells the night before, & that noncombatants were moving out as fast as they could. This statement would hardly have been manufactured at C. or R. If it's true these visitors must have come from the Monitors, & the Monitors must have got nearer the City than I thought they could. It's apparently authentic, & it gives particulars, "15 eight inch Parrott shells", beginning at Midnight of Sunday; but I doubt.

G.F. Allen very seriously ill with dysentery of a bad type, but Horatio A. do'nt seem alarmed about him to night.

Long talk with G.W. Blunt & others at Club. — It seems certain that the Riot of July has damaged Seymour & his friends seriously, in this City. It has stirred up also a feeling against *Irishmen* more bitter & proscriptive than was displayed by the most thorough Native American partizans in former times.

No wonder. The atrocities those Celtic devils perpetrated can hardly be paralleled in the history of human crime & cruelty, and were without shadow of provocation or excuse.

Aug. 27. Nothing much later from Charleston, but there are a few farther details of our operations up to Monday noon. Sumter is pulverized. The shells thrown into the City seem to have emanated from a land battery in the marsh to the left of Morris Island. So Collins is told by an officer who came here on the Arago to day. Beauregard protests against these shells as barbaric. So would rats protest against terriers no doubt, if they could speak, and the Pediculus family against brimstone. Who was it that took the pretended grievances of South Carolina out of the domain of law & reason, and first appealed to brute force? Wonder what Beauregard & Jeff: Davis think of the massacre just perpetrated at Lawrence in Kansas by *Quantrill* & his gang of amateur border-ruffians — arson & murder inflicted wholesale on a peaceful settlement of non-combatants.

San: Com: is doing a good work most thoroughly on Morris Island, under Dr Marsh.

We have a long job there — no end of forts & earth works to reduce before we are absolute masters of the City & it's approaches. But Bache says the extinction of Sumter enables us to close the harbor against Blockade-runners. If we can do that, & destroy the town & the shipping at it's wharves with incendiary shells, we need not put ourselves into a perspiration about Fort Moultrie, & Fort Ripley &c &c &c. I suppose another attack has been delivered before this upon Fort Wagner, or perhaps on the newly established James Island batteries. Gov^t^ has been engaging civil surgeons for service in that quarter.

Aug. 28. From Charleston we have Gillmore's official Report of the demolition of Sumter. He says it is destroyed for all purposes of offence or defence, & that he shall pay it no farther attention. We have also the statement that Gillmore has occupied both Sumter & Wagner. It seems tolerably direct & authentic, but is not believed.

At U.L. Club to night, Barney the Collector tells me of an interview between Gen. Dix & *Waterbury* during the Riot Week, how the latter tried a little treasonable talk & how summarily

Dix snubbed & suppressed him. According to Barney, this wretched little Copperhead advised Gov. Seymour to take command of the State Militia, & to forbid their firing on the mob, and also to "forbid" any interference by U.S. troops. In other words, to "intervene" against Government in aid of the Riot. Wonder whether the Secret history of that atrocious business will ever be truly written. Wonder if Fernandy-Wud's departure to Canada, or to Europe, or to whatever region it is that he has transferred himself & his scoundrelism, were in fact a prudential move, as some say it was. Many believe that Government holds proofs of F. Wood's guilty connexion with Richmond & Charleston, & has warned him that his disappearance will promote his health. Perhaps. I hope not, for Government would be immensely strengthened if any prominent New Yorker were legally indicted for treason, fairly tried, deliberately convicted, oratorically sentenced, & formally hanged. If there be legal evidence against Wood he might be made most useful to the Country in this way — so useful that one would almost forgive the mischief he has been doing us for so many years.

Aug. 31. Dined with Agnew at Maison Dorée, and went with him to Van Buren's, where was the Surgeon General. He sails in the Arago tomorrow for Hilton Head & goes thence to N. Orleans, under orders from the War Department. He thinks it's the first step in a scheme of Stanton's to supersede him & he is probably right. Stanton shook him by both hands when he bade him good bye, & it is generally understood at Wash^{n} that that mark of cordiality is the invariable precursor of some stab or blow at it's recipient.

Hammond says the regular regiments now in this City are destined for Texas — but under *Joe Hooker* instead of *Sickles* — that Mexico means to recognize the Confederacy, & will be thereupon invaded, & that the prophets of Washington predict war with *France*. Not at all unlikely.

Sept. 1. Tuesday night. Found myself, on awaking, under sustained fire from a sick headache of twenty inch calibre, & lay abed till two o'clock, when a shower-bath & a cup of tea enabled me to stagger down to N° 823 & attend to a little San: Com: business. Home again at 6. Murray Hoffman called. I went down at 9 to U.L. Club, & spent an hour there.

Talk with Gen: Reid, introduced by M[r] Collector Barney. He has been serving under Grant. Has seen raw regiments of niggers under fire, & thinks they behave as well as white folks.

Many rumors — of skirmish, & of Raid, & of impending battle in Arkansas, but none of them worth recording. We are rather depressed by our slow progress toward the reduction of Charleston. Gold rises. We forget that the siege of Troy lasted ten years, tho' Troy had no sand-bag works & no rifled guns.

Report that Jeff. Davis has ordered the Conscription of 500.000 slaves wants confirmation badly. It would be equivalent to a decree of emancipation, & would give the Peculiar Institution it's coup de grace.

Our draft (in N.Y.) has terminated peaceably. I fear it will not be a "miraculous draught" & that Gov[t] will get far fewer men than it needs.

Every one at the Club full of deep sincere regret for Geo: Allen's death. He is universally lamented.

My thoughts keep constantly reverting to that grassy hillside, & I find myself wondering whether it be really true that he is under it. — No longer ago than Thursday night, the 20th, he was at the Club, in his usual health & spirits, presided at meeting of Com: on Admissions, & was full of kind enquiries about Ellie & the children.

Sept. 2[d]. Newspaper gabble about the "backbone of the Rebellion" being "broken at last" is abundant & nauseating. I dread premature insolent jubilations as a tempting of Providence. We have gained most important results since 1st July, of course, & God be praised for them, but the Herald &c talk in a strain that would be reasonable if we had taken Charleston Mobile & Wilmington, dispersed Lee's Army, & occupied Texas, & if Jeff. Davis & 100 of his chief Rajahs had been severally committed to await the action of the Grand Jury. — G.C.A. has returned from Newport, where he has been staying with Geo. F. Jones. There has been much sickness at Newport, chiefly dysentery & disorders of that class. Bradish died of dysentery. M[rs] Eleanor Strong has survived a most severe & perilous visitation of Cholera Morbus or some such thing. D[r] Barker says she came very near dying.

Prof: Bull Anthon found a Regiment of regulars, the other day, *squatting* on one of the vacant blocks of Col: Coll: property on W. side of 5th Av: about 50th St. & accosted a tall sergeant.

Prof. "By whose authority, sir, have you taken possession of these premises?"

Sergt. "By *Abe Lincoln's* authority, G— d— you. What have you got to say about it? Sa-a-a-ay!"

The Profr subsided & walked down town.

Sept. 3d. Thursday. Another blank day, in the usual ruts. Journalizing languishes, & it's unprofitableness is specially manifest. The proverb is reversed in our case. "No news is *bad* news" from Charleston & from Chattanooga. There was a story in the street this morn'g that Gillmore had evacuated Morris Island, being shelled out by the rebel batteries on James Island. It is apocryphal & improbable, but stocks went down & Gold went up to 131. A tight money-market & rumors of a new Government loan are quite sufficient to account for this. Nobody pretends to believe the Morris Island story, & nobody knows of anybody who believes it. But it's high time for a Disaster. We have been winning battles & reducing strongholds so long that a Disaster must be at hand if there be any truth in the Doctrine of Chances, & anything fortuitous in the "fortunes of war".

Dined with G.A. this aftn. — Lincoln's little letter defending his War-policy is very good, a straightforward simple honest forcible exposition of his views, & likely to be a conspicuous document in the history of our times. There are sentences that a critic would like to eliminate, but they are delightfully characteristic of the "plain man" who wrote it, & will appeal directly to the great mass of "plain men" from Maine to Minnesota. I think this little letter a brilliantly successful move. The squirmings of the World & Express are painful to behold.

Visited *Barnum's* this aftn. His Aquaria have just recd a large accession of fish from Bermuda. Many of them very curious & beautiful.

Sept. 4. Friday. We have news from Charleston Harbor to the 31st. Not very weighty, but looking like slow steady progress. Our Iron Clads were then "abreast of Fort Moultrie", & Fort

Wagner was silenced. Certain "rifle-pits" in it's front had been carried & we had taken some 70 prisoners. A reconnoissance by night is said to have ascertained that the Obstructions in the channel can be managed. Guns had been mounted on Sumter (which takes a deal of killing) but seem to have been speedily dismounted again. — Why do'nt Dahlgren try "a big rush" up to the City with his fleet? — [Echo answers "Probably because he knows more about his business than you do, and thinks it would not be judicious."] — From Knoxville & Chattanooga we have little gleams of information, very faint, but favorable. If Rosecrans & Burnside succeed, Rebellion will be sorely damaged.

Weather is cool & lovely. Gold up & stocks down. Death of old Greene C. Bronson. Dined with Van Buren & Agnew at Maison Dorée. — Club afterwards, & G.C.A.

Sept. 8. Burnside & Rosecrans seems to have grabbed Eastern Tennessee without serious opposition. Rebel-dom asserts itself only in the Chattanooga region, & the decisive battle of this War may perhaps be fought there. But we have reports this afternoon from "authentic" deserters that the troops of Bragg, Buckner, Joe Johnston & C° are demoralized, mutinous, deserting in squads, fleeing to the Mountains, watching & waiting for the Old Flag. May be so. May be not.

On Morris Island we hold our own, & perhaps gain ground. But the shattered casemates of Sumter "still live", & require more pounding. The pluck & endurance of the handful of traitors that continue to hold it are admirable.

At 823 this aft^{n} with Agnew & Knapp. Discussed the grave question of filling Olmsted's place. Agnew wants Dr Newberry. I rather incline toward Jenkins. Dr Steiner has certain qualifications for the place. Dr Douglas has not.

Sept. 11th. We have much good news to thank God for. The tide of National Success keeps rising, without check.

Wednesday we heard, but hardly dared believe — that the Rebels abandoned Fort Wagner & "Battery Gregg" last Sunday night. The news is fully confirmed. Gillmore holds all Morris Island. His guns are in full view of Charleston which is now confessedly at his mercy & within very easy range. Much remains to be done before all it's detached harbor defences are reduced, but the valiant Beauregard, alias Peter Toutant, may very possibly spike his guns, scuttle his iron-clads, & withdraw his men to help Lee or Bragg, before ten days are past. Our Monitors, when last heard from, (Tuesday, I think) were pounding Rebel batteries on Sullivan's Island & had just blown up a Magazine in Moultrie.

Yesterday's papers announced that the "formidable Mountain stronghold" of *Chattanooga* is given up without a fight. Rosecrans is in full possession of it, & E. Tennessee is liberated & redeemed & rescued at last.

To day's papers, read on the Mary Powell's forward deck, with Dr Cogswell, & gassy Alfred Pell, told us that a rebel force of 2000 at Cumberland Gap has surrendered — that the Arkansites have abandoned their state capital (Little Rock) — & that Gen: X has routed Gen: Y (Rebel) driving him across Bayou Z. I do not remember the names. Sitch is Glory.

Evacuation of Chattanooga generally received as a decisive confirmation of reports that the Rebels are dispirited & demoralized in the S.W. & as proof that there is no *fight* in them. But the felon-chivalry may have given up East Tennessee in order to concentrate it's resources for an irresistible attack somewhere else — e.g. on Washington. It would be a desperate move, like the Sacrifice of a Queen & two Castles to secure a Checkmate dimly worked out twenty moves ahead — & would do Rebeldom special mischief by strengthening the "submissionist" or Reconstructist minority, which Southern newspapers begin to recognize & at which they scold as if it were not by any means insignificant. The indications therefore on the whole favor the opinion that the "Backbone of the Rebellion" is badly cracked, tho' not yet broken.

Yet it seems unprecedented & unlikely that social & political questions so grave as those we are fighting about, & involving all the destiny of so vast a territory should be settled by a Single War. No issues of like importance to mankind have been submitted to Trial by Battle since the Saracen invasion of Western Europe was beat back by Charles Martel. And this too is a Religious war. Two antagonistic creeds are struggling for possession of half a continent. For Mahometanism is nearer the common faith of Christendom than is the modern advanced type of Southern Christianity, so called. By their fruits ye shall know them. A church that inculcates Anti-Christian Ethics & makes crime & oppression a paramount duty, is to say the least no better than one founded on Anti-Christian dogmas.

Southern vaporings about "*Infidel*" Abolitionists, (meaning by Abolitionist every body who objects to Slavery whether on moral or economical grounds) seem to recognize this essential antagonism between the two Religions. — tho' Southern Editors & Orators habitually use bad language & call names in such a loose random hysterical way that one can hardly infer anything from their words, except spite & rage & bad whiskey. There is much "fousel oil" in most of their lucubrations.

Sept. 12th. We have undergone a repulse in Charleston Harbor. Boat attack on the ruins of Sumter beat off with loss, as, it seems to me, anybody might have known it would be.

People grumble at Dahlgren, & call him a *Marine McClellan* — i.e. a brave & capable man but over-cautious, unwilling to encounter risks.

Bennett comes out against Govr Seymour. A good sign. The sagacious old rat knows when his ship is unseaworthy.

Sept: 23. News Monday night that *Rosecrans* had been badly defeated at "Chittamauga Creek" — if that's it's name — & had fallen back on Chattanooga, after a two days' battle. It looked like a grave disaster & perhaps it is, but later news looks better. He has certainly had a severe fight, suffered heavy loss, & encountered a serious check. But Rebel dispatches speak in subdued tone. It was probably a desperate but indecisive conflict, & every battle in which the Rebels come short of complete victory is equivalent to a Rebel defeat just now.

At 823 this aft^{n}. Our San: Com: agents with Meade's army call for a large consignment of *Chloroform*, which was sent them. The call is suggestive of movement & battle in Virginia. Lee seems tending to fall back, step by step, toward the field-works before Richmond. Some portion of his Army has been withdrawn Southwestwardly & helped Bragg contest Rosecrans' advance into Georgia.

Sept. 25. No precise information yet as to the result of Rosecrans' late battle. People take it for granted that it's all right, but I have misgivings, & our bits & scraps of intelligence from that quarter do not improve as they come in, but rather tend to assume a well-defined blue tint. I guess it will turn out that we were badly beat, but that it cost Bragg so dear that he cannot follow up his victory, and that Rosecrans is rapidly receiving reinforcements. The Rebellion cannot afford victories of that sort.

From what Rosecrans told Captn Keteltas when he gave him his furlough, it seems certain that R. expected not only to occupy Chattanooga but to penetrate well into Georgia without a battle, & that he was confident that the bulk of Bragg's army had been sent to *Charleston*. This looks a little as if he had been out-generalled — for Bragg's army seems to have been on the spot in full force, & with a large detachment from Lee's army to help it.

Dined at Dr Bellows' yesterday, with the Surgeon General, Agnew, Van Buren, Norris of San Francisco, Dr Bell of Louisville (terribly shattered by recent illness & reclining on a sofa all dinner time) Dr Chapin — who is very entertaining — et aliis. Hammond has just returned from Charleston Harbor & is off for the West & N. Orleans to day. He lauds & magnifies the work of the San: Commission on Morris Island. Says Gen. Gillmore told him he had now accomplished all he undertook to do when he went there — viz: to drive the Rebels off Morris Island & to silence Fort Sumter. The programme was that the iron-clads, when no longer endangered by the plunging fire of Sumter, would finish the job. But Dahlgren hesitates about encountering the hypothetical obstructions & submarine torpedoes of the inner harbor, & is grumbled at, as over-cautious. The Sec: of War assures pretty Mrs Hammond that he never dreamed of ousting her husband from the Surgeon Generalship. May be so. His instructions to Hammond for his Western tour certainly look as if he were not to be displaced. Perhaps Stanton has been a little enlightened within the last month. A letter that appeared in the Herald some ten days ago purporting to come from an Assistant Surgeon of Volunteers, but in fact written by *Col: Chas. G. Halpine*, is said to have made a sensation in the medico-military circles of Washington, & to have satisfied Stanton that his manipulation of the Medical Bureau was *watched*.

Sept. 26. News from Meade's Army is suppressed. This confirms the hints of our San: Com: Agents that some important movement is going on. Whatever it is, it do'nt look like an advance on Richmond, for detachments from Meade are going West by Baltimore & Ohio R.R. probably to strengthen Rosecrans. It seems certain now that Rosecrans was badly beat at "Chickamauga". But he still holds Chattanooga & commands Eastern Tennessee. If he can maintain his hold on that vital centre of Rebeldom, his defeat is unimportant — but I fear his communications will be endangered, & he will be forced to fall back.

I have forgotten to register for the benefit of Posterity, the funniest incident of the Riot Week — gravely detailed to Ellie a fortnight ago by little Elbridge Gerry. You are doubtless aware, O Posterity, that Gerry lives with old Goelet, his uncle, in the big oldfashioned house on the corner of Broadway & 19th St. with a big court-yard around it. Old Goelet's business is the receipt of Rents & the investment of capital. His relaxation is the culture of Gallinacea. Everybody that passes his courtyard stops to look through the iron railing at his superb peacocks, golden pheasants, silver pheasants, California quail &c &c &c. — Well, Gerry was telling all the great things he did, & all the tremendous things he was prepared to do, last July: how he armed the servants, & barricaded the windows. He is a very grandiose young man. "One of the great objects at which I aimed" said Gerry, "was to make the house as little *conspicuous* as possible." — "But" said Mrs Ellie "your house is always conspicuous: the beautiful birds in your courtyard always attract people's attention". "Ah" — said G. "I provided for that. Just as soon as the disturbances commenced, I sent for my Coachman, & *I ordered him to pull out all the Tails of all those birds.* — It is really quite remarkable" proceeded Gerry "but the new tails have not grown yet, and whenever my peacocks hop up on the fence they always lose their balance & *teeter* over forward".

Sept. 28. At 823 this aftn were Dr Bellows & Dr Agnew. Scandlin & McDonald our San: Com: Agents, captured at Gettysburgh & just released from their Richmond prison, give an interesting account of their hard experiences in Secesh-dom. They were allowed to go out at intervals & air their lousiness in the streets of Richmond. A sentinel was at every corner, &

no man woman or child could walk a single block without a Pass. Everybody was on short commons & distrusted everybody else. Rebel officers told them that half the people were longing for the restoration of National Rule. Which story I think doubtful.

Rev: Young asked for leave of absence. Wants to go to Europe for six months because his health is impaired by diligent performance of parochial duty. Also he belongs to two "Commissions" appointed by the last Gen: Convention — one to revise the Hymnbook, & the other to negotiate terms of alliance & intercommunion with the Russian Church (which project will never come to anything) & he wanted another six months to attend to these two jobs, in England & in Russia. I demurred to sending a Southern Sympathizer to represent the Church abroad, & to my agreeable surprise, almost every one present expressed the same feeling, & more strongly than I had ventured to do. Swift instantly withdrew his motion to grant the leave asked for, and very sharp things were said by Cisco Youngs Skidmore & others. (Gen: Dix, by the by, said nothing one way or the other.) I moved to table the application instead of declining it, so that the Rev. Young could have an opportunity to assert his loyalty if he pleases, & to prove it, if he can. But he can say nothing to the purpose. He has been comparatively decent & quiet of late, but for months after the war began he was an offensive blatant supporter of the rebellion, & last winter he had a pet batch of arrested Rebel presbyters from New Orleans living in his house. He is rather clever too, & his talk about our public affairs, with Oxford sons of Russian Archimandrites, would do us harm, more or less, especially coming from one officially representing (in some sense) the American Church at large, & connected with the first parish in the Country. So I shall not help him to go abroad. If he wants six months holiday let him spend it in this country which is quite as salubrious as Canterbury or Moscow.

Sept. 29. To night Dr Bellows & Dr Agnew here, & also Dr Jenkins. We miss Olmsted & Gibbs, each a substantial loss to this community. There was much good talk over the supper table from 10 to 12.

D[r] Marsh, San: Com: Inspector from Port Royal & Morris Island is in town, & I discoursed him at length this aft[n] at N[o] 823. His Report most interesting & important, but it's too late to record it's details. It is to be received cum grano salis, for Marsh's personal equation is a most appreciable element in the computation of the value of his statements. He does not tend to over-value his own services, or to over-state his confidential intimacy with Gen: Gillmore & his relation as patron & protector to Gen: Gillmore's medical staff. His work on Morris Island has done the Commission the greatest credit. But he is possessed by a demon of criticism & cavil, & depreciation.

He says among other things that we are farther from Charleston than we were six weeks ago. The "Swamp-Angel" battery has been knocked to pieces & its position cannot be recovered for the present. It was nearer Charleston than is Cumming's Point wh: we now hold. Gillmore does'nt shell Charleston for the sufficient reason that his guns will not carry so far. He can do nothing more without heavy re-inforcements, which are promised him. Without the iron-clads we could not hold Morris Island forty eight hours. He is now erecting huge curtains & traverses to protect his force from the Guns of James Island & Sullivan. He has made artillery practice at long range a specialité & understands it as well as any living man. But Marsh evidently thinks his capacity as a General below the average. Our assaults on Wagner were ill planned & murderously bungled. Etcetera: etc: etc:

Jenkins is fresh from a visit to Culpeper, Meade's headquarters. His advance is on this bank of the Rapidan, some eight miles farther South. His force about 45000. Two divisions have just been withdrawn from him. One has gone West over B. & O. R.R. under Gen: Joe Hooker. It's officers grumble at serving under him. The other may be going the same way, or may be going South. Transports are waiting at Alexandria, for somebody.

Oct: 1. This ev'g to Club — Large assemblage, & a speech from a Rev: Englishman, D[r] Massie, who is here to represent the Anti Southern feeling of England. He seems a sensible venerable old Codger — white as to his hair, nut-crackery as to his countenance, accurate as to his diction.

Oct. 2[d]. D[r] Marsh tells me that about half an hour after our repulse from Fort Wagner, an Ohio L[t] gave him this little incident of the assault. The L[t] was climbing the scarp, preceded by a S.C. recruit of the 54th Mass: under a galling fire, when the Nigger dropped. He stooped & asked "Are you hit?" He was answered "Yes Mas'r, *I'm done gone* — but go ahead & do'nt mind stepping on me". The L[t] "did'nt mind" & pushed forward, trampling on the prostrate body. Such stupid soulless brutes are the black peasantry of the South!!! "None of them dam Niggers shall speak to me, be Jasus". "Modern Physiology, my dear sir, has, as you must be aware, demonstrated the essential inferiority of the black race, & proved it to be Anthropoid rather than human". Certainly. Why not? The negro can be taught reading & writing & the first four rules of Arithmetic, to be sure, & he is capable of keeping a hotel. He can fight like a hero, & live & die like a Christian. But look at his Facial Angle, sir, & at the peculiarities of his skeleton, & you will at once perceive that his place is with the Chimpanzee & the Gorilla, not with *man*. Physical Science is absolutely infallible you know. No matter what the Church or the Bible or human instincts or common sense may seem to say on any subject, Physical Science is always entitled to overrule them. It's very true that the Science of 1863 has reversed or modified about 250.000 of the decisions it gave twenty years ago; but that makes no difference. That's the Advance of Science. Geology & physiology & M[r] Darwin & Prof: Oken &c &c &c are fallible as against each other. They can squabble among themselves, & can abolish on Wednesday the infallible truths they agreed to promulgate on Tuesday. But their voice is conclusive, for the time being. If they adjudge my respectable friend *Downing* not to be a thriving dealer in Oysters & a vestryman & a brother, but merely an intelligent Anthropoid Ape, we must accept their opinion. If they discover that all men, birds, beasts, creeping things, fishes, plants, & trees, have been somehow "developed" from Amœbas Naviculæ & fungi, or from some still lower germ, by a process of Development & Natural Selection, that would require more years than I could express in Arabic numerals on 100 of these pages, we must gulp down the miracle, because it is a scientific proposition. If they find an old bone in a mud-flat we must accept their inference that men began to live two million five hundred & sixty seven thousand years ago.

Oct: 11th. Went to Washington by the usual unavoidable R.R. Monday 5th inst. H. Binney & Chas J. Stillé boarded the train at Philada. Our ride presented no incidents, unless it might be the lovely glimpses of the arms of Chesapeake which the R.R. traverses — beautiful bays, bordered by golden autumnal woodland. Genteel seceshdom has it's home along their sequestered shores, and waxes fat on soft-shell crabs & canvas-back ducks. But Maryland Seceshdom is nearly played out. It will soon be what *Jacobitism* was in England sixty years ago, or seventy, — the sentimental tradition of a few old families. A new order of Society is coming there, and the Patriarchs must clear the track.

Our session at Washn lasted till Friday night, and was highly satisfactory. Full Reports came in from East & West. We spent sometime in chasing the "igneous fatuous" of Executive Organization that led poor Olmsted thro' so many thickets & bogs. We succeeded at last in putting on paper a scheme that he would pronounce loose indefinite & unsystematic, but which is as near completeness & precision as the nature of the case admits. It may perhaps work, & that is more than Olmsted's complex laboriously elaborated paper programmes ever did or could. Newberry was satisfied, & we left him I think with all the soreness produced by his jars with Olmsted & with the Exec: Com: worked out of his bones.

We chalked out much work. An appeal to the public for more money must be issued at once. A Sanitary Com: periodical is to be started here, like Newberry's Western "Reporter". Bellows is to go to the Pacific Coast & if possible stir up the pure minds of the Californicators to the extent of another ½ million.

Visited the Convalescent Camp near Alexandria Thursday aftn. A lovely drive. From beneath the ruins of the Old Virginny Civilization, as manifested in desolate old houses & barns stripped of half their wood for fuel & shanty-building, the germs of the New Order are springing up. There are "Government farms" nicely fenced, & worked by gangs of

Contrabands — good roads newly cut — substantial bridges, & other Signs that the Vandals of the North are at work. This "Convalescent Camp" has long been a most scandalous insanitary nuisance & offence. But our remonstrances & petitions have prevailed & it is now a model of neatness & order. It looks like a model New England village, with its long rows of comfortable white huts or shanties, it's wide streets, well drained & perfectly policed, it's pretty enclosures, & evergreen groves. The men (about 8000 — it can accommodate 12000) looked orderly & cheerful.

We gave a grand dinner to Seward Friday night, at Willard's. Fifteen altogether. Sat next the Sec^{y}, and am satisfied there is more of him than I supposed. He is either deep, or very clever in simulating depth, & discoursed of public affairs in a statesmanlike way, as I thought.

Prof: McCulloh of Col: Coll: has sent in his resignation, dated *Richmond V^{a}*!!! He "has gone over to the Dragons" and we are well rid of him. He has probably been offered a high price to come South & take charge of some military laboratory, having high qualifications (so says Prof: Bache) for work of that kind. What a pity this sneak did not desert six months sooner, when poor Geo: F. Allen was still with us, & W. Gibbs had not gone to Boston.

Dr Heywood of Louisville brought in a favorable report from Rosecrans' headquarters. His Army does not suppose that it has been defeated or repulsed. It fought it's battle of Chickamauga for the possession of Chattanooga, & though severely handled in the contest, it holds Chattanooga & expects to hold it.

Oct. 12. I went down to a Tr: Ch: Vestry meeting. Rev. J.F. Young's application for leave of absence (laid on the table at last meeting) was taken up. I moved to decline it, & made a speech in support of the motion — a very superior style of speech indeed. Swift & Cisco spoke on the same side. That wretched prating pragmatical Tillou, & honest wrongheaded Benjn Bob Winthrop opposed, because there was no technical proof of Young's disloyalty. The Rector read a letter from Young, asserting himself loyal. It was a somewhat equivocal ambiguous letter, but it's professions of loyalty were very remarkably strong, to come from a man who talks as Young does about "*your fleet*" being unable to open the Mississippi, & "*your Army*" being badly defeated at Chancellorsville. It lowered Young in my opinion. The Rector affirmed Young's loyalty. Clergymen are clannish, & always uphold each other. I acquiesced in a motion to lay the matter on the table again,— so it is still undecided.

If the Vestry grant this application, I will resign, but I do'nt expect it will be granted. As the Rev: applicant has taken his passage for the 1st Nov: & the Vestry does not meet again till the 2[d] Monday of that month, & as he married a wealthy old maid a few years ago, & is therefore independent of the Vestry, it is whispered that he will resign his Assistant Minister-ship. Hope he will.

Oct. 13. What little War-news we have is not star-spangled. Meade has fallen back to the Rappahannock. Of course the movement is merely a masterly change of base, and brings Meade (strategically) much nearer Richmond, but it is liable to misconstruction. — Rosecrans' long line of communication is threatened & bothered. — Gillmore & Dahlgren were to have made a combined attack on something, Sunday. If they did, I guess we shall hear that they were repulsed.

State Elections came off to day in Ohio & Pennsylvania. Their result is as important as that of any battle delivered since this war began. If it shew a Copperhead majority in either of those States, the National cause will be sorely damaged. We shall know tomorrow. Deus salvam fac Rempublicam!

Oct. 14. We are all jubilant over the good news from Ohio & Pennsylvania. The tail of the National Copperhead is out of joint. Ohio pronounces against that pinchbeck Martyr to Free Speech, Vallandigham, by a majority estimated at near 100.000. Curtin's majority in Penn[a] is less multitudinous, but 'twill serve. *McClellan* has lowered himself sadly by an ill-advised letter supporting Judge *Woodward*, Curtin's copperhead–Anti-administration–Peace-on-any-terms opponent. I guess the McClellan pipe is nearly smoked out, and that McClellan is henceforth "out of this Story" — to quote the delightful "Saga of Burnt Njal" as translated by M[r] Dasent. He may be a good general, but he is a bad citizen — doing all he can — ignorantly I hope & believe — to weaken & embarrass Government & to help the public enemy. I think his name is losing day by day the potency it had a year ago, & that he is slowly settling down into obscurity. This miserable political letter of his, followed by the defeat of his Candidate, gives him a heavy downward shove. *He has lost the next Presidency* by want of common-sense, by inability to see things as they are, & by misplaced confidence in men like S.L.M. Barlow & ex-Gen: Fitz-John Porter.

News from the Rappahannock & from Chattanooga not much, & not at all fluorescent — nowise brilliant or luminous, but rather suggestive of failure. In Charleston Harbor the *Ironsides* has been assailed by a *Torpedo*, the explosion of which upheaved & hurled upon her decks such a mass of water as actually extinguished all her fires! She seems to have survived the Shock & to have sustained no permanent damage.

Oct. 17. Sat: — A summer day. At U.L. Club to night are apocryphal despatches posted on the bulletin board that there has been a great battle at Chattanooga, result unknown, & also that Lincoln has issued a Proclamation calling for 300.000 volunteers. — I am profoundly disgusted. Here has the Court of Appeals been *reversing* the judgment in Young v. Brush, the plainest clearest & simplest of cases, as I've always thought. With a judiciary like ours, it seems criminal to advise a client to take any legal proceeding whatever, for it's result is a matter of pure chance, unless (as probably in this case) it be determined by some nasty outside intrigue.

Meade has fallen back to Centreville. There has been a sharp fight at Bristoe's station, terminating favorably but no general engagement has occurred or is expected.

Oct. 18. No war-news to day. Reports that Lee contemplates a third *cis-Potomac* Maryland campaign are discredited. Meade's position at Centreville & on Bull Run supposed to be strong. How will all that region be infested by tourists fifty years hence! The affair at *Bristoe's station* was a victory. We held the field & captured guns colors & prisoners. The credit of our success is attributed to *Warren*.

Oct. 22^{d}. To night at Acad: of Music, with Ellie, Gen Dix's handsome buxom bouncing daughter Miss Kitty, Jem Ruggles, G.C.A. & *Johny.* We had Mrs Little's box. *Macbeth* for the benefit of the San: Com: — with Charlotte Cushman & Booth — a strong cast. Immensely crowded house. The Com: would have made $10.000, but for the fact that the seats were bought up by speculators instead of being sold at auction as they should have been. They were selling at $20. each in Wall St. to day.

The performance excellent. The sleep-walking scene particularly intense: indeed Miss C.C. is the best Lady Macbeth I ever saw — beyond all comparison. Macbeth died very game — his finale was made very effective. MacDuff was an importation from the Bowery.

Rosecrans is superseded by Grant! The change astonishes every one — it's alleged reasons are still more startling. Opium-eating — fits of religious melancholy — & gross personal misconduct at Chickamauga are charged by newspaper correspondents. There has certainly been something queer & unexplained about his disappearance from the field during a critical period of that battle, but I cannot give up Rosecrans till something is clearly made out against him. — [Banks & Franklin seem established at the mouth of the Rio Grande?] — In V^{a} Lee is falling back, & we hear this aft^{n} that Meade is ordered to follow him up & force a battle. If so, we shall soon be conjugating the verb To Lick in the passive voice, indicative present. — But to night I bought five cents worth of Extry-a-Herald containing a blind apocryphal story of a Rebel raid on *Chambersburgh.*

Oct. 24. Gen: Lee has brought his army off without a battle & recrossed the Rapidan probably. The roads & bridges behind him are destroyed so as to make rapid advance by Meade impossible, & Lee will probably send off large reinforcements to Chattanooga or East Tennessee. I think we shall never reach Richmond by that line.

Oct. 26. Drudging tediously all this ev'g over a San: Com: paper. It should have been in press a fortnight ago, but is not half finished yet. Uphill work, & the product will be lifeless &

leaden. — Ellie is at N° 24 nursing Jem — & G.C.A. who just looked in for a moment thinks we ought to *send for Mrs Ruggles at Delhi.* I half think so myself.

No war news. I am now in one of my periodical phases of discouragement about our prospects & disgust with things in general — especially with that odious offensive Snob & Donkey G.T.S.

Oct. 30. Jem Ruggles continues gravely ill, but is in no danger I think. Ellie spends most of her time with him at N° 24 & uses the experience she gained in Hospital ships in the James & York. His mother comes on to night from Delhi.

At Agnew's till about midnight. *Stand'g Com.* of *San. Com.* met there, discoursed & devoured. Wolcott Gibbs was added unto us. He likes his position at Harvard, & the people about him, but says (what I was surprised to hear *him* say,) that tho' there is more mental activity & culture in Boston than in N.Y. there is *less mental health.* No doubt he is right. Poor Mrs Paulding's case is utterly hopeless he says, but she may get through the winter. Sorry to hear from Dr Bellows that Mrs Geo: Schuyler is sinking fast under uterine cancer. An admirable woman, inheriting somewhat of the genius of her grandfather, *Alexander Hamilton.*

To night's War-news important. Gillmore's batteries have reopened on Sumter Moultrie & Johnson. — The rebels seem to have been crowded & manœuvred out of certain snug positions near Chattanooga, from which they threatened our fearfully long & vulnerable line of communications. They have given up "Lookout Mountain". A sharp battle has been fought on their left, which is claimed as a victory for Hooker.

Last Tuesday Miss Charlotte Cushman dined here — also Bellows Van Buren Agnew & Dr Weston. The tragedienne is a cultivated woman & made herself most agreeable. She looks far better off the stage than on it. Her performances of Macbeth at Boston N.Y. Washn &c have brought the San: Com: some $8000.

Nov. 1. News that Gillmore has tossed a few more incendiary shells into Charleston. How English newspapers will howl & whine over Yankee barbarism; — quite oblivious of the havoc English projectiles made among East Indian palaces

& the shops & houses of Sebastopol a few years ago. I am confounded & bewildered by the ignorance & prejudice of educated Englishmen of the best class (as e.g. the University men & young barristers who write for the Saturday Review) as manifested in writing about American affairs. One of it's contributors recently defined Burnside's execution of certain Rebel officers caught within our lines, disguised, & recruiting for the Rebel Army, as "the murder of officers enlisting subjects of their own Government on their own territory." This article went on to investigate the causes that have produced the degeneration of an Anglo-Saxon race to the stage of barbaric cruelty & inhumanity reached by our Northern people & manifested in their conduct of this War. The sagacious investigator thinks "climate" has something to do with it, — or may have, — but that the true reason lies deeper. There has been an immense emigration into America. Emigrations are generally short of women. Hence, alliances between new settlers from the Old World, & Oneida *Squaws.* Hence a large infusion of "Red Indian" blood into the population of the North. Which unquestionable fact fully accounts for the fiendish atrocities & ruffianly brutalities Northern soldiers love to perpetrate & Northern communities approve — & also for "the milk in the Cocoa-nut."

Nov: 3. Tuesday. Election Day. Only State & County officers to be chosen, but the result is of National importance. It will determine whether the reaction for Gov^{t} extends to New York. I think it does, & that we shall cut down the Copperhead vote even if we fail to carry the State. The City is beyond hope. The seat of Sam: Jones, Duer, & Oakley is pretty certain to be disgraced by McCunn. I stood in queue an hour & a half this morn'g in 19th St. waiting to get in my vote. All the respectability seemed to have turned out & was voting one way. Not a "friend" of Seymour's was visible. Many blackguards are afraid to vote for him, lest they should be put down for the next draft.

Have just come from U.L. Club — where I left an eager crowd waiting for returns which come in slowly & indicate that we have lost the City, as was to be expected, but by a greatly reduced majority.

Nov. 7. Election turned out as I expected. The State repudiates Seymour by about 30.000 majority. The disloyal vote of the City is greatly reduced, & that nasty sewer-rat McCunn gets in by only about 1600. This change from last year's vote is a thing to be thankful for, but not to crow over. Anything short of substantial unanimity on the question before us is a public disgrace. — But this fall's grand reaction, East & West, in support of Nationality will do much good & shew Copperhead leaders, like Seymour & the Woods that disloyalty is bad policy. It extends to every State. Every election has been a vote of confidence in Government & in the National cause — except in N. Jersey, & even in that benighted region Copperheadism loses ground. Kentucky goes right by 50.000, & Maryland votes for unconditional Union & immediate emancipation! The world certainly moves. — There are other signs of promise. An eminent Arkansawyer, one Gantt, a slaveholder & lately in the rebel service, comes out with an address to the people of his State declaring his conviction that the Rebel Cause is hopeless & urging return to the Union & the Abolition of Slavery. This may amount to nothing, but it is certain that if such a movement should be able to attain respectable dimensions in any Southern State, it would carry everything before it. Even in S. Carolina itself, a Union & Emancipation party would be irresistible if it were allowed to exist till it could stand alone. Rebel leaders perfectly understand this — & Southern rulers have understood it for the last 30 years & acted accordingly.

It seems certain that Richmond Petersburgh & the region round about are suffering badly for want of food.

Things in general look pretty well — but a serious reverse at any one point would change everything.

Russian Ball Thursday night was well managed & successful. E. & I joined Gen: Dix's party at his house — & went thence in great glory — staff & all — half a dozen captivating creatures in epaulets — nice Mrs Blake & Miss Kitty. I like all that family very much. They seem up to the standard of the Genl & the Rev. Morgan D. & that is saying a great deal. — The crowd was dense. Shoddy largely represented. I could find no one I cared to discourse, & soon sank into depths of boredom. The common phrase "bored to death" is no hyperbole, but represents a very possible contingency.

Nov: 9. Monday night. Wintry weather for Nov^{r} — but there is sunshiny news from Army of Potomac — which is now making one of those periodical oscillations across N.E. Virginia of which there have been so many — (on the forward swing now) — On Sat: it encountered the enemy in force on the Rappahannock, & drove him in the most creditable manner, carried his works with the bayonet & took guns & near 2000 prisoners.

Trinity Church vestry to night. Rev. J.F. Young's application for leave to go abroad was taken up. The Rector backed it strongly, I regret to say, because he had much faith in Rev. Young's efforts to promote Anglo-Americano-Muscovite Intercommunion. Gen: Dix thought Young's letter equivalent to a declaration of loyalty or quasi-oath of allegiance which might reasonably satisfy us — so he went the same way. Tillou supported Young in a long speech — just as if he were arguing a special demurrer in the Common Pleas — & Sam: Davis delivered a long rambling eulogy on the Rev: applicant. Cisco & Ogden & I opposed. We said that the man's sympathy with Treason was notorious — that it was certain he would do harm abroad — that his talk, be it's weight more or less, would tend *pro tanto* to counteract the efforts of Agents sent by Government expressly to enlighten English people about our affairs. But the motion was carried. Davis, E.M. Young, old Verplanck, Dunscomb, Gen: Dix (!) Skidmore (!) Caswell, Benjn Bob Winthrop & Tillou voted aye. Cisco, Ogden, Sackett, Curtiss, Henry Youngs & myself voted no. Ayes & noes were called for & recorded. This vote is disgraceful & I have been inwardly vowing an immediate resignation all the way up in the Omnibus. I shall be sorry to leave a board in which I have sat sixteen years & for which I have worked hard — but I do'nt want to belong to any concern that sends Secession Agents to England, or to be exposed to Tillou's oratory.

Nov. 12. Thursday. Indian summer. Still toiling heavily over the dreary San. Com. "Appeal" which grows on my hands. It will have to be a general abstract of all we have done & are doing. Hard writing is apt to produce hard reading. This will be about as lively & agreeable as a stale codfish. Pity one should work so hard to effect so little.

Library Com: of Col: College met at my office this morn'g. M[r] Jones as twitchy & tetanic as usual. — M[r] Derby & Eloise in town & staying next door. — Spent an hour to night at monthly meeting of U.L. Club. Unusually full & business-like. Signs of a disposition to have the Club do something more than furnish a convenient smoking room for a knot of loyal men — . Committees appointed to keep volunteering — raise funds, & regiments.

Yesterday dined here M[rs] Georgey Peters, Robinson, & Henry Brevoort. Robinson has experienced a change of heart & laid aside his former filthiness of copperhead conversation. He says he voted the Union ticket last week. — Surprised to find Brevoort an advanced Spiritualist mesmerist clairvoyancer, hypnotist biologist &c. He talks of these subjects intelligently, & apparently with full conviction of their reality.

Prices are rising fast — bad for mortgagees & for all who depend on fixed incomes. We shall soon be even as the F.F.V.s of Richmond who go to market with their money in their baskets & come home with its purchases in their pocketbooks. Insolvency draws nearer daily. Never mind. I dare say I shall get along with it when it comes at last. Only let us succeed in asserting our National existence. Many insolvents of my acquaintance seem to get along somehow & to have, on the whole a rather particularly good time. Workmen & workwomen of almost every class are *on strike* (& small blame to them) & among others the City R.R. drivers. So our facilities for getting up town & down are diminished, all omnib*i* being overcrowded. In the Coal Region of Pennsylvania the strike is combined with organized resistance to the Draft & has attained serious dimensions. It has doubled the bill for coal annually rendered me by M[r] Henry Reeve, & is in fact a Copperhead insurrection that holds two or three counties. The insurgent strikers are mostly lewd fellows of the baser sort, & Irish at that, & are of course committing all manner of murderous brutality. Paddy has not done much to entitle his race to our sympathy & affection during the last six months. Pen. Hosack tells me more about this than has appeared in the newspapers. He comes fresh from the Seat of War, where are mines in which he holds an interest, & he came away very quietly, being warned that his stay in those parts might be dangerous.

Cisco & others object strongly to my resigning off Trin: Ch: Vestry.

Ellie is spending the ev'g at Mrs John Sherwood's, with whom Mrs Carson is staying. Mrs C. is a daughter of old Petigru, (or Pettigrew) the distinguished Charleston lawyer who stood out, faithful among the faithless, as a Union man among the disunionists of that treasonous City, till his death a few months ago. He was too eminent & respectable to be lynched, so his death was in the course of Nature. His daughter inherits his loyalty. It has cost her all her property & she is absolutely destitute, supporting herself by the help of her friends & by her amateur talent for art.

Nov: 17. Sent for to Dr Van Buren's last ev'g, whereby I was prevented from going to Opera with Ellie & M^r & Mrs Wm Schermerhorn & little Miss Fanny S., now a young lady of 17. Opera was Trovatore, & no loss. Went to V.B.'s & waited there awhile till Bellows Agnew & Van Buren came in. It then appeared that we are fired by the example of Chicago, & that a great Union Metropolitan International Cosmical World's Fair has got to be got up in N.Y. in aid of the San: Commission. Proceeds not less than ¼ of a million. We proceeded to preliminary measures. Circulars & newspaper editorials were devised or written & lists of names made out. We propose to convoke a great feminine Wittenagemote or Hen Parliament at the Union League Club House next Saturday. I do not believe it will amount to much. Dr Van Buren came in from poor Miss Martha Coles. She was at Cornwall this summer. He reported her in terrible trouble from rupture of some internal tumor. Peritonitis. V.B. thought her case hopeless, & she died this morn'g.

Temple wo'nt soon forget our walk up town from Wall St. Sat. aft^n & the little fishes & the little Aquarium tank I bought for him. — A great & decisive battle said to be at hand in front of Chattanooga. Perhaps. From the S.W. corner of N. Carolina we have a legend of 5000 men, deserters from the Rebel Army, & White trash, who have organized in the mountains, licked a rebel force sent out against them, & marched off to East Tennessee. Good luck go with them. — Famine at Richmond seems a settled fact. I've no objection to have "the runagates continue in scarceness" but this is very bad for our poor fellows in prison there. They are dying of starvation. San: Com: has obtained leave to send a consignment of food suitable to men in their condition, & Gov[t] is sending clothing & ordinary rations. Strange as it may seem, Gen: Neal Dow writes that these supplies have not been gobbled up in transitu by the Chivalrics, but have actually reached their destination. But for a great many they will come too late. There is reason to believe that this famine is caused not so much by actual deficiency of hog & hominy as by the unwillingness of V[a] farmers to sell anything for which they must be paid in Rebel paper. Want of lively faith in the value of Rebel currency implies of course scepticism as to the ultimate triumph of the Rebel cause. — A British squadron has just been shelling a Japanese city of 180.000 inhabitants & laying it in ashes. With what refinement of humanity *they* make war, compared with us bloodthirsty Yankee barbarians. The Squadron proceeded to attack certain Japanese coast batteries — but the batteries were not silenced & Britannia had to haul off badly punished. Ca'nt say I'm very sorry.

Nov: 21. Thursday night, E. & I with Bellows & his wife & daughter went to Brooklyn Academy of Music. I rode outside, on the box. Rev: H. Ward Beecher delivered an address about his experiences in England. Proceeds of the performance for the benefit of the Sanitary Commission. As representatives of the San: Com: we were received with distinguished consideration, admitted thro' the stage door, shewn into the "Committee Room" introduced to the Rev. Orator, & accommodated in a Special proscenium box. The house was large & intelligent. Capital address & enthusiastically applauded. Most agreeably disappointed in *Beecher*, whom I had supposed to be a cross between Friar Gerund and Geo. Francis Train. His matter & his manner were excellent — I never heard so good a popular address.

Beecher stands up for the English People & maintains that we have their sympathy. His speech was an argument against the bitter Anti-anglicanism now prevalent. He says that tho' we are hated by the Aristocracy, the Establishment, the Universities, the "plutocracy" & the larger portion of the leading Non-conformists, the great mass of the people is with us.

Sorry to learn the death of Miss Alice Jones, at *Paris* — M[rs]

Rebecca Jones' daughter — . Geo. Winthrop Gray also dead. He was old Griswold's son-in-law. Old John Allan too, at a very advanced age. What will become of his superb collection of illustrated books & bibliomaniacal oddities?

Burnside has had a fight near Knoxville, E.T. Result not yet fully known & not promising.

Nov. 22. Meeting of ladies yesterday at U.L. Club house, to organize for the proposed Metropolitan Fair. Ellie is to be a Directress or Manager, & Grand Treasurer also, I believe.

Battle seems imminent at Chattanooga. It's result will be weighty, perhaps decisive.

Nov. 25. Wednesday night. Thank Heaven for good tidings from Chattanooga! They are not very definite as yet, but there is no doubt that Bragg is beaten with heavy loss in guns & men, after several days of sharp fighting. Burnside holds his own at Knoxville. He has 22000 men, according to Col. Jem Strong, & Foster who is about to relieve him will probably bring reinforcements. If Bragg be forced back, as seems likely, Longstreet, who is operating against Knoxville, may find himself in a tight place.

Col. Jem dined here — (his handsome wife could'nt come) & Geo. Anthon. We went to the Opera picking up Miss Kitty Dix on the road. First performance of Gounod's Faust. It is prettily put on the stage, but it's music seems not much above commonplace, so after two acts I "cut" & came home to work. Listening to second rate music is a most unprofitable way of spending one's time. — The Col. sets off on Monday to join Foster at Knoxville. This war has made a man of him — would I were in his boots.

Last evening H.W. Beecher spoke again at our Academy of Music. Proceeds for benefit of San. Com. The tickets had been put too high, $3. for reserved seats, & it was a vile rainy night — rebel weather — so the house was thin, & the net proceeds will not exceed $2100 — or about half what we counted on. The speech was admirable & well received. I adjourned with Van Buren to Dr Bellows', where were the orator & some half dozen others including Mrs Harriet Beecher Stowe, whom I found very bright & agreeable. Her brother is also a most interesting talker. We departed early after a slight supper.

Ellie is appointed Treasurer of the grand Metropolitan Fair. Heaven help her!

Nov: 27. Friday night or rather Sat: morn'g. The good news from Chattanooga amply confirmed & more than confirmed. Bragg's defeat is a rout, & Grant telegraphed at 10 A.M. this morn'g 60 guns taken at least, & every sign of flight & disorganization. He is pushing the shattered rebel columns hard, & there is probably much terrible swearing this minute among the Chivalry at several points far south of Chattanooga. God be praised for this victory, which looks like the heaviest blow the country has yet dealt at Rebellion.

Thence to San: Com: rooms, 823, with Johny & Temple. Collins in a twitter about a dreadful blunder D[r] Bellows was making — viz: publishing his clever N.A. Review article with all its slashing attacks on M[r] Sec'y Stanton as a document of the Commission — "N° 76". It would have been a most horrible blunder. "The Dominie" with all his tact sagacity and energy needs watching. Left to himself he can do the greatest mischief. Got this set straight this ev'g.

Thence with the boys to a place high up Broadway to buy some *turtles* for their two Aquaria, & thence home. G.C.A. dined here & went with E. & Jem R. to hear *Faust* again. I went to Agnew's. Stand'g Com. meeting of S.C. & a slight supper as usual. A great deal of business done. Our work was protracted over the supper table till midnight.

Bellows preached a sermon yesterday that aggravated & offended many who heard it. Dont exactly know what position he took, but it is called disguised Copperhead-ism — sympathy with the Rebellion — &c &c &c. If he's a Copperhead he is singularly wanting in the Wisdom of the Serpent.

Meade's Army again reported in motion, & across the Rapidan. It seems to have a grand opportunity just now. The nation needs one or two splendid victories by it's *Eastern* armies to offset those gained in the West. Western sectionalism is already an established fact, & it may become no less mischievous than Southern sectionalism. All our Western S.C. correspondence foreshadows this danger. Chicago & Cincinnati feel sore because the Commission has thus far held no session at the West.

Dec. 1. Voted this morning at Charter Election. It's a triangular duel between Orison Blunt, who is a decent citizen & the "Union" candidate — Gunther, equally decent, but supported by Peace Democrats & Copperheads, — and BOOLE, a disciple of F. Wood, a chief operator in "the Ring", and reputed a very clever corrupt swindling Scoundrel. I thought his chance far the best, but at nine this evening full returns were received at U.L. Club, where I was with G.W. Blunt, Chas King, Col. Howe & others. Διος δ'ετελειετο Βουλη — which means that during the day Boole "was all the time undergoing his accomplishment" — "force of the imperfect tense" — as Bull Anthon used to translate it — or in other words "his finish & quietus". He is *beat* & *Gunther* is Mayor by about 6000 plurality in a vote of 70.000. Well — a Copperhead is perhaps as good as a thief, but it's a melancholy reflection that if Union men had not voted for Gunther, as the only way of defeating Boole, they could have elected Blunt. — I find people at the Club & elsewhere full of wrath about this extraordinary sermon of Bellows'. It must be that it is misunderstood. Not more than ten days ago we were all lamenting his indiscretion & ultraism in consenting to preside at a series of meetings to be held under the Auspices of the most advanced Abolitionists, intended to create a feeling in favor of a proclamation of Emancipation every where — Border States & all. This caper of his — or this misconception — as the case may be, will do the San: Com: & this projected "Metropolitan Fair" in it's aid, serious damage, which we can ill afford now, with a balance in bank fast falling below $90.000. — Thank Heaven, by the by, I finished up that dull dreary labored paper of mine, last night, & gave it to Dr Jenkins this aft^{n} to look over.

I fear Meade may be in trouble. He has cut loose from his base to follow *Lee*, who has fallen back to a strong position & shews fight. Our information about their movements for the last two days is imperfect, & it looks badly "in spots". People are anxious. Some think Meade will dodge round Lee's flank & try a race to Richmond with him. It would be a most ticklish & perilous move. But he must either do this, or fight at seeming disadvantage, or fall ignominiously back, *re infecta*.

Dec. 3. Thursday. Weather still wintry. Col: Coll: Library Com: meeting in Wall St. this morn'g. At No 823 thereafter. Poor Dr Jenkins' little two year old boy, his only child, has been roughly handled by Diptheria, & is now assailed by membranous croup, & I fear, in Extremis. From the San: Com: office to Mrs John Sherwood's in 32d St. Left with her the draft of a Circular about the proposed Fair & sundry papers beside. After dinner Agnew came in, & we held council over the list of men to be invited to help the undertaking. We must take in copperheads, I think, like Belmont & Willy Duncan. They will work the harder for the sick & wounded because they are in a minority of opposition to the War & to Government. — Johny has been embargoed at home by sharp sore throat since Monday. It seems cured this ev'g, but Peters tells E. it looked very like *Diptheria*! Temple & Louis will probably experience a hostile demonstration from the same disease. May it be as readily repelled & controlled.

Meade has fallen back to "Brandy Station". Guess he will be relieved, — but by whom? His whole movement has been rather incomprehensible.

Edge writes from England that English feeling about us improves — & quotes Tempora mutantur — "the Times is changing."

Dec: 6. Friday night our S.C. committee met at Dr Bellows. The Dr expatiated to us about his Thanksgiving Day discourse that has stirred up such a hornets' nest. He says the proposition he asserted was this. "Ours is a Representative Government, & must be guided by the average instincts & wishes of the People — not by the aspirations of it's more advanced intelligence & principle. The People wants to see the Rebellion squelched, but cares comparatively little about the Slavery question. Hence it is probable that our trouble will be settled without the absolute destruction of Slavery, & that the restored Union will include Slaveholding states tho' Slavery will be shorn of it's political power, & in a declining moribund condition." If this be all he said, it's very gratifying & encouraging that people are in such a fume over so moderate & reasonable a proposition.

Mr Ruggles got home Friday morn'g from his Statistical Congress & Anglo-Græco Church mission Safe & sound, &

unchanged save by the eruption of a grizzly moustache that is rather effective. He dined here yesterday with Mrs R. Mr Derby, Jem, & Blackmore. Blackmore is a Britisher — one of the Agents or Solicitors employed on our side in the *Alexandra* case in the Court of Exchequer — & seems a cultivated thorough-bred man. He came over in the *Scotia* with M[r] Ruggles.

War news little or none. We are daily tossing twenty shells or so into the City of Charleston, but make little progress toward reduction of it's harbor defences. There is uneasiness about Burnside & Knoxville. Our latest information from East Tennessee is nearly a week old. Congress meets tomorrow. There are rumors of intrigue about it's organization that may do immense mischief.

Dec. 7. Gave Johny a dose of Latin after dinner. "Columbæ et Gallinæ sunt Aves" & the like. Spent most of the ev'g drilling Ellie in her novel duties as Treasu*ress* — how to endorse checks — how to write receipts &c &c.

Eloise tells me this aft[n] that old H.B. Rogers of Boston talks enthusiastically of Ellie's work on our Hospital transports at White House & in James River 18 months ago. "She knew everything & could do everything & was'nt afraid of anything. She is really a wonderful woman." — "Bully for E.!" — Rogers had abundant opportunity to estimate the value of her work.

Rev: Bellows continues to receive pepper — vide to night's Post. — Nothing later from Knoxville.

Dec: 11. Friday — opened with a leaden gray sky & nipping air that foretold snow. It appeared at two, and has been coming down moderately ever since. [Snow-storm N[o] 2.] — Weather windy & cold of late, and not improved by the abominable dust-storms that have prevailed, and which are due to the recent work on new City R.R. tracks through so many Streets & Avenues. A walk down Fourth Avenue has been a dirt-bath.

Longstreet has retreated from before Knoxville — thank God — & was at last accounts retreating toward V[a] or N. Carolina. We still hold East Tennessee therefore, and maintain a firm paralyzing benumbing grip on a vital central "pneumogastric" nerve-plexus of Rebel-dom.

Wednesday night Dr Bellows here, Dr Van Buren, Dr Agnew & Dr Jenkins. Sanitary Council, & a season of refreshing at the supper table. Jenkins' little boy is likely to be saved after all — a narrow escape for poor Jenkins.

Visited by the unknown author of "the New Gospel of Peace", which has been attributed to a score of people, myself among them. The Cincinnati San: Com: Fair people had written to his publisher, Tousey, to ask for the original MS. that they might make merchandize thereof — whereupon Mr X.Y., the Evangelist, came to me to say that our "Metropolitan Fair" could have it for the asking. I closed with the offer, for the MS will bring money. Tho' the squib does not seem to me very particularly clever, it has hit the average popular taste very hard. 70.000 copies of the first part & 40.000 of the second, have been sold. The author is [ ]. Who'd have thought it!

Pres'dt's Message & proclamation of conditional Amnesty to the rebels, certain classes excepted, finds very general favor. Uncle Abe is the most popular man in America to day. The firmness honesty & sagacity of the "Gorilla Despot" may be recognized by the rebels themselves sooner than we expect, and the weight of his personal character may do a great deal toward restoration of our National Unity.

Rebeldom has just played us a pretty prank. It's audacity is wonderful. Sixteen "passengers" on the peaceful propeller Chesapeake which left N.Y. for Portland last Saturday, took possession of her during her voyage, killed some of her officers & crew, put the rest ashore near St Johns, & then steamed off with their prize in triumph under "Confederate" colors. A whole Armada has been sent in pursuit, but they w'ont catch her.

There is an almost universal feeling that Rebellion has received it's death-blow, & will not survive this winter. It is premature, but being coupled with no suggestion that our efforts may safely be slackened, it will do no harm. The soi-disant "Chivalry" shews no sign of disposition to back down, & is as rampant blatant & blustering as ever. The most truculent & foul-mouthed bravoes & swash-bucklers of the South feel a certain amount of discouragement, no doubt, but they generally keep it to themselves. There will be no enduring peace while the class that has hitherto governed the South continues to exist. They are almost universally given over to a reprobate mind & past possibility of repentance. Southern Aristocracy must be dealt with as the Clans were after 1745. Parton's life of *Butler* (a readable book) tells how that General treated their case in N. Orleans. Even his remedies were too mild, but they come nearer what is required than any others' yet administered. That book will do much to raise Butler in popular favor. It paints him as of that Jacksonesque type of beauty which we especially appreciate & admire. Parton colors very high & tries to make a demigod of his hero, but I have always thought Butler among the strongest men brought forward by the War.

Dec. 13. Dr P. brings news of a bulletin at U.L. Club announcing that A.H. Stephens, Vice Pres^{dt} of Rebeldom, has just presented himself once more at Fortress Monroe, with a couple of colleagues, as "Peace Commissioners", that Butler refused to receive them in any official character, but offered to hear what they had to say as prominent citizens of Secessia — that they thereupon went back again, in a huff, sending a vindictive Parthian shaft behind them in the shape of a notification that they would no longer allow supplies to be sent our starving prisoners at Richmond.

If they have done this, it wo'nt much help their cause abroad. But that's a small matter. Government should notify them that inasmuch as they have declared their inability to give their prisoners rations sufficient to sustain life, their refusal to allow us to make up the deficiency will be followed by the Execution of ten Rebel officers in our hands *per diem*, till such refusal is revoked. — Message of Jeff: Davis, "Anti President", to the squad of malefactors now gathered at Richmond, and styling themselves members of Congress from Kentucky Tennessee Missouri &c, is long and doleful & dull — a melange of lies sophistry swagger lamentation treason perjury & piety. He admits that Rebellion has been drifting to leeward during the past year, but refers his gang for consolation to the boundless capacities of the Future. He is moral, also, and objects to any action inconsistent with the letter or the spirit of "the Constitution we have sworn to obey". This is cool. He and probably the majority of his pals & councillors in Congress assembled had held not less than twenty offices apiece, before they concluded to rebel. How many hundred broken oaths to uphold another Constitution were represented on the floor while this pious Message was being read? Could all these several perjuries have been combined in one Colossal Act of blasphemy, I think the Earth would necessarily have opened & swallowed the perpetrator. Jeff's Act of hypocrisy is (time place & presence considered) of like enormity though less criminal & black. I wonder the assembled Peers of Secessia were not startled by a vast resounding guffaw from the Powers of Nature, reverberating from the Chesapeake to the Alleghanies. Jeff: D. has out-brazened L. Napoleon himself.

Dec. 15. Yesterday dined here Mrs David Lane, Mrs Jno Sherwood, R.G. White, Griswold Gray & Agnew — a Committee on the "Metropolitan Fair".

Memminger's Report has appeared. He is "secretary" of that vast void, the Rebel Treasury. He reveals a fearful condition of vacuity & insolvency, & reminds one of Mr Micawber in "David Copperfield" expatiating on his own private impecuniosity. The difference between them is that while Micawber bewails a deficiency of the circulating medium, Memminger is suffering from it's excess. Among his people a Dollar is represented by about a peck of Confederate Treasury notes, & circulates with extreme difficulty, for Southern Railroads are nearly worn out & unequal to the transportation of Army Supplies. So Memminger is in grand choler and proposes certain measures for financial relief that seem frantic & impracticable & unavailing if practicable. This paper is a confession that the Confederacy is *mired*. It may struggle out, for it has the fury & the energy of a cornered mad cat — but it is in a tight place. Foreign financiers will hold Memminger's statement and his propositions equivalent to a General Assignment by a mercantile firm. — Reports of Union feeling in S. and W. Arkansas so multiply that we may begin to believe it exists there & is not only appreciable but important. So too in Texas, though not yet so distinctly manifested. If a Reaction be once fairly established at any Southern point, it will spread like fire in a cotton-factory, & the lawless vengeful half savage Southern people will have a fearful settlement of accounts with their Aristocratic rulers. The Rebellion may be crushed that way — or may not.

Dec. 19. Stopped on my way up town this aft[n] to see John Wolfe's fine picture gallery, on exhibition at the old Dusseldorf rooms, & to be sold at auction next week. It's a good collection. There's not a picture in it that I positively covet, but all are above average merit. Their sale is a domestic tragedy. They are to Wolfe only not quite so precious as his wife & children. He had built a fine house on Madison Avenue with a fine large room for his collection just before the War broke out. Being a merchant with extensive business connexions at the Sunny South, he suffered, of course, from the reluctance of Chivalric Southern debtors to pay what they owed a mere Northern mudsill, and this sale is thus made necessary. — Thence to N[o] 823. Letters from Paris announce the organization of a "European Branch" of San: Com: at Paris, under presidency of Rev: D[r] McClintock. Rather important. What a "big thing" San: Com: is getting to be, with all these great "Fairs" at Chicago Cincinnati & Boston, & with it's great money receipts & it's recognized position as an Auxiliary to the Army system! When we began it's work in June /61 we used to talk of what we could do if we could only hope to secure fifty thousand dollars for our Treasury. I have already received about $920.000, & our Branches at Boston, Philad[a], Cleveland &c &c have doubtless received as much more. After dinner, gave Johny a dose of Latin. This is the first of his studies in which he seems interested & anxious to make progress. He wants to go on & get ahead of his class during the Xmas holidays. — Then to M[rs] Ham: Fish's. That lady sent for me to discuss certain questions about the "Metropolitan Fair". Her drawing-room was very nice. There was the ex-Governor and his wife & pretty blonde Miss Susy & one or two young ladies beside, & a general aspect of wealth & refinement agreeable to behold. Discoursed M[rs] F. about the fair, & M[r] F. about the approaching election to fill the vacant Col: Coll: Professorship. He is non-committal as to his own views. Hope Lewis Rutherfurd will make him vote right.

Last Wednesday night with Ellie Johny & Temple to Acad: of Music, & heard Der Freyschutz once more. It's among the loveliest of operas. Poor little Temple was as white as a sheet when the curtain fell on the grand pyrotechnic tableau of the third act. It's a pity Anschütz's Season should come to an untimely end, as it does next Monday. He made a blunder in taking so large a house, but only two cities have a larger German population than N.Y. and it ought to sustain a German Opera.

Nothing material in public affairs except the recapture of the Chesapeake and Lincoln's last joke. He has had an attack of *varioloid*, & told some condoling friend that the disease was rather a subject of congratulation. "For the first time since he became Pres'dt, he felt he had something to *give* every man who called on him." — The N.Y. Herald has discovered within a day or two that Gen[l] Grant is to be next President, and expatiates on his claims & merits in slashing slangy editorials. It's former pet, McClellan, seems forgotten. Grant is certainly our most successful General, and might probably make a good President, but that the Herald takes him up so earnestly is against him.

Dec. 21. Report this aft[n] (thro' Rebel channel) of terrible disaster in Charleston Harbor. "The Ironsides & two Monitors disabled" in an effort to pass the obstructions of the inner harbor, probably. This would be a great National calamity, equivalent to the raising of the siege of Charleston. Let us hope that the story is a Rebel lie.

Dec. 23. Wednesday night. Steady cold weather, but clear & bracing. Down town late this morn'g, with slight sick headache, but worked efficiently. At 823 with Agnew & Bellows, & with them again to night at Van Buren's. Master Willy V.B. is convalescing — thank God, for his father's sake. We have had matters of some interest before us, & especially the great case of M[r] Sec'y Stanton *vs* the Surgeon General — and we concluded to night that we must at once begin operations on the Surgeon General's behalf. My belief is that they have been delayed too long already. We propose to open the campaign with an address to the President by the Sanitary Commission,

& perhaps, to follow this up with a Circular to a few leading Congressmen which is already in type & has been signed by Agassiz Peirce Hill & Longfellow of Harvard & by a lot of eminent N.Y. & Boston doctors. It may be a serious struggle. The first gun will be fired in the next (5th) N° of the "Bulletin". It is an anonymous letter purporting to come from an outsider, asking information as to the meaning of the Surgeon Gen'l's banishment to Knoxville, which letter I concocted last night. Agnew read it to Van Buren & Bellows this ev'g, and they heartily approved it without knowing who wrote it — which fact titillates my vanity quite agreeably.

Prof: Rood called just after dinner & spent half an hour with me in the dining room. I never saw him but once & had quite forgotten what he looked like. He impresses me most favorably, & seems a real man, honest, unaffected, straight-forward, & full of enthusiasm & earnestness.

The alarming story of Naval disaster at Charleston is not confirmed & is discredited. But I do not believe it possible for Gillmore & Dahlgren to silence the works that defend Charleston harbor without a land force of 50.000 men, & regular approaches.

Dec. 24. Xmas Eve. Bitter cold. News of a successful Cavalry foray by Gen: Averell in S.W. Va. To Trinity Ch: at 3 — "the Childrens' Festival", with Xmas tree &c as usual. Church very full. E. was there with Mrs Dick Hunt, Johny & Temple & Miss Puss. Service rather unusually satisfactory. Some of the music was positively good, the first of the two "Carols" for instance, & a very fine crescendo of simple chords, accompanying the last clauses of the chanted Creed. Dix made the children a nice little address, exactly what it should have been. — Thence to 823 where Agnew & I as Stand'g Com. dispatched some matters of importance. I begin to be seriously alarmed about our finances. Our disbursements for to day (including drafts of which Newberry notified me by telegraph to night) are nearly $22.000. These will leave not more than $40.000 in the treasury.

Hard at work with E. after dinner arranging presents — Johny's silver watch, & Temple's wonderful R.R. train &c &c

&c. Mary sends me a sumptuous bronze inkstand, & dear little Miss Puss a dear little pincushion worked by her own pretty little paws. C.E.S. & Mrs Eleanor, Jem Ruggles & G.C.A. supped here on roast oysters as heretofore.

Trin: Ch: lit with gas for first time this aft^{n}.

Dec. 25. No material change in public affairs. Belief grows stronger & stronger that Secessia is moribund. But she has Satan for her backer & bottle-holder, and he is full of resources. It seems conceded & certain that Rebel finance has utterly broken down. Can great Armies be maintained in the field by a Community without a currency?

That illconditioned vicious pragmatical brute J.A.S. J^{r} has just undergone an Experience that may do him good. At a wedding party supper the other night (at Chas A. Heckscher's) he proclaimed, in presence & hearing of several McClellanizing Army officers, that "Of course no *gentleman* ever did or ever could accept a position on McClellan's staff." Whereupon his host grabbed him by the collar & marched him to the street door. He apologized next day. His friends say this indiscretion should not be remembered against him because wholly due to temporary "Sur-excitation alcoholique". Perhaps. But he is an ugly fellow, drunk or sober.

Dec. 29. Tuesday. Warm & clear, after two days of detestable chilly rain-storm. Nothing very new. These premises pervaded by the San: Com: "Metropolitan Fair". Ellie finds her duties already arduous.

Sorry to hear this aft^{n} that poor young Willy Van Buren has had a relapse, & is again in a very bad way. Agnew thinks he wont recover.

Signs of reaction & reconstruction seem to multiply in Arkansas Louisiana Florida & elsewhere. It is difficult to estimate their value, or to be quite sure that they exist at all. But we had few if any stories of the kind a year ago.

Charleston had a very merry Xmas. 130 shells had been thrown into her, up to afternoon Church time. Her newspapers reluctantly admit serious damage, houses burned & lives lost. A pretty performance for Xmas day. Snap-dragon in earnest. But she deserves it all. Sowing the wind was an exhilarating Chivalric pastime. Shelling Anderson out of Sumter was pleasant. Reaping the whirlwind is less agreeable. To be *shelled back* is a bore.

Dec. 30. Wednesday. Fine weather. Mrs Lane, Mrs Sherwood, Macdonough, White & Bellows spent the ev'g here in council over the *Fair*, with the Treasuress. I sat apart, representing the galleries, & throwing in applause & groans at intervals. The debates were interesting. The Male Committee wants to hold the Fair in a building to be put up *by the City* on the "Palace Garden" lots in 14th St. — & to be used afterwards as an Armory for the 22^{d} Regiment, wh: already occupies part of the ground. Griswold Gray is manipulating the Board of Supervisors in a rather blundering way, & the plan smells of jobbery. The other locality — the "Manice building" (Bway & 6th Av:) seemed to find favor to night.

Dec. 31. Thursday. A dull dingy leaden day, with a chilly watery North wind. Snow-spitting began 2 P.M., but I walked up town with G.C.A. in full faith that the prospect of a snow storm was past. Spent an hour or two in diligent work at N° 823. Dr Jenkins was there, just returned from a Western tour of Inspection. His report is satisfactory. Thence home at 5 P.M. through a vehement snow-storm — [N° 3] — It seems to have turned to rain now.

Agnew says Van Buren's boy is doing badly, & all but absolutely past hope of recovery. God help poor V.B.

Agnew has his personal troubles, too. His wife gave him a little girl-baby a week ago, & has since had symptoms that look like puerperal fever. He is manifestly anxious about her.

A.D. 1863 is now in extremis. It has proved a far better year for the country than it promised at it's birth. If it's nascent successor prove half as propitious to the National cause, it will witness the downfall of Rebellion. So, at least, things look *now*. But only a very bold man can prophesy for a whole year ahead, in these times.

1864

Jan. 1. By these presents I wish a Happy New Year to all mankind except Jefferson Davis & his gang. To them I wish virtue enough to withstand urgent daily temptations to hang themselves.

Routed out of bed early (for me) to look over certain papers which Knapp had thought important enough to be sent on from Wash^{n} by special Messenger. They were about the Surgeon Gen'l's case. Knapp had shewn our letter to the President (N° 73 — protesting against the S.G.'s removal without a hearing) to Nicolay, the Presdt's private Secretary, who raised certain objections to it, & dissuaded Knapp from handing it in. Knapp sent on a Statement of Nicolay's views. They were founded on considerations of official propriety & Etiquette. In a "*Gold-stick*-in-waiting" point of view they were perhaps entitled to respect. But they did not convince me, nor have they convinced any of the Committee. We telegraph Knapp to hand in the letter, & shall follow it up *totis viribus.* But we shall fail. Stanton is a strong man. He has made up his mind to commit this injustice & we can hardly hope to prevent him.

Jan: 2. Long session at N° 823. Coming home at 6, I find poor Ellie in bed. She had been out in the cold wind, on "Metropolitan Fair" business — & coming home half frozen, had something like a chill, & is now feverish & suffering from neuralgic pains, with some trace of sore throat. I have sent for Dr Peters. She is in the best spirits, & very full of her day's work about the Fair. Sorry to say that Mrs John Sherwood has made herself slightly ridiculous by her most gassy circular. It is Oriental Bombast of the lowest type. Had I seen it before it was printed I should have assumed the right to suppress it. — Gov: Seymour has undertaken to remove our efficient Police Commissioners for making a "partizan" report about the July rioters, his particular "friends." He is an unprincipled politician, & I believe he deserves the infamous place he will occupy in our history. The validity of this official act will be contested.

Jan: 4. Staid at home all day looking after Ellie, still in bed, & visited by fever again toward evening. At supper were Mr Ruggles, Gen: Van Alen, Dr Peters &c. Much excellent talk from Mr R. — The ex-Genl seems a blower, & generates gas with fearful facility.

To day like yesterday till ev'g when a spitting of snow began. The streets are whitened by Snow storm N° 4. It does not threaten to be heavy. Poor Ellie is still prostrate, but was free from fever at eight P.M. Very bilious & forlorn down town — but I like the Trinity School decision better the longer I look at it. At 823 with Agnew & Bellows. After dinner & after an hour with Johny of Volunteer drill in Latin, went up to Agnew's for a 2^{d} Standing Com: session. On my way up town met old Dr Valentine Mott, evidently just from Van Buren's — stopped him & asked after poor Willy. He said "Falling off since morning — prospect about as bad as it can be." Agnew who was with him last night had previously told me the boy was all but dying this morning, so I fear the case is beyond reasonable hope.

Long business meeting with Agnew, Bellows, & Dr Jenkins. No supper, in consideration of the peculiar position of Agnew's household. Much discourse of our financial prospects, which are not satisfactory.

Knapp telegraphs that he gave our Letter about Hammond to the Pres'dt — who said his impression was the Surgeon Gen'l would have a trial. Very good. That is all we can ask.

Jan: 5. Long aft^{n} meeting at N° 823. Robinson dined here — Cram's partner — a rapidly mollifying Secessionist. This time last year I did'nt want to have him in my house, tho' he's an unusually well bred intelligent young fellow. But the progress of opinion in these days is rapid. The Copperhead of last week is the Abolitionist of to day. Robinson has the apology of Virginian birth or family. Thankful to say that Mistress Ellen was well enough to be with us at the dinner table, & afterwards, awhile, in the Library, whither Robinson & I adjourned to look over sundry books. Horace Binney came in, & we had a very satisfactory talk over S.C. matters.

Arch^{bp} Hughes is dead. Pity he survived last June & committed the imbecility of his address to the Rioters last July.

That speech blotted & spoiled a record which the Vatican must have held respectable, & against which Protestants had nothing to say, except, of course, "Babylon", "Scarlet Woman", & "Antichrist." — Gov: Seymour's Message is understood to be a most Copperheady Manifesto. Very likely. He seems strangely blind to the signs of the times. I supposed him sagacious & politic, tho' utterly base & selfish & incapable of any patriotic National impulse. But the manifestations of his malignity are those of a boor, & not of a subtle politician.

Jan: 7. Thursday. Still this cold grey weather. There is every promise to night of more snow. Met Geo: Griswold this morn'g, by appointment, & we called on Gen: Dix to invite him to become Pres'dt of the U.L. Club, vice Robt B. Minturn resigned & gone to Europe. The Gen: "will think of it" & probably say *no* at last. He is scrupulous about joining any organization that has any sort of *political* aspect, while he is in Gov^t^ service. Apropos of *Clubs*, the General Election at the Century comes off next Saturday, & old *Verplanck*, it's founder, & it's President since it was first organized 17 years ago is to be scratched, as a *copperhead*. So are Edwd Cooper & Appleton the bookseller who are on certain standing Committees. Sorry for Verplanck, but *fiat justitia*. Geo: Bancroft is put up as opposition candidate. Wm C. Bryant would have run better, for most people hold Bancroft an erudite ass. The opposition will be strong but probably unsuccessful. It will have my reluctant vote against Verplanck.

Down town. Called on by Richd Grant White & Frothingham of Brooklyn, about *Fairs*. There are many funny incidents in the history of the "Metropolitan Fair" which I have no time to record. "Miss Leonora Jones" who got into the Exec: Com: of ladies, somehow, is now reported to be not only a very disagreeable old maid, but a suspicious character, & is (according to *Acton*) under surveillance by the *police*. Pleasant. Told White to take the responsibility of leaving her name off the printed list. Then there is the delectable mess about poor Mrs John Sherwood's high-falutin' Circular, about Queen Victoria & Prince Albert & "Humanity" as "a greater than" Queen Victoria &c &c &c — & how people guffawed over it, & how visitors on New Years Day asked the lady who *could* have written that ridiculous circular — & how it was decided privily to suppress it, & how Mrs Fish & Mrs Lane spent a morning in burning up a cord or two of printed copies. All that is funny, but it's a sore mortification to the poor lady, whose *role* is to be clever & to have a literary salon & put little pomes into the Atlantic Monthly & be intimate with Everett & Longfellow. She is really intelligent & cultivated. How could she have made such a goose of herself?

At half past one Wm Schermerhorn & I with our tetanic librarian Mr Jones had a Col: Coll: Library Com: meeting in my office, & at two, I went into Wm Betts' office for a meet'g of the Com: on "School of Mines" — Betts, Edwd Jones, & myself. We were harmonious. I took Jones to the office of the *Copake Iron works* (Nassau St.) & introduced him to Egleston, & then went up town to 823 where I had three hours of work over San: Com: affairs. Our financial spasm was relieved yesterday afternoon, temporarily at least, by drafts for $50.000 from California, & the Commission has now about $90.000 in bank. But our expenses for December were $64000, so this is a mere palliative. — Home at six.

Jan: 8. Friday. Snow storm N° 6 lasted till noon, when the sun came out & it became a fine specimen of clear cold still bright winter weather. At 823 this P.M. was a great Philad^{a} map-publisher, one Smith, with his engraved fac-simile of the Emancipation Proclamation — (of it's original draft, I mean). He proposes to give us fifty cents for each copy sold, using that arrangement as a stimulus to buyers. This offer, coming from an expert in the art of canvassing & advertising on a large scale, is an important indication of the hold the San: Com: has got on the public.

After dinner to Dr Bellows'. We read over the draft of Ordronaux's labored Report on pension systems & provision for Army Invalids. It is valuable, but ponderous & polysyllabic. At half past ten the Doctor became insensible, under the section of "Military Colonies", so I glanced over the rest of it in silence. The Doctor woke up & we talked over the question of publishing, when I came off.

Poor Willy Van Buren still hangs by the eyelids, alive, & nothing more. Agnew is worried about his wife, who does not come up as she should after her confinement, & is restless & feverish &, as I suspect, rather seriously ill, tho' A. makes no fuss about it. He did not keep his appointment at Dr Bellows' to night. Our S.C. session at Wash^{n} next week will be a queer transaction, without Gibbs Agnew or Van Buren. Each will probably be kept away by the grave illness of a member of his family. Gibbs will be watching Mrs Paulding's death-bed, & I fear poor Van Buren will be watching his son's, if poor young Willy live till next Tuesday. Judge Skinner of Chicago is also telegraphed "very low" with some sort of fever, so he cannot come, and J. Huntington Wolcott of Boston has some ailment or other that will keep him away. Dr Howe can think of nothing now but the duty of giving aid & comfort to Freedmen, so he wo'nt come, & he will not be missed. I fear this meeting will be discreditably slim.

Jan: 9. Nothing noteworthy at N° 823 this P.M. At Century Club to night was Annual Election & a great crowd. 176 votes polled, an unprecedented number. It was understood this morn'g that Verplanck had been advised by his friends not to run, & had decided to decline a re-election. But unfortunately for him & for his personal friends like myself, he did not so decide, so I had to vote against him. The result was Verplanck 61, Bancroft 110, scattering 5. Considering Verplanck's popularity & his long identification with the Club, & Bancroft's foibles & snobbishness, this is an encouraging sign. Twenty people said to me to night — in substance — "How unpleasant it is to vote for a snob like Bancroft, & against my old friend Verplanck! But Verplanck's copperhead talk is intolerable". I think our U.L. Club has done something toward educating people's moral sense up to this point.

Verplanck means to be & tries to be a loyal patriotic citizen, after his kind. But he is naturally incapable of warm hearty generous impulses, except in his personal relations, and (like the Bourbons) he "learns nothing & forgets nothing". He does not see how times have changed & how fast they are changing. He looks on the great National Movement that is growing stronger every day & already controls the conduct of the War, just as he looked on the ravings of the little knot of philanthropes & infidels that constituted the "Abolition Soc^{y}" twenty five years ago.

I did not stay to learn the result of the contest as to members of Committees. It was doubtless in favor of the Opposition ticket & probably by majorities larger than Bancroft's. If so, Pierson is elected in place of Wm Kemble, — Wm J. Hoppin displaces W.H. Appleton, the bookseller, — W.T. Blodgett succeeds Wm E. Curtis, — C.E. Whitehead, Irving Paris — Henry Peters Gray, Thos R. Foster — & Eastman Johnson, that most venomous reptile, Edward Cooper.

Willy Van Buren *died* at 3 this morning, aged 16 years & 10 months. Though I had seen but little of the boy I feel this deeply, through my respect & positive *affection* for his admirable father. Then there is something so especially sad & *unnatural* about death at that age — of developing energies & aspirations. The dying baby or very young child seems just going straight back to God — home again after a visit. But the stripling or maiden seems entitled to a period of work & probation, as connected with Humanity, — as part, & the loveliest & most loveable part, of mankind. Poor V.B. will, I fear, be quite heartbroken. The boy would be alive & well now, no doubt, but for an imprudence while convalescing. He had advanced to a diet of champagne & roast oysters, & was daily gaining strength, & so one morn'g when no one was by, he got out of bed & put on his clothes. The consequence was a fainting fit, & a *relapse*. Agnew's educated eye saw the result a fortnight ago. He told me there was an "undefinable kind of look" about the patient that forbade hope of his recovery.

Jan: 10. Sunday. Clear & not quite so cold. A sharp headache kept me at home & in bed this A.M. After dinner Mrs Ashmore came in from Van Buren's, & said the D^{r} would take it kindly if Ellie & I went there. I had not dreamed of intruding, & had even hesitated before sending V.B. a very brief note just saying that we felt for him most sincerely. But of course E. put on her bonnet at once, & we went to the house. Poor Van Buren received us with an affectionate grateful simple straightforwardness that was most touching. He never appeared more nobly than in his deep sorrow, & selfcontrol, & thoughtfulness about others. I came near breaking down, when he interrupted himself in something he was saying about Willy, to ask "How are *your* young people, by the way?" — There was not a word of religious commonplace, but Christian hope & resignation seemed latent in everything he said. With all his self command there was a nervous quickness about his speech — & a restless way of going off now & then to see to some trifle, that shewed he was under intense excitement. We went up stairs to *the Nursery*, where poor Willy "lay in State" in his coffin, with lighted candles, heaps of flowers, & a picture of our Lord at his head. His handsome mother was there, pale & sobbing, & wandering about. She was a friend of E's in their schoolgirl days, & they met like sisters. It was miserable to see her caressing the cold face, & bringing me a card photograph to shew how different *He* used to look, how attenuated he was, & how much he must have suffered. This visit was a new experience to me. Such visits are apt to be inflictions. Icy reserve & conventional sanctimonious commonplace make them formal unreal oppressive & painful. But in V.B's bereaved household there was a kind of frankness & openness to sympathy — a freedom in the confession of grief, & a heartiness in the reception of kindly meant words, that made the hour we spent there none the less painful, perhaps, but certainly one of true genuine human feeling. — Thence we walked up the 5th Av: to Agnew's, for whom I wanted to leave a note. Mrs A. is better.

Jan: 11. To 823, & then called at Dr Peters', understanding that Mrs Lily Clymer wanted an escort as far as Baltimore. She is a very charming little lady, but I was not deeply grieved to learn that she had changed her mind, & that I am not to enjoy her society for nine hours of R.R. travel tomorrow. — Being at the headquarters of Æsculapius, I thought I might as well bring Sanitary Science to bear on my own case, so I got myself *re-vaccinated*, with reference to the smallpox said to be prevalent at Washn.

Jan: 16. Sat: night. Home, after ten hours of R.R., but without special discomfort, except the atmosphere of my car, wh: was "typho-malarial". Hot stove, packed crowd of passengers, & no ventilation. I should be thankful that I'm not spotty with jail fever. A cloudless winter day, moderately cold. Read Cha[s] Reade's "Very Hard Cash", a novel of the Special-Abuse-Corrective school. It is aimed agst alleged defects in the Lunacy-system of England, & with all it's faults & extravagance is the best thing Reade has produced this long while.

Ellie & her chickens are well thank God. Johny has'nt yet returned from drill, but I have seen Lewis, sound asleep in his nest, & Temple, just after his bath, who rushed up to me in his *cutty sark*, with his little bare legs, & hugged me to the verge of strangulation. E. has gone with M[rs] Georgey Peters to French Theatre — my return this ev'g being unexpected.

To Wash[n] Tuesday morn'g by the usual R.R. — Agnew, Wolcott of Boston, & Harris on board. It was our first experience of the new arrangement that takes people round Philad[a] instead of carrying them by horse car thro' it's monotonous streets. We got to our journey's end two hours behind time. The delays & detentions were intolerable. But near us sat a lady with two children, both lovely, & I established a sentimental intimacy with the elder, a perfect little gem of a roley-poley blue-eyed curly-wigged creature some six years old, & we got on famously together. Agnew found that the Mamma was the wife of a certain D[r] Stark, an acquaintance of his, attached to a Wash[n] Hospital, & introduced himself. When we left the cars I escorted the younger lady & had the pleasure of turning her over to the arms of her lucky papa. I hereby record her name — Miss *Julia Something Stark* — wondering whether the whirligig of time will ever bring me within hailing distance of this beautiful child, again.

Willard's absolutely worse than ever — crowded dirty & insufferable. Agnew & I were put into one room in an obscure corner of the top-story, accessible only by an enterprising & difficult escalade. It had the advantage of being traversed by certain steampipes, connected with a large iron tank in the garret. They leaked, & gave us the benefit of an atmosphere warmed by escaping steam & flavored with oleaginous vapors, also of a persistent noise "as of a hidden brook in the leafy month of June" & somewhat as of frying sausages, likewise. Dinner next day abominable — especially in point of attendance. Waiters a crowd of "*What-is-it*"s — or perhaps refugee field hands, incapable of being *enlisted* even as teamsters, cooks, or military boot-blacks.

I shifted my quarters that night to N° 244 F. St, where I got a good third story room, & a comfortable bed. I took my meals "out" — at Buhler's restaurant — a vile place (hippopotamus & cassowary served up as beef & turkey) — & yesterday at "the Occidental", a degree or two better???

Our session was satisfactory, tho' Van Buren & Gibbs were missed. We elected Chas J. Stillé a full member. Bache & Newberry & Bp Clark were with us.

Yesterday I called on the Surgeon Gen'l at his house in K. St. He has just returned from Nashville & still suffers from the effects of his very serious fall down stairs. He can only walk on crutches, both legs being still paralyzed below the knee, but is gaining ground slowly, & profoundly interested in the minute scientific observations & experiments he is making on his own case & diligently recording. Highly characteristic of the man. So is his talk about his feud with Stanton. The Sec'y is manifestly hesitating before he pushes the case farther. Our letter to the President & the Circular to Members of Congress (whereof more hereafter) shewed him that there was a hornets' nest in that bush, & that if he stirred it up he might get stung. So being politic as well as arbitrary he told a Senator to tell a Surgeon to tell H that he would abandon the persecution, if H. would consent to let by-gones be by-gones. To which H. responded that he would be glad to do so, if the Sec[y] would *apologize*, but that if the Sec[y] would'nt, he must have a Court Martial. From what Will Winthrop tells me (Theodore's brother) who is attached to the Judge Adv: Genl's office, there will doubtless be a Court, & probably an unfriendly one. The S.G. gave me an outline of the case, & on *his* showing it is plain enough of course. He proposed to try his own case, without counsel, against which preposterous course, I gave him advice gratis, most emphatically.

As to the Circular. It was signed by Agassiz & Peirce of Harvard, among others, & they were at Wash[n] last week attending a session of the National Acad: of Sciences. Stanton was asked to meet them at dinner, & replied, Stantonically, "Meet them at dinner! I'd rather send them both to Fort Lafayette!!!" But when the Wise Men heard this, their hearts failed them and their knees became as water, because they had given offence to a great Mandarin & a Cabinet Member — so they declared it was all a forgery & a fabrication. They never signed the Circular, or did anything else that could be displeasing unto so sweet a Prince — God forbid they should presume to take on themselves to do this thing! Did the Honorable Sec'y suppose they did'nt know their place? Of course they knowed their place. Were they not even as dead dogs before an Hon: Sec^{y}? Of course they were — and that's *my* opinion too.

This accounted for a mysterious telegraphic paragraph in the Times & Herald last week. But as I had seen the well known autographs of both Peirce & Agassiz to this document, with my own proper eyes, & knew that Gibbs had asked & obtained their signatures, I was at a loss to guess what they meant now. On enquiry it appeared, that V.B. had added to their signatures their respective academic titles or office in full, Prof^{r} of this, & Prof^{r} of that, in order that Congressmen might know what manner of men they were appealed to. Both these enlightened personages declared they "never signed their names *that way*", & that these therefore were not their signatures!

I think it highly probable they will have a lively time with W. Gibbs when they get home to Cambridge!

Spent last ev'g pleasantly with Foster of Conn: & his wife.

Col: (D^{r}) Hamlin — a nephew of the V.P's. — seems a remarkably clear well informed man. Much pleased also with a Col: Andrews, of Marietta — an intelligent man with a tawny leonine beard — who has seen much service & talks strategy & geology. — Boston sends us $50.000 from the proceeds of her Fair. This makes the Treasury comfortable. — I see clearly that the Commission is more generally recognized & appreciated than ever before. Senator Foster praised & magnified it as having become a great Power in the land. Which I think it *be* — but my rôle is to depreciate & diminish when I hear people talk that way. — This, by the by, may be our last Session at Wash^{n}. Talking with Bishop Clark in that crowded stye, the lobby of Willard's, & exchanging condolences over our respective experiences of dirt discomfort & inattention, I asked him WHY we should expose ourselves to these torments? What do we gain by meeting "near" the seat of Gov^{t}, that would not be more than counterbalanced by the advantage of meeting elsewhere & shewing ourselves to our *branches*? The Prelate rec[d] the suggestion as a shark gobbles a porgy, & brought the subject forward next day. After much discussion, we agreed to hold a special meeting at Philad[a] in March, & our quarterly meeting at some point West of the Alleghanies — probably Cincinnati — whereat D[r] Newberry rejoiced greatly.

At Gettysburgh, Lee used the Cupola of the Seminary, while his Hospital flag was flying from it, to reconnoitre the field, and from that position went out the order for the final attack, which failed as it deserved. So Stillé was told by a theological student who was in the Cupola when Lee & his staff came up there with their glasses. *Sich* is Chivalry. Lee would not have done this five years ago. Bad company has degraded him. No gentleman can fight two years to sustain the right of men to flog women, without damage to his moral sense.

Jan: 17. Intercepted Rebel Correspondence is entertaining & instructive. Rebel Agents abroad are making & losing great sums in their blockade-running lottery, while their people at home suffer & starve. It is curious to observe how freely these agents of the "Confederacy" talk of assigning to Louis Napoleon Texas, or even Louisiana & Arkansas & everything West of the Mississippi, as a bribe that might at last induce one Power of Xtendom to recognize the Confederacy, & a new nation of women-floggers. Their first principle is the right of every State to secede, whenever it pleases, but they are ready to make any State a Colony of a foreign power if the interests of their dirty rebellion will be thereby promoted.

Jan: 22. Friday night. Decent winter weather. A rather busy day in Wall St. Gold keeps going up in an alarming way. It would be deplorable if a financial collapse should force us to lay down our arms. Afternoon with Rev: M. Dix, & Cisco at Trinity Church discussing the "Chancel organ" question, on which we are a Committee. Guess we'll make that project go. — Thence to 823 Bway, — where were Newberry & Bellows, just from Wash[n].

The Surgeon Gen'l's Court Martial is sitting. It refused an adjournment to allow him to bring on his most important witness (A.K. Smith) from Little Rock. But Hammond thinks well of the Court & sees no symptom of prejudice or partiality. I do not expect an acquittal, tho' I am confident his case is honest & good. Some impulsive blunder of his will probably spoil it, & Stanton is an ugly adversary.

Went off by myself after dinner & heard Boieldieu's *Dame Blanche* (in German) at Acad: of Music. It is a bright sparkling pretty opera, & I hope I may hear it again. The composer has worked in sundry phrases from old Scotch melodies, quite effectively, & has stolen from Haydn, as most composers of the second rank used to do, until the new generation arose which knows not Haydn, & do'nt know enough of music to be aware that his conceptions are worth stealing. — Stopped at M^r^ R's, for E. on my way home. Nothing talked of now but the *Fair.*

Extracts from Rebel newspapers that are produced in our own, are unusually interesting. The proposal to put every male adult into the Rebel ranks, to make Jeff. Davis practically Dictator, to repudiate the "Confederate" debt, & then to raise a few hundred millions by direct taxation, makes Southerners open their eyes wide. There are complaints and protests and signs of recalcitration. The statistical & chivalric De Bow himself — whilom Apostle of Slavery & First Gent in Waiting to the late King Cotton — has been suppressed & locked up, because of an Article — in which for the first time in his life he uttered a little common sense. North Carolina is particularly disgusted, and wants to know *why* N. Carolinians should be legislated out of their houses & into the Army by "members of Congress" from Kentucky Tennessee Missouri Arkansas & Louisiana, who are fugitives from the States they profess to represent, and whose legislation is inoperative as against their own nominal constituencies. It is a pertinent enquiry. But Jeff: Davis has his foot on the neck of N. Carolina, & will be little embarrassed by Editorials. Conscription will be vigorously pushed, & there will be a desperate convulsive effort to overwhelm us at some weak point — probably in East Tennessee, where Longstreet seems offering battle already. A Captn Leggett (one of the Whitestone & Westchester C^o^ Quaker family) who was at 823 yesterday, & seems intelligent & trustworthy, is just from Knoxville & says our men there & at Chattanooga are in most fearful destitution, on much less than ½ rations & with no hospital supplies at all.

Hammerstein told us something of the state of things there, Sunday night, but it seems far worse than I supposed. We have been straining hard to get supplies forward, but transportation cannot be had, in any way or on any terms. Wagon trains are impracticable over the mountain roads, & the one line of singletrack R.R. on which Grant's Army depends is unequal to the movement of ordnance stores alone. The road is worn out. Trains traverse it at the rate of five miles an hour & run off the track on an average twice a day. The Country is stripped, & it's loyal population is perishing for want of food. What immeasurable misery this causeless Rebellion has brought on our people!

Thank God, the signs of reaction & reorganization grow Stronger every day. "Healthy granulations" appear in the mangled tissues at last. Barring military disaster, we may expect to see Free State Governments established in Arkansas & Louisiana before next May. Maryland & Missouri are fast developing into Free States, & I think Kentucky & Tennessee will not be long behind them. But the Rebellion is not yet suppressed, by any manner of means, & we have yet much hard work to do. God prosper it! Amen.

Jan. 24. The confidence every one seems to feel in the speedy downfall of rebellion surprises me. We shall have the hardest fighting of the War before next June. Suppose the Rebels move their Seat of Government from Richmond to Columbia, & send the bulk of Lee's Army to reinforce Longstreet & Bragg, leaving a small force in fortified camps to retard Meade's pursuit through a difficult & desolate country. They would hazard the loss of V[a] & N. Carolina, but they might annihilate our Army in the S.W.

Jan: 25. Am just from a Session at D[r] Bellows' with "the Dominie" Agnew Van Buren & Jenkins. Poor V.B. is grave & sad, & there are new lines in his face that look like traces of a fortnight's stern self-control & suppression, but he is as kind & courteous & thoughtful as ever. We sat from 8 to 12 & did much business. *Inter alia* was the question whether we should advise the Managers of the "Metropolitan Fair" to permit no "Raffles". We decided it in the affirmative. Agnew thinks Raffles immoral & sinful, not merely *malum prohibitum* but *malum in se*, & holds that a man endangers his eternal salvation by combining with nineteen other men to take a five dollar chance apiece for a hundred dollar bronze or picture. Bellows thinks we shall on the whole make more money by taking high moral ground, & securing the sympathy of "unco' good" rich men who think raffles wicked. I think that a movement in aid of the National Army fighting for the Law of the Land against Rebellion ought not to raise money by machinery which is forbidden under penalties by statute & which is punishable as a misdemeanor. V.B. acquiesced in this view of the case, so our conclusion was unanimous, & I think right. Giving tithes of mint & cummin does not prevent our attending to weightier matters.

Jan: 27. Nothing authentic from that vital centre of contest, the region of Chattanooga & Knoxville. Should we win another important battle there, & dispose of Bragg or Longstreet, Secesh-dom would be manifestly moribund, & Peace probably close at hand. But I count on no such good luck. We may be thankful if we escape grave *retarding* disaster at that most critical point. Indications elsewhere are good. It seems certain that Arkansas is reorganizing herself as one of the United States, under an Anti-Slavery Constitution. The fact is momentous. Our Western world has moved since 1860! Our lavish expenditure of life & of money has not been in vain. It has established Freedom in Arkansas & Missouri & Maryland & half Virginia, & paralyzed the grasp of the Slaveholder in Kentucky & Tennessee & Louisiana, & all along the Southern coast. It has already made a vast area, equal to that of many European states, *free-soil*, & opened it to free labor — an immense result. No one should complain of his prospective insolvency, when he thinks of what the War has purchased for mankind — to say nothing of "Beati pauperes".

It is very certain the world is moving. In after dinner talk last ev'g, Jem Ruggles avowed himself a thorough-going "d—d Abolitionist". A marvellous revolution. Fred. Sheldon said that Clitz confesses a like change of heart. He voted for *Breckinridge*, & was a strong Pro-slavery Democrat, when the war began, but he sees now that Slavery has got to be abolished everywhere & anyhow, Constitutionally or unconstitutionally.

Jan: 29. M[rs] H. Fish sent for me this morn'g, & I called on her on my way down town to discourse of The Fair and the great ethical question of *raffling* or not raffling. She is in a state of mind. Everybody is in a state of mind. I think the Stand'g Com: of the San: Com: had better back out of the Controversy as gracefully as it can.

Feb: 4. The "Metropolitan Fair" becomes interesting. It's Administration brings up a great Ethical question — viz: is *Raffling* Sinful? The Stand'g Com: of San: Com: discussed it fully ten days ago, & decided to advise the Managers of the Fair to exclude & prohibit Raffling. I acquiesced, not very heartily, for it seemed to me that there was more fuss about the matter than it deserved. Afterwards I saw M[rs] Fish & others, & found that our advice was likely to offend sundry efficient & valuable people who were working for the Fair, so I wrote a note to Bellows Tuesday, begging him to do nothing about it, offer no advice, & allow the San: Com: to occupy a position of neutrality. But he sent the letter I had previously signed to both Managing Committees yesterday morning. R.G. White tells me to day that it came before the Gentlemen's Committee last night, was respectfully received, & was responded to by a resolution that the Com: does not yet see sufficient reasons for prohibiting a feature that is recognized by usage as appropriate to all "Fairs" intended to raise money for humane charitable or religious purposes. What the Ladies' Committee will do about it I do not know & cannot guess. I predict they will agree with the Gentlemen.

Dr Bellows was stimulated to his perhaps rather premature action by intelligence that certain of our city clergy are in a state of hyperæsthesia about the sinfulness of "Raffling" & are signing a paper, that is to be published, denouncing the Metropolitan Fair & the Sanitary Commission for seeking to raise money by criminal unchristian wicked agencies. I fear this intelligence is too true. If so, it sadly lowers my respect for our clerical teachers & guides.

"Es ist kein Pfafflein noch so klein
Er möchte gar ein Päbstlein seyn"

If these gentlemen decide to issue their threatened Protest & Circular, they may diminish the proceeds of the Fair, & reduce the amount of aid & comfort thus provided for our

Camps & hospitals fifty per cent — perhaps even more. But they will damage the cause of Religion in this Community at least as much. Men who value religion & morality quite as much as they do or can, will be ready to make war on them, & from a strong position. They undertake to discourage & to denounce a great work of Charity & patriotism because of a twopenny scruple about the morality of games of chance, because it's channel does not conform to the mathematical line they approve. They use their official position to keep succor from reaching men in hospital & on the field, because it is to be raised, in part, by agencies they deem technically unlawful. It is the old — old question, — with reverence be it said — of healing men on the Sabbath Day. If the intensely rightminded & religious clergymen who threaten to go out of their way to interfere in this matter be equally sensitive about any uncharitable word or harsh judgment or selfish act on their own part, & equally ready to denounce any symptom of love of wealth, a position that may appear in members of their respective congregations — if they habitually condemn from their pulpits the stock-jobbing operations that enable Mr A. to pay the rent of Pew N° 25, & the gambling in gold — or cotton — or Petroleum — the profits whereof are received by M^r^ B's pastor, & daily eaten & drunken by that Rev. Gentleman and his household, as part of his income from Pew N° 26. — if, in short, they carry out their principles with any evidence of effort at consistency, then is there not a word to be said against them. But if they come short one iota in the weightier matters of the law while thus offensively volunteering "tithes of mint & Cummin" against our undertaking in the interest of charity & humanity, they belong to the class designated in the Four Gospels as *Pharisees.*

Heaven help us. The Clergymen of our day tend to make us unbelievers. *Per contra*, however their stolidity & folly is a standing proof that Xtianity & the Church are supernatural & Divine. No human device could have been sustained for so many generations by such half-hearted insincere blundering blockheads.

Feb: 6th. Sat: night. Mild weather. An inefficient headachy day. To night at a concert at Mrs Macaulay's in Madison Av: — the first of a series intended to raise money for the *Fair*. Chas Kuhn dined & went with us. The rooms were well filled. Programme included a lovely trio of Mendelssohn's (by Scharfenberg, Burke, & Bergmann) & a great deal of trash. I came away before it was over. To Century Club too late to hear Bancroft's Inaugural address — to U.L. Club too late for a speech by Gantt, the repentant rebel of Arkansas — & to Av. A & 25th St. too late for anything but the finale of a great fire that has destroyed the "Empire Works", but was still blazing very brilliantly.

Feb: 8th. Monday night. Winter continues bland & amiable. Also there are no more scarlet-fever patients in this household as yet. — Last night Rood & Joy were here, with M. Hoffman, G.C.A., Mr S.B.R. Wolcott Gibbs et al. Satisfactory session, & much good talk. Today's news is an "advance" of the Army of the Potomac, across the Rapidan. Guess it is only a strong reconnoissance.

Feb: 10. Ash-Wednesday. Cold winds have prevailed these two days, with warm sunshine, & the weather has been that of March with an extra chill on. But to night is genuine winter. — biting cold — & as I walked down town & Eastward after dinner, the drop of post-prandial coffee that lingered on my nuisance of a moustache, became an icicle before I reached 2d Av: — Nothing very new in Wall St. or at No 823. Dr Anderson, an eminent Presbyterian clergyman belonging at San Francisco, who has been spending some time in the S.W. at Chattanooga & elsewhere, & seems clearheaded & honest, says that talk with scores of deserters from the Rebel army has satisfied him that "the bottom of the Rebellion has come out" & that the worst is over. Perhaps. We have hard fighting yet to do, anyway. His opinion is confirmed by the report of our S.C. Inspector at Point Lookout (cor: Potomac River & Chesapeake Bay) where is a great Camp of Rebel prisoners. He gives us (contraband) information of a full Regiment of recruits from this camp, wh: he has just been inspecting, & which he pronounces *first rate.*

Feb: 11th. This cold-snap continues. To night is very frosty. Little or nothing for my journal & no sufficient reason for lugging it out — unless it be that *Nihility* is itself a fact to be registered. Have just glanced thro' Vol: 2 of Count Gurowski's Diary. He is Thersites still — not κυνος ομματ'εχων however, for his blue spectacles have won him the title of Gig-lamps & Count Goggle-owski. As to the κςαδιην δ'ελαφοιο, it's but justice to say that I believe this savage merciless censor of everybody & everything would be in the field & at the front but for his age & his obesity.

He growls, as we all do, at our slow progress towards suppression of Slavery & Rebellion. Is not this because he keeps his eyes fixed on the hour hand of the clock? Look *back* at July 1861, & then look where Maryland Missouri & Arkansas stand in 1864, at West Virginia, & at the Mississippi relieved from Rebel Strangulation. Our progress has been beyond what we had any right to hope for, three years ago, in spite of the blunders he attributes (very justly I suppose) to McClellan, Scott, Halleck, et al. He is humiliated because Rebel generals — Lee, Jackson, &c, shew energy superior to ours. But did he ever try to bag an infuriated tom-cat? If he ever did, he would do well to remember that he found the job troublesome, & that he did not feel inclined to give the tom-cat higher rank than his own, on the scale of being, because of it's difficulty.

To night there was an Organ performance at Trinity Chapel. That instrument has been completed at last, & it's builders, Hall & Labagh, wanted it exhibited. It was on the whole a dull performance, but it included two or three striking fugues & "toccatas" by Bach. Thence to U.L. Club — where were Gens Burnside, Hancock, & Anderson, with other militaires, & quite a crowd.

Old *Gurowski* holds Lincoln & all his ministers & Generals (except Wadsworth & one or two others) knaves or fools or both, & scolds more viciously, & in worse language than any Russian Count I've lately heard of. Many of his points are strong, but his style & temper are those of an enraged Tartar Khan, full of raw horse & bad liquor. This book will exert little influence. His epithets for the Woods Barlows Brookses & all that race of vermin, are various, novel, pungent, & sometimes unsavory. He deplores the probability of Lincoln's re-election & thinks Stanton the man for the time. So do'nt I. Anyway that probability grows stronger daily.

Feb. 13. Sat. night. Fine day. Spent it in bed, tormented by sickheadache. Obvious cause a most elaborate dinner at Union Club last night with Van Buren Agnew Bellows, Knapp,

Jenkins, & Anderson & [ ] of San Francisco. Anderson is the leading Presbyterian parson of California — a benevolent sensible old gentleman, & a worshipper of the San: Com: — He was to sail for home to day, an enthusiastic missionary in it's Cause. Much interesting discourse of the Jo Semiti valley with its magnificent precipices & unequalled Waterfalls — and about recent letters from Olmsted at Mariposa. He says you must walk a mile at least from his shanty to find a "Grizzly", but that the little brown bears circulate in front of his door every ev'g. "Last night" he heard a revolver shot, & immediately thereafter one of his subordinates came in for a call & took a seat & a pipe. O's attention was attracted by a singular clawing & sniffing outside the door, & he asked what it meant. "Why" quoth the visitor "I reckon it's a Bar. I just took a crack at him, & missed, & it 'pears like he's tryin' to git *in*." — The village Cemetery is just behind Olmsted's quarters. It's inmates are 29. Of these *one* died a natural Death — all the rest of bullet or knife. "The rude forefathers of the hamlet" must have had a rough time, in their day.

E. has just come in from "Metrop: Fair" Concert N° 3 at Mrs Gardner's just below here — & has hurried to bed with severe sickheadache.

G.C.A. dined here. Much talk about what I should do in a certain contingency, about as sensible as a discussion of what should be done if an aerolite as big as Calvary Church tumbled down into Gramercy Park.

Feb: 15. 823. Raffling question creates much talk. — A long string of parsons sign a protest against the Fair in yesterday's Times. Tyng, Canfield, & Cotton Smith the only nominal Churchmen on the list. Technically right, for "Raffles" are prohibited by positive law — but it strikes me as a symptom of Pharisæism — that they should go out of their way to denounce this, when they leave so much else undenounced. The solid conservative feeling of the Community against raffling is to be viewed in a very different light. Mrs Ham: Fish & her committees will have to give it up & the sooner they do so the better.

Our columns in the S.W. are moving & Newspaper Strategists are racking their brains for good guesses at the plan of the coming campaign. But in E. Tennessee, Secesh has the initiative, & threatens Knoxville again. The Army of the Potomac is mired and stationary, as usual. There must soon be hard fighting in the Gulf States. Secesh would prefer to fall back, concentrating — it's true policy. But the morale of it's army is too low to bear this process. With a little more discouragement, such as retreat & abandonment of territory would produce, the cohorts of Bragg & Johnston would be disorganized by desertion & mutiny. So Secesh will have to fight. Defeat on a large scale will be damaging to us, tho' not irreparable, but to them it will be final & fatal.

Feb: 17. Busy down town to day over various matters — (resisting death by frost, among them) — Afterwards at 823. Money still comes in from the Pacific coast to sustain the San. Com. — Another $50.000 received from San Francisco yesterday. That chrysogonous City is pledged for $25000.00 per month during 1864, & has paid up it's first four instalments. Our monthly expenses for 1863 averaged $48.532.17. So we shall need farther contributions. We shall probably get them from the Brooklyn Fair (Feb. 22^{d}) & the Metropolitan Fair (March 28th) — Dwight Johnson at 823 this aft^{n} tells me the cash subscriptions to the former are $120.000. Deducting say $10.000 for expenses, & $30.000 to be set apart to sustain the local ["Branch"] work of accumulating stores & supplies, $80.000 is left for my Central Treasury, to which must be added the hundred or two thousands that seem like to be raised by the Fair itself. We cannot yet foresee how the N.Y. Fair will turn out. This nasty "*Raffling*" question — & the question whether sufficient area has been secured, are embarrassing.

Feb: 18. G.C.A. dined here. Spent the ev'g with him in the Library. Rehearsal going on, down stairs, for the next "Metropolitan Fair" Concert, Sat: night. Poor Ellie! What toil has she undergone in securing her "amateurs" & her "professionals".

No war news — except that there are signs of a large Rebel raid into Pennsylvania.

Feb. 21. Sunday. Weather moderates. At Trinity Church Vinton halloed at us from the pulpit for three quarters of an hour, vainly striving to make commonplaces forcible. — Temple released from Quarantine to day, & at the dinner table once more. Kate was allowed to return to her appointed place at the Sunday ev'g tea table where we have missed her for some time. Afterwards, Laurence Williams, Mr S.B.R., Dr Peters, M^{r} & Mrs Peck of California, C.E.S., Blake, Robinson, & others appeared. They were received in the little "Blue room" for the parlors were untenantable, being filled up with the chairs, stage, & other lumber of last night's concert — "Metropolitan Fair Concert N° 3."

The concert was crowded, very hot, & "delightful". It was also successful to the extent of near $500. at $2 a ticket. My personal position was not well defined for I was uncertain whether I ought to behave as host, or as proprietor of a concert room. The assemblage was made up of "nice people" nearly all of whom we knew. — The programme was poor stuff, well enough rendered. At it's close came a novelty, to the credit whereof that ingenious & enterprising person Mrs Ellie is entitled. This was the sudden introduction of "Bryant's Minstrels" for a Part 3^{d}, in full costume, with black faces, preposterous shirt collars, banjos, bones, & all their paraphernalia. They performed with great spirit & effect, & gave us good honest melodies that were refreshing after the feeble trivialities of Donizetti & Co. We hob-nobbed together afterwards, in the dining room, over whiskey & cigars & I found them apparently respectable intelligent fellows enough.

Their appearance was a surprise, & the supplementary programme was not distributed till just at the close of Part 2^{d}. So they were introduced as privately as possible. They double-quicked through the hall & up stairs, & streamed into the Library, where C.E.S. was enjoying a quiet cigar & Speke's book on the Nile. Imagine his consternation when this Ethiopian horde invaded the premises. It was as if his reading had evoked a swarm of Mzarami or Myamuezi. Burke was equally amazed when he went up stairs after his violin fantasia, for his hat & coat, & found the library in possession of this swart gathering. He thought he had stepped into Pandemonium.

One of these Ethiops tells me that "Dixie's Land" — now established throughout the Country as a most energetic & vigorous Volks-weise, & a really fine original popular melody — was written by [ ] & produced in Concert saloons a year before our troubles began. It's words did not then refer to the South or "Dixie" or to Mason & Dixon's line, but to the children's game of "I'm on Dixie's land & Dixie ca'nt come" &c &c wh: I played at Whitestone 30 years ago. The idiotic song now associated with the melody was got up in the summer of /60 when North & South were taking hostile attitudes.

Feb. 22. Monday. Overcast, & threatening rain. It's too mild for snow. Quite a crowd assembled in Broadway & Wall St. at noon to listen to the Chimes of Trinity in honor of Washington's Birthday. — Up town to 823, where I find Bellows & Agnew & good news from across the Atlantic. Home, dressed & went with E. to dine with Mrs C.E.S. They went to opera — (Puritani). I came here & worked a couple of hours with Egleston over School of Mines. We had a Com: meeting on that subject at two, at Betts' office. Prospects of the School are good. Rumors from Grant & Sherman of battle & victory, but they are untrustworthy.

Feb. 24. Wednesday. Blandest weather, with one or two little April showers. Busy down town, mainly on a proposed circular about the proposed School of Mines & a hypothetical $20.000 "proposed" to be raised by subscription. Afterwards at 823. — No end of cackle & jaw about this "Raffling" controversy. Every one occupies a high moral position — or else a stately personal position of offended dignity & more or less of Xtian forgiveness of injury. The blonde curls of that "rather elderly Ophelia" Mrs Ham: Fish tend to become Ophidian like Medusa's. But one should speak of her respectfully, for she is an excellent woman, though liable to fits of ferocity. — Mr S.B.R. spent most of the ev'g here, talking Atlantic Dock Stores, Columbia College, & the State of the Nation — and then I turned out for an hour's stroll in the moonlight, & inspected the progress of the building that's going up for the "Metropolitan Fair" on 14th St.

News from *Sherman* is anxiously looked for. He is making a most enterprising & splendid, but hazardous, move — marching from Vicksburgh, by way of Jackson, Meridian, & Quitman, straight for Mobile, as we suppose, there to cooperate with a naval force. He is detached from his base, & "in the air", moving by forced marches & probably without a siege train, & breaking down bridges behind him as he advances. If he find himself at last in front of strong field works covering Mobile, he may come to grief, but his undertaking savors not only of audacity but of genius. When last heard from (thro' Rebel reports) he was at *Quitman*, 100 miles or so North of Mobile. This was on the 18th. — At other points, I see no sign of progress.

Political caldron begins to bubble. *Lincoln* will not be renominated unanimously. The Tribune comes out for a new man — for Chase, or possibly Frémont. On the other hand many old Democrats, like Cisco & the Cuttings, do strongly Lincolnize, & I should bet on Uncle Abe. It may result in a triangular duel between Chase, "radical" — Lincoln "moderate", & McClellan or some other extinct fossil "conservative". But the "conservatives" must nominate promptly or there will not be enough of them left to make a "Convention". Public opinion is "a-marching on" with seven league boots, & the politicians observe it's progress with lively personal interest. The Hon: Jas Brooks, for instance, has just ratted again, & made an abolition speech, congratulating the Country & mankind on the death of Slavery. Wonder if he supposes that anybody believes a word he says. The N.Y. Herald crawled the same way some time ago. Probably the Woods, & Win: Chanler, reptiles of the same genus, will soon be squirming after them.

The change of opinion on this Slavery question since 1860 is a great historical fact — comparable with the early progress of Christianity & of Mahometanism. Who could have predicted it, even when the news came that Sumter had fallen — or even a year & a quarter afterwards, when Pope was falling back on Washington, routed & disorganized? I think this great & blessed revolution is due, in no small degree, to A. Lincoln's sagacious policy. But I do wish A. Lincoln told fewer dirty stories. — What a marvellous change it is! Henry Clitz — Walter Cutting — Jem Ruggles — avowing themselves D— Abolitionists, & my little Lewis singing after dinner, Sundays,

"John Brown's bodies lies a-*modrin'* in the graves".

just as if it were the "Star-Spangled Banner". Abolitionism established in the District of Columbia, & triumphantly rampant, under State laws, in Maryland & Missouri! *Mirifica Opera Tua.* God pardon our blindness of three years ago! But for our want of eyes to see, & of courage to say what we saw, the South would never have ventured on rebellion.

Feb: 26. An energetic day in Wall St. and at 823. Walked up Broadway and 7th Av: to parts unknown, looking for eligible vacant blocks on which temporary buildings can be put up for the *Metropolitan Fair.* The 14th St. building does not contain a quarter the room that will be wanted, and I fear it is already too late to secure additional accommodations. It gives an area of 55.000. sq: feet all told. Brooklyn occupies an area of 45.500, & the managers are suffocating for want of room & lamenting their want of foresight. We need four times as much space as Brooklyn.

Visited the Brooklyn Fair yesterday. A very pretty & lively spectacle, but the crowd was such that I could see no details, & could have bought nothing, had I wanted to. — Last ev'g with Ellie & Mr Blake to Artists' Reception at Dodworth's building on 5th Av. in which G.C.A's School flourishes. Pleasant ev'g, but the collection of pictures exhibited was small trash.

Grant is advancing from Chattanooga on Tunnel Hill & Dalton & seems doing well so far. Reports that Sherman is at Selma, Alabama, & that a naval attack on Mobile is in progress, are untrustworthy.

Feb: 27. Batch of bad news. Gunboat Housatonic sunk by some devilish torpedo in Charleston Harbor, & serious disaster in Florida somewhere west of Jacksonville. Gen: Seymour is badly defeated, with heavy loss of men guns & stores. Details suppressed, & avowedly by Govt order — all private letters stopped. A most stupid proceeding this seems, tempting every one to magnify the mischief. But we got a letter from Dr Marsh, our Chief Inspector in that quarter. He estimates our casualties at not more than 2000, & attributes the defeat to the treachery of guides professing loyalty. Anticipating trouble from the too ready reception of these villains, he kept our San:

Com: stores well in the rear, & thus prevented a heavy loss. So he reports, and he is a very sagacious old gentleman.

This is bad, but it is not the first licking we have received — nor is it probably the last we shall get — and we have somehow or other made very substantial progress since the war began.

Feb. 28. Report that Sherman has occupied *Selma* gains strength. The Florida defeat is a serious disaster, but John Brown will continue "a-marching on" nevertheless.

Feb: 29. Monday night. Dirty weather. Mrs Week's funeral, 10 A.M., at Ch: of Annunciation, 14th St. Thence to Egleston's — 5th Av: — to go over the proposed Circular about the Sch: of Mines. He shewed me some fascinating minerals. Dodecahedrons and planes of cleavage must be delightful to people who understand Crystallography, — wh: I *do'nt.* But there is, for me, a specially weird uncanny interest & sentiment in fine crystals. They seem poems of the *Past* & of Death, just as flowers are the Poetry of the present & of Life. — Then tried to find W. Blackstone, whom I wanted to consult as to the possibility of large temporary structures in season for the Fair. Sought him in Laurens St & at the Mechanics' Exchange in Pine St. & elsewhere, in vain. Death of Thos Tileston. He was Pres'dt of the Phœnix Bank & all the Wall St. flags were at half mast. He died last night, of disease of the heart, without a moment of premonition.

Home at 3½ to witness the first Rehearsal of "the Two Buzzards" an absurd amusing little farce or "Comedietta" that is to be included in the series of Private Theatricals in aid of the *Metropolitan Fair.* Performers Mrs Blake, Miss Teresa Meert, Rice, Major Charley Dix, & Talboys. The two ladies acted with much spirit & freedom, but the men were paralyzed by self-consciousness, & mere sticks. They will do better next time. — Mrs Gen: Dix assisted as spectatress — also Mrs Eleanor, M^rs^ McVickar, Hoppin, R.G. White & al.

Long satisfactory session with Master Johny, after dinner, over Latin & Algebra. He does very well indeed.

No War news, except that our unlucky Army of the Potomac is said to be executing a Movement. If so, it's movement is probably Andante mæstoso — slow, & destined to cause mourning. I fear that Army is paralyzed by the McClellanism impressed on it when it was organized two years ago. McClellan's voluminous Report, just published, will not raise him in public estimation. Considered as a historical essay, or as a bit of autobiography contributed to the history of the war, it may have it's value, more or less. But as the Report of a General to his military superior, it is worthless, or worse, & will do him harm. It's publication blights whatever hopes his friends may have entertained of making him President.

March 1st. Sent for by the "Brooklyn Fair" people to give information on certain points, so I waded off thro' the slush, crossed the ferry in the fog, & spent a couple of hours in the Bn Acad: of M: — Was recd by Stranahan, Dr Farley, & other magnates of Brooklyn, with great respect, as Treasurer of the illustrious San: Com:, & my explanations seemed satisfactory.

Afterwards at 823. Home. Visit from Van Nostrand, etc:

March 2. Found Prof: Bache at No 823, with Bellows & Agnew. We decided to request old Dr Satterlee U.S.A. in writing, to inform us what he means by his habitual loose talk about the San: Com: being "a swindling concern" & the like.

No authentic war news. Rumors from Meade are favorable, as far as they go. They indicate heavy cavalry expeditions to Lee's rear, by both flanks. Anxiety is felt for Sherman's column.

To night by invitation to a Convention of Boss Carpenters at Clinton Hall (Astor Place) to organize a concerted movement in aid of "Metropolitan Fair". They wanted some representative of the San: Com: to be present & give explanations as to the objects methods & results of the Commission. I got Agnew & Jenkins to attend also. They were solid respectable intelligent public spirited men, as it seemed to me. Jas Renwick was Chief Manager. I was called on for "a few remarks", & favored the assemblage with an unpremeditated harangue, that they must have found rather dull — but then there was a good deal of it. Agnew also spoke with spirit & effect, & we left the meeting busy over a subscription paper.

March 3. That plucky little Captn Ash of the 5th Cavalry has been distinguishing himself by a bold & successful attack on a Rebel camp on the Rapidan or some other river — but there is no news of general importance. This is bad, if only for it's bad influence on public feeling. We are in danger of a period of discouragement weariness & soreness, like that thro' which we struggled from Antietam to Vicksburgh.

March 4. That Copperhead Willy Duncan having called here last night to consult about a certain matter connected with the Fair, of some little delicacy & importance, & communicated his difficulties to M[rs] Ellie, I thought it expedient to see Cisco on my way down Wall St. & take his opinion — Cisco being among the most sagacious advisers I know. The situation is this. Certain officers of her Majesty's [ ] Reg[t] at Montreal are addicted to private theatricals, & give M[rs] Duncan to understand that if invited they will come here & perform in aid of the Fair. Of course this is kind & creditable to them. Such performance would be inter-nationally emollient, moreover. But is there danger of any popular Anti-Anglican insult to a set of British swells — of anything like the Forrest & Macready row of /49? Any such demonstration would be unutterably shocking & mortifying. Is it worth while to run the least risk of it?

Talked it over at length with Cisco — afterwards with Duncan. We agree in thinking it safe to accept the offer informally made by these gentlemen, provided there be abundant precaution & vigilance.

March 6. Strolled down to N° 823 at 2 P.M. to look after my report as Treasurer — to the San: Com: meet'g at Philad[a] next week, which I fear this very virulent cold will forbid my attending. Made my way with difficulty thro' the dense crowd that filled Union Square — for the First *N.Y. Negro Regiment* was receiving it's Colors at the Union League Club House. It has been organized by aid of subscriptions got up in this Club. A second regiment of black N. Yorkers will soon be sent off under the same auspices. Our labors of a year ago have born fruit. The N.Y. Club has done something for the Country. From the windows of 823 I saw this regiment march down Broadway, after a spirited allocution by Cha[s] King. The Reg[t] was "black but comely" & marched well. Gen: Wadsworth, who was in the office, said it was not below the average of new regiments. Both side walks & all the windows were full of applauding spectators. There was hearty cheering & clapping & waving of handkerchiefs, & I neither heard nor heard of any expression of sound constitutional conservative disapproval. Which is sad to think of!

This march will be the subject of cords of historical paintings before A.D. 1900. The flag presentation with Cha[s] King & Col: Bartram in the foreground, is destined to spoil many acres of canvass. I have seen two memorable marches down Bdway, viz: this one, & that of the Seventh Regiment in April /61. This transaction had far less *material* sublimity. The immense concourse was wanting, & so were the vague sense of awe & the fearful anticipations of coming woe, & the *new* thrill of National life and of patriotic resolution that stirred all the throng, that cloudy windy afternoon. It is among the most solemn memories of my life — thus far. But I think yesterday morning's phenomenon — Ethiopia marching down Broadway, armed drilled truculent & elate, was the weightier & the more memorable of the two.

March 8. Stopped at N[o] 2 Great Jones St. (Metropolitan Fair office) on my way down, & discoursed M[rs] Lane & M[rs] D.D. Field, & Miss Nash, & M[rs] Alex: Hamilton J[r], all very charming, & all as busy as bees, — M[rs] Ellie among the busiest of the whole hive. The Ladies have failed to convince their inert & stupid masculine colleagues that the "Fair" will be a disastrous failure, & a disgrace to N.Y. without at least four times the area yet secured for it. They were despondent, & wanted — or said they wanted — to announce thro' the newspapers that the Metropolitan Fair was given up & would not come off at all. I suggested an appeal to the Stand'g Com: of the San: Commission which expressly reserved the right to decide between the two committees — male & female — in case of disagreement. The suggestion was well received. I was promptly served with written notice of disagreement — & of appeal — & telegraphed as promptly to Philadelphia, where the San: Com: is in session. I ought to be there in person but I am made deaf & voiceless & altogether inert & useless by this miserable cold.

It kept me from the regular Col: Coll: meeting yesterday aft[n]. I hear from M[r] S.B.R. that the Board approved the action of the Committee on "School of Mines", & voted vehement thanks to me for sending the College a little collection of minerals several months ago. Wm Betts moved the resolution, & made certain statements about my admirable personal traits of character, for which I'm much obliged to him. King's resignation as *President* was formally accepted (to take effect after next commencement) under a heavy fire of complimentary speechification from B^{p} Potter & others. Potter, Bradford, & Betts were appointed a Committee on the question of the succession.

To night at U.L. Club. Committee on Admissions. — Kilpatrick's Raid was dashing & creditable. Tho' he did not harry Richmond, he came *near* doing it. Poor young Col: Dahlgren is a serious loss however. As to the "Orders" found in his pocket, about which Richmond papers are raving so vindictively & murderously, I think they were concocted in Richmond itself "to fire the Southern heart".

The Great Brooklyn Fair has been a splendid triumph of public morality. Let Tyng & Spring rejoice. There was no "raffling" & nothing was disposed of by chance or lottery. The Brooklyn people (who are mostly Down-Easters & very smart) substituted an ingenious & absolutely unexceptionable process for the raffles & the Xtian gaming tables Tyng & Spring used to wink at when used to raise money for Sunday-school libraries & the like. People "subscribed" for an article. Each paid up his $5.00 or $10.00, and when the "subscription list" was full the names of all the "subscribers" were put into a hat, & one was drawn out. But the person thus drawn did not thereby "win" the article, or become it's owner. *O No!* He was merely selected by chance as the man to decide which one of all the subscribers was in his judgment the most meritorious pious patriotic public-spirited praiseworthy person, & as such best entitled to the prize. His nominee or appointee took it as a testimonial of the respect & affection of the whole corps of "subscribers". It is a striking illustration of the universal prevalence of *Selfishness* in the human heart that the person whose name was drawn actually decided in every case that *he* was the most meritorious &c person in that crowd, & walked off with the property. All the others acquiesced most good naturedly. But that does not affect the *Principle*. Brooklyn Fair has been a glorious protest against Gambling!

March 14. At 823, an important session. The sudden death of Rev. T. Starr King makes it necessary for Bellows to go to California for six months, to look after King's congregation and the interests of the Commission. So he thinks & he may be right. He is telegraphed for, most urgently. — Then Van Buren will probably go off to Europe next month for a short spell of leisure — & if he do so, *Agnew & I* will be left to run this great machine! It's a rather grave prospect.

Trinity Ch: Vestry to night. Nothing very material done, tho' we sat late. Nominations agreed on for two vacancies. I hoped C.E.S. would have been one of them, but he got only 3 votes. That wrongheaded Henry Youngs bustled about insisting that the new men should be taken from the congregation of S[t] Johns, & I did not think it decorous to urge the claims of a kinsman. — By the by, C's unlucky papa has been for some days at the point of death at Cincinnati, with typhoid pneumonia, & C. has been hourly expecting a telegraphic summons to the funeral. But the patient is reported improving to day.

The Ladies of the Metropolitan Fair have taken the providing of additional Space into their own hands. I saw Mayor Gunther on their behalf Friday morn'g, & he approved & signed a "joint Resolution" authorizing a large Structure on the N. side of Union Square. It was begun this morn'g. San: Com: guarantees payment of it's cost, by vote of Stand'g Com: during the Philadelphia session. Strange that I, with two or three other New Yorkers, should have the right to decide questions so large — confided to us somehow or other, nobody can exactly say how or by whom. This Brooklyn Fair — the "Metropolitan Fair" — & the "Central Fair" at Philad[a] may very possibly put more than a million into our Treasury, for Agnew & me to use at our own sweet will during the next six months. It seems a most irrational & improvident arrangement. But it works & works well. At "Olustee" in Florida our agents had 700 wounded men on their hands for two days, & provided for them, the Medical Staff being wholly without medical stores of any kind.

Lt Gen[l] Grant supersedes Halleck as Commander in Chief. Probably a judicious change. Halleck abides at Wash[n] as Chief of Staff — wh: seems equally judicious. — Fitz-John Porter has recently gone to Colorado Territory, as an agent of Eastern capitalists to inspect certain *mines.* Whereupon (according to the newspapers) the Coloradians held a mass meeting — of the Vigilance Committee & Vehm-Gericht type, — and requested F.J.P. to depart from among them & quit those "diggins". — Poor F.J.P.! That his conviction & Disgrace should have been deserved seems incredible. But one damning fact is unexplained & undenied, so far as I know. He lay still for hours listening to the guns of a disastrous battlefield, without an effort to help his comrades.

March 16. Very pleasant reports of our work at "Olustee", Florida, in a grateful General Order printed at Jacksonville & in letters from Seymour's Medical Director and others of the Medical Staff. San: Com: seems to have given the wounded all the help they got — and the Medical Bureau confesses it had none to give them. This comes in very *apropos* to meet Dr Satterlee's malignant official mendacities about the ability of Government to do all that is needed, & the folly of any outside movement for "Army Relief".

March 18. Gen: Grant seems for the present in command of the Army of the Potomac as General-in-Chief, without displacing Gen: Meade. He will doubtless do or try to do something decisive in Virginia. But the road to Richmond is a *passage perylous, whereon have perysshed manie good Knyghtes.* E.g. Syr Scott & Syr McDowell, Syr McClellan, Syr Burnside & Syr Hooker, — to say nothing of Pope the Incredible Knyght, & Meade "Le Noir Faineant" for the last 8 months. A terrible ordeal for Grant. His patch is whitened by the bones of popular reputations that perished because their defunct owners did not know how to march through Virginia to Richmond. I hope Grant may possess the talisman — "the seal of Solomon" — that raises its possessor to capacity for his place, however large.

March 21. Monday. Atmosphere like iced vinegar, as it has been for a week. Perhaps it's because of the weather that this tyrannous cold has dominion over me so long. Up 5th Av: this morn'g to call on Mrs Will: Astor, & get instructions for drawing her will (not her husband but a testamentary paper) — The great hideous $100.000 Townsend-Sarsaparilla-Spingler house on the other side of XXXIV St. has just been bought by A.T. Stewart, who has razed it to the ground & tells W.A. he is going to lay out one million on a new white-marble Palazzo — I suppose it will be just ten times as ugly & barbaric as it's predecessor, if that be conceivable.

This is a sign of the times. Another is Jerome's (not the Saint but the stockjobber) grand $80.000 stable with the private theatre for a second story, wherein the private Theatricals "in aid of the Metropolitan Fair" are now being daily rehearsed. The whole city is bubbling & fizzing with the Fair & the San: Com: — I wonder people are not worn out with it & that the words San: Com: do not produce the effect of a heavy dose of Tartar Emetic.

Up town rather early — paralyzed & aching with this horrible "cold". Important conference at 823 with Agnew Jenkins & Bellows. Dinner. A half hour's indoctrination of Mr J.R.S. in Latinity, & then to T.C. Vestry meeting at Trinity Chapel Schoolhouse. Nothing noteworthy, except a fuss raised by Ja^{s} G. King about the proposed monument to Bishop Onderdonk. He had heard there were to be certain symbols on the monument — lions & snakes (know not exactly what) that would somehow commit Trinity Church to the assertion that Onderdonk's conviction was unjust. Nothing came of it.

Talked with G.M.O. after the meeting about College affairs. He paid me the compliment of a frank expression of opinion on a matter in which I'm personally interested. — Certain of my friends keep themselves very busy in this C: Coll: business. I fear they will compromise me in sundry ways, & also that they will get me the credit of being an office seeker *now*, & a defeated office seeker next June.

Death of poor Fred: Leavenworth. He went to the dogs at last, but he had his good points. He narrowly missed being a valuable gallant officer. He was in the Army at Chattanooga, for some time as Captn or Lt: — Was said to have been cashiered for habitual drunkenness, tho' when he called on me last summer he said he was "absent on leave". That was our last interview. He was then rather tight, & looked whiskey-&-waterlogged, boozy & bibulous, & as if he had been tight for a great while & wanted to borrow ten dollars or so.

March 22. To night Stand'g Com: of San: Com: met here. Van Buren — Agnew — Bellows — also D[r] Secretary Jenkins — & M[rs] Ellie assisted at a modest supper table, 10 P.M.

Queer incident in the *Hammond* Court martial, communicated by H. to Van Buren — While he was off at Knoxville, under those mysterious orders of the Sec: of War, a large number of papers & letters disappeared from the files of the Surgeon General's office — nobody knew how. When charges were presented against him, Hammond found to his dismay that the abstracted documents were mostly quite essential to his defence — especially his correspondence with a D[r] Cooper, Medical Director at Philad[a]. Cooper, when put on the stand swore emphatically that he never wrote or received the letters that make up this correspondence. A few days ago Hammond received an anonymous note, stating that it's writer was in possession of these missing papers, & would deliver them up for a consideration viz: $1500.00. He complied with the conditions I suppose, but at all events a package was left at his house containing most of them. One, of special importance, was missing. The Anonymous personage wrote that it had been stolen from him. But Hammond thinks that on the evidence he has thus secured he can convict Cooper of wilful perjury — and also that he was sent to the West to give [ ] an opportunity of ransacking his office & stealing his papers, so as to leave him defenceless against a conspiracy to ruin him. There are certainly signs of very sharp practice by *somebody*.

March 24. Bellows goes off to California 4th April. Agnew & I will have to run this great San: Com: machine for the next six months, unless Van Buren can be persuaded to relinquish his projected visit to Europe — which I should hate to ask of him.

March 26. Easter Eve. The most vehement N.E. storm all day. Expected to see the "Fair" Buildings now half finished on Union Square prostrate — but they were still erect at half past 5 P.M. & the wind has gone down since then, tho' it's still overcast, & there is no Easter moon.

Treated my cold to a carriage down to Wall St — where I was much driven by work & visitors, & had to sally out into the weather repeatedly, to the wetting of my feet & the inflaming of my cold. Among my visitors was Jas. H. Frothingham, Treasurer, with a check for $300.000.00 — ¾ the net proceeds of Brooklyn & L.I. Fair. Also Dwight Johnson, a good deal annoyed because Frothingham had asked me to deposit this sum on interest with the Nassau Bank Brooklyn, of which F's father is President.

To Law School Com: meeting 2 P.M. 6 Wall St. Nothing worth noting. Talk afterwards with Gouv: Ogden about the Comptrollership & other matters. To N° 823. Then G.A. dined here, & at 8 I went to Van Buren's for a com: meeting. Agnew Bellows V.B. & I. Gen[l] Keyes looked in at supper time & squelched our discussion of the important question whether we can do anything indirectly toward helping Hammond in the ruinous cost of this Court-Martial, which has already been sitting nine weeks, & but just got through with the case for the prosecution. I am clear we can do nothing for him directly — out of the funds of the Commission. This Court is said to have cost Government $250.000 already — a heavy sum to be assessed on the Country for the gratification of Stanton's personal pique & spitefulness — & rather oppressive on the Surgeon Genl with his pay & allowances of $3500. per annum.

March 28. Monday. Mild weather. Have been staggering all day under the sequelæ of yesterday's headache, viz: sore bones & general stupefaction. Worked hard in Wall St. nevertheless. Stopped twice at N° 2 Great Jones St (head-quarters of Metropolitan Fair) & inspected the building on N. side of Union Square. It is now nearly under cover. The quantity of gossip intrigue & personal pique that grows out of this Fair & it's hundred Committees is stupendous & terrible. Vast controversies have arisen, and immense issues, but I have not time to define & record them. My general impression is that the Executive He-Committee has thus far proved a mere incumbrance to the Executive Com: of Ladies. Griswold Gray Ch'man of the former, & Lloyd Aspinwall, seem like to come out of the transaction without laurels, & with positive damage. They have somehow affronted the ladies — whose husbands & brothers will of course side with them & adopt their views. Gray means well, but he is a mere successful trader, without culture or refinement, who has spent the best years of his life making money at Canton or Hong-Kong, & comes home to be petted by young ladies to whom he gives grand ostentatious dinners & suppers at Delmonico's, and fivehundred dollar baskets (or colossal structures) of flowers now & then.

March 29. *Bache* writes, (with politic obscurity, & diplomatic non-committal vague phrases) letters that shew that he expects Stanton's hostility to *San*: *Com*: to be about exploding at last. He is perturbed — anticipates some serious crisis — & talks of "withdrawing from any responsible position" in connexion with the S.C. if there is to be a row. He is a most wary old practitioner and will not stand by the San: Com: a single day, if he think himself thereby likely to endanger his influence with the Administration as Chief of the Coast Survey. I suppose him to be perturbed & alarmed by something or other that has been brought out in the Hammond Court Martial. I cannot guess what it is, but signs & tokens from several quarters indicate that some attack on us is coming, probably inspired by Stanton's malignity & wrongheadedness. We are invulnerable — except possibly as to the arrangement for furnishing supplies to the Hospitals of Washington & it's vicinity, which was adopted while I was laid up last May & June. I have always maintained that this undertaking was unwise & wrong — no matter how practically beneficent — because it made the Com: a recipient of public money — buying mutton & poultry & vegetables in Penn: & Maryland for which it was to be reimbursed from the "Hospital funds" of Wash^{n}. I know the system has saved these hospital funds 25 per cent at least on the cost of their extra supplies but it has mixed us up with money transactions, that can be misrepresented & which I wish had never occurred.

March 30. Dick Hunt called, in a great tantrum about flags — decorations — Coats of Arms — &c &c &c. A full & accurate report of all the controversies, cross-purposes, jealousies, tribulations, heartburnings, manœuvrings, affronts, &c &c &c that are produced in the progress of the "Metropolitan Fair" & its x + y Score of Committees would be as hard to write as a precise definition of each & every one of the wiry eddies that swirl & react on each other at the foot of Niagara.

At Trinity Church, 4 P.M., to meet the Rector — for discussion of the "accompaniment organ" question. Cisco, the 3^d^ Committee-man, was detained at the Treasury. We agreed on a plan, which seems likely to work, viz: to put the proposed instrument into the second story of the North "robing room", cutting an opening for it thro' the Chancel wall.

823. Much work of importance done, especially as to purchase of antiscorbutics for the West. Large powers given Dr Newberry. Nothing new as to the storm we are awaiting from Washington. I expect to find the Commission assailed some fine morning by a concentric fire from about forty "Administration" newspapers, East & West, as dishonest imbecile & disloyal — If so, we must roll up our sleeves & "sail in".

April 1st. At 823 from half past three till near 6. — Standing Com of S. Commission met here at 8, & others of the Commission were with us. Bellows Van Buren Agnew W. Gibbs, Dr Jenkins, Knapp, Prof. Bache, Judge Skinner & McCagg of Chicago & Ellie & I sat down to our usual supper at 10 but kept steadily at business till after twelve, tolerating no talk that was out of order. (I forgot to count in Bishop Clark.) We disposed of much work. Bache's intimations of something wrong & alarming at Washington turn out to be moonshine. At least he professed to know of no threatening signs in that or any other quarter. That politic old gentleman is rather hard to follow. He talked oddly to night — as if he thought of resigning his Vice-Presidency in case Mr Bloor were transferred from the Wash^n^ to the N.Y. Office! It's very possible he "sees a hand we cannot see" — that of Sec^y^ Stanton to wit — doubled up & ready to give us "one on the nob." But every other indication is that we are exceedingly strong at Wash^n^ just now — & much respected in view of the Presidential campaign just opening (politicians take it for granted, of course, that we are disposed to use our large machinery for political ends) — and also that the Surgeon General's case is progressing favorably, & that nothing has been brought out by the prosecution that reflects on the honesty of the Commission. Nevertheless we shall probably send E.H. Owen to Wash^n^ next Monday to look into the case professionally & advise whether we are called on to do anything.

We are in collision with the "Gentlemen's (?) Committee of the Metropolitan Fair." They were appointed as auxiliaries to the Ladies, & as their advisers & aids in business matters which ladies could not be expected to deal with. But they have seen fit to thwart snub insult & override the Ladies' Committee in the most disgusting offensive & low-bred way. Their general course has been snobbish & stupid. They have shewn want of manners, & of appreciation of the magnitude of the undertaking. Their chairman, Griswold Gray, is a well meaning fellow enough, but a mere rich tradesman, without substantial culture or refinement, & his colleagues are mostly of the same stripe — men like Lloyd Aspinwall, whose bank accounts are all they can rely on for social position & influence. So far as I can discover, this Masculine Committee has been a positive drawback & damage & nuisance & calamity. By the original organization of this Fair with its binary system of Two Committees, male & female, the right was reserved to our Stand'g Com: (San: Com:) of coming in as umpire in case of any difference of opinion between them. Such a difference arose about a qu: concerning tickets of admission, & Bellows being appealed to by the womankind called me in to make a quorum of the Stand'g Committee, & we agreed on a letter to the Gents (yesterday morn'g) most courteous in tone but distinctly adopting & assuming the policy preferred by the women. This letter was laid before the "gents" at their meeting last night. It made a shindy. After much debate they resolved that it be *returned* to Dr B. & it was so *returned* accordingly under cover of an official note from "Richd Grant White, Sec^{y}". I regret this. Dick White should have resigned his Secretaryship & cut off several fingers of his right hand rather than consent to make himself responsible, personally or officially, for this piece of insolent monied dirtiness. But I fear he is in fact a "poor shoat". I had thought he might make a good letter-writer & "literary Secretary" for the San: Com: during Dr Bellows' absence in California, but he is clearly invertebrate & unavailable.

April 2^{d}. Philharmonic Extra-Concert in aid of Metropolitan Fair. It was a new experience to me — there were not 150 people in all the vast auditorium. But Eisfeld & his battalion came manfully up to their work, and gave us the glorious ever-new

Fifth Symphony [C. Minor] in grand style. Eisfeld seemed to lead with a special dash and freedom, I thought, & wielded his baton half recklessly, emphasizing fortes & pianos & changes of time, as if he meant to say "This is a preposterous absurd transaction altogether, but never mind. Let us give this little knot of people their allowance of Beethoven, & pepper with it. Here goes for a real jolly rendering of the C. Minor!" The performance was a little rough here & there, but it brought out the great features & contrasts of the Symphony most distinctly & beautifully. The transcendent *energy* of the 1st & 4th movements were made splendidly conspicuous. There is nothing comparable to the outburst of that finale. It always makes me feel as if the roof of the concert room were in danger of being blown off. There were two American overtures also — "Columbus" by G.F. Bristow & "Hail Columbia" by one Hohnstock, both creditable productions, notwithstanding a certain amount of clap-trap.

Coming up town thro' the weather, I observe that the 17th St. Fair building is brilliantly lit up. They have a gang of men there working all night. Detmold by the by has resigned. A most excellent man, & he has worked indefatigably for the Fair these two or three months, but he has somehow made himself generally odious. If this Fair be wound up without any memorable calamity & catastrophe I shall be thankful. What I most dread is *fire*, & I have been prosing & writing to everybody about the necessity of precaution against that danger, for a month past. Suggested a preventive to *White* (architect of the 17th St. Shingle Palace) this aftn, which he cordially approved & said he would provide — viz: a little embankment of earth or sand or rubbish of any sort all along the base of the structure, sufficient to prevent any malignant devilish copperhead or sympathizer from poking a little lump of cotton, or of rags, saturated with camphine under the floor through the crevices of the rough wood-work. Richmond papers would laud and magnify any such transaction, & there are many beasts in this community who would like to be concerned in it, could it be safely done.

While G.C.A. & I were taking our glass of whiskey & water after the concert, enter Senator Foster & his wife — enquiring for Ellie. She was at a meeting of the "Dramatic Committee".

They left two very valuable "albums" of photographs and autographs, for the Fair.

Poor Johny has met with a severe affliction. His eldest pet killy fish — the patriarch of his aquarium, that he brought all the way from Newport a year & a half ago was found the other morn'g wrong side up, it's career of usefulness having been abruptly terminated, without warning, during the night. Johny cried himself into a sickheadache. What strange delicate sensitive unaccountable organizations children are, & how wary their elders must be if they want to avoid "offending" them! I fear I am not one tenth part as vigilant as I should be in my dealings with these three splendid little boys of ours — tho' I honestly try to do my best for them.

The War languishes & makes no progress. People naturally turn their thoughts therefore to questions of finance — taxation — & prices, and wonder whether gold will not soon be at 200 & butter a dollar a pound. I believe Gen. Grant is working in his new place "Ohne hast, ohne rast", purging the Army of the Potomac of disaffected McClellanists in high command, & bringing it's *morale* into training for hard work in its next campaign agst "Lee's Miserábles" — Stanton seems trying to interfere & thwart the Lt General. So people say. If he is doing so, I hope Grant will tender his resignation & tell the Country the reason why.

April 4th. Went at 10 A.M. to the "Fair" buildings in 14th St., & spent a couple of hours there. The spectacle was interesting, but fatiguing to the spectator. A vast crowd of well dressed men & women — our "best people" — were working their fingers to the bone, arranging & sorting material, directing decorative operations, receiving acknowledging unpacking & distributing to their appropriate departments, contributions from the four quarters of the earth. It was the busiest human ant-hill I ever saw. My self assumed mission was to confer with the Police Department, & the Fire Department about the fearful possibility of *Fire* — panic — & slaughter. — They seem fully aware of this peril, & have taken special precautions against it. Suggested one or two extra precautions that were favorably received. When I introduce myself as "Treasurer of the San: Com:" I find every suggestion I offer cordially treated.

To Wall St. & then walked up town with G.C.A. Grand parade & military spectacle in honor of the opening of the Metropolitan Fair. We inspected the column from the side walk of Astor Place. Gen: Dix tells me to night that 11000 men turned out, & that this was the largest parade that N.Y. Island has seen since 1814 when a large numerical force was assembled here to repel an expected invasion. Most of the warriors of this aftn's pageant had been under fire. Many of their regimental flags were tattered & torn by rebel bullets. — After dinner to the Fair — calling for Mrs Gen: Dix & Mrs Blake. Everything brilliant & handsome — a fine spectacle, creditable to the City & its dependencies. Crowd large but not oppressive. Police omnipresent & civil. They caught four or five pickpockets, red hand, & marched them backward & forward thro' the building with placards round their necks, defining their vocation in large capitals, & then haled them off to their appointed place. Poor devils, how shame & brazen impudence contended for the mastery in their mean faces! Some of our softhearted women thought the transaction "painful" & "cruel" & "humiliating" & "too bad," but to my coarser sense it seemed a very goodly spectacle.

The ceremony of "inaugurating" the Fair went off well. For Dr Adams' opening prayer — Gen: Dix's speech, & Mr Choate's reply I refer posterity to tomorrow's papers, where they will doubtless be found verbatim. Both orations are said to have been good but they were inaudible to me. I did hear the bass-part of the Hallelujah Chorus however — which was bellowed into my ears by a battallion of Bull-bassi extinguishing & drowning the ensemble.

That *he*-Committee is made up of louts & cubs, & of a powerless minority of decent well bred men, like Marshall O. Roberts & Acton the Police Commissioner. They made no provision for receiving Gen: Dix to night, & he had to get in as he could & find his way to the platform for himself. Nor was any place assigned to the ladies of the Executive Com. — to their intense mortification. Mrs Astor, Mrs Belmont, Ellie, Mrs Lane &c were almost tearful about it — while that indomitable Mrs Jno Sherwood, & that iron-clad little Miss Catharine Nash (what an appropriate sister in law for Agnew!) were not in the least tearful but rather tended toward grimness. As I heard some one remark to night, "I would'nt be in Griswold Gray's boots for twice his assets." Gray, Lloyd Aspinwall, Detmold, Dick White, &c, have certainly shewn themselves in all this business, not to be thorough bred men. They may be severally most respectable & most useful & valuable in their several spheres. — but they are *gentlemen* only in a conventional acceptation of that term.

White came here last night. I did not feel inclined to cut him — but I turned him a cold shoulder by formality of reception. He's a decorated flamboyant *Gent.* I hate to throw him over, for he has a certain amount of culture, & is generally underrated & slighted — & was blackballed at the Century three or four years ago — I never knew exactly why. But he is clearly a second rate fellow. I had intended to get him the position of "Literary" — or Correspond'g Sec^{y}: to our Stand'g Com: during Bellows' absence (such an officer must be got somewhere) but it cannot be done. Both Agnew & Gibbs are "down upon" him to a surprising extent.

Called on Bellows last night in 20th St. & bade him goodbye with sincere regrets. We shall miss him sorely these coming six months — for he is most useful & efficient. He has his foibles, & they lead many people to underrate him. Tho' public spirited energetic & unselfish, far-sighted & wise (never foolish if he give himself time to take counsel with slower men, like Van Buren Agnew Gibbs or myself), he is conceited & he likes to be conspicuous. But what a trifling drawback it is on the reputation of a man admitted to be sagacious active & willing to sacrifice personal interests in public service, to admit that he knows after all that he is doing the Country good service, & that he likes to see his usefulness made manifest in newspapers.

Mr S.B.R. dined here — & returning from the Fair at *XI* after a fearful bother about Carriages, — I found G.C.A. here, having spent the ev'g at Wm Schermerhorn's.

April 5th. At the Fair (14th St.) from 10 to 12 while Ellie, aided by her financial staff was endorsing & arranging $25000. in checks for me to deposit for her in Bank of America. Very active in Wall St. — Uptowned & inspected the 17th St. Union Square Shingle Palace, with W. Gibbs, after a diligent session at 823. It promises well. It's general effect will be better than that of the 14th St. Centre. But it cannot possibly be ready for "opening" before tomorrow night.

After dinner with Johny to the 14th St. Fair Building. Crowd & heat were fearful & will doubtless visit Master Johny with a headache tomorrow morning.

April 6th. Had to wait a long while in 14th St. this A.M. while Ellie the Treasuress was endorsing the pocket full of checks I carried down to the Bank of America. It was a pretty sight — the throng of well dressed people — the showy decorations — the stalls or counters loaded with all sorts of things — & especially the shoals of nice women with their graceful *diagonal* broad blue ribbons (a *line* generally wanting in our womens' costume) all working in such deadly earnest.

Tho' so much humbug, vanity, ostentation, & emulation are inherent in all Fairs, there is a very deep feeling below them all in this instance, & it's visible manifestation on so large a scale with accessories so brilliant, appeals to one very strongly indeed. I confess it made my eyes fill, this morning. Thank God for the hearts & the heads He has given the women of the Country, & the men too — after making every allowance for the baneful existence among us of vermin like the Woods & Brookses, & Win: Chanler & Marble & Gov: Seymour & J.G. Bennett — & of purseproud snobs like G.G.G. —

Down town & up again. Session at 823. Gibbs Van Buren Agnew Jenkins & I. Agnew brings forward a very large proposition — viz: to buy 500 acres of land near Saratoga, where he has just been making a tour of inspection with Knapp — put up a Sanitarium for disabled & discharged soldiers — a Hotel des Invalides — sufficient for (say) 100 men & to fund about $300.000. for it's endowment. Much can be & was said in favor of the scheme, but my first impressions are strongly against it.

After dinner with Ellie to "opening" of Union Square Department of the Fair. Dense crowd of course. We met in a little box of a room appropriated to the Ladies' Committee, & filed off to the stage or platform in the large room at the Eastern end of the building, at 8. I took in Mrs Pres'dt King or Mrs Sherwood, I forget which. King presided. Rev: Morgan Dix made a brief prayer. Mr Ruggles made a speech, inaudible to me, but well received by those whom the laws of acoustics permitted to hear it, & said to have been felicitous. Orchestra played the Overture to Der Freyschutz (blessed be the memory of it's composer!) King made a brief final allocution, & the meeting adjourned, & the Concert went on. Put Ellie & Mrs Sherwood into their carriage for the first of the Private Theatrical nights at L.W. Jerome's theatre — & then went down to the 14th St. Department with Rev: M. Dix, & spent an hour or so as pleasantly as heat & crowd permitted. Dix is certainly a Brick of the first quality. I never knew a more genuine man, or one who can be cultivated with more pleasure & profit. —— The Union Square buildings are far more effective than those in 14th St. Their architect, *White*, has done his hurried job wisely & well. Dick Hunt has put all his taste & all his indomitable energy into their decoration, & has produced a series of most artistic & splendid interiors at little cost. The "international department" at the W. end, is quite gorgeous with its banners & escutcheons, its fountain & it's shew of flowers.

Who dreamed two years ago last June that the poor little Sanitary Commission would ever make such a noise in the world?

Heaven grant the *Fair* may pass off without any memorable catastrophe from fire or crowd — & that Ellie may not be harmed by this long period of excitement & hard labor! She is & for months has been steadily working under a terrible pressure of steam. — I have estimated the proceeds of the "Metropolitan Fair" as probably not far from $700.000. But there are bets on a *million & a half*, & all the indications of the last three days point toward something larger than I anticipated.

— tells me that Agnew has been in a dreadful state of mind because people were at work in these Fair buildings last Sunday. Evangelical doctrine certainly sanctions the keeping of a brute beast out of the pit in which he has come to grief on the Sabbath Day. Surely we may by analogy feel authorized in bringing help twenty four hours sooner to dying *men* by working on the machinery that is to produce such help, even tho' we have to sacrifice Sunday to the saving of their lives.

Agnew is among the best & purest men I ever knew, but how like Presbyterians are to the Pharisees of 1800 years ago in all their tendencies & characteristic habits of thought!

April 7th. At 14th St. this A.M. early to get Ellie's checks & cash for deposit in Bank of America. About $37.000 I think. Took a carriage with John H. Gourlie & drove first to the N.Y. County Bank where he deposited the proceeds of *sales* & *admissions*. My deposit was of *contributions*. He is Chief of E's financial Staff & a most efficient officer. Got into the "Art Gallery" before the doors were opened to the public. It's a splendid collection of pictures, probably far the finest ever exhibited in this City. This being the first "fifty cent day" the crowd was most oppressive, & obstructive. The Ladies will have to restore the price of admission to a dollar next week, or sales will be impracticable. — At 3½ to meeting of Col: Coll: Committee on the Course at Law School. Bradford, Rutherford, Potter & I. G.C.A's letter about qualifications for admission finds great favor, & it's suggestions will probably be recommended to the Board for adoption. Important session at 823. After dinner Mr S.B.R. appeared, & we spent an hour in the "Knickerbocker Kitchen" of the Fair — on 17th St. Ellie too tired with her days work to be with us, or even to come down stairs to dinner.

April 8th. Some approach to Spring weather. Took a carriage from 14th St. again this A.M. & by way of precaution carried a stalwart policeman with me to Bk of America where I made a heavy deposit to the credit of the *Fair*.

How Ellie works! — At Agnew's to night for weekly Committee meeting, where important questions were up. I had to come away rather prematurely, suffering sharply from a swelled face — faucibus tumefactis — the post mortem revenge of a defunct old molar for injuries unknown. It died a natural death without any caries it could have blamed me for neglecting.

April 10. Our S.C. people at *Brandy Station* are notified to send surplus stores & impedimenta to the rear. This indicates a move, but Dr Steiner (who was in town yesterday) thinks it cannot be made for a week. To day's heavy rain must delay it three days at least.

Congress is doing bravely with its Constitutional Amendment abolishing Slavery. Think of Reverdy Johnson sustaining & advocating it! John Brown's "soul's a marching on" — double quick.

There has been a lovely little performance in the House. One Harris of M^{d}, made an elaborate speech recommending that the Confederacy be "recognized" at once. A motion was made to expel him, & a considerable majority voted for it, but not the two-thirds required. [affirm: 81, neg: 58] Thereupon a resolution was introduced declaring Harris "an unworthy member of this House" & that he is "hereby severely censured". *Carried* — 92:18. Good for the House. Fernandy Wood was one of the 18 of course — so was Winthrop Chanler — & with them voted John V.L. Pruyn, whom I have respected & esteemed for twenty years, but neither respect nor esteem any more. It is interesting to observe how eager such members of the Opposition as can see beyond their own noses — even Cox of Ohio — were to set themselves right before the People on this question, & to desert poor Harris, in hope of saving the moribund Old Democratic Party from the death & decomposition that seem to await it.

April 11th. Wallack very kindly gave a performance of "The Follies of a Night" this ev'g, to let Ellie & the other amateurs who are to perform it in a day or two, see how it ought to be done. E. brings home the "Dramatic Committee" & others to supper — and they are now arriving in frequent force. Discoursed nice Miss Louisa Anderson a moment in the Blue Room, & White & Charley Bristed have just bolted into the Library by mistake, but I ca'nt help E. receive her guests — "swell-head" that I am — so I listen to the sound of revelry below, & scribble here, tenderly fingering my hypertrophied fauces now & then in quest of some sign of suppuration — "which there aint any".

April 12th. Tuesday night. Chill easterly weather continues to reign, as I hear — for I have not ventured out of doors. A rather rough experience with my gibbous left jowl, which was in bolder relief than ever this morning. Dr P. looked in at noon, "cruel only to be kind", & gave me an excruciating dig with his lancet, bringing out a little matter, & much blood. After 15 minutes repose & a second inspection, he thought that if I had no objection it might be as well to enlarge the incision, so he ripped up an inch long of inflamed sensitive tissue. The sharp pain of these two little specimens of surgery lasted only a few seconds, but it was followed by about an hour of grave suffering — of sensations such as a red hot grape shot lodged in one's jaw would probably produce. Went to bed in despair, with a dose of morphine, did'nt sleep, but was dreamy & uncertain of my whereabouts, till six P.M. when I rose & girded up my loins, & went down to the dinner table, for a little milk toast & "spoon victuals". E. was laid up in the dressing room, worn out with her morn'g's work in 14th St. But she dressed & has gone to to night's *private theatricals.*

April 14. Gold has been oscillating madly to day. It reached 187! God help us. Things look very bad, but better men than I have died beggars, & we must endure every trial cheerfully if our National Struggle can only be fairly fought out to the end.

April 15. Friday. Weather comparatively decent. Twice at the Fair. Drove thence in the morn'g with a jolly policeman, carrying some $25.000 to the Bk of America, for the *Treasuress.* Asked my companion if some of the people on the sidewalk would'nt suppose I was in his custody. — to which he replied "Well — I reckon most on 'em think so, of course." — On my afternoon visit I invested a small amt in the only article of the Russian Department that I cared for — viz: one of the marvellous pictures of the Madonna & Child that are found in every Russian habitation, from the palace to the peasants' shanty. It's a most interesting symbol, representing not only the daily λατρεια of so many millions of men & women, but also as coming down to us unchanged through a thousand years & more of faithful adherence to "old Custom" in art, like certain usages in China.

Agnew Van Buren & Jenkins here to night. An agreeable session. But I find myself in a minority of one on this proposition to establish Sanitaria or Hotels des Invalides for the *permanent* maintenance of discharged invalid soldiers. They are sorely needed. *States* cannot supply them for many reasons, — relations between disease & climate among others. Pulmonary invalids should be sent to an inland Sanitarium, patients shattered & disabled by typhoid malarial disease to some "Home" on the seaboard. State institutions cannot thus discriminate. Government does nothing. Can we do anything?

I fear not. Any considerable appropriation of our funds to this object would be a misappropriation — misapplication — breach of trust — constructive fraud — as it seems to me.

Bad news from Fort Pillow & Paducah. The Rebels seem to have out-generalled & beaten us once more, & badly.

April 16th. Sat: Easterly wind & a cloudy sky. But Burnside says all loyal men should pray for a week longer of foul weather & bad roads to prevent some movement or other by the Rebels. Why is the initiative not with us?

A very blue day, for many reasons. I was out of bed disgracefully late. Gold keeps at about 170 & Exchange was bought to day at 200! Insolvency is imminent. Congress is inefficient. The Country seems drifting to leeward. I dread the newspaper attacks & queries & criticisms to which the San: Com: is about to be exposed on it's receipt of the proceeds of this *Fair*, & I have my doubts & difficulties about this question of our establishing Sanitaria. Everything looks black and "Life is a Failure" to day.

G.C.A. dined here, tete a tete with me. E. & Johny & Temple were at a "childrens' matinée" from 4 to 8 in aid of the Fair of course. After dinner G. & I adjourned to the 17th St. Department & spent a couple of hours there very agreeably, discoursing many of the nice women & pretty young girls — as e.g. Mrs Dick Hunt & Miss Louisa Barnewall — who are so hard at work behind their respective Counters. Cram & his wife were there with a nice looking very young daughter of Gen: Meade's, who married Mrs C's sister.

Bull Anthon's motto for the flag of the next Black Regiment — "Nimium ne crede colori".

Bostonian joke about Whiting, now in high place in the War Department & doing his duties most creditably, but while practising in the Hub of the Universe enjoying little reputation, & that bad. "First he got *on*, then he got *honor* & at last he got *honest*."

April 18. Monday night. O Jupiter, how much there is to do, & how feebly I am doing it! — Saw A.A. Low this morn'g & Jonathan Sturges about our San: Com: Advisory Finance Committee. Also Wm H. Aspinwall. He is full of the plan, which public opinion is pressing on us, of funding part of the proceeds of the "Metropolitan Fair" for a Hotel des Invalides, or two, and made a magnificent suggestion on the subject, *en grand Seigneur*. If we will set apart half a million or so for that purpose, he will turn over to us lands & buildings (ci-devant factories easily convertible to this new use) which must be worth $100.000 at least. It is very clear that we have got to meet this question, & it seems likely that we shall be compelled to fall in with Aspinwall's view, unless a great battle or two & the manifest urgency of calls for relief on the field divert public attention from the subject. That such battles are close at hand seems certain. The next two months are to be most momentous.

To night memorable for Ellie's *debut* at L.W. Jerome's sumptuous Private Theatre in 26th St. This was the third night of the "season" of Private Theatricals under the auspices of the Dramatic Com: of the Metr: Fair. Tickets are in great demand at $5. the whole transaction being highly distinguished, aristocratic, & exclusive. House was full & everybody in the fullest tag, i.e. men in white chokers & women in ball costume. The spectacle was brilliant & pretty. First came "The Follies of a Night," with handsome Miss Isabel Rogers for Duchesse, & Ellie as Mlle Duval, her lady in waiting. The men did very well, especially young Chas Fearing. So did Miss R. I trembled for Ellie, but she was perfectly self possessed & went thro' her subordinate but difficult part with wonderful grace dignity & spirit. Her attire was most elaborate, & she looked lovely, quite eclipsing her Duchess as I thought, & so did others whose speech I overheard. I was glad I took Johny with me to witness his mamma's triumph, & hear the applause she received. The whole performance was strikingly *elegant*. Ladies & Gentlemen have certain advantages over professionals, to compensate for their inexperience & their lack of stage training.

The second piece "The Dead Shot" was well rendered, but over-acted, as I suppose farces must be. Talboys was intensely funny & enthusiastically applauded, but I think Jem: Ruggles the better actor. He does'nt exaggerate & is comic without ceasing to be a gentleman. Miss Meert & Mrs Harrison (daughter of Anson Livingston) did their work in the most dashing style — but *I* thought Ellie on the whole, queen of the performances, & I was not alone in my opinion.

April 20. Wednesday. Just from the Fair, which I find much more crowded than on any former visit. It closes next Saturday, I am happy to say. — Call on Major Halpine this A.M. at Dix's headquarters. He is about leaving the service, by reason of ill health, & there is talk of making him a paid "literary Sec'y" of the San: Com: about which step I *doubt*, tho' he is an unusually clever man.

There was bad news this morn'g, another disaster had taken place, at least as damaging as Olustee & seemingly still more discreditable. The opening of this fearful campaign seemed to promise ill. But to night, in 3^d edition of the Post, is report of a second day's fight on the same ground (somewhere this side of Shreveport in the Red River country) in which we retrieved our fortunes, routed Secesh-dom & took 20 guns. May it be true!

April 22. Wm Travers dined here with G.A. — We went with Ellie to Jerome's theatre. I stopped at his house in Madison Av: & had the honor of escorting T's pretty young daughter, & her grandmamma Mrs Reverdy Johnson. The first piece was "Circumstances Alter Cases" in which Mrs C.E.S. took the chief part. Her acting was spirited, but seemed to me harsh & ungenial. The piece itself however is inexpressibly foolish & unnatural, inconsistent with even the conventional "Nature" that is met with behind foot-lights. Then there was a *Contretemps.* The valiant Charley Hutton whose part required to be on the stage nearly all the time announced at 6 P.M. that he could'nt play because old Ja^s Benkard (his father's partner) died yesterday. As he attended the one P.M. Rehearsal this seemed generally held rather rough practice, and H. who has always been a little spoiled & is frequently accused of giving himself airs, came in for a large share of inverted benedictions. I should have liked to see Mrs C.E.S. when his defection was made known to her!!! Edwd Anderson "read the part", literally, with his book in his hand, & did it very well, considering the awkwardness of the job. — Came off at 9 & attended a SC/SC i.e. Stand'g Com: of San: Com: at Van Buren's. — Prof. Bache was with us.

Coll: Com: "on Honors" at Betts' office to day — twopenny business.

Our neighbour Mrs D.D. Field died this morn'g after 10 days illness, of bilious remittent. According to newspapers both Mrs Field & Mrs Kirkland sacrificed their lives to over-work at the Fair. Both certainly worked very hard, but I doubt whether the death of either can be traced to this cause.

Fair continues crowded, & its receipts are very large. Whether the final tottle will get up to a million is still uncertain, but it will not fall very far short of that sum.

Wall St. simmering with rumors. Fighting at Plymouth N.C. Rebels repulsed, but certain of our gunboats sunk — We may have to evacuate Plymouth — Longstreet moving down the Shenandoah valley — Lee crossing the Rappahannock or the Rapidan with 160.000 men — (do'nt he wish he had them!) — Transmission of news from Washn stopped by Government — &c &c &c. All this sent up gold sadly. — Well, thus much is certain, that the struggle of the campaign now just opening will be fearful, & it's results momentous. What if we fail?! Has this people faith & virtue enough to persevere after another season of failure or even of *partial* success?

Dr Jenkins, just returned from Washn brings back many important items of contraband intelligence about the Army of the Potomac & of the Cumberland, wh: I wo'nt record. Good & hopeful on the whole. — But we are not yet quite ready & every day's postponement of the coming fight will be a great gain to the Country.

April 23. Sat: Loveliest Spring weather, but a dismal day. More bad news. Disaster in N. Carolina, & prospect of yet farther damage, & news from New Orleans looks like positive unmitigated defeat on the Red River. May this tide of ill-luck run out before the great struggle in Virginia begins!

Called on Mrs Wm Astor & read her the draft of her will. [N.B. . . . . . . ?] — Called on by J.J. Post in Wall St. & walked up town with G.C.A. Received to day proceeds of Albany "Sanitary" Fair — $80.000, minus $15000. to be refunded the Albanians for their local work in getting up & forwarding supplies. Good for Albany. Tho' personally insolvent, I am quite flush, for the present, in my official character. —

After dinner & after Johny's hour of drill on Amabo & Amavi, took Ellie to 14th St. Fair building. We ensconced ourselves in the "Floral Temple", a harbor of refuge from the dense crowd, mostly plebeian, of this final ev'g. Mrs Ritchie was there, in full blown splendor, nice Mrs Geo: Betts, Mrs Thorndike, Mrs Robt Cutting, Mrs Ronalds (one of our prettiest & cleverest women), her most sumptuous fairhaired beautiful sister, Miss Something Carter, whom I do not know at all, but whose presence is most worshipful to every one who appreciates a first class *blonde* — also Mrs Gallatin, Mrs Gentil &c &c &c. Had to struggle thro' the crowd, like a fly in a pitcher of molasses, on sundry errands for the ladies — which were successfully achieved. At 9½ came the so-called *announcement* of the vote on the Sword presentation, to Grant or to McClellan. The mob cheered madly & frantically over & over again for each candidate alternately. Asked forty people what was the result. Their contradictory answers were about equally divided. Rather guess McClellan has prevailed. It does'nt matter much. The suggestion of this vote came from Tiffany, & does credit to his inventive faculty. It will add near $20.000 to the proceeds of the Fair. Brought E. off at 10. Thank Heaven the Fair is ended, & that Ellie is not yet broken down & seriously ill.

April 24. Gen: Grant gets the sword after all, & by some 15000 majority! Good. "Dignum et justum est." The Union League Club subscription, & other subscriptions, in Grant's favor, had been held back, — judiciously — to the last moment. Belmont & Barlow looked in during the aftn, satisfied themselves that McClellan was ahead, put in a little thousand just to give him a handsome majority, & went off. I hear they are full of wrath & confusion to day. I am glad of this result, from no partizan feeling, but because Grant is in command & "little Mac" is'nt, & because McC's success would have tended — pro tanto — more or less — to weaken Grant, in the estimation of his soldiers & of the people.

It seems clear — or rather, *probable* — that Burnside's command has gone to Alexandria, & is to constitute Grant's reserve. If so, the programme is *probably* that B. is to hold the defences of Wash^{n} with 35000 or 40000 men, and thus enable G. to *turn* Lee's entrenched position on the Rapidan without endangering the National Capital. A promising plan, if Burnside's force be strong enough to hold our field works against an assault by Lee's whole army. — But if Lee try that game, cannot Grant turn short round, follow him up & put him between two fires?

April 26. Weather has been wet & muggy, & is not yet settled. Visited Fair buildings — the process of dismantling & denudation of goods goes on rapidly — & Ellie works & endorses checks in the Treasurer's room like [of course] "Marius amid the ruins of Carthage". Busy down town. No good news from N. Car: or from the S.W. — This campaign opens with evil portents.

Charley Fearing dined here yesterday & we went to Jerome's Private Theatricals. "The Ladies Battle" — a very pretty piece, vilely played. Every performer was either stage-y, or a stick — so I came off early.

In the Hammond Court-martial, the evidence is closed. The Surgeon Gen'l is to present his defence May 3^{d}. From all I can learn it appears that there is nothing in the case to compromise the San: Com: & that the prosecution has failed on every point. E.H. Owen however (who called on me to day to settle the judgment in Allen v. Schuchardt wherein we got an *affirmance* from the Supreme C^{t} at Wash^{n}) thinks there is a weak point in the defence as to a certain little contract for blankets. Four of the eight members of the Court are understood to be positively hostile to Hammond, & I am confident the finding of the Court will be short of full acquittal, at best, and that Hammond will thereupon resign in a huff, unless Van Buren can keep him within the bounds of reason.

April 27. Long talk with Cisco this morn'g at the Treasury, anent certain Tr: Ch: matters, on which we are of one mind with the Rector — & afterwards about public finance. All depends, he says, on the result of this campaign. Grant's failure or mere partial success will ruin us. His talk rather dyed me blue. I cannot bring myself even to hope for decisive victory by the Army of the Potomac — under any chief.

Ellie's second appearance on any stage was this ev'g — at the Theatre San Jeronimo, in the "Follies of a Night". Cast as before, house crowded, performance even better than before. Miss Isabel Rogers & Fearing, the most conspicuous personages, acted with more spirit & freedom, and Ellie went thro' her part with the utmost grace & delicacy of perception — looked & acted charmingly, & had a bouquet hurled at her by some unknown admirer — the first demonstration of the kind I have heard of as occurring in Aedibus Hieronomycis — no — Hieronomycensibus, or Hieronomycalibus.

All this work is for a good & patriotic end — but the spectacle of lavish luxury to night was a little suggestive of fiddling while Rome is in full blaze at it's four corners. Raising a million by a Fair & by auxiliary concerts & private theatricals for Army Relief, is good, & creditable to the Community, but I should like to see somewhere, a trace of the savage indomitable resolution, as of forty thousand tomcats concentrated in one beleaguered Corner — the ready endurance of privation — the reckless disregard of consequences — that are shewn by the cruel semi-barbaric treacherous leaders of the Rebellion — or rather by their people.

Long discussion this aft^{n} at 823 about the proposed removal of the 17th St. Fair building to the Battery, to be used as a "Home" & perhaps as an experiment also in the way of providing for discharged & permanently disabled men — if we can get the consent of our most honorable Civic authorities. White was with us — a clever architect, full of suggestions & expedients.

Letter from Binney about our device for a San: Com: *Seal.* He suggests a design that has been adopted by the Managers of the Philad^{a} Fair. I d'ont like it. It brings reality & fancy into too close contact & contrast, & combines them in proportions too nearly equal. Hoppin's sketch is imaginative or ideal, with a mere suggestion of the practical — of the actual suffering of the battlefield, & is certainly far the more artistic of the two.

April 29. Friday. Fine weather. Most of the morning spent in laboring over the complications of Income tax Return. At two, our Advisory Finance Committee came in, by appointment — viz: A.A. Low, Jonathan Sturges, & Jn° Astor — a very worshipful trio of financial magnates. Jenkins was there, bringing with him a cord of accounts vouchers &c from N° 823. The Committee rec^d general statement of our way of doing business very favorably, dipped a little into the books & papers without shewing any sign of captiousness, & agreed to appoint a confidential accountant to go over the whole mass of figures. They advised also against withdrawing our $300.000 from the Nassau Bank (Brooklyn) for investment in Cisco's demand notes — because the Commission would probably want to use the money so soon that the additional 2 p: c: int: was not sufficient reason for moving the deposit.

Dined here to day Miss Isabel Rogers (la Duchesse de Chartres) Jem Ruggles — Edwd Anderson & Charley Fearing. The young lady is most charming. Had to go to Agnew's for a Stand'g Com: meet'g at 8, from wh: I have just walked home with Van Buren, under the bells of midnight.

Yesterday Ellie and I dined in state at John Astor's, with M^r and Mrs Carson Brevoort, Pinckney Stewart, M^r and Mrs Henry Day ("Lord's Day") — Cunards — Goold Hoyts &c &c. Sat between Mrs Cunard and Mrs Camilla Hoyt. That lady grows stouter than is becoming, but her face is among the most splendid specimens of physical beauty — of form & color — I have ever seen. She is absolutely gorgeous to behold, tho' without much expression, if any. A model of her superb head in wax, under a glass case, would be just as good as the original.

April 30. No news from Virginia. Our San: Com: Relief Corps is largely strengthened, & we are making heavy purchases of supplies. The collision must come soon. It will be nearly decisive. I fear it will be fatal. God help us!

May 1st. Mr S.B.R. came in at dinner time, just from Washington. Seward had sent for him, to advise about a Report — or something — as to a proposed line of telegraphic communication with Europe by way of Behring's straits & Asia.

Afterwards appeared W. Gibbs. Both R. & G. had much to say about the College & the Presidency. I believe my own personal position on that question is understood — at least I hope so. I am sure it's an honest well defined & unselfish position.

To night dear little Kate here as usual — & C.E.S. At supper D[r] Peters, M[r] S.B.R. D[r] Aleck Mott, Sidney Ashmore G.C.A., little Gerry, *Rice*, Robinson, Jem Ruggles, Charley Fearing &c &c &c. That rather dubious D[r] M. wants Ellie to enlist in some plan for private theatricals in aid of his 51st St. Military Hospital, but I strongly advise her to have no finger in that pie. D[r] M's administration may have been all right. I take it for granted it was & is. But it has stirred up most bitter feud, in which private character is freely assailed, & charges of stealing are put forward agst Mott (as I hear) by ladies formerly engaged in helping him. It's a dirty business, & Ellie must keep out of it.

May 8th. Got home from Wash[n] last night at eleven, after a day of weariness & starvation. A leather sandwich put into my stomach between Baltimore & ϕilad[a] was my sole aliment, & accounts under the circumstances for to day's *infernal* visitation of acute nervous restless sickheadache, & the heavy deadly somnolence that followed it's partial relief.

News. Stanton's telegram to Dix, in our last extra, indicates Battle on the largest scale, & *victory.* Meade's Med: Director reports to Barnes, acting Surgeon Gen'l, that 6 or 7 thousand wounded men are to be sent into Wash[n]. We have held the field, therefore. It would seem that Lee was forced to leave his intrenchments & attack, that his attack failed, and that the woman-scourging Chivalry was beat back with loss. But all our information on this point is vague. From the Peninsula we learn that Butler's & Baldy Smith's "change of base" from Williamsburgh & West Point to the right bank of the James has been successfully executed. Strong naval force coöperating. Butler holds Petersburgh. [?] Sherman is moving from Chattanooga (that appears aliunde — by telegrams to Dr Newberry) taking advantage of Longstreets withdrawal from the S.W. to reinforce Lee. Sigel, with Hooker (or more probably Couch) is marching up the valley of the Shenandoah & threatening Lee's communications. It is long since our National prospects have looked so bright. But we may be fearfully "disillusionated" tomorrow morning, and find that an assault on Richmond has been repulsed & that Grant & Meade are falling back on Washington, or "changing their base" to Fredericsburgh & Aquia Creek.

Monday, 2^{d} inst:, by R.R. to Wash^{n}, with Gibbs & Agnew. Pleasant ride enough. Woods & fields brighter & brighter with blossoms & greenery as we went Southward. The orchards of Maryland lovely with apple & peach blossoms, & all the woodlands "a glad light green" contrasting with the red foliage that had survived the winter, & the dark coloring of cedar & pine trees. A heavy shower came up at sunset & we reached Wash^{n} amid pouring rain. Drove to N° 244 F St. where comfortable rooms awaited us, enabling us to eschew *Willard's*. We slept at 244, & took our meals "out" — at Gautier's & Buhler's. — Steiner, Knapp &c, estimate Meade's force 125000: Burnside's 20.000: Sigel's 16000: Butler's 40.000 at least. *Quien sabe?* Everybody's utter ignorance about everything connected with the campaign, a most encouraging fact. Another is the relentless refusal of passes to the front. — *Tuesday (3^{d})* the Commission met, Bache in the chair. He has grown so deaf as to make an inefficient Chairman. We were in small force, did only a little routine business, & adjourned early. With Bache & Gibbs to Navy Department. Adm: Davis, a most elegant urbane courteous old gentleman — but reported to be sly & selfish & ambitious of succeeding Bache in the Coast Survey, tho' a mere sciolist. — Thence to Smithsonian. Went thro' the rooms with it's Superintend^{t}, Prof: Henry. It's museum is magnificent, but the laboratory & the working rooms look shabby dusty listless & feeble. *Wednesday (4th)* Loveliest weather. Spring manifested in ideal perfection. Genial warmth & bracing wind. The shady & the sunshiny side of the street each delightful. I crossed & recrossed F St. & 14th St. & Penn: Av: in voluptuous enjoyment of the change. Trees budding & visibly developing from hour to hour. The air full of little *cottony* pellets thrown off from the "American poplar", copious as the flakes of a January snow storm. Reports were (from our Inspectors) that Meade's headquarters at Brandy Station broke up, & the Army of the Potomac *moved* at 12 last night, or at 3 this A.M. — Warren was to make a nocturnal movement & surprise the Rebels at Germanna Ford.

Surgeon Genl Hammond's defence was read yesterday. It seems conclusive, but Stanton will probably prevail against him. Hammond is confident of acquittal, but his anticipations are untrustworthy.

News from F[t] Monroe W. ev'g of advance & coming battle, so we sent Knapp off to Baltimore to charter a steamer, & she was on her way down the Chesapeake by 2 Thursday P.M. heavily freighted with life saving stores. Our ev'g session was interesting. Agnew brought forward the report of his Committee in favor of establishing at least one Sanitarium or Hotel des Invalides on a small scale. I was obliged to oppose the measure, because this is not among our legitimate functions. We are appointed to look after "Sanitary interests" of the National Forces, and have, strictly speaking, nothing to do with any man discharged from the National Army. Binney backed this theory of our duty quite emphatically, & raised the question whether our system of "*Pension Bounty & back pay*" agencies — which we have just been extending & enlarging, were not outside our proper sphere. We decided to take advice of Counsel in N.Y. & Philad[a]. Whom can we consult in N.Y.?

Thursday — 5th. — Long session. Grant is wholly detached from his base, with 10 days forage & 15 days rations. Rumors abound, but there is no trustworthy intelligence. The general absolute ignorance of Grant's plans & movements is a good sign. The Commission adjourned this (Thursday) ev'g.

Friday morn'g I spent mostly in letter-writing. At half past nine P.M. Agnew & I went to Gov[r] (Senator) Morgan's by appointment, & with him to the War Department for an interview with Sec[y] Stanton. Our object was to tell that terrible Turk in substance this. "M[r] Secretary, the Com: will have x + y dollars to spend for the aid & relief of your army & the promotion of it's efficiency during the Campaign now just opened. Your cordial sympathy & cooperation will add fifty percent to the value & effect of every dollar we spend. We know we do not enjoy the light of your favor. On the contrary, quite the reverse. You habitually denounce us & our work, & commonly talk of the Commission as a 'swindling concern'. Will you please tell us what you mean by it — why you hate us

— & what we can do to appease your august disapprobation & secure for our unpaid unofficial unrecognized private exertions for the benefit of your Army, the neutrality — at least — of the War Department — ?"

After a little dangling in the Antechamber, where we discoursed Chauncey McKeever, Genl Augur, & Senator Harris, we "sailed in", to run Stanton's batteries, under protection & convoy of *Morgan*, who had no occasion however to "shell the woods" or open fire at all, during our two hours session. Our reception was on the whole rather grim — such as a medieval Saint would have vouchsafed to the D—l, on receiving a call from that functionary. We presented the resolution of the Commission appointing a Committee to wait on the Sec^{y} — on hearing which the Sec^{y} remarked "Well, Sir???". Agnew proceeded thereupon to state from memoranda he had prepared, an outline of our work & our expenditure, which Stanton interrupted — with inexpressible venom & viciousness of manner. "I do'nt perceive any mention here of what you must have paid for your scurrilous attacks on me & on the Administration thro' the public press." We could not guess what he meant, & I humbly asked for light. We found that he referred to an article in an early N^{o} of the "Bulletin" [signed "A Republican"] urging that the Surgeon Gen'l ought not to be displaced without a Court Martial or an investigation in some form. We submitted that this article discussed fairly & temperately a question bearing directly on the efficiency of the medical service, & reminded him that it simply recommended him to do what he did a month afterwards. Then he brought up the memorable Circular of last January. We said this was no act of the Commission, & that the Commission was in no way responsible for it. But Stanton said he had proof that it had been laid on the desks of members of Congress by "our agent in Wash^{n}" — as to which fact we had no knowledge & could say nothing. He dwelt with ferocious delight on the disgraceful conduct of Peirce, Agassiz, & Hill "whose signatures had been *fraudulently obtained* — by whom he could'nt say" —

It occurred to both A & myself to tell him of the affidavits now in N.Y. describing the deliberate reading of that paper & the careful consideration of it's purport, after wh: these gentlemen signed it — but it also occurred to us both that it would be unwise to shew our hand, & inexpedient to waste time in a squabble about details. So we took the Secretary's fire with serenity & his manner became less insolent when he found we were not much frightened. Then he attacked our Pension & back pay system as not within our proper sphere, but this position (tho' his only strong one) he finally abandoned, admitting that the work was useful & important — forced upon us in a manner — & subject only to a technical objection.

Next came a savage assault on our Hospital supply system, kept up at Wash^{n} during the past year (but now wound up, I'm happy to say.) "We had gone into the marketing business — made ourselves a trading association. Hammond's order that Surgeons get their extra supplies thro' this channel was a gross violation of law — because all purchases were required to be by contract." There we *had* him. It was clear the Sec: of War did'nt know what a "Hospital Fund" is, or the regulations applicable to it's disbursement. We enlightened him on this subject. He gasped & staggered, but soon came up again, & insinuated rather than asserted that the Commission had made money by the operation. "On the contrary, Mr Sec'y, our books & vouchers shew a balance against us of from 5 to 10.000 dollars." Whereupon the Sec: hit out viciously — but rather wild. "Then that amount of money has been lost — so much of the People's bounty wasted in this job." — Our answer was obvious. This balance represents so much contributed to the hospitals, just as directly & effectually as if it had been used to buy them it's equivalent in chickens, fresh eggs, & butter. The Com: has turned over the stores it bought & charged the hospital fund their cost price & no more — thus saving that fund not merely the profit of the middle man but also the expense of transportation &c. Of course the Sec^{y} saw this, but he did not choose to say so, & changed the subject. — Agnew — who shewed great tact temper & presence of mind throughout — said "Well Mr Sec^{y} these criticisms are, after all, just what we have long wished to have the Department give us. What we want is the establishment of such relations with you as will secure our receiving your views & suggestions from time to time, and we shall of course &c &c

always listen to your advice with &c &c". But this was among the things S. did not happen to want & he withdrew himself at once — like a startled land-tortoise, or an irritated Actinia. "You must execute your great trust in your own way, & on your own responsibility. I cannot advise you about it." So our interview ended at last, the Sec^y taking leave of us with more Civility than he had previously shewn.

He went out of his way more than once to declare his unbounded admiration & undying passionate affection for the Commission. He found fault only with the conduct of certain of it's members or officers. He had done & always should do all he could to support & strengthen the Commission itself. Strange — for he must have been aware that we knew this to be as big a bouncer as any that has passed over the telegraph wires during the last three years. It so demoralized me that I instantly replied "with effusion" that we could'nt possibly doubt it.

I was amazed by the discovery of our importance, & that the Secretary of War keeps himself thoroughly posted as to our movements & doings. Whenever he referred to any publication, he rang in his messenger & said "Ben! get me — so & so — of the Sanitary Commission" — which the faithful but seedy creature did with admirable accuracy & promptitude. He failed only once, when he brought in a copy of the "Medical Times" instead. Whereupon the Secretary d—d him, & sent him back — soliloquizing, as it were, *sotto voce*, "It contains *another* attack on me — I suppose the Commission got *that* up, *too*." He was wrathful, also, over certain publications (I do not know what) in Engl^d which he evidently credited to us, & about the authorship whereof he designs to "*have an investigation*". This innocent design he announced in the tone with which a magistrate would notify a man charged with murder that his alleged *Alibi* would be sternly scrutinized.

On the whole, this interview was a good thing — tho' without direct tangible result. We drew Stanton's fire & can estimate his weight of metal. It is not very heavy. He hates us cordially & would destroy us if he dared — but he fears our constituency. Public favor is the breath of his nostrils.

He is not a first rate man morally or intellectually. His eye is bad & cold & leaden & *snake-y*, even when he is most excited.

His only signs of ability at this conference were remarkable memory & capacity for details.

Pending our conference the long lean lank figure of *Uncle Abraham* suddenly appeared at the door. Agnew & I *rose.* Stanton *did'nt.* Lincoln uttered no word, but beckoned to Stanton in a ghostly manner with one sepulchral forefinger, & they disappeared together for a few minutes, going into a side room & locking the door behind them. We saw A.L. in the telegraph room as we entered the office, waiting for despatches & no doubt sickening with anxiety — poor old codger! But it's shameful so to designate a man who has so well filled so great a place during times so trying.

May 9th. Thank God, Grant's Victory seems established. Prisoners were taken on both sides. We lost one or two guns, & I do not hear that we captured any. But Lee is retreating & Grant is after him. Lee can hardly be making for Richmond. He no doubt means to fight again, on the "North Anna" or at or about Hanover Court House. He shews no sign of demoralization. This battle of Thursday & Friday, nameless as yet, was a severe & close affair. Had not Lee retired it would have been called a drawn battle. He seems to retire with his men well in hand, drawing us farther from our base & our supports.

That fine old fellow, Genl Wadsworth, received a rebel bullet in his brain while leading his command into action. "Happy whom He finds in battle's Splendor". We have lost a brave & useful man, but this is just the death W. would have ordered of the destinies, had they consulted him on the subject.

During our vestry meeting Gen: Dix received & read the President's announcement of success & recommendation of public thanksgiving. If this good news *wear* a day or two longer, there should be a special service in Trinity.

Banks has come to grief. He is held responsible for our defeat & disaster in the Red River Country & is condemned & denounced by everybody. Gen: Canby supersedes him. People say he ought to be court martialled & shot — poor Banks! Why will men of ability & reputation in civil affairs let themselves be deluded into the notion that they can handle armies?

At our Vestry meet'g to night Neely was elected to succeed Hobart. Question of salary left undecided.

Well — Heaven help the country & send us good news to-morrow! I think I would consent to be publicly executed in Union Square next Sunday, after morning service, if that ceremony would ensure success to Grant & Butler. Should their campaign fail, as it well may, our prospects public & private, are gloomy.

May 10. Tuesday. Very bright & hopeful feeling seemed to prevail all the morning. Every report, authentic or otherwise, was favorable. Sherman & Thomas were in successful conflict with Joe Johnston in the Chattanooga & Dalton Country. Butler & Smith had cut the Richmond & Petersburgh R.R. — isolating Beauregard's forces. They had taken Fort Darling. Grant & Meade were steadily driving Lee. The only question was whether Grant or Butler would be first in Richmond.

But at Union League Club to night — where was much people — the tone of talk was grave and subdued. No one seemed particularly jubilant or sanguine. The sad news of Gen: Sedgwick's death (he was picked off by a sharp-shooter at Spottsylvania) is depressing, and then Lee shews such obstinacy & tenacity after his alleged defeat, & our losses are so heavy! Twenty thousand men hors du combat already — & the work only begun. — Heaven help us!

Agnew went to the front this ev'g.

May 11. Wednesday. Little light from the morn'g papers, & that not particularly roseate. Their Editorials are full of glowing prophecies about the moribund Rebellion & the "doomed" city of Richmond, but that style of talk is stale & profitless. Their letters & despatches justify no vaporing. We seem to be holding our own — that's all. Were the case *reversed* however, we should certainly feel more profoundly blue than we have felt this long while. If Grant were falling back toward Washington, fighting bravely & taking advantage of every defensible position, & Longstreet were in Maryland with from twenty to forty thousand men, feeling for a weak spot in the defences of the Capital, & rebel gunboats controlled the lower Potomac, & some rebel chief were marching *up* the Shenandoah valley (as Sigel is marching *down* the same) I think we should feel ourselves in a very tight place.

May 12th. Thursday. Overcast — wind N.E. News up to 8 A.M. yesterday rec[d] this morn'g is of most severe fighting on Tuesday, without disadvantage to us. Grant's despatch to Stanton, of that date, looks well, & looks all the better I think for it's moderate tone, and absence of anything like strong statements of success. These fearful battles seem mere hard pounding on both sides. Both shew wonderful endurance. Which can endure longest? Everything depends on the Answer to that question. There are intimations of Strategy to be used on Lee's flanks & in his rear, but I put no trust in them.

To night's reports are of continued battle yesterday — a rebel brigade captured, 12 guns taken, spiked, & abandoned, (by us) & the rebel left "crushed." This may or may not be true.

May 13. Van Buren & Jenkins here to night from 8 to 12 on Commission business, of which we did a good deal. M[rs] Ellie with us at the supper table, yearning to go to the front once more & work with Miss Helen Gilson at Belle Plain or Fredericsburgh. But it wo'nt do. Our relief force is doing splendid service in Virginia just now & on a larger scale than ever.

News from that fearful arena at & around *Spotsylvania Court House* is good, & has kept improving up to about three P.M. when our latest tidings came, & our last Extra was issued. If these tidings be true, Grant & Meade have achieved what looks like material & perhaps decisive results, crushing & driving the larger portion of Lee's line of battle & taking 30 or 40 guns & several thousand prisoners: Lee is out of Ammunition & on short rations: The R.R. lines that connect him with his base are cut or threatened. All this may be true. God grant it is! But we are so schooled in adversity that we presume all good news apocryphal. Ingalls sends a jubilant telegram. "You may bet your pile" on complete victory, & Ingalls is a grave business-like quartermastering officer, not ordinarily liable to sanguine spasms of exaltation. His despatch appears in this ev'g's Post, 3[d] edition. From Butler & Baldy Smith, operating on the right bank of James River, our intelligence is good, tho' indefinite & obscure. They would seem to be threatening Petersburgh rather than Richmond, & to have cut the R.R. that connects the two cities.

May 14. Sat: — Dull showery day. Morning papers overflow with glad tidings of great joy. That Lee is retreating [probably towards Gordonsville] terribly punished & much dilapidated, and that Grant is following him up, are propositions that can be safely filed away in the pigeon-hole of History. It seems not impossible that Lee may be disorganized & annihilated by Grant's relentless pertinacity in pursuit. Our newspaper *Jominis* profess to consider the rebel Army of Virginia as good as destroyed already. Therein they err grossly, no doubt. But while they thus over-state the immediate result of this campaign, they talk less of "Peace within 30 days" than after any former victory. This is encouraging, as a reflex symptom of the general feeling. It shews that the People is patient, steady & resolute, & does not forget how much work has yet to be done — even in this hour of jubilation over what looks like decisive success.

The Bulletin boards of the Post & Advertiser — 2 P.M. — were not dispiriting. Sherman holds *Dalton* after a fight in which he took 12 guns & 5000 prisoners. Schofield has beaten a rebel force out of E. Tennessee into North Carolina, viâ "Bull's Gap", & is following up his victory. The killed & wounded Lee leaves behind him are 35000. Among our prisoners is reported the notable Maryland renegade *Bradley Johnson*. Longstreet reported dead & Lee severely wounded & in Richmond. All this looks well but I do not believe that Lee's Army is yet so demoralized as to be incapable of fighting, & Grant's force must be sorely reduced by the casualties of this terrible week of Battle.

May 15. Whitsunday — a day of public thanksgiving for National Victory — and a happy personal anniversary beside, so it has been a threefold "Fest der Freude", tho' chilly & rainy. Special thanksgiving in the services at Trinity, & generally in the City Churches as I hear. Vinton pinned one or two sentences about our Armies on a Sermon evidently written before Grant's success, & it was too manifest that they were interpolations.

To night G.C.A. Walter Cutting & Mr S.B.R. here at supper.

Not much news. "Sheridan" (who is he?) reported to have made a most brilliant raid in Lee's rear, tearing up miles of

R.R., burning bridges, retaking prisoners, & destroying locomotives, cars, & commissary stores that Lee cannot well afford to lose. To night we hear of a despatch from Stanton to Dix that "Sheridan" is on the right bank of James River, with Butler, and that Grant made a reconnoissance yesterday which disclosed that Lee was retreating Westward — on Gordonsville, I suppose. I hope this may not tempt Grant to move on Richmond until he has put Lee beyond all power of doing mischief. Also, that very valiant rebel J.E.B. Stuart is said to be killed. Also, Sigel is at Woodstock, wherever that is, & censured for tardiness. It's said he should have traversed the Shenandoah valley, & been rolling Dutch thunder on Lee's flank & rear a week ago. *Quien sabe?*

All the prospect of this Campaign is splendid beyond our hopes. But will it last? When McClellan moved into the abandoned works of Yorktown, when Vicksburgh was surrendered, & when Lee fell back beaten & shattered after Gettysburgh, we felt sanguine & triumphant as we do to night. But the Rebellion survived those disasters & may survive this. Another day or week may alter all the aspect of affairs & change our confidence to despondency.

May 16. Long session at 823 this aft^{n} with Dr Vinton Judge Binney & that rather slippery Chas Gould. They are a Com: of Conference from the New England Soldiers' Relief Association on the proposition to consolidate their establishment with the "Home" we contemplate setting up for our "Special Relief Work" in this City. I was sole representative of the Commission in this Conference, for Van Buren was doing a little vivisection on some wretch or other, Agnew is at the front & Jenkins in Wash^{n}. We got along harmoniously enough.

At T.C. Vestry to night. (25th St.) We disposed of the question of clerical salaries by voting temporary donations to Weston &c. Tillou was as troublesome as usual, & wasted much time. He is an incorrigible nuisance. I had to interrupt him in a flamboyant speech about St George's chapel Beekman St & the ancient memories that consecrate it's site, & so forth, by the enquiry whether there was any question before us. There was not — So Tillou subsided & somebody moved an adjournment, wh: was fortunately carried, nem: con:

Not much war news. Burnside seems to have fought on Friday, without decisive result. Reports from Sherman & the S.W. do not look ill. Butler seems investing Drury's Bluff & Fort Darling. Gen: Dix had no despatch from the War Department at 9 P.M. Among the lying rumors recognized as such to day are that Stuart & Longstreet are killed & that Grant has taken 40 guns. He reports 18. Also that Lee is retreating. He seems to be grimly holding a strong position on one of the monosyllabic confluents & constituents of the Mat-ta-po-ny. I greatly fear that *Ash* is killed — a fine spirited enterprising ambitious young Cavalry officer who used to come here a year ago.

May 17. Tuesday. Unsettled weather & oppressively warm. With Ellie at 10 to N° 2 Great Jones St. where I had the satisfaction of receiving from her & from John Gourlie, Chairman of her Finance Committee, One Million of Dollars for the San: Com: the same being "on account of" proceeds of the Fair. There will yet be a little balance of $100.000 or so to be paid over whenever we have time to attend to trifles & settle questions about small change.

Thence to Wall St. & then to Wm Betts' office, where I had to sign my name 264 times to diplomas (in duplicate) certificates &c for the benefit of our Law School class now just graduating. Walked up town with G.C.A. & met Van Buren at 823. — After dinner to Trinity Chapel where Higbee preached before the Law School class aforesaid. The sermon was worthy of him, full of deep thought & large practical views, & manifestly an utterance from the heart, not from the lips alone. I have seldom heard him preach much more effectively.

Sorry to say that the feeling down town to day is despondent & bad. There is no news from the front to justify it, but people have taken up with an exaggerated view of Grant's hardly-won success in opening the campaign & now, finding that the "backbone of the Rebellion" is not "broken at last" into a handful of incoherent vertebræ, & that Lee still shews fight, "on the Po" or elsewhere, they are disappointed disgusted & ready to believe every rumor of disaster & mischief that the wicked ingenuity of speculators can devise & inculcate. C.E.S. has been an especial croaker. G.C.A. & I had to tell him he was making an M.S.B. of himself. Poor M.S.B!

The meeting of ladies called at Cooper Institute yesterday to consider questions of private economy, & of reducing the export of gold for foreign luxuries, was very funny. Would there were time to record it's details. The Εκκλησιαζουσαι broke up in something not unlike a row. Old M[rs] Gibbs, charging with an umbrella on some English woman who presumed to "make a few remarks" and bidding her "subside" as not entitled to address or advise "the women of America" must have been a grand spectacle. I hope we may have Historical painters able to do it justice.

Poor M.S.B. is never lively or earnest in talk about National affairs, except when discussing some National disaster or some vague rumor thereof, the truth of which he always takes for granted. Under such circumstances, he is always fluent in speech, & copious of important suggestions as to what might could or should have been done. But if you ask him to give the Country the benefit of his great acquirements on any Constitutional question, at the cost of half an hour's work — or to do his duty as a citizen, & *vote* at any election, he declines doing so, because "he has nothing to do with public affairs". He's an ιδιωτης. With all his professed — & real — interest in our National cause, & all his learning ability & high character, he has done no one thing, & made no one effort, to help the Country, during all these years of struggle, tho' he might have done so much.

May 18. Wednesday. No material news from Grant or Butler. Sigel is having a rough experience on the Shenandoah, & is beat with the loss of 5 guns. Per contra certain successful "affairs" are reported in Western Virginia.

Copperheadism perpetrated a most flagitious act of Moral High Treason this morning, thro' the agency of the World & the Journal of Commerce. Those papers published a fictitious proclamation by the President that the situation in Virginia, our defeats in Louisiana (Banks to wit) & our failure to reduce Charleston compelled him to call for three hundred thousand more men, & to suspend all aggressive operations till they should be enlisted & drilled into efficiency. This bogus despatch was announced to be a forgery on every bulletin board by 10 A.M. but it did it's mischievous work & sent gold up to 184. At U.L. Club to night with M[r] Ruggles, I rejoice to hear that Gen: Dix has taken possession, under *martial law* of the offices of both papers. Public feeling will sustain him. In Wall St. this morn'g capitalists lawyers & sober citizens in general seemed inclined to prosecute the Journal of Commerce under the provisions of the Code of Lynch. Exasperation was intense, & it seemed taken for granted that this forgery was the work of Sam: Barlow.

May 19. News from Virginia very good but not entitled to the least credit. Offices of World & Journal of Commerce still occupied by squads of men with guns & bayonets. A very grave proceeding & involving very grave questions, but no one should criticize it now, or until Lee is driven south of Richmond. Perhaps Constitutional doubts about the action of Government will then be in order. — The Obituary record of to night's Post includes the name of Thomas Colden Cooper — Tom Cooper, my old College Classmate — Captain in the 67th N.Y.V. — who fell while leading his command on the 6th inst. "in the Wilderness". Poor Tom Cooper! From my recollection of his College ways I can well believe he was doing his work with courage & with reckless audacity. He was not a bully, as some of us used to call him nearly 30 years ago, but brave & resolute, tho' often on the wrong side. His special friend & ally in our class M[r] F.A. was his superior in physical strength, & was I think recognized even in those days as coward & bully. Had an interview with him yesterday or day before, the first for many years, getting his certificate as Commissioner of Deeds to a satisfaction-piece signed by me as subscribing witness. He *would* write the certificate as if I were party instead of witness — & acknowledging instead of proving the paper. I tried to explain his mistake, & he assented blandly to what I said, & always kept handing me the document as fully disposed of. His mind seemed gone, poor fellow. He has lived pretty hard I fear. So did Tom Cooper, more or less, but he has died in his duty — given his life for his country, & his Countrymen should forget his past short-comings whatever they were.

May 20. Friday. Very busy day. Nothing new from Grant. Am just from Union League Club, whither I went at 10 in pursuit of knowledge, after writing letters here all the ev'g. These are fearfully critical anxious days. Their most trifling memories will be interesting hereafter, the destinies of this Continent for centuries depend in great measure on what is now being done & suffered a few hundred miles South of 21st St. The howl of a newsboy may at any moment rise on the midnight air, announcing an Extra with news of National success or ruin. — At this very minute, it may be practically settled, at or about Spotsylvania Court House, whether American development is to be controlled by the ideas of New England & New York or by those of South Carolina & Mississippi — whether an Algerine Slave-ocracy is or is not destined to bear sway from the Lakes to the Gulf & from the Atlantic to the Pacific for generations to come. Is'nt it strange that one can make even a pretence of going through with the petty duties of common life, while these tremendous issues are *sub judice* —?

Grant holds his own, for aught I know to the contrary. But the general current has been setting strongly against us, ever since last Feby. There are Olustee, the Red River failure, Plymouth N.C., & Fort Pillow — etc: — And it would seem that *Butler* has come to grief in his operations against Fort Darling & Richmond.

It all looks grey & blue & bad, but *In Te Domine Speravi.* Eternal Right & Justice are on our side, & they cannot be permanently defeated, no matter how many guns they may have lost to day or may lose tomorrow. They must triumph at last, & they *will*, perhaps not in my time, but most surely & inevitably in God's own good time, hereafter. Treason for the sake of woman-flogging may prevail for a season, but we may be sure it's reign will be shortlived, for "the Lord God Omnipotent reigneth" now & forever. Vide Handel.

May 21. Sat: Warm, & to night a little shower. No news at U.L. Club half past 10 P.M. Agnew & Jenkins, just from Belle Plain, Fburgh, & our lines generally, bring reports that are not positively discouraging, but far from star spangled. Grant

& Lee are playing a nearly even game. The former has been fearfully punished, & Lee no less, as we suppose. Agnew's account of the hospitals of Fburgh, & the miles of waggon trains of shattered suffering men, & the horrible sights & sounds of the crowded pier at Belle Plain, where hundreds of men lay wounded & helpless on the planks waiting their turn, & shrieking with terror as the unruly mule teams passed between their lines, lest they should be trampled under the feet of the beasts or shoved off into the water, would have set up Edgar A. Poe for a month. Such are the "horrors of war" and the fruits of Treason.

Long session of Com: on Law School at Mr S.B.R's office this P.M. Thence to N° 823 as usual.

Have been wrapped in dismal thinkings all day, & sorely tempted to the sin of disordinate anxiety & discouragement. But I kept my qualmishness to myself & talked large of the Situation & the prospect.

I *was* provoked this morning, when M.S.B. volunteered the cheerful observation "I have just been talking with Mr Silliman" (that ass Ben S. to wit) "& he says he sees nothing that can possibly save us from utter ruin." This was in M.S.B's best tone, of solemn gladness, as it were, like that of an Early Christian remarking that the Proconsul would undoubtedly order his execution before night. I replied that Silliman's views were always valuable, but that I thought Jeff: Davis could well afford to pay him $50. a week in greenbacks, to go about & express them. It is infamous. Were I Gen: Dix I would send Silliman & M.S.B. to Fort Lafayette, & lock them up together in the same casemate to groan at each other. After a week's experience of that treatment they could safely be discharged, cured of croaking.

C.E.S. is at Milford, Penn:, trout fishing — happy man.

Why did not Government call for 200 000 more men, six months ago? They could have been got, and they might have been now strengthening the Army of the Potomac, enabling it to achieve decisive victory & averting the calamity of another unsuccessful campaign. But criticism is easier than administration.

We are working on a very large scale in aid of Grant's Army, & making our mark there, as it seems to me. We spend $650 a day for river transportation by steamers barges & schooners chartered by Knapp. We are running 50 or 60 wagons with 4 & 6 horse teams — & employing from 150 to 200 Relief Agents, all to some extent skilled laborers, & twice as many teamsters servants & contrabands. — But I foresee a fearful time at hand of newspaper queries "What has become of all this money?" that may irritate me to suicide. No matter, if the money have been so used as to help save the Country. Deus salvam fac Rempublicam! To be an instrument of that Divine purpose, however indirect & obscure, is honor enough for any citizen of the 18th Ward. If I can promote that great end by my relations with the Sanitary Commission, my character may take care of itself. — & I will cheerfully submit to any amt of suspicion & denunciation.

May 23d. Monday. Resplendent weather. Spent the day mostly in San: Commissioneering. No end of letters & bother. Ev'g same way viz: at Dr Van Buren's. Saw old Dr Mott this morn'g anent the proposed investigation at Annapolis. He is interested & agrees to go, but cannot just now, because of a slight dissection-wound which he is just getting over.

News from Sherman good, from Banks bad, from Grant obscure but not discouraging. Stanton's last published despatch to Dix, coupled with telegrams recd at 823 to day & with the fact that Knapp is going up the Rappahannock in one of our supply steamers with a heavy cargo of stores & with the vague reports of success that I hear of as prevalent down town late this afternoon — all these things being put together seem to indicate that Grant has slipped quietly around Lee's right flank without a serious engagement, and that both are moving toward Richmond, side by side, Grant having the inside track, but Lee moving probably with fewer impedimenta & therefore faster: — that there will be a decisive battle in the region of Hanover Court House: — that Grant will establish his base on the Rappahannock below Fredericsburgh, perhaps at Port Royal: — that &c &c &c. — We shift our supply stations from Belle Plain to Aquia tomorrow, or perhaps did so to day. The R.R. from A. to F. is restored or nearly so, & I suppose the hospitals of F. are to be cleared out with all convenient speed.

We agreed to night on large Antiscorbutic purchases, ($25000. worth of pickled cucumbers & preserved tomatoes) anticipating that the Army of the Potomac will be on our hands within a month in the same condition in which we found it at Harrison's Landing July /62 — every man sickening from exhaustion & hard work on the monotonous diet of fighting rations, hard tack & salt pork to wit, & craving an onion or a raw potato or a hatfull of sour crout, as an old drunkard craves his gin.

Van Buren looks fagged & worn & means to take a week's holiday at Saratoga. Finding of Hammond's Court Martial has now been in Stanton's pocket for a fortnight, & is not yet disclosed. The Sec'y declines to inform enquirers what it is. Does he thus delay because it is not what he would have it, or only because he takes a malignant pleasure in keeping the Surgeon General in suspense as long as he can? Nobody knows. The decision if for the prosecution on a single point will be a public calamity, for Hammond tho' impulsive in speech & somewhat coarse in moral and mental texture, has made a most honest & useful Surgeon General. No one in the Medical Staff could replace him. He proposes to wait a week longer, and then if the decision be still kept back to have it called for in the Senate.

The martyred newspapers — World & Journal of Commerce — have been ungagged, and the former vomits acid bile most copiously. Two or three of it's editorial columns are occupied by a letter to the President, full of protest & fury, signed Manton Marble — (the name of a mercenary renegade) — suggesting, inter alia, a parallel between Uncle Abe Lincoln & *Charles the First*! One might as well compare dirty little penny-a-lining Marble with Catiline. Will this most novel suggestion tempt Honest Old Abe to cultivate a peaked beard & long curls & to extend his shirt collar into a wide area of ornamental lace? Will he set about writing an *Eikon Basiliké* in view of his possible dethronement by a Convention & an Election now at hand, & will such publication (should it ever appear) be discussed & fought over by literary critics, & its genuineness affirmed & denied with profound research & ingenious argument, a century hence, by scholars who have been unfortunately unable to discover any more useful work for their scholarship to do?

May 25. Wedn: Down cast & despondent all day. It must be because of this dull grey damp weather, for the stream of bad news flows less freely just now. Grant has made a brilliant flank movement, & advances doggedly. But Lee shews like resolution, acknowledges no defeat, and maintains a grim & dangerous front.

Called on Gen: Dix this morn'g & yesterday, in Bleecker St. He looks anxious.

Ellie's cousin, Mrs Cadwallader from Marietta Ohio, dined here this aft'n: & seems a nice warm hearted loyal woman. Her daughter, Miss Ella, was here last Spring or early last Summer. —After dinner to U.L. Club, where I discoursed Cyrus W. Field about telegraph lines, &c. There are stories that our advance holds Hanover C.H. & that Jeff: Davis has fled from Richmond with the "archives" of his Rebel pseudo-government in a Carpet bag. Which stories I see no reason to believe.

That demagogue, traitor, & scoundrel, Horatio Seymour, who is (for our sins) Governor of this State of N.Y. publishes a letter to Mr Dist: Att^y^ Oakey Hall [Arcades Ambo] bewailing the lawless violence lately perpetrated on the World & the Journal of Commerce, & requesting him to get everybody responsible therefor duly indicted as soon as may be. The Governor's official sense of the danger of violating law has improved since the memorable riots arsons & murders of last July. He dealt with rioters houseburners & murderers more kindly then, addressed them as his "friends", & said nothing about promoting any action against them by Grand Juries. But his "friends" of the Canaille were working for the Rebellion then, & against the Country. They were entitled to a degree of consideration which the National Government cannot expect — from H. Seymour. Their violations of law were to be tenderly treated — but those of the Administration though technical & not murderous must be sternly resisted.

Seymour has blundered again, as men without *principle* are apt to blunder. Even War Democrats denounce him for seeking to commit "the party" to a position agst Government.

He is a miserable creature. I know no man whom the elegant popular appellation of "Squirt" is more felicitously appropriate. And he is a squirt of small calibre. This letter of his is contemptible. But he might use his official position to do vast mischief, if he has the *pluck*. Thank Heaven he has not got it.

May 26. Thursday. Fine rain & pelting showers, by turns all day, with high wind that has made it hard to manipulate one's umbrella. M[r] Derby in town, & dined here. He returned from his European tour some 10 days ago, cured of his nervous dyspepsia — has seen everybody & everything that the most enterprising of Bostonians could possibly see in the short space of four months — and gives an interesting report of the policy & the talk of Secessionist Americans abroad and of Secessioniphilite Englishmen.

After dinner to Agnew's. Standing Com: of San: Commission. Prof: Bache & Wolcott Gibbs with us.

War news looks favorable. Lee seems falling back on a position between the North & South Anna rivers — or perhaps to Hanover Junction. Some think he will not stop till he has burrowed in the field works of Richmond, but I do not. There is much fight in him yet. May God deal with his host & with him, according to the righteousness of their cause, and according to the justice or injustice of the misery their bullets have inflicted on so many thousand National soldiers & Northern homes.

May 27. Friday. Pleasant weather. Grant still goes *Vorwärts* as obstinately as old Blücher, & has crossed the "North Anna" after a sharp conflict, in which field works seem to have been stormed in a style creditable to any soldiers. Lee is probably between the North Anna & the South Anna. People think he means to fall back on the strong forts of Richmond, but people may be wrong. It's reported — tho' not yet officially, that the finding of Hammond's Court Martial is against him. It is a calamity, if the report be true, but I have expected no other result. His displacement would almost justify us in renouncing our title of "Commission" & our nominal relations with Government, going on with our work as a private Army relief Committee, without even quasi-official character, & making open war on Stanton. I should seriously consider the propriety of doing so, but for the aid & comfort that would be thereby given to Copperheads & opponents of the Administration.

May 28. Fine day — Not the least bit of news from the front, which is annoying. There are those who think Lee means to give Grant the slip, leave him to knock his head against the entrenchments of Richmond held by some 30.000 men, & then to rush up the Shenandoah valley with the rest of his Army, for a raid into Pennsylvania — or a dash at Washington. That plan would hardly work. Grant is a wary practitioner, & has a good cavalry force, & holds the interior line. Well — Heaven save the Country in it's sore distress!

Left Wall St. early & took Johny & Temple by the horse cars to Coney Island, not yet infested by it's summer crowd of human scum. We spent a couple of hours strolling on the beach, & the boys waded in the surf & rejoiced greatly. Home to a late dinner. Ellie has gone to a pic-nic at Dobbs' Ferry with Miss Kitty Dix &c & has not yet returned — tho' past due. (11 P.M.) — Called on Gen: Dix after dinner, & had a walk with him & a talk concerning the proposed "Home" on the Battery, wh: was highly satisfactory. — The Beach has wholly changed since last Septr. Inlets & *Dunes* have disappeared.

A brilliant feat of engineering has saved our Red River fleet (iron-clads, "tin-clads" &c) from destruction or capture. It's coöperating land force was retreating, but the fleet was cut off by low water on certain rapids or "falls". A dam was built across this great river, within a fortnight, the water was raised on the rapids, & the fleet brought down the river without loss. Canby relieves Banks, & it's to be hoped will do better. *Buell* — a valuable officer — is mustered out of service for refusing to take a subordinate position under Canby. So it's said. No punishment is too severe for an officer who declines any duty, in these times, because it wounds his personal dignity & is a breach of military etiquette. — — Signs multiply that Lincoln will be renominated & re-elected. But the election is still five months off. His re-election seems to me on the whole most desirable.

Gold reached 189 to day! We are in a bad way, unless Grant or Sherman soon win decisive victory. But I see no symptom yet of debility in the backbones of loyal & patriotic men, or, in other words, of the *community* minus Peace Democrats, McClellan-maniacs, mere traders & capitalists, & the brutal herd of ignorant Kelts & profligate bullies & gamblers & "sporting men" that have so large a share in the government of our Cities.

It is remarkable that every "sporting man" & every disreputable character, every employé of a gaming house — a policy shop — or a Lupanar — is sure to be full of wrath against Abolitionists, to despise the Administration, to rate Southern pluck & capacity for fight far beyond our own, & to canonize McClellan as a martyr. Old "Hingland" takes the same view of the situation. I am thankful to be cured at last of the Anglophilism that has oppressed me ever since I was a boy & made me forget or underrate my own people & my fathers house.

May 29. News from Grant. He retired across the North Anna, but moved quickly down it's left bank, & down that of the Pamunkey, crossed it, turning Lee's position, & held Hanover, (*not* Hanover C.H.) some twelve miles from Richmond on Friday. If this series of bold movements succeed, Grant will be held a great general. Should Lee be forced to cross the James River, Rebeldom will totter to it's base. God grant it!

May 30. News continues very good. May it prove *true*, also. Grant reported advancing, & close to Richmond. There has been battle in Georgia resulting in our favor. "Rebel loss 2500, ours 300." Wonder whether these figures be strictly accurate!

G.A. dined here, & Wm Schermerhorn looked in to discuss the advantages of summer quarters at *Quogue*. To the League Club — but got no news. Gold reached 191 to day! U. L. Club people think Lee will not risk a battle outside the forts of Richmond, but will burrow in them & stand a siege. I think otherwise — that he will fight, & fight hard, & fall back on his earthworks if beaten.

May 31. Tuesday. Decidedly hot. Rather a busy day. Call for the —th time on Mr Street-Commissioner *Cornell*, who is as hard to see as the cross lines on any known diatom, but saw him at last, and found him accommodating, & disposed to do all we want about the proposed "Home" on the Battery.

Gen: Dix brought news of a despatch from Stanton. Attack on Grant repulsed, & Grant in possession of the outer works of Richmond. The news colored the evening. I suppose this "outer line of works" however to be merely some series of outlying rifle pits meant to cover skirmishers, seven or eight miles from the City, & forming no part of it's substantial defences. What has become of Lee's Army does not appear.

June 1. Wednesday. More decidedly hot. Concerned about Johny who came home from school to day, rather feverish & suffering acute pain in the left side & abdomen, & has since been in bed. D[r] Peters saw him before I came up town, & did not appear to think much of it, but tho' the boy is cooler & easier, this pain & tenderness on pressure have an ugly *inflammatory* look.

No news from Grant, up to 10 P.M. at U.L. Club. Sherman's advance at *Dallas*, 20 miles from Atlanta after another successful round with Secesh under Johnston.

Cisco says that M[rs] *Grant* & a party of her friends came down town the other day to see the Treasury building, & that he escorted them through it. The lady is a simplemannered plain quiet woman. "Is the General anxious?" — "O no, not at all; the last aft[n] he was in Wash[n] he spent a couple of hours on the floor playing with the baby." "He is confident of success then?" — "Entirely so, of course: he knows it's his destiny to take Richmond". — In reply to some suggestion about the White House & the next Presidency, the lady said most emphatically that her husband would not think for one moment of accepting a nomination.

By the way, the "Cleveland Convention", or Conventicle, has nominated Frémont & John Cochrane for P. & V.P. — If Grant take Richmond & Sherman take Atlanta, Lincoln's renomination by the Baltimore Convention is a tolerably sure thing. — "Letter to a Whig member of the Southern Independence Association" by Goldwin Smith of Oxford is among the best essays on this Revolution, so far — but it will make no impression on Shabby old Shop-keeping England. Her position among nations is to be estimated now only by the value of her assets in pounds sterling. The England I have venerated for so many years is dead — of fatty degeneration, & hypertrophied Ledgers.

June 2. Thursday. Johny much better, & nearly free from pain. Thank Heaven, for Peters says it was a nice question yesterday whether he would not have a case of enteritis to deal with. Don Giovanuccio wants careful handling a day or two yet, before he is out of the woods. — It's a clear cool night, after a raw rainy morning. — Nothing new in Wall St. except that my heart was rejoiced by a letter from that excellent fellow, Wm E. Dodge Jr with a subscription list & checks *totting up* about $2000.00 for the Col: Coll: School of Mines. This renews my dying hopes. It is but a trifle to be sure compared with what New Haven people are doing for a like object, at Yale, & an infinitesimally minute trifle considering the resources of N.Y. — which would be poured forth at our call had the community any respect for the College or any confidence in it's management.

Nothing notable at 823 & nothing in the Evening papers. But at 9 P.M. came an Extra. Grant to Stanton, & Stanton to Dix report that at 5 P.M. Tuesday Sheridan's cavalry attacked Fitzhugh Lee's Chivalry & an Infantry brigade under Clingman, at Cold Harbor (on the James? Maps are silent.) and drove them: That Sheridan holds the position: That Wright's corps (the 6th) was marching to support him: That Baldy Smith (from Bermuda Hundred) "must be" close upon Wright: That Lee was moving in force on the same point yesterday, 10 A.M., & that Warren is to attack the column in flank. — That there has been a successful encounter near Hanover C.H.: — and that Burnside is within a mile & a half of Mechanicsville. It would seem that Grant's line extends from Hanover C.H. to Mechanicsville, facing *West*ward (an auspicious omen) & that Lee means to stand the shock of battle, & to retire by his right flank within the works of Richmond in case of defeat. A hazardous programme. But my strategic view of the situation may be all wrong. — To U.L. Club with G.C.A. at 10. Found no farther news from Grant, but an obscure telegram about a most important order for Retaliation issued by Butler, and about certain Rebel iron-clads on James River licked & repulsed by a Monitor. All these premonitory symptoms of detailed information look well, but Heaven save us from the folly of premature crowing & avert the projected mass-meeting next Saturday for the glorification of Grant & the passage of resolutions about his "triumph." Triumph indeed! He has got himself into a position from which he can deliver a battle at advantage, & has shewn, I *guess*, most uncommon ability in so doing. But *the* battle is not yet fought. I remember our exuberance when the lines of Yorktown were abandoned, & the *Merrimac* was blown up, too distinctly to tolerate anything like jubilation until we know that Richmond is held by the National Army, & that Lee & his woman flogging host is south of the James.

June 3. Friday. Wholesome sunshiny weather, & an active day. Agnew & I in the library to night as Stand'g Committee of San Com: — Van Buren is at Saratoga — Jenkins at *White House.* — Little news to day, but good. Grant & Butler have been severally successful in small encounters (comparatively small) with the Jebusites & Ammonites. Baal seems losing ground day by day just now. — At supper Agnew gave E. & G.C.A. (who dined here & spent the ev'g down stairs) many most interesting details of his late experiences in Virginia. — Johny continues improving & convalescent, but must be kept very quiet a day or two longer.

I am shocked to learn from the newspapers that Cisco resigns his important position under Government. I suspect that his health obliges him to do so — for he has been laboring under some pulmonary trouble these two years. It is a National disaster.

June 4. The Grant mass-meeting on Union Square is reported to have been large earnest & grave. Perhaps Union Sq: will be held a classical locality by our great-great . . . . grandchildren, & awaken historical associations.

Bulletin from Grant in this ev'g's papers announces a fight that began early yesterday morning. He attacked, & was successful at every point, but "without decisive results". The moderate tone of all his despatches is a most favorable sign. It indicates that he is a man of *business* & *work*, that he knows the worth of facts & of results accomplished, and the importance of results not yet attained, & that he cares little for talk or for *telling* bulletins. I begin to rate Grant very high. He seems earnest & capable: stronger than Burnside & Hooker, more singleminded than *McClellan.*

McClellan went into this work intending to do his *professional duty*. So did poor Fitz-John Porter. Both have come to grief, because they were blinded to the situation of affairs by old West Point traditions & by the professional sympathies of the old Military service before 1861. Neither saw the case & the duties the case imposed on him, from a National point of view. They thought more of the good old Democratic party — of the infamy of Abolitionism, & the provocations of the South — of the worthlessness of volunteer Generals compared with genuine West Pointers — & of their excellent but perhaps a little misguided West Point & Army friends, such as Lee & Albert Sidney Johnston, — than of the great National Cause. Grant & Meade seem free from this mischievous taint — thank God.

June 5. Grant sends another comfortable despatch. Another collision, in which we have not come off second-best. Lee's Army, tough as it is, must be wearing out under this long series of obstinate conflicts. So must ours, but then our recuperative power is far greater. He has the compensating advantage however of being on the defensive, & of strong works into which he can retire when no longer able to keep the field.

To night Mr S.B.R. here, G.C.A., Gerry, a young Mr Lawrence who seems cultivated & pleasant — (a Col: Coll: man) — Barry — Dr Peters — Walter Cutting — Murray Hoffman, & his brother Major Wickham H. who returned yesterday after two years & a half of service under Butler & Banks. He was Cock of the supper table, of course, & had much to tell us of men & things — & I'm sorry to say that much of his talk must have delighted young Robinson — also present — whose blood is Virginian & at least 75 per cent traitorous. The Major denounces Banks: says he is without capacity for service civil or military: that he has no qualification for high place save his imposing "deportment": that every officer of Government at New Orleans, Baton Rouge, &c &c, is stealing & swindling: that the "Union men of Louisiana" who are organizing a new State Government are, each & all, in Government pay: & that our service in the region of the S.W. is paralyzed by the corruption & profligacy of our officials, who are making money out of cotton, or trying to make it, & loading their consciences with a new breach of public trust every day. He reports Banks' life notoriously profligate, that he worships habitually at the most notorious houses of ill-fame, & that Col: Frank Howe during his late visit to N.O. officiated as Banks' purveyor, or Sir Pandarus. If Hoffman believe these atrocious stories, he should have kept them to himself. — Among the officers we have lost in this unprecedented series of obstinate combats is Col. Peter B. Porter of Niagara — a gentleman of wealth & culture — a good fellow — & a true patriot. He was not long married.

June 6. At 823 with Agnew. Letters from Rev: Bellows at San Francisco. He is recognized as a notability by all the notabilities of that region, is having a great time, feels "*fine*", holds the late Stan King (whom I take to have been a clever Unitarian pulpit orator, an earnest efficient advocate of National principles, & a most valuable friend & supporter of the San: Commission) to have been the Apostle of civilization & Xtianity (?) on the Pacific coast, & magnifies his own office as Stan King's temporary locum tenens. But under all this are signs of uncomfortable consciousness that "Progressive Xtianity" ought not to be so dependent on individual talent — that it wants a system & a Church.

After dinner Gen: Dix came in, then G.C.A. & Willy Hovey of Boston, one of our Wash^{n} employés now here on duty. Ellie made his acquaintance & learned to like him much, during her Peninsular campaign of /62.

News from Grant & from Sherman to day continues hopeful.

June 7th. No news from Grant or Sherman. Discouragement has prevailed to day, slight but distinctly marked. It is due to the arrival of fuller reports of *Friday's* battle — a short but sharp conflict — . Tho' we failed to drive Lee across the Chickahominy, Secesh came out of the fray second best, & our lines rested at last far in advance of their original ground. It is not the very best result, but it is good, & far better than many things we have suffered during the last three years.

English newspapers have heard of Grant's progress as far as Spotsylvania Court House. They are bothered by the news. Their faith in the final triumph of those dear chivalric slave-breeders & girl-floggers is unimpaired of course, but they are pained to discover that Grant, tho' a Northern General, must be admitted to possess a certain amount of military ability — that men in the National Service can fight almost if not quite as well as the "*patriot legions*" of the South. [Eheu, John Bull & England, "quantum mutatus ab illâ Angliâ" that I used to venerate as the leader of mankind] They think our battles, day after day, & night after night, without exhaustion, rather remarkable & interesting, as compared with the history of European campaigns. By a curious coincidence with this discovery, the British Government seems to have decided on *buying* the much debated *Laird Rams*, instead of letting them steam forth from a British port to *butt open* our blockade. If Grant's campaign be blessed with victory, old *John Bully* — that Great Briton — will be most respectfully & truly our obliged & obedient servant.

June 8. Wednesday. Unusually agreeable day. With Ellie at half past 10 to Gen: Dix's, & thence with him & M[rs] D. & Miss Kitty & M[r] & M[rs] G.T. Blodgett, & Blake, & two of the General's staff to his fast little steamer the Henry Burden which took us up the East River to Hart's Island, where we landed, & inspected Quarters, kitchens, & storehouses, & the Gen: reviewed a corps of recruits — good material but not yet quite perfect in drill. Thence to David's Island. We went thro' part of the great group of pavilion hospitals, & saw, of course, much that was sad. Everything in perfect order. Hospital gangrene prevails, but is met by external applications of free Bromine, with entire success. An important surgical discovery.

Home at 6.30 having run down the Narrows just below Fort Lafayette, to give the ladies a look at that Bastile.

To night Binney here. G.C.A., Hasket Derby the οφθαλmologist, & Miss Louisa Anderson.

Ev'g papers give Stanton's latest bulletins. Nothing new with Grant. But Grant reports that the Richmond papers say that Gen[l] Hunter (Sigel's successor) has defeated the Rebels in the valley of the Shenandoah, killed their General Jones (stationed at West Point in /50 I think) & occupied *Stanton*. Excellent if true, & a vast improvement on Sigel.

Baltimore Convention admitted the "Radical" delegation from Missouri, excluding the "Claybank" or "Conservative" contestants, & nominated *Uncle Abe Lincoln* by acclamation.

Well & wisely done — *me judice.* Who will be nominated as V.P.? Either Hamlin Dickinson or Andy Johnson of Tennessee, probably. I should prefer Johnson. Mrs Dix says the Genl was asked to be a candidate, but declined.

Johny seems convalescent. Regret to hear that poor Joe Bridgham is an inmate of a Rhode Island Lunatic Asylum & probably a hopeless case of "softening of the brain". So says G.C.A. — Frémont's nomination by the Cleveland Schismatics seems to attract little attention. Their choice of a cypher like John Cochrane as their candidate for V.P. is a confession of weakness. What will the Democrats do? Will they try to over-bid their opponents by nominating some ultra *Anti-Slavery & War to the Knife* man, or allow their party name & prestige to be used by their Peace-mongering brethren? They have a difficult game to play. Should they adopt the former policy & decide to be Democratic in principle & reality as well as in name, they may endorse Frémont. That would be a revolution indeed! But Frémont is not nearly as strong as he was in /56, & will run badly. Who could be brought forward as a "Peace" candidate? Should Grant's campaign fail disastrously, McClellan stock might revive, but his name has lost much of it's power, & it would be hard to make him an available candidate for any office. That pipe is probably smoked out at last. Gov: Seymour would like to run as representative of a platform of treason & National disintegration, but his dallyings with the beastly rioters of last July could be used against him with fatal conclusive effect, I hope.

June 9. Baltimore Convention nominates *Andy Johnson* for V.P. *vice Hamlin* dropped. Very well. Unanimity of these nominations encouraging. But it disgusts the *World* newspaper, which condemns & denounces both Lincoln & Johnson as mere plebeians, utterly ungenteel, & excessively low. The World's editorial would make an effective L. & J. campaign document. I suppose a certain amount of disapproval & abuse by *Marble & Hurlbut* of the *World* & by such like coprophagous insects to be as honorable as the Victoria Cross or the Order of the Garter. Of course it's amount would have to be almost inconceivably large, it's authors being so despicable, but these renegade Copperheads dignify & ennoble every loyal American by every epithet of indignity they apply to him.

No War news, except that the Commercial says Butler is about undertaking some great movement. I fear it will be a failure. Gold 197!!! — People are blue. They have found out somehow that Grant will never get into Richmond after all. They may be right but I do not see why they think so. Certain well meaning friends of mine in Wall St. help depress public opinion & raise Gold by going about bleating like forlorn desolate stray lambs. — Take —— for example. His daily talk, when I ask the news, is "Ba-a-a-a! Snooks says he knows Grant's losses have been per-fect-ly tre-mendous. Ma-a-a-a-a! Captn Sniggelfritz who used to be on Genl Schweitzer Käse's staff you know, told me at the Club last night that he thought things did not look well at all — Ba-a-a-a-a" & Da Capo. Sometimes it takes the form of lament over the increased price of Beef, like "Woman wailing for her Demon Lover", or of a grunt about the Internal Revenue Income Tax, but it's always "*incivisme*", & mischievous, more or less. Such *incivisme* does more harm than Marble's or Hurlbut's or Sam: Barlow's because it comes from loyal men & uttered depresses loyal men far more than mere Copperhead utterance.

June 13. Monday. Home again, after a fleeting pleasant glimpse of green fields, wooded hillsides & living streams at *Cornwall.* The Mary Powell took us thither Friday afternoon. We were Ellie & I, Johny, Temple, G.C.A., & Mistress Annie, E's Quartermistress General. Up the river against a lively cool N.W. wind, wh: prevailed during our whole visit & made Cornwall utterly unlike the verdurous stewpan wherein I sweated & stifled & groaned last Summer. Very cordially received by Roe at 7 P.M. — entered on possession of good quarters & ate a vast supper. Spent my time mostly with E. & the two children, walking & driving. Johny concentrated himself on the capture of "Shiners" & Crawfish for his Aquarium, & brought a drove or school of aquatic live stock to town in a large tin pail. Pleasant drive to the "Mountain House," so called, which stands nearly on a level with the crest-line of Butter Hill & overlooks a gorgeous landscape. — Pleasant walk to *Plum Point*, where Johny & Temple & I swept the river with fire from a "parlor pistol". Our practice was rather wild, but I think we could have hulled a three story house at 25 yards every time.

To night to Tr: Ch: Vestry meeting, wh: fell thro' because Verplanck is out of town, & Dunscomb, the other Warden was ill. I hear he was attacked yesterday by something wearing a disagreeable paralytic aspect. Talking of paralysis Prof: Bache has improved so far as to drive out, but Agnew says that *Brown-Séquard* (now of Boston) has been called in & thinks badly of the prospect. Brown-Séquard has been employed by San: Com: to go to Wash[n] & lecture to Army Surgeons at the Smithsonian on *Tetanus*, which is reported rather prevalent in Military Hospitals. He saw Bache on his way thither thro' this City, & I suppose he is among the first authorities on all diseases of the nervous system & brain.

Much business at 823 this P.M. Agnew Jenkins & I. A cord of big Bills examined & passed. We are spending money fearfully fast, but I believe, to good purpose, and from present appearances our disbursements for *June* will not much exceed $150.000. *May* cost us over $262.000! Apocryphal War news most abundant these four days. Newspaper reports, official telegrams, & our San: Com: correspondence indicate one or two facts as established. Grant is destroying his communications with White House & changing his base once more — to James River. Hunter's success in Western V[a] is fully confirmed & may prove important. Butler has been taking liberties with the city of Petersburgh V[a], which would have been more completely successful had Gillmore's coöperation been more energetic.

It's a blessed sign that Richmond papers seem in a special fit or orgasm of rage fury spite brag & insolent indecency just now. The extracts we get from Southern newspapers seldom fail to be significant. They illustrate or indicate the mental & moral tone that Slaveholding has given to our Southern Aristocracy — falsely so called. *Kakistocracy* rather. They far out-Herald the worst extravagancies of J.G. Bennett — or of Capt[n] Bobadil — with their "thrasonicall huffe-snuffe". These Southern gents are a strange compound of Tiger & Turkey-cock — Roman & Chinese — Gorilla & monkey. Never did people fight so hard & brag so consumedly.

Talked much with Gen: Cullum on our way down. He appeared well: talks as one in earnest: seems free from McClellan malaria: & recognizes brave soldiers & good generals outside the charmed circle of West Point & the Regular Army. He says Irishmen fight well, but "Dutchmen" from Sigel down are good at running & good for nothing else.

By the by, the proportion of Keltic & Teutonic surnames in the daily newspaper lists of casualties is extremely small & of those who bear (or who bore) these surnames, very many must have been born Americans. But the Richmond papers & the London Times would sneer at our Armies — "made up of hireling foreign scum" — just the same, were every name on our muster-rolls pure Saxon or Norman.

June 14. Tuesday. Clear & cool. Nothing new in the Street called *Wall*, nor at 823, except that our plan of putting up a "Home" on the Battery seems like to fail. Genl Dix thinks all the available ground will be needed for Government buildings.

June 15. Wednesday. Fine weather. Busied with high Finance this morn'g. Shifted our $900.000 loaned to Cisco from 5 to 6 per cent notes, Cisco waiving the notice to which he is entitled, & behaving like a brick about it. Also opened an a/c for San: Com: with Fourth National Bank, by a deposit of $50.000 withdrawn from Nassau Bank Bklyn. Morris Ketchum, Pres'^{dt} of this 4th Nat: Bk agrees to allow us 4 per cent int: on our balances — & A.A. Low, Sturges & Jno Astor (our Auxiliary Finance Com:) formally approve the arrangement.

Worked at home this ev'g. At half past ten D^{r}. — appeared, escorting E. home from a call at his house, & just stopped a moment in the dining room to light a cigar. I foresaw the inevitable result. An hour of the cruellest boredom has but just ended. How *can* a valuable intelligent useful man allow himself to become such a nuisance? There he sat — uttering prosy platitudes — to which I responded at intervals with the briefest assent. He was utterly without suspicion of his profound afflictiveness & never dreamed & I hope never will that I was saying to myself all the time "OH what a Bore you are! Why wo'nt you go away *now*, & let me go up stairs & finish my Case for Counsel about Pension systems & Sanitaria? Do please take up your hat & go away. Your views about McClellan & Grant & Lincoln & Butler are irrefragable, but for mercy's sake go aw-a-a-ay! I'm trying to be civil & urbane, but I can not stand this much longer. How can you be so blind to the suffering you are inflicting on me? May every blessing hover round your path through life, but do be merciful, stop this maundering, & *go home.*" He went at last.

Very weighty news was posted on the bulletin-boards before noon to day. Grant "changed his base" to James River on Sunday. He has crossed that river & his headquarters are at *Bermuda Hundred.* Part of his force marched to White House & so round by water, down the Pamunkey & York, & up the James. This movement has been effected without molestation. That is it's most remarkable feature. After closely hugging the Rebel lines for a week Grant detaches part of his Army for a long roundabout detour, disengages the rest of it somehow, slides it along Lee's front by a most critical flank movement, & takes it across a difficult river. Yet Lee makes no attempt to follow him up or to destroy his divided army in detail. I do not understand the Situation. Either Lee has made some demonstration of which we are not informed, *or* he holds Grant's move a false one & disinclines (like Napoleon) to disturb him while making it, *or* he is weaker, & more seriously exhausted by these five weeks of fighting, than we have supposed.

Can he contemplate parrying by a rush on Washington? Hardly; for every R.R. on which he could depend for transportation has been destroyed.

Richmond is probably most vulnerable from the South.

R^t Rev: Leonidas Polk, a Bishop of the Catholic Church, & also a Major General of the Rebel Armies that fight against the right of the Poor man to his own wife & children, is reported killed. I confess I hope the report may be true, tho' Polk's generalship has done his Woman-flogging Cause no great service. The sooner such a "Bishop" is killed the better.

Killed or not killed, has any Bishop ever run so shameful a career?

June 16. At U.L. Club awhile this ev'g — smoked a cigar in the balcony & watched the rockets & beautiful fire balls "red white & blue" that formed part of the ceremonial of the great meeting on the South side of Union Square. Lounged about the rooms afterwards, discoursing Geo: W. Blunt & Cyrus

Field — cum multis aliis. Tone of feeling at the Club is good — quiet hopeful, even confident, but subdued & moderate, prepared for either fortune. So it is generally — tho' Batrachians like to dwell on the fact that Grant is now several miles of linear distance farther from Richmond than when he was on the Chickahominy. Βςεϰεϰεϰϰεϰεϰεξ ϰοαξ ϰοαξ So croaks — e.g. — C.E.S.

"Little Mac" [very little — Napoleoniculus] delivered himself of an Oration yesterday at West Point on the occasion of the founding of a monument to the memory of Regular officers, thereby inviting comparisons between himself, the late Pericles, & the contemporaneous Edwd Everett. It's a dull speech, and the squirms of a latent Copperhead are dimly apparent here & there, under a pile of commonplace flowers of rhetoric. McClellan was serenaded by the Cadets thereafter, & some of them called for three cheers for G.B. M^{c}C. "*our next President*", which cheers were given. Col: Bowman & Clitz looked on & listened & let it pass. The official "visitors", then also looking on, were much offended by this "affront to the Administration". One of them, a nephew of Andy Johnson's, avowed his intention of going straight to Washington & making an official report of Clitz & Bowman's scandalous misconduct. But that most clever little fascinating Mrs Bob Le Roy, who is staying at the Point & likes Clitz, got hold of this Tennessean & talked him over to such an extent that he afterwards declared he did not know whether he stood on his head or his heels & was not sure he should make any Report after all.

Sorry to hear that Clitz has been jilted by some Ohio girl — is soured thereby — makes himself most unpopular at West Point — & (what's worst of all) has relapsed into Copperheadism, of which filthy disease I thought him radically cured last summer.

Bulletin placards at 2 P.M. looked well, & so do the Ev'g papers. Sheridan's foray West of Richmond seems successful. Grant comfortably established on his new base. Fighting in the direction of Petersburgh — result unknown.

June 17. Friday. Grant *has taken Petersburgh*, before the ink was dry wherewith its flatulent editors were recording their triumph over the failure of a late demonstration against that "gallant little City", & their full faith in it's impregnability against "Lincoln the Baboon" & "Butler the Beast" & all the hordes of "Yahoo-land." Heaven be praised. This leaves Richmond and Lee's army but one line of R.R. (Richmond & Danville) & it's very possible Sheridan has cut that line before now. If so, Lee must come out & fight — retreat to the S.W. — or surrender, for his magazine will not carry his Army thro' many days of siege.

It may be very wicked of me, but I think with great satisfaction of the wrath & fury prevalent to night in the traitorous households of Petersburgh, & of the liberties our National soldiers are probably taking in the region across the James, among aristocratic seats of low-bred secessionist Aristocracy, now for the first time enjoying the after-taste of Rebellion without cause.

Weather sultry & hazy. "The maiden with white fire laden whom Mortals call the Moon" was riding full orbed in a cloudless sky as I walked down Fifth Av: from Agnew's, but she looked coppery & erysipelatous, & her fire was not white at all, but as that of a phosphorescent disc of decomposing Smoked Salmon.

At Agnew's Rev: D[r] McClintock & M[r] Bowles were with us, & we had an uncommonly interesting talk about the position the prospects & the possible results of our Branches at London & Paris. We decide to help them to fuller development. Also we shelve D[r] *Steiner* who seems impracticable & not efficient & put Douglas in charge of our work with the Army of the Potomac.

June 20. Monday. Fine weather, but hot. Ellie went to Philad[a] this A.M. with her brother Jem, to inspect the "Great Central Fair". Philad[a] impudently threatens to beat N.Y. not only in the architectural & artistic features of it's Fair, but in the am[t] of cash thereby raised for the San: Com:! It's proceeds are already hard on a million.

Our cackle over *Petersburgh* was premature. What we did on Wednesday was merely to storm a difficult line of field works, capturing prisoners & 16 guns. Ethiopia by the by took 6 of the 16 & came up to the scratch in the best style. On Sat:

we attempted another line, & failed. Hence long faces in Wall St. this morn'g. Bulletin Board of the Commercial announced (3 P.M.) a Rebel raid into Penn: & "rumors" of a disaster to Grant. Nothing about either story in the Ev'g Post, & both are discredited at U.L. Club to night.

June 21. Tuesday. Gold has reached 200 at last! Another long visit from X this morn'g. At 823 this aft^{n} Agnew & I with *Knapp* despatched much business. We send a supply steamer to City Point (on James River) Friday or Thursday, & I may go with her, to see the Elephant, if certain Wall St: work can be postponed.

News from Grant not unfavorable.

Long walk this ev'g, bringing up at 47th St. where was a great fire. The *hay depot* of the Harlem R.R. C^{o} was burning up. The depot covered nearly the whole block between 47 & 48 Sts Fourth & Lexington Avenues, & made a splendid blaze.

June 22. Wednesday. Ellie returned from Philad^{a} to night, safe & sound: has had a good time: reports the "Central Fair" very brilliant, & young Bowles, whom she met there, & who is to be our San: Com: agent in Paris, a decided Brick.

Hot weather. Walked up with G.C.A. Nothing new at 823, except that our Inspectors at City Point are told confidentially by the Q^{r} M$^{r's}$ Dep^{t} that James River will be our base "all summer". Our new propeller, the "Commander" is delayed in coaling, & cannot be got off for a couple of days.

Gold has run wild under the Act of Congress meant to suppress speculation therein, & has been privily sold at 230!!! Pauperism probably awaits me, & better men than myself. Let it come. I have lived much more than half my allotted term in ease & comfort much beyond my deservings, & have no right to complain. Only let us all do our utmost to uphold the National cause, & let us not be disheartened by fear of poverty. News from the front is not much, — not bad — on the whole, as far as it goes, perhaps rather encouraging.

One of our Generals is said to have made a significant remark after our successful assault on the outer works of Petersburgh last week — viz — "I now see that Black Soldiers will fight. The Question is settled, & *the War is over*."

At U.L. Club awhile to night. Delano, Captn Marshall, H.A. Coit, Otis Swan, &c were there, — also John Jay. He complains of Lincoln's re-nomination, & talks like an Ass — far less reasonable than Balaam's. His vocation is to be factious & fractious & to fight the battle of a protesting minority. He cannot abide the policy of the Administration because it seems to aim at abolishing slavery, instead of endeavoring to unite all parties in an effort to save the National life. A strange position for him to take.

June 23^{d}. Thursday. Piping hot. At 823 this aft^{n} I find "my apple cart upset." Our new propeller the "Commander" will take *four days* to reach City Point, & I fear I cannot spare so much time. Sorry for it. I had a vague project of taking Johny with me, & shewing him something he would remember all his life.

G.C.A. dined here. Walked up 5th Av: with him to Agnew's, who was'nt at home. The boys have enjoyed an hour or two after dinner these two or three days, with fire crackers & pin wheels. Messrs Ernest Cox (Son of Rev. A.C.C.) Georgey Grant (son of a copperhead, I believe) & Jemmy Harper, son of a great publisher, have assisted, burned their fingers, & enjoyed themselves.

Another interview with X this morn'g. I advised him 1st to hold his tongue & suppress himself while this controversy is pending. 2^{d} to employ a detective to ferret out the whereabouts of his abducted child — 3^{d} to retain either Jem Brady or Henry Cram. His counsel are too respectable & estimable & hightoned to fight his battles successfully against the bitter unscrupulous opposition he has to encounter. He asked me to get him the name of a skilful & trustworthy detective & I did so this aft^{n} from Mr Police Commissioner *Acton*.

His case is among the most extraordinary & amazing on record. His wife confessed to him that she was impelled to this intrigue by *jealousy* of her very beautiful younger sister, to whom his brother paid some attention, & whom it was reported he was likely to marry. This young lady is now engaged to a brave & valuable officer. Heaven help him! I should deplore any alliance with the household of his betrothed. X's wife tried to poison herself. It was represented as an accidental over-dose of laudanum, at the time, but she confessed it's object afterwards. This was when her paramour decided to accept a Commission, & join the Army. When she revealed her guilt, she confessed herself *enceinte* & not by her husband. She suffered a miscarriage soon thereafter. Her family is now trying to prove that one of the conditions on which X stipulated to condone the adultery was his wife's submission to processes intended to produce an abortion!!! I look on this case with dismay. It seems to me one of those great public scandals that have sometimes been the forerunners & patents of revolution & calamity to the community in which they occurred — like that of the Duc de Praslin for instance. I see no way of avoiding full publicity, should both parties survive three months longer.

June 24. 8 P.M. Hot — & disgusted. I greatly fear Grant finds himself blocked, & is about making a move that looks like retreat. His losses have been most severe. And it is said there is a bad feeling among his rank & file that they have been fought & worked enough for the present. The failure of this Campaign would be profoundly discouraging & disastrous. Could we survive it? These are evil days, & worse are coming I fear. But this flagitious Rebellion *cannot* be destined to triumph. If the People hold out a year or two longer, the Country will be saved. But I live in dread, day by day, of a sudden sweeping fatal epidemic of discouragement & *fatigue* that will change the whole look of affairs & drive us into a disgraceful short-lived peace.

But I do not talk this way — All my croaking is strictly confidential — between myself & my journal.

With Agnew this aft[n] to visit our new *propeller* — the *Commander* — on wh: it seems likely I shall be moving toward James River tomorrow.

11.30. Agnew Van Buren & Jenkins here in Stand'g Com: — Ellie came in late from her yachting party. I propose taking Johny with me on our voyage — at his earnest prayer — but not without misgivings. He will be at least as seasick as I — & then there are the chances of sharp-shooting — torpedoes — flying field batteries &c, for we are going into the heart of the enemy's country, & thro' miles of hostile river-navigation, more or less dangerous. But he is wild to go — his mother wants him to go — and the voyage & the glimpses of an Army in the field will be such a precious memory to him. Agnew thinks it altogether best to take him with us.

July 4th. Monday. Home at 8 A.M. — Hot day. Usual firecrackering in full blast. All well at home — thank Heaven.

Sat: 25th June. A most Collar-wilting day. With Johny to No 823 Broadway — final arrangements made: thence to propeller "*Commander*", foot of 10th St. N.R. Off at [ ]15 P.M. Hotter & hotter. Not till we were well down the Narrows did we cease groaning & begin to breathe freely. Our Captn, *Petrick*, obliging & kind, & anxious for our comfort, but not efficient, & ignorant of the Coast. Mate a jolly hirsute ruffian. Steward the embodiment of all stewardly virtues. Engineer (Peck) an exceedingly respectable person. Propeller seems a steady sea boat. All her appointments are good save her boiler & engine, which are *too small*. She makes not more than six or seven knots, even under sail. Our table very good, & reinforced by stores of our own providing. "We" were Agnew, Johny & I, Rev. Mr Greenleaf, an amiable simple minded young Presbyterian Dominie of Piermont (surprised & pained to find that there were no "professors of Religion" among the deckhands, & that some of them were actually addicted to profanity) and *Captn Lord*, late of the Army of the Cumberland, who has seen much service in the West, & suffered much in Libby Prison. He left the service because of illness — is in our employ — went down as supercargo, — was very useful, & seems a valuable man. A very pleasant party it was. — We run pleasantly past Sandy Hook, with its fast developing lines of grim fortification & the Navesink Hills — watch the sun, setting behind the caravanserais of Long Branch — & turn in at last. "Off Barnegat Light", according to the Skipper, but knowledge of localities is plainly not his strong point. — Greenleaf was a protegé of Agnew's & a goose.

Sunday 26th. Running slowly down the coast, wh: is sometimes wholly out of sight. "How fearfully hot it must be in town" (& so it was). Watch ships, & an occasional sharkfin sailing slowly along. Rev: G. a little qualmish, but the sea is like a millpond, & no one else experienced the suspicion of a qualm. General voracity. Up at 5.30 A.M. for a cup of strong coffee, & breakfast well at 9. Bluefish lines brought out, & two tied to the taffrail. Agnew doubts whether they be legitimate on "the Sabbath". Some 16 chose to be caught, big fellows mostly, & we ichthyophagized morn'g noon & night for the rest of the voyage. Johny's line took it's full share. He finds favor with all on board, behaves like a brick, takes charge of the Live-Stock department, & devotes himself to feeding our half dozen sheep & our 9 doz: chickens. The latter had a rough experience. They were cooped too closely, & began on Monday to die of *coup de soleil.* Copious affusions of ice water restored all but half a dozen, & then they wandered about the decks laying what the Mariners termed "soft shell eggs", got into the rigging & every where else, & now & then attempted suicide by jumping overboard. Some of these were saved by the most heroic exertions, with buckets & by divers from the deck.

Short but most grand thunder squall — without rain — at 6 P.M. Clouds black & threatening — sea inky black — & then a white line of foam visible three miles off (toward shore) & coming swiftly toward us.

Off Hog Island Light 9 30 P.M., *teste skippers.* We consult charts, estimate our speed, & venture to doubt. Skipper positive, & we shall reach Hampton Roads by 9 tomorrow — *Sartain.*

Monday 27th. 5.30 A.M. Hog Isld Light off our Starboard bow! Skipper much humiliated — last nights luminous phenomenon must have been a ship's light or else "Jinkatig" Light, & he does not know how he could ha' made such a curious mistake. Nor do we know. — 8 A.M. the two lighthouses on "Smith's Island" 9.30 Cape Henry — a dismal coast line. 2 P.M. — Hail the guard ship off Fortress Monroe & anchor. Send a boat ashore for a Government James River pilot. Heat for the next two hours most horrible. I inwardly execrated my folly in coming hither, & felt that a few hours more would surely make me a gibbering maniac. Another heavy squall came & others followed it at intervals till dark, interposing a grateful shelter from the fierce sunshine. Pilot arrives. *Jameson* to wit, & up Anchor. Pass the three turreted *Roanoke* — gunboats — the wreck of the Cumberland — Newport News — & anchor a mile above *White Shoal Light.*

Most gorgeous & terrible sunset — leaden black solid clouds — so solid that they looked as though they must be in act of dropping to the earth — flying streamers of grey vapor beneath them, torn & twisted & ravelled out. With these were mingled spaces of glowing fiery blood red light. Just above the setting sun, a thin curtain of rain caught it's rays, & shone crimson like an Auroral column, or a shower of blood. Intense shafts of lightning came every moment to the horizon from the huge leaden masses of cloud that were slowly marching Southwards. It was a *battle sunset.*

Pilot full of discourse — local information — anecdotes of a long life spent in perils of the sea, & for the last few months in worse peril among our false brethren of the South. We looked up to him, & listened admiringly, & drew comparisons between him & our amiable skipper to the disadvantage of the latter. He was "equus marinus" — an old salt — a Marine Leatherstocking — & how lucky we were to have secured him!

Tuesday, 28th. Cooler. Off Jamestown Island 8 A.M. — Ruined church a pregnant illustration of the difference between North & South. Had this building with all its historical associations been this side the Potomac & reduced by time or accident to it's present condition, how easily could any amount of money have been raised to preserve or restore or rather to rebuild it, for only the tower is left, or rather the stump of it's tower. Note in connexion with this the numerous brick chimneys that one constantly sees in Va, standing alone — the wooden house having been deserted & gone to decay. I took them at first for "horrors of War", but in nine cases out of ten they are no such thing.

These people have long been tending toward barbarism. Had they been let alone, I believe that they would, except in their cities, have retrograded to the Nomad stage, & lived in patriarchal tents, before many years.

9 A.M. Past the mouth of the fatal Chickahominy — draw near to *Brandon* — are passing Sandy Hill (or Point) Plantation. Pilot suddenly discovers shoal water. Next minute we run into a tenacious mud-bank, under full sail & 30 lb of steam, at the top of a rather full flood tide. Back the engine. She budges not. "We must wait for to night's flood". We are 400 yards out

of the channel, & within 300 yards of a nicely wooded shore — an eligible position for sharpshooters. Our force is 5 deckhands & our armament one revolver. Rebels were in force ten miles above, last Friday. — Pilot is the most mournful instance since the late N. Buonaparte of the instability of human grandeur. Every nose from the Captn's to that of the Steward's boy is turned up at him. He is berated & denounced & retires to his solitary stateroom. The crew talked of putting him ashore & of throwing him overboard in a tone not wholly jocose, & so did the Captain & every one else. He never regained his lost position. At long intervals he appeared & vouchsafed a professional remark, but he was invariably snubbed & went back to his hole again. [& was dismissed the service of Gov^{t} when we got back to Fortress Monroe.]

Boat sent up at once to "Wilson's Wharf" where was an armed flotilla. At 12 appears the *Tin-clad* Young America — two guns — acting Ensign Lasher in command — supervised by Lt J.A. Jackaway of gunboat *Dawn*, who took up his quarters with us.

So far as I can learn our position was just this. If we were unprotected the circumambient guerillas would have been not unlikely to open on us & make us uncomfortable. They could easily have kept us below with small arms & might have sent out boats to attack us. It was possible also that a light battery might be sent down, but that was not probable, at least while we were in communication with the Y.A. & the rest of Captn Simmons' force at Wilson's wharf was ready to drop down the river on hearing guns.

Waiting for the tide, we went ashore in the aft^{n} with the two Naval men & a foraging party. "If you've revolvers with you, gentlemen, you had better take them of course". As we had but *one*, a supply was sent on board — also half a dozen rifles with their appurtenances. We saw no seceshers — nor any bipeds save certain idiotic contrabands. Country most lovely — vegetation rich — fields fertile but neglected — everything seedy & run down, though this spot was unvisited by War. Visited a spacious wealthy looking mansion that had been the abode of some F.F.V. household. It was uninjured but deserted, & every stick of furniture gone. The evergreen wreaths & crosses of last Xmas still adorned the walls of one room.

Barns & stables were rickety. Queer slovenly makeshifts every where — e.g. the well-rope was an old *seine* twisted up & kept in proper form by pieces of twine at intervals. Return after a pleasant walk thro' woods glowing with trumpet creeper, & swampy spots lovely with flowers, unknown to me. The blue-jackets brought off potatoes & squawking chickens which they had bought & paid for — as they said.

6 P.M. Flood draws near. Tinclad Tug makes fast aft, & tries to haul us off. Two hours of trial & tribulation in vain. Jackaway on our stern bellows at Lasher & occasionally curses him *sotto voce*. Lasher gets his boat on the bottom too, in a convenient position for a raking fire from the shore. The Lieutenant boards her & by long straining gets her afloat at last. It's clear the "*Commander*" must be lightened, & our supply boat the Wilson Small (previously sent for) comes alongside at 10 P.M. I am up till daylight, helping Lord in the work of shifting some forty tons of cargo — wherein Johny assisted.

29th, Wednesday. The Small goes up to Wilson's Wharf at daylight, lands stores, & returns at 9.30. Agnew went with her & thence to City Point to secure a stronger tug-boat. Morning flood very slack. No use trying with so little water. General disgust. At 12 appears Army gunboat Genl Jessup. Lt Marjoram commanding. I board her & bring the Lt back to dinner — dine wine & cigar him into a cordial ally. He goes back to Wilson's Wharf at 3.30 promising to return. Then down comes the *Dawn*. Captn Simmons comes on board with several of his officers — a very genial party. All go forward to have the pleasure of giving the *Pilot* a piece of their mind — officially, pilot being in employ of Government. Pilot receives much pepper. —

Heavy thudding of big guns audible Petersburgh way —

The Jessup returns at sunset & makes fast along side. Young America makes fast astern. Of course we shall get off *now*. Any expression of doubt is regarded as an indication of disguised rebel sympathies. Pulling sets in at nine. Captn Lasher comes to grief again — fouls his screw with his own hawser — reverses his engine, & tangles his screw up the other way with that attached to our kedge anchor, on which we had established an auxiliary haul. Then he *grounds*. Jackaway goes off in wild despair — & at last gets her afloat, but with her screw & engine still disabled. Both gunboats anchor near us, & we are advised to maintain a special extra watch all night. "Which we did it" — but nothing happened.

30th Thursday. Our storeboat Elizabeth alongside at 6 A.M. Discharging cargo all day — & lightened our "Commander" of everything in the upper hold. Screw of the *Young Am*: cleared at last — after hard work by men toiling up to their necks in water. We issued certain bottles of whiskey for their comfort & restoration. The powerful sidewheel tug *City of Troy* (a Quarter Master's boat) appears, with Dr McDonald. Heavy guns near Petersburgh very audible during the afternoon. Fire in the evening, supposed to be the nigger quarters on the *Allen* plantation — fired by a boat's crew from the Jessup. A little before midnight the *C. of T.* takes hold astern & the Elizabeth aids on our port side. After ten minutes straining, *off we slide at last.* Io Triumphe! We are towed to an anchorage having blown all the water out of our boilers to lighten the ship. Drink of Congratulation all round — & to bed.

Friday. July 1st. Up at day break with Johny & Dr McDonald & up the river by the "*City of Troy*" leaving the Commander in charge of Lord to turn over the contents of her lower hold to the Elizabeth & then return to N.Y. for another cargo of pickles & onions & curried cabbage. Most sultry. Below Harrison's Landing, where a force of Cavalry raiders lately crossed, the air is black with innumerable *turkey buzzards* — indeed these foul birds are visible everywhere on the banks of James River. Pass the Rebel Atlanta, now converted & a loyal iron-clad, lying off Fort Powhatan. She looks like an ugly customer. City Point at 9. The waters swarming with transports — hospital boats — tugs — gunboats — light steamers & all manner of river craft. — Land in a scene of matchless dust confusion (apparent at least) & activity. They are repairing the R.R. — Wagon trains are moving every way — gangs of contrabands following mounted leaders — who carry remarkably long riding whips — (honi soit qui mal y pense) — docks are being built — officers riding about — & the usual nebula of stragglers, disabled men & army followers is all pervading. Everyone desperately in earnest about something. The shore is lined three deep — yes, *six* deep with barges &c — steamers are screeching — corrals of mules braying — but I can do no justice to the sights & sounds of the place. All this is on or beside a strip of river shore.

Back of this is a bank covered with fine trees & shrubs that were green once but are now ash-colored & grey or "Cow-calf" colored — among them are tents of the same neutral tint. To your right, on the bank, there is a refreshing bit of warm color, the flag of *Grant's* headquarters — Looking still farther you make out dimly through the yellow dust-saturated air, the outline of a long series of pavilion hospitals where 6000 sick & wounded men (too sorely hurt or too ill to bear transportation) are stifling as they breathe the sluggish heavy current of dust that keeps pouring in upon them. High up against the blue sky stand great columns of coppery dust — hardly moving & shifting their vague outlines slowly, like thunderheads on a summer ev'g.

Join Agnew & proceed at once to our headquarters (San. Com.) viz: sundry barges moored on the mud bank of the shore — a festering expanse of filthiness. In all respects a most "insanitary" arrangement. Our men are so full of their work that they neglect themselves. No wonder more than 20 of our Relief corps have broken down & gone home within so short a space. There is everything to produce disease, not only in their work, but in their food & quarters. It is disgraceful & murderous. We gave Douglas (in charge) our views about it, & shall do so formally in writing — with definite orders for reform — so far as reform is possible. The situation is bad enough *per se* — & cannot be changed at present — but precautions can be taken against disease — & there are none now. The San: Commission needs a new San: Com: to look after the health of it's small army of field agents & our Executive Committee must undertake the work instanter. — With Agnew to Gen: Grant's headquarters, taking Johny with us that he might enjoy a sight of *the* great man of the day — perhaps of the age. Heaven grant it! Headquarters camp is pleasantly situated on top of the bluff, among fine old trees, near the house of a runaway rebel named Eppes. Ingalls has set up his quartermastering offices in the building. It has been riddled & made nearly untenantable by shot & shell — having been used as a trap to decoy some of our men under fire by a story of some sick lady in it who wanted the attendance of a surgeon from our fleet. Such is the story. Ingalls had three little niggers *fanning him* & looked like a Rajah. — Call on Captn Janes — Gen: Rawlins (Chief of Staff) & to Gen: Grant's tent. Most cordially received. Talk with him about transportation of *vegetables* to the front — &c &c. He's a man of few words, but gave us clearest assurance of his readiness to help our work, & of his intelligent recognition of it's importance. Whenever we want facilities of any kind we must come straight to him, or send Dr Douglas, & he will "see us through". Our discourse lasted some 15 minutes. We made it as brief as possible, tho' the Genl professed to be quite disengaged. The impression he makes on me is favorable. He talks like an earnest business-man — prompt clearheaded & decisive — & utters no bosh. As we were leaving something was said about encouraging enlistments, & the need of more men. "I think we shall want more men" said Grant "but there will be no difficulty in getting them". — His staff says his losses have been less than the estimate with which the Campaign began! — that Richmond & Petersburgh are nearly *insulated* & cut off from R.R. communication with mankind — that it must be many days before these roads are repaired — that all the carts & wagons that can be raised are doing their utmost to carry in supplies — & that the results of these raiding expeditions are worth ten times their cost in men & *materiel.* — Also that the black troops fight well — & make no prisoners. "Dont know how it is — we have made no enquiry — somehow they give the Provost Marshal nothing to do. I suppose they have to kill their prisoners before they can take them. When they go into action they yell 'Fort Pillow!' But it is queer they do'nt take any prisoners, tho' they fight so well". Very queer indeed.

Agnew Greenleaf & I set off for the front at 12 in a wagon with four horse team. Frightful heat. Dust unspeakable. After poking about at & around Gen: Baldy Smith's headquarters awhile we came unexpectedly on my very estimable young cousin Capt: Horace Binney, & were made much of — taken up to the top of an adjoining house — fed — & shewn all that could be seen. Our position — near our extreme right — overlooked a wide area of smiling landscape. The spires of Petersburgh rose from a sea of foliage at a distance of a mile & a half. Nearer us, three lines of newly up-turned earth could be traced at intervals among the trees. From the two farther, & from other points, little puffs of smoke were breaking out, & there was a crackling sound, like that of the squibs now going off in the streets, sometimes rather sluggish & comparatively infrequent, & then rapid & multitudinous as when a pack of crackers is fired at once. Every two or three minutes came the smoke & the boom of a big gun from one side or the other, & every fifteen minutes a special Parrott ("the Petersburgh Express") went off with a crash — & a whoo-oo-oosh — & a shell burst in the City near the R.R. bridge. We were near enough to see the little spirts of dust thrown up by the sharp-shooters' bullets as they struck the ground a little in advance of us. It would seem we can take the City whenever we like, but it would be too hot to hold us while certain outside Rebel works continue to command it. Back to City Point, & long discourse with Douglas &c. I meant to have taken Johny to the front, but am glad I did not. He was a little headachy in the morning, & the heat dust & discomfort of the drive would have surely made him ill. I have seen the Army smothering in mud before, but never, till now, stifling in Dust. Drought & travel have done their work on this region, & pulverized the soil to a "potency" (as the homœopaths would say) beyond what I had dreamed possible. Miles & miles of what were meadow & cornfield are now seas of impalpable dust, of unknown depth, & heated to a temperature beyond what the hand can bear. Through this, & over such roads as are still defined & distinct, though equally dusty or even worse, passes all Grant's enormous transportation. Every horse raises a convoluted cloud of ropy smoke, that comes up to his belly, & trails away behind him for half a mile. A drove of cattle or a mule train creates a fog so dense that in passing them this aft^{n} our *leaders* were invisible. Tho' our teamster knew the ground perfectly, he had to stop within a mile of City Point, on the boundless area of naked yellow dust, limited only by the circumambient haze, & traversed by wagon ruts in every direction, & ask which way City Point lay.

There were curious effects of mirage, such as one reads of. It was easy to imagine that the surface of fine powdery sand, cut up by hoofs & wheels was a rippled sea beach, & looking a little farther out into the fog, the effect was that of a shallow & waveless lake or sea within a quarter of a mile. When one got a glimpse of a distant road, the dust was like mist rising from a river & as the sun shone on the denser base of the fog line, there seemed to be gleams of the river itself.

Sat: July 2^{d}. Came off in Gov^{t} steamer Keyport for Wash^{n} at 10 A.M. Hot day. Crowds of discharged & invalid soldiers. Most of them dirty & noisy. Many brought off souvenirs of the war — e.g. little boxes with growing plants. One was carefully tending a lovely little bit of a fawn no larger than an Italian greyhound, captured in the Chickahominy swamp.

We all spent the night on deck, & got what sleep we could on chairs. Happily it was mild & still as we ran up the Chesapeake. Johny takes kindly to a little bit of roughing.

Yesterday 9 A.M. at Washington. Spend the day in council with Knapp over important matters. Off at 6½ by R.R. Sleeping cars new & good & I got thro' the night very comfortably — So did Master Johny. —

Fire crackers as usual all day. Assisted at ignition of wheels & Roman Candles after dinner. Gen: Dix & Mr Ruggles came in awhile. Was X examined about my experiences in V^{a}. Dix thinks Grant "sanguine". He certainly does not err that way himself!!!!

I am very glad I made this expedition. Agnew & I have (especially A.) done substantial service.

July 5th. Tuesday. Hot. Rose headachy feverish & in a state of diarrhæa, quite unusual with me & continuing all day. Is it because I sat up late last night, after closing my journal, to draft certain regulations for the better conduct of our affairs in Virginia, or am I slightly poisoned by the atmosphere of that malarial mudhole at City Point? Should not wonder if I were, tho' my sojourn was so brief.

Down town nevertheless to confront an accumulated pile of letters that would fill a bushel basket. — Walked up town with — infelicissimo. The *habeas Corpus* for the recovery of his little Alice has been pushed, & has got into the newspapers. Members of his wife's family, — her father & two of her sisters — have been examined as to their knowledge of her present whereabouts. They are profoundly ignorant on the subject. — Good news. The pirate *Alabama* sunk by the *Kearsarge*, off Cherbourg, after an hour's hard fighting. Much work at N° 823 — home late to dinner. Conference with Mortimer Thomson ("Doesticks") whom we retain as our agent to look after the newspaper press. — At U.L. Club to night — Mr S.B.R. Pres'dt Barnard, Chas E. Butler, Hutton &c. —

July 7. Thursday. Cloudy & muggy. Find myself still oppressed with this pestilent diarrhæa, nauseated, & a little feverish. Did not go down town this morn'g. Went up to 49th St. at two P.M. to keep an appointment with Dr Torrey & Egleston & inspect the incipient collections of our School of Mines. Spent a couple of hours there agreeably. The Nucleus of a Cabinet contains many splendid things. The Collection I bought a year or two since seems well worth it's cost, & the extraordinary stalactites (of *pyrites*, *blende* &c), bought at the Fair, are especially interesting. — Thence to 823. — Home & down town to Fulton St. for a sultry session with Trinity Church Stand'g Com: — Poor old Dunscomb inexpressibly stolid & senile & slow.

July 8. Friday. Wet morn'g, followed by mugginess: unwholesome weather, as my bowels bear witness. More discourse with X —. Poor fellow — he finds some unaccountable kind of comfort in talking this wretched business over — & over again. Old Mrs Cutting Walter C's "old lady" dead at 90 & upwards. So is Chas McKnight's pretty wife, who was Miss Louisa Champlin. No trustworthy War-news. The raid into Maryland still obscure. Some think Lee has sent half his Army North. I do not. Others hold this a mere cattle-lifting foray. The last story is that the Cateran are retreating. At 823 this aftn & at Agnew's to night.

Bidwell's latest groan. "Well Mr B" said I "do you think the destruction of the Alabama rather unsatisfactory and discouraging?" "*Why, of course it is*", quoth B. "We have not *caught Semmes*, and besides, all our commerce is destroyed already." What can one do with people who talk that way? — *Edge* writes me from London, just setting out for Cherbourg, where he is about investigating the details of that fight, for embodiment in a pamphlet to be reprinted here. Saw Randolph on the subject this aftn. —

I dislike writing what looks like brag, but I believe the work of the San: Com: with the Army before Petersburgh may materially influence the result of the Campaign & the destiny of the Country. Fifty thousand pounds of antiscorbutics issued daily to an army that has begun to shew symptoms of scurvy, slight but generally diffused, are no insignificant contribution toward keeping up it's health & efficiency.

July 9. At 823 this aft[n] as usual. To night at Soc[y] Library awhile to look through magazines, and to U.L. Club. G.W. Blunt tells me *Bache* is recovering but slowly from his late shock. Many contradictory rumors about the invasion of Maryland — e.g. that they have occupied Frederick — that our forces are retreating — that three Rebel corps are across the Potomac — that they are marching straight on Baltimore — that a corps has been detached from Grant's army to meet them — &c &c. I am sick & sore with long anxiety about the War. God send us Victory & Peace! There can be no lasting Peace without Victory & thorough subjugation of Southern barbarism.

Seymour — that Judas — seems deliberately endeavoring to bring this state into collision with the National Government, on questions growing out of the closing of the Journal of Commerce & World offices, but I doubt whether he possess the pluck to carry out his purpose. He is destined to unutterable infamy. — The European conference about Denmark has accomplished nothing & hostilities are recommencing. I shall be sorry to see that plucky little old kingdom & nation destroyed, but prospects are bad. England scolds & blusters & pours out Billingsgate on Prussia. When has England respected the weakness of a hostile Power or refrained from using all her brute strength against any foe, however feeble, for the maintenance of her pride or the extension of her trade? She *may* decide to intervene & save Denmark, even now, but I think she will not. She can make no money by the operation, & War would be inconvenient while the precedent she has set of fitting out *Alabamas* to prey on the Commerce of a friendly power is fresh in our memory. I hope she may conclude to ally herself with Denmark. The navies of Austria & Prussia will find themselves largely reinforced by Teutonic privateers that have somehow managed to escape from American ports, & England will taste in legitimate war the treatment she has given us in our struggle with Rebellion & Slavery —

July 10. Sunday. Bad news & threatening worse. Morning papers announce official despatch that Gen: Wallace yesterday engaged the rebel invaders, 20.000 strong, on or near the Monocacy, M[d], that he was beaten & that he is falling back on Baltimore. An extra at two P.M. reports great agitation in Baltimore & hurried preparations for defence — also untrustworthy stories that the Rebel advance is at Ellicot's Mills & also at other points. Gen: Dix looked in awhile this aft^{n} & talked blue — *more suo.* He gave me his opinion of that cold-blooded Caitiff Gov: Seymour with considerable freedom of expression. — This is an ugly business — but I do not think Secesh likely to take Baltimore. Wallace *seems* falling back without loss of guns & with a force not demoralized — & falling back on field works, on a city of 200.000 inhabitants, many of them enrolled as militia, & many of them Roughs whose hate of rebellion is vindictive beyond anything we see farther North. They may fight well behind street barricades. What is more important, he will probably find reinforcements there, & gunboats. The Roanoke & the Atlanta should both be hurried thither at once. Even the Secessionizing Aristocracy of Baltimore will be disinclined to see battle & murder brought home to their own front-door-steps & disposed to keep War outside their City.

Worse than this raid, a thousandfold, is the financial trouble that threatens to crush us.

At home all day, with this malarial diarrhæa not yet quite cured. Miss Puss, Murray Hoffman, Lawrence, C.E.S. & Mr S.B.R. here to night. Since the Kearsarge destroyed the *British* Gun-boat Alabama, I observe that we are more furiously Anti-Anglican than ever. We have long had abundant reason to hate England & Englishmen, but I do not see why the happy result of this combat should increase our animosity. It was a happy result indeed! Suppose the Anglo-rebel-pirate-Slaveship had sunk or captured the Kearsarge! The Alabama was to all intents & purposes a *slave ship* sent out from an English port — manned by English seamen & by gunners from an English practising ship, aided by an English tender (the "*Deerhound*", of the Yacht Club, which took off our prisoners to the *nominally* neutral jurisdiction of England) & sustained by all the moral support English sympathy could give her.

Report that Grant is about making a new move, of the most daring character, & that we shall get great news from Petersburgh & Richmond tomorrow or next day. Perhaps. We shall see.

July 11. Monday. Most horribly hot. I guard my journal, as I write, with blotting paper, to receive the drops of perspiration. Were I a public-spirited Millionaire, I should present Central Park with a bronze statue of myself as a "Perspiring gladiator" & make it the centre-piece of a fountain, with a minute jet issuing from every pore. I feel as if all the watery part of my blood were pumped out of me, & my blood discs were rustling & shuffling along like dry discs of card paper. What's very bad, I've a swelled face again.

News from Maryland does not improve. R.R. & Telegraph communication with Baltimore & *Wash*^{n} is cut. Rebel cavalry are burning & laying waste within four miles of Balt: — Balt: seems resolute & ready to defend itself. Cisco has a story that Gen: Franklin, ordered North with his Army Corps (the 19th) was gobbled up, on a R.R. train near Perryville. Gunpowder Creek & Bush Creek bridges said to be burned. In short, that Old Dragon is let loose & has power given him for a time & times, but not for always, as I believe.

July 12. San: Com: met to day at 823 Bdway & to night at Dr Van Buren's. Stillé, Newberry & Knapp with us. Came off early this ev'g, tormented by tumefaction.

Nothing material from M^{d}. We are concentrating force there, & I hope the worst is over, but it is still a critical situation.

July 13. Miserrimus. Tortured by this face-ache & by the heat. Dr Peters & his lancet out of town, & Van Buren is attending a San Comical session to night. I attended awhile this aft^{n}, but had to come away. Down town I got through with an appointment that could not be broken. Blake dined here. Tells me Dix has a telegram from Baltimore that there has been a successful combat near Washington — an unofficial despatch that arrived at two this aft^{n}. Ev'g papers publish no material news, but plenty of details that look well. Blake says moreover that Judge Russell will *dismiss* the criminal charge against Dix of unlawful interference with the *World* & the *Journal of Commerce*. Dix seems to have shewn much tact forbearance & sagacity in dealing with that perilous business.

July 14. Waked thro' last night, under the pain, tingling, & malaise produced by my want of physiognomonical symmetry. Learn with dismay that Van Buren was summoned to Saratoga early this morn'g. Down town reluctant, stopping at Everett House to see Judge Clark Hare of Philad[a] — who is full of the militia question but not fuller than it's importance deserves. Did a certain amount of work in Wall St — not a large amount. San: Com: session 2 P.M. at 823. Had Agnew here at half past five, & he brought his "bistoury" to the rescue, producing much blood & a little matter, & some slight relief. I fear there will have to be another surgical interference, for my face is still tumid & tense, as hard as a green apple, as sore as so much raw flesh, & so inflamed that it looks semi-transparent like a spheroid of red-hot iron.

At San: Com: session again after dinner. We adjourned finally at 10. Much having been done that was designed to promote more perfect internal organization — which we sorely need.

July 16. Sat: — Hot. Ellie marched on Quogue yesterday morn'g, with an immense baggage-train in charge of Q.M. John Nolan (the waiter) & arrived safely, as I learn from that functionary on his return, to night. I was too cruelly tumefied as to my *fauces* to go with her, or to go out of doors at all, & spent the day paging material for some three more volumes of San: Com: "Documents" & arranging them for the binder. My countenance spent the day swelling & tingling till toward night, when the baleful little abscess *exploded*, so to speak, spontaneously, & I felt better. But it is still uncertain whether I am through with this trouble.

Talking of explosions, there was a destructive fire yesterday noon among the big storehouses below Brooklyn Heights wherein was much nitrate of soda or saltpetre or both. Their combustion was most gunpowdery & frightened all South Brooklyn, blowing in windows, & bringing down plaster ceilings all through an extensive region. Here, in 21st St., I distinctly heard, & wondered at, the dull heavy prolonged reports that seemed to jar the atmosphere, if not the house. — & apropos of the same subject, our Agent (San: Com:) D[r] Stevens, just from the front tells me we are *mining up to the Rebel works* in front of Petersburgh & that there will *positively* be "something decisive" there "next week." He had no business to tell me this, & so I mildly suggested to him. — Down town late to day — stopping at 823.

Nothing special. Gold has fallen to 250, & there is a tight money-market. Sherman has crowded Joe Johnston across the Chattahoochee & must be very near *Atlanta*. The rebel Kerne are withdrawing from M^{d} with their plunder.

July 18. Monday. Drought & heat still prevail, to the discomfort of all farmers. Consolatory that the South shares the general damage. One of Grant's staff said, when I was at his head-quarters, that fearfully as the Army was suffering from *Dust*, he prayed there might be no rain for just one week longer. Such delay would utterly destroy the corn crop of V^{a}. — My Tumefaction still prevails likewise, or is going away by the slowest stages. It kept me from going to Quogue this morning. Did a little business in Wall St. & a good deal at 823 and dined with Agnew at U.L. Club, for the first time. A good dinner but unconscionably dear.

To night Mr Binney here & Mr Ruggles. — Nothing new from *Sherman* or *Grant* — and Time is so costly a commodity! But a long letter from Dr Douglas this aft^{n} gave us a page of conflicting camp rumors that concur in indicating some important move by Grant as close at hand. General Orders, as to transportation &c, point the same way. There are predictions that Grant will suddenly change his front and march straight down into the Carolinas to put himself in rapport with Sherman — leaving Lee to follow him or to move northward at his discretion. Not very likely.

A Richmond paper takes tremendous moral ground against the Kearsarge for using her chain cable to shield her boiler & engine, in her fight with the Alabama. It was most "unchivalric". "Any Knight of Chivalric times who had thus secured himself an advantage would have had his spurs hacked off in the tiltyard & been hanged on the highest of gibbets" &c &c &c. There is an element of childlike simplicity in the audacious unscrupulous ruffianism of these bravest but most unchivalric Rebel desperadoes, that is positively touching & love-able, if not pitiable. Their brag over success & their lament over failure are like those of very young boys. It was not unchivalric for the iron-clad *Merrimac* to sink two of our wooden frigates! — nor for the Alabama herself to burn & destroy a score of unarmed merchantmen — . Long years of slaveholding & slave breeding, woman-flogging & baby-selling, bullying, vaporing, & swaggering, have made our deluded Southern brethren to differ from the rest of mankind. They are an alien race as the Seminoles or the Japanese. It cannot be assimilated & restored to its' old place — but it can, with God's help & blessing, be suppressed & subjugated. If it cannot, our National cause & life are lost.

July 21. News in town is that Hunter & Wright have overtaken the Maryland Raiders, retarded in their flight by the weight of their plunder — have recaptured "300 wagons loaded with grain" & taken x guns & x + y prisoners. — A good whiff of wholesome news, & seemingly credible. — Also that Joe Johnston has withdrawn within the defences of Atlanta, & has made a vigorous unsuccessful sortie on Sherman, & that our cavalry is operating between Atlanta & Augusta. I trust Johnston's retreat may be compulsory rather than strategic, that he is not luring Sherman onward from his base, as Napoleon was lured to Moscow, & that he is playing no deep game in concert with Lee. Probably not, but the situation is critical.

July 22. Friday. Much cooler. Down town & at 823 as usual, & dined thereafter with Agnew at Maison Dorée. Came home, & at seven, Ellie reported herself, most unexpectedly, being in sudden need of certain dentistry. With her to Delmonico's, 14th St., where we dined again, — I assisting as spectator. Edwd Anderson (Prof: H.J.A.'s handsome son) joined us. Home — & to Agnew's, for San Comical Stand'g Com: session. Jenkins & Knapp also present. Knapp shewed the first sign of human weakness & imperfection he has ever revealed to me, in his sensitiveness & annoyance about Dr Douglas' assignment to an independent department at City Point. It was a very mild symptom. Had it appeared in any one else, I should have noted it as an instance of singular freedom from mere personal & official feeling. But a claim or grievance founded on rank or etiquette, however plausible, seems base & selfish when it comes from Knapp. Returning, spent half an hour in the dining room with E. & Wm Travers — the most genial sunshiny & prosperous of men. Except the cure of his *stammer*, what has he to wish for that an average mortal can expect?

Old Joe Kernochan dead. One Copperhead the less.

July 23^d^. To day's atmosphere unwholesome. People seem discouraged, weary, & faint hearted. They ask plaintively "Why do'nt Grant & Sherman do something?" . . . "How can we raise 500.000 more men under Lincoln's last call?" . . . . And so forth. Such is the talk not only of Copperhead malignants, but of truly loyal men with weak backbones. Mrs Eleanor is free from qualms of this sort. All her feminine vehemence is directed against timid loyalism — & some of it against her husband, who moans, & likes to quote the moaning of others. To be sure a stiff upper lip can be maintained in these days only by the liveliest Faith, such as removes Mountains — (would that mine could remove a few field-works I could mention!) But I will not let myself doubt the final issue. What farther humiliation & disaster, public & private, we must suffer before we reach the end, God only knows — but this shabbiest & basest of Rebellions cannot be destined to triumph.

"Es *Kann* nicht seyn, Kann *nicht* seyn, Kann nicht *seyn*!
Sehst du, es *Kann nicht*?"

For these are the first of mankind who have rebelled for the sole purpose of destroying their own Nation. Ambitious men have rebelled that they might get their Country into their own hands — classes have revolted to secure political rights, real or imaginary — Colonies, to secure National existence — conquered races (Poland &c) to recover it. Catiline wanted to be First Consul, or dictator, *not* to destroy the Republic. The Balmerinos & Kilmarnocks of 1745 sought to restore an exiled dynasty, not to disintegrate the British Empire. The Despards & Thistlewoods professed to seek the public good. The glory of France — one & indivisible — was the watchword of Paris in it's worst hour of revolutionary madness. Till these days, no rebellion or revolutionary party — so far as I know — ever said, with these caitiffs of the South "Go to, let us create civil war that we may break up our Country and destroy it, so that it may no longer have place among Nations. We have no grievances: we are not oppressed. We are & long have been the governing party: we can continue to govern for indefinite years to come — but never mind that. We, a portion of the people of the United States, maintaining certain questionable social institutions of our own, & finding that a large portion of our fellow-citizens regard these institutions with a certain degree of disfavor, & being defeated in an election (in which we had deliberately taken measures to secure our own defeat that so we might provide ourselves a pretext for getting into a passion) — We therefore, as aforesaid, decide that our Country shall *exist no longer* — though it's destruction cost blood enough to float our Navy."

Had they been sincere in their talk about grievances that justified Revolution, they would have taken a very different course. Their platform would have been something like this. — "The Northern States — or People — have violated the Constitution of the U.S. to our damage, and thereby put themselves 'out of law.' *We* are the U.S. The flag, the Constitution, the Army Navy forts & Capital of the Country belong to us. A. Lincoln is a usurper, & his Congress an illegal assemblage. We the U.S. will proceed as we lawfully may, to amend our Constitution according to our own views of political justice, and to recover our Capital. We will then invite our rebellious unconstitutional Northern fellow citizens to repent & return to their allegiance within sixty days. If they decline, *we, the U.S.*, will make war on them or let them go, as we shall please." It seems to me unaccountable that these wily astute conspirators failed to see the vast accession of strength they would have gained by taking this position. For they never dreamed that the exercise of their alleged "right of Secession" was anything but a declaration of War. They never expected to be "let alone". Every State act of Secession was coupled with appropriations of money to buy arms & prepare for an inevitable appeal to battle. They knew they were bringing Civil War on the Country, and it is an illustration of the reckless lawless temper engendered by Slaveholding, that they over-looked the importance of professing to fight for the Constitution & laws of the Country, & chose to avow themselves *Rebels.* Had they taken the other course, I believe their traitorous Northern Allies, Vallandigham, F'nandy Wud, Barlow, Belmont & Co would have been able long before this to paralyze the North.

They may do so, as it is. There are whisperings about Peace Negotiations, that are alarming. Goose Greeley (Horace) has been mixing himself up with an "unofficial conference" at Niagara — that impudent adventurer "Colorado Jewett" assisting. Southern traitors & their Northern confederates may use Peace demonstrations so as to commit the South to nothing but to do the North infinite demoralizing harm at the coming election. I trust Southern arrogance & insolence will prevent Jeff: Davis & Co from playing *that* card. It would be more damaging than the retreat of Grant or Sherman. I long for Peace, but "Dona nobis Pacem" comes in at the end of the Mass, & is appropriate only at the *conclusion* of an Act of Divine Service, ritual or belligerent. The *Credo in unum Deum, Patrem omnipotentem*, the Father of all men, black & white, has to be intoned before you reach the joyous Prayer for Peace. You must profess your faith in the brotherhood of mankind as children of One Father before you have a right to ask to live undisturbed by Evil Men.

July 26. News from Atlanta looks well, though not yet clear & positive enough to forbid the *World*'s cavilling & doubting & suggesting that "something is probably kept back". Hood, Joe Johnston's successor, seems to have attacked Sherman on Wednesday & again on Friday last, in great force, & to have been beat back with loss numerically more than double ours. But Genl McPherson fell — one of our best officers. We seem to occupy part of the City or of it's defences — not clear which. It was under fire Saturday, & Hood was apparently burning his depots & withdrawing. All this comes thro' several & distinct despatches (not official however) & there are no counter stories of disaster. If it be true, Rebellion comes out of this round with a very black eye. It seems also that a raiding column of accursed Abolitionists has defiled that great City Montgomery Ala: — Per contra, we hear this aft^n that Crook Averell Hunter & Co have come to grief in Western V^a & that another foray into Maryland is imminent.

July 28. Rec[d] this ev'g from Edge at London, advance sheets of his pamphlet on the Kearsarge & Alabama combat, wh: I must get reprinted here at once.

Nothing from Atlanta, except that we seem working with the Spade. Lee has certainly made some kind of movement on the James River. There seems to have been a "muss" there. The demonstration was, apparently agst Butler at Bermuda Hundred, & agst Harrison's Landing. Result unknown. Visit from my client, old Clemens of S[t] Louis, this morning. I have had dealings with him for twenty years, but never saw him before. He's a fine old Western gentleman (Kentuckian by birth) of seventy & upwards, & a millionaire in right of his late wife, who was a *Mullanphy*. Erect, keen, formally courteous in speech, & vigorous, tho' nearly blinded by *cataract*. He was an old "Henry Clay Whig" & I was surprised to find him a thorough-going uncompromising loyalist & hater of Rebellion.

July 30. Sat: — Oppressive heat. — Van Buren sent for me this morning. He is just from Cazenovia, a pleasant & cheap, but hungry boarding place. Letters from Hammond, who tells the D[r] that Chauncey McKeever has seen the record of the Court Martial, & that the judgment is of acquittal on every charge, but that Sec'y Stanton has thus far prevailed on Lincoln to keep the findings in his pocket, & to let the Surgeon General continue under arrest. Bad for Lincoln if true.

Death of *M[rs] Arabella Barlow* (who was *Miss Arabella Griffith*) at Wash[n] of typhus, announced in last ev'g's Post. She was ill when I was last at Wash[n], poisoned by disease contracted during her Hospital work at Fredericsburgh & Belle Plain. She did great service there. She was a very noble woman. Since her marriage she had lost her high-faluting-Elizabeth-Barrett-Browning habits of thought & of talk, & become genuine & real.

A Rebel Cavalry raid — possibly on a large scale, has crossed the Potomac & occupied Chambersburgh P[a]. Will these feeble fat Pennsylvanians ever learn to establish a militia system & do a little to protect themselves? I almost hope *Harrisburgh* may be harried — the lesson would be so useful. — At Atlanta the

Rebel Gen: Hood claims a victory. I rather think he lies. Untruthfulness is characteristic of his Tribe. Southerners seem unable to perceive any virtue or value in veracity. But the silence of the War Department gives a certain color to the Rebel story.

Grant has had a fight on this side James River, seemingly successful. "Four" or "six" guns captured, & prisoners.

Busy to day, & fearfully bored & hot, arranging about Bank "accommodations" for the San: Com: — I had been too dilatory in calling for payment of loans to Cisco. Our bank account had run down, & a great sudden freshet of bills from Baltimore & Wash^{n} had made us nearly insolvent. Effected my negotiation, after much sweat & anxiety, and a remittance of about $30.000 from California came in at noon to strengthen our credit & put us on velvet again.

July 31. Sunday night. Hottest day of this burning Summer, according to my sensations, if not by the thermometer. Have staid within doors till to night, steaming with perspiration & vainly dawdling over H. Greeley's History of the War, Vol. I. At two o'clock came an *Extra.* News important, the precursor possibly of decisive events. At 4 A.M. yesterday Grant's mines in front of the 9th Army Corps were sprung, & one of the Petersburgh redoubts was blown up. Heavy firing was instantly opened along the whole line, under cover of which the 9th Corps carried two lines — or else one line — of entrenchments "with severe loss". The latest despatch purports to have been written yesterday aft^{n} & reports that we are in line of battle — only an artillery duel so far — & that a general engagement is impending, forced on Lee by Grant's strategy. I suppose Grant's move to the N. side of the James may have been a feint, for the purpose of withdrawing part of Lee's force from Petersburgh to Richmond. Well — it's safe to say that matters might look much worse than they do. Atlanta is probably at least as vital a point as Richmond, & I think we have established a firm grip on both. The former is the nerve centre of Rebellion, the latter it's right arm. Charleston it's organ of generation. — Strolled down to U.L. Club this ev'g & found Mr S.B.R. there, Lieber, Wm Hoppin, G.C.A. &c. Discourse of the Petersburgh news & of poor Mrs Arabella Barlow. I am not sanguine about Petersburgh. We have no right to expect speedy victory in this War, or to ask that Rebellion be suppressed till we have suffered more than we yet have done by way of atonement for the many years of servility & of anæsthetic processes applied to our moral sense, without which the South would have never dared rebel.

Aug: 1st. Monday. I am an incarnate Shower — of perspiration. O for thirty seconds experience of those grand rollers that are breaking this minute on Quogue beach. This dry heat suggests Zahara. At Van Buren's awhile this ev'g. He takes his family to Easthampton tomorrow. Afterwards with C.E.S. & G.C.A.

No news from Petersburgh this morn'g. But we have news by the aftn papers. Grant has delivered his grand *coup*, and has *failed.* He exploded his mines, opened his batteries, & pushed forward his columns, but had to withdraw them, or to let them withdraw themselves, with severe loss it would seem. Never mind. Attacks on Vicksburgh, Port Hudson, & *Sebastopol* failed ignominiously, but all three fell at last. Copperheads, sympathizers & traitors will rejoice over this news, but their joy may yet be turned to mourning — & the Country saved.

Heat lightning all the ev'g. There is now distant grumbling of thunder, & some hope of rain.

I am consoled for Grant's repulse by what C.E.S. tells me of the way in which the crowded passengers of a N.R. boat, of whom he was one, received certain violent talk by a casual copperhead. The man had a narrow escape from lynching. But for the presence & squeals of his wife he would have been roughly handled.

Aug: 2. Tuesday. Hotter. At 823 this P.M. When I took off my coat, & sat down to my daily routine of signing receipts, looking over cash-book, & the like, my forehead *dripped* all over my papers. There was abundant promise of a thundershower this aftn but it was not kept. The air seemed cooler for an hour — but the heat has returned now, in fullest force. Dined with C.E.S. at Maison Dorée.

People keep up their spirits about Petersburgh very creditably.

Knapp telegraphs death of three of our Relief Agents, including Prof: Hadley of "Union Theolog: Seminary", of overwork. Others very ill. — Rebel Raiders, under the valiant

McCausland, have been treating themselves to a little chivalric pastime, by burning up the unresisting & most pacific town of Chambersburgh — P[a]. A very "knightly" sport. Rebel towns & hamlets may have reason to rue it, before this game is played out. If these feeble inert Pennsylvanian borderers are thus harried, we are plainly justified in applying the torch to the homes of avowed secessionists in V[a] & Georgia. This savage violation of the usages of war, committed by order of a Rebel Chief, & not by uncontrolled stragglers, justifies — fully — Retaliation — Devastation — & Extermination. "Only those & nothing more."

Aug: 5. Friday ev'g. To Quogue by 8.30 A.M. train Wednesday. Find there has been a welcome visitation of heavy rain all along the E. half of L.I.

Find Rev. Morgan Dix the life of the house — keeping everybody entertained — (*dont* I envy him his social faculty!) — introducing "Croquet" — leading the simple *games* that make the ev'gs pleasant &c &c. The General, his papa, arrived last night.

Gen[l] D. brought up a rumor that Grant was about giving up this Richmond & Petersburgh job & coming back to the Potomac! A most lamentable result it would be. To day's papers refer to the existence of this rumor. It is founded on the notion that our repulse last Saturday has revealed to Lee the fact that he is able to hold his lines with part of his force, & that he will therefore certainly detach the rest of it to take Washington. I am no strategist, but I think it improbable that Lee will venture on that move.

Aug. 6th. Sat. Showery morn'g & a hot day. Have just returned from a sultry stroll, & a visit to the Club, where I find no news. — Collins at 823 this P.M. — He has been spending a couple of days at City Point. Says Grant was so certain of succeeding last Sat: that he had made all his arrangements for moving head-quarters into Petersburgh, and that his disgust at this failure brought on a sharp bilious attack. Collins was on the mail boat when it was fired on from near Harrison's Land'g. There was no little consternation on board. Telegram that one of our young "Auxiliary Relief Agents" has been picked off by a guerilla shot from the banks of James River.

It seems quite clear that this last attack on Petersburgh failed because of somebody's criminal bungling — & that "somebody" ought to be court-martialled & shot. But nobody will be. Whether "Somebody" is Meade or Burnside, I do not know.

Most seriously perturbed by what I hear, from independent trustworthy sources, about the increasing prevalence of Discouragement, & of aspirations for Peace "at any price". Our slow progress — bothered finances — & difficult recruiting can be endured or remedied, but if the National backbone become diseased, & degenerate into cartilage or gelatine, we are a lost People. Peace dictated by a Rebel General at Albany or Boston would be less humiliating. Calm dishonorable vile submission, with half one's strength still unemployed is worse than fighting it out, & getting pounded to death at last. Let us hope for better things. Could we but inspire our People with an hundredth part of the earnestness & resolution the Rebel leaders shew, all would be well, & that right early.

Aug: 7th. Sunday night. Long walk to night, bringing to at U.L. Club, where were Mr S.B.R. & *Botta*, who has a story that *Grant* has gone to Harper's Ferry, taking the bulk of the Army of the Potomac with him, & giving up Richmond & Petersburgh as a bad job. Perhaps. I am tending toward a desperate frame of mind, & feel like going South in disguise, as the modern Charlotte Corday & shooting Jeff. Davis. This desperation is mainly due to a fit of dyspepsia, now ravaging my inward parts. I acknowledge value received therefor, having dined on Roast Onions — a forbidden fruit, on wh: I seldom venture except when solitary & alone, as now.

Aug: 8. Monday night. Hot & hazy. Drought seems reinstalled. The sun was a red rayless disk from 5 P.M. till he disappeared. One of the bluest of many blue days. C.E.S. spent Sunday on a visit at Throg's Neck, where he fell in with Franklin & Baldy Smith. Both Generals think themselves aggrieved by Grant or Government or somebody, & both talk dismally of everybody's incapacity, of the failure of this campaign, and the gloom of the military situation, East & West. All which C.E.S. detailed to me with a Ghoulish gusto worthy of Bidwell himself. But there seems a woful plausibility in the evil prophesyings of these discontented Chieftains. If Grant's progress be effectually barred, & Lee can hold Richmond & Petersburgh with a quarter of his Army, why should he not send off the other three quarters to harry Pennsylvania, or (if he be wise) to reinforce Atlanta & compel Sherman to a retreat like that from Moscow fifty years ago?

φευ φευ ελελευ — Ullaloo — Ochone — Ochone — Οιμοι — ω ποποι — O Abraham, Uncle of thy People, why didst thou not provide a trifle of two hundred thousand more men in season for this crisis?

Then, as if this were not enough, the Political Caldron is seething — as it were much Nitric Acid in contact with boundless copper filings. There is fearful evolution of irritating offensive gas — & Heaven only knows what compound will be generated by the furious reaction of which we now see only the beginning. Peace Democrats & McClellanites are blatant. McClellan, it's said, will accept no nomination except on a War Platform. Good for McClellan. But I guess the Vallandighams will control the Democratic nominating Convention, & that we shall have a well defined struggle next fall between those who want to fight for our National life, and the Northern friends of the Rebellion. A momentous struggle it will be! How well I remember an aft^{n} in Wall St. *in 1842* — when I turned over the pages of the just published "Poems on Slavery, by H.W. Longfellow" with Henry Cram, both of us rather sniffing at the book as a remarkable avowal of "Abolition" sympathies by a poet a scholar & a gentleman, & how we were amused by the impractical sentimental notion embodied in it's last stanza. (The identical copy is before me now. Much has changed since that October afternoon.)

"There is a poor blind Samson in this land
    Shorn of his strength & bound in bonds of steel,
Who may, in some grim revel, raise his hand,
    And shake the pillar of this Commonweal,
Till the vast Temple of our Liberties
A shapeless mass of wreck & rubbish lies."

Longfellow may have been a prophet after all. — Wolcott Gibbs, D[r] Jenkins & D[r] Douglas here to night. Much business done. Our (S.C.) relations with Army Surgeons in Army of Potomac need looking after. I fear some of it's Medical Staff (e.g. one Lowenthal) pervert the supplies we issue.

Aug: 9. Tuesday. Sultry muggy dog-day weather. Am just from a session of Com: on Admissions at U.L. Club. We perspired freely & passed a few new names, that of C.E.S. among them. Gleams of light to day — destined to be delusive & short-lived, I fear — like the effulgence of a decomposing lobster. We have certainly smitten the Raiders, or Invaders, whichever they are, on the Upper Potomac — and Farragut has passed the outer Forts of Mobile Harbor, probably after a severe fight, & captured at least three ships or steamers of the Rebel flotilla there. It's Admiral, Buchanan, is a prisoner, all but one leg, carried away in action. Farragut is "approaching the City". We get this news thro' a despatch to Richmond from little Maury, now a traitor & a Major General. His despatch contains not a single word of brag — but he says the Monitor Tecumseh was sunk. We seem to have landed a force (under Asboth?) to take Fort Gaines in the rear. This looks well, but there are no doubt heavy earthworks around Mobile itself, & it's said our iron-clads draw too much water to reach them. And how is Farragut to get out again, if he be repulsed?

Aug: 10. Fearful heat. Savings Bank Trustees sat this aft[n], perspiring horribly. After adjournment, to 823. This ev'g Binney came in, & we strolled out to the U.L. Club, where we sat an hour and watched the rockets & fireworks of the McClellan mass-meeting. It's stands & oratorical centres were on the 14th St. side (the *South* side) of *Union* Square, but there was much promenading & processionizing round the square with no end of lanterns, torches, Roman candles & bands of music. [10.15 P.M. There goes a prolonged roar from the assemblage, that is impressive. Can Geo: B. have condescended to appear in person?] The legends on lanterns & banners indicated no favor for the "Peace Democracy". This is a symptom of health, & good as far as it goes. But no doubt many of those who carried them assisted at the riots of last summer, & would like to repeat that little performance. As the columns passed our windows, they groaned heartily for the "Shoddy Club" & the "Abolitionists", & I thought a volley of paving stones no unlikely phenomenon. Sam. Barlow & C° have spent a great deal of money on this meeting, & it will probably prove to have been successfully managed — "a most imposing spontaneous demonstration by the People". — The Herald is playing a game I do not understand, attacking McClellan & asserting *Grant's* superiority in generalship & in availability as a candidate.

Aug: 11. Thursday. Have spent the day perspiring energetically & doing little beside. Heat is fearful — literally *inclement*, or merciless. — At 823 this aft^{n}, & to night at Monthly meeting of U.L. Club, where was a creditable gathering, for such weather. — Last night's McClellan meeting seems an insignificant affair. No one of any weight or influence took part in the proceedings. The speakers were mostly obscure third rate men. "Democratic" leaders kept away. The tone of the speeches & of the Resolutions inclines toward a Vallandigham, or Peace-at-any-price, platform.

Good news from Mobile by Rebel despatches to Richmond. They refer to our "victory over" their ironclads (of which felon fleet only one seems to have escaped) and inform us that Fort Powell has been evacuated & blown up & Fort Gaines surrendered under circumstances discreditable to it's chivalric commandant, a "hightoned Alabama gentleman", Anderson by name. He is evidently in bad odor just now with his chivalric military superiors, & suspected of cowardice or treachery. Poor Anderson. — Per Contra, people talk darkly of the *failure* of Grant's campaign, & of Sherman's.

Aug: 15. I find no material war-news in town — only farther details of Farragut's victory in Mobile Bay. That transaction gains by closer acquaintance. The veteran Admiral *lashed in the foretop of his flagship*, for wider range of view, & sending down his orders through a speaking tube, is a new feature of Naval War. How England would brag & blow about a like procedure by Nelson or Collingwood! Sorry to learn that T.A.M. Craven commanded the Monitor *Tecumseh*, & went down with her, shattered by a submarine chivalric torpedo.

Aug: 16. Tuesday night. Rather cooler. That is, my shirt collar did not collapse & wilt down into a wisp of wet linen, till I was half way down town. Stopped at the office of Treasurer of Metrop: Fair to leave E's MS *Report*, for the printer, and at Savings' Bank — this being my week of nominal attendance. At N° 68 find that C.E.S. has gone to Saratoga, to escort Madame home. Poor Charley McKnight called, for counsel about his Will, which needs change now that his beautiful wife is dead. She was his guide and governess — his reliance & mainstay, in all his affairs.

To 823 — then for dinner to Maison Dorée, — then home for a cup of coffee. Turned out for a walk at eight, but was warned home by a threatening thundercloud in the N.W. — Nothing has come of it, as yet.

Grant is again reported to have begun a grand strategic move, of the deepest & deadliest character. Do not know what it is, but one of it's elements is a canal that is to cut off a great bend of James River. May it prove more prosperous than his *mine*!

The great Election of next Novr looks more & more obscure dubious & muddled every day. *Lincoln* is drifting to leeward. So much is certain. There is rumor of a move by our wire-pullers & secret unofficial governors to make him withdraw in favor of Chase, or somebody else, on whom the whole Republican party (if such a thing exist) can heartily unite. Frémont's nomination is coldly received here, tho' it may find favor in Missouri. John Jay (!!!) & a few others are denouncing Lincoln for making Abolition of Slavery the object of the war, & insisting that he ought to aim only at Restoration of the Union with or without slavery. A strange position for J.J.! But he is by nature factious — unable to work with others — or to accomplish anything. — His only talent is that of criticizing & retarding the efforts of his own friends & allies to carry out his own principles. There is talk of a movement to get A.L. to withdraw, so that some one may be nominated on whom all National men can unite. But A.L. the venerable, probably "dont see it" — "Not if this Court knows itself, & she think she do", as he would probably say on receiving the suggestion.

Aug: 17. C.E.S. just from Saratoga, & Agnew with whom I dined at M.D. & who is just from New England & the Northern & Western parts of this state agree in a bad report of the general feeling. Great complaints, even by the most loyal men, of the shortcomings & mistakes of Government: and the "Peace Democrats" loud & truculent in threats of vengeance on Black Republicans & abolitionists & in talk about revolution & repudiation of the War Debt — all which will do them no good. That blatant traitor Walter Church is the representative of this school. "Maledicti Pacifici" just now. It is satisfactory to know that these scoundrels have no love for the popular hero McClellan, but denounce him & Uncle Abe alike.

Agnew, generally so hopeful, is deeply darkly hideously *blue*. Thinks both Grant & Sherman on the eve of disaster for want of men — because the Administration is afraid to go vigorously forward with the draft, lest it lose a few votes next November!

Grant seems doing well with his last move. Nothing new from Sherman or Farragut. Sheridan may be about delivering an important battle in the Valley of the Shenandoah — that "dark & bloody ground."

Aug: 18. A little less hot, but the weather is still oppressive. It is not at all clear to me why I have brought out this very valuable Record, for I have nothing to put in it. Nothing new on these premises — at *Bank for Savings* — at 68 Wall St. at 823 Bdway at Maison D. (where I dined) or at Soc^y^ Library where I brought up after my ev'g's stroll — unless it may be that Knapp sends in a long formal letter, complaining of our action in taking the Army of the Potomac out of his immediate charge, & making Dr Douglas Superintendant of our service at City Point. He has much to say about his official position & his "self-respect". We live & learn, & sometimes learn what we would rather not know. I had supposed Knapp to be exalted far above any paltry feeling like this. But it seems he is made of common clay after all. Two Ideals smashed within 60 days, Knapp & M^rs^ — X— , to wit. Very bad & demoralizing.

Aug: 19. Friday. Deeply darkly hideously blue, & for a despicable reason enough.

At 823 this aft^n^ as usual. Resolved to drop one of our Agents, Rev: Van Ingen of Western N.Y. who is suspected of being a jackal of Seymours, & of serving him as a spy in the Army of the Potomac. Dined with Agnew & brought him home for a cup of XXX black coffee, pending which symposium Mistress Ellie presented herself. She came from Quogue with Morgan Dix to see her excellent old grandmamma, who tho' still up & "about" seems slowly settling down. After a good talk over things in general we took her to 24 Union Square, & then I went with Agnew to his house for another Committee session & a little bit of *Surgery*.

My swelled face of last month has never quite subsided, & a new abscess has lately formed working toward the *outside* (a new experience) with some little pain & increase of swelling. Agnew opened it, & the pleasing performance will probably have to be repeated.

Pauper et miserrimus! I see no bright spot anywhere. Rebeldom is beginning to bother Sherman's long line of communications. We may expect to hear any day that he is fighting his way back to Chattanooga & that Grant has bid Richmond good bye. I fear the blood & treasure spent on this summer's campaign have done little for the Country. This is the kind of talk to which I respond with "thrasonicall huffe-snuffe" (vide Stanyhurst) whenever I hear it, but it certainly has a dismal plausibility. — Then these infernal Peace mongers — how busily & malignantly they are working to spread their own foul disease of baseness & disloyalty, & how omnipotently they will be despised & execrated hereafter! They are moral lepers necessarily but unfortunately allowed free range & permitted to do what they can to infect the whole community. Whether they succeed or fail they will be gibbetted in the History of these Times, & no one despises them, even now, more heartily than the Rebel leaders for whom they are humbly pimping. They have not yet corrupted the People to the point of Surrender, but the People may be deluded into electing some so-called War-Democrat who will betray the Country.

Lincoln's blunder in his Letter "to all whom it may concern" may cost him his election. By declaring that "Abandonment of Slavery" is a fundamental article in any negotiation for Peace & Settlement he has given the disaffected & discontented a weapon that doubles their power of mischief. It's wonderful what an ill savor the word *Abolition* has acquired during our long period of constitutional subjugation by the Slave holding

Caste. One would think it a good word, & likely to be popular with a free people, but it is'nt. I never call myself an Abolitionist without a feeling that I am saying something rather reckless & audacious. So it will be for this generation at least. People have not yet learned the lesson these three years should have taught them. They need more flogging, & seem likely to get it.

The nomination & platform of the (pseudo) Democratic Convention — Chicago, 29th inst. — are anxiously looked for. Can the two wings of that Party — the Peace Democrats & the War Democrats — work together at all? Is not *schism* inevitable? Will the Convention nominate some obscure man & run him without committing him or his Party for or against the War?

McClellan, the inevitable, is talked of as nominee. So is Grant. Iscariot Seymour is in active squirm & wriggle for the nomination. Being an adroit scoundrel he may get it. The names of Millard Fillmore & Franklin Pierce have been indecently exhumed. Should either be nominated I shall expect to meet some great re-vivified Lizard or Saurian, from the "Lias formation" (?) marching along Quogue Beach some fine morning on his way to Washington, to report to the Chief of the Smithsonian Institution. Then there is Judge Nelson, a learned lawyer & full blooded Copperhead, but he would not make a good popular available candidate.

If the Chicago Sanhedrim have sagacity & patriotism enough to nominate John A. Dix, I believe he will be elected. Many "Republicans" would vote for him. Possibly I should do so, tho' I object to "swapping horses while you are crossing a river" (vide Facetiæ by A.L.) But Genl D. is too honest & true to find favor with politicians. Even if they recognize his availability, the question remains, for every one of the gang "Cui bono? Suppose he is sure to be elected, what good will his election do me? He wo'nt give me a foreign embassy or anything else for supporting him in Convention. So I had better support the claims of the Hon: Judas Jobbinger, who knows how to take care of his friends."

Aug: 22. Monday. So the Surgeon General is found guilty on every one of the charges — dismissed the service, & declared "incapable" &c in the usual formula! An unrighteous finding I believe — but what can we, or anybody, do about it?

Hammond will probably appeal to the public. He will hardly get fifty people outside the circle of his private friends to read & digest several cubic feet of evidence for & against him. But a well written statement of certain matters outside the trial might be made very damaging to the Sec: of War, & if Hammond could smite him under the fifth rib, he would be fully consoled for his own downfall. [What a brute of a Pen this is!]

A most sultry day. To night promises a thundershower, & is made bearable by a lively sea-breeze. Yesterday was a day of steady quiet uninterrupted rain — a novelty in these times.

I'm still Blue — more properly black & blue.

At meeting of Com: on School of Mines this morning, Dr Torrey announced that Gouv: Kemble has presented the school a collection of minerals, purchased for $6000.00. Long life to Kemble! This sets us on our legs. Egleston posts to Baltimore (where the collection lies) to take possession of it. We authorized Torrey & Egleston to go on at once, under Barnard's supervision, to set up their metallurgical furnaces, & other Cantrips. The outside subscriptions now on deposit in the Trust Co ($2400.00) will pay for them. Again I say Vivat Kemble! Let us pass Resolutions about Kemble.

With Knapp Agnew & Jenkins at 823. Long session. Knapp's official & personal dignities — both — are sorely outraged by the restrictions we have imposed on the Washington office. I'm very sorry for it. — Raining hard now. I have been obliged to close the window & shut off the sea-breeze, & oh how hot I am. — News from Sherman does not look well, tho' it is of no great importance. Grant has made a new move, extending his left, & occupying the Weldon R.R. Lee was compelled to come out & attack. Sharp fighting. Results rather mixed in quality. We have lost heavily, but seem to hold our new position — a position it much concerns Lee to recover, if he can. — Ellie returned to Quogue Sat. aft^n, escorted by Jem R. — Our neighbour Rev. A.C. Coxe is invited to become Assis^t Bishop of Western N.Y.

"O General McClellan, he is the man.
He licked the Rebels at Antiet*an*" is a popular song now. One hears it's very good Keltic melody whistled everywhere, as just now by someone whom it helps defy the rain. A various reading devotes this lyric to Grant, & makes him "lick the Rebels wherever he can" — which is equivocal praise.

Aug: 23. At 823 I find a letter from *Hammond*, full of fight. He has published a Card announcing a Review of the Case, & is not in the least cast down. His promised Appeal to the People will need careful revision by some clear cool eye, or it will do him yet farther damage. He sends on a copy (official) of the *finding*. Am glad to see that the adverb "*corruptly*" & other words & phrases in the Charges & specifications are expressly excepted in the finding as not proven. So he stands convicted of little more than the technical sin of purchasing supplies too freely & not in the way technically sanctioned by some Act of Congress half a century old. His conviction looks like a base tyrannical outrage on Law & Right effected by the vast power of the man at the head of the War Department who hates Hammond, & whose hates are as implacable & unscrupulous as they are bitter & dangerous.

The N.Y. Times published a savage editorial about Hammond this morn'g, but without Raymond's knowledge, as I hear. It is to change it's base tomorrow, & be more moderate.

Aug: 25. Thursday. Bitter hot. Not much to write about. Visited N.Y. Hospital by Mrs Eleanor's invitation (dined with her yesterday) & walked thro' the Military Wards with her. Fine fellows — sorely wounded or diseased — but as usual patient & plucky. Told one of them that if I had only suffered what he had for the Country, I should be the most unbearable swell in N.Y. — which did tickle & arride him. They all give great glory to the San. Com. — Mrs Eleanor has done for the last two years & is still doing noble self sacrificing work at that Hospital. She spends some eight hours there every day.

Van Buren returned from East Hampton. Saw him this ev'g. Has raised a full beard, — no improvement.

After being severely repulsed in his attacks on our new position across the Weldon R.R. Lee seems to have given that up as a bad job. So far well. But Lieber tells me to night in confidence that he receives most gloomy letters from Halleck. I rank Halleck among the least of small potatoes, but he knows more about the state of affairs than I do. The Peace faction grows more & more rampant & truculent. I predict that Belmont &

Barlow will manipulate the Chicago convention into nominating McClellan on a non-committal platform, & that if elected he will betray the Country.

Aug. 26. Friday. Wasted most of the morn'g in pursuit of a substitute. It is still not quite certain the Draft set down for 5th Sept. will come off, but if it should not, or if I should not be conscripted, it would still be erring on the safe side to have sent a man into the ranks — tho' $700.00 is a jolly price to pay for the privilege. God knows how gladly I'd serve in person, but my nearsightedness makes me worthless for Military duties proper, & I believe I'm doing the Cause more service here in N.Y. than I should if detailed as a Hospital steward or the like. — So I proceeded to a rather "shady" law-office in Broome St. where I found an Invalid — a very respectable fellow, with whom I made my arrangements. The candidate for glory was outside, with another Invalid (one-armed) mounting guard over him, & all four of us proceeded to the office in the Park, where he was duly inspected & promptly *rejected*. I was not very sorry, for he was a most scurvy loafer, a Kelt of the lowest degree, probably a hod carrier in embarrassed circumstances & just convalescing from a bad drunk. — This will prevent my going Quogue-ward tomorrow, for I must, if possible, provide a substitute & "get out of the Draft" before leaving town. It is some consolation to remember that if I went thither in my present grim & gloomy frame of mind, my arrival would doubtless turn all Mr Foster's milk sour. — To night Agnew Van Buren & Jenkins here, & V.B. brought in Hammond who's staying at his house.

Hammond is as jolly as possible — even under these adverse circumstances, and full of the pamphlet he proposes to issue. Heaven send him grace to write it with only a moderate degree of intemperance, & wisdom to choose some judicious friend to help him. He talked over the evidence. His statements agree with my recollection of his printed defence & of Bingham's (the Judge Advocate's) very bitter & partizan Reply. The mental processes of the majority of the Court (which seems to have stood 5 to 4) must have been most peculiar when they decided on their finding. It was doubtless under pressure of Stanton — whom I take to be among the severest of our many public calamities, and by far the worst of our prominent politicians. He seems to me thoroughly *corrupt*, not in the ordinary sense of the term, for I do not think he could be bought with any amount of money. But his judgment & his patriotism — if he have any — & his conscience — be the same more or less — are hourly corrupted by his vindictive tyrannical temper, and his intolerance of any opinion but his own. I believe he would crush the most valuable officer in the service for expressing a doubt as to any point in the policy of his Department, & I fear his moral sense is not strong enough to make him scrupulous about the means to that end. He seems to me corruptible & corrupted by his abundant hates & his uncontrolled self-will, and the result of their action is quite as bad for the Country as if he were venal.

Nothing material from Petersburgh, Atlanta, Harper's Ferry, or Mobile. It is rather comforting to study the map of Virginia however, & the system of RRoads that centre at Petersburgh & Richmond. Our grasp of the Weldon R.R. must be a serious bore to Lee. It cuts the line that could & should have been cut at Wilmington N.C. two years ago.

It looks more & more likely that the Chicago convention will nominate McClellan by acclamation next Monday & adopt an obscurely worded doubtful non-committal programme of Resolutions under which the Nominee will be able to disintegrate & destroy the Country like a gentleman & a Statesman. If so, they will try to appease the Peace Democracy traitors by nominating some Vallandigham or Seymour for V.P. They may win — tho' Heaven forbid! for the Administration has damaged itself fearfully of late. I fear the World & Express do not lie (for a wonder) when they say the Post office is no longer safe. Jenkins told us to night that his recent letters from *Hammond* seemed to have been tampered with.

Aug: 27. Sat: In the house nearly all day with severe headache. It seemed unprovoked, for we had no supper last night. Toddled to 823, & to dinner (M.D.) at four, & visited the Club to night in search of farther news. Unsuccessfully.

Aft^{n} papers report a severe engagement on the 25th, when Lee made a third attempt to recover the Weldon Road. The reports are partly official, but obscure. The sum appears to be that we were driven back with heavy loss of prisoners (God help them!) but still hold the Road, that the Rebels left the field, & their dead & wounded, & that their loss was unusually large. It is received as good news, & I think rightly. Lee's repeated efforts to drive us from our new position seem to shew it's importance, & that while it is held, Grant has his finger & thumb on the aorta of Richmond. If we had a spare column now to move on the Danville Road! But

"If wishes were horses, beggars would ride.

If wishes were fishes we'd have some, fried". That exquisite & epigrammatic embodiment of Wisdom in verse is among my very earliest recollections.

Lincoln manifestly loses ground every day. The most zealous "Republican" partizans talk doubtfully of his chances. Sorry for it, tho' it would be great gain to the Country to unseat Stanton. Symptoms of an "independent" movement to nominate Gen: Dix. Mr S.B.R. talked it over with the Gen'l. last night. He would probably *go in*, for a free fight, if nominated by any respectable party or organization. But getting up any such machine is a large job. I suppose the very best thing that could befal the Country next Novr would be the election of so honest & able a man as Dix to the Presidency. I know he veered about between /48 & /56 in his views about certain matters & has been abused therefor. But no one ever questioned his integrity or his patriotism.

Aug: 28. Sunday night. Continuation of headache & a wretchedly dull day within doors tho' everything outside looked bright & bracing, for it has grown cooler. Tried vainly for an after dinner nap, & went to U.L. Club this ev'g, where were Mr S.B.R., Lieber, Coit, the inevitable G.W. Blunt, Gov: Andrew (Mass:) Frank Howe & Hon: Isaac Sherman, *cum aliis*. Talk rather good. A despatch came in announcing that Richmond papers say Fort Morgan is "in possession of the enemy". Another (from Tribune office) that there is nothing new before Petersburgh. Lieber told me in great confidence a large story about a "reliable gentleman" who has arrived in town from N. Carolina via Nassau & is now on his way to Wash^{n} with overtures to Government from the "Union men" (?) of N.C. Georgia & (I think) Alabama proposing to pronounce for the Union & rebel agst the Rebellion, if they can be assured their States will be readmitted as States. I put no faith in the story & less (if possible) in the hypothetical Emissary & his constituents. — Lieber told of his going to Church at Charleston S.C. just after the Nullification fuss there, & taking up a prayer-book on the margin whereof he found pencilled opposite the Prayer for the Pres'dt of the U.S. "D— the Scoundrel." — And of a talk with Calhoun, who became furious when Lieber suggested that one of our National wants was a National Name. He said we were not a Nation & that this want of a name was conclusive proof of it — that we ought not to be a Nation, & that if a name could be devised & generally adopted comprehending the aggregation of States, it would be a public calamity. I suppose that up to 1861 the maleficent names in our history are Arnold, Jefferson, Burr, & above all Calhoun. Lieber thinks we should try to revive the old Norse appellation of *Vinland*. I rather like *Alleghania*, shortened to *Alghania*, & that we should call ourselves *Alghans*. But Calhoun's views may be dismally verified within six months, which will save us the trouble of considering questions of a name for the Country by abolishing & extinguishing the Country itself. — General impression to night that McClellan will surely be nominated at Chicago, and that he will not run well. I think A.L. would find him a most troublesome antagonist.

Aug: 29th. Monday. To office of Provost Marshal of my District this A.M. (Capt. Manierre's) where after waiting an hour, I purveyed myself a substitute — a big "Dutch" boy of 20 or thereabouts — for the moderate consideration of $1100.00. Thus do we approach the almshouse at an accelerating rate of speed. My *Alter ego* could make a good soldier if he tried. Gave him my address, & told him to write me if he found himself in Hospital or in trouble, & that I would try to do what I properly could to help him. I got myself exempted at this high price because I have felt all day as if some attack of illness were at hand & as if it might be unsafe to leave my liability to Draft unsettled.

At Wall St. & at 823 as usual & a solitary dinner at Maison Dorée. Home for a cup of coffee, & then to U.L. Club, where I spent an hour or two in talk over the premonitory symptoms of the Chicago Convention. They look well for the Country, & ill for the Democratic Party. The Convention has appointed a Committee on Resolutions, of which Vallandigham & F. Pierce & other Pediculi of the same species are members. If this action indicate the policy of the Dem: party the Country is safe — for the People is not yet so degraded & disheartened as to tolerate it. We are not yet prepared to listen to proposals for Recognition & Disunion.

Brought Dr Peters home with me. I've been troubled these three days with severe acute pain in the right side & in the back — quite serious when I make certain muscular movements, cough, or draw a long breath. Cannot account for it, unless it is because I stumbled Thursday or Friday aft^{n} going up the stairs of 823 & may have incurred some strain or sprain in my effort to save myself from falling. It's accompanied by no symptoms — unless it may be two sudden turns of dizziness that I experienced on my way to Wall St. from the Prov: Marshal's this morning. I was almost obliged to seat myself on the nearest door-step. It was very bad & suggested Softening of the brain!!!

Sundry Resolutions have been moved in this Convention which it will not easily dispose of without committing itself to one side or the other of the great question (underlying all others, even that of Slavery & Abolition) — Are we a Nation & a People like France & Spain & England & Scotland, or a mere agglomeration of independent provinces with no *Country* at all?

Sept: 2^{d}. Friday. To Quogue Tuesday 30th. Tore myself away this morning, & returned to lonely old N° 74 at half past seven this ev'g.

Nothing noteworthy in Tuesday's journey but the plague of musquitoes in the R.R. cars. All the passengers thumped themselves from Jamaica to Riverhead as if they belonged to some new order of Flagellants. Never knew musquitoes to invade a moving train before. Found Ellie & her squad of Infantry well & jolly. Spent my daylight hours on the beach mostly with Johny & Temple & a Maynard Rifle. Johny & I improve in our practice.

Chicago Convention has nominated McClellan. That was expected. But the baseness of the "platform" on which he is to run was unexpected. Jeff. Davis might have drawn it. The word Rebel does not occur in it. It contemplates surrender & abasement. If McClellan consent to be it's representative, he condemns his name to infamy. So shameful an avowal of dishonor has never been made by any Political party North of the Potomac — nor even South of it. Gen: Dix thinks McC. will decline a nomination on such terms. We shall see. I have little faith in McClellan's principles. I could write at least a page of indignation about the insult these Chicago Resolutions have inflicted on the Country, were it not rather late, & were I not rather tired. If the People should endorse them next Nov^r^, the Country is not worth saving; the title "Citizen of the United States" is equivalent to that of Coward, faineant, Serf & Craven, & I will emigrate, & become a citizen of some community of Gregarious blue baboons in South Africa. It's a hopeful indication however that Gen: Dix (who does not love the Administration) denounces these Resolutions as shameful & scandalous. He tells me there will be no draft next Monday. So I expected. But I do not regret the $1100.00 I paid for a substitute. The big Dutchman therewith purchased looked as if he could do good service.

Sept: 3^d^. Sat: Glorious news this morning — viz: *Atlanta taken at last*!!! It comes in official form, seemingly most authentic, but there are doubters who distrust it, and the appearance of no additional intelligence since morning gives a certain plausibility to their scepticism. So I suspend all jubilation for the present. If it be true, it is (coming at this political crisis) the greatest event of the War. It would seem that Sherman moved to the South of Atlanta, leaving one corps to guard his communications, & cutting off Hood's: that Hood thereupon left his entrenchments, gave battle, & was beat — more or less — & that pending the battle this reserve corps walked into the beleaguered City by it's back door. We shall probably know more tomorrow. God grant our first news prove true.

A very busy day. Letters, & a Complaint, *Cryder* v. *Slocom*, founded on a Contract for sale of a big house on 5th Av:.

Dined with G.C.A. at Maison Dorée. Glad to learn that all but the most inveterate malignant Copperheads denounce & repudiate the Chicago "Platform". Even the *Herald* condemns it. They say McC. will come out with a letter repudiating it, & consenting to run as an "independent candidate". This may be part of a politic scheme intended to secure the votes of both Peace & War Democrats. McClellan is in the hands of Belmont & Barlow, & I fear they can manipulate him as they please. — At U.L. Club to night, watching for news. None came. Told Mr S.B.R. that I would be glad if he could somehow hint to his special friend Hon: Wash: Hunt, member of the Chicago Convention, that he was not particularly wanted as a visitor on these premises, Sunday ev'gs or weekdays, or at any time.

Sept: 5. Monday. Two days of cold Easterly Storm. Thank God, the fall of Atlanta is fully confirmed. We hardly dared believe it till to day. It's importance both moral & military is immense. Hardee is said to be killed, and two less notorious Rebel generals. He is no great loss to Secessia. Hood seems to have destroyed much rolling stock & stores, wh: he could not carry off. — We have news that the rebel privateer *Georgia* has been bagged by the Niagara (her name makes the event a coincidence, for I suppose Sherman's success gives us mastery of nearly all that State) & there is some reason to fear a complication with England, as the Georgia was sailing under British colors. — Dined with Agnew after a busy day. He is over-worked, & may be in danger of breaking down, wh: would be a grave misfortune. — The general howl against the base policy offered for our endorsement at Chicago is refreshing. Bitter opponents of Lincoln join in it heartily, & denounce the proposition that the Country should take it's hands off the throat of half-strangled Treason, go down on it's knees before it's prostrate but insolent enemy, & beg it to do a little friendly negotiating. The audacious infamy of the Chicago traitors seems likely to produce a reaction, & make the Administration party vigorous & united once more. Friends of Govt have been somewhat languid & disheartened for a couple of months — always on the defensive, & apologetic in the tone of their talk. *Chicago* has put new life into them.

"Is all our travail turned to this effect?
After the slaughter of so many peers,
So many Captains, gentlemen, & soldiers,
That in this quarrel have been overthrown
And sold their bodies for their Country's benefit,
Shall we at last conclude effeminate Peace?"

Lord, help us, and save us from *Ourselves*, our own deadliest enemy! —

How it rains & blows! Surf on Quogue beach must be grand tonight.

Sept: 6. Tuesday. Easterly storm continues, cold grey & sour, so I went not to Quogue this P.M. as I meant to do. Deplorably down hearted & blue all day long. But at two o'clock a comfortable announcement appeared on the Com: Advertiser bulletin. John Morgan's raiding force in Tennessee has been attacked & routed, & their hard-riding moss-trooper of a General is killed. He was an enterprising mischievous bandit. G.W. Blunt says tomorrow's McClellan *ratification meeting* on Union Square ought in decency to be postponed "on account of a death in the family".

Belmont tells C.E.S. who returned from Newport this morn'g, that McClellan's letter of Acceptance will be most satisfactory, even to the most resolute "War Democrats" & will secure his Election. He may succeed in mystifying people with plausible generalities & commonplaces. If he take his stand on the Chicago Platform without some attempt at a protest, my faith in his honesty & loyalty will be shattered. Major Halpine (Miles O'Reilly) tells —— that he & Jem Brady & others are urging "little Mac" to say in substance "I accept the nomination, and I adopt the platform. I want negotiation — armistice & Peace, as badly as anybody. My policy will be to expedite them by a very vigorous prosecution of the War, which must soon put us in a position to negotiate with advantage for settlement, reconstruction, & pacification". Halpine is a very shrewd fellow, & on the fence till McClellan shall distinctly define his ground. He wants to support him — which he can do most efficiently — provided McC. set himself right & repudiate the Vallandigham wing of his party. He thinks the defeat of Lincoln would give the

Rebels "a canoe to come ashore in" — that we cannot hope they will consent to scuttle their own ship & founder at sea, even after many calamities like the loss of Atlanta — that they are tired of war & will come back if we do something that looks like compromise. Perhaps. It would be a most hazardous experiment.

A new danger looms up, larger & darker every day. It is nothing less than Civil War in the N.W. States! They are honeycombed by secret societies working in aid of the Rebellion & controlled by reckless desperate traitors for whom the gallows is far too good. The navigation of the Mississippi is still closed to ordinary trade, & that fact enables these "Knights of the Golden Circle" (more properly Caitiffs of the Hempen Circle) to spread disaffection among Western farmers & tradesmen. Both parties seem to be arming. — — — The great Experiment of Democracy may be destined to fail a century sooner than I expected, in disastrous explosion & general Chaos, & this our Grand Republic over which we have bragged so offensively may be cast down as a great millstone into the Sea & perish utterly — and all this within sixty days from the date of these presents. So much for traitors, demagogues & lunatics! All the South & half the North are absolutely demented. Neither Lincoln nor McClellan is strong enough to manage so large & populous an Asylum. Who is? Satan seems superintendant *de facto* just now.

Old Fuller wrote, 200 years ago, when Civil War was ravaging English homes, "Our sins were ripe. God could no longer be just if we were prosperous."

At U.L. Club to night. Com: on Admissions. No quorum. Proposed breakfast in honor of Prof: Goldwin Smith of Oxford.

Sept: 8. Political indications furnished by our Quogue family are encouraging. A fortnight ago Blake & Charley Lawrence expected to stump the State for McClellan. But the Chicago Platform has changed their views. They cannot support McClellan. No matter what he says in his letter of acceptance. If he accept the nomination he is bound by the resolutions that define the policy he is nominated to represent — & how can his co-nominee for the Vice-Presidency (Geo: H. Pendleton, an avowed Peacemonger) & members of Congress & Governors of States, nominated by the same Party Convention or by affiliated Conventions be disposed of? Must they each & all write letters denouncing their own Party principles, or explaining them away? Blake insists that Lincoln possesses neither ability nor honesty, but cannot oppose him, *now*. He undervalues Lincoln — but no matter. Lincoln is an honest man, of considerable ability (far below the first grade) but made odious by the vagaries & the arbitrary temper of Mr Secretary Stanton. — As for McClellan — approved by Vallandigham & the London Times, & the Asylum burning Rioters who hurraed for him in July /63.

Sept: 9th. Friday. Agnew & Jenkins in the Library to night, & G.C.A. & C.E.S. at the supper-table.

McClellan's letter of Acceptance in the morning papers. Will it help him much? It is made up of Platitudes floating in mucilage, without a single plain word against Treason & Rebellion. It has no ring of true metal, and no suggestion of magnetic power in word phrase or thought. But it is artfully drawn & may do it's work, especially if Grant or Sherman be badly defeated any time before November. It's artificers know how to face both ways — to use language for the concealment of thought — and to humbug & seduce the Sovereign People — as well as any Demagogues in History. Wonderful to consider how much study has been expended on every word of this lamentable lifeless epistle by at least a score of eminent politic experienced Copperheads! It's flatness is due, in some degree, no doubt, to the labor it cost, but still more to it's constructors' ignorance of any sincere patriotic purpose. McClellan wrote none of it. I suppose him far more honest than the Scoundrels who are using him, but he is as Putty in the hands of Barlow & Co. and the majority of that set would rather see Jeff: Davis President to day than "Abe Lincoln".

Said one of the Orators at last night's Ratification meeting — in substance — "When we have elected McClellan, we will bring back the Prodigal Son to his home, & tell him we have subjugated the Common enemy that alienated us, & caused all these calamities" — viz: the opponents of Slavery extension into the Territories, whom it is convenient to call Abolitionists. In other words — Let us carry this Election & then hang

Horace Greeley & H. Ward Beecher, & put ourselves wholly under the feet of the "prodigal" woman-flogging fire eating law-breaking member of the Family.

Where in all history is one to look for a Political Party base enough for a comparison with our Copperheads?

To change the subject abruptly: — Talboys says that Miss Bell Perry (M[rs] Belmont's sister) who lately married Tiffany of Baltimore — both being pretty well stricken in years — can certainly count on a peaceful & happy life — because the couple will never have any little Tiffs!!! — Rev: Bellows has been making a San: Com: speech at San Francisco, & told his audience inter alia, that he had the minutes of our Standing Committee's daily meetings sent to him by every steamer because "*when the cat's away the mice will play.*" Very cool indeed. Want of self-appreciation is not among "the Dominie's" faults. Confound his impudence! — Gold *falls*, tho' still about 230. Stream of recruits to the front reported steady & large. Rumors from City Point are hopeful. Rebels said to be massing on our left for another effort to dislodge us from our position on the Weldon R.R. which position is said to be strong in men & in field-works. Private letters to 823 indicate that Grant is stronger than is generally thought. The largest estimate of his force is 117 000, including 7000 in hospital, of whom a certain Number, more or less, will become fit for duty every day. But we rather discourage the transmission of information on points of this sort by our Inspectors. — Now that Atlanta has fallen, Rebel newspapers discover that it was not worth holding, & declare that Sherman's occupation of it is quite a blow to the "Federal" cause, & equivalent to a Rebel Victory. Nothing is so characteristic of Southerners as *Brag* — self assertion — tall talking — & loud lying. Were they thoroughly squelched & subjugated tomorrow, they would say & swear that they never dreamed of establishing an independent Confederacy, & that they had been fighting for "the old Flag" ever since they opened fire on Fort Sumter. — Rumors continue of overtures by the State of Georgia or by somebody professing to represent that *soi-disant* Nation for her return to the Union. These rumors are so persistent that I begin to think some dim shadow of some small fact may have set them going. Any move that way by even a respectable minority of any one "Seceded" State would probably give Rebellion it's coup-de-grace. But I fear the slaveholding Aristocracy is still omnipotent in every Southern State.

I say, with Marat, "O Peuple babillard, si tu savais agir!" One month of honest hearty enthusiasm & work, like May 1861, would secure our National Triumph. But we are in danger of perishing from faintheartedness & internal discord.

Sept: 12th. Last night Gov: Andrew here, among others. He talks confidently & hopefully. Also that dubious cosmopolite "M. Harrisse" the Cynic philosopher of Quogue. He seems a diluted Gurowski — a learned Pig like the expatriated Count — much less learned & a little less swinish. "I do desire we may be better strangers."

McClellan's Letter, tho' so meek & mild is too martial to suit the *Extreme Left*. Vallandigham denounces it. The "Daily News" & the yet more openly traitorous "Metropolitan Record" insist very logically that McClellan, having walked off the Chicago Platform, does not represent the Democratic party & is a mere independent candidate. They want the Chicago convention called together again to nominate somebody else. It looks like serious discord in the Copperhead camp. But party rule & lust for office will bring back the recusants.

Johny took his first plunge into *Cæsar* after dinner. Did it creditably.

At 823 this P.M. we had to reprimand our Washington office (F.N. Knapp) for disobedience of orders.

At U.L. Club, 9 P.M. tone of talk was most jolly & hopeful. G.W. Blunt, H.A. Coit, F. Sherman &c &c &c &c see all things couleur de rose.

Sept: 13. Tuesday. Rather an unfruitful day. Weather acrid & cool as an iced crab-apple. Cloudy sky & bustious North wind. Good news from Maine. Her state election, like that of Vermont, sustains Government & shews that the advocates of National Suicide gain no ground in the East. This recalls the old campaign song of 1840

"O have you heard from Maine — Maine — Maine?
Have you heard from Maine?

She went *Hell bent* for Governor Kent." — "Tippecanoe & Tyler too" etcetera. Near a quarter of a Century ago. Think of it! — There are indications that Grant is moving — extending his left — and also that Lee is massing his forces for another effort to free the Weldon R.R. — It seems significant that the ev'g papers have no telegrams from City Point. A great & decisive battle may be fought in Virginia before this week ends. There will be a murder grim & great, for Lee's hungry cohorts will fight their best. Hundreds or thousands of men, enlisted to maintain & enforce the law of the land will perish by the violence of masterful rebels. Our Copperheads — Anti-administrationists — Peace Democrats — & their candidates & leaders — McClellan & Geo. H. Pendleton — Win: Chanler & F'nandy Wud & C° — are answerable for the death of every national Soldier who dies in his duty. For it is only their factious Opposition that keeps the Rebellion alive. Were we united Jeff Davis himself would beat a parley. Wash: Hunt, Barlow, Belmont &c are the Rebels' last hope.

At 823 with Agnew & Jenkins. Much business. Fear we must throw *Knapp* over — but it's a great pity. The Wash^{n} office is utterly insubordinate & unruly. At U.L. Club to night, & a long walk.

We had to record something like a plain vote of censure on Knapp this P.M., and as he is already in a state of hyperæsthesia & wounded dignity, it will probably make him resign. We ought never to have appointed him an Associate Secretary. He was admirable as Superintendant of Special Relief but is incompetent to run the Washington office, which is fast becoming chaotic under his slip-shod government. Moreover, strange as it seems, we hear that he "seems to have lost all interest in the business of the Commission". If he has, it is because of the wound we gave his official feelings, when we ordered the Chief Inspector at City Point to report directly to the Standing Com: at N.Y. & not thro the Assoc: Sec^{y} at Washington, & when we put a check on his wild way of purchasing supplies at Washingt^{n}. Who could have dreamed that that best of men, F.N.K., so wholly free from selfishness, so single minded & devoted to duty — a combination, as I have often thought, of Mark Tapley & Tom Pinch (vide Martin Chuzzlewit) could be upset by these wretched little personal piques & morbid suspicions of affront?

Sept: 16. Coming up town this aft[n] I perceived Der Freyschutz announced on the bills for to night, & remembered with disgust an uncontrollable San: Com: engagement at Agnew's, & that Temple had been asking twice a day since we came home "Papa, are they going to play D.F. again *soon*?" So I concluded to give him & two of the servants a treat, & sent him to the Acad: of Music in charge of *John* & *Lizzy*. They have got back, & Temple has gone to bed. John says they had a good time & pronounces the music "splendid" with an emphasis that indicates sincere appreciation. I guess my five-dollar greenback bought a considerable aggregate of enjoyment.

At our San. Com. Session were Agnew, Van Buren, & Jenkins. We decided, among other things, to put D[r] Parrish in charge of the semi-monthly "Bulletin" & to publish it henceforth in Philad[a]. After we had got thro' with the business of the ev'g, Jenkins asked a hearing, & proceeded to state that he had now been General Secretary just a year, & that he considered his administration a failure. He was satisfied at last that he had not capacity equal to his duties as our Chief Executive Officer, & wanted to bring his deficiencies to our notice. This was said in the most single-minded candid honest way. We told him frankly that he was mistaken; that the embarrassments of the last three months were caused by a vicious organization & by insubordinate officials at Washington & elsewhere, & that he would come to the same conclusion if he took a blue pill to night & a few quarts of Congress water tomorrow morning. — Walked down town with Van Buren. Singular & silly performance of our neighbour Rev: A.C. Coxe at Easthampton, refusing to speak to a certain R.C. priest who happened to be in the same boarding house, or to let him pass a plate at the dinner table to any of the Coxe family. The priest thus tabooed was a respectable decent-mannered person, & this seems the extremest case of Papaphobia of which I've heard for some time. Coxe by the by will accept the office of Assist: Bishop of Western N.Y. So says his nice refined looking little boy, Master Ernest, Johny's special friend & ally.

Spent last night looking over proof sheets of first half of ci-devant Surgeon General Hammond's pamphlet. It is too long, but he will not shorten it, and rather vehement & intemperate, but I have weeded out some of the hard words. It will not be generally read, but it will furnish texts for damaging Editorials against Stanton in Opposition newspapers. He deserves them, & Hammond has been treated most oppressively & infamously. But I hate to be anyhow privy to any attack on the Administration just now.

Farragut has pushed his gunboats to a point within shelling distance of Mobile. But we have indications that the coöperating land force is to be withdrawn, & transferred to the other side of the Mississippi.

Rev: Geo: Potts, pastor of the meeting-house corner of University Place & Tenth Street, dead. Softening of the brain. He used to be one of those wonderful theologians who hold, with Bishop Hopkins, that breeding black children & selling them is the crown of Christian virtues. But I hear he came to a better mind a year or two ago.

Horatio Seymour renominated at Syracuse as Governor of New York. If any Democratic nominee can be beat he can.

Sept. 17. Sat. Nothing new. Finest possible weather. At U.L. Club to night, & strolled about awhile with G.C.A. inspecting the outskirts of the great McClellan meeting on U. Square, & the tributary streams of banners, lanterns, transparencies, Roman candles, & rabblement, that were flowing up 4th Av: & Broadway. Govr Seymour's friends of July /63 turned out in force. Meeting very large & showy with its lights & fireworks. It's appliances cost a large sum. Belmont must have bled freely.

Strange to see these working-men carrying banners on which Lincoln is held up to ridicule as a "Rail-splitter". *Swinish* is the appropriate adjective for the Multitude. Even our comparatively intelligent Mechanics (or many of them) are too brutally stupid to see that L. is their representative & is fighting their battle against "Little Mac", the Champion of sympathy with & concession to a rebellion that asserts the rightful supremacy of Capital over Labor.

The *Peace-at-any-price* party is holding it's little conferences, & considering whether it shall Bolt or not. It's open hostility would do McClellan little harm. But there will be no Bolt & no nomination of any one pledged to recognize Rebel independence. Wood & Wash: Hunt & their respective tails will sneak back into the ranks, after making a few wry faces, & will support the patriot who locked up the Maryland Legislature — the General whose soldiers shattered the columns of our brethren at Malvern Hill. That was an unconstitutional proceeding to be sure, & seems at first sight to have tended toward strengthening Abolitionism. But the General had nothing to do with it — for he swears he *cannot remember* whether he was on the field or on board a gunboat miles away. His lieutenants have better memories, & swear he was on the gunboat & *not* with his soldiers. I do'nt see why Wood & Co should make much fuss about swallowing McClellan. There is a very small modicum of War in his concoction, & abundant tenderness for treason.

It's certainly hard to vote for sustaining an Administration of which Stanton is a member. He is a ruffian, and will always abuse the power of his great place to purposes of arbitrary vindictive tyranny. His adulators may possibly dishonor the memories of the Earl of Strafford & the Duke d'Alva by comparing him with them — but the part he would play if he dared is that of Doctor Francia, Dictator of Paraguay, or of the Committee of Public Safety during the Reign of Terror. Still it is a plain duty to uphold Lincoln, even with this millstone round his neck, as against the Chicago Platform, McClellan, & Pendleton. Pendleton is as rank a traitor & secessionizer as Vallandigham himself. Tho' he is nominated only for the Vice Presidency, the President is mortal.

"An Apoplexy, catarrh, or cough o' the lungs"

may carry off the valiant McClellan any day, and then V.P. Pendleton would be Pres'dt of the United States, & John Doe would become charged with the duty of conducting the case of Richard Roe. "Ab omni stultitiâ et dementiâ, Libera nos, Domine".

"Mac." will carry this city by a great majority, but it will be made up, in great measure, of what Milton calls "the ragged Infantrie of Stewes and Brothels, the Spawn & shipwrack of Taverns & Dicing houses," & of ignorant emigrant *Gorillas* (Gov: Seymour's "friends") to whom our fatal laws concede the right of suffrage, for abuse & mischief.

It is certain however that many weak-backed men of respectability will go the same way, as, e.g. Ham: Fish & W.H. Aspinwall.

Sept: 19. Monday night. Ellie came to town this morning for a couple of hours in Gen: Dix's government steamboat — made me a visit in Wall St. (thereby causing the Coll: Committee on School of Mines to lose the benefit of my counsels) & returned on the Powell this afternoon. She looks very well & enjoys herself at Cozzens'.

Busy day. No news except that the well-managed raiding party that bagged nearly 2500 beef cattle on the banks of the James has been pursued in vain & that its booty will reinforce the Rebel commissariat. — Also that the Mexican *Cortinas*, probably finding Imperial Mexico too hot for him, has declared himself an American citizen, crossed the Rio Grande with 2000 men & 16 guns, driven the rebel garrison out of Brownsville, & announced that he holds that place for the National Government.

Last night Agnew & Jenkins came in with a Report of *Bloor's*. Bloor has been grumbling for some time because his salary was not raised, & his furloughs lengthened. In this Report he relieves himself by an attack on the Standing Committee. It is not intelligible (for B. delights in dignified diplomatic circumambulatory phrases) & is wholly gratuitous, but it is manifestly a deliberate act of insolence & insubordination. So we instructed Dr Jenkins (who went to Wash^n^ this morning) to dismiss Mr Bloor incontinently, unless he give us a full withdrawal & apology in writing.

Walked thro' Central Park yesterday aft^n^ with G.C.A. The lower Park is finished now, all but the Trees, which have twenty years of work before them yet, & is certainly most attractive & creditable. The Structures — bridges &c — are all good, some of them very good. Strange that of all these various elaborate structures not one should be an absolute monstrosity. Dick Hunt & that scamp Wrey Mould are clever architects.

A cold storm set in last ev'g, but stormed itself out during the night, & to day has been sunshiny *ab extra*, tho' internally livid & Cholera-blue. — — — Mr S.B.R. has just looked in a moment. There is a projected Lincoln "Ratification Mass-Meeting" intended to counterbalance the great McClellan mass-meeting of Sat: night. He (Mr R.) thinks it politic to postpone this meeting a fortnight or so, for the sake of a great victory which somebody says Genl Scott thinks must happen within that space.

Sept: 20. Tuesday. Fall weather cannot be finer than this. It has been worthy of the news to day brought us. The howl of "Extry-a Herald" resounded thro' Wall St. at one o'clock. Extras are not common now. Their appearance indicates something of gravest importance, & I sent out for the news with fear & trembling. *Gratias Deo* for what was brought back. Sheridan attacked Early yesterday & after fighting all day drove him twelve miles with the loss of 2500 prisoners, 5000 killed & wounded, & five guns, pushing him into Winchester & through it & out of it, & promising to resume his pursuit this morning. Hurra for Sheridan & Sherman! If Grant can but do as well as his lieutenants have done, the Rebellion will be "played out" before November. The military value of this victory is great, but it is worth still more as influencing the Political campaign, & contributing to the determination of the fearful issue that campaign is to decide, — Nationality or Anarchy. It will be known in history, I suppose, as the battle "of *Berryville*" or of "*the Opequon*". It is priceless under any name.

Walked up town to 823 in a state of positive exaltation & jubilation, humming over to myself reminiscences of the most triumphant & resolute Mass-music — Glorias & Credos from Haydn & Mozart — a frame of mind unknown to me for several months. Worked with Agnew at 823. Jenkins is diverted from his expedition to Wash^{n} by this news & goes west from Baltimore on the B.&O. R.R.

Dined with Temple & Lewis. Soc'y Library — Reviews — G.C.A. who came home with me & sat awhile.

According to G.C.A. Rev: Dyer reports R^{t} Rev: Hopkins of Vermont in bad odor with his people. Dyer says the Bishop is hooted at as a traitor & an apostle of slave-breeding throughout his diocese. This confirms Miss Jay's story. She spent last summer at Burlington V^{t}, & was driving into town one day, when she saw the Bishop walking the same way. She asked her driver to stop & pick him up, but he drove on. The lady repeated her request, & the driver said "Well marm I do'nt want him in *my* carriage. He aint noways respected about here. It would'nt do for me to be seen drivin' him round".

I feel comparatively jolly to night, for the first time this long while, & inclined to say with somebody in *Beaumont & Fletcher* "I have money & meat & drink beforehand till tomorrow at noon. Why should I be sad?" The wisest thing *Sydney Smith* ever uttered was his maxim "*Take short views.*" Wish I could act on it.

Sept 21. Wednesday. No incidents to day except that Henry Nicoll called at the office on certain business, & that in the course of our talk it appeared that the Chicago platform has converted him. He & his fathers have always been stubborn Democrats, & tho' loyal enough he has never loved this Administration, but he is an uncompromising thorough going supporter of Lincoln. — At U.L. Club to night after a long walk. Mr S.B.R. there. He applies Burns' lines to the Devil to Wash^n^ Hunt & the other Chicagoners

"So fare ye well, auld Nickie Ben! [qu: Ben. Wood?]
O would ye take a thought and men'
Ye aiblins might — I dinna ken —
Still hae a stake.
I'm wae to think upon yon Den,
E'en for your sake!"

A dismal den of political infamy (& without offices) it will be, unless this People be stricken with judicial blindness & a mania for National Suicide. Historical infamy is inevitable, any way. The destruction of our armies, & our conquest & subjugation by the South would be less shameful to us as a People than a public endorsement of the Chicago Platform & the election of a coldblooded traitor like Pendleton to the Vice Presidency. God defend us from such dishonor. I am not sure we the People are wise enough & patriotic enough to defend ourselves from it.

Sheridan seems doing much to help our defence. His victory of the 19th grows bigger & brighter as we learn more about it, & about his way of following it up. It was a hard-fought battle, decided at last by a heavy cavalry charge. That is a new feature in our battles, I think. Another new feature is that he seems to be pushing the retreating enemy vigorously — even as Blücher after Waterloo — & was when last heard from near Strasburgh, 30 miles from his original position. No victorious army, Rebel or National, has heretofore made what seemed a prompt effort to secure the fruits of victory by pressing on the heels of it's retiring adversary. — E.g. Beauregard after Bull Run & McClellan after Antietam.

Richmond papers (before the 19th) brag & bluster of course but there is a trace of anxiety mingled with their savage *thrasonism*. One of them urges non-combatants to leave the City because there is a remote possibility it may be shelled. Grant is certainly being reinforced, & largely. Whence I know not. Dr McDonald reports the arrival of 10 transports at City Point one day last week, & of 6 the next.

The irrepressible Col. Frank Howe had a story at the Club to night of a McClellanist haranguing a crowd in the bar-room of the National Hotel Washington, in the highest altitude of enthusiastic oratory — "Oh gentlemen if I had but the wings of a bird that I might fly through the length & the breadth of these glorious but now disunited States & proclaim to them in a voice of thunder that the Constitution is to be preserved & that George B. McClellan is to be our next President, and that" — Here one of the audience broke in with the very audible suggestion of "Oh *shut up*. You would'nt fly thirty rods before somebody shot you for a *Shite-poke*". — Solvebantur Tabulæ Risu — & that speech ended prematurely.

Sorry to hear from Blunt, to night, (G.W.), as from Prof: Torrey the other day, that *Prof: Bache* is failing. Brown-Séquard & other physicians who have seen him diagnose disease of the brain — softening or some other morbid condition — & the disease seems progressive. He is too *irritable* now to receive his friends or attend to any business. It's a hopeless case, I fear, & this kind genial but most politic old gentleman will assist at no more sessions of San. Com.

Sept: 26. I had a Tr: Ch: Vestry meeting to night, which I could not shirk. Attended it — but there was no quorum. Not displeased, for this enabled me to go to Van Buren's where was a special session of the Stand'g Com: of S: C: — to wit Van Buren Agnew & I. We had business of importance. Our people at City Point expect a battle within a fortnight. Grant's reinforcements average 4000 a day, raw men mostly. Jenkins writes from Harper's Ferry & Winchester. We send large consignments to that quarter, & to City Point. Also we expunge M[r] A.J. Bloor's name from our roster, on which it has stood long & honorably. Sorry for it. But quite independent of the insolence of his late Report (for which he makes no apology, but which he tries to explain away by verbal criticism) & more than sufficient to justify his dismissal, are matters that have come to light since last Sunday. *Malum Ovum.* He may try to avenge himself by a public assault, for he has a *cacoethes scribendi* but whatever he writes is so verbose, polysyllabic & obscure, that it will do us no great mischief.

Find Johny returned safe from Point Judith, where he has had the grandest time with Hector the Newfoundland, & the blackfish & Eel he fished for. — Temple & Lewis seem all right. God bless them all three, and their mamma, and may she be safe at Cornwall!

Signs & tokens multiply. Rob[t] J. Dillon, always a Democrat, no longer in active political life, but always finding fault with Government & magnifying the South, in a slimy underhand way, says "Lincoln is *sure* of re-election". Perhaps the word has been passed through the Democratic ranks to talk that way & tempt supporters of Government to false security — but that is an improbable stroke of subtlety.

Poor old General Scott is quite infirm, and very gracious. He answered my reverent enquiry as to his health & my congratulations on his apparent improvement since I saw him last (he looks much better than in the summer of /63) "My health sir is on the whole good. It is true sir that I am at present suffering from a *suppression of urine*, but it is without pain sir, — without pain." He is a delightful compound of strength & weakness — a grand old General & a good man, kept down from his due place in public respect by petty foibles.

Friday — about 9 P.M. — I was sitting & smoking on the piazza with Talboys, when a youthful vender of newspapers appeared, & said "Express & Post sir?" Returned an indolent negative. Had read the *Post* on my way up the River. "*Fourth* Edition sir, on'y ten cents." "Well let me have it" said I with a sense of reckless extravagance in a small way. Nothing new of course that's of any importance, but there may possibly be some scrap of news in the 3^{d} & 4th Editions beyond the intelligence conveyed by the 1st & 2^{d}. What a ten cents' worth I secured! Was such news ever bought so cheap? Sheridan attacked Early's retreating column at Fisher's Hill, an "impregnable" position near Strasburgh — Thursday the 23^{d} 4 P.M. — doubled up it's left flank & assailed it in front. Early ran. Left some 20 guns behind him. Seems to have been utterly broken routed & demoralized. — Genl Scott says "Sheridan's two battles seem to me to have been among the *most finished* affairs of this War". The Genl defines them accurately as an artist in tactique & strategy.

To night's reports — Sherman's communications endangered — Arkansas & Missouri threatened. Also that Mobile has surrendered to Farragut's gunboats. D'ont believe it.

Sept. 27. Tuesday night. Weather rather warm again. As I brought an incipient cold-in-the-head home with me yesterday, I tried a mild dose of morphine (5 drops) last night. Agnew says it sometimes makes a nascent *coryza* "*abort*" — an elegant verb now much used by Doctors. It seems to have checked the development of the cold, but it has kept me in a wretched state all day. — C.E.S. reports most favorably of Johny's conduct during the Point Judith expedition. He was most tractable & obedient, patient in his fishing, good-natured, & plucky — rather an acquisition to the party than the encumbrance & nuisance I feared he would be. He *Began Greek* to day, & I drilled him a little on the Alphabet after dinner.

Much work with Agnew at 823 this P.M. — Report of our Committee appointed to investigate the treatment of prisoners by the Rebels. The Report leads one straight to conclusions inexpressible in ordinary speech. It confirms the findings of the Congressional Committee on the same subject. These findings needed confirmation. They were incredible till confirmed by the investigations of men quite outside the Political field, such as Dr Mott, Dr Delafield & Gouv: M. Wilkins. —

This report will have a position in History. It establishes the proposition that Jeff: Davis' Policy is to starve & freeze & kill off by inches the prisoners he dares not butcher outright. To cut their throats at once would be more merciful, but the proceeding might alienate outsiders, perhaps even Englishmen.

Safer & pleasanter to destroy them by slow torture, especially as they are thus kept available for Exchange, & the shattered semi-idiotic wreck of a Northern boy can thus be made useful in restoring to the Rebel ranks some prisoner who has been gaining flesh & strength & efficiency ever since he was captured. God grant this war may last till these fiends are exterminated from the surface of God's earth, no matter what insolvency it may bring on *me* for one! The Noyades & Fusillades & Republican Baptisms of the French Revolution were acts of Mercy & Charity compared with the lingering death Secessia is inflicting — deliberately & with murderous malice aforethought — on thousands of prisoners of War. We *cannot* retaliate, it is said. But why can we not & *should* we not take a dozen or a dozen score aristocratic rebel Colonels & Majors, & subject them to the same treatment & regimen which our soldiers have to endure when in rebel hands?

After dinner with Johny & Temple to *Acad: of Music — Don Giovanni* done in German, & rather badly done. Mme Johannsen is hardly equal to Donna Anna's music, & Karl Formes [Leporello] is not what he was six years ago. But I enjoyed the ev'g much. Johny's criticisms are sensible. The Ghost or Statue is on the stage too long, & talks too much. The *Deus ex Machinâ* should never make himself chargeable with garrulity or with a tendency to prose.

Gen: Phil: Sheridan has knocked down Gold & G.B. McClellan together. The former is below 200, & the latter is nowhere. But a reverse or two before Novr would bring him up again. With gold goes down the price of dry goods pork & flour.

It seems well established that during these late battles our men cheered for Lincoln, & the Rebs hurraed for "little Mac". They feel by instinct that he & his supporters are the allies & friends of Rebellion, & help it by a "fire on the rear" of the Army, from Boston Cincinnati & N.Y.

Sept. 28. Wednesday. Weather unsettled. No letter from Ellie, but long R. Grant White reports her safe & well at Cornwall. No material news about the War. Early seems still skedaddling up the Valley. It's said that Sheridan has been strengthened with 20.000 men from Washington (our letters from Winchester

& Harper's Ferry say nothing about it) and that Sherman has detached a corps from Atlanta to operate in the direction of Lynchburgh. — At 823 this aft^{n} with Agnew & Van Buren. After dinner to T.C. Vestry meeting. Nothing of much consequence came up. We adjourned at nine, & I betook myself to U.L. Club where I discoursed John C Hamilton & an intelligent loyal Col. McKean from the Northern parts of this State.

Sept. 29. Thursday. Showery — then clear & steamy & sultry — then cooler & pleasant enough. Annoyed by the failure of any letter from my dear little wife. GOD save her Majesty! I hope she is not ill, and so prevented from writing. — Wall St. & 823 as usual. Letters from Dr Marsh at Morris Island, and from one of Gen: Foster's staff urging us to send supplies to prisoners in Charleston, & assuring us that there is every reason to believe the Rebel authorities will faithfully & honestly apply them to the relief of our men. Clothing is urgently needed. Many of these poor fellows are in absolute nakedness. We (Agnew & I) sent the papers to Van Buren for his opinion. I think we shall have to risk it & send the supplies, but I have very little faith in the promises of these cruel treacherous caitiffs. Their very peculiar "Chivalry" is devoid of honor & humanity.

News this morning that Sheridan's advance cavalry occupies Staunton V^{a}. To night, that Grant has made a move on Richmond, seemingly successful as far as it goes, carrying works on the Newmarket road, & taking some 15 guns. The operation, whatever it is, still in progress at date of his despatch, & a column in motion *toward Richmond*. Weighty news may be looked for hourly. There have been tokens for several days of Lee's intention to shorten his lines by abandoning Petersburgh. This move may expedite the contraction.

The "overtures by the State of Georgia" for a separate peace & return to the Union, about which so much has been said, are now pretty generally understood to be bogus & bosh. Glad of it. Propositions from "Vice Pres'dt" Stephens & Gov: Brown & Robt Toombs would probably be made in bad faith, & meant only to embarrass the Administration, divide the North, & help their friends McClellan & Pendleton into power. While

Sherman Sheridan & Grant keep up their present rate of progress we can do without Peace Overtures. But I am horribly afraid the tide will turn & there will be some fearful disheartening reverse before November.

Gen[l] Dix has come out strong against the "Chicago Platform." *Good* for Dix!

Sept. 30th. Friday. Rain till 3 P.M. Letters from Dame Ellen Strong. She is well, but finds Cornwall slower than Quogue — wh: I readily believe. — After 823 this aft[n] I met Johny by appointment & went with him down town to a West Broadway shop, & bought him a pair of lovely squirrels, designated by the intelligent Dutchman at the head of the menagerie as "Fox Squirrels" from N. Carolina. These exiled secessionists are jolly goodnatured fat & intelligent unlike their fellow countrymen. They were brought here after dinner, & the half hour Johny spent in their society before going to bed was a beatific experience. He squealed with delight at intervals. I suppose a little money laid out in gratifying a child's fancies produces more positive enjoyment than if spent in any other way.

Agnew here to night. We two make a quorum of the Stand'g Com: of the Sanitary Commission, & we two decided on applying quite a large sum to the relief of Union prisoners. Agnew & I *are the Sanitary Com*: just now, & will be till D[r] Bellows comes home. Our powers are large, and our responsibility for their prudent exercise very grave. — After Agnew's departure, M[r] S.B.R. came in, to talk of Diocesan Convention — proposed division of Diocese &c &c &c.

Oct. 1st. Sat. I fear this cold storm is not promoting Ellie's happiness at Cornwall. Attended meeting of Diocesan Standing Com: at Trinity Church 2 P.M. D[r] Higbee, Morgan Dix, Eigenbrodt, old Floyd Smith, & the sagacious Strong. Helped create one Bishop (of Kansas) and a small batch of Presbyters. Then walked up town thro' by-ways on the West Side — & at 823 found Collins returned from Baltimore. San: Com: seems doing a specially good work in the Hospitals of Winchester &c. — Century Club to night. Monthly meeting. Prof: Rood & Prof: Joy, Rutherfurd, Van Nostrand, Henry Winthrop, Haseltine &c. Also Win: Chanler, the "Honorable", but I dodged that traitorous second fiddler to Fernando Wood successfully, & saved myself the humiliation of speaking to him. — Grant & Sheridan seem doing well, thank God. May they continue to prosper. The Rebels have fought the battles of the last ten days without much sign of vigor. Can it be that their rank & file are discouraged & demoralized?

How the City of N.Y. is disgraced by Mayor Gunther's message vetoing the Common Council Resolutions for an illumination in honor of our late victories. Prudence compels the N.Y. World itself to denounce him.

Oct: 6. No war news of importance. Grant seems doing well. Cisco tells me this ev'g that he goes for McClellan "as a choice of evils". Sorry for it. He ought to know better, but I suppose he has private griefs agst Lincoln.

Oct. 7th. Sedulous in Wall St. — also for a couple of hours at 823. To night at Van Buren's for our weekly ev'g session. There were V.B., Gibbs, Jenkins, & myself of the Committee & McCagg of Chicago, who happens to be in town & was invited to sit with us. Letters from Bellows, who is on his way home, & likely to be here within ten days &c &c &c. Much business done. Jenkins goes to City Point tomorrow, taking McCagg with him.

Tidings from the war are good as far as they go. Grant seems extending his left S.W. of Petersburgh & to have got within a short distance of the Southside R.R. thereby compelling Lee to a corresponding extension. If Lee be out-numbered as we suppose he is, this extension must sooner or later attenuate his lines to dangerous weakness. — The attempt to cut-off Sherman's communications seems to have failed. There has been hard fighting at or near "Allatoona", & Rebeldom seems to have been badly punished. If I could only be sure that faction Copperheadism & party sympathies with Southern treason had not so demoralized the North as to make it lay down it's arms next November, I should feel sanguine of National triumph at no distant day. Our most dangerous Public enemy is not Jeff: Davis with his Army, but the party of malcontents &

home-traitors represented by "little Mac"clellan & Pendleton, H. Seymour, Vallandigham Cox & Co.

Jeff: Davis has been making a queer oration at Macon, G[a]. I should take it for a fraudulent invention, did not Southern newspapers quote & condemn it. Surely the oration & the newspaper comments cannot all be forgeries together! Seward & Stanton are hardly equal to so bold a stroke as that would be. If this *be* Jeff's latest utterance, he confesses Rebellion a failure — admits it crushed — declares that it has called out it's last man — deplores the "absence without leave" of many thousand men who have deserted their rebel regiments — and howls for old men & boys to volunteer & defend the Confederacy against Sherman & Grant. This speech would be a *cognovit* — & a surrender — but for the hopes still left to Rebeldom by the possibility that their allies may get control of the North, next November. God grant we may be true to ourselves & to our *Duty*.

Oct. 8th. With *D[r] Marsh* at 823. Yellow fever is fearfully prevalent in N. Carolina.

News from before Richmond this P.M. Butler's lines attacked yesterday 6.30 A.M. in great force, & I suspect, surprized. Kautz's cavalry driven back, with loss of guns. Birney pushed forward thereupon, checking the attack, recovering the ground lost, & possibly more ground, & Butler's despatches claim a victory, & loss to the enemy far exceeding ours. I am glad "*Butler the Beast*" has fought a battle & won it. But even a drawn battle is a victory just now, for Rebeldom is exhausted, out-numbered, & suffocating — teste Rebel newspaper articles, General Orders, & Jeff: Davis' Macon speech.

On my way up town treated myself to a "Bunsen's Burner" & a few inches of *Magnesium* wire. Ignited the latter in the flame of the former after dinner, to the great delectation of Temple & Lewis.

Oct. 9. Sunday. November weather — far too cool for poor Ellie's comfort at Cornwall, I fear. Johny's sick headache kept him in bed this morning, and was so severe that I staid at home to watch him — on picket duty, as it were, against the possible assault of some grave illness. But he was able to join Temple &

Lewis at the dinner table, & spent a pleasant afternoon in the society of his Squirrels.

After dinner M[r] S.B.R. came in, bringing *Judge Selden* to look at some of my old books. The Judge is fervent in patriotism, & in zeal for the restoration of our degraded Profession to it's due place. He expects much from Col: Coll: Law School. May he not be disappointed! — Is quite sure Lincoln will be re-elected. — God grant it! — & laments his own want of early training, & his inability to read Latin & Norman French. Tells me that one of his earliest legal recollections is a brief of my Father's for some motion before a Vice Chancellor at Rochester or thereabouts, in 1829 or 1830, on some question about a Bill of Supplement or of Revivor. —

Then came in my darling little Miss Puss — whom I have not seen these three months. The dear child is almost a young lady now. I kiss her with reverence already. A year or two hence she will be *Miss Kate Strong* — a stately maiden in spreading crinoline.

At tea time Gen: Dix came in, & spent an hour in the dining room & the library. Also *Collins* with a telegram from Jenkins about a contraband paragraph in the San: Com: Bulletin (last N°, not yet distributed) wh: I decided to have suppressed — tho' the reprinting half this number will be costly. Also Murray Hoffman & G.C.A.

Oct. 10. Monday. Cold. War news not much but of a good sort. Sheridan seems to have harried the Valley of Virginia like a Viking. Poor young Meigs' murder by bush-whackers was avenged by burning all the houses within five miles. Probably they were not many, & the sacrifice to the *manes* of this brave promising boy cost little. — Visit from Hammond this morn'g who wanted advice about a school for one of his children. Recommended G.C.A. — Hammond's defence is out. Reads better than I expected, & has made a favorable impression. He has been shamefully treated, but there is just a little bit of ground for hoping that the tyranny of the Sec: of War will soon be overpast. Delafield Smith (U.S. Dist: Atty) told D[r] Van Buren this morning that Stanton's course was nearly run, & I find Gen: Dix & Cisco in possession of the same story this evening. Heaven grant it may be true! The appointment of a good man in his place would strengthen the Administration most appreciably. — At 823 this P.M. — Agnew missing, so I could do nothing. Long talk with D[r] Marsh who ca'nt get transportation to Newbern. Yellow Fever and a congestive "country fever", still more deadly, are making havoc there. Our troops in that quarter have ample supplies, so the Quartermaster's Department holds it safest to keep the infected district insulated, and to send down no boats from this post or from Fortress Monroe.

Home, & finding Johny still miserable with headache & general discomfort, walked down town again & brought D[r] Peters back with me. He diagnosed nothing worse than sickheadache, derangement of the stomach, & the like. I had feared some ugly typhoid fever might be at hand. Poor Johny was able to come down to dinner but was wan & wilted, & retired after dinner to lie down in the society of his beloved squirrels.

Went to Tr: Ch: Vestry meeting. Nothing important came up. Barely a quorum. Sorry to miss *Edmund M. Young*, one of the most valuable of my colleagues in that body — a member of the Century — & a useful public-spirited disinterested active member of the Community. A special loss just now. *He has died* very suddenly — of typhoid fever — of Bright's disease — of "hemorrhage from the kidneys" or of something else. His death is a misfortune to Trinity Church & to the public. — After our Vestry meeting, to U.L. Club. — Binney came in. Brought him home with me. He returns to Philad[a] tomorrow in time to vote. That State election is an event of the first importance. It's result will go far toward deciding whether Lincoln or McClellan shall be *president* for the next four years — whether this Nation choose to assert itself & live, or to lie down in the gutter & *die*, by an abject act of National suicide. Binney is hopeful but not very confident.

Oct. 11. Dispatched much work at 823 this aft[n]. After dinner to Club. Com: on Admissions sat, & passed on a score of names. Coming down stairs from the Committee room, we find the lower rooms crowded with members waiting for news from Penn. Bulletin up announcing Union gain in Philad[a] & prospect good. Cheering in the street from a circum-ambient procession, the vanguard of which entered our front door to exhibit a lantern bearing the legend "*Pennsylvania safe by 20.000 majority! How are you, Little Mac?*" — Most "important, if true", but let us see what tomorrow's papers have to say. If that great State have in fact expressed decided disapproval of the proposal that we lie down in the mud to be kicked by Jeff Davis, spit upon by England, & ruled by F. Wood, our chance of escaping calamity & National infamy next November is doubled.

Our friend Bishop Clark has been making a fool of himself at Newport — writing a political pamphlet that Belmont and W[m] Beach Lawrence praise, & which his loyal friends have hardly saved him from the sin of publishing. Hoppin tells me to night that loyal Churchmen in R.I. were beginning to look darkly on their Bishop — that invitations to dine were growing fewer, & that he preached a vigorous War Sermon last Sunday morning. I supposed his spinal column to be made of sounder stuff.

11.30 P.M. — G.C.A. just rang at the front door to announce that the Penn: news is confirmed, & that Indiana & Ohio are reported (by despatch from Tribune office at the Club) to have *gone Union* by great majorities. May it be true! If these state elections have come out right, thousands of men like Ham: Fish, Gouv: Ogden, Cisco, &c &c &c, will review their decision to vote for McClellan & *Pendleton*. Waiters on Providence, like Ja[s] Gordon Bennett, will declare they have always been on the winning side, & the Administration will be *sustained* — unless some great military disaster occur before November 8th, & a period of discouragement set in.

Oct. 13. Wall St. & 823 as usual, & to night at meeting of Club. Reports from our Committees on Enlistment. They have done the country substantial service, and the Club was not organized in vain.

Results of the October elections not yet quite clear. Ohio & Indiana are all right, but the "Home vote" in Penn[a] is very close, & both sides claim it. The Army vote will carry the state for the Administration however — for the Army is Republican ten to one. On the whole, things look well for Abraham, but Penn[a] disappoints me a little. — One of the commonplaces of Republican talk is that the exhausted Rebels are only holding out in hope of McClellan's election, and that if they see four years more of Lincoln & War coming, next November, they will instantly collapse. I doubt. The pride & rage of their leaders makes surrender unlikely under any circumstances. We have got to destroy their military force & occupy their territory. When that is done & after a year spent in doing military execution on Bush-whackers & guerillas, we shall have Peace.

Hon: old Roger B. Taney has earned the gratitude of his Country by *dying* at last. Better late than never. I had begun to fear he was a *Struldbrug*. Even should Lincoln be defeated he will have time to appoint a new Chief Justice, & he cannot appoint anybody worse than Taney. Chase may very possibly be the man. Curious coincidence that the judge whose opinion in the Dred Scott case proved him the most faithful of slaves to the South should have been dying while his own State, Maryland, was solemnly extinguishing Slavery within her borders by voting on her new Anti-Slavery Constitution. (There seems no doubt it has been adopted). Two ancient abuses & evils were perishing together. The tyrant's foot has rested so long on the neck of "Maryland, my Maryland", that she has undergone an organic change of structure, making it necessary for her to continue under that pressure, or in other words loyal to the National Government. The Confederacy will have nothing to say to Maryland as a free state.

Oct: 14. Friday. Ellen went to West Point this aft[n] with Johny for a day or two, to see what a little change of air will do for him. She goes to Rider's — the Point proper — not Cozzens', so Don John will have a chance of observing the outer manifestations of Cadet life. Agnew thinks his indisposition merely an aggravation of his habit of sickheadache, connected with the change in his constitution that ought to come before long. Hope it is nothing worse.

Com: meeting at 823 this P.M. & another to night, on these premises. The next session of the Commission promises to be stormy. Knapp is full of wrath over the restrictions the Committee has put on his well meant extravagance, & means to attack the Committee & hurl them from their place as Robespierre & Couthon were overthrown.

Grand rumpus at the Club meeting last night after I left it. The Executive Committee reported & recommended for adoption a preamble & resolution, whereas-ing the infamy of the Chicago Platform & inferring the duty of the Club to use it's influence & means to promote the election of A. Lincoln. There was some little disposition to table the Resolution at first. That oracular donkey, Rev: Osgood, thought it's passage would convert the Club into a mere political machine. John Jay, who is always a stumbling block in the way of his own hobbies, by some inscrutable mysterious law of his factious nature, thought so too. There was a lively debate. The supporters of the Resolution had it all their own way & the resolution was carried at last without audible dissent. But I hear that a few members talk of resigning. Let them depart in peace. A "Mere Political Machine" indeed! What subject of human thought & action is higher than Politics, except only Religion? What political issues have arisen for centuries more momentous than those dependent on this election? They are to determine the destinies — the daily life — of the millions & millions who are to live on this continent for many generations to come. They will decide the relations of the laboring man toward the capitalist in A.D. 1900, from Maine to Mexico.

Oct. 15. Sat: Fine weather. Nothing important to note except that it is doubtful whether the Marylanders have adopted their Free-State Constitution after all. Tried twice to see Morgan Dix this aft^{n}, but in vain. I want him to refer me to some good country-clergyman with a young family, a nice wife, & a small income, who would like to take Master Johny as a boarder for a few months, letting him spend most of his time in the open air, & giving him a little dose of Latin now & then, just enough to keep him from losing the little he has got. A Boarding school would be very bad indeed. Saw Dr Peters afterwards, who heartily approved this plan. So does Dr Van Buren with whom I talked of it this ev'g. He sent for me to consult about Dr Hammond's affairs. The case will be ventilated in the Senate this session — tho' I see no action the Senate can take upon it — unless it be a resolution disapproving the findings of the Court-Martial. Bradley of Wash^{n} (Hammond's Counsel) advises him by letter to keep his pamphlet Statement back till after the Election. Sound advice. It is in fact an accusation against the Administration of gross injustice & oppression. If generally circulated just now, it would displease Republican Senators.

Walk to night, & look in at Club, seeking news & finding none. Mr S.B.R. looked in before dinner. Just returned from Washington. Abraham the Venerable says to him "It does look as if the People wanted me to stay here a little longer, & I suppose I shall have to, if they do." He presented a certain Hon: or Rt Hon: Mr Stopford (son or nephew to the Duke or Earl of Something) to our Chief Magistrate, who made a favorable impression on the Son of Albion. The Briton is good enough to "think your President has been strangely vilified". Blessings on the magnanimous Mother Country! — "England, with all thy faults, I love thee still". This swell probably expected to find Mr Lincoln receiving visitors in his shirt sleeves, smoking two cigars at once, blowing his nose with his fingers, & cutting his toe nails with the biggest of bowie knives.

Oct. 18. Weather is lovely. To night at Dr Bellows'. He has returned from the Pacific coast & appeared at 823 yesterday aftn. To night there were also Van Buren, Jenkins & Agnew. The Dr delivered a most instructive & entertaining monologue on his observations & experiences of the last six months in California, Oregon, & Washn Territory, held the floor without much interruption from half past seven till five minutes ago (11.30 P.M.) and was not in the least tedious or prosy. He has gone deep into the philosophy of California manners & morals, & his view of the probable future of the Pacific states is not discouraging. He expatiates on the *Jo Semité* valley — the marvellous Trees — "the Cascades" of the Columbia &c &c. Olmsted is living in great state & dignity as chief of Mariposa. Our (San: Com:) hold on California seems fully confirmed.

Matters political & military look hopeful. Elections in Maryland & Penn: have apparently come out right by small majorities. The Copperheads try to crow over Penn: but it dies in their throats. News from Grant & Sherman is satisfactory, but I suppose the War Department is in no hurry to give the Public, just at this crisis, any news but such as is hopeful. "A great Battle" between Sherman & Hood is reported "imminent". Hood has got into Sherman's rear, & is in the region of Dalton & Resaca, & has failed in the object of his movement, which was to cut off Sherman's communications. It is possible he may get cornered, and come to grief.

Oct. 20. Thursday. LAUS DEO. Another victory by Sheridan. News came at noon to day. Early's successor, the redoubtable Longstreet attacked our Shenandoah Army at day-break yesterday, between Strasburgh & Winchester, with alarming vigor. He had probably been reinforced from Richmond. By twelve o'clock we had been driven four miles down the valley, with loss of guns, and prospect of disastrous defeat, which might have cost us the Campaign & the Election. At this stage of the transaction, *Sheridan* appeared on the field from Winchester, on his way back after a visit to Washington. Then the tide of battle turned. The retreating lines were halted and formed again: the Rebels were repulsed, and at three o'clock Sheridan became the assailant, & drove them back thro' Strasburgh, with loss of forty three guns! He seems a brilliant practitioner, and our best fighting General. There are few cases in history of battle lost, and suddenly restored & converted into complete victory, within six hours, by the advent of a Commander, "Sicut Deus ex machinâ". Of course the affair may look otherwise when we learn more about it, but our intelligence is official, and this looms up *now* as the most splendid battle of the War. — Either we fight better of late, or the Rebels fight worse. Probably both propositions are true. They began the War after long preparation with an army of sturdy semi-barbarians officered by a wild aristocracy of the knife & revolver, recognized as natural leaders. We were taken by surprise. Our soldiers were peaceful farmers & mechanics: and our officers were selected by the dice box of pure democracy. Their Generals were in deadliest earnest. Some of ours, (one, at least, who held supreme command at a most critical period) were not in earnest at all. So the hard fighting of our earlier campaigns, when on anything like equal terms, was on the whole to the advantage of Rebellion. I think this state of things is changed now. Our Armies have been educated & trained by bitter experience. Theirs are becoming weary & disheartened. National Salvation *may* be nearer than we think. But jubilation is premature. We have still hard battles to fight — doubtful & dangerous questions to settle —

Nothing very notable at 68 Wall St. or 823 Bdway. Weather fine. Johny enters his *Teens* to day — this is his 13th birthday. He still abstains from School & work, but seems better. Meeting of Library Com: (Col: Coll:) at 68. Rec^{d} a telegram from

Knapp at 823 & authorized purchase of $10.000 worth of supplies for the hospitals of Sheridan's Army, in addition to our stores at Winchester & Harper's Ferry. None too much to provide the "Supplementary" relief that's needed, no doubt, by thousands of brave men, lying mutilated, lacerated, & in misery this minute. Victory at *Cedar Creek* cannot have been recovered without fearful cost. And the Medical Bureau is as worthless now, as it was three years ago. Surgeon Gen'l *Barnes* is an amiable non-entity.

At U.L. Club awhile this ev'g. Discoursed Captn Marshall, Chas. E. Butler, Parke Godwin &c. Godwin is disposed to protest against confidence in result of *Election*. He does not despond — but maintains the necessity of hard work by all loyal men. That is sound doctrine. Every symptom now apparent is unfavorable to the aspirations of G.B. ("Gun Boat") *McClellan* & of "Peace & Surrender at any price" *Pendleton* — but the damnable traitors who support them may be keeping some revolutionary movement in reserve for the day of Election. The best thing I know of Stanton is that he wanted to send *Gov: Seymour* to Fort Lafayette in July /63, and that his colleagues of the Cabinet, & Lincoln himself, hardly kept Stanton from doing it.

I would walk several miles to see Seymour duly & lawfully hanged — as convict of treason. He is an avowed traitor, or *traitoro-phile*.

Oct. 21. Friday. Pleasant weather. Long session of Stand'g Com: of S.C. just concluded. Bellows Agnew Van Buren Jenkins & I. — Ellie, who had been dining out, came in, radiant, to our mild Supper. A second dispatch from Sheridan improves on his first. He drove the Rebel rear-guard from Fisher's Hill (just below Strasburgh) and has taken *fifty* guns. Among them however are some twenty *re*captures — guns we lost early on the 19th.

Oct. 22. Sat: A juicy morning, grateful to water fowl, but disagreeable to featherless bipeds. Weather still unsettled. Johny went with C.E.S. this morning to Point Judith for a couple of days' sojourn. That young scamp has actually been *smoking* on the sly — the premature ruffian! — and has been duly &

severely lectured therefor. — Nothing very special in Wall St. Heard the *Eroica* rehearsed at Acad: of Music, with Ellie, a slovenly performance, but the strength & beauty of the Symphony were apparent nevertheless. I suppose it excelled by no extant orchestral work, but the peerless C. *minor*. From beginning to end it is an intense manifestation of that highest Art which cannot be embodied in rules or Canons of Art. No critic can analyze it's wonderful power, and tell why this or that passage is so pungent, & burns itself so deep into one's memory, & recurs to one so often, solacing a walk up town or a Rail Road ride. So Shakespeare. "Come unto these yellow sands" cannot be scientifically distinguished from doggrel, and in "Hark, hark, the lark at Heaven's gate Sings" English grammar is sacrificed to rhyme. But those two songs live and are loved, & long will be, because there is in them the same occult vital power that inspires the *Eroica*. I admit however that I do not yet appreciate a certain *scratch-cat* passage in the first movement — and the doleful long-lingering *Fugue* in the second. But fault-finding is ungracious. Is there anything, in all music, instrumental or vocal, fuller of pathos & majesty — more touching sad & stately — than the melody that occurs toward the close of the 4th movement? It is stronger even than Elvira's "Non ti fidar, o misera" in Don Giovanni, heartbreaking as that is. It seemed, this afternoon, to embody in music the wail of the ten thousand Northern homes that are proudly sorrowing for sons brothers & husbands sacrificed to save the country. It is among the noblest of musical conceptions.

At 823 as usual this afternoon, and at Club to night. G.W. Blunt gives a bad account of Prof: Bache's health. Dr Lieber talks of probable row & riot here at the Novr election, & is uneasy because the Democrats are so desperate. But they have no principle — no convictions — no Idea — to fight for. They are struggling only for possession of the official crib. To be sure there are among them many Southern refugees & desperadoes. But the Democratic party as a whole will not try to get up a Row. It's leaders are none too good, but they know better.

Oct. 23. Sunday. Ungenial weather. Mrs Eleanor & Gen: Stahel sat with us at Trinity. Burrowed in the Second Part of Faust after dinner, & to night there were here Miss Kitty Dix — &

Miss Puss — & Murray Hoffman, G.C.A. Rice, Gerry, Charley Post &c.

Bad Lapsus Linguæ by G.C.A. in talking about a walk in Central Park, & the embry° Zoological Garden there. "There are lots of deer & six foxes, & three bears, & four *Pessaries* — *Peccaries*, I mean." — By the by Johny's squirrels have found a loose bar in their cage — & broken prison, & are ranging through the garret eating up Trunks carpetbags & other valuables. They run out occasionally on the flagstaff that projects from the garret window, & sun themselves there. — Promise of foul weather to night. I'm off for Wash^n tomorrow.

Sheridan reports himself pursuing the routed rebels up the Valley, that they are throwing away their arms, & that considerable bodies of them are breaking up & taking to the mountains. This looks as if the character of the War were changing. So does a late article, quite elaborate, that appeared in some Richmond paper. It says in substance "We *have no Cavalry*, tho' the South is a people of horsemen. We have only mounted men, useful as scouts & skirmishers, like the Cossacks, but unequal to conflict with the masses of trained Cavalry the Yankees have somehow been able to put in the field. Most of them have actually thrown away their sabres. They always run when attacked by Yankee horse. They are not worth their cost, and three fourths of them should at once be dismounted & put into infantry regiments." A significant confession. It would seem that the estimate generally received at the beginning of the War, of the qualities & relative value of a Northern & a Southern soldiery, was just & true, but that it's truth was not developed till both armies had experienced three years of battle. In July 1861 a Northern Mob & a Southern Mob came into Collision at *Bull Run*, and the North was routed. In 1864 Northern veterans are meeting Southern veterans in Georgia & on the Shenandoah, and *the case is altered*. The Southern gent, with his familiar friends the bowie knife & revolver, fought better than the Northern farmer or clerk, handling a deadly weapon for the first time in his life, & astonished to find himself actually called on to use it for the purpose of killing another man. But after all these campaigns the Northern soldier is free from this disadvantage. He has become reconciled to homicide in fair fight. His deficiency in early homicidal education is cured. That inequality being removed, the superiority of his Northern pluck, endurance, & intelligence, over the fitful, ferocious valor of the Southern Savagery, begins to tell. The New-England mechanic is competing now, on equal terms, with the Poor White Slave of Georgia & the Carolinas, both having enjoyed equal opportunity of learning his business, in the job of War. I prefer to bet on New England — & the North.

But we *may* elect McClellan next Nov[r], & then all these considerations will become worthless. Historians of our Decline & Fall will devote their most carefully written chapters to the question what might this Country not have done or become, but for it's vote for National Suicide Nov. 1864!

Oct. 31. Monday night. A most anxious unhappy day. — But before going into that subject, let me register the notabilia of last week's San: Com: campaign at Washington.

Thither Monday, 24th, by 8 A.M. train. Woods still in full autumn beauty. Ride as dreary & tedious as usual. B[p] Clark joined me at Baltimore, & his lively talk helped me through the last two hours. He seems indisposed to commit himself as to his present views on public affairs. Probably they are of no great importance to anybody. I detected nothing worse than a little pardonable uneasiness about the duration of the War.

At 244 F. St. I found a good room awaiting me — (poor Bloor's quarters) — & a Commissariat department fully established for the benefit of this session; so we all breakfasted & dined together. The Experiment is not wholly successful, but it is an improvement on feeding at Willard's or at Buhler's cockroachy restaurant, and our symposia tho' plain & frugal were jolly.

Session closed Friday night, or rather Sat: morning. There were Bellows, Agnew, Newberry, Clark, Harris, Binney Stillé (whom we added to the Standing Com:) & Wolcott of Boston. Also a very strongminded Miss Abby W. May, an Elect lady from the patriotic womankind of Boston, who had invited us to invite her attendance. She was attentive interested & silent — but her presence obliged us to "go into Executive Session" now & then, for the discussion of sundry personal questions, & to "clear the galleries" (the sofa in the corner, to wit.) — Then we lit our cigars.

We had several matters of this class to pass upon. Knapp had two grievances. First there was the cutting off Grant's Army from his Diocese as Sec'y for the Eastern Department, by order of the Standing Committee, & the carving out of an independent Department within his jurisdiction, the head of which (D[r] McDonald) reports directly to N.Y. & not through him. This action of the Committee was unanimously confirmed. Our experience of July & June /62 was decisive on that question. During that Peninsular campaign all the resources of the Washington office were drawn off to Yorktown White House & Harrison's Landing, & the general service of the Commission went to the dogs. — Secondly: Knapp found fault with our prohibition of purchases except on authority from the Stand'g Com. — a restriction made necessary by his unbusiness-like warm hearted philanthropy. I brought in a Resolution, which was adopted, authorizing such purchases in case of emergency, & not exceeding certain amounts. That is probably well disposed of.

Knapp brought in a letter Friday night, proposing a change in our organization — that we appoint a new Sec[y] for the East, & make *him* head of a new Department, viz: that of "Special Relief" E. & W. Referred to a Committee. Suggestion promises well. He has won all his honors in the work of Special Relief, & his administration as Eastern Sec'y is a failure.

Gen: Grant wrote us for copies of the Report on Rebel prisons to be sent to Gen[l] Lee. We appointed a Committee on my motion (for the sake of perfecting our record, but with no hope of accomplishing anything) to visit City Point & see whether the Rebel authorities could be shamed into allowing us to send supplies to our starving men in their wicked tyrannous hands, and agents to distribute them, and protect them from misappropriation. The President authorized the Com: to make the experiment — but just as it was setting off for James River, news came that the Rebels had themselves made overtures that way!!! So Bellows Stillé & Wolcott concluded to postpone their journey — especially as Grant was just making a movement, & was likely to be too busy to attend to them. [N.B. This movement failed, and was a worse failure than the newspapers indicate]. I believe these Rebel overtures are due to this Report by men like Dr Mott, D[r] Delafield &c, known abroad as entitled to credence & respect & free from all partizan taint. Lee, Davis & C° see that it is likely to raise a howl throughout Xtendom against their barbarism, and hasten to open negotiations on the treatment of prisoners. — It is a most important paper. Significant that Lord Lyons asked Bellows for copies to distribute in England.

We had an interesting visit to the *Military Cemetery* — near the old "Soldiers' Home" where Uncle Abe has his summer quarters. 6500 walnut headboards painted white, numbered, & recording the name Company & Regiment of the dead soldier sleeping below. These ghastly shapes crowd the beautiful greensward. — Suppose the chivalric & "venerable Edmund Ruffin" who fired the First Gun on Sumter could have seen this sight in trance or vision the night before. Would he have touched off his piece without misgivings?

We adj^d^ Friday night. Sat: morn'g Agnew & I took M. Hoffman J^r^ across the River by Georgetown Bridge. We inspected Fort Whipple — Arlington House — Convalescent Camp — & Freedman's Village — & drove back to Wash^n^ by 3 P.M.

Nov. 1st. Tuesday. *Dr Van Buren* made a careful examination of Johny this morning. I called on him to night & got his report. Thank God it is favorable.

Looked in at Cooper Institute to night. Meeting of the *Anti-Chicago* "War Democracy". Dix — F.B. Cutting — Moses Taylor & C°. Dense crowd. Judge Pierrepont was making a speech — inaudible from my position on the outskirts. It seemed well received.

Gold rising fearfully. Military news not specially brilliant.

"Maryland — OUR Maryland" — became a *Free State* to day, and fell into line with her Northern Sisterhood.

Nov. 2^d^. Stand'g Com: of San. Com. to night at Dr Bellows'. Newberry with us. The moment election is over we must declare War agst the Medical Bureau, wh: has been steadily retrograding for six months. If we were to proclaim what we know of it's general inefficiency & recklessness & of it's murderous non-feasances in the Valley of the Shenandoah, the facts could be used by Copperheads so as seriously to weaken Lincoln's chance of re-election. Of course we must hold our peace a little longer.

The N.Y. World scolds venomously over last night's meeting of "War Democrats", and is very hard on Gen: Dix. He is nobody, and a tool of the Administration besides. McClellan stock is low just now — though Gold is high — & the News and World are therefore roaring their loudest.

Nov: 3^d^. Nothing notable in Wall St. or at 823. Seward telegraphs Gunther the Mayor to beware of a conspiracy to *burn* this and other Northern cities on or about Nov: 8th. — The Community is infested by Rebel refugees & sympathizers. There are doubtless Rebel agents among them, eagerly watching their opportunity to do mischief. *Seymour*'s "*Friends*" are ready to emerge from their tenement houses & cellars & suburban shanties, & from every gambling shop & brothel in the City, whenever there shall be an opening for pillage arson & murder like that of July 1863. But I predict no serious breach of the peace next week, tho' Rebeldom & Copperheadism are cornered & desperate, & none too good to bring fire & knife into the streets of New York & Philadelphia, if their wicked cause could be helped thereby, or even for the mere gratification of their malignant spite against us.

It looks as if the Administration would be sustained by next Tuesday's Election. God grant it!

Nov: 4th. At 823 this afternoon. Bellows tells me that Gov: Morgan tells him "he considers the election *over* — & won". May he be sustained by the result! This prognosis of a coming election is as trustworthy as that of any Political practitioner I know. N.B. The N.Y. World is disgusted with Bellows — says he is making "Lincoln speeches" at "corner groceries" (meaning thereby the Cooper Institute) & that if the Sanitary Commission do not get him out of it's Presidency forthwith, it will be universally recognized as a mere "Black Republican Club."

Meeting of Com: on School of Mines at Wm Betts' office this morning. Prospects very hopeful.

After dinner to U.L. Club — & thence with G.C.A. to inspect the grand Union torch-light procession. It was large, enthusiastic, and most brilliantly pyrotechnic with it's rockets &

roman candles. What is more important, it was made up of *voters.* There were comparatively few boys of sixteen & upwards. Perhaps the Secesh majority in this city may be less than people expect.

Belmont has been publicly invited in the newspapers to take up a bet of two to one that Lincoln will be re-elected. He replies by offering to bet that *if* L. be re-elected the war will last through his term of office, & that if McClellan be elected there will be peace & reconstruction. Very significant as to Herr Belmont's (or Schönberg's) views of the case. The "Democratic" party must be short of strong men when it has to put this Dutch banker at the head of it's Executive Committee. I have a sort of respect for him as being beautiful Mrs Belmont's husband, but he is in fact a mere successful cosmopolite adventurer & alien, who has made money as the agent of foreign capitalists, & has no real affinity with our Country or People. They *do* say, moreover, that he is a Jew, half-converted & conforming outwardly — a political Joannes Pfefferkorn — (vide Epist: Obsc: Virorum). — Do'nt know about that, but his setting himself up as one of our guides & governors is a piece of audacious impudence, whether he be Jew or Xtian.

Nov: 5. The City is full of noises to night. There is a grand McClellan demonstration in progress. Little Mac was to "review" his hordes of Celts & Rebel sympathizers, in person, from the balcony of 5th Av: Hotel. I have still respect enough for him left to believe that he must feel himself in a horribly false position. A general who commanded at Malvern Hill & Antietam in /62 must be tempted to doubt his own identity when he hears "Gov: Seymour's Friends" hurraing for him in /64.

Hope our confidence in the result of next Tuesday may not be premature. Certainly everything promises well. Copperheads are disheartened & comfort themselves with prophecies that the streets of N.Y. will "run with blood". If they do, I guess Copperheads will contribute their share. We shall not be taken off our guard, as we were a year ago last July.

Nov: 6th. Gen: *Butler* in town. He commands the U.S. forces here, reporting to Gen: *Dix.* I hear he proposed issuing an order last night that all officers of State militia regiments report to him. Dix objected, and Stanton was telegraphed for a decision. Such an order would be disregarded by Seymour's Copperhead Colonels, and they would have the law on their side. It would promote collision with "State" authorities. But Gen: Butler's personal presence next Tuesday will do no harm. The rabble of New York is not generally well informed, but it knows Butler's name as suggestive of vigorous action against Rebels at New Orleans & elsewhere — action hampered by very few scruples about form & legal right, and thus far successful. The World & News & Express have raved about Butler "the Beast" — the tyrant — the lawless minion of a profligate administration, till such of their party as can read print regard him as the Covenanters regarded *Claverhouse* — a wholesome fear & dread of Butler underlies all the Rebel & Copperhead denunciation of his corruption & abuse of power. It is quite natural that rats should hold terriers unconstitutional & scandalous.

Nov: 7th. At U.L. Club to night. Rooms crowded. Predictions of success tomorrow, and that there will be no *row*. Heaven preserve us from National *felo de se*! Lincoln's re-election will strike more terror to the heart of Rebellion than the fall of Richmond itself.

Nov: 8. *TUESDAY*. So this momentous day is over, and the battle lost & won. We shall know more of the result tomorrow. Present signs are not unfavorable.

Wet weather, which did not prevent a very heavy vote. I stood in queue nearly two hours waiting my turn. A little before me was Belmont, whose vote was challenged on the ground that he had betted on the election. The Inspector rejected it — unwillingly — & Belmont went off in a rage. Very few men would have been challenged on that ground, but this foreign money dealer has made himself uncommonly odious, & the bystanders, mostly of the Union persuasion, chuckled over his discomfiture. Wonderful to relate, Bidwell voted, for the first time since he came to N.Y. twenty six years ago. C.E.S. — G.C.A. — & I had severally belabored him on the subject of his obstinate refusal to vote, & had represented it to him as a constructive fraud, an omission to use a power given him in trust not for himself alone but for the community.

This Election has been quiet beyond precedent. Few arrests, if any, have been made for disorderly conduct. There has been no military force visible. It is said that portions of the city militia regiments were on guard, at their armories, and that some 6000 U.S. troops were at Governor's Island & other points outside the City. But no one could have guessed from the appearance of the streets that so momentous an issue was *sub judice*.

Found myself headachy, & did little in Wall St. — Walked up town with G.C.A. to 823. After dinner to U.L. Club. Great crowd there. G.W. Blunt & Col: Howe conspicuous — receiving despatches every five minutes.

In this City the Democratic strongholds have enlarged their copperhead majorities, but the total majority seems not to exceed 35.750, which is less than was feared. News from Westchester C° looks rather ill, but there is not much of it. Philadelphia reported to have improved upon last month's state election. Baltimore & Maryland right by a large vote. Indiana d°. Gain in New Jersey. Massachusetts all one way. Prospect good in Connecticut. — G.C.A. has just looked in, on his way homeward from the Club. Says the feeling there is that Lincoln is certainly re-elected, but that this State is doubtful — & is claimed at the Copperhead headquarters by 5000 majority. That would be a serious offset against the results of victory. I hope better things. River towns like Rhinebeck & Newburgh are said to have given Union majorities. The Rebel majority in Brooklyn is but small, and the Western Counties have compensated for this City before now. May they save us another two years of *Seymour*!

Nov: 9. Wednesday. Laus Deo! The Crisis has been past, and the most momentous popular Election ever held since ballots were invented has decided against Treason & Disunion. My contempt for Democracy & extended suffrage is mitigated. The American People can be trusted to take care of the National honor. Lincoln is re-elected by an overwhelming vote. The only States that seem to have McClellanized are Missouri, Kentucky, Delaware, & New Jersey. New York, about which we have been uneasy all day, is reported safe at the Club to night. The Copperheads are routed — "Submersi sunt quasi plumbum in aquis vehementibus." Poor "*little Mac*" will never be heard of any more, I think. No man of his moderate calibre ever had such an opportunity of becoming illustrious & threw it away so stupidly. Notwithstanding a certain lukewarmness in the National cause, his instincts & impulses were on the whole right & loyal. Had he acted on them honestly & manfully he would have been elected. But his friends insisted on his being *politic*, and he had not the strength to resist them. He allowed Belmont & Barlow to strike out of his letter of acceptance a vigorous sentence declaring an Armistice with armed Rebels out of the question, and to append to it it's unmeaning finale (which imposed on no man) stating that he assumed the views he had expressed to be what the *Chicago Convention* really *meant* to say in its treasonous Resolutions. *Fuit* McClellan, Napoleoniculus. Five years hence people will wonder how such a fuss ever came to be made about him.

A very wet warm day. Copperheads talk meekly & well. "It's a terrible mistake, but we have got to make the best of it, & support Government." The serene impudence of this morning's "*World*" can hardly be matched. It says the mission of the Democratic party for the next four years will be to keep A. Lincoln from making a dishonorable Disunion Peace with the South. So a gentleman who has just received a sentence of four years in the State Prison might (if cheeky enough) inform the Court & Jury that their unjust decision would oblige him to be especially careful during his term that Law & Order were maintained throughout the State & that no Crime failed to meet prompt punishment. — The "World" is moreover uncommonly proud of the "Democratic masses" — (Gov: Seymour's friends — the liquor dealers — roughs — & brutal Irishry of the City) because they committed no disorders yesterday *though* so easily tempted to make a general row by the offensive & insulting presence of Gen: Butler with sundry regiments to back him. This is as absurd & preposterous as *Fagin* would be if he delivered a Eulogium on the high moral principle — the reverence for the rights of property — displayed by *the Artful Dodger*, in declining to pick any pockets in an eligible crowd, though much aggravated & incited to larceny by an uncommonly large & vigilant force of circumambient Detectives.

Wrote letters in Wall St. Thence to 823 after a brief attendance as witness before Nicoll Referee, in Mason v. Ring. G.C.A. dined here, & we proceeded to U.L. Club, where was much folk. Discoursed Gen: Banks among others. It would seem that Wm E. Dodge is defeated by James Brooks — that most coprophagous of Copperheads — in this Congressional district. A great pity, but Dodge's election was hardly hoped for. Would we were quite sure that Seymour is beaten. John Astor says he thinks Seymour's election would be more mischievous than McClellan's, and he may be right. Seymour and McClellan are weak men, but the latter means well. Seymour's instincts are all evil. He is quite as bad as Fernando Wood.

Report that Sherman has burned Atlanta, and is marching on Charleston. Do not believe it.

Nov: 10. Thursday opened wet and warm but cleared off at noon. Nothing startling at 68 Wall St. or 823 Bdway. To night at Stand'g Com: of T.C. Vestry. The Rector with us — as matters were to come up affecting the Clerical Staff. We prosed over them till 10 o'clock, so I did not attend our San: Com: meeting at Agnew's. N.B. Bellows has just come near getting us into a pretty scrape by a Circular drawn up without due consideration. It was fortunately suppressed before any of the 10 or 15000 copies had been sent out.

Election returns improve. N.Y. seems secure by from 5000 to 7500 — Seymour running a little behind his ticket — and Missouri is claimed for the administration, leaving poor McClellan only three states. If his wife & her mother Mrs Marcy had not allowed themselves to be talked over by Belmont & Barlow, and brought household influence to bear upon him, he would not be in this Plight. They prevailed on him to disregard Gen: Dix's earnest advice, and to try to ride two horses — Peace & War — at once. Should not wonder if the old Democratic party were killed with it's candidate — tho' it has immense vitality. It would be curious if that old & potent organization should die of this Election — the result of which has been in great measure determined by the fireside talk of an amiable young wife & a strong minded mother-in-law. That party can hardly survive another four years of Exclusion from office under the National Government & in almost every State.

It's extinction would be a great blessing. It has been an ancient imperium in imperio with it's own settled rules usages & traditions of political immorality, not worse perhaps than those of other Parties, but better established, more powerful & more fruitful of public mischief.

Nov: 11th. Friday. Weather cooler, & clear till this ev'g, but unsettled still. No material news — except that it is positively asserted that Little Mac has resigned his Commission in a pet, & by way of spiting an unappreciative People. Why not call him Little Mac*k* after his prototype who distinguished himself at Ulm as McC. came near doing just before Malvern Hill? — By the by, the most infamous paper of the last four years appeared in yesterday's Daily News — viz: a congratulatory address to our Mayor, Gunther, (an abject Copperhead) on his refusal to approve a resolution of the Common Council recommending illuminations in honor of Sheridan's victories & the fall of Atlanta. It fills two columns with treason & baseness. Chas O'Conor signs it (& it's evidently his handiwork) Horace F. Clark, S.F.B. Morse, Tucker the Surrogate, John W. Mitchell, Hiram Cranston, John McKeon, Richd O'Gorman, & a lot of others (mostly unknown to fame) among whom is the urbane *Wm Betts*. May their names be remembered! I shall find it hard to meet Betts, after this at our College Committees on the Law School & the School of Mines, without letting him know that I think him as infamous as his very small capacity can make him. This flagitious document bears date Oct. 20th, but was suppressed till after the Election — an unconscious compliment to the honesty & patriotism of the People. It should be remembered however that Betts inherited a large amount of treasonable impulse thro' his wife — a descendant of the Col: Beverley Robinson of the last century, who was mixed up with Arnold's treason. Betts got his social position by his marriage (I believe he was an adventurer from Jamaica or some other British Colony) & he has dutifully adopted the anti-American traditions of his wife's family. Fortunately he has no more weight or influence than his cat. He is an attorney & conveyancer of small calibre, with a small amount of literary culture & scholarship, on the strength of which he looks down upon the community at large with a supreme disdain. He knows the difference between a Hexameter & a Pentameter. The American People does not know it, & on the whole does not much care about knowing it, having questions more pressing to consider & knowledge more important to gain, just now. So Betts regards the struggle of these three years as a Sage would look on a battle between two street boys — but always with a feeling in favor of Disunion & against Nationality.

Enough of him. I have given him more space than he deserves. — At U.L. Club to night. Majority in this State promises to exceed our hopes. This Election, peacefully conducted in a time of such bitter excitement, & with a result quietly recognized & acquiesced in by a furious malcontent minority, is the strongest testimonial in favor of Popular institutions to be found in History.

Nov. 12. Sat: Uncertain weather: shower drizzle & sunshine by turns. To night there is a thin uniform cloud under the sky, and the Moon shines as through ground glass, darkly. This morning spent at *Breakfast*, (U.L. Club), in honor of Prof: Goldwin Smith of Oxford. About 70 sat down. I was between Wm C. Bryant & Lieber, & of course had an agreeable time enough. After a period of deleterious deglutition came speeches. Chas Butler, John Jay, Genl Butler, Evarts, Geo. Wm Curtis &c — and the Prof: of course. He is a tall thin grave man, and speaks slowly but accurately, with intonation a little monotonous but agreeable. He is evidently a scholar & a thinker. Gen: Butler's speech was telling, though a little artificial or stage-y in delivery. Rev: A.C. Coxe spoke — made certain very good points — and shewed his usual want of tact. Avowed that he had little sympathy with the English Liberals (of whom Prof: Smith is a representative) said he was "not a political clergyman" and that "he never voted." This little dab at political clergymen brought the Abbé Bellows down on him, & when Bellows' turn came he delivered an opinion that "Cocks that did'nt fight and did'nt vote ought not to crow." Quite smart, but not in the best taste.

Lieber says he wants to have the event of Tuesday known in history as "*The Great & Good Election of /64*". He is always saying Things.

To night to an adjourned monthly meeting of Century Club, for election of members. Attendance large, as it was understood our minority of Copperhead members meant to black-ball Parke Godwin of the Ev'g Post. He was triumphantly elected. Ned Bell, Marbury, Wm E. Curtis &c could not muster half the one third required to defeat him.

Poor pretty little loyal Mrs Belmont, whom Ellie met to night at the Concert in aid of that everlasting "*Nursery*", declares herself made very unhappy by newspaper flings at her husband.

Nov: 13. A distinguished delegate to the Chicago Convention expatiated to *Blake* (a fortnight ago) on the dignity & weight of that body. "It was made up, sir, of the most loyal & influential Democratic leaders from Illinois — from New York — from New England — from Ohio — from *Canada* — In fact it represented the whole Democracy." Quite true, no doubt. Had fewer *Canadian* Democrats (i.e. plotting Southern refugees) assisted at that Convention, it might have adopted a more patriotic platform, & its Party might have escaped absolute annihilation.

"Please to remember the *Eighth* of November,
Copperhead Treason & Plot.
We know no reason why Copperhead Treason
Should ever be forgot." &c.

This Election of last Tuesday is quite as important an event in our history as the miscarriage of the Gunpowder Plot in that of Great Britain. Both indicate progress the same way.

Nov. 14. Monday. Cold. Rebel newspapers disapprove Lincoln's re-election. C.E.S. took R.R. for Washington this aft^n^, & goes thence to City Point with Burnside.

Nov: 15. Clear moonlight after a day of the foulest weather. A spitting of snow began the performance, & soon changed into rain that seemed several degrees colder. A *very* lazy day. Jem Ruggles dined here, & a very nice intelligent Col. McMahon of Gen: Dix's staff who has seen much service in Virginia. Ellie went with them to the opera.

What shall we do with poor Johny? This period of enforced idleness seems to strengthen all his worst points of character. Thoughtless disobedience — negligence — forgetfulness are growing on him. I have to be severe with him, & I do so hate it. I am blue to night.

Rebel Editors & Congressmen are in great heat over the question whether they shall arm a few thousand slaves, offering them *freedom* as a reward for a certain term of military service. The chief objection to doing so seems to be that they would thereby admit that freedom is a boon to the field-hand, whereas Slavery is his highest blessing & emancipation a penalty, & a curse, instead of a reward. The policy proposed therefore violates first [Southern] principles. They do'nt want to stultify themselves, but necessity will probably outweigh logic in the end, & their most sacred & inviolable theories will have to be violated. The most pious pirate would consent to raise the Devil to help him when in extremity — but the Devil is not to be depended on as an ally. *There* is the real stress of the question. When Cuffee is armed & equipped & under orders to march on Maryland, he will be very apt to march at double quick, & perhaps to march back again in the pay of the "Gorilla Despot" & under the Command of "Butler the Beast-Fiend," or some other myrmidon, Hessian, "miscegenator", Vandal, cut-throat & horse-thief.

Nov: 16. Wednesday. Clear & cool. Diligent in Wall St. Gold falling — inopportunely, as I had $16000.00 worth from California (San: Com:) to dispose of. Why it falls is a mystery. Some say it's because Gen: Butler talked about offering an amnesty at 5th Av: Hotel Monday night. But the Southern newspapers are, if possible, more truculent & thrasonical than ever, & more earnest than ever about the necessity of dying in the very last ditch if it can be reached, and of dying in any ditch rather than give up — now that they know of A. Lincoln's re-election. The air is full of rumors that Sherman has made a grand movement from Atlanta. Nobody knows what or whither. They are severally contradicted, but I shall not be surprised if something important has in fact created them. Sherman *may* be striking out for Augusta, Montgomery, Mobile, Savannah, Charleston or Lynchburgh.

With Ellie to night to Convention of delegates from Soldiers' Aid Societies affiliated with the *Women's Central Association* & convened at Cooper Institute. This was the preliminary meeting of the session, which is to continue tomorrow, for business. About 100 societies represented. Large Room of the Institute at least 2/3 full. Rev: Hitchcock presided. I had to take a seat on the platform with the Nobs. Knapp made a Speech — d° Bellows, & very effectively — d° a certain wild East Tennessean Col: Ray Hawkins, who has been wounded eight times, & employs his time while he is recovering from his last wound (in the leg) in stump-oratory. He is well qualified for it. None of his wounds involved the lungs or windpipe, for he is a Boanerges. His grammar is loose, but he has the root of the matter in him, wants our *Malignants* thoroughly disposed of, & our National Sores radically cured, that our Peace may be enduring when won at last. His oration was less finished than the finer efforts of Isocrates, but it *told*.

Nov: 19. U.L. Club to night. A hundred or more of it's members came together to meet Lt Cushing who finished the rebel Ram Albemarle, with a torpedo boat, in the waters of N. Carolina, thereby not only doing the country most substantial service, but shewing the most distinguished personal gallantry & daring. He blew up his own boat with the hostile Ironclad, & saved himself by swimming. According to our abominable National usage, somebody had to make "a few remarks" on the occasion, & John Jay was happy to make them, & belabored this modest boyish looking young hero with ten minutes of eulogy. He blushed & looked uncomfortable, but made his inevitable reply, simply & briefly, & passed this ordeal as creditably as the other, which I dare say he found hardly more trying. He seems a most charming young fellow — handsome, intelligent, & dignified in his bearing, tho' very young (twenty two) & looking much younger. Hon: John Sherman of Ohio was also present, & he had to make a "few remarks" too, of course. What he said was much to the purpose, & the ev'ng was uncommonly satisfactory.

Yesterday Laurence Williams dined with us — he's on a visit to N.Y. from his pastoral retreat at Batavia. He appeared well. Marriage has done him good. — Afterwards San: Com: at D^r

Van Buren's. Knapp & Gibbs with us, but poor V.B. was laid up with a swelled face, & we saw nothing of him. We worked hard from 8 till midnight. Knapp was put at the head of the new Department of Special Relief East & West, ranking as a third Associate Secretary. Dr Douglas will probably succeed him as Assoc: Sec^y^ for the East. He should never have been taken from his peculiar field of "Special Relief". That work of mercy was devised by him: it suited him, & in it he gained his reputation. His administration as Head of the Washington office has been an admitted failure, & he is relieved from that place on his own motion.

Gold down to 218. Rumor that Gen: Gillem has been smitten by that blackest of traitors, Breckinridge, at Bull's Gap. Spero meliora. Sherman's whereabouts & object are not yet revealed. It is commonly supposed that he has cut loose from Atlanta & his communications, and is moving Southeastwardly. It would be a most bold & hazardous undertaking, resulting in splendid success or tremendous disaster. Stanton continues ill & is off duty. The story still runs that he is to succeed the late Taney, & that Butler is to take the War-office. I think Stanton would do the Country most service as Ambassador Extraordinary to the Court of Heaven. But he would be less calamitous on the Bench than in the Cabinet.

C.E.S. still at City Point. Burnside said to have resumed Command of his old Corps. Quod felix faustumque sit, but I fear that Burnside, though among the best & purest of men, is a third rate General.

Nov: 20. Reports from Sherman, more or less authentic, (probably *less*), place him 70 miles South of Atlanta on the 14th, "advancing toward the Savannah River", eating his way, living on the country, & leaving a track of desolation behind him. May God prosper his march, & help & comfort the homes which Right & Justice, whose Minister he is, oblige him to lay waste! It is sad to think of the misery Rebellion has brought upon Rebeldom, of the many thousand households it has ruined, & is starving. They have brought it on themselves in the great majority of cases. The father or brother was a sturdy masterful Rebel, or (in the Border States) a swearer of oaths of allegiance, murdering National Soldiers, & his own neighbours if suspected of National partialities, on the sly. The wife or sister was a blatant noisy vulgar vixen, vehement in treasonous talk, chewing snuff, & doing her utmost to encourage her male friends to fight hard for the destruction of their country. They deserve no sympathy. But think of the poor little children, who do not know good from Evil! Think of the thousands of little people, each "like an angel, with bright hair", who have pined & wasted & perished under privation & exposure inflicted on them by this war. Think of them, & then say what doom can meet the deserts of the wicked men who forced war upon us, in mere arrogance of self-will. Treason so groundless & gratuitous cannot be found in the history of man. The children have to suffer for the sins of their fathers, — poor little souls. But the Nation should execute Justice on the guilty all the more sternly because their crime has inflicted so much suffering on the innocent.

Nov: 22. Tuesday. Sunshine, a notable phenomenon this fall. Most industrious in Wall St. — C.E.S. has returned from his visit to the front with Burnside, & has of course seen more in a single day than most people would learn in a week, & talked to more Generals, from Grant down, than I have time to enumerate. Grant declares he does not know on what point Sherman is moving. — ["Over the left" — "In a horn"]. "Sherman's orders were indefinite. He was merely directed to move into the Bowels of the Enemy's Country." Whereupon somebody remarked that we should in that case hear of Operations & Evacuations before long. Grant was nervous & anxious — unusually so, according to Burnside — in consequence of telegrams from Sheridan that the enemy had disappeared from his front, and reports from Rebel deserters that all rolling stock had been moved westward from Richmond, & that Lee reinforced by Early was contemplating a grand attack on our lines. On the other hand we have reports from City Point of issues of rations & ammunition indicating a forward movement from our side. But C.E.S. says it was believed at City Point that such movement would be postponed ten days or a fortnight, inasmuch as many furloughed military voters are still absent from their regiments, tho' they are pouring in day by day, and that when the bulk of these men have returned to duty, the two ends of Butler's "Dutch Gap" Canal will be blown out, & there will be a combined assault by land & water. The lines in front of Petersburgh are said to be very thin, & we expect it to be abandoned any day for the sake of concentration of Lee's force.

Burnside wants a Command, & called on the Pres'dt about it. C.E.S. & Tom Goddard were present at the interview. Lincoln said he must wait & consent to be under a cloud a little longer. He must not resign. Burnside seems to acquiesce. C.E.S. is full of admiration of his unselfish magnanimous disposition. He reports Meade unpopular & morbidly sensitive about his personal reputation. E.g. — when directed by Grant to issue a certain order Meade demurs because "if this move succeed, you will get all the credit, but if it fail, I shall have to bear all the newspaper criticism". Bad for Meade if true. Perhaps utterly untrue. "I tell the tale as 'twas told to me".

C.E.S. reports the Army of the Potomac, & of the James, in the best possible heart, & highest confidence, according to his observation.

At 823 this P.M. — An anxious discussion. Renewed it with Agnew at U.L. Club this ev'g. San: Com: is in trouble. I fear we must throw overboard either *Knapp*, or *Jenkins & Collins*, to save the ship from foundering. Very unfortunate, but these men cannot work together.

Coming home, find Bankhead here — of U.S.N. — a very fine officer — calling on Mrs Ellie. He told all about the sinking of the Monitor, which he commanded on her last voyage. — Yesterday Clitz & G.C.A. dined here, & Clitz told us the story of his wound at Gaines' Mill, & how he fell into the hands of certain old West Point friends & chums perverted into Rebel officers, — how kind & sympathetic they were — & how unlike their treatment were his experiences when transferred from their hands to those of the tyrannous caitiffs who rule that infernal Libby Prison. — Notes of this story, taken down just as he told it, in the simplest way & without epithets or emphasis, would be worth an unknown sum to any publisher of A.D. 1900.

Nov: 23. No news on Bulletin Boards or in ev'g papers except that Richmond papers are said to report that Sherman's column has bagged a batch of Rebel Legislators, somewhere in Georgia.

At 823 this aft^{n}, & to night at Dr Bellows' with Agnew, Van Buren, & Gibbs. Jenkins not present, by request, being interested in the personal embroilments & jealousies we had to discuss. There are three grave questions now before us, each requiring much sagacity & a large range of view for it's decision. First, there is this miserable but most perilous disagreement & discord among our chief officers. *Second*, the apportionment of our expenditure, & the settlement of it's monthly amount, which is necessary inasmuch as we have probably seen our best financial days, & can hope for no more Millioniferous Metropolitan Fairs. *Third*. Our policy of peace or open War with the Medical Bureau, which has relapsed nearly to it's condition of three years ago. It has already opened a campaign against us in the N.Y. World, which has published two editorials against us evidently inspired by Copperhead hostility to Bellows as a recent speaker in support of Government, but using material as evidently furnished by Satterlee or some other representative of the fossil fogyism of the Bureau. We were mostly occupied with the first of the three, & agreed on a new disposition of our staff: sending Jenkins to Washington. It is a mere palliative at best, postponing the inevitable explosion a month or two. But Jenkins will probably refuse to try the experiment & decline all farther official relations with Knapp. Jenkins thinks himself unequal to his work — naturally enough, for his rôle is altogether exceptional & indefinite — & this makes him morbid dissatisfied & irritable. If he resign whom can we put in his place? Dr Douglas & Dr Parrish were talked of. Douglas declines the *Associate* Secretaryship, but might consent to become General Secretary.

My chief anxiety is about Collins' possible defection. He is certainly cross-grained & crotchetty, but without a lieutenant of his unquestionable honesty & accuracy, I should not dare to make myself responsible for the really large & complex money operations of the Commission, as its Treasurer, and I do not see how we can replace him. I shall have been the depositary of near four millions of trust money before this work is wound up, — if I live so long — an hundred fold more than I ever dreamed of handling when I consented to take the treasurership. I take it for granted I shall be charged with stealing some of it, & I do'nt very much mind the prospect for myself. But I do'nt want the name of Johny's, Temple's & Lewis' Papa mixed up, twenty years hence, with vague rumors of "something wrong about that great Sanitary Fund", and a thoroughly trustworthy aid like Collins is my chief dependence & reliance against such rumors. With him to help me I am sure I can squelch them just as fast as they spring up. None have sprouted yet, thank God.

Nov: 25. Friday. Fine day: winter with circumstances of mitigation, sunshine, moderate temperature, & a quiet atmosphere: Indian summer frappée. Littell the Boston publisher called in Wall St. about the cheap edition of the Report on Rebel prisons which he is getting out, and for the expense of which he is raising money by subscription. A single Bostonian — A.A. Lawrence I think — agrees to pay for three or four thousand copies to be sent to England. Littell wants to be enabled to send a copy to every clergyman & every newspaper editor in the Northern states. He thinks it will influence the coming campaign on the Anti-Slavery Constitutional Amendment question, as displaying most clearly the barbarizing & brutalizing effect of Slavery on Slaveholding communities, and says he knows Eastern copperheads who have apologized for every crime Rebels have committed, but now confess Rebel treatment of our prisoners inexcusable & criminal beyond precedent.

Up town early, at Egleston's request, to visit School of Mines now fully at work — with 29 pupils!!! Everything looks well, save our account with the Trust C°, which is much too small. Our $2400.00 is nearly used up — & at least $3000.00 more is needed for indispensable outfit & equipment. Can we get an appropriation from the College? The School seems managed by Egleston, Barnard, Vinton, & Chandler, with the utmost energy economy & judgment. With a little judicious stimulation & nutrition it can be developed into a most important centre of practical training in science. O for $50.000! — D^r

Haight, Dr Dix, & Mr S.B.R. were there, with Egleston & Chandler.

From 49th St. to 823: then home: & after dinner a San: Com: [Stand'g Committee] session — viz: Bellows, Jenkins, Agnew, Gibbs, Van Buren, Stillé. Mainly devoted to discussion of our relations with the Medical Bureau, & of the propriety of undertaking a Congressional campaign in the hope of promoting reform in the Bureau, & preventing Barnes' confirmation as Surgeon General. We incline that way — tho' Van Buren declares he will not go to Washington on any terms, and Agnew has crotchets I do not understand. Our application to Barnes for authority to renew our Inspection of Hospitals is formally disapproved by order of the Secretary of War on the ground that official Inspectors were appointed by the Act of /62. This is a subterfuge, for the Corps of Gov[t] Inspectors has notoriously proved a nullity. They have no authority, their reports & recommendations are studiously ignored, and they are systematically snubbed. Stanton's policy as to the Sanitary Commission almost makes me wish myself a Copperhead & a traitor, that I might freely deliver myself of my opinion as to a member of the Administration whom duty compels every loyal man, in these critical days, to uphold or at least to tolerate, & silently to acquiesce in as a necessary evil that will doubtless be somehow overruled to good ends in the course of God's good Providence. But his arrogant Official discouragement of aid from the unexampled bounty of the People, through the Commission, in his duty of saving the lives of our soldiers & economizing the lifeblood of the Country, is a crime almost without precedent. It's sole provocation (that I can discover) is some little squabble with Bellows in /62, when Bellows called on him to object to the appointment of one Tucker as an Assist: Sec'y of War — because the said Tucker was reported corrupt & untrustworthy.

No definite news from Sherman's column. What gleams of light we get from Rebel newspapers indicate that it is "marching on" — D[r] M[c]Donald's letters from City Point state that Monitors & gun-boats, stationed there, *have gone up James River*, and that a movement is at hand such as would have come off on the 19th, but for the long spell of rain that broke up the roads.

Nov: 26. Sat: In bed till near six P.M. — my interior devastated by sick headache of the most virulent type, even as the inward parts of Georgia are, and with God's blessing will be, ravaged by Sherman's columns. It would seem from Rebel newspapers that he is bothering Macon & Milledgeville — that there is perturbation at Savannah & Charleston. These papers talk as truculently as usual. If the people of Georgia will but turn out, they can retard Sherman's Anabasis & perhaps destroy his army as Burgoyne's was destroyed in the old time before us. Quite true — but will they turn out? All we know of his situation & progress is from Rebel authorities, & is favorable as far as it goes. But this march of 300 miles through a poor & hostile country is a most daring & dangerous move. It may end in fearful failure.

G.C.A. dined here, and spent the evening. He tells me that according to the talk of N.Y. Club men, the Harlotry of the City is largely reinforced by Southern refugee women who were of good social standing at home, but find themselves here without means of support, & forced to choose between starving & whoring. Mortal man will never know the whole amount of sorrow, suffering, bereavement, devastation, & crime, for which the Secession conspirators of A.D. 1860 are answerable. It seems a just retribution on the Southern Slaveholding Chivalry who have been forcing their female slaves — black, mulatto, & quadroon — to minister to their pleasures, that their Rebellion should drive their wives & daughters to flee northward & prostitute themselves to Northern "mudsills" — plebeian "Yankees". All the North is full of these refugees male & female. One of them tried to seduce Burnside the other day at Washington, & nearly succeeded — but as she was turning down the gas he remembered "Molly" [Mrs B.] and fled the room. — These scoundrels tried to burn the City last night. I heard the melancholy bell of Calvary Church tolling the alarm again & again at short intervals during our San: Com: session, but did not know what it meant. They fired the old U.S. Hotel ("Holts' Hotel" of 30 years ago, corner of Fulton & Pearl Sts) — the St James Hotel — Barnum's Museum — the St Nicholas — the Laffarge — the Metropolitan — Lovejoy's (twice) — the Belmont House (Fulton St.) — Tammany Hall — the Howard House — & the "New England Hotel" cor:

Bowery & Bayard Sts. This morning they tried to fire the Astor House & the Fifth Avenue Hotel. To night Calvary Church bell clanked awhile, but I do not know why. All these incendiary efforts have been made by unknown lodgers securing rooms, saturating their beds with camphine, depositing a stick of Phosphorus to promote combustion [which it would'nt] & then disappearing. If any of them can be caught red-hand, I should be in favor of hanging them up, without Judge or Jury. Their proper treatment is *Lynch Law*. They should be killed the moment they are caught. — This incendiarism has done but little mischief so far — less than $10.000 worth, all told.

Nov: 27. Sunday night. Fine weather, but the sequelæ of yesterday's sickheadache kept me within doors. Ellie went to Calvary Ch: where Rev: Coxe introduced a thanksgiving for our escape from conflagration, & then called on "the Dix's" — or Dixes — which she is usually doing when the Ds are not calling on her. She could not have an intimacy I should prefer to theirs. Gen[l] D. says he fears most of the incendiaries have made good their escape to Canada, but that he has one or two men in custody who are supposed to be in the Plot, & who are to be duly interrogated. He has published certain orders about Military Commissions, & summary execution immediately on conviction that ring like true metal and will do good.

To night, G.C.A. here, *Vatable* (a *Guadeloupean* — a great friend of Miss Kitty Dix — & an intelligent gentleman-like young man) Harris of Providence — M[r] S.B.R. & Robinson. Since the election Robinson's copperheadism has assumed a mild type, & become "benignant" — to speak as Doctors would of a case of smallpox or scarlet fever.

This Rebel attempt at arson was grave & perilous. It shews that they are desperate, & we should be most thankful that it failed. By all human calculation it should have been successful, & should have destroyed half the City. It's atrocity is unexampled in the history of modern war. The nearest approach to it, I remember, is in the State Trials — 1776 or 1777 — when one Hill was convicted of firing the Rope House at Portsmouth Dock, England, at the instigation of M[r] Benj[n] Franklin & M[r] Silas Deane, agents of the Rebel Colonies. That was a comparatively legitimate transaction. Any agent Rebeldom can secure who is willing to work his way into the Brooklyn Navy Yard under false pretences, & fire its storehouses, must of course expect to be treated as a spy if he fail & be caught. But he is attacking & seeking to destroy only certain depots of public property belonging to — what he considers — his public enemy. These scoundrels sought to fire private property — great caravanserais crowded with women & children — many of whom must have perished had any one of their dozen wicked arsons succeeded. — This attempt to weaken New York by private fire-raising was actually made by the "CHIVALRY" of the South! Why should we be surprised? They flog their women, & sell their children, & kill prisoners entrusted to them in the course of war, by slow torture of starvation & maltreatment. It is quite natural that their emissaries should cross our borders under false colors, & do a little work as incendiaries & burglars, in aid of their wicked cause.

Nov: 28. Overcast, with prospect of rain. At Trinity Church awhile this morning with old Verplanck & Sam[l] Davis, Committee on Monument to the late Rector. It's artist, Brown, with us. It is now finished, and our business was to choose a place for it. Brown preferred the space on the S. side of the main entrance, under the organ loft. I thought the W. end of the South Aisle better, but yielded of course to the judgment of an expert, and we ordered it accordingly. Chancel organ is nearly complete, & it's tone seems good, as far as one can judge. Cutler, the Mus: Doc:, is in great exaltation over the instrument, and expects to do great things with it. Orders are given to admit nobody to the Church tower & spire without a written pass from some one of the Vestry or of the Clergy of the Parish. Visitors average about 30 on fine days, and any one could so use a little phosphorus dissolved in bisulphide of carbon, or in turpentine, on the woodwork of the stairs, as to gladden the chivalric soul of Rebeldom.

At 823 this P.M. Long session over Thanksgiving Day Collections sent in to San: Com: — Why wo'nt people stop giving & let us retire?

Dined here that little gem of a Miss Nettie Craig, her brother Sam: [anserinus], and Jem R. — They went to Niblo's ("Corsican Brothers") with Ellie. Jem seems to like the young lady.

I wish he would make up to her & marry her, for she is a very noble little personage.

I had an appointment at U.L. Club, & spent the ev'g there. — F.H. Delano — that old "foozle" McCurdy — Van Nostrand &c &c.

Our news from Sherman, thro' Rebel channels indicates that he is marching on — ploughing a deep furrow, many miles wide, thro' Georgia, & destroying a vital nerve-system of R.R. — that he has passed by *Macon* — has harried *Milledgeville* — & is threatening *Savannah*. But Rebel Editors judiciously keep back most of their information about his movements, & what scraps of intelligence we get from them reach us thro' a distorting refracting atmospheric stratum of falsehood & bluster. What scoundrels they are! Good men & true women are to be found South of the Potomac, but I firmly believe the Southern Rebel Community, as a whole, to be more base, cruel, wicked, & Anti-christian than any recorded in Modern History. Think of their treatment of their Prisoners! Think of their attempt at arson in N.Y. last Friday night!

Nov. 29. Tuesday. Mild weather. Nothing to record. Diligent in Wall St. & at N° DCCCXXIII. Our official discords are tending to heal. Bellows has gone to Boston, so Agnew & I are remodelling the whole Executive System of the Commission. Jenkins must go to Washington. Knapp must consent to be his lieutenant, and give up the notion of ruling an independent Bureau of Special Relief. We shall not need to repeal any past action of the Committee, for this new Bureau was to go into operation when a new Assoc: Sec'y for the East was appointed, and we shall simply omit to appoint. We must take responsibility — I think the Commission will sustain us.

At U.L. Club to night. — Emmet — Osborn — Marshall — Butler &c &c. Rebeldom is sorely perturbed by Sherman's march S.E.ward. But Rebel newspapers are sure he will be destroyed before he can reach the Coast, "if every man will only do his duty". They comfort themselves also with the reflection that his movement is really a retreat, tho' it does not look like one when superficially considered — being the *wrong way* . . & that he is in fact driven out of Atlanta. So Napoleon drove the Allies out of Leipsic toward Paris.

I am satisfied the South is thoroughly rotten, & the Confederacy a mere shell. It's a white hot crust, that can burn the fingers that try to break it, but there is nothing to support it — nothing below it's surface. It's weakness lies mainly in the utter debasement of it's Poor Whites. The original fire-eating, revolver flourishing, aristocratic "chivalry" of 1861 is nearly used up & worn out. The material to replace it is scanty. RailRoad tracks & rolling stock are in like case, & still harder to replace, for there is no crop of young rails & locomotives growing up to an age that fits them for service. And there seems reason to believe — though it's a horrible suspicion to record — that a large class of Southern women has been Demoralized & corrupted by the War. Not only in N.Y. but at Nashville, Cairo, New Orleans, Washington, &c, I hear stories of Southern ladies whose husbands & brothers are in the Rebel Army, & who live by the profits of Sin. It is said that Sherman decided to order all inhabitants of Atlanta to leave their homes mainly because he knew the health & efficiency of his soldiers would be seriously impaired if any women were left in Atlanta! This seems incredible, but all the foundations of Southern society have been shaken or destroyed for three years & upwards. Unsettling of social institutions & habits always produces crime of every grade — (and hence in part the moral guilt, now unappreciated, of "mere" political offences, treason & Rebellion included) — and Plantation life has not tended to give Plantation ladies a specially keen sense of the sanctity of womanhood or the guilt of unchastity. They have been familiar with the practice of stripping & flogging female slaves, & more or less aware that black & mulatto concubines gave comfort to their husbands & their friends. Fornication, adultery, & Rape are features of the Institution for which their men are fighting. They themselves are in danger of starving. They cannot work (Heaven forbid) & to beg they are ashamed. So Sexual Sin is really no such weighty matter after all. "We have seen women stripped & scourged — we have known or taken it for granted that our partners in the *German* left us for the embrace of some woman whose purity or impurity was matter of utter indifference to us, because, whether Negress, Mulatto, quadroon, or Octoroon, we regarded her not as a woman but as a slave & an animal. We are women — are hard up — & must have a little money. After all, fornication & adultery are venial sins. Perhaps these female creatures were women. They lived thro' a period of prostitution, — let us try the experiment".

Nov: 30. A positively hot day! Incendiary attempts are renewed, & people talk darkly of Vigilance Committees or Martial Law — find fault with Gen: Dix & wish Butler were here.

Newberry telegraphs to 823 that there has been "heavy fighting" in Tennessee, & calls for supplies. We have no such intelligence from any other quarter. — Nothing from Sherman. Grant is believed to be awaiting results from Sherman's move. There is a story that Grant has detached a large force by water to cut the Charleston & Savannah R.R. & cooperate with Sherman's advance, but it is safe to disbelieve all stories.

12. P.M. — Ellie has just returned from an operatic ev'g (Faust) with Miss Kitty Dix, Col: McMahon & Rice. McMahon says a man was arrested this morning who is probably a party to the Rebel plot of house-burning, and that Gen: Dix has ordered a *Military Commission* — I hope it may be true. — N.B. Poor little Lewis tumbled down stairs this morn'g while I was at breakfast, and ensanguined his dear little nose, and howled lamentably for some time — but seems to have suffered no permanent damage. How fast he clung to me, & with what a mute appeal for protection in his fright!

Dec: 1st. "Extray" at noon to day, announcing victory at Franklin, Tennessee, (18 miles South of Nashville) yesterday. Hood's Rebels attacked Schofield (one of Thomas' Lieutenants) at 4 P.M., fought till dark, & were defeated, losing "6000 killed & wounded" & 1000 prisoners — our loss only 500. The news confirmed by official despatch in evening papers. The result very probably overstated but it looks like substantial success at a most important point of conflict, and any serious check is a disaster to Hood. Thank God. — Rebel papers tell us nothing definite about Sherman, & talk of his movements only in the style of vague bluster & brag with which a N.Y. Bowery boy mentions the movements of his adversary. Richmond "is going to bust Sherman's eye — sure — now you may bet high on that I tell yer, & no mistake. Sherman aint no account nohow." But the Rebel press has no victory over him to announce, thus far.

Dec: 4. Sunday. Fine weather. Vinton's sermon admirable for it's brevity. Carried Egleston up town with us to 10 Fifth Av: & then dismissed the carriage, & E. & I walked home. This ev'g M[r] S.B.R. — Talboys &c. Talboys just as clever as he used to be eight years ago. Spoke of a recent experience in a bath-tub, when "he was so cold he did'nt know which was tin, & which was Talboys." — No material news from the Seat of War. We know little about Sherman — but that little looks well. He seems to have crossed the Oconee, & to be striking at Savannah. Much depends on this daring march of his, and on the battle *Thomas* will probably deliver at some point near Nashville.

Yesterday — a nasty wet day — went with Ellie to Acad: of Music & heard that most brilliant & effective Symphony of Mendelssohn's rehearsed again. It is full of talent. G.C.A. dined here & spent the evening.

Friday, Egleston, Chandler, & Vinton, of the School of Mines dined here, with Jem Ruggles. A most satisfactory session. Vinton made a great impression. Ellie enthusiastic about him. He left the service, in consequence of a wound received at Fredericsburgh, having risen to the rank of Brigadier General, & shewn distinguished merit while in the Army. He is fluent vivacious clever & earnest — somewhat like Dick Hunt. Three young men so accomplished in science & so full of self-devotion & disinterestedness would be hard to find in New York.

Dec: 5. College Board met at two. Not a full meeting. Our Chairman, Ham: Fish was kept away by illness. He is threatened by a visit from Enteritis — so Rutherfurd tells me. I doubt if we lost much by his absence.

Mr S.B.R. was in the chair — *vice Pisciado* — and said a forcible word or two. This may prove our most important meeting for ten years past. Dicite Io Pæan, et Io bis dicite Pæan! Hooray! I see an annual corps of skilled engineers & metallurgists going out to develop our mineral wealth, now so wastefully used — but on which we must so largely rely for payment of our swelling National Debt — or, in other words, to defray the cost of saving our National Life. I see capitalists & Stockholders in mining companies enlisted in the cause of the College. I see a splendid collection of all manner of Minerals, including the most magnificent quartz crystals, the loveliest agates, the most resplendent "Elba ores", the greenest Malachites & the biggest Beryls. I see Pterodactyls & Ichthyosauri & Megatheria. What do'nt I see? Much of my vision is "out of sight" I fear, like that of the heroine of "The Critic" when she raved about the Spanish Fleet. — But the prospects of this undertaking are reasonably good. — At 823 this aftn — Agnew & Jenkins. Letters from Newberry, not very hopeful about affairs at or about Nashville. — At U.L. Club to night. Ellie at Geo: Bancroft's, to meet Goldwin Smith. Jem R. came home with her. I want him to read up on the Law of Mines & qualify himself to become a lecturer in the School — on "*mining legislation*". —

Dec. 6. Tuesday. Weather warm & variable, varying between damp & wet. Voted at Charter election, all by myself. Small vote polled. Gave mine against our neighbour old Gerard as School Commissioner. We want no Copperheads in office, high or low. President's Message seems characteristically sensible & straightforward. Chase said to have been nominated & confirmed as Chief Justice of the Supreme Court. Not a bad appointment. We hear nothing about Sherman or Thomas.

Dec. 7. At 823 this P.M. Dr McDonald (from City Point) tells me Grant is quietly establishing heavy guns in a position four miles from Richmond & will soon be pitching shell into that nest of Treason. Nothing from Sherman, about whom there is deep anxiety. Pres'dt's Message is well received.

Dec. 8. Thursday. A windy night, & growing colder, after a cold day. Much concern felt about Sherman. His failure would be a fearful calamity. Even Richmond papers seem not certainly to know what has become of him. Perhaps he will never be heard of again, like King Arthur & Don Sebastian. He should be very near the coast by this time, unless he has come utterly to grief. The most common guess is that he is marching on Savannah, but the occupation of that city is worth little to us. I hope he may be striking for some point a little farther North & treating South Carolina to a taste of what her traitorous folly & fanaticism has inflicted on nearly every other Rebel State.

Dec: 9th. At 823 this P.M. & to night at Van Buren's, with Agnew Jenkins & Dr Parrish —. Suggested a plan for putting our protest against the mismanagement of the Med: Bureau on record — (for the sake of our own credit hereafter, not with any hope of doing any good —) by formally calling it's attention to the suffering & waste of life caused by the want of *splints* on the field — & then — our suggestion being of course ignored — by asking Congress to legislate — which it of course will not take the trouble to do. A series of such moves, each directed against some flagrant abuse, & each made public at the time, may stir up the people at last to demand action & reformation. Surgeon General Barnes seems to behave as if his object were to demoralize the Med: Bureau & destroy it's usefulness. He is sending all his best men, like Cuyler for instance, off to remote posts, & studiously assembling all the worst subjects of the Medical Staff at Washington & putting them in the most responsible places.

No positive intelligence from Sherman. Rebel newspapers report that he has been badly defeated at this point — repulsed with heavy loss at that point. His march is a failure. He shews himself at last irresolute. He has manifestly lost his head, if he ever had any, & does not know which way to turn. His army is disorganized, men & animals are worn out & exhausted. But "on Mr X's plantation we saw y horses, apparently of fine stock, that had been wantonly slaughtered by the invaders"!!! Why did the invaders slaughter these noble *anomiles*, & why did they not put saddles on their backs, if the National Rosinante were used up? — "The roadside thickly strewn with corpses of negro women & children" murdered by these Ogres from Yankeeland. There must be Southerners capable of believing such stuff or it would not have been written. That they exist is a damaging piece of evidence against Southern Civilization. Rebel Editors are generally bragging & blustering their loudest. But one of them, quoted in to night's Post, says that Sherman will be "at Savannah by the 9th".

Dec. 10. Grant has been making a strong demonstration on his right — down to the Nottoway River. Object & result unknown.

Dec. 11. Nothing decisive from Sherman even yet — nothing at all indeed. But bad news travels fast, and if he had met with disaster we should know it before this, thro' the Rebel newspapers.

Dec. 13. Tuesday. Cold sunshine, with intervals of cloud & snow-spitting. Discoursed Howard Potter concerning School of Mines. He will take hold. Visit from Collins who reveals a prank of Knapp's that decides me as to his unfitness for his place, and the necessity of deposing him unless we can devise some system of checks & safeguards more cunning & stringent than our present rules. I have esteemed Knapp as highly as any man I ever knew, but he is recklessly insubordinate, — I fear he is tortuous surreptitious & suppressive of truth, (tho' never for selfish ends) and capable of pious frauds. He has been selling certain of our horses, which was right as he had been ordered to lessen the cost of our wagon trains. But he keeps the proceeds ($900.00 or so) in his own hands instead of putting them forthwith into those of Bowne the Cashier, as he should have done, (or rather, he instructs Culyer, the Chief Clerk of the Wash^{n} Office to retain them) and these funds are thus withheld from the Cashier since 28th Nov^{r}. — With part of them he proceeds to buy a couple of Hospital wagons. All which is utterly irregular & wrong. But — what's much worse — he applies to the Stand'g Committee for leave to buy them, *after they are bought*, saying nothing about these facts. I will have no farther official relations as to money matters with any man who behaves in this tricky disingenuous way, were he Howard & Florence Nightingale welded into one lump of philanthropy & beneficence.

Chess with Johny & Temple after dinner — bless 'em both, not forgetting dear little Lewis, & may all three get well through this winter which looks as if were to be keen & savage, & a trial to little people. — Afterwards to U.L. Club. Rooms crowded. Goldwin Smith there. Old Erastus Benedict made a few remarks. So did the Oxonian. So did *Barnard.* I heard none of their eloquence, choosing rather to look over the handsome collection of American books presented to Smith & displayed on the reading-room table.

Sherman *seemed* within 25 miles of Savannah when last heard from. Warren's move toward Weldon *seems* to have been successful, if it's aim was to break up 15 or 20 miles of Petersburgh & Weldon R.R. — At 823 this P.M. was Hon. R.J. Walker talking over certain matters connected with his generous gift to the Commission of blank thousand dollars' worth of pictures purchased by him in Germany & Italy. He tends a little toward prolixity & prosiness. Dwight Johnson also there.

Dec. 14. Thaw, & the nastiest slop, but to night grows colder and ice makes again. Bank for Savings trustees met in Bleecker St. this P.M. & thence I went to 823. A long letter goes from Bellows to Knapp by to night's mail, informing him of our dissatisfaction & its grounds and that we will accept his resignation. I did not think Bellows had the strength so to deal with a near-kinsman & friend, but I am most heartily sorry about Knapp. I fear he will refuse to go down from his Secretaryship to his old place in our Special Relief service, & that the Commission will lose him, but it cannot be helped, if we do. He is utterly unfit for the post he now holds, tho' he was, & still might be, priceless as a subordinate.

G.C.A. called to night. He has sold his 39th St. house, finding it much too far up town for comfort, and sold it at a profit.

Sherman was, when last heard of thro' Richmond papers, within *five* miles of Savannah, "with a large force in his front, & a great battle imminent & every prospect of our (Rebel) complete success." — About $15000.00 worth of supplies ordered South, coast-wise, this aft^{n}, to meet him. Rumored repulse of Hood — very doubtful. The St Albans Raiders & bank robbers *discharged* by the Canadian Court, for want of jurisdiction. Whereupon Gen: Dix issues a stringent order to military authorities along the Canada frontier, bidding them be watchful & militant, & requiring them in case of another raid to pursue the raiders across the line. This is right, & sustained by British precedent in the case of the Caroline, when American sympathizers were aiding Provincial rebellion. It may lead to complications & war with England, but we must take that disaster, if it come, as in our day's work. It's a great inducement of course to Southern Refugees & agents in Canada to repeat the St Albans experiment. But I think the Canadian government is honestly trying to prevent it's repetition.

Dec. 15. Bulletin boards announced at two P.M. that Sherman *took Savannah* on the 10th. The news comes by way of Philadelphia, & is bogus, as is most Philadelphia news. But to night's Post gives us official tidings that Sherman was just outside Savannah on the 12th, all right, & in communication with Admiral Dahlgren. Laus Deo!

Dec. 16. Friday. Grey cold day. Plentiful deposit of snow from last night's storm. To night a vile small rain is freezing as it falls, & the side walks are covered with a moist vitreous film. Nearly tumbled down half a dozen times on my way home from Bellows' just now. Important session. Gibbs & Stillé were with us, & we stuck close to business from 8 to 12.

Miss Helen Stanley, an intelligent pretty brunette (at Quogue last summer) dined with us, as did also Jem Ruggles & Major Charley Dix. To day's news important. Thomas attacked Hood in front of Nashville yesterday & drove him, taking 1000 prisoners and 16 guns. This was reported last night, but not believed. It comes officially now. Battle would probably be renewed to day, but we have no later tidings. — Nothing whatever from Sherman. Butler has left City Point with his whole force, Ethiopians excepted, gone down the James, & sailed from Hampton roads with a great Naval escort, for parts unknown, Wilmington most probably. The latest of the facetiæ generated by the War is that Butler ordered an offending officer before a Court-Martial, which found him guilty & sentenced him to *two years hard labor on the Canal at Dutch Gap*! Whereupon Butler disapproved finding & sentence, dissolved the Court, & bade the Culprit go & sin no more.

Dec: 17. Saturday. Gratias agimus Tibi! Glad tidings from all quarters. Official despatch as to the second day (16th inst:) of fight before Nashville. Hood worse clawed than on Thursday the 15th, driven from one position after another, with loss of thirty guns & many thousand prisoners. He must be much cut up. Thomas has been deliberately & steadily seducing him into a tight place, & has assailed him at last in overwhelming force. Newberry's letters satisfy me of this. We had not less than 63000 men engaged yesterday & day before besides the garrisons of Murfreesboro' &c. Thomas commands 100.000 men at least. Canby has been helping him by cutting Hood's R.R. communication with his base, in which work certain Nigger regiments did themselves credit. Stoneman is making a stir in S.W. Virginia. Sherman has stormed "Fort McAllister", the stronghold commanding Savannah Harbor which was vainly shelled by our iron-clads 18 months or more ago. Probably Savannah cannot long hold out. Rebellion has bad luck in Dec: A.D. 1864. May it not be so very bad as to lead to a reaction & a run the other way!

G.C.A. dined here, & after dinner Wm E. Dodge Jr, Egleston, & Chandler came in. We had a council in the Library, & adjourned it to a slight supper in the dining room, over *School of Mines*. Dodge & G.C.A. are "Associates". Much work settled (as to Committees &c) & much more planned.

This morning to Philharmonic Rehearsal — by sloppy slippery streets, under a dull grey sky. Mendelssohn's Symphony. Overture to Zaüberflötte, very lovely. "Overture to King Lear" by Berlioz, mere rubbish & *rot*. Shakespearean Overtures by galvanized anthropoid Parisians are becoming a nuisance.

Dec. 20. Tuesday. Clear for a wonder, & keenly cold. Citizens of N.Y. have seventy days of meteorological brutality & outrage to expect before the winter of /64–5 goes away. At 823 this aftn I find myself running the San: Com: machine all alone. Bellows & Agnew were summoned to City Point by Telegram from Fay that arrived yesterday. It was obscure & alarming. "Grave charges against officers of the Commission, demanding immediate investigation". We concluded that some of our people had been getting the Com: into a scrape with the military authorities — so B. & A. posted off this morning most unwillingly. To day comes a letter from Fay, more plain-spoken than his telegram, & indicating that he charges M[c]Donald, Chief Inspector at the City Point station, with drunkenness & immorality. — I do'nt believe a word of it. — D[r] Jenkins is at Boston on business for the Commission, & Fra[s] Fowler, his excellent Assistant, is off duty, poor fellow, having just lost his only child by scarlet fever, or it's sequelæ.

News continues good. Stoneman reported to have whipped Breckinridge. Hood is in full retreat & Thomas is after him. A despatch from Newberry dated to day (later than anything from that quarter in the newspapers) calls for hospital stores by express, and says "Our Agents from the front report Hood's men dispersing in the woods". Very likely an overgrown story, but that Hood has been routed with great loss of material & men, and that Thomas has bagged 5/6[ths] of his artillery & many thousand prisoners, at comparatively small cost, seems quite certain. — At U.L. Club a little while to night. There is danger from discord & faction in that institution.

Dec. 21. Union League Club to night — special meeting. Proposed act of Incorporation discussed & approved. Proposition to change name to "National" or "National Union" Club voted down. It would have been better to adopt the former title at first, & I urged it at that time. But the Club has done a certain amount of public service under it's present title, and we may as well keep it for that reason.

Dec. 22. A fearful superfluity of Cold. Sunshine, but no more thaw than there is at the North Pole this minute. It's growing colder still to night. — Spent the day busily. Found time to call on Torrey at his office in the Treasury building to talk over my pet project of a separate incorporation of the School of Mines, wh: I rejoice to find meets his hearty favor. Carry it out, & the School will have a chance. Had we six men like Torrey among the Trustees of the College they would be well worth six hundred thousand dollars to it's lifeless Board. Walked up town, chilled through, & at 823 find Jenkins safe back Orientis partibus — & a despatch announcing that Bellows & Agnew are at City Point.

With Ellie & Johny to Winter Garden. Booth as Hamlet. He does it well — very well — his readings are good & carefully studied — his bearing is that of a gentleman — even in his difficult ambiguous dealings with poor dear Ophelia. Possibly he *over-does* a little now & then.

Notable that the grave-diggers facetious remark that Hamlet's madness would do him no harm in *England*, for "there the men are as mad as he" — brought down the house. — — — N.B. Shakespeare uses words as nobody but Beethoven has ever used musical notes — conveying the most intense impressions in the most unaccountable way.

What news we get is good. Thomas is following up his Victory, & Hood is unable to make a stand anywhere. Foote of Mississippi has been letting off a doleful speech in the Rebel Senate — the purport whereof is that the Confederacy must soon come to grief, and that he means to return to private life. Details come in of Sherman's grand Adagio movement thro' Georgia, & most interesting they are. That seems to have been among the best & boldest conceptions of the War, and to have been most triumphantly executed. Savannah is fully invested now by land & water. Rebel newspapers have not the least misgivings as to the safety of that City. Even if it should capitulate, or be stormed, nobody need be much concerned. Indeed the surrender of Savannah — should strategic considerations lead thereto — would probably give the final blow to the Yankees.

Dec: 24. Xmas Eve. This ruffianly weather is a little milder since afternoon. I trust it's harshness may not have nipped either of the boys into pneumonia or diphtheria, as yet undeveloped. To night is overcast — with lively promise of a rainy Xmas. Tackled A.W. Bradford in Wall St and converted him fully to my School of Mines project. To Trinity Church at 3 P.M. The annual childrens' Festival & Xmas Tree. Crowded congregation. Every body in a pleasant kindly form of mild excitement. The many voices of those poor children, singing their little Carol on the eve of Christmas Day, touch one deeply. Ellie was there with the boys & dear little Kate. It was little Lewis' first experience of Church since the day of his Baptism. Ellie tells me Temple held him on his lap & took care of him all thro' their drive down town. There is a most rare & lovely element of helpfulness & unselfishness in that child's nature.

At 823 I find no news from Agnew & Bellows. To night presents have been coming in & going out as of old, — in spite of war & sorrow — and according to ancient usage Charley & M[rs] Eleanor, Jem Ruggles & G.C.A. supped here on roast oysters.

Judge Vanderpoel told me on my way up town that *Curtis Noyes* was stricken down by paralysis yesterday morning on getting out of bed, & is dangerously ill. His overworked brain has brought this on him, for he is not yet sixty years old. It ends his career, tho' he may probably survive this attack.

N.Y. World publishes a savage editorial against the San: Com: this morning — one of a series. Collins thinks that Agnew's friend & patient "Private Miles O'Reilly" writes the attacks, hoping that he may be engaged by the Commission to answer them. Halpine is a Bohemian & a Free Lance & a professional member of the Press-gang, but I do not believe he would descend to work quite so dirty.

Yesterday Ellie & I dined at Gen: Viele's in 28th St. Also Admiral Farragut & wife, Mrs Jessie Frémont; Ja[s] T. Brady: Fred: Sheldon: Dr Barker: Geo: Bancroft: Belmont: Pierrepont Edwards: John Van Buren: Wm C. Bryant: & Genl Dix. A queerly mixed assemblage, characteristic of our hostess, tho' she is much toned down now, & is quiet, having outgrown her oddities. She retains much of her cleverness & originality however. As I sat between Sheldon & Jem Brady with the Admiral just opposite & M[rs] Teresa Viele next to Brady I had a better time than I usually have at these solemn feasts.

No one would recognize the Admiral by acquaintance with his portraits. I know his photograph well, but when I saw him talking with Belmont, before dinner, I asked Gen: Dix what was the name of that naval officer. Tho' I knew Farragut was to be present I never dreamed it could be he. I find him a most jolly conversible genial old boy — clear headed, well informed, & perhaps a little dogmatic — not much. He does not talk shop, so we gained no insight into the Counsels of the Navy Department. He seems fond of science, tho' professing to know nothing about it, and to be an uncommonly sharp observer of Nature, making up no theories of his own but fond of using what he has seen to upset the theories of others, however generally received. He announced himself sceptical to night as to certain geological propositions enunciated by Viele (when half a dozen of us were tippling Clos de Vougeot after the ladies had gone upstairs), did not venture to deny them, but had observations of his own which he thought justified him in declining to believe them. I think Farragut is built on a large pattern. His Wife is young looking & attractive though not pretty at all. Her manner is most kindly simple & cordial. — — — Fred: Sheldon is the first man I have seen who gives Kingsley's queer fanciful "Water Babies" story the credit I think it deserves.

Dec: 25. Christmas & Sunday. Fine bright mild day, for a wonder. Trinity Church with Ellie, Johny, & Temple. Great crowd. Standing room hardly to be found, and hundreds of people went away discouraged. The musical part of the service did "D^r^" Cutler much credit. The Te Deum & Jubilate were better sung than such dull worthless compositions deserve, and the Anthem ("Comfort ye my People" — "Every Valley" — "And the Glory of the Lord shall be revealed") was nobly rendered. I trembled for the pretty choir-boys when they took up that terrible fugue, but they stood up to their work like little bricks. That fearful phrase "And all Flesh shall see It together" was brought distinctly out, and made itself felt with all it's awful grisly suggestiveness. — After Church Ellie drove up to Curtis Noyes' to ask after him and found the bell-pull *swathed in crape*! He died at half past eleven this morning, having undergone a second stroke or shock of paralysis last night. This is a public loss, for Noyes was an able learned & honest lawyer, and that breed is nearly extinct. He was ambitious and hard and cold. But he was lavish in his bounty to a clan of poor relations. He had scholarly or literary tendencies, too, outside his professional studies, & has often talked to me about delivering a lecture or lectures on the illustrations of English Law in Shakespeare. Poor Noyes! I am very sorry to lose him. This City cannot spare men who have been talked of as possible candidates for Taney's place.

Old Ja^s^ W. Wallack also reported dead — of gout. And Col: May, of some disease of the heart.

To night came in dear little Puss — & her papa — & G.C.A. & Murray Hoffman J[r] — Willy Graham — one Van Kanderbeek (?) a Dutch or Belgian attaché, & an agreeable cultivated person. — &c. An *Extra* went screeching through the streets at 7 P.M. It announced the surrender of Savannah & of Wilmington (I'm told) on the authority of a "very reliable" contraband, or Southern Union man, who has sought refuge within our lines, & brings this story *with* him from Richmond. — *Bogus.* — Do'nt believe it. When *Wilmington* is choked, the whole Confederacy will be asphyxiated, and perish. I cannot hope for that result quite yet. But it must come, sooner or later, in God's good time. There are already signs of demoralization at Richmond. "Senator" Foote ("Hangman Foote") seems to have ratted. Hood's Army is so shattered, that the Rebels have no substantial force East of the Mississippi, except at & about Richmond.

Dec: 26. Monday. Xmas Part Second: the secular holiday & festival. Foulest weather: copious warm rain, not rained out even yet. It made little difference to me, for I rose sickheadachy at half past eight, tried to dress, & was driven back to bed, where I tossed wearily till afternoon. Agnew came in, just returned from City Point. Fay's charges against D[r] M[c]Donald & D[r] Swalm have been thoroughly looked into and proofs have been taken. As I supposed Fay had discovered a mare's nest.

N[o] 24 dined here this aft[n] — viz: M[r] & Mrs S.B.R. — Mrs Ruggles the elder (that ancient lady as bright & kindly as ever) Mrs Bostwick & Miss Mary & Jem R. — After dinner we enjoyed looking over Gustave Doré's wonderfully grotesque & clever "History of Holy Russia".

Poor Curtis Noyes' death was unexpected ten minutes before it happened. His "hemiplegia" seems to have suddenly extended itself so as to paralyze the respiratory muscles. He became unable to speak soon after his first seizure, but was conscious through most of the first day, and knew his wife & his daughter, little Miss Emily. Poor little lady, her drawing room will not be as bright with great baskets of flowers, next New Years Day, as it was the last.

Great news to day — official & indubitable. Savannah surrendered to Sherman last Wednesday, with 120 guns, storehouses full of cotton worth eighteen millions, and some hundred prisoners. Hardee stole away with the bulk of his army — 15000 more or less — through some unguarded loophole of retreat. But the City is reclaimed, & occupied by the National Army. It's people seems quite resigned to the change, and we have secured a new & most valuable water-base for operations in the Gulf States & in S. Carolina. Laus Deo! So much for Sherman's desperate enforced retreat to the Coast, and for the braying & bragging & outre-cuidance of all Rebel newspapers. Their statements have ceased to affect me at all, when favorable to their own wicked cause. They out-lie any Northern paper I know. Never knew such freedom & boldness in lying as theirs. Woman-flogging & baby-selling must blunt the moral sense of the *Vendor & Castigator*, tho' otherwise as chivalric as Sir Lancelot or the Black Prince. Lying & scolding, & slow starvation & torture of prisoners, seem the habits "Southern Chivalry" is best calculated to develop.

Dec. 27. Tuesday. Another vile drizzling slimy day. Not much to note, though I have been industrious. Bellows & Agnew reported at 823. They found our work at City Point well & economically conducted. They had a long interview with Grant just after dinner. B. thought the General might have taken "just a little too much soup". According to his judgment much of Grant's strength lies in his singleness of purpose, his entire devotion to his work, his freedom from political aspirations, & his readiness to avail himself of the talent & energy of any subordinate without pausing to consider whether his own personal renown may not be thereby endangered. He spoke of Sherman, frankly & naturally, as "altogether our best General" — and as "loose at Savannah", giving Bellows to understand that this march through Georgia was Sherman's own conception, and that Sherman's next move would be at his own discretion. Very good for Grant. If not only able, but unselfish & singleminded, we may hope much from him. He says Hood is smashed & powerless for the present — that he expects little from the Wilmington expedition (he seems to hold Butler rather cheap) — that there is much despondency at Richmond just now, and that he is on the look-out for Jeff Davis trying to pass our lines in disguise on his way to Europe. He made this statement seriously, & says that every Refugee, in breeches or petticoats, is scrutinized with a view to the chance of detecting a fugacious Confederate Rebel pseudo-president! Perhaps a delusive dream, from wh: we shall wake unpleasantly.

Dec. 28. From D[r] Adams' preaching house to N° 823. Bellows Agnew & Van Buren there, & a discussion about Hammond. He feels hurt & aggrieved because the San: Com: has made no public fuss about his unjust conviction & dismissal. Bellows & V.B. are disposed to make fight, but I fear it would do no good to Hammond, & hurt the Commission.

After dinner, Johny & I had our usual Chess, with Temple for spectator & advisor, while Ellie read Mendelssohn & Weber in the music-room. I ca'nt afford to play with Johannes quite at random any longer. — Then to U.L. Club, hoping for farther news from Wilmington, but found nothing distinct or trustworthy. This afternoon's vague rumors of repulse & disaster are not confirmed, and grow less credible. We have no information but through Richmond papers. They reveal that Fort Fisher was vigorously attacked Christmas Eve; that the attack was vigorously maintained Xmas day, & that Butler had succeeded in lodging some 10.000 men between this Fort & Wilmington itself — which movement is distasteful to them. A certain alleged hypothetical "torpedo boat", carrying x + y tons of gunpowder, either has or has not been successfully exploded close to *Fort Fisher*, & knocked it's casemates & embrasures into *pi*. Probably *not*. I never thought that device promising. — Geo: W. Blunt is ready to bet that *Fort Fisher* falls, & blockade-running into Wilmington is finally suppressed before next Monday. May he be, in fact, as sagacious & infallible as he thinks himself! If we can close the harbor of Wilmington, we shut off the Slave-breeding & woman-scourging Rebels from the illicit aid *England* has been giving them ever since they rebelled, and but for English sympathy & comfort this most flagitious of rebellions would have collapsed & perished long ago.

Dec. 29. Thursday. Sunshiny day, but to night overcast, & blowing. Bad for Porter's Armada. We generally believe that move to have *failed*. Morning papers leaned that way, and it seems settled that Butler's land-force had to be re-embarked with loss. But to night's Post (3[d] edition) says the bombardment was still going on, at last accounts. Their date is not disclosed.

Agnew has been conferring with *Marble* of *The World* about his attacks on the San: Com: & calling him to account. Marble can only say that somebody or other told him so-and-so. His gross broad charges of fraud & corruption among our agents, & of great fortunes made by some of them out of their relations with the Commission have nothing tangible to rest on, though his renegade Copperhead paper has published these charges just as if their truth were notorious, and agents of the Commission were generally conceded to be as profligate as members of the Common Council of N.Y. — Agnew is more or less prejudiced in Marble's favor. I am not. Marble seems to me one of the dirtiest of our dirty dogs.

Dec. 30. Standing Committee of San: Com: here to night. Bellows, Agnew, Gibbs, Van Buren, Jenkins. We despatched much business, & discussed our relations with the Sec: of War & the late Surgeon General, at great length, over a very modest supper-table. Mrs Ellie intervened Sicut Dea ex Machinâ, pending our symposium, took her seat as the Hon: Member for the Opera House, & her share in the Debates — a most ornamental accession. How pretty she did look!

We were repulsed at Wilmington: that is clear. May this not be the beginning of a turn of the tide, & a run of bad luck! There has been want of concert between Army & Navy, it would seem, & Butler has gone back to the James River, more or less damaged — probably *more*. The fleet seems disposed to stay & try a little longer, but we can hardly hope it will accomplish anything. We must trust to Sherman to squelch Wilmington by a northward march from Savannah, calling at Charleston on his way. Announcement by *Savannah* newspaper of Hardee's abandonment of that City & it's probable occupation by the National Army is peculiar in it's tone. It counsels submission to a "magnanimous" enemy that is likely to hold the place "for an indefinite period". Talk so moderate by a Southern Organ, on the eve of coercion by Yankees mudsills & Abolitionists is something new. Perhaps the ancient trading rivalry of Savannah & Charleston accounts for it. If that feeling be strong enough to counteract or mollify the general Southern rabies, it can be used to great advantage. — I guess our failure at Wilmington is more than counterbalanced by Burbridge's and Stoneman's success in destroying the Salt works & Lead works of S.W. Virginia. Each is vitally important to the Confederacy. It's Ordnance department at Richmond lately issued an order requiring Soldiers to economize bullets picked up on the field, & to discharge captured muskets into earth-banks, so as to secure their lead. But our newspapers say little about this, & expatiate at length on the alleged short-comings of Gen: Butler & Admiral Porter.

Dec: 31. Sat: — A climate like this is fit only for a community of penguins & white bears. Another snow-storm all day long, and (till night) thawing as it fell, & flooding this corner of the universe with ice porridge. Now the thermometer is falling & the porridge has solidified: the snow has suspended it's visitation for a time, the sky is leaden, & the N.E. wind wails dismally.

Uptown with G.C.A. to lunch on Welsh rabbits at Ayliffe's in Bleecker St. Ayliffe is Chimer or bell-ringer to Trinity Church. His pot house is said to make Welsh Rabbits a specialité. It certainly supplies a first rate article, & very good beer likewise. I am prepared to make a most favorable Report to the Vestry on the exertions of it's Agents in this department. This was my first genuine Welsh Rabbit for near twenty years. — G.C.A. dined here & spent the evening. Chess with Johny & Temple.

At 823 this aft[n] were Bellows Agnew & Gibbs. Seward wants *30.000* copies of the Report on Rebel treatment of prisoners for circulation in England. It should be translated into French & German & scattered over Europe. Hovey resigns — a great loss. He wants to enter the *School of Mines* next fall, & to rub up his Mathematics meanwhile. Knapp also expects to resign before next Spring — his "Self-respect" being damaged by sundry orders of the Standing Committee. But he will not resign if I am a prophet & he have common-sense. He has done great service & won high honor in the Special Relief Department of the Commission. He is not so silly as to renounce his place in the Commission's staff, merely because he is found to be without certain "business" qualifications for work in another department — as far out of his line as the presidency of a Bank would be outside that of Florence Nightingale.

Told Cram of the queer prayer at Noyes' funeral for Noyes' household servants. Cram said "Why he must have meant *little Gerry* [Elbridge J.] — If I had been Gerry, I should have got up & asked — Look here — are you praying for *me* or for the Cook & the Chambermaid?"

Thus passeth away into History this memorable year 1864. Much has been done toward destroying Rebellion in these twelve months. It is far weaker to night than it was a year ago. God aid our efforts to put it down & establish Unity and Peace, this coming year as the last! DEUS SALVAM FAC REMPUBLICAM. — and may God bless & preserve my wife and our three little boys! — — Success to the San: Com: & to the School of Mines! — For one result of the coming of this New Year we may certainly be thankful, in advance. *Seymour* will no longer be Governor of this State. We are fairly entitled to assume it impossible that his successor — Fenton — (tho' we know but little about him) can prove as base maleficent & disgraceful as Seymour. The less said about *him* the better for us. Let us hope Historians will overlook his official existence, & ignore the disgrace he has inflicted on the State of N.Y. — If he be not forgotten, he must be named in the same category with Benedict Arnold & Aaron Burr. From Horatio Seymour & his tribe, during A.D. 1865, et in secula seculorum — Libera nos Domine.

1865

Jan: 2. I think N.Y. day visiting has been rather less generally attended to this year than usual. The streets were bad for pedestrians, & a hack cost $30.00!! — Then our repulse at Wilmington has produced more depression than it should, considering that Nashville & Savannah & the Salt works & lead mines of V^{a} can be offset agst it.

Jan: 4. News from Savannah *possibly* of first rate importance. It's Mayor, & sundry Civic notables, seem to have been prominent at a public meeting that passed resolutions declaring that community subject to the laws of the United States, praising Gen: Sherman, deploring farther War, averring that by-gones should be by-gones, & calling on the Govr of Georgia to convoke a convention that shall restore his state to her lawful & constitutional relations with the Union! Did this meeting represent any respectable minority of Savannites? Or was it got up by Sherman? If genuine, it is an event of the first order. One *Arnold* is or seems to be Mayor of the City, & his name will give the sons of Belial who write for newspapers at Richmond much occasion to blaspheme.

Jan: 5. Richmond papers (especially the "Sentinel" Jeff: D's peculiar mouth piece) are blue & dismal. They lament prevailing Discouragement, & endeavor to cure it by discussing the advantages of emancipating Cuffee & making a soldier of him, & then asking France Spain & England to be kind enough to receive the Rebel States as Colonies! Of course these measures are mentioned "only as a man in good health talks of his will." It can obviously do no harm to think of what the Confederacy could would or might do, if it should meet any serious reverse hereafter — though it is hardly necessary to say that everything is now most uncommonly serene & all the future most hopeful & brilliant. Etc: Etc: — This is stimulus & encouragement of most inferior quality. The most sanguine & Chivalric Rebel in Richmond must have needed six drinks instead of five after being *thus* cheered & upheld by his morning paper. What a falling off is this from the bluster of every Editorial bravo in Secessia four years ago!

The signs of healthy reaction in Savannah are stronger than they seemed. A certain respectable minority at least declares publicly for Peace & Re-Union, & so commits itself on that side as to be without hope of mercy should it fall hereafter under the paws of the Rebellion. And there is no shew in Savannah of the furious spite & inveterate hatred encountered by the Army when it occupied New Orleans. This may be the germ of an entirely new Southern party. *May* be — & may be not. If a movement that way go on & gain strength for a month or two, it will become irresistible: Jeff: D. will be quite pardonable should he quake in his boots, and the President Cabinet Congressmen & Chief Counsellors of Secessia will do well to cut & run. But I do not hope for this. The Chivalry is too passionate & arrogant — the miserable "poor whites" too ignorant & degraded — & there is no middle class to be guided to reaction by Common sense. Still, the kindly submission of Savannah alone is a weighty fact. — if it be a fact.

Jan: 6th. Bellows called for me after dinner, interrupting a game of chess with Prince John (to Johny's regret, for his position was quite hopeful) & we waded up the 5th Av: to Agnew's, held our San: Com: council, & waded back at eleven. Many interesting letters & reports produced by Jenkins, especially a report from one of our Relief Agents (Hoblit) who accompanied Sherman's column on it's memorable march to Savannah. He seems to have had little to do. The Army took care of itself & of it's sick & wounded. It's ambulances & medical stores were abundant & well managed. It lived on turkies & chickens, fresh beef & pork, sweet potatoes, honey, & sorghum molasses, & carried droves of milch cows with it for the benefit of it's invalids. The land it traversed was flowing with milk & honey, & all manner of good things. Hence I deduce (1st) farther proof of the barbarity & cruelty of Slave-ownia in starving it's prisoners at Andersonville Millen &c, & (2d) a doubt whether the farmers & planters of Georgia, whose barn-yards, pig-pens, & store rooms unwillingly issued all these delicacies, are likely to feel much love for National soldiers or for the Union, in the name whereof their homesteads have thus been harried. But the grip of Richmond officials may have been as bad, or even worse.

Jan: 7. Bellows at N° 823, & afterwards Agnew, horribly disgusted because D[r] B. has given a certain D[r] Fisher an official letter of recommendation without first consulting his medical colleagues — the said Fisher being a low-caste practitioner. D[r] B. is too apt to do this sort of thing without due pause. Fisher it seems wants Gov: Fenton to make him superintendant of the State "Soldiers' Relief" establishment in Howard St.

To Century Club to night, where I put up the names of Prof[r] Egleston & Vinton, but the vacancies are so few, & the nominations so many that their chance of immediate election is bad. Thence to U.L. Club awhile & thence back to Century with Dodge & Roosevelt for a conference about their plan for a corps of *Commissionaires* to be made up of Invalid soldiers. Dodge is certainly among the best men we have. He must spend nearly all his time in undertakings for the public good — in which he is most useful, without the least self-seeking or ostentation, keeping himself always in the background as far as may be. His manners are refined & attractive. He is likely to become a very prominent man. — Discoursed Tuckerman about Sch: of Mines — also C.E. Habicht, from whom I extracted a pledge to get us a suite of mineralogy & metallurgy, from Dannemora & Falun, & other *Berg-werke* of Scandinavia.

War-news not much, but promising. Successful raids & forays, destroying rail-roads & locomotives & *materiel* of War. We have reduced the Richmondites to the necessity of paying six dollars a pound for beef, and the "Sentinel" says they are starving. May "the runagates continue in scarceness" till they repent & return to their duty. Another expedition agst Wilmington seems under way. A large force has been put on transports now lying in James River. Would it not be well to postpone that move till this tyranny of stormy weather be overpast?

Jan: 8. People seem to hope much from a reactionary movement in Georgia: may they not be disappointed! — Richmond papers find fault with the conduct of the war. The swashbucklers who edit them still use the old formulas of truculent swagger & "huff-snuff", but one can detect a change in their tone. They seem tending toward an acknowledgement that Subjugation is not a mathematical impossibility, but merely an improbable disaster — easily averted if every body will only do everything. This may be premonitory of Collapse. Let us hope it is, though such hopes have been so often disappointed.

Jan: 14. Sat. To Wash^{n} Tuesday the 10th. Pelting rain all day, & a doleful ride. Sky bluish gray, fields livid with melting snow, or ochreous with Jersey mud — altogether, a dismal collocation of red white & blue. Took refuge in one of Anthony Trollope's novels ("The Bertrams") a good quiet story — & at half past six emerged from the depot into the National mudflats. Made my way to 244 F. St. where a comfortable room awaited me. Bellows, Jenkins, Binney, Stillé, Harris, & Newberry there — also Dr Gould of Cambridge & Dr Parrish. Skinner & McCagg of Chicago appeared next day. Our session ended yesterday morn'g. It's business was mostly routine — hearing Reports &c, of which several were important. We appointed Knapp general superintendant of Special Relief, *under the Gen: Sec'y*: Jenkins, but declined to create a separate Bureau or Department of Special Relief. This will I trust appease Knapp's wounded dignity. We cannot afford either to lose his services, or to give him an independent position with money to spend.

Weather at Wash^{n} was cold but sunshiny & genial. Left it at 7.30 last night with our three Western Colleagues & Gould. My berth in the sleeping car most unfavorable to slumber. Waked uncomfortably all night — caught cold from a slender current of air that found its way into the hot illventilated car — & got home at *eleven* this morning — hours behind time, — tired jaded & sore.

It was snowing hard, but that's over now. Found myself too thoroughly stupefied to go down town — dozed in the library — sent John to Wall St. for letters — went to 823 this aft^{n} to make entries of cash receipts. — Dined here this aft^{n} a fortuitous concurrence of Dr Newberry, G.C.A., Mr S.B.R., & young *Vatable*. The 3 first names staid till eleven, & got off much good talk.

War news. Butler relieved. Symptoms at Savannah continue good, — healthy granulations seem trying to form at that & other points in Georgia. — Hon: Henry S. Foote tried to flee from Richmond & cross our lines, but was grabbed *in transitu* by the Rebels. They are welcome to keep "Hangman Foote". His wife succeeded in absconding & is at Wash^{n}. — *Spinner* told Knapp yesterday in confidence (Spinner of the Treasury Department, whose autograph gives greenbacks their value) that the expedition from City Point went to *Wilmington* & was reinforced by a detachment from Sherman's corps — that the aggregate, 18000 strong, was doing well, that Porter's fleet was fully re-furnished with ordnance stores, and that we were "*nearly*" in possession of *Fort Fisher.* Perhaps. Also Perhaps *not.*

Authentic story about E.B. Elliott, whilome Actuary to the San: Com:. He has much talent for mathematics, & a great faculty of working with entire concentration on abstract questions, but is quite without common sense. He called on Dr Woodward U.S.A. to find fault with certain blanks Dr W. has been issuing to Army Surgeons calling for information as to the medical history of the War. — "Dr W." said Elliott "I have looked over these forms of yours very hastily, but I am shocked to discover at the first glance omissions in your list of diseases, that must deprive the returns of all scientific value". Woodward regrets to hear it, & begs for particulars. "Why, Sir, in your catalogue of Fevers — malarious, typhoid, &c &c &c, you have overlooked & omitted a most important form of Fever — a fever, which according to foreign statistics constitutes 8.2376948" (or whatever it may be) "per cent of the aggregate of febrile cases. What will foreign statisticians think of us if we publish returns founded on so imperfect a classification??? I have studied the subject thoroughly & exhaustively, and feel it my solemn duty to warn you that this oversight destroys the worth of all your work". — "Gracious goodness" — said W. — "You do'nt mean it — do tell me what species of Fever has been forgotten." — "Why, *Puerperal Fever*", said Elliott — "& here are the tables that shew the percentage" &c &c &c. "But Soldiers cannot have Puerperal fever" quoth Woodward. "I dont see why they are not as much exposed to it as Civilians" replied Elliott — & Woodward told him why, in very vigorous Saxon English. Elliott fled in consternation. —

Missouri is a Free State, if a Constitutional convention can make her free, by a vote of 60 to 4! Tennessee drifts fast the same way. Kentucky & Delaware feel the current & will soon be drawn into it. Certainly John Brown is marching on. What a *Nunc Dimittis* would the valiant honest old man have sung under the gallows tree had he foreseen this day!

Jan: 17. Tuesday. Another snow storm disgusted me this morning, & has kept me disgusted all day. Far worse annoyance grew out of a mistake as to the registry of $25000.00 Gov[t] Stocks belonging to Eloise's trust estate, which prevented my drawing her interest to day. It will cost much trouble to set this right, if it can be done at all. Eheu — eheu — eheu. — But at noon came Extras, & glad tidings. *Gen: Terry stormed Fort Fisher Sunday afternoon, taking 1000 prisoners (2500, according to another story) among whom are General Whiting & Col. Lamb, Commandant* of the post. He lost only 500 men, tho' the defence seems to have been dogged, & the struggle lasted seven hours — from 3 to 10 P.M. Gratias Agimus Tibi. — If I understand the topography of Wilmington Harbor aright, this ties up the last of the Rebel æsophagi — stops any considerable supply of material aid to Rebeldom from without.

"A voice of weeping heard & loud lament" at Liverpool, Nassau Island, the Bermudas, & wherever sordid Englishmen have been fattening on the profits of their blockade runners. "Ay de mi, Fort Fisher!" — This is bad for Butler, coming so close on his signal failure — his re-embarkation, after a landing had been effected, — and his half-mutinous farewell to his command, when he was relieved from duty. I guess he is finally shelved, & his military career ended, but he is a tough subject.

Jan: 19. We occupy the long-coveted "Pocotaligo" in Charleston & Savannah R.R. Fuller accounts from Fort Fisher shew that it's reduction was a most gallant affair, of wh: both Army & Navy may be proud. Southern newspapers of last week were in a hysterical state, of "prostration with excitement", denouncing Jeff: Davis & his cabinet & his congress-men as imbeciles, drawing comparisons between their Armies & Sherman's to the great disadvantage of the former, & between Lincoln & Davis to the disadvantage of the latter — "Lincoln is a blackguard, but he is disinterested — patriotic according to his lights — and able, or at least willing to be guided by able advisers. On the other hand, look at *Richmond*." — This heavy blow will not quiet their nerves!

Jan: 20. The street was full of stories that Wilmington had capitulated — that there was somewhere or other great news from Sherman — & that old Blair's journeys to Richmond are to bring about negotiations & Peace & Union. May there be no negotiations formal or informal with the Davis pseudo-government! To open them in any shape would be the worst of blunders, and I think Lincoln knows it. The fall in gold seems to me rather due to the drum of discord & demoralization within the Confederacy — manifested by the wild talk of Rebel Editors & Congressmen. They are frightened & furious. Closing Wilmington Harbor is probably a "blessing in disguise", they say — & all their late reverses are insignificant, if their People will only come up to their work & cease being discouraged & disposed to acquiesce in Yankee rule. They admit their communities disheartened, & that there is a strong party among them hostile to the Richmond Junta & not unfriendly to prospects of "reconstruction".

At Van Buren's to night were Agnew, Bellows, Jenkins, C.J. Stillé, & Blatchford of Boston, who is to go to Wash^{n} as Jenkins' chief of staff. I fear Knapp is not fully appeased, & may resign. Hope he will do nothing so foolish. Our San: Com: Agents did good service at Fort Fisher.

Jan: 21. To night with Johny & Temple to "Broadway Theatre". *Solon Shingle* was not quite so funny this second time. But "*The Live Indian*" was excruciating. Laughed myself sore. — Hon: Geo. P. Marsh contributes to treasury of San: Com: $500.00, being proceeds of copyright of his very able work "Man & Nature". Work is unequally paid in this world. This 8 vo of 550 pp: full of thought & research brings it's author $500.00. Success in developing a batch of Petroleum Wells gives some Snooks or Snobkins an income of $25000. per annum.

Jan: 22. Burnside dined with C.E.S. to day. Just from Washington. Is promised a command forthwith. Says *Grant*, whom he met at Wash^{n} is the happiest man he has seen for many days. It is thought best that Sherman should not take Charleston, unless it be quite necessary to have a water-base at that point — because it will be impossible to save the City from utter demolition if once occupied by our men, and it's destruction would injure us at the South & abroad. I do'nt see it in that light myself. But we can postpone the question till Charleston is within our grasp, which it is *not*, as yet. Burnside says *Butler* had just got thro' with his evidence before the Com: on the

Conduct of the War, or with that branch of it which proved that Fort Fisher was impregnable, when the news came into the Committee room that the Fort had fallen! — He uttered an ejaculation of delight, but has been "much chop-fallen" ever since. Poor Butler! I should fully acquiesce in his being shelved, but for the joy it gives all Copperheads. What they so heartily approve must be wrong. — We get no material War news to day. Everything still looks most hopeful. Everybody thinks Rebeldom in *articulo mortis* at last. Grant himself tells Burnside he looks for no more serious fighting, & Burnside's only fear is that the Rebels may give in before we have shewn them that we can drive Lee out of Richmond. May all this sanguine feeling not prove premature! — I think old Blair's coming & going between Richmond & Washington shew that there are negotiations for a settlement, or efforts to open such negotiations. They may do the greatest mischief, but I have faith in Uncle Abe's sagacity & honesty, & in Stanton's vindictiveness. They will favor no pacification that leaves the sources of this War still open, & the Slave-ocracy (Δουλοκρατεια?) in existence, to recover it's strength & rebel a second time. They know that Peace & Union cannot be secured without utterly squelching Slavery & Slaveholders. — Blair's unofficial diplomacy will probably produce no result — unless the story be true that he was charged with the duty of informing Jeff: Davis that the Gov[t] of the U.S. would put no obstacles in the way if he should feel inclined to take a foreign tour for the benefit of his health. I wish J.D. would abscond to foreign parts, for we should not hang him if we caught him. We should let him run, & he would be a U.S. Senator again within a year or two.

Jan. 24. At U.L. Club to night. M[r] S.B.R. just from Washington reports every one there full of confidence & spirit, except Butler.

The Rebels have blown up Fort Caswell. Our victory in Wilmington Harbor gives us 162 guns. But Rebel newspapers are more outrageously thrasonical than ever. If brag, bluster, "huff-snuff" & loud talk were batteries & regiments, we should be in a bad way. They rather over-do their swaggering, and there are signs of perilous discord in the Councils of Secessia. A strong & bitter Anti-Davis party seems growing fast.

Jan: 25. News from City Point that a flotilla of five Rebel rams or gunboats came down James River before daylight yesterday, & opened fire on our depots there. They were answered by our batteries. One of them was blown up, & the other four retired — two of them much clawed. Whether they succeeded in doing any mischief does not appear. *Farragut* said to have gone down to take command of our naval force on the James. All this in 3^d Edition of Ev'g Post, & in condensed telegraphic shape. It may turn out to have been a damaging move on a point supposed perfectly safe. We shall see.

Jan: 26. Cisco tells me that, according to Senator Sherman, Genl S. has once more cut loose from his base, leaving Foster in command at Savannah, and is in full march with the bulk of his Army, on Raleigh N.C. — May this promenade be as fortunate as that from Atlanta! They called that "a constitutional" from it's good effect on the health of the men. Heavy reinforcements from the West are on their way to Grant, and many look for the speedy abandonment of *Richmond*. But I have heard prophesyings of the same tenor and effect, several times already. — Certainly the results of the last six months are most brilliant & star spangled, and the immediate future looks brighter than it has looked for four years. *Thank God for all.* But let us not be too confident. A run of ill-luck, or an embroilment with France about Mexico, may yet change the whole prospect, & bury us in discouragement once more. — Curious article, from a Richmond (or Charleston) paper, published this morn'g. It says "If the Yankees *do* whip us (supposing it possible) we shall be the strongest power on Earth. Just look at the Navy we should control. England would lose commerce & colonies & Ireland within ten years. France would be kicked out of Mexico & probably out of Algeria too. *Our two armies* could over-run Europe". &c &c. "What fools Lord John Russell & Louis Napoleon have been not to help us!" — This out-crop of an unconscious *National* instinct is interesting, especially as it is coupled with the most hysterical extravagance of invective against the North. This is still the staple of every S. Editor. — They exhausted the vocabulary of Billingsgate & the phrases of bluster & braggadocio long ago, but they keep on repeating themselves, & trying to intensify the expression of their hate & spite, & to write themselves traitor & bully yet more legibly, if possible — But.

"Before the curing of a strong disease,
Even in the instant of repair and health,
The fit is strongest. Evils that take leave
On their departure most of all shew evil."

It seems to me reasonable to look for most important events within the next thirty days. If Terry has been strong enough to move straight on Wilmington & grab the lines of R.R. that converge there, the supply of rations to Lee's Army is already troubled & checked. If he be compelled to take a new position, can he do it at this season without ruinous sacrifice of material of War? — Perhaps his unsuccessful naval foray down James River was a desperate attempt to do a little mischief with his gun boats before abandoning them to their fate, or blowing them up. — Perhaps — Perhaps — & Perhaps *not.*

Jan: 27. Am just from San. Com. Standing Com: session at Bellows'. — Jenkins just back from Washington. We talked over poor Knapp's fancied grievances, & came to the conclusion that if he will be foolish enough to leave us we must let him go in peace. He is not the first good earnest & disinterested man that has been bewildered by that delusive unmeaning word *Self-respect* & misled by pride & selfishness disguised under that title to abandon his usefulness & sacrifice his duty. It is a most doubtful & dangerous word. How many of us have any right to respect or reverence ourselves? I have no such right, for one. There are millions of far better men — thank God — but there are few so very good as to be able to set up their own Personality or Self as something worth preserving from disrespect at the cost of duty, or at any considerable cost.

Jan: 28. "Peace rumors" growing out of old Blair's excursions to Richmond have died — easily & without pain. Their death has sent gold up to 220. Rumors of the Evacuation of Richmond survive, in a weakly condition. — Walked up town with G.C.A. who dined here & spent the ev'g. Stopped on our way at the Van Amburgh Menagerie. An interesting establishment. There's a dogfaced baboon there, with cheek pouches, & orange colored patches on the seat of his pantaloons, who engrossed much of our attention. I have always thought the *Tiger*, with his sullen glare of malignity, & the fearful power latent in his muscles, the worst & most manifest form of total depravity to be found in the Fauna of this period. But this brute of a baboon was depraved below all the Felinæ. He was in continual aggressive demoniacal activity, & his little bits of eyes always watchful for a chance of mischief — his strong muscular paws always ready to grab & tear anything put within their reach. A *cane* & a *handkerchief* offered for his inspection were dragged within the bars of his cage & torn to bits. When at rest he seemed studying to affront his spectators by making the vilest faces at them, & every now & then he picked up a handful of rubbish from the floor of his den, & hurled it at some individual of the crowd with malice worthy of Apollyon himself. Whenever not thus engaged, he was executing a savage barbaric up-&-down dance — of swagger & defiance. He seemed to me the type or embodiment of a Rebel Editor or Congressman. The nature office & destiny of the Brute creation is a great mystery.

Jan: 29. A point made by Gov: Andrew is worth noting, though it seems to tell in favor of State Rights. He says the Nation must have been destroyed in /61 but for the State organizations of the North, for Rebeldom then held the Federal — or, National, — Machinery under it's undisputed control. The States saved the Country (if it is to be saved) in spite of all the power & influence of it's National organization exerted to secure it's disintegration, by old Buchanan & C°. — N.Y. Mass: &c &c possessed powers they could use to save the Nation, even though Washington was in the hands of traitors & of sympathizers with Treason. — There is something in it, perhaps. Consolidation "pure and simple" has it's disadvantages.

Jan: 31. Certain bogus news knocked down the gold market this morning. "Mobile was evacuated. A.H. Stephens & a brace of Rebel Senators were at City Point on their way to Wash^{n} as Peace Commissioners". The 4th Edition of to night's Post tends a little to confirm the latter story. — If it be true, the Commissioners should be received with an Apage Satanas! Lincoln's weak point is softheartedness — over-estimate of the worth of human life. Witness his most shortsighted course of clemency toward scores of deserters & bounty-jumpers pardoned after conviction — each pardon costing the lives of a dozen honest & true men in the Field. There is no telling what folly he might commit if approached by a party of subtle dishonest Southern agents with illusory offers of settlement & Peace. Let us hope he will not be led into temptation & will not lead the Country into a Southern trap.

Feb: 1. The Constitutional Amendment prohibiting Slavery within the United States passed the House yesterday by a Vote of 119 to 56; a little more than the required Two-Thirds. Sundry Democratic members helped it, but James Brooks & Winthrop Chanler voted *no*, as might have been expected of them. So did John V.L. Pruyn, I am sorry to say. The Senate has already passed on it, but three fourths of the States must endorse the Amendment before it can become part of the Constitution. Unless affairs change greatly for the worse within six months, it will surely be ratified. The current sets steadily that way. — Witness this vote as compared with the last, 95 to 65, when the measure failed for want of a 2/3^{ds} majority. No one expected it to prevail in this Congress. — Who thought four years ago that John Brown would march so fast? And here has the Supreme Court of the U.S. just been admitting a colored person one of it's Attornies & Counsellors, on motion of Charles Sumner!!! I can scarce believe the Ev'g papers. The dust that was Roger B. Taney must have shivered in it's tomb when the motion was granted, and Sumner must have felt an acute but pleasing titillation in all those portions of his manly form that were contused by the Hon: Brooks' chivalric bludgeon, nine years ago come next May.

Feb: 2. There is no longer any doubt that A.H. Stephens & Co are somewhere within our lines, & propose talking about peace with Lincoln or any one else who will hear them discourse on that subject. The discussion will be an abstract one, & can lead to nothing, except perhaps to entangling our representative in his talk & putting us in a false position. Better have kept them out. I hope & almost believe that Uncle Abe's straightforwardness & sagacity will prove a match for the craft & subtlety of the Devil or the Confederacy, but these unofficial unauthorized negotiations can do no good, & may do harm.

Last Saturday Review considers Butler's failure at Fort Fisher conclusive proof that Earth works can be made absolutely impregnable, & is much comforted by our repulse there. — The finest specimen of British self-conceit I have yet seen is in a late *Blackwood* ("Papers by Cornelius O'Dowd" or some such thing is the title of the article). It's author thinks these wretched Northerners are fighting only because they thereby attract the attention of England, and that if English newspapers had ignored the squabble it would have ended long ago. But that while we Britons condescend to watch the row, &, as it were, to form a ring, the Yankee canaille will keep fighting, surprised & delighted to find itself an object of curiosity & of interest (partly compassionate & of course wholly contemptuous) to US Great Britons.

Feb: 3. Lincoln is at City Point this minute, talking Peace with A.H. Stephens & his two colleagues, who deserve hanging for treason, if ever men deserved it, & Stephens above all, who has sinned against the clearest light. This negotiation will come to no good. It is undignified for Lincoln to make a long expedition for the purpose of arguing with a little delegation of conspirators representing an armed & truculent rebellion. But if the palaver had to be held it will be less mischievous at City Point than at Washington, where these wily Legates *a latere* Diaboli would have contrived to open privy communication with copperheads & with invertebrate National men & with political caitiffs of every grade from that of Fernandy Wood up. The claims of the Rebellion & of the Nation seem incapable of compromise or adjustment by concession. The first principle of the latter is Union — that of the former is Independence of the Rebel States & their recognition as independent. These positions are irreconcilable by logic or rhetoric or negotiation. One or the other must be established by physical force. This is self-evident, unless our information as to Southern feeling, mainly derived from Southern newspaper articles & reported debates in Rebel legislatures & houses of Congress, be defective. It may be defective — Rebel Congressmen & Editors & legislators do their public writing & talking under a tyrannous pressure. Lincoln may know of subterranean movements toward Peace & reconstruction which justify him in consenting to hear what the Rebel delegates have to say. I hope so, but his consent looks like a weak blunder.

Feb: 6. Peace Negotiations seem to have proved a failure. *Laus Deo*. Lincoln & Seward have come back to Wash[n] *re infectâ.* Gold rises, of course, and that is bad, but nothing could be so bad as a parley with Rebeldom.

Feb: 7. Poor Walter Cutting, (Robt L.C's son), who's on Augur's staff, is in Agnew's hands, & Van Buren's, having met with a strange & painful accident. While inspecting pickets around the field works at Washington his horse ran away & plunged into a pine wood. A straight slender spicula of dead branch came into contact with his eye & penetrated to the very rear of the "orbit" or whatever is the name of the ocular cavity, striking it's wall close to the point at which it is entered by the optic nerve. Our enlightened Medical Staff allowed him to stay a week in Washington, & did little or nothing for him, & the inflammation grew so severe at last, that he had to come home on sick leave. A. & V.B. have dug out a dozen or more pieces of wood lodged within the cavity, and the chances are he will lose the eye. To make matters worse, he undertook to inflate an air cushion (for the relief of certain bumps & bruises he experienced when knocked off his horse) tho' he had been warned to eschew the use of pocket handkerchiefs & to be on his guard against temptations to sneeze — and this muscular strain ruptured certain inflamed tissues, & did him serious harm.

No trustworthy war-news. Rebel newspapers report Sherman as aiming at either Branchville S.C., Augusta, or Charleston, they know not which. Our daily Reports (at 823) state that Lee is supposed to be detaching part of his force to oppose Sherman, & that we are sending guns to the front, both right & left, & carrying all patients back to the Base Hospitals. If Lee be weakening his Richmond Army to defend the Carolinas,

Grant may feel strong enough to attack Richmond. But it's unlikely. — More rumors that *Mobile* is evacuated. They come from deserters — "reliable gentlemen" & "intelligent contrabands", & are primâ facie untrue.

Feb: 8. Grant's left moved on Sunday, & is reported to have repulsed three rebel attacks with brilliant success & no serious loss. Whether the demonstration was more than a reconnoissance in force, does not yet appear. But at U.L. Club, where I spent the ev'g with G.C.A., it's said that Gen: Davies (Judge Davies' son) is expected home to night, having been wounded, tho' not severely, *on Monday*. If this be true, & if the fight *were* continued on Monday, the non-appearance of despatches & the absence of all information about it, look unpromising.

Savings' Bank Trustees met this P.M. — At 823 thereafter as usual.

Not so clear but that the "Hampton Roads Conference" has done good after all, by silencing or converting Peace Democrats. Fernandy Wood has changed his base, & made a speech breathing battle murder & sudden death, & protesting against all talk of Pacification till peace is won by force of Arms. Opposition papers incline the same way, & say in substance, more or less distinctly, "Since the South refuses to negotiate about Peace, except on the basis of Recognition & disunion, there is nothing left but to fight it out". Strange they have been so long in coming to that conclusion. It has been self-evident for three years. The course of Southern leaders is unaccountable. They are astute experienced politicians & subtle negotiators. They must see that an offer to compromise would divide & paralyze the North, & that in the discussions to which it would lead they would get the ascendancy & be able to make their own terms of settlement, & secure the means of ultimate Disunion & independence. Probably they dare not trust their own people, & fear that if negotiations were once opened, they would be forced to consent to reconstruction, & would forfeit place & power.

Feb: 9. Thursday. Exceeding cold. There was fighting S.W. of Petersburgh — near "Hatchetts Run" (?) — Monday. Results "mixed". We held the positions gained on Sunday, but one division was stampeded in attempting a farther advance. Meade commanded in person. His reputation tends to wane. Interesting rumors from Mexico this afternoon, but only rumors. "*Duke Gwin*" seems to have cut & run, & is on his way to Europe. Cisco tells me to night that the (more or less) Hon: Foote, (whilom Rebel Congressman) is spending to night in Eldridge St: Jail under Gen: Dix's protection. Foote has abandoned the Confederacy & come within our lines, but Dix is instructed to keep him in ward till he leaves the Country, as he refuses to "take the Oath". He has had a long talk with the Gen: — says the Rebel Cause is hopeless, & that the Southern people know the fact, but are so mastered by the Richmond despotism that they can make no demonstrations toward reunion & peace. But Foote is a malcontent, & with a specially sore head just now.

Feb: 12. Richmond papers are said to report that Sherman has taken Branchville, & that Charleston is to be abandoned.

Tried to comfort myself under our wintry circumstances by reading D[r] Kane's books.

Feb: 13. Southern newspapers & mass-meetings at Richmond are full of fury & thrasonism, somewhat factitious perhaps, but certainly most passionate & shrewish in Expression. "It's all right *now*" say these Rebel "organs" & "our success is assured at last, *if every man will only do his utmost for our cause*". So said Napoleonizers when they heard of Waterloo. These Rebel voices speak truth. If *every* man South of the Potomac & the Ohio be ready to sacrifice *everything* for Seceshionism, the National cause must fail. If M[rs] Dombey could have been induced to "make an effort" that lady would have survived. — At a certain stage of every war, weariness & discouragement become important elements of the problem. The failing party may bluster about its possible achievements, were it rid of fatigue & despondency, but it's talk of those drawbacks — it's recognition of their influence, shew that it is in *extremis*.

Feb: 15. We must soon get weighty news from Sherman & S. Carolina. James' Island, not more than two miles below Charleston has been occupied in force. Branchville & Columbia are threatened, & the former seems to have been abandoned.

If so, Charleston is said to be made untenable. Sherman seems to divide up his army in a perilous way — but he knows his business better than I do. There is a strong & out-spoken call for *Peace* in N. Car: — *Peace* on any terms, if not the very best then the best obtainable — & evidence of mutinous feeling against the Richmond despotism. The Rebel army appears to share this yearning for Peace. May I live to see this Civil War so ended as to vindicate the Right — but may it not stop short of that, even tho' it's continuance send me to the Alms House. Peace prematurely patched up is the mother of battle & murder. "Maledicti Pacifici" may under circumstances, be just as true as the converse proposition in the Beatitudes.

Feb: 16. Will Lincoln pardon or reprieve that scoundrel Bell or Beall, sentenced by Court-Martial to be hanged next Sat: at Governor's Island, as spy, pirate, guerillero, and thief? Ja^{s} Brady has gone to Wash^{n} to plead for his client, & Lincoln describes himself rightly as "chickenhearted" on questions of life & death. But mercy would be wicked in a case as flagrant as this. The ruffian in question is bold & adroit, but no one is entitled to much sympathy who tries to "serve his Country" by putting obstructions on R.R. tracks, & exposing scores of women & children to mutilation or death, that he & his confederates may rob the Express car in the confusion, & thereby weaken their Enemy. — Mercy is good. God knows we all need all we can get of it. But it is good only in it's relations with Justice, & Mercy that wholly ignores Justice is probably quite as bad as Justice without mercy. We should probably be stronger to day, & our record would be clearer, had we from the first regarded every rebel as a Criminal, & recognized the guilt of Treason, proceeding to extremities only in aggravated cases — e.g. against Army & Navy officers who had thrown up their Commissions to take Rebel service, using the education they received from their Country without price, for their country's destruction. The unscrupulous barbaric Richmond clique would have ordered *Retaliation*, no doubt — but our position would be far better defined. — The Arago which arrived here yesterday aft^{n}, heard heavy firing as it passed Charleston Harbor on Sunday. A severe bombardment was in progress. Perhaps our new lodgment on James Island has become effective.

Feb: 17. Gen: Dix tells me Lincoln has postponed the execution of Beall, the pirate & spy, as predicted. We treat rebels traitors spies & assassins with unprecedented delicacy & mildness. It seems wrong, but the fact may have important bearings on the future course of history.

No definite War-news, but Sherman seems to have taken Branchville S.C. — a very vital ganglion. — The *Raleigh Progress* & the *Charleston Mercury* publish remarkable Editorials. Their sound is as the dying howl of a suppressed ram cat with a shattered spine. The former demands Peace, on any terms, — the best obtainable — but Peace NOW. Both indicate helplessness — utter inability to oppose Sherman's advance — Both denounce & vituperate Richmond & Jeff: Davis as savagely as they ever abused Washington & the Illinois Baboon — & both seem to look sideways at Subjugation & Reconstruction as possibilities that can no longer be ignored. — Per contra the N.Y. World, carrying out it's policy of disheartening & discouraging, thinks that when we have taken Charleston Wilmington & Richmond, & occupied all the Rebel Seaboard, the War will have but begun in earnest. Lee will withdraw to an interior position — entrench himself in the Western strongholds of Virginia & the Carolinas, & bid us defiance. Perhaps.

Feb: 19. *Columbia, the Capital of S. Carolina was abandoned by the Rebels & occupied by Sherman on Friday last.* It was abandoned under such pressure that the Rebels destroyed even the sorely needed medical stores in depot there. A few loyal shells seem to have entered the traitorous little town an hour or two in advance of the National Army. So testify the Richmond newspapers. *Columbia* has been pouring sanious purulent treason into our National veins for twenty years. It has been only less prominent & conspicuous than *Charleston* in bringing this murderous war upon us, & probably quite as deleterious a centre of poison to our National life. May there be cogent Military Necessity for scratching Columbia S.C. off the map of N. America!

Feb: 20. Monday. Mild weather. A busy day. Rec^d^ $520.000. & upwards, for San: Com: being proceeds of Philad^a^ "Great

Central Fair" held last June — & spent some time over telegrams, statements, forms of receipts & letters to Binney & Caleb Cope. Philadelphians are a fussy folk compared with New Yorkers. But they have done great service to the Country & the San: Com: too, in these latter years. Conference with Cram about Pete's troubles. — At two came an Extra — "*Evacuation of Charleston!*" Grant telegraphs Stanton that Richmond papers say Charleston was abandoned last Tuesday. We are of little faith, and do not fully receive these good tidings, tho' officially announced. Washington is said to accept them with jubilation, but we distrust them, & can shew reasons for the scepticism that is in us. We have Rebel news later than Tuesday, of skirmishing South of the City. Of course this may have been designed merely to cover the withdrawal of the Garrison.

At U.L. Club to night. Diverse opinions as to the Charleston report. Drake DeKay here — promoted to be Lt Col: for good conduct at The Wilderness & Spottsylvania C.H.

Feb: 21. Tuesday. Yesterday's doubtful news confirmed by the Fulton, which left Charleston Bar Saturday night. Charleston was entered and occupied Saturday morning, and the National flag floats over the ruins of Sumter. — The Chivalry did not stay to exchange shots with mudsills, but flitted Friday night, after firing their cotton-storehouses. As they left behind them only niggers & white Trash — (the Aristocracy having been gone some time) — they naturally & pardonably overlooked the fact that certain ordnance stores were lodged with their cotton, and an *explosion* killed some hundred or two, more or less, of their "Citizens." At last accounts the conflagration was still lively. Perhaps our people were unable to suppress it. Who cares? — Dahlgren thereupon steamed up the Harbor, & Gen: Gillmore followed him, and the detachment on James Island crossed the Ashley River & took possession of the place. — 200 guns are captured in the Harbor Forts. The City is mostly in ruins.

My deluded Southern friends — who would hear of no Compromise four years ago, "not even if you had *carte blanche* to dictate its terms", and who shook hands with effusion, & drank cocktails, in Charleston bar-rooms on the night of April 12th /61, after you had fired the Southern heart & hurled a proud & scornful defiance at Abe Lincoln & his Northern

Scum, by beginning a causeless Civil war, & who telegraphed in the exuberance of your jollity to Washington,

"With mortar cannon & petard,
We tender old Abe our Beau-Regard"

— what do you think about *that day's job* now? But I suppose a large majority of the young gentlemen who got more or less gloriously tipsy that memorable night are in their graves before this. Heaven forgive them their share in the colossal crime that has cost so many lives. Wiser cooler & better men might have been as blind mad & criminal had they grown up as members of a Slaveholding caste, in a womanflogging & baby-buying Country.

Of course the whole city has been lit up with flags all day. Long meeting at two, of sub-Committee of Com: on School of Mines. Betts, Rutherfurd, Fish, Jones, & I. — Much of our talk deplorably dense & fatuous — but the result, on the whole, not unsatisfactory, & we report in the course of red-tape, to the "Mother Committee" on Thursday, & then it will report to the Board some of these days.

And now, as we unanimously declare, *the Back-Bone of the Rebellion IS positively broken at Last.* So have I seen Johny after dinner, cornered, disorganized & trembling on the verge of Checkmate, when a careless move of mine has enabled him to pounce on a Castle or a Queen, & restored his game. I tremble for the events of the next 60 days!

Columbia & Charleston are abandoned of course in order that every available man may be brought into the field to oppose Sherman. They are sacrificed for the sake of concentration. Territory — cities — ports — prestige — warlike material that can no longer be replaced by blockade runners — all are less important than men enough to meet Sherman & Grant on even terms. There is a story (& many receive it) that Lee is about to give up Richmond, & fall back on Lynchburgh or thereabouts. This policy indicates that the Confederacy feels itself under severe pressure — but if so, the policy is wise. It may bring on one (or two) great battles — and the result of a great battle cannot be surely foreseen.

But the Confederacy with it's broken lines of R: R: will not easily *feed* it's Armies when they are massed together on the hungry & thinly settled Eastern slopes of the Alleghany Ridge.

Then there seems to be increasing discouragement among Lee's soldiers. They desert to our lines at the rate of 70 per diem, as reported. If half we hear be true, his army is like a *Prince Rupert's Drop* — kept together by pressure, & eager to disintegrate itself & disperse into fragments, the moment that pressure is removed at a single point. Lee's orders against straggling are said to be of unusual severity. Every man found half a mile from his camp to be arrested & taken to headquarters. The morale that requires so stringent a remedy will not be improved by news that Columbia & Charleston have been subjugated by the Yankees.

Feb: 22. More tidings of success. Fort Anderson, an important stronghold on the right bank of Cape Fear River, has fallen. At last accounts Army & Navy were moving steadily on Wilmington. May our gun-boats get there unscathed by torpedoes! —

Eruption of Flags over the City to day is positively confluent. Houses & stores, churches, public buildings, & omnibus horses all decorated. Nothing like it since the glorious uprising of 1861. We are celebrating Washington's birthday & the Fall of Charleston together. U.L. Club illuminated to night.

Feb: 23. Mild cloudy weather. We underwent a chill this morn'g, due to a Report of some check, repulse, or disaster, experienced by Grant. But the report came from Philadelphia & was therefore prima facie doubtful, and nothing has appeared to confirm it. So we hope & believe it was a weak invention of stock operators & dealers in gold.

Feb: 24. At 823 this P.M. & to night at Bellows' for our usual weekly meeting. Decided to hire premises in Grove St: for a "Home", with a strong squint toward the long talked of project of a *Sanitarium* — the beginning of a Hotel des Invalides.

I fear Ellie's grandmamma's long life of usefulness is near its' end. She seems failing, & is harassed by a distressing Cough. — Mrs John Sherwood has lost *both* her little twins by acute bronchitis. — Pretty little Miss Charlotte Higbee became Mrs Oscar Schmidt yesterday at Grace Church. They were married from my sister's — next door. — Rebel newspapers call the loss of Charleston "a blessing in disguise", and say that God is unquestionably "fighting on their side" though just at present "*with His Vizor down*"!!! A fine & startling piece of Chivalric Anthropomorphism. — Knapp tells me to night of a lively description given him by one of Sherman's staff of his jolly roystering march through Georgia — the glorious foraging — the constant surplus of turkeys & roasting pigs & beef cattle. He wound up by saying "In fact, sir, it was the *d—dest pic-nic* the world ever saw!" — Gen: Dix succeeded in getting Beall the Spy & "raider" hanged on Governor's Island to day — in spite of Lincoln's scruples.

Feb: 27. No news of Sherman. How much depends on his march! If it succeed & he meet no serious check, I shall think Rebellion moribund. Rebel newspapers still attitudinize as truculently as ever. Their audacity is amazing. But they *over-act* when they represent the *loss of Wilmington* & Charleston & Savannah as cause of congratulation & a crowning mercy that assures them of triumph at last. Meanwhile Lee's indomitable veterans are deserting their colors in the most unchivalric manner. Nearly 100 come into our lines every day, and others doubtless slip off the other way. Mrs *Carson*, who has been denounced abused cursed repudiated & insulted by her ferocious Charlestonian mother & sisters for four years, receives a bland letter from them, full of hope that our little differences may soon be adjusted & an era of good feeling return. R^{t} Rev: Coxe gets a letter from some Georgian Presbyter, which he thinks inspired by Bishop Elliott — a tentative letter somewhat to the same purport, & apologizing for the schismatic course of Southern clergymen as forced upon them by circumstances.

Feb: 28. Nothing yet from Sherman. News from his column is most anxiously looked for. He knows what he is about — but his troubles are only just beginning. Beauregard & Co must soon be able to scrape together force enough to shew fight.

Newspaper correspondents at *Charleston* & *Wilmington* expatiate on the display of Union feeling in both towns. Whoso will believe, let him believe — & be sold.

March 1. Agnew & Van Buren at 823 this aft^{n} — organizing a "Relief Corps" of Medical students for the coming campaign.

D[r] Peters at U.L. Club to night — just returned from a seven weeks exploration at Beaufort Savannah & Charleston, with Surgeon Clymer U.S.A. He seems to have made good use of his opportunities, & has much to tell that is interesting. He visited Sumter the day after the Rebels left it. Conflagration & rifled cannon have left about ¾ of Charleston standing, but the City is dead. Only low-caste whites & their Ethiops remain there. "Obstructions in the Harbor" have been a delusion for many months. There has always been an opening half a mile wide through the piles that barred the channel. This opening *was* obstructed with rope-net entanglements, but they were carried away by tides & currents, & the rebels got tired of replacing them.

Many of the better-most, blue-blooded Savannites still abide in Savannah. Of these ⅓ Secessionize strongly. The rest hate *U.S.A.* and *C.S.A.* — the Nation & the Rebellion — more or less impartially, & pant for peace & for the restoration of law & order anyhow & on any terms. — Peters supposes Sherman to be striking for Wilmington as a new base — with 60.000 men as a *minimum* estimate, & thinks Beauregard cannot confront him with more than 30.000.

March 2. Nothing from Sherman. There seems to be a panic in Richmond. Rebel Congressmen have gone away & the Rebel Congress gets a quorum only with difficulty. Richmond newspapers are protesting against giving up that town as utterly suicidal.

March 4. Sat: Like yesterday — copious rain, but the sun shewed himself early in the afternoon — too late however for the grand procession mass-meeting & jollification that were to have celebrated the progress of our Arms. That solemnity is put off to Monday. Would it were put off without day. Premature jubilation is unlucky, & we might better save up our fireworks till rebellion is finally smothered — or till Lee abandons Richmond — or at the very least, till we know where Sherman's Army is. Rebeldom can still fight, & whatever can fight may win a campaign or two.

Abraham the Venerable entered on his second term this morn'g. Have but glanced at his brief Inaugural. It seems strongly flavored with Anti-Slavery doctrine, but most fresh & real & unconventional. Perhaps ranked as a *great paper*, hereafter.

Stand'g Com: of San: Com: here this ev'g. Bellows, Agnew, Van Buren, Stillé, with Wolcott, Jenkins, & Knapp. Appropriated $100.000 for immediate investment in battle-field stores. Made progress with organization of our little Hotel des Invalides in Grove St. The lease of it's building has been taken in my name. We have published an advertisement announcing our intention to use funds for that object, and thus get around Prof: Dwight's opinion as to the trusts on which our funds are held.

My nephew Henry Derby dined with us. He is studying medicine & seems a fine intelligent young fellow.

No war-news, which fact is equivalent to good news. We should not be slow to hear of any check or disaster to Sherman through the Rebel papers. They seem in the dark as to his designs & his present position. But they tell us very briefly of Staunton being threatened by a force — which must belong to Sheridan. How did he get down there through the mud?

March 5. C.E.S. came to convey Miss Puss home. He had just received a telegram announcing that Bob Le Roy died at Philadelphia this morning! He has been on Gen: McCook's staff for about two years, serving with diligence & credit, and wholly free from excess in drink (if not strictly abstinent,) & was in Philad[a] on a short furlough, suffering from diarrhæa. While there, the old hereditary morbid appetite got beyond his control, & he experienced a prolonged *drunk*. It does not appear to have been a case of D.T. but this spree probably killed him. Requiescat in Pace. For his shortcomings others were in some large measure responsible. These two years of self control & self denying discharge of duty should go to the credit side of his own private account. — Peters brings news, officially promulgated he says, that Sheridan has taken *Staunton* V[a], bagging many prisoners, Gen: Early among them!!! If this be true, & if Sheridan be strong enough to push on toward *Lynchburgh*, & if Sherman be doing well in N.C. — *then* is Lee in a very tight place.

March 6. Monday. The news of Early's defeat & capture by Sheridan was telegraphed by Grant to Stanton & by Stanton to Dix. But as it rests on nothing but the hearsay of deserters and refugees, I receive it as not yet proven. — At Bank for Savings, & came down thence by hack with the weekly money box, dropping Ham: Fish (Attend'g Committee for this week) at the Astor House.

To day's grand jubilation was a splendid affair, more so than it would have been if held on the 4th, for there are Anti-Lincolnites who would have kept aloof lest they should seem to do honor to Lincoln by making the day of his re-inauguration a festival. The crowd was enormous. Even Wall St. was thronged with Brooklinites from the Wall St. Ferry. From the Park to Madison Square all N.Y. seemed in the streets at the windows or on the housetops. We saw great crowds in the Spring of 1861, & when the Prince of Wales honored us with a visit, but that of to day seems to me bigger than any of them — perhaps because the impression is more fresh. The procession was three hours & a half long — i.e. in passing any one point. I saw portions of it. — After dinner spent an hour at Union Square looking at fireworks. The jets of fire balls — red white & blue — a dozen or twenty in the air at once — were very brilliant & beautiful.

All this extravagant exuberant rejoicing frightens me. It seems a manifest omen of mishap.

Sorry to say that Andy Johnson — Vice Pres'dt of the Nation — whom I have held in great respect for four years past — seems to have been disgracefully *drunk* last Saturday, & hardly in a condition to take part in the inaugural ceremonies of the new administration. He has given the "World" & the "News" lamentable occasion to blaspheme. — Those newspapers denounce & deride the Inaugural address delivered by A.L. — It is certainly most unlike the Inaugurals of Pierce, Polk, Buchanan, or any of their predecessors — unlike any American state paper of this century. I would give a good deal to know what estimate will be put on it ten — or fifty — years hence.

March 8. Wednesday. Wet ev'g after a fine day. Poor Bob Le Roy's funeral was at Trinity Church 10 A.M. Ellie went with me — that true little woman never forgets an old friend. I was glad to see so many in attendance.

Poor fellow, he came home on furlough a fortnight ago, having suffered since June from Camp diarrhæa of unusual severity, but seemingly not at all pulled down by it. Gen: McCook spoke of him as among the bravest & coolest men he ever knew, & as having utterly abstained from stimulants while on his staff. Poor Bob spoke of his own reformation — lamented the prevalence of drunkenness among officers in the Army, and referred to himself as a living proof that the habit could be broken up, no matter how far it had gone [he had suffered at least two attacks of D. Tremens] — A day or two after, while he was waiting at a R.R. depot to receive Mrs C.E.S. & escort her to her hotel, the morbid appetite came on him suddenly with a force he found absolutely irresistible. This is what he stated on his death bed. He went involuntarily to the nearest grocery & swallowed two or three glasses of whiskey, one after another, & then adjourned to his Club to continue the treatment. Mrs C.E.S. found her way to her hotel without escort as best she could, & Bob returned to his father in law's house while the family was at dinner — his wife included, & dropped on the rug before the dining room fire. He was carried up to bed, and resumed the same practice next day.

March 9. Remittances of gold from California & Oregon required attention, as my invaluable Lieut: Treasurer Collins is still absent at Newberne. Talk with Cram & Pete, who is downcast & weak about the knees & blue & nervous. An affid^t was read on a motion to postpone the trial of the divorce suit, which sets forth a little of it's secret history & is not unlikely to be pounced on by newspaper reporters. — To School of Mines, where I spent an hour. — then to 823 where was Marcus L. Ward of Newark, & also Mrs Hoge & Mrs Livermore of Chicago, who are here working for the Great N.W. Sanitary Fair that is to be opened next June, & to surpass all Fairs that have been held since the Universe was a Universe. They are fearful & wonderful women, whose horsepower is to be expressed in terms of *droves* of horses. We send a first class propeller to Wilmington Sat: as the Uncas does not yet return from her last trip, & we cannot delay supplies to that point any longer. I should go with her, but for this confounded School of Mines. The next fortnight is a critical period in our accouchement of that bantling, & I ought not to go away.

Egleston & Chandler spent the ev'g here, settling drafts of certain circulars.

All reports tend to confirm the story that Sheridan licked Early very fearfully somewhere near Staunton V[a] about a week ago, but we get no despatches from Sheridan. Perhaps he has taken a lesson from Sherman & is pushing for Lynchburgh or some other point without trying to keep his communications open. Nor do we know anything about Sherman. I trust he may not have got himself mired in N. Carolina.

March 10. Richmond newspapers are in a special spasm of fury, beyond any fit they have yet suffered. We must not attach too much weight to what these sensitive excitable hightoned chivalric creatures rave when in nervous exaltation — whether arising from patriotic or from alcoholic stimulus. But this particular paroxysm certainly resembles the death flurry of a whale. The Editorial utterances are violent desperate incoherent hurried objectless. They amount in substance to this — that there is somewhere a class of "whipped seceders" & "whipped croakers" who desire subjugation, & have an appetite for infamy: that these caitiffs want Davis to abdicate, and their pressure is sufficient to make it worth while to expend much bad language on them: that they will not succeed in their base designs because Southerners never — never — *never* will be slaves, & because "our women" ought to take up their broomsticks & drive these wretches into the James River — &c &c &c. There are certainly signs in Secessia of incipient decomposition. The Rebellion has at the very least another year's fight in it — but it may die of inward disease within 30 days. — I trust it will not die too soon, & that it will be Killed, not merely "Kilt". I long for Peace, but only for a durable Peace — of material that will wear. John Bright writes F.M. Edge that he hopes our War will not end till it's work is done, & he sees the case aright.

The Rebel hosts continue to be seriously drained by desertion. Not less than fifty deserters have taken refuge within Grant's lines every day for many weeks past, & their average number is probably nearer 100 than 50. Companies come in, led by their company officers. All tell the same story, of compulsory service, hardships, failure of pay & of clothing & of rations — and of general despondency. The Confederacy has "gone up" they say, — "we all know it, & we know it is useless to fight any longer — " Lee's soldiers would throw away their arms & disband tomorrow, if they dared. And so on. Such statements made by deserters are worth much "less than their face". But when made by hundreds, & corroborated by the actual desertion of thousands at imminent risk of life & with certain & conscious loss of honor, they are worth a great deal. It is likely, moreover, that for every rebel who flees within our lines, two flee the other way & take sanctuary in the hill country or the "piney woods", supporting themselves by levying contributions on all & sundry, as Sovereign powers so far as their own personal Sovereignty can be made practically available, & thus carrying out the doctrine of Secession to it's ultimate legitimate results. Many counties of Virginia, the Carolinas, & the Gulf States are said to swarm with these banditti, & they are admitted to be even more savage & reckless than the Vandal hordes of the North.

The Rebel Congress seems to have reconsidered it's refusal to arm the Slaves, & to have decided, reluctantly & by a very close vote, that there is no help for it — and that Cuffee must be conscripted & made to fight for his Chivalric Master. So much for the visions of glory the South saw in /60! — This sacrifice of the first principles of the Southern social system is a confession of utter exhaustion — a desperate remedy & a most dangerous experiment. And the experiment is tried at least a year too late. It will take six months to drill & equip any considerable Corps d'Afrique, and Sherman Sheridan Thomas & Grant are likely — with GOD's blessing — to give Rebellion it's death blow within that time. But the measure has it's immediate effects. It disgusts & alienates many Slaveholders & many fanatical theorists about Slavery and it is received as an affront by the Rebel rank & file — an affront that justifies desertion. They will feel it not only as an affront, but as a disheartening surrender of the principle for which they have fought.

March 13. War-news on the whole very good. Yesterday's story that the column moving from Newberne on Kinston & Goldsboro', repairing the R.R. as it advances, had been attacked & forced back with heavy loss, is reported to day to be an exaggerated account of an affair of outposts. We also hear that Bragg attacked in earnest on the following day, & was badly beaten. But this is Philadelphia news. A despatch from *Sheridan* reports that he has occupied Charlottesville, & was when he wrote between Lynchburgh & Richmond, tearing up R.R. tracks, smashing canal locks, destroying the James River Canal, living off the country, & having a "high old time" generally. This is bad for Lee. There can be no great reserve stock of bacon & corn in Richmond, & Sheridan has cut a vital channel of supply. I should be glad to hear that Sheridan had ordered a bonfire to be made of the University of V^a^ at Charlottesville, a pestilent fountain of Anti-National theories, in which young men have been educated to become traitors, for thirty years past. Sherman's column seems to have left devastation behind it, as it marched thro' S. Carolina. Very deplorable, is it not? My view of the matter is like that of the lady whose poodle bit a piece out of her brother's leg, & who said "Poor little thing! I trust it will not disagree with him!" I am concerned only lest a month of pillage fire raising & general licence in S. Carolina should have impaired the morale & efficiency of Sherman's soldiers. If the report be true — (& it rests on rebel statements alone) — there have been doubtless scores or more probably hundreds of domestic tragedies in that state. Opulent old homesteads have been burned. Women & children have been made beggars. But think of the misery brought on thousands of households throughout the whole Country by this wicked wilful Rebellion for the sake of Rebelling & for no other sake & for no grievance or wrong whatever, & then of the part S. Carolina played in getting up Rebellion. If the words Justice — Punishment — Vengeance — be anything more than articulate sounds without meaning, it was right & just — "vere dignum et justum æquum et salutare" — that South Carolina be harried & laid waste. I know that Vengeance is a Divine attribute, but Armies are among the instruments Divine Providence uses to punish guilty communities, just as Judges Jurors Sheriffs & hangmen are organs of It's vengeance on individual malefactors.

March 15. Yesterday brought tidings from Sherman at last. At Laurel Hill N.C. the 8th inst. & "all right." — Gold dropped. To day at noon came news that he was at Fayetteville N.C. & had opened communication with Wilmington. This let gold down to 174⅛. A very deep descent & sudden fall. It almost makes me suspect that Operators have farther information of an esoteric nature. — Bragg has retreated across the Neuse. Sherman seems steering for Raleigh. If he get there safe, his entry may be the signal for a hearty counterrevolution. Loyal men abound in Raleigh & are kept quiet only by Davis's bayonets. And if Bragg stay where he is, he may find it a tight place. He will probably make for Raleigh, too, with Schofield after him. All which looks very nice & hopeful, but let us put off exultation a little longer.

Moreover the morning papers say that there is sore panic in Richmond, & that the Evacuation of that Pseudo-metropolis is positively in progress at last. This must be the 750th time we have been so informed, on the authority of "escaped prisoners" or "reliable gentlemen" or "intelligent contrabands". I should not think the story worth noting had I not a scrap of information from a disgusted N.Y. Secesher wh: tends to confirm it. The scrap of information is second hand of course (for I have no relations with any vermin of that species) & may be quite worthless. Probably it is so. But the report is not unlikely to be true. For both the Lynchburgh & the Danville R: RR: seem endangered by Sheridan's enterprising movements. At last accounts he was within twenty miles of Richmond, breaking things, & making great disturbance. If these roads or either of them be cut, Lee will be forced to choose between surrender, starvation, or a battle at great disadvantage. Even if he can hold them both, they must be hardly sufficient to bring him subsistence, now that the James River Canal is "busted up". Lee is a wary old practitioner, & may think it prudent to get out of Richmond while he can, lest he be shut in there & compelled to surrender his Army with his capital. The capture of that City would be of immense *moral* value to us, but I do not see that the place is worth much in a strictly military or strategic sense.

March 17th. Friday. Dined yesterday with C.E.S. — Convives Gen: Burnside, Gen: Dix, Tom Goddard, Griswold Gray & G.C.A. Most agreeable session. What a noble generous magnanimous fellow Burnside is! He may not be a great Captain, but he seems to be among the truest & best of men. — This dinner caused to day's sick headache, & kept me in bed till 6 P.M. Ev'g at Dr Bellows (S. Com: of the Commission) with Van Buren, Chas Stillé, & Gibbs.

Rumor to night of fighting before Petersburgh. There have been premonitions of battle there for a day or two. If Lee has attacked Grant's entrenchments, the odds are against him. Anything short of overwhelming victory is equivalent to defeat. But Lee's prudence boldness & skill make him always an ugly opponent, & if there is a battle, I shall be glad to know that it's well over.

Particulars of Sherman's progress from Savannah to Fayetteville shew that it was almost undisputed, & that he took or destroyed some 60 guns & great quantities of ammunition &c, abandoned by the fugacious Chivalry. — Gold keeps tending downward in a spasmodic way — it falls far, in a couple of hours, & then partially recovers itself by an upward jerk. I hear it touched 154 to day, & that the market closed at 166 or thereabouts.

March 18. At 823. $11.000 in gold from San: Francisco. Sold the draft at 64. No War news: no fighting around Richmond. Davis sends his Congress a Message, almost equivalent to a *Cognovit* of failure & ruin. — Southern newspapers are unhappy about the conflagration that destroyed Columbia S.C. when the Rebels walked out & our Army walked in. It would seem to have been caused by the firing of cotton stored there & to have been suppressed at last by the exertions of our soldiers. But it is attributed to Sherman's "*unprincipled Diabolism*".

March 19. No tidings from the Field, but we get sundry details of Sherman's march through South Carolina. South Carolinians seem to have behaved as a "whipped" people. They never dreamed of War within their own borders as a possible consequence of their arrogance & their treason of four years ago, and they meet invasion now by hanging out table cloths from the windows of their chivalric chateaux inscribed with the legend "Have Mercy on us". Charlestonians are elbowing each other in crowds around the Provost Marshal's office for the privilege of swearing fidelity to Government. Their oaths are not worth much, but their eagerness to swear shews what they think of the prospects of their Confederacy — or conspiracy. South Carolinian brag was good & effective, in Congress & in Conventions, but the pluck and endurance of Virginia, ravaged by War, rank her people far above the braggarts & faineants of Charleston & Columbia.

March 21. Great dismay in Wall St. Gold down to 156. It touched 152, I hear. So stocks are down & mens hearts fail them for fear of a revulsion & collapse. U.S. Securities can be bought for less than their face, taking accrued interest into account. This fact will throw cold water on the new 7–30 loan, a curious consequence of our late triumphs & of the general conviction that Rebellion is stricken with death.

Fifth Av:, from 49th St. down absolutely thronged with costly new equipages on their way to Central Park this bright bland afternoon. It was a broad torrent of vehicular gentility, wherein profits of Shoddy & of Petroleum were largely represented. Not a few of the ladies who were driving in the most sumptuous turn-outs with liveried servants, looked as if they might have been Cooks or chambermaids a very few years ago. — Blake was here this ev'g, a good talker.

News to night that Sherman or Schofield or both together have taken Goldsboro' N.C. Not unlikely per se, but it comes to us on the authority of certain scouts of Sherman's alleged to have reached City Point, whereas it ought, if true, to come thro' Newberne & Morehead City. I am therefore philosophically sceptical on the subject. Sheridan seems to have put himself in communication with Grant, & to be taking a breathing spell. He will probably strike out again soon, S. or W., for another job like his last.

Jeff: Davis' "Message" seems of graver & more doleful import the longer it is looked at. "Was ne'er prophetic sound so full of woe". — He tells his Congress that he & they & all Rebeldom are in desperate case, & that it is difficult to imagine a worse extremity than theirs, and urges remedies that are not only desperate but impracticable & that would be ruinous if practicable. His Congress has dispersed without administering these remedies or any of them. Strange this paper should have been published. Some say he means to resign & run — having no doubt put away a pot of money in London or Paris — & to become an illustrious exile, & that this manifesto is meant to justify his abdication. — Let him run if he will. I hope he may get off safe, for if we caught him we should not hang him & our omission to do so would be discreditable. Whatever may be Jeff's pious intentions, Lee doubtless intends to risk a battle or two for Raleigh & Richmond & we must not forget that he may win — and that any fight that could be even plausibly misrepresented as a Rebel victory would bring 20.000 rebel deserters back to their colors. — N.B. Richmond papers report that two negroes convicted of burglary have been pardoned on condition of enlisting, & have been mustered in accordingly. Pretty well for the Chivalry that has been howling these four years about the scum & the riff-raff — the runagates & jail birds — that make up the National rank & file. Scornful dog never ate a dirtier pudding.

March 23. Jeff: Davis' Congress, being snubbed by that Potentate in his last message, & charged with responsibility for all the present troubles of the Confederacy, "jaws back" thro' a Committee-Report adopted just before adjournment (*not* on ayes & noes), "Sasses" J.D., and says it's all his fault. As between J.D. & his peers, I believe myself quite impartial, like the spectator of the fight between Skunk & rattlesnake — & I think that on the face of the papers, "Congress" has the best of it, & J.D. gets a black eye. Anyhow, Satan is certainly divided against himself, & that is a hopeful sign, and besides, the decorous dabs administered in these official documents, & at this critical time, could have been produced only by sharp division & bitter discord. Richmond must be a nice place for a quiet man, just now — somewhat like Jerusalem when Titus was battering her towers, & her citizens cutting each others throats. "The haughty echo" of the guns that drove back the Star of the West from Charleston Harbor in Jan: 1861 [vide Charleston newspapers of the period] has not done reverberating yet, but the sound has become a bore to the surviving chivalry of that city. The heavy shot then fired have *come back* crashing & smashing through the roof trees of S. Carolina & of the South generally & through close columns of brave foolish young Southern sons & husbands & fathers, as the big stone that the reckless tipsy Irish gentleman (in one of Crofton Croker's admirable Legends of the *South* of Ireland) hurled into the Enchanted Cavern of Knock-fierna came back into his own face, knocked him senseless, & spoiled his beauty. What a deplorable wicked mischievous murderous blunder it was! — & how unaccountable! After thinking over the matter for years, I cannot understand why the Conspirators conspired & cannot make out the grounds on which they justified Rebellion, or (if they object to that term & insist that Secession from the Union was a right to be exercised by any "Sovereign" State at it's own pleasure, with or without reason) on which they justified the unsettling of the established order of things with Civil War as an inevitable consequence. I suppose the solution is to be found among the consequences of Slave-owning —

March 24. Friday. Gusty, with snow squalls. Gold 148, & this & that & the other Gold operator reported to have "gone up". Regret for their failure will be confined to themselves & their creditors.

San: Com: session here to night. Bellows Van Buren Jenkins. Agnew still in N. Carolina. Jenkins gives no good account of Knapp's ways at Washington — thinks him cunning evil-disposed, & untrue. It seems incredible this should be his character, but I fear he is not the embodiment of singlemindedness & unselfishness I used to suppose him.

Jenkins has just had a long semi-confidential talk with Whiting of the War office, & certain of our Western Agents have held like discourse with high officials of Thomas' Army, as to the coming campaign, & the points at which we should set about accumulating supplies. Their letters & reports, read to night were interesting. As far as they go they confirm Whiting's statements, which are generally none the worse for a little confirmation. Taken together they are encouraging. Sherman & Schofield are about 100.000 strong. Grant 140.000. Sheridan has 15.000 cavalry in S. Virginia. Hancock (or Torbert?) a like force at Winchester & some 8000 infantry beside. Thomas is 150.000 (I suppose this means our whole force from Nashville & Knoxville to N. Orleans.) He is to send 50.000 toward Lynchburgh & Danville, the Winchester column moving in concert up the valley, & is to command in person a column of 40.000 marching on Selma. The Department thinks it quite likely that Lee will have to capitulate without a battle. The draft & the volunteering thereby stimulated have already mustered into service nearly 100.000, & of these 30.000 are now under arms. We are 100.000 stronger than this time last year.

I hope all this may be true. If we have near 400.000 men in the field, Secessia must be outnumbered two to one, at least, to say nothing of discouragement, discord, financial collapse, & the closing of Rebel ports to supplies from abroad. May we get through the next sixty days without any serious reverse or blunder!

March 25. Sat: — Rebels report engagements somewhere near Fayetteville, & Sherman defeated with vast loss in both. As Sherman was routed — baffled — beaten — demoralized — stuck in the mud — manœuvered into a tight place — checkmated — hurled back with scorn — &c — &c — &c (on paper) at least 250 times while he was marching cheerfully thro' Georgia & S. Carolina, I see no reason to believe these reports. But they make me uneasy. I think it will turn out either that his advance has experienced one or two checks, more or less serious, or that he has suffered heavily in pushing the enemy out of some position — probably entrenched. — Tribune's Wash^{n} correspondent gives us sundry specially authentic disclosures from Richmond, warranted true by the Editor, including the verbatim report of a private talk between J. Davis & A.H. Stephens. Also the minutes of certain evidence given by Lee before a "Congressional" Committee of Enquiry. Lee is made to testify that he cannot hold out where he is till midsummer — that his Army would decompose if moved out of Virginia, & that according to the best judgment the Confederacy is past saving. Quicunque vult decipi, decipiatur. It's very possible Davis Stephens & Lee may have said or sworn all this, but I do not believe this correspondent knows it any better than I do.

At Philharmonic Rehearsal 3 P.M. — Beethoven's 9th Symphony (the *Choral*) of which I have not heard a note for about five years. A rough performance.

———

At 823 thereafter. Long letter from Agnew at Wilmington about our returned prisoners. 3000. Many of them idiotic from months or years of starvation & exposure, unable to remember their own names, without sense of modesty or decency, brutalized past restoration by the politic cruelty of Rebels who call themselves Chivalric. Shall we ever begin to deal with Rebels as they deserve? I hope not, after all, for it would be a fearful office to entrust to mortal man.

March 26. Vinton at Trinity Church this morning. Despatch from Schofield in morning papers (21st I think) indicates nothing unfavorable. He was within hearing of Sherman's guns, & Terry moving north from Wilmington, had almost put himself in communication with both columns. — From City Point the news seems more important. Lee made an offensive move yesterday & failed; — played out a Knight at least, if not a Castle, & lost it. That is to say, he suddenly attacked & carried one of our field works at daybreak or a little before it, but was promptly driven out again, *minus* 3000 killed & wounded & as many prisoners. Our loss about 800, & none of our guns disabled. This large haul of prisoners looks a little like demoralization among Lee's rank & file. If this affair have cost Lee 6000 men, it is a heavy blow & sore discouragement to the Army of Richmond. — — Ellie had a long talk with Senator Foster this aft[n]. He has just returned from a visit to Charleston & Savannah & has much to say that is interesting & instructive. — Rood shewed us this ev'g photography taken by Magnesium light. — *Kennedy* was hanged yesterday, on Governor's Island, as a guerilla & spy, by Sentence of Court-Martial for his share in the Rebel effort to burn this City last Nov[r]. It is satisfactory that he confessed just before he was hanged. His end was not edifying but the reverse. He died "sae rantingly, sae dauntingly" as the old Scotch song has it — & though he did not "play a spring & dance a fling — Under the gallows tree", he sang a verse from some reckless Irish ditty the moment before he was run up. McMahon & Stoughton said last ev'g that his conduct & demeanor indicated intense nervous excitement & consternation at the prospect of death, which the wretched man was trying to conceal by swagger profanity & indecency. But the poor devil has gone to his account — has suffered for the sins of his fathers & his brethren & for the vices of the social system in which he was reared or "raised". He has been hanged by the neck till he was dead, & has undergone the uttermost infliction & visitation of Mortal Finite Justice. Infinite Immortal Justice & Mercy will surely & fully redress all wrongs done on Earth. Let us not insult the memory of this miserable scamp. We have done our duty by him. If there were latent good in him God knows it, & it will not be forgotten.

March 27. To day's news from Sherman Schofield & Terry looks well. Their two *defeats* lately announced by Richmond papers look like insignificant affairs of out-posts in which Sherman & C° got the mastery, & after which they marched on, pushing Johnston Hardee Bragg & C° before them. It's not at all improbable that we have taken possession of Raleigh N.C. before this, & if so North Carolina will soon be a penitent petitioner for leave to come back to the Union under a reorganized State Government cordially approved by at least half her people. Results of the fight before Petersburgh on the 25th seem to have been satisfactory. Not only was Lee beaten back with loss of some 6000 killed wounded & prisoners, & nothing to set off against that loss, but we seem to have gained & to hold certain rifle pits or field works of Lee's.

I must record the movement of two *Chips*, because they shew which way the tide is setting. I. The Baltimore correspondent of the N.Y. World — a bitter secessionist — who has long been prophesying Woes to the Country & victory to Jeff: Davis, over the signature of "Druid", writes that within a few weeks or months "the Confederacy must cease to exist. It will no longer have a Government an Army or a Capital. It's leaders made several mistakes at the outset, and among others this, that the cause of Self-government and Freedom must be destined always to prevail." Does this statement invite one to vehement cachinnation or to profuse nausea????? — II. Recent debates in House of Commons. Palmerston & Disraeli &c of one mind with Mr Bright, commending the energy & discretion of Lincoln's administration under the most trying circumstances, & the most creditable spirit it has shewn in all it's dealings with Foreign Powers!! — Poor mean shabby fallen old England restores us the tribute of her shopkeeper's civility & compliments the moment she discovers that we may win our unpromising law-suit after all, "come to our own again", & be a profitable customer or an expensive enemy next year.

March 28. Gold seems to have stuck fast in the neighbourhood of 154. The prophets of Wall St: prophesy that it will not soon sink much lower. They hold that we have discounted Victory, that the late rapid decline represents the common belief that Rebellion is as good as dead already, and that gold will stay where it is for some time after Rebellion is actually defunct & gibbeted in chains as a warning to posterity. I do not think so. The wisest financier can only guess how it will be, for the equation is too complex & includes too many unknown & variable quantities — too many chances & contingencies — to be worked out by human wit.

The fray of the 25th before Petersburgh was no small affair. Had Lee's veterans fought as they fought last May it might have been a bad business. But after their first brilliant & successful dash at our line they shewed little sign of their ancient pluck & tenacity. When once inside "Fort Steadman" many of them seem to have withdrawn into bombproofs in spite of their officers, & thus to have secured an opportunity to surrender by dint of great resolution. Lee cannot afford many experiments like this. It must have cost him ten per cent of his available force. But what can he do? Grant has him by the throat. Sherman, reinforced by Schofield & Terry, was at last accounts threatening Raleigh N.C. & steadily approaching the last duct that brings nutriment to the garrison of Richmond.

March 29. Agnew made a long & most interesting Report (verbal) on what he did & saw at Newberne & Wilmington. Our supplies sent by the "Chase" reached Wilmington just at the right moment & saved scores of lives. His account of the condition of hundreds of returned prisoners — founded on personal inspection — is fearful. They have been starved into idiocy — do not know their own names, or where they are, or where their home is. Starvation has gangrened their extremities — destroyed their instinctive sense of decency, — & converted them into irrational atrophied moribund animals. No Bastille & no Inquisition Dungeon has ever come up to the Chivalric Rebel Pen for prisoners of War. I do not think people quite see — even yet — the unexampled enormity of this crime. It is a new thing in the history of man. It infinitely transcends the records of the Guillotine, & concomitant Noyades & Fusillades. The disembowelment & decapitation of all the men women & children of a Chinese city convicted of rebel sympathies is an act of mercy compared with the politic slow torture Davis & Lee have been inflicting on their prisoners, with the intent of making them unfit for service when exchanged.

I almost hope this War may last till it become a War of extermination. Southerners who could endure the knowledge that human creatures were undergoing this torture within their own borders, & who did not actively protest against it, deserve to be *killed*.

March 30. At 823 were Bellows, Van Buren, Agnew & I, & a clear & valuable Report from the physiological Dalton, who accompanied Agnew to Wilmington, on the condition of our returned prisoners there. We ordered it printed.

Gold touched 149 to day. Military matters are as they were. Sherman's army is taking a rest at or near Goldsboro' & trying on it's new shoes. Lee has made another push at Grant's lines — a small affair compared with that of the 25th — and took nothing by his motion. Sheridan is on the rampage somewhere South of the Appomattox. A column from Thomas seems moving Lynchburgh-ward. We are closing in upon Richmond but Lee has his back to the wall, & will fight like a rat in a corner, if his men can be kept to their work. I do not believe it possible for him to carry his Army to Danville or Lynchburgh if he wants to. His only hope is in the chapter of Accidents. Something may turn up. Richmond editors keep up their spirits however, and also their Vocabulary. One of them calls Sherman a "Blustering Bluffer" — whatever that may be: — no doubt something horribly offensive. Another admits that the Confederacy has been in a bad way for some time, & is in a rather tight place just now, but takes comfort in the thought that the movements of Grant & Sherman have been devised by old Scott (!) and that Scott being a Virginian, it is really "the South" that took Savannah Wilmington & Charleston. That is optimism carried to it's highest perfection. Some one told me the other day a story of a New England farmer whose two disreputable sons had been severally sent to the State Prison. His friends called to condole with him — & he "allowed" that it was a dispensation & a trial, but not without features of compensating good — for "after all, *come night, you know where they be*". — Lincoln & Sherman have visited City Point & held Council with Grant. Hence comes a swarm of "Peace" rumors. I believe & almost hope they are unfounded. "Peace" with the miscreants who perpetrated or acquiesced in the horrors of Libby & Andersonville sounds like "Peace" with the powers of Hell. The harrying of Virginia & S. Carolina is but an instalment of their deserts — not enough to keep down the interest. Whenever these most cold & calculating of all inhuman & merciless savages choose to lay down their arms, I suppose we must receive them back to the privileges of citizenship, but till they do so let us know them only as subjects for hot shot & cold steel, & their territories only as "food for the sword & the torch" [which phrase is a quotation from a Speech of Jeff: Davis' four years ago, in which he mentioned Northern Cities] & let us beware of polluting ourselves by treaty or negotiation with them. May War be made on them till they are exterminated, no matter what it cost me & my children.

March 31. Gold 151. News that Mobile was attacked on the 21st. Result not yet known. Also that Grant opened an important movement at 3 A.M. the 29th. Sheridan seems to have marched toward Dinwiddie C.H. backed by a strong infantry force. Object probably to cut the "Southside R.R." & perhaps to draw Lee out of his forts. I hope this rain may not have spoiled the party. We may expect weighty news any minute. There has already been a lively little collision, of which the rebels had the worst. Tho' all the chances are in our favor, I am anxious, for we are in a premature state of jubilation that invites disaster.

Agnew opened more of his budget from Wilmington & Newberne. He tells us Sherman's officers say that *their campaign was made possible by the order of the Rebel government that corn be planted instead of cotton*. Four years ago the army could not have been fed. As it was, they marched through a land of groaning corncribs & granaries, & their men & their animals entered Savannah in better flesh than when they left Atlanta. A notable statement. Agnew brought with him & took to his house a Col: Morse, of a Mass: regiment, wounded at Bentonville N.C. who tells this. Among the Rebel forces engaged in that fight was a S.C. heavy artillery regiment or brigade that had been holding the defences of Charleston Harbor, and came away with Bragg. It was made up of the most chivalric S. Carolinians with blood bluer than indigo, & shewed the utmost pluck & audacity, but being without experience of business in the field, got into a bad place between two fires, & was awfully cut up. When our parties went out to bring in the wounded, many of the officers of this regiment insisted on being left to die rather than be "touched by a d—d Yankee". One of them when in *articulo mortis*, & almost blind, kept picking up pebbles & trying to throw them, feebly, in the direction from which the voices of the Relief parties came to his dying Ears. *Rhett*, the Col: or Brigadier of the command was made prisoner, taken to Slocum's headquarters, & treated with distinguished consideration & courtesy. But he was so supercilious & puffy that Slocum & the Staff found him an intolerable bore, sent him off to the rear, in charge of a Sergeant — having first made him formal overtures for the purchase of his new boots at $100.000.00 in Confederate paper, and (when that proposition was indignantly declined) at $10.00 in greenbacks. The Sergeant who marched this "high-toned" chivalric personage to the rear, saw the poltroonery that underlay his swagger, & being doubtless a practical humorist, told him as they walked together thro' the pine woods "Of course you know, Sir, that we generally hang men like you, now, that is, men who talk your way — particularly men who belong to S. Carolina. Hav'nt you read the general order? Strange you hav'nt seen it, Sir, but that's the rule now. We generally hang 'em about two miles farther on, Sir. We'll be there in a few minutes now Sir. Will they hang you Sir? O I do'nt know nothing about that. We'll see when we get there." This produced a paroxysm of abject fright entreaty & submissiveness that nearly cost the valuable life of a S. Carolinian.

From observation at Wilmington Agnew thinks the Southern "masses" an effete people, unable to take care of themselves, now that their Slaveholding Lords & magnates are gone. A "local Committee" at W. is feeding 4000. Wilmingtonians on rations issued by government. The White trash of even N. Carolina is helpless & imbecile, unable either to work or to re-organize the community.

April 1. Sat: Most unamiable March weather. Noon brought an Extra. Despatches from Grant. In substance — "Hard fighting yesterday. We took the Boydton plank road, lost it, recovered it, & hold it. Also took four battle flags." Not bad as far as it goes, tho' it leaves much to the imagination. Lee cannot afford indecisive battles, and this is unlikely to be anything worse. But it's an anxious time. Spent the morning mostly in nervous wandering from one bulletin board & Newspaper office to another: but in vain, & have just (half past ten) left the U.L. Club, hoping later news might come there, but none came. It will be discouraging if Grant fall back, *re infectâ*. Are we sure Parke can hold our field works, & protect City Point & the Army R.R? He is stripped of Cavalry. Grant knows what he is doing, but it is certain he has divided his force, which is primâ facie, a false move, and it seems to me that this move could have been more safely made when the column from E. Tennessee was making itself felt at Lynchburgh, & Sherman was within supporting distance. But I confess myself, very willingly, not qualified to sit in judgment on Grant's strategy. As Sherman is freely giving officers furloughs till the 20th inst: it would seem he expects to stay where he is till then.

According to C.E.S. who has returned from City Point & the front, after three days there, our officers say the Rebels have clearly lost heart, that they fight coldly, run readily, & surrender joyfully. To be sure, this hard pounding on the 31st looks unlike it. — But he talked with a Major Miller of Gen: Tidball's staff, who was bagged by the Rebels during the "Fort Steadman" fight. Their commanding officer ("a Louisiana Tiger, G— d— you") instantly demanded the Major's overcoat watch money & horse, which were surrendered, & hailed the orderly who was taking off the quadruped. "Recollect now, that's *my* horse, do'nt you go & turn him over to anybody." After this business transaction, the Major asked his captor's name & rank, received the answer above quoted, & was ordered to the rear. But it "rained blue beans", as the Germans say, & also iron cocoa nuts & watermelons, all along the way to the rebel lines, — the fire from both sides was a "feu d'enfer", & the Major's guard preferred taking him into one of the bomb-proofs of Steadman & waiting there till the storm should abate a little. The bomb-proof was already crowded with Rebel Soldiers. The Major proceeded to call the attention of those nearest him to a few leading facts. 'The Confederacy had gone up. If they went back to their own lines & took him along, it would be unpleasant for him, but would it be a good thing for them? They would have to do more fighting & probably be bagged at last. Whereas, if they were only in *our* lines, they would be well treated, & get not only abundant rations, but twenty dollars each for their arms & accoutrements'. They listened eagerly, but did not like to *desert*. "Very becoming & proper" said the Major, "but why ca'nt I take you in as *my prisoners*?" The suggestion was rec[d] with favor, so he formed them in column by threes, & doublequicked them into our lines, *204* men, each with his musket.

April 2[d]. Fine weather. There is reason to hope this day may long be remembered. To Trinity with E. & the two boys. After service (communion) we asked Gen[l] Anderson (of Fort Sumter) to ride up with us, and stopped at the Tribune office to look for news. There was an extra with a despatch from Lincoln, at City Point, to Stanton — brief but weighty. Read it to the General, & his *Thank God* was fervently uttered & good to hear. At four o'clock came another extra, with another despatch dated 11 A.M. to day, from which still farther success may fairly be inferred. Since then, lots of "authentic rumors", all rosecolored & utterly untrustworthy, but nothing official which makes one a little uneasy about the general result of the great battle that has doubtless been fought to day. I well remember our first tidings from Bull Run, & the woful news that came a few hours after them. A Victory just within reach may so easily be turned into a defeat by so many accidents. *Spero Meliora*. We shall soon know.

To night dear little Katinka as usual. Afterwards, C.E.S., Murray Hoffman, D[r] Peters, M[r] S.B.R.

After studying our imperfect maps of the Petersburgh country in consultation with C.E.S., who has just come from the front & is strong on localities, I cannot make even a tolerable guess as to the relative position held by the two armies, or the outline of the battle. Lincoln reports prisoners & forts taken, & several batteries. That is tangible — all the rest is shadowy. Our lines now extend from Hatcher's Run to the Appomatox. At what points? Grant "ordered an attack along the whole line" & "both Wright & Parke got thro' the enemy's lines" (despatch of 8.30 A.M.) — Does this mean that Parke carried the works in his front? If so he must be in Petersburgh. Sheridan's cavalry, "the 5th Corps & part of the 2d are coming in from the West on the enemy's flank, & Wright is already tearing up the Southside R.R." — (despatch of 11 A.M.) — It is all a muddle. One construction of these despatches is that we are actually between Lee & Petersburgh. A dozen others are equally plausible. May God send us good tidings tomorrow!

April 3d.

PETERSBURGH and RICHMOND!

Gloria in excelsis DEO.

Monday. New York has seen no such day in our time, nor in the old time before us. The jubilations of the Revolutionary War & the War of 1812 were those of a second rate seaport town. This has been metropolitan & worthy an event of the first National importance to a Continental Nation, and a cosmopolitan City.

The morn'g papers disclosed nothing decisive. There were two short despatches from City Point, giving later news of yesterday's great battle, which looked well, but I omnibussed down town expecting only to learn during the day, more positively, that the South Side R.R. was cut — that Lee had returned to his intrenchments badly punished, & that it was confidently expected that he would have to evacuate them at some future period. Walking down Wall St. I saw something on the Commercial Adv: Bulletin Board, cor: Pine & William Sts, & turned off to investigate. I read the announcement "Petersburgh is taken" & went into the office in quest of particulars. The man behind the Counter was slowly painting in large letters on a large sheet of brown paper, another *Annunciation* for the board outside. — "RICHMOND is" — "What's that about Richmond" said I. — "Anything more?" He was too busy for speech — but he went on with a capital C. & a capital A — &c till I read the word, CAPTURED.!!!! Finding that this was official, I posted up to Trinity Church to tell the Sexton to suggest to Vinton to ask the Rector's permission to set the chimes going (*which was duly done*) — When I came back, all William St. around the Advertiser office was impenetrably crowded; & people were running together in front of the Custom House (ci-devant Merchants Exchange) where Prosper M. Wetmore & Sim: Draper were getting up a meeting on the spur of the moment. An enormous crowd soon blocked that part of Wall St., & speeches began — Draper & Hon: Moses Odell & Evarts & Dean (a proselyte from Copperheadism) & the inevitable Wetmore &c &c &c severally had their say, & the meeting, organized at about 12, did not break up, I hear, till 4 P.M. — Never before did I hear cheering that came straight from the heart — that was given because people felt relieved by cheering & hallooing. All the cheers I ever listened to were tame in comparison because seemingly inspired only by a design to shew enthusiasm. These were spontaneous & involuntary & of vast "magnetizing" power. They sang Old Hundred — the Doxology — "John Brown" — & the Star Spangled Banner — repeating the last two lines of Key's Song over & over & over — with a massive roar from the crowd & a unanimous waving of hats at the end of each repetition. I think I shall never lose the impression made by this rude many-voiced Chorale. It seemed a revelation of profound National feeling, underlying all our vulgarisms & corruptions, & vouchsafed to us in their very focus & centre, in Wall St. itself. I walked about on the outskirts of the crowd, shaking hands with everybody, congratulating & being congratulated by scores of men I hardly know even by sight. Men embraced & hugged each other — *kissed* each other — retreated into doorways to dry their eyes & came out again to flourish their hats & hurra. There will be many sore throats in N.Y. tomorrow. My only experience of a people stirred up to like intensity of feeling was at the great Union meeting on Union Square, April 1861. But the feeling of to day's crowd was not at all identical with that of the memorable mass-meeting four years ago. It was no less earnest & serious, but it was founded on memories of years of failure, all but hopeless, & on the consciousness that National Victory was at last secured, through much tribulation.

Ellie appeared in Wall St. full of her projected visit to City Point with a pleasant party, on *Arthur Leary's* Steamer. Dear little Kate — in charge of her maid — rushed into the office to say that her Papa must instantly go out & buy a flag for the adornment of E. 22^d St.

To Col: Coll: meeting at two P.M. Much done — but nothing of value. Thence to 823. — where I learn that that valuable & single minded officer, Gen: Potter is most severely, if not mortally, wounded. He was to have married Miss Abby Stevens. I hope the report overstates the mischief. The family of his betrothed has disgraced itself — were I in his place I should prefer death to marriage with a sister of Mrs P.R.S. of J.A.S. J^r & of Mrs L.H. — But beautiful Miss Abby is not responsible for the doings of her household. Poor young lady! This is doubtless a bitter night for her.

After dinner to U.L. Club. Vast crowd, enthusiasm, & excitement. Meeting organized up stairs, Captn Marshall in the chair & "a few remarks" made by a score of people. Honest downright old Judge Vanderpoel was very good. "Gentlemen" said the Judge "I tell you that for years before this Rebellion we at the North lived under the tyranny of the Slaveholders. I see now that when I was in Congress almost every important vote I gave was dictated by them & given under the plantation lash. I confess it with shame, & humbly ask pardon of this meeting & of all my fellow-countrymen". — Ham: Fish was at the Club — never saw him there before — beaming & gushing & shaking everybody's hands with fervor. Two years ago he talked nothing but discouragement & *practical* disloyalty. But (as Sydney Smith irreverently said of Bishops) "If you want to know which way the wind blows, *throw up H.F.*"

It seems like a Fourth of July night — such a fusillade & cannonade is going on. Thus ends a day *sui generis* in my life.

We shall long remember that the first troops to enter Richmond were *Niggers* of Weitzel's corps. It is a most suggestive fact. — It's said there were abundant signs of Union feeling in the City. Lee Davis & C° are supposed to be making for Burke's Junction. Lynchburgh or Danville is doubtless their proposed harbor of Refuge. May Sheridan's Cavalry be fresh enough to deal with them according to the example of Blücher after Waterloo. The Government of the "Confederate States" has become nomadic. It's Capitol & its Departments of State & of War are probably in a dirty damaged worn-out R.R. car, & its "Seat of Government" probably rests on the saddle wh: Jeff: Davis bestrides.

April 4th. Tuesday. Dullish weather, but this ev'g is clear. Ellie set off for City Point on the steamer George Leary, with a large pleasant party. Mrs Paran Stevens & Miss Fanny Reid, John Van Buren & his pretty daughter Miss Annie, Capt: Comstock & his daughter, Arthur Leary, Griswold Gray & Col: Stoughton. Wish I could have gone. I consented with sore misgivings, but she had earned this little spree by her faithful service on Hospital transports on the Pamunkey & the James in /62. — And I fear she & her party will be disappointed after all, & unable to visit Richmond.

Broadway is a river of flags. — Poor Frederick Winthrop was shot thro' the lungs & is dead. He rose from the ranks to a brigadier general's brevet. He was a cousin of Theo: Winthrop's — & brother of Frank Winthrop, with whom I walked up town after the Coll: meeting yesterday. — It's said another despatch came last night, after Howard Potter had left town, announcing the *death* of Gen: Robt Potter. To night's Post mentions the report as probably true. God help poor Miss Stevens! — At Life & Trust C° meeting this morning — & at 3 P.M. to meeting of *Kenzua* C° Directors at their new office 36 Wall St. To night at U.L. Club, looking over the collection recently bought by the Club of foreign books & tracts on the Rebellion. Nearly all one way, of course.

No news from the front up to half past one. Everybody was sallying out to look for news every ten minutes & coming back disappointed and wondering whether something had'nt gone wrong. At last came announcements on bulletin boards, & an Extra with despatches. They indicate that Lee is damaged & demoralized. The Country is full of stragglers. We bag prisoners in large handfulls. Lee's course is marked by abandoned artillery & by burned or charred wagons & caissons. Great store of war-material found at Richmond, including R.R. rolling stock. — Unofficial statements are that we have 15000 prisoners at City Point — that Fort Darling & the rebel ironclads on the upper James have been blown up — that the Union feeling of N. Carolina is so star spangled as to be actually oppressive — that Sherman's men are so cocky & Johnston's Rebels so depressed that three of our foragers commonly form in line of battle when they encounter not more than thirty seceshers, & always drive them. Also, however, that the communication between Goldsboro' & Sherman's base is thought to be just a little endangered by Wade Hampton's Cavalry.

Guns popping off in every direction to night. A salute of 100 guns fired at the foot of Wall St this morning — & another in front of U.L. Club to night.

Surely the Slaveholders' Rebellion, with it's capital lost, it's best army defeated, it's soldiers demoralized, it's people broken spirited, & its ports closed to contributions from sympathizing Britons, & its President & chief General both running for their lives, cannot sustain itself or claim to be called a Nation, much longer. But Heaven save us from overtures of Peace & reconstruction for the next six months. May Pharaoh's heart be hardened yet a little longer!

April 5th. Wednesday. Fine weather. Hope E. may be safe & well at City Point. "O my leanness, my leanness!" How frightfully poor I am! My bank a/c is visible only under a 1/12 inch object glass of superior defining power. Never mind — we've got Richmond.

Sorry to hear of Bishop DeLancey's death. Thus our neighbour, Rt Rev: Coxe becomes Bishop of W.N.Y. & not merely Assistant.

Gen: Potter's wound tho' severe is not necessarily mortal. So Brown Brothers are told by telegraph. He has already survived one desperate wound, from a musket ball that went clear thro' his body, taking off a suspender button in front & another behind. So he has a precedent for surviving this. We cannot yet spare officers of his merit & capacity.

Spent most of the ev'g cramming young Ogilby. He has waked up, perhaps because I gave his Rev: papa a gentle hint that he needed a little stimulus, & his examination this ev'g was quite creditable. But he does'nt know much.

Despatches are still bright. They report Lee's Grand Army crippled & in great measure disorganized. Unless newspaper correspondents lie most exorbitantly, it is used up & done for. Many think Lee will now confess farther fight mere waste of life, & give it up. I do not think so. Slaveholders' arrogance is a powerful tonic, even in cases of absolute collapse. And it has the property of dilating the pupils & impairing vision, so that the patient does'nt see the signs of adverse Destiny. No. To give the devils their due, there is no back out in the breed of Lee & Davis. Their prototype is Milton's Satan. — But what can Lee now undertake with any reasonable hope of success? Of course there are chances & accidents & possibilities, but what move can he make without ten chances against him for one in his favor? Suppose he succeed in uniting his shattered army with Johnston's. Grant will bear down on him from one direction — Sherman from another — Thomas from a third, & either is probably his match. Suppose he try another dash on Washington — there are 20.000 men at Winchester, & twice 20.000 could be sent North by water to meet him. — A grand march for Texas? His army would melt away long before it got there, & the Mississippi is patrolled by National gunboats. Then there is the moral influence, on Rebel Armies & on the masses to which they look for reinforcement, of last Monday's event. Their capital, the gage of battle for four years, the central prominent object of the War, has fallen at last — tho' Charleston & Savannah & Wilmington had been given up for it's sake, & in order to carry out a grand strategic policy of concentration, that was to squelch the braggart Sherman & the overrated Grant & the fiend Sheridan. It's fall lowers the vital forces of Rebeldom 50 per cent at least.

April 6. To day's news is good & full of promise. Lee is retreating perforce toward Lynchburgh. He cannot make for Danville, or try to join Johnston in N.C. because Sheridan & Grant are moving on a parallel line South of his, & are seemingly ahead of him. He has been obliged to take the wrong side (the North bank) of the Appomattox. We were last ev'g, at "Jettersville", "Black & White Station", & Burkesville, where the two R.R's cross — This is an important position. Sheridan sent word to Grant yesterday, that "if we exert ourselves" we can capture or break up what is left of Lee's army, but we can hardly hope for a "crowning mercy" so signal as that would be. Cisco tells me however that Gen: Dix thinks Sheridan will do it.

At Richmond we have taken several hundred guns, some say 500. Jeff: Davis made a moonlight flitting Sunday night, & is believed to have taken a special train for Danville. Like the missing Massa, in the "Year of Jubilo"

"He saw the smoke 'way down the river, where the
Linkum gunboats lay,
And he picked up his hat, & he left very sudden,
& I 'spec he's run away!

But however fast he run, the curses of widows & orphans North & South will keep up with him — & ten times as many of them as waited on Robespierre at the guillotine. He is responsible, beyond any other man or score of men for the devastation & the carnage of this War, the only Civil War in history without the excuse of a grievance to be redressed. He is responsible for the murder of thousands by slow torture of exposure & starvation, deliberately inflicted, with politic purpose, at Andersonville & Libby. If criminality be measured by the consequences of crime, there has been no criminal so worthy the extremest penalty man is authorized to inflict on man.

Gen: Davies (under Sheridan) has taken 5 guns, 200 wagons, & prisoners at "Farne's" Station or X roads, or some such place, not down on the map. — Gen: Lee's wife abides in Richmond. Her son Fitz Lee is reported killed. So is A.P. Hill. Very valiant Rebels both — bold able distinguished malefactors. The Davis household seems to have been run off by R.R. several days before Richmond fell. Whither will they go? I hope the poor woman & her innocent children may not come to grief.

April 7. Dingy & drizzly. Entered Walter Cutting, just after breakfast, with funny news enough. Our friend D[r] Peters has been in correspondence with an ugly quarrelsome dentist named Gunning, about a contemptible two-penny question whether the latter did or did not shirk paying his share of what was due to a hackman for a drive down Broadway one night during the riot week of /63. The dentist issues a pamphlet on the subject. N.Y. World gets hold of the pamphlet & Editorially condemns the Doctor, & lugs in the U.L. Club, apropos of something or nothing, observing that of course any one called on to do anything that devolves on him as a *gentleman*, can plead in bar that he is a member of that organization. Doctor having lost his temper goes to dentists house, horsewhips dentist, & gets his face badly scratched by dentist's wife daughter & servant-gal, who came to the rescue. Dentist thereupon has Doctor held to bail for assault & battery — so Walter & I went down to Jefferson Market Police Court & did what was needful. The Dentist deserved his licking, but the D[r] has been shockingly indiscreet in sundry of his doings. He can take care of himself & his patients in matters of pathology, but in the ordinary affairs of life he needs counsel.

At noon came more good news. Lee's Army again routed yesterday. More guns & waggon trains captured, & several thousand prisoners, among them Kershaw & Ewell & half a dozen Rebel generals beside. Sheridan confident that Lee with the debris of the "Army of Northern Virginia" will soon be bagged. Later came despatches that they had been bagged, but this was unofficial, & I do not believe the story. But there is abundant ground for believing Lee's army so damaged & dislocated that it is no longer to be counted an important element in the War. It's debris may *possibly* reinforce Johnston, but it can do no more as an independent force. — Grant & Sheridan have followed up it's retreat with admirable energy — not feeling bound by the precedent the great McClellan set after he won Antietam. — There was vast jubilation in Wall St. in spite of the lowering weather. But two such days as last Monday can hardly occur in one lifetime, certainly not in one week. The more I think of that day the more impressive & memorable it seems to me.

April 8. Grant telegraphed at noon from Farmville (?) 16 (?) miles N.W. of Burke's junction that he was still pushing Lee toward Lynchburgh & away from Danville. He expects to bag

Lee & the remains of Lee's Army. Blessed are they who expect nothing. — Letters at 823 this P.M. indicate that Sherman will soon be in motion again, aiming probably at Weldon. They were written without notice of Lee's defeat & the fall of Richmond, but the movements of stores by the Q.M.'s department confirm their statements.

April 9. Sunday. Not a word from the army. This naturally makes one a little anxious. Nor have I yet any news from Ellie & her party. I rather infer from her silence that they have penetrated to Richmond.

LEE and his ARMY HAVE SURRENDERED!
Gloria in Excelsis DEO. Et in Terra
Pax *hominibus bonæ voluntatis*

April 10th. Monday. A series of vehement pulls at the front door bell slowly roused me to consciousness, soon after I turned in last night, & routed me out of bed at last. Made my way down stairs in my dressing gown, half awake, & expecting to find Ellie, returned from her James River trip. But it was G.C.A. come to announce The SURRENDER — & that the Rebel Army of the Peninsula, Antietam, Fredericsburgh, Chancellorsville, the Wilderness, Spotsylvania C.H. &c &c &c has ceased to exist. It can bother & perplex none but Historians henceforth for ever. It can never open fire again on loyal men, or lend it's powerful aid to any cause, good or bad. There is no such Army any more. GOD be praised!

To bed again, but sleep was difficult. Up early — stimulated thereto by the enthusiasm of John R. Strong Esq: who was hallooing all over the house, hurraing for Grant & "singing of anthems" after a fashion, i.e. making well meant efforts to chant "John Brown" & "the Red White & Blue". Find the correspondence between Grant & Lee in the morning papers at the breakfast table. It is creditable to Grant, who opened it, & not discreditable to Lee. Lee made a decent show of coyness, & wrote quite a large number of notes. He was not altogether prepared to admit his position quite hopeless. But he accepted Grant's terms at last. They are most generous. Officers & men to be paroled, officers retaining their side arms & private property. My first thought was that Grant had been too liberal, & should have waited a day or two longer, when Lee would have been without ammunition & without rations, & ready to surrender at discretion. But I was wrong. Grant understands his business. Every officer & every private who goes home on parole under this arrangement will report — for his own credit's sake, — that the surrender was unavoidable, that the Confederacy was overmatched — fighting, useless waste of life — the Rebel cause hopeless. Each will be a fountain of cold water on whatever pugnacity & Chivalry may yet survive in his own home & vicinage. Thus ends Grant's most memorable campaign of eleven months.

Binney came in after breakfast. Then to Wall St. where appeared at noon tidings (unofficial & not to be counted upon) that Sherman has occupied Raleigh N.C. & a column of Thomas' army penetrated far into Alabama, & burned Selma. If untrue, they are merely premature I think, facts a little irregular as to the accident of Time "Φαντασματα θεια, και σκιαι των οντων."

It has rained hard all day — too hard for jubilant demonstrations out of doors. We should have made this Monday something like 3[d] April 1865, I think, had the Sun shone, & could we have congregated in the Streets without umbrellas. Guns have been firing all day, in spite of foul weather.

Will or will not Johnston follow Lee's example? He is in a very tight place. Where is J. Davis? Why have we no proclamation or manifesto from the fugacious chief of Rebeldom, Jeffersonus Augustulus?

Two letters from Ellie. She was all right, safe & well, when they were written. The later of the two was written in a parlor of the abandoned Jeff: Davis Palazzo at Richmond, Friday last.

April 11. Tuesday. Cloudy. No farther tidings from Ellie — & none from the Army. Our appetite for news has been gratified with such powerful stimulants of late, that a single day without intelligence of great victory or gain somewhere seems a disappointment. —

To Trinity Church at half past twelve. A meeting of business men yesterday resolved on a *Te Deum*, & arrangements for a service of thanksgiving had accordingly been made, so far as they could be made on such short notice. Found the Church already packed, and made my way up the crowded S. aisle, as certain marine molluscs bore into sandstone. Encountered Miss Kate Wolfe & handsome Miss Mary Ulshoeffer, & got them chairs from the Vestry room. Service began a little after one o'clock. The Church was then jammed to its utmost capacity, & (I am told) there was a dense crowd at all it's doors. It was an irregular special service, conforming to no rubric, but the great assemblage joined in it heartily. The "Lesson" was *the Beatitudes.* Vinton made a very short & very judicious little address from the pulpit, enforcing the duty of forgiveness & Charity. In alluding to the President he used terms that do his insight credit — "Wise — merciful — resolute — Christian", or their equivalent. Many loyal men hold Lincoln a sensible commonplace man, without special talent except for story telling, and it must be admitted that he sometimes tells stories of the class that is "not convenient" & does not become a gentleman & the holder of an exalted place. But his weaknesses are on the surface, & his name will be of high account fifty years hence, & for many generations thereafter. — The Choir had been largely reinforced, & did well, considering there had been no time for Rehearsal. The *Te Deum* was called I think "Clarke in *A*", but it is unimportant whether it was Clarke in A, Timkins in B., or Snooks in C. — I have heard it scores of times, — a decent succession of lifeless chords, like all the English Church music I know. But the old Gloria in Excelsis — the old chant — familiar to me since boyhood — was taken up by a thousand voices, sustained by both organs. It was most touching, noble, awe-ful, to hear. The "nave-organ" played the assemblage out of Church with Handel's Hallelujah Chorus, Hail Columbia, & the Star-Spangled Banner, *fortissimo.*

To N° 823. Much work there. May we hope to wind up soon, & muster ourselves out of service? — After dinner to U.L. Club where I presided over Com: on Admissions. Copperheads of two years ago, & men who supported Seymour & McClellan last fall are applying for admission. We rejected half a score of them this evening. Barlow & Belmont, O'Conor

& Betts will soon be sending in their names I suppose. We are discovering now, with some surprise, that everybody, little Ned Bell included, has been an "Uncompromising Union man from the very first." What a pity we had not known this a year ago. We should have been saved much uneasiness.

People hold the War virtually ended. It looks so. Lee is out of the game. Napoleon could hardly save Joe Johnston's army. There is no other Rebel force worth mentioning between the Atlantic & the Mississippi, & none can be raised but by miracle. Kirby Smith's banditti may yet stand a campaign or two in the Red River country, & Texas. But their war-*materiel* must soon give out, and cannot be replaced: they must be disheartened by the failure of Eastern Rebellion: and we can put an overwhelming force in the field against them, with Grant Sherman & Sheridan to lead it. There are chances & changes & complications of course, that no one can foresee, but I think there is no salvation for Rebeldom within the range of ordinary human prevision.

When Joe Johnston is disposed of, Lincoln should announce by proclamation that from & after the — day of — next, the Confederacy will be no longer practically recognized as a Belligerent Power, & that men thereafter taken in Arms against the Country, will be treated as criminals, & not as Prisoners of War. He might properly do so forthwith, for the so called Confederate Government seems to have abdicated, & to be concealing itself with intent to avoid the service of process. That Power is reported to have emerged from a R.R. Car at Danville, V^a^, Monday evening (3^d^ inst:), represented by Davis Imperator & two of his Pals, all three dusty deliquescent & much demoralized. Since that date we know nothing of it. It has made no sign, published no notice that it's place of business is changed, issued no manifesto of any kind. It's silence at so critical a time seems to shew that it considers itself defunct, & so very defunct that it is not worth while to keep up appearances, & go to the expense of a Galvanic battery. We quite miss our daily extracts from Richmond papers by the by. Those periodicals have been galvanizing the Confederacy into a ghastly simulation of aggressive truculent muscular vitality, but their editors have fled, no one knows whither, & I for one D'ont Care.

A rather lively *theoretical* controversy has arisen of & concerning J.D. viz: Shall we hang him, when & if we catch him, or shall we let him run? Weight of opinion is clearly for hanging him, but he will save his neck somehow. Justice requires his solemn public execution; Sound policy would probably let him live, in prison or exile. I should vote to hang him.

"We'll hang Jeff: Davis on a Sour Apple Tree
As we go marching on"

This Choral Promise & vow, so often repeated by so many thousand soldiers & civilians should be performed at the first opportunity. Bidwell has long predicted that Jeff: when finally cornered would kill himself. The best disposition Destiny can make of the Scoundrel would be to let him be grabbed by some one of the organized bands of deserters & refugees who hold the hill country of N. Carolina & Virginia. They would award him a high gallows & a short shrift & so dispose of a troublesome question.

Even the World & the Daily News say that Secessia is now conquered, crushed, subjugated, & under our feet. They whine for forbearance & magnanimity toward their friends & fellow-conspirators. To be sure we should be as merciful as we *safely* can be. The punishment already inflicted on the Southern People is fearful to think of. The Death of their best (or worst) & bravest: Devastation: the breaking up of their social system: general destitution: the bitterest humiliation of the most arrogant of mankind: the most splendid & confident expectations disappointed — universal ruin bereavement & shame — these are among the terms of the Sentence God has pronounced & is executing on Rebellious Slaveholders. Never, in modern times at least, has so vast a territory been so scourged.

April 12. Stanton reports *officially*, but only as probably true, that we have taken *Montgomery* & *Selma*, Alabama, & that *Lynchburgh* V[a], long bragged over as impregnable, has succumbed to "a *Scouting party under a L[t]*" — The woman flogging Chivalry seems to have little fight left in it. — We have got into a mess with Portugal. One of our ships has been fired on by the Belem forts & a man was killed. This was to prevent us from following the pirate *Stonewall*, & enabled her to get safe to sea. Portugal will probably beg pardon when she hears of the turn things have taken in Virginia. Hope so, for we can do without any more War for some time. Should the Portuganders stand on their dignity, we will refer it to a Committee, say Rhode Island & Vermont, with *power*, leave the subject in their hands & let them polish off Portugal.

Report that Gen: Rob[t] Lee is coming here. Confound his Southern impudence. If he come, I hope some woman who has lost a son or a husband in Virginia, will horsewhip the renegade traitor deserter & scoundrel. But there are flunkies in N.Y. who would overwhelm him with civilities.

April 13. To night at U.L. Club. Monthly meeting, & large attendance. The great collection of newspaper cuttings &c from 1860 to this time, made by one Townsend, & forming some 54 huge folios, was on exhibition there.

Weather cool & clear. Leading Virginians seem moving toward "reconstruction" with the approval of our military authorities. The General Assembly (or Legislature) of V[a] is invited to assemble at Richmond, under safe-conducts. This looks well. Despatch from Stanton read at Club to night, announcing that the draft is stopped, & that the military & Naval establishments will soon be greatly reduced! Not a word yet from the absconded Government of "the Confederate States of America". Where is it hiding? What Southern hamlet or swamp has the honor to be the Capital of Rebeldom to night? Thank God for the undeserved mercy He has shewn this People.

April 14. At Bellows' to night with Van Buren Agnew & Gibbs. No special War-news today. Tho' I believe "the Backbone of the Rebellion IS broken at last", there is probably some life left in it's extremities, & the San: Com: cannot yet disband itself. Mosby's guerillas are reported to tell our people that tho' Lee has surrendered, Mosby's "independent Companies" have not surrendered & do'nt mean to. We hear nothing from J.D. but if we did it would doubtless be to the same effect. He will be a traitor either fighting or intriguing against us, till his last breath.

N.B. The Chivalric & hightoned Gen: Lee seems to have played *Grant* a trick. While they were negotiating for a surrender he stated his force to be twenty or thirty thousand men; he could not be more exact because they had been so hurried & driven since they began retreating that no morning reports had been made. On this statement (probably true) he got the most generous terms, as a *wholesale* purchaser. But when the contract came to be executed next day, there were not more than seven or eight thousand men to be paroled. All the rest had somehow smuggled themselves off during the night, many of them no doubt making a beeline for the standards of Joe Johnston. Perhaps Lee's force was so demoralized that he could not have prevented it. In that case one would think he would have frankly told Grant he could not carry out his bargain & would have offered to consider it annulled. It does not appear that he made such offer. Every gentleman & every business man of fair repute would have made it under analogous circumstances, but Lee though the most gentlemanly & soldierly of gentlemen & soldiers (according to the N.Y. World) is a *Southern* gentleman & soldier. Southern faith will be a by-word yet, like Punica fides.

April 15. Sat: 9 A.M. *Lincoln* & *Seward* assassinated last night — !!!

The South has nearly filled up the measure of her iniquities at last!

Lincoln's death not yet certainly announced, but the 1 A.M. despatch states that he was then dying. Seward's side room was entered by the same or another assassin, & his throat cut. It is unlikely he will survive, for he was suffering from a broken arm & other injuries, the consequence of a fall — & is advanced in life. —

Ellie brought me this news two hours ago, but I can hardly *take it in* even yet. — Eheu A.L.!

I have been expecting this — I predicted an attempt would be made on Lincoln's life when he went into Richmond — but just now, after his generous dealings with Lee, I should have said the danger was past. — But the ferocious malignity of Southerners is infinite & inexhaustible. — I am stunned, as by a fearful personal calamity — tho' I can see that this thing, occurring just at this time may be overruled to our great good. — Poor Ellie is heart-broken, tho' never an admirer of Lincoln's. We shall appreciate *him* at last.

Up with the Black Flag now!

10 P.M. What a day it has been! Excitement & suspension of business even more general than on the 3[d] inst: — Tone of feeling very like that of four years ago, when the news came of *Sumter*. This atrocity has invigorated National feeling in the same way, almost in the same degree. People who pitied our misguided brethren yesterday, & thought they had been punished enough already, & hoped there would be a general amnesty including J. Davis himself, talk approvingly to day of Vindictive Justice, & favor the introduction of Judges Juries Gaolers and Hangmen among the dramatis personæ. Above all there is a profound awe-stricken feeling that we are as it were in immediate presence of a fearful gigantic Crime, such as has not been committed in our day & can hardly be matched in history.

Faulkner, one of our Kenzua directors, called for me by appointment at half past nine, & we drove to the foot of Jane St. to inspect apparatus for reduction of gold ore by amalgamation, which he considers a great improvement on the machinery generally used for that purpose. Returned up town & saw Bellows, to advise about adjournment of our San: Com: meeting next week. — Thence to Wall St. — Immense crowd. Bulletins & Extras following each other in quick contradictory succession. Seward & his son Fred: had died & had not. Booth (one of the assassins, a Marylander, brother of Edwin Booth) had been taken & had not. So it has gone on all day. To night the case stands thus.

Abraham Lincoln died at twenty two minutes after seven this morning. He never regained consciousness after the pistol ball fired at him from behind, over his wife's shoulder, entered his brain. Seward is living, & may recover. The gentleman assigned to the duty of murdering *him*, did his butchery badly. The throat is severely lacerated by his knife, but it's believed that no arteries are injured. Fred: Seward's situation is less hopeful his scull being fractured by a bludgeon or slung shot used by the same gentleman. The Attendant who was stabbed is dead. [is not]

The temper of the great meeting I found assembled in front of the Custom House (the old Exchange) was grim. A Southerner would compare it with that of the first session of the

Jacobins after *Marat's* death. I thought it healthy & virile. It was the first great patriotic meeting since the War began at which there was no talk of concession & conciliation. It would have endured no such talk. It's sentiment seemed like this — "Now it is plain at last to everybody that there can be no terms with the Woman flogging Aristocracy. Grant's generous dealing with Lee was a blunder. The *Tribune*'s talk for the last fortnight was folly. Let us henceforth deal with rebels as they deserve. The Rosewater treatment does not meet their case". I have heard it said fifty times to day "These madmen have murdered the two best friends they had in the world", & it is quite true. — I heard of three or four men, in Wall St. & near the Post office, who spoke lightly of this Tragedy, & were instantly set upon by the bystanders & *pummelled*. One of them narrowly escaped death. It was Chas E. Anderson, brother of our friend Prof: Henry Ja^s A., father of pretty Miss Louisa. Moses H. Grinnell & the police had hard work to save him. I never supposed him a Secessionist.

To Trinity Church vestry meeting, specially called, at 3½ P.M., at the rebuilt vestry office, cor: Fulton & Church. A series of resolutions read, drawn by the Rector. — They were masculine & good, & were passed nem: con: tho' Verplanck & Tillou were in their seats — Copperheads both. Looked at the record of our action when Washington died, 66 years ago. It was a mere resolution that the Church & Chapels be put in mourning. Our resolutions of to day went, naturally, much farther. I record to the credit of Gouv: Ogden whom I have always held cold hearted & selfish, that he broke down in trying to read these resolutions, could not get beyond the first sentence, & had to hand them back to the Rector. There was a little diversity of opinion whether we should put our chancel into mourning tomorrow, being Easter Sunday, or postpone it a day longer. We left it to the Rector's discretion. — No business was done to day. Most shops closed & draped with black & white muslin. Broadway is clad in "weepers" from Wall St. to Union Square.

At 823 with Agnew Bellows & Gibbs. — G.C.A. dined here. With him to U.L. Club. Special meeting & dense asphyxiating crowd. Orations by Geo: Bancroft & by Rev: (Presbyterian) Thompson, of the Tabernacle. Both good. Thompson's very good. "When A. Johnson was sworn in as President to day" said Rev: Thompson "the Statue of Liberty that surmounts the Dome of the Capitol, & was put there by Lincoln, looked down on the City & on the Nation & said — our government is unchanged — it has merely passed from the hands of one man into those of another. *Let the Dead bury their Dead. Follow thou Me.*" — — — Burnside tells me this morn'g that he ranks Johnson very high.

Jeff: Davis has at last issued a manifesto. It is from Danville, before Lee's surrender, & is full of fight.

April 16. Sunshiny morning, followed by heavy showers. To night clear & cold with Northern lights in the heavens & a harsh but healthful wind blowing down toward Richmond & Raleigh from the N.W.

An Easter Sunday unlike any I have seen. Drove down town very early with E. Johny & Temple. Nearly every building in Broadway & in all the side streets, as far as one could see, festooned lavishly with black & white muslin. Columns swathed in the same material. Rosettes pinned to window curtains. Flags at half mast & tied up with crape. I hear that even in second & third class quarters, people who could afford to do no more, have generally displayed at least a little twenty five cent flag with a little scrap of crape annexed. Never was a public mourning more spontaneous & general. It is like what we read of the demonstrations that followed *Princess Charlotte's* death, but with feelings of just wrath & aspirations for vengeance that had no place then.

Trinity was never filled so full, not even last Tuesday. The crowd packed the aisles tight, & even occupied the choir steps & the choir itself nearly to the chancel rails. The outer doors, by the by, were in mourning, & the flag on the spire edged with black, pursuant to my suggestion yesterday. Within the church the symbols of public sorrow properly gave place to those of *Easter*. When we came to the closing prayers of the Litany, Vinton proclaimed "I bid you all unite with me in prayer for all the bereaved & afflicted families of this land, & especially for that of *Abraham Lincoln*, late President of the United States, recently destroyed by assassination", & read the proper prayer for those in affliction. He then prefaced the usual prayer for a sick person by a like bidding "for the Secretary of State & the Assistant Secretary of State, now in peril of death from wounds inflicted on them by an assassin". The effect of these formulas introduced into the service was telling. The Anthem [Hallelujah Chorus] represented the Ecclesiastical aspect of the day, & was admirably well done. Vinton's sermon, or rather address, was far the best I have heard him deliver. Extemporaneous, as he told us afterwards, when Ellie asked him for a copy. He blended the Easter sentiment with that of public grief most skillfully, or I should rather say by presenting suggestions of deep-lying Truths that harmonized them. He brought out clearly the thought that had occurred to me, & to many others: viz: Perhaps Lincoln had done his appointed work. His honesty sagacity kindliness & singleness of purpose had united the North, & secured the suppression of Rebellion. Perhaps the time has come for something beside kindliness mercy & forbearance, even for vengeance & Judgment. Perhaps the murdered President's magnanimity would have been circumvented & his generosity & goodness abused by Rebel subtlety & falsehood, to our lasting National injury. Perhaps God's voice in this tragedy is "Well done, good & faithful Servant. Thou hast done thy work of mercy. To others is given the duty of Vengeance. Thy murder will help teach them that duty. Enter thou — by a painless process of death — into the joy of thy Lord".

Southern barbarism has largely promoted our ethical education. What should we have said four years ago, of Vinton earnestly enforcing on us the duty of hewing (Southern) Agag in pieces before the Lord, not from personal animosity, but as a sacred obligation to be neglected only at peril of Divine punishment, public & private? The whole service was a new experience to me. Men & women (poor Ellie among them) were sobbing & crying bitterly all around. My own eyes kept filling, & the corners of my mouth would twitch now & then, in spite of all I could do.

To night Osten-Sacken, little Kate & her papa, G.C.A. & Col. Howe with a pocket full of telegrams from Washington. Seward & his son seem doing well. Sorry to say that neither Assassin has yet been caught. There are reports that our policy at Richmond is to be changed, that the proposed convocation of Virginia rebels will be discouraged, & that some of them will be held as hostages against farther attempts at assassination of Presidents & Cabinet officers.

There is intense exasperation. I hear of a dozen households whose Keltic handmaidens have been summarily discharged for some talk of rejoicing at Abe Lincoln's death. The N.Y. Hotel was protected by policemen last night & to day, on it's proprietor's petition. The President's funeral is to be Thursday next. Gramercy Park Hotel dismissed a batch of waiters to day, at Howe's instigation, for blind foolish Keltic talk approving Lincoln's murder. *Horace Greeley* — the advocate of Pacification & Amnesty — is as unpopular as Gen: Lee. — Directed my waiter to stop the Tribune. There are hopeful signs that the Community may be ready at last for action against its Barlows, Larocques, Belmonts, & Duncans.

April 17. Monday. Clear & cold. Very busy in Wall St. & at two, to Col: Coll: meeting. A little progress made in the ancient undertaking of the "New Statutes". Did any one of the Pyramids take so much time to build? Also we passed & ordered published a series of resolutions on the assassination. Barnard drew them. They are plain spoken & radical enough, declaring this atrocity, like the attempted incendiarism of last Nov^r^ & the systematic starvation of 60.000 prisoners of War, due to the brutalizing influences of Slavery. They seemed diffuse, & too abundantly peppered with Vehemence of adjectives — but it is hard to find words too strong for this case. Betts & Zabriskie recalcitrated of course — doubted — demurred — & did not like the resolutions a bit. But they passed without a division. — Thence to N° 823, making arrangements for the S.C. Session at Washington, for which I expect to leave town tomorrow.

All over the City people have been at work all day draping street fronts — so hardly a building in Wall St. Broadway, Chatham St. Bowery, & 4th Av: is without it's symbol of the profound public sorrow. What a place this man, whom his best friends have been patronizing for four years as a well meaning, rather sagacious, kind hearted ignorant old codger, had won for himself in the heart of the People! What a place he will fill in History! I foresaw most clearly that he would be ranked high, as the Great Emancipator, twenty years hence, but I did not suppose his death would instantly reveal — even to

Copperhead newspaper Editors — the nobleness & the glory of his part in this great Contest. It reminds one of the last line of Blanco White's great sonnet — "If Light can thus deceive, wherefore not Life?" *Death* has suddenly opened the eyes of the People — (& I think of the world) — to the fact that a Hero has been holding high place among them for four years, closely watched & studied, but despised & rejected by a third of this community, & only tolerated by the other two-thirds.

To M[r] S.B.R.'s after dinner. He's laid up with very severe cold, that has threatened to become inflammation of the lungs. He says "the one consolatory fact connected with Lincoln's death is that *he cannot pardon his murderer*". Seward's throat was saved from the assassin's knife by the wire apparatus applied by his surgeons to his broken jaw. He is said to be improving. Fred Seward is a little better, has recovered consciousness in some degree, & may yet survive. An Extra announces to night that *Sarratt* or *Sarrant*, the loup-garou or two legged wolf who made his murderous way to Seward's sick room, has been captured. God grant it. — Mobile has fallen — & there is a great "take" of guns & prisoners, but the news is hardly noticed. At U.L. Club to night are reports that J. Wilkes Booth has been traced to "Port Tobacco" — that important arrests of his brethren in conspiracy have been made — & that Rev: Fra[s] L. Hawks stated last week, in reply to some one who spoke of a general pacification as at hand, that "Something would occur in a day or two that would prove that notion a delusion." Is Rev: F.L.H. too good to have been an accessory to this crime? Should it be proved on him, I would walk ten miles to see him hanged, & pay fifty dollars for a front place at the execution. — But it is to be presumed that these reports are all groundless. — We have a story also that Sherman & Johnston were in negotiation about surrender last Friday. May that negotiation have been prolonged till tidings of the murder were brought to Sherman! — Edwin Booth, the actor, reputed an honest & loyal man is said to be in the deepest affliction & humiliation over his brother's crime, & to have declared that he will never appear in public again. He is in town & has sent for Bellows, to come & see him to night, as a spiritual adviser. *Marie*, little Lewis' nurse, who used to take charge of poor Booth's little *Edwina*, called at his house, as she often does with Lewis (who was quite a pet of Booth's, it seems,) but found only signs of consternation & misery. None of the family could be seen. M[rs] John Sherwood told Ellie to day that she knew the late M[rs] Edwin Booth, (a very charming admirable young woman, who died some two years ago) & once asked her about the several members of her husband's family who had appeared on the stage. The lady spoke kindly & affectionately of them all save & except this wretched caitiff J. Wilkes Booth. *Him* she declared the most false malignant wicked man she had ever known, & this astounding declaration she made so frankly & earnestly as almost to take away poor M[rs] Sherwood's breath. Such is her story.

How the South — & *especially* Southern women (sorrow & shame & deep disgrace to Womanhood — but it's true) will exult over the news of Lincoln's murder! But this stage of febrile excitement & exaltation will be brief. It will last only an hour or two, & then will come a stage of "depression" & "anxiety" & fearful looking forward to the terrors of a Judgment to come, — a sense that the time for "conciliation" & "reconstruction" is past & gone, that their own agent & representative has stricken down the olive branch vainly tendered them so long, and that they can now hope for nothing but to be dealt with as a breed that *cannot be domesticated* — feræ naturæ — mischievous vermin. The scoundrels have murdered the only man who stood between them and the Execution of National Justice.

April 28. Friday night. The best part of an expedition even to Richmond itself is the getting home again & finding E. & the children safe & well — as I did at 6 P.M. D[r] Vinton's nice son Frank was dining here, & there was reading from Haydn's 2[d] & 6th Masses & Mozart's N[o] 1, after dinner, that refreshed me after my day of Railroading. — To night's papers announce that Johnston has surrendered everything from Raleigh to the Chattahoochie on the same terms that were given Lee. People will grumble. Sherman opened these negotiations several days ago, & bungled himself into sore disfavor. His popularity is gone for the present. — — Within the week died our eminent neighbour, old D[r] Mott — and also Rev: D[r] Creighton of Sing-Sing. — Little business has been done in town these ten days. — Never I think has sorrow for a Leader been displayed on so great a scale & so profoundly felt. It is very noteworthy that the *number of arrests for drunkenness & disorder during the week that followed Lincoln's murder, was less than in any week for very many years*! The City is still swathed in crape & black muslin. —

Tuesday: 18th. To Wash^{n} by early train. Called for Rev: Bellows, & then we picked up Miss Louisa Schuyler & drove through two miles of silent black-draped streets to Jersey City Ferry, where we found Wolcott Gibbs & Agnew & his sister-in-law Miss Nash (a chief engineer of last year's Metropolitan Fair). We were invited to take seats in the special car set apart for the delegations on their way to *the Funeral*. There were Moses Grinnell — Col: Howe — Chas H. Russell — John Jay — Wm E. Dodge — Judge Pierrepont — &c &c &c — also Gov: Andrew, with Adams & Ritchie of his "staff". A generous lunch was provided at noon, & the car, being "select" & not overcrowded, was comfortable — so our journey was less afflictive than usual. — Read a sensation novel — "My Uncle Silas", reprinted from Fraser's (or somebody else's) Magazine. — [On my journey home today I read another sensation novel, some seven years old, of another class, æsthetically maudlin, called "Charles Auchester" — hysterical hyperflutinations about Music]

In Copperhead New Jersey few buildings public or private shewed sign of public mourning. But Baltimore was all in black. The humble shops & houses, past which the train runs, displayed almost without exception some little black rag, & every street we looked up as we went along was a vista of flags & drapery. I am told the traitorous mansions on Monument Square & the aristocratic quarters generally were profuse in weeds of woe. Perhaps they were put on as mere matter of prudence — perhaps Baltimore aristocracy sees that the cause it favors is hopeless now, & finds in this great Crime, committed in the interest of that cause & stimulated by Southern teaching, a good opportunity to change it's front.

We entered Wash^{n} on time, for a wonder. Everywhere like insignia of sorrow. I got a breezy room high up among the higher ranges of Willard's, by special favor, for the City is very full. — San: Com: met in F. St. 8 P.M. — Jenkins was plainly unhappy nervous & unstrung. He had no quarterly Report. Had tried to write his Report, but had been in a state of "mental torpor" that made it impossible. Three ladies attended our session, — Miss Schuyler & Miss Nash of N.Y. & Miss Abby May of Boston.

Wednesday — 19th. Bright cloudless day. All places of business closed, of course. Learned that members & officers of the San: Com: (& of the soi disant X^{n} Com: also) had places on the official programme & were expected to attend the ceremonial in the East Room — a privilege eagerly sought by all sorts of people, but not solicited or invited by any of us. We went in a body to the office of the Sec^{y} of the Treasury in the Treasury building. A delegation of our "Christian" friends reported at the same place including that Evangelical Mountebank & philanthrope Mr G.H. Stuart of Philad^{a}. They were an ugly looking set, mostly of the Maw-worm & Chadband type. Some were unctuous to behold — others vinegary. — A bad lot. — A little before 12 we marched to the White House, thro' the grounds that separate it from the Treasury, were shewn into the East Room, & took our appointed place, on the raised steps that occupied three of its sides — the catafalque with it's black canopy & open coffin occupying the centre.

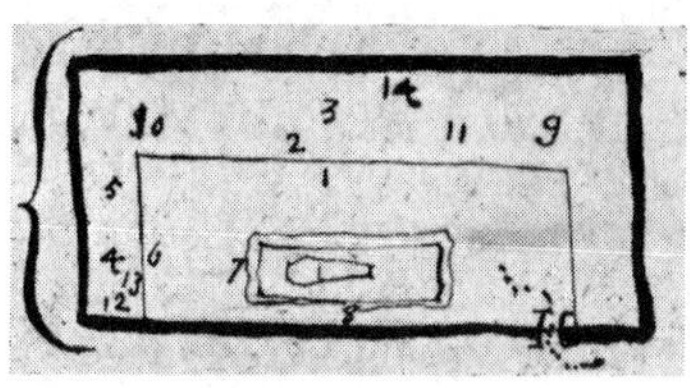

[1. Johnson — Preston King — Hamlin — Cabinet officers — 2. C.J. Chase & Supreme Court — 3. Diplomatic Corps — 4. N.Y. delegations — 5. San. Com. 6. Grant, Farragut &c — 7. Officiating clergy. — 8. Reporters — 9. Heads of Bureaux &c — 10. New England delegations — 11 Western d^{o} — 12. Pallbearers — 13. Judiciary of the district. — 14. A small party of ladies.]

I had my last glimpse of the honest face of our great & good President as we passed by. It was darker than in life, otherwise little changed. Personages & delegations were severally marshalled to their places quietly & in good order. — the diplomatic corps in fullest glory of buttons & gold lace, — Johnson & the Cabinet — C.J. Chase — many Senators & notables — Generals & Admirals — Grant, Farragut, Burnside (in plain clothes) Davis, Porter, Goldsborough &c. — about 650 in all. The appearance of the assemblage was most distinguished. Most of those present were men of visible force & mark, with whom the bedizened diplomats contrasted unfavorably. The latter looked like gorgeously liveried flunkies. Of the religious service the less that is said the better, for it was vile & vulgar. "Bishop" Simpson's whining oratorical prayer most nauseous. When this was finished the coffin was lifted, & the assemblage followed it silently reverently & in perfect order. All that was perfectly & admirably arranged & executed, and it was all most solemn & decorous, save & except the spoken words.

So ended the most memorable ceremonial this Continent has ever seen. I count it a great privilege to have been present. There will be thousands of people ten years hence who would pay any money to have been in my place.

After standing nearly four hours we were too tired for a march in procession to the Capitol. So we slipped off, & Gibbs & I watched the latter half of the funeral cortege as it moved thither along Pennsylvania Avenue. A great body of Freedmen brought up the rear, marching in well-ordered ranks, & looking quite as respectable as the Caucasian civilians who preceded them. — — — We dined at Welcker's (Buhler's) & held an ev'g session.

Two incidents in the East Room were worth noting. — The Italian Minister (who looked like a green & gold scarabæus on it's hind legs) leaving his place to march across the room & shake hands with Grant in a very marked way — & Johnson stepping quietly up to the side of the coffin & looking down a few moments, solemnly & thoughtfully upon the dead face. A subject for some future Delaroche.

Thursday. 20th. Wet day & wholly given to business. After ev'g session adjourned there was a conference about Jenkins. Knapp & he dislike & distrust each other so thoroughly as to neutralize each other, & demoralize the Wash^{n} office. Jenkins is among the best & most unselfish of men, but he has little executive ability. He knows it, & the knowledge frightens & paralyzes him. He wanted to resign six months ago. We decided to let him know his resignation would be accepted now. Newberry should succeed him, but he declines the appointment. Knapp would not do. We must take J. S. Blatchford who has been long in our service at Boston, & for the last few months, at Washington. He is efficient & accurate, but so formal in manner & quiet in speech that I have not rated him very high. — We called at Seward's to day. He is doing well.

Friday. 21st. "Executive Session" — i.e. the three ladies locked out. Jenkins resigned. Sorry for him. He shewed himself morbid & sore. He thinks Knapp has ousted him by some subtle intrigue, a great mistake. Blatchford elected & accepts.

Bellows Stillé Binney & I waited on Andrew Johnson, Gratiâ Dei President, at 2 P.M. by appointment, at his temporary Executive chamber in the Treasury building. Before it's door hang the two flags that decorated Lincoln's box at Ford's theatre that fatal Friday night. One of them shews a rent several inches long made by the assassin's spur as he leaped down on the stage. We discoursed Maunsell Field a few minutes while waiting for admission to our Audience. Field was present during Lincoln's last hours. — Being admitted we find fat Preston King & a couple of military men with Johnson. Graciously received. Bellows said a few words as to who & what we were, & the Pres'dt replied in substance that he knew all about the Commission & would further it's operations by all means in his power. We made our interview as brief as might be. Most favorably impressed by Johnson. The "incoherency" of 4th March is doubtless correctly accounted for as an accident, for he looks utterly unlike a free drinker. He seems dignified urbane & self possessed — a most "presentable" person. Heaven prosper his handiwork.

Left cards for Seward. He is improving. Mr Fred. S d°, but not out of danger. Our San. Com. session closed to night.

Agnew brought away many anecdotes of Lincoln, after a talk with Dr Stone, his friend & physician. The story of his *Dream* the night before his death, as retailed in the papers, is true. It was of a "fine ship entering harbor under full sail". He had had that very dream before every great National success — before New Orleans, Gettysburgh, Fort Fisher, Charleston &c &c, & he was certain he should hear of some great piece of good news within forty eight hours. — A poet could make something out of that. — When one McKim, a notable abolitionist, complimented him on some thought or phrase in his Emancipation Proclamation, L said very simply, "Well I should be a quack if I accepted any praise for that. It was Chase gave me that notion."

Sat: 22^d April. Morning unsettled & showery. At 2 P.M. with Newberry, [Johannes Neubrigendis,] to Gov^t mail boat the "City Point" & down the river, stopping at Alexandria. Great crowd. Overcast, but before we had gone far there was a narrow strip of clear sky along the western horizon. This brightened first to amber & then to topaz as the sun drew near it, & the loose ragged blue-grey clouds above it were lit up at last with the most gorgeous irregular lines of fretted ruby light. It was a glorious sunset, followed by a stern N.W. Wind that sent us early to our state rooms. At one A.M. there was a knocking at state room doors & general commotion. Everybody tumbled up & turned out. A picket boat had brought us to, & was lying along side. Officers came on board & searched every state room, for Booth or some of his accomplices but in vain. We were all inspected & called on to shew our papers.

Sunday, 23^d. Up early. Stopped at Fortress Monroe, & then proceeded up James River. N.W. wind severely cool. Newberry shivered all day. Lower deck crowded with African warriors. They uttered a prolonged screech or yell as we met each boat load of crestfallen "Johnies" on their way down. At City Point we transferred ourselves to the "Red Jacket" a boat of lighter draft, & went forward. "On to Richmond" at last (vide N.Y. Tribune of June & July /61, passim) after four years of hope deferred. The upper James is but a mean river. It's rapid waters are lager-bier color. It winds & twines in the most aggravating tortuosity, & is rich in bars & shoals. Great stagnant lagoons flood the low lands. But the rank luxuriant vegetation of it's banks, & it's series of wild swamp & forest scenery are worth seeing. The geological Newberry pointed out many deposits of Diatomaceous earth in the stratification of it's banks. Never was little river so lavishly fortified & defended. Field works everywhere, from the impregnable Fort Darling down to little redoubts each with a single big gun. Three or four lines of obstructions — piles — serving also as bridges. Torpedoes — their site indicated by buoys with little red flags. Timbers of booms, one end still anchored on shore, sway slowly about. Wrecks everywhere, sunken skeletons of burned iron-clads — steamers pontoon scows etc: — Dutch Gap Canal seems traversed by water. The Regenerated Richmond of 1875 will finish up that job & save itself seven miles of crooked navigation. — Land at Rocketts 7 P.M. — We found the "Spottswood Hotel" after a march of a mile & a quarter at double quick, mostly through the burned district, a wide area of ruin, still smoking. Just before we got there, we heard a familiar voice behind us. It was a small newsboy, evidently an enterprising emigrant from Wall St. or Chatham St. tearing madly up "Main St." & yelling "Ere's the New York Tribune and-a-Errald!" I looked at him with profound respect as a missionary, & a harbinger of civilization. — Find the Hotel rather full, but we got a room, & what was called tea & after a short stroll thro' the silent sombre streets, went to bed. Many secesh officers on parole infest the public rooms of the Spottswood. They are in uniform, but they have no other clothes. They have been ordered not to appear with their side arms, on penalty of arrest. They are silent & downcast. The sight of the greyback uniform & buttons seems to irritate our officers, whose feeling against Rebeldom has become bitterly intensified. They now seem to regard Rebels as mortal enemies: unscrupulous, malignant, faithless, & unfit for any treatment but stern suppression. Had they but begun to do so three years ago!

Monday 24th. Cloudless & cool, but direct sunshine even in April is far more potent at Richmond than at N.Y. — After breakfast we proceeded to the San: Com: office on Broad St. & spent an hour or two there. One Williams in charge. As there are very few sick or wounded in the military hospitals, he is issuing medical stores to civilians on medical certificates. The office was crowded with applicants, mostly women in black, with baskets. They were receiving Northern charity with little shew of gratitude, much as a hungry sulky illconditioned hound accepts a bone, uncertain whether to gnaw the donation or to bite the fingers of the donor. The women were arrogant & sour, but there were poor little children with wan faces & pitiful stories of sick mothers, & of privation & misery endured for months. *We decided to stop these issues*, pursuant to the resolution adopted last week. It seems hard & cruel, but providing tea & sugar for sick rebels is no part of our legitimate work, & it strengthens Southerners in their delusions about their own supreme dignity & the duty of Yankees to take care of them. — Long walk out of town to *Jackson* & *Winder* General Hospitals (Rebel). They provide for 5000 patients & are well organized. Talked with Rebel surgeons & patients, & found abundant evidence to confirm what we heard in Wash^{n} — viz: that while our men were dying by the thousand of slow starvation on Belle-Island & in Libby Prison, these Hospitals were lavishly supplied — more abundantly than ours. Their Hospital Ration was just double ours. They had dairies — ice houses — & a great staff of official "matrons" with assistants. They had fewer luxuries — jellies oranges &c — than our patients, but a more liberal issue of subsistence. Talked with many of the patients, Tennesseans, Louisianians, & Carolinians. All looked well fed & had suffered no recent privation. All "wanted to go home" — "hoped there would be no more fighting" & shewed no sulkiness. — The (Reb:) Dr Hancock in charge (associated with our Dr Quick) felt the same way, very strongly. Asked him if he'd ever happened to hear of Willy Alston. He said yes "he died in my arms in that room, Aug: 11th, of pyæmia after amputation at the shoulder joint." It may be some other W.A. — for the name is common in S.C. After returning we walked thro' the ruined district & along the riverside, looked at Belle Island & the rapids — talked with Natives, middle class people who denounced & d—d Jeff: Davis with the most heartfelt sincerity of manner — & looked for bookstores. All burned up.

After dinner went thro' that execrable *Folter-Haus*, Libby Prison, now being cleaned out — saw Turner's ugly mug peering out of a hole in the door of his underground cell. — Walked to Rocketts, & explored the hilly suburb in it's rear. Lovely view of the City & down the river. Home & early to bed, in profound sick headache. Newberry had walked me nearly off my legs.

Richmondites are cowed & broken in spirit. The only utterance of seceshdom I heard was from a party of little boys in an out of the way street, who hurraed for Jeff: Davis as Newberry & I walked by, then set up a song — how

"Jeff: Davis rides on a whi-ite horse
And so does General Lee".

The former is running away as fast as he can, & the latter is living on rations issued by our charitable Government. I hope he will go abroad & stay there. He can take service under the

King of Dahomey, who sells his prisoners of war into slavery, or the Emperor of China, who disembowels them. No power, (now that the Confederacy has exploded,) can be found that starves them to death, so Lee will have to put up with a milder discipline & a more "humanitarian" rule than he has been used to.

Saw not the least sign of the spite & fury manifested by the women of Nashville & New Orleans when the vandals entered those cities, but perhaps the most aristocratic & blueblooded of the daughters of Richmond kept within doors.

Charming exhibition of "State feeling", *in extremis*, by a lantern jawed F.F.V. in a decomposing coat & a stovepipe hat of other days, whom I discoursed at a corner near the "*Capital*". I told him I did not recognize that building — thought it had a cupola & colonnades — had seen what I supposed were engravings of it on "Confed:" notes. He replied that *that* was the Capital at Montgomery Alabama, & added with inexpressible dignity "But *our* Capitol is engraved on some of the Confederate paper, too, I assure you sir." As I had just been buying about a cord of this paper for 50 cents, I did not see that this was much to brag of.

Tuesday 25th. More explorations of the city & its surroundings. Grand Review by Genls Ord & Devens. Lines extended near the whole length of Main St. — black regiments & white, alternating like the keys of a piano. Newberry & I sat in a shady place on the pretty Capitol grounds & watched the performance, the intervening block or two of buildings having been burned down. It was a most significant spectacle. Opposite to us — i.e. on the other side of the gravel walk, sat a boy of 18, in the uniform of a Rebel captain — an olive complexioned Southerner with features that suggested Jewish blood. He was gazing over the ruins of the Rebel capital, on the long line of victorious regiments parading in triumph, with their bands playing, & their men bursting out into cheers now & then — regiments of liberated Slaves among them, & he did not look as if he liked the spectacle! Occasionally he would give us a furtive sideglance, such as a subjugated wild cat in a cage gives a spectator whom it would bite if it dared. It was a look of malice & of curiosity, & said "I wonder what those two d—d Yankees think of all this. I wonder if they are fully aware that it would give me the highest gratification to cut their throats."

Dined frugally at San: Com: office & went down the River at 2 P.M. on the "Trumpeter". Pleasant voyage. Land at City Point 5 P.M. & find quarters for the night on our S.C. barges. Benson J. Lossing & Greble of Philad[a] (L[t] Greble's father, of Big Bethel memory) were guests of the Com:, & after a good plain supper we spent the ev'g in good talk. — Our work at C.P. seems systematic & efficient, tho' it is growing smaller. I fear D[r] McDonald is wearing out.

Wednesday 26th. Warm. Newberry takes our tug & steams over to Bermuda Hundreds to look for the famous "Bermuda Clay," but returns without any. Off for Wash[n] 10 A.M. in the George Leary. Many Refugees from Richmond & Petersburgh on board. Americans & Germans — Amster-"dam Dutchmen", & Rotter "dam Dutchmen" (vide Blackwood) — All most bitter agst J.D. & seceshers. "Ah-h-h" said one of these Teutons pointing to a whiskered grey-back, "I hate dem man like Schnake! Day before dey wot you call evacuate Petersburg, I pay $360.00 for von Horse, & I pay some of mein debts, too. I vish I had invest all mein monish dat way, a-a-ah! Mein Gott, it ish no goot now!"

To Wash[n] 8 A.M. Thursday too late for day train to N.Y. Spent day at 244 F St. dining & breakfasting with Newberry at Welcker's. City full of reports about Booth & Herold. Question settled at last by a Surgeon who had seen Booth lying dead & Herold in irons on one of our Monitors off the Navy Yard. How shall we dispose of what Booth has left behind him? I say embalm the carrion with the costliest antiseptics, & hang it in chains.

Interrogated on the train to day by an officer of the Invalid Corps — & produced papers to prove my identity. Very glad Gov[t] is so watchful.

May 1st. I look daily for the assassination of some high officer of Government. Examples of that crime are apt to be contagious. Herold & the others now in custody, should be sentenced, if convicted, not merely to death, but to some preliminary process of ignominy that will go farther than capital punishment to discourage the morbid taste for notoriety & conspicuous martyrdom which may tempt fools to imitate them. They should be subjected to a pro formâ flogging in public, or exhibited at 25 cents a head in an iron cage for a week or two, & then be very privately hanged.

We begin to receive to day the rebound of the fall of Richmond from across the Atlantic. Albion is disappointed & disgusted of course — but her newspapers think we may come out all wrong, & Slavery may triumph somehow, even yet, — which would be consolatory to Albion. They suggest, among other comfortable theories of the next campaign that Lee, being now rid of local engagements, will be able to invade & subjugate the North at last. English Newspapers from the Times down have certainly proved themselves lying prophets. All their predictions for these four years have been utter failures. No circle of spiritualists was ever more completely exposed & disgraced by an investigating Committee than the Editorial Corps of Great Britain has been by the progress of events. The news of April 3d opened their eyes a little. We shall hear within a week or two that they have been opened yet wider, & that even the Toriest "organs" begin to see us from a new standpoint, & to talk of us with mitigated indecency. — Thank God that the loyalty & affection I used to waste on England, years ago, have been transferred to my own Country & People.

I think England has outlived everything that gave her a high place among nations, & is governed now by but one single motive power — to wit, love of money. If so, her downfall is not far off, and before many generations have passed away, London will be as Savannah, & Liverpool as Charleston.

May 2d. No War news. Is there any War? There is military occupation to be completed, & military rule to be confirmed & perfected: there are banditti to be hunted down, & traitors to be unearthed, but I see no War this side the Mississippi. Kirby Smith & Magruder may try a campaign in W. Louisiana & Texas, but (unless we get into a quarrel with Mexico & France) it will be a bad business for them & for the people among whom such campaign is conducted. This sudden cessation of War — apparent at least, & unhoped for six months ago — gives me a strange sense of *vacuity*. War & Rebellion have been the one great subject of my hopes & fears every hour for four years past. I feel strangely to night, & hardly recognize myself, from the absence of anxiety about McClellan — or Buell — or Burnside — or Hooker — or Grant — from a new sense of indifference to the devices of Beauregard Bragg Lee & Joe Johnston.

May 3^{d}. Report that J. Davis recently abandoned a R.R. train in N.C. menaced by Stoneman's cavalry, & is like to be caught. Possible but not probable. Ellie took Johny to Cornwall this aft^{n} for a period of sanitary rustication, carrying off little Lewis also. I expect her to return with Lewis tomorrow, but Johny is to be an absentee till we leave town for the summer. We shall miss him. It's a hateful necessity. His headaches are less frequent of late, & I hope a few months of country air will set him right & enable him to take up his books again next fall.

Called at N° 24 to night. Mr S.B.R. is still in bed. I hope this "bronchitis" may not be a graver matter than his people seem to think. His medicine man, Whiting, is (*me judice*) second-rate. He is in good spirits however & seems rather better than when I last saw him, Saturday ev'g.

I reluctantly confess it probably the best thing for the country that J.D. make good his escape to foreign parts with the specie he borrowed from the Richmond banks a day or two before he evacuated Richmond. Catching him & hanging him would be a national luxury, but it would be enervating. Our good-natured People would feel that Justice was satisfied, & would instantly begin treating Southern rebels with hyper-charitable magnanimity, & inviting them to resume their old place & crack the Plantation whip. For the same reason we should be thankful that *Booth* was not captured & hanged. Let us dispense with judicial vengeance on individuals, for the sake of keeping the people up to it's more important work of so dealing with the subjugated South that it will not be tempted to set up another Rebellion in a hurry.

May 4th. At 823 this P.M. was a preliminary meeting to organize an Auxiliary Board to take care of our Experimental "Home" or Hotel des Invalides, 45 Grove St. Wm E. Dodge J^{r}, Geo: F. Jones, Colden Murray, C.E.S., a brother of Egleston's, Bellows Agnew & I, & a younger brother of Agnew's. Result satisfactory. Spent half an hour thereafter in the New Academy of Design, cor: 23^{d} St. & 4th Av:. Interior very good. Collection for the year includes sundry very fine things, of which the most striking is a noble *Jo Semité* landscape by Bierstadt. — Ev'g. Stand'g Com: of the Diocese at the house of McVickar the Venerable, 32^{d} St. — thence to Stand'g Com: of Trinity Church.

Lincoln buried to day. I suppose it would be hard to find in history an instance of mourning for a ruler so spontaneous heartfelt & general, & so conspicuously manifested. New York is still draped in black. Business was suspended here for ten days after the murder. But the strongest evidence of the depth of popular feeling is the fact that there were fewer arrests in the City for drunkenness & disorder during that time than during any like period for many years past. Another significant fact is the demonstration of public favor shewn the Societies of black men that joined the funeral procession of the great Liberator. There could be no cheering of course, but I am told the crowded side walks & windows all along the route were white with waving handkerchiefs. Times have changed since July /63! This gigantic crime damages the Public Enemy more than the National Victories. It has broken the back bone of that vile spirit of ruffianism & savagery engendered even here at the North by years of partnership with a race of knife bearing woman flogging petty profligate rake helly despots.

A weighty Proclamation by the President appeared this morning. It announces that the authorities have evidence of the Complicity of Jeff: Davis, Geo: N. Sanders, Jacob Thompson & others in the plot for the murder of Abraham Lincoln, and offers a reward of $100.000 for the arrest of Davis, and smaller rewards for the arrest of the others. An important State Paper for Historians of the next Age. I cannot suppose it was lightly issued, or without substantial grounds for it's averments. If there be such grounds, even tho' legally & technically defective, Rebeldom is not only dead but d—d. It's name will be a stink & an abomination to Xtendom for centuries to come. The averment seems incredible. But it is certain that Gen: Joe Johnston's negotiations with Sherman were conducted under the eye of Davis Breckinridge & Co. They were contemporaneous with the Murder. Davis knew the terms of pacification then provisionally agreed upon would never be ratified by Lincoln. It would seem he must have known that Lincoln would not long stand in the way. The assassination plot appears to have included Johnson Grant & Stanton. Davis may have counted on such general dismay following the removal of these three & of Lincoln & Seward by one blow, & on such weakness & irresolution on the part of their successors, that this Peace programme, endorsed by Sherman, would be promptly ratified, and the South left in condition to rebel again next fall. There is certainly some reason to believe that the Rebel authorities knew of the Conspiracy. — Very many arrests have been made. The parties are to be tried by Military Commission, it is said. Some of them are reported to have collapsed & turned States-Evidence.

May 5th. At Bellows' this ev'g. Mrs Lane, M^{rs} D'Oremieulx &c a delegation from the Women's C.R. Assoc^{n} were with us — also Stranahan & his wife representing our Brooklyn auxiliaries — for conference as to what we would have them say to their affiliated Aid Societies. We decided on a Circular asking the Aid Societies to keep up their organization & their work till July 4th. We shall see the position better than we now do by the middle of June, & can then determine whether their services are still farther required. After the ladies withdrew we took action on various matters, generally toward reducing our working force & winding up our operations.

No War news. I believe a few more Generals have surrendered, but it attracts little attention. Our information from the country across the Mississippi is still imperfect, but from Richmond to New Orleans healthy granulations seem multiplying. Prominent Richmondites civil & military are taking the oath. The paroled rank & file seem to rejoice in the prospect of peace on any terms. Many of their officers are still sour & malignant, but that feeling will wear out. Some of them will emigrate, more of them will be submerged by the flood of social revolution & reconstruction, & will never regain position or considerable influence. This young Country heals up it's wounds very fast. Rebeldom may break out again here & there within the next ten years, but it's spirit & power will not survive from this our 1688 to a "Forty five". That would be 67 years hence, or A.D. 1932! All Slavery questions will be dead & in ashes, long before then. Slavery will be what the Salem Witchcraft epidemic is now. The Southern states will have been then long regenerated by a new immigrant people, a new social system.

May 6. Sat: Chilly rain, winding up with a thundershower, this ev'g. At monthly meeting of Century, & afterwards at U.L. Club awhile. We have a queer story to night of judicial investigations, at Bermuda, of the doings of certain hightoned Southern gentlemen who have been buying up the clothes of defunct yellow fever patients, saturating other clothes with the same infection, & boxing up the dry goods for shipment to this City next summer, with intent to get up an Epidemic in aid of the Confederacy. A *Dr Blackburn* said to be the leader of the movement. The report needs confirmation. It would be incredible on it's face if it charged so devilish a design on anybody else. The prisoner-starving, woman-whipping, hotel burning, fanatics & assassins of the South are capable of anything base subtle cowardly & murderous. — It's said the trial of the Assassination conspirators is to be opened Monday, before a Military Commission, & to be public. The proceedings will be watched with interest. There is uneasiness lest the proclamation declaring Davis &c privy to the crime should have been issued without sufficient evidence to justify so grave a charge. The Administration is unlikely to have made such a blunder. But legal evidence of complicity is not to be looked for. We cannot expect Government to produce a commission or power of attorney signed by Davis authorizing Booth to murder Lincoln and Seward. But the question will be settled in history — as in the case of James II and William — by moral evidence such as no Court would allow to go to a jury, and these trials may bring it out & put it on record. It is quite certain that the little gang of Southern leaders was troubled with no scruples that would prevent it's instigating the murder of anybody. It may be impossible to prove that Davis & C° directed this murder. It may be they did not direct it. But I think it will appear that they knew a blow was to be struck, and tried to profit by their early information.

Where is J.D.? We have a very authentic statement that the R.R. train that carried his stolen specie was burned, and the specie pocketed by a mutinous escort. Another report — equally authentic — places him, when last heard of, at Greensboro' N.C. eating & sleeping in his R.R. car, because the Greensborites would not admit him to their houses. All which may or may not be true. One thing is certain. $100.000. reward for his capture — in greenbacks — will be a sore temptation to insolvent Carolinians & Mississipians, however chivalric & Southron.

May 7th. Sunday. A beautiful day. Trinity Church with E. & Temple, & E's nice little Western cousin Miss Ella Cadwallader. To night Gen: Dix here. Morgan, D'Oremieulx, Miss Ella, & Miss Josephine Strong. — Gen: Dix says he has known of this alleged *yellow-fever conspiracy* for some time, & that there is proof of it in his office — and Dix does not say such things lightly. The venom of the Southern reptile is something fearful & wonderful beyond finite understanding — unfathomable past finding out. This story, true or false, is mere cumulative evidence. I am a convert to Democracy and Free Institutions. Tho' imperfect & bad, they are better & bear better fruit than the aristocratic slave selling Institutions that have prevailed at the South & are approved by the aristocracy of England. Let England's stately old manor-houses & seats of ancient families perish, with all their memories & their treasures of art. Their destruction will be good for mankind, even tho' brutal weavers & operatives be the Destroyers. English aristocracy has shewn itself unworthy it's great trust. It has devoted it's powers to the upholding of the worst tyranny known to Modern Xtendom. The sooner it is destroyed the better — whether by French Invasion, Irish outbreak, or the more peaceful process of so called "Reform".

May 8. England seems shocked by the murder of Lincoln. Assassins are always unpopular in England, specially so I suppose, because of memories of the Gunpowder Plot, & of a century spent in agonized dread of Spaniards & of Jesuits. So Booth & C° will find small favor in Albion, even tho' their crime was committed in the interest of Southern Slaveholders. English newspapers are tearful over Lee's surrender. It's "an untoward event." England's omission to intervene & help the Rebellion was a "blunder & a crime" for which it is to be feared "we or our children will have to pay". "We might have done so much for *civilization* & *free institutions* at so little cost." Grant has shewn "tenacity" & the resources of the North seem really remarkable, but let us praise & glorify Rebeldom for having maintained slavery so long against such enormous odds & without reasonable prospect of success. Up to this time these sagacious newspaper organs of Albion have been insisting that Rebeldom was manifestly unconquerable & must prevail at last.

May 9th. After dinner Agnew called here, & we drove to 45 Grove St. for 2d meeting of Trustees of proposed "Sanitarium". Moved that G.F. Jones be chairman & that the nascent establishment be styled — "The *Lincoln* Home — or Retreat or &c &c wh: was approved. Had to come away before adjournment for meeting of Com: on Admissions of U.L. Club. We sat late. Tendency is to make the test of eligibility more stringent.

Gold 136 or thereabouts. Signs of pacification are multiplying. Grass plats are being laid down, & temporary recruiting shanties demolished, in the Park (i.e. the City Hall Park) which has been a desolation these four years. Sundry Army corps are moving on Alexandria & Harrisburgh to be paid off & mustered out of service.

May 11th. There is much dissatisfaction because the Assassination plotters are tried by a Military Court & not by the ordinary public methods of criminal law. Tribune Times & Post are of one mind with the News & the World on this matter. There may be reasons for the course adopted of which we know nothing, but it seems impolitic & of doubtful legality. I hope nothing will be done to revive discord at the North. We have an era of good feeling now. Copperheads are silent even if still unconverted. It's a golden age after four years of Iron preceded by a long period of Pewter & Pinchbeck. May it last unbroken, at least till we are fully reconstructed & Southern Congressmen return to the bosom of Willard's Hotel. Then we shall have trouble again — of course.

English newspapers are full of comments on the assassination. It has clearly produced a feeling in London Manchester Liverpool &c never before created by the death of any foreign ruler. Hearty sorrow & indignation seem universal throughout all England. After reviling Lincoln for four years as a bloodthirsty clown, Albion has suddenly discovered that he was a merciful honest wise Ruler — & that his death is a calamity to mankind. Now that he is dead & gone, her Editors can afford to admit that he was a great & good man. But they prove to their own satisfaction that our success in putting down Rebellion was wholly due to his sagacity & honesty, and that the Country must come to grief without him, & with a "drunken mechanic" as his successor. They grasp at any straw of hope for their friends the slavedealers. To do them justice, they admit — or some of them admit — that this assassination — the Hotel burning plot of last Nov^{r} — and the robbery & murder plot at St Albans V^{t} do no credit to the Cause in the interest whereof those atrocities were perpetrated. More atrocious than all of them together has been (I think) the starvation, on system, of 60.000 prisoners of War.

May 14. Sunday. Morning papers interesting — Imprimis. *J. Davis has been bagged at Irwinsville Georgia!*

2do. Kirby Smith hears of Lee's Surrender but thinks it of no consequence, & proclaims his intention to fight for the Southern cause in Texas & Louisiana. Meetings are held & defiant resolutions passed in that benighted region. A Texan *Flournoy* pronounced a eulogy on Booth as the Brutus of America! — Reporters admitted yesterday to the trial of the assassin at Wash^{n} — their report of little interest. A passage of Arms occurred between a member of the Court & Reverdy Johnson — of counsel for some one of the caitiffs on trial. It shewed no high sense of dignity & propriety on the part of the Judge. But Hon: R.J. has lost caste sadly of late, & no one will regret that he got snubbed.

In bed all the morn'g with some sick headache. At tea time C.E.S. came in with dear little Kate, & the latest news of Jeff: Davis' capture. Being alarmed by the approach of our cavalry, that potentate arrayed himself in M^{rs} D's crinolines & ran for his life — "ad salices" or rather to the piney woods, even as fleet Camilla scoured the plain. The stalwart nymph made good time & her pursuers were about abandoning the pursuit, when they perceived that she wore long boots, & that her "action" was masculine. So they put more vigor into their chase, & brought her to at last. She produced a bowie knife, but gave it up on perceiving that the Genius of Columbia had revolvers. She was duly secured (& I hope ironed) protesting agst the want of magnanimity displayed by Government in not letting her get away.

What a subject for a grand Historical picture! *This* is the "Last Ditch" that has been talked of so long! The sons of Belial have made themselves merry for years over the story of Lincoln's entry into Washington disguised in a "Scotch cap & long Cloak". Jeff: Davis' race in petticoats will offset that legend. He has made himself ridiculous in his ruin. Had he got off in female disguise, like Charles Second, & Charles Edward, & Lord Nithsdale in 1715, & Sir John Falstaff, the laugh might have been on his side. But a fugitive potentate in a hoop skirt, running for his life with a party of Northern mudsills at his heels, surrendering at last for want of wind, & escorted to headquarters in his preposterous costume, & unable or unwilling to kill himself, or at least to kill some one of his captors & so to redeem his absurd position & dignify it with some trace of a Tragic element, is a mere figure of fun, to be grinned at for many generations. He has lost all chance of beatification as Heroic Martyr or Confessor. It will be safe to hang him.

Bowles (just from Paris), Lee, Col: McMahon, Graham &c here this ev'g. Much good talk around the little supper table.

McMahon, who is on Dix's staff, accompanied the funeral cortege of Lincoln from this city to Buffalo. He says nothing in all this unprecedented manifestation of public mourning has impressed him so much, as the sight that was frequent along the line of the R.R. of some solitary husbandman laying down his spade or hoe, or stopping his team, half a mile away, taking off his hat, & remaining uncovered while the train passed by and as long as he was in sight. No Prince — no Leader of a People — was ever so lamented as this unpolished Western lawyer has been and is. His name is Faithful and True. He will stand in History beside Washington, perhaps higher.

May 15. There is a universal guffaw over J.D.'s involuntary abdication of his high place as Hero, Champion, Patriot, & Statesman, & his appearance in the new character of Comic Gentleman, running thro' bush & thro' briar, in the cumbrous disguise of hooped skirts that were the separate property of Mrs Davis. His declaration after capture that he had thought Government too magnanimous to chase *Women* — & his wife's suggestion to his captors that they had better be careful or Mr Davis would hurt them, provoke much laughter. So does Barnum's telegram to Stanton offering $500.00 for the petticoats in which J.D. was captured. Barnum is a shrewd business man. He could make money out of those petticoats if he paid $20.000.00 for the privilege of exhibiting them.

May 16. Tuesday. "A day Æstivall". Decided premonition of hot weather. Fervent in business down town. N.B. One need'nt rejoice so violently over the Fall of Gold. I drew $900.00 interest from the Treasury this morning, which brought some $1180.00 in greenbacks. Last summer it would have brought about $2500.00. But the price of beef and mutton is just what it was, so the Fall of Gold merely accelerates my march toward the Almshouse.

823 this P.M. — To night at 45 Grove St. Elected Jem Ruggles, Thos H. Faile, & Wm Bowles Trustees of the "Lincoln Home". Dr Marsh with us. Kennedy has given the establishment some costly & valuable furniture — that came to him from his brother James. We elected Kennedy Pres'd^{t}. Our policy is to turn the institution over to the gentlemen we have associated as Managers & get it fully into their hands as soon as may be. — From Wash^{n} I hear pretty directly (from Sec: McCulloch thro Ben Silliman) that Government has decided on it's policy toward Rebel leaders. A few will be punished — probably very few — & most of them will be given their choice, to leave the country or stand a trial for treason. This choice was tendered Foote a day or two since, & he prudently transferred himself to Canada.

May 17. Wednesday. Very warm. Bowles with us at 823 this P.M. His parts of speech are marvellous, & would be past endurance if one forgot his energy & patriotism. Another long letter from poor Edge who is offered the Secretaryship of the English Reform League, which advocates "Manhood Suffrage" & wants to take the office. But he is in debt £440. & that fact stands in his way. His debts have been incurred in fighting our battles by a series of effective pamphlets & he thinks we on this side should help him. So we should, but raising the money would be uphill work.

He says the effect of Lincoln's murder on English feeling toward this Country astonishes him. Southern sympathizers hold their tongues, & the cause for which Lincoln died stands at last with Englishmen where it ought to have stood these four years. One of his statements is very remarkable, viz: that tho' the words Democrat & Democracy have heretofore been almost as odious, even to English Liberals, as Abolitionism & Abolitionist were in this country before /61, they are now freely & openly adopted by the Reform party. If so, the influence of America on England is far more direct & potent than I ever dreamed, & the sympathy of English Aristocracy with any movement likely to divide & destroy us — even with a Rebellion for the sake of Slavery, is fully accounted for. — Another notable symptom is Mr Punch's frank self-condemning Palinode. A more manly confession & recantation could hardly be written, and it is the finest tribute to Lincoln's memory that has yet been framed in verse. It would be ungenerous to consider whether it is prompted by perception that the tide has turned. Let Mr Punch have full credit for it, & it entitles him to a great deal.

Law School Commencement to night, at Hist: Soc^y^ rooms. Address by Judge Daly was acceptable. Alumni Oration by one Richards fair. Valedictory by Kernochan very good in style matter & delivery. The award of prizes (by Committees of outside lawyers ignorant of the names of the authors of the Essays & Examination papers submitted to them) did not at all correspond with my expectations, founded on the vivâ voce examinations.

Evidence taken on the trial of the Assassins becomes interesting. One of them, at least, seems legally proven an abettor of Booth's — . What is far more important the authorities at Richmond & the distinguished Rebel Refugees in Canada, or some of them, are already branded as accessories, by evidence insufficient for a petty jury, but quite enough to secure a verdict against them from Public opinion & from History. The Conspirators had visited Virginia & Canada. Somebody had put large funds at their control. Plans of arson & murder were freely talked of by Rebel officers as in progress, and the words "On detached service" were habitually used to designate the status of the men assigned to the execution of these villainies. It is certain that Rebel leaders have proven themselves none too good to instigate the murder of Mr Lincoln. We know that they have deliberately starved & tortured thousands of their prisoners to death or imbecility — that they have employed men to fire crowded hotels in peaceful Cities & to throw R.R. trains off their tracks, & thus to destroy scores of non-combatants, women & children included, for the sake of depressing & discouraging the North. The Yellow Fever Plot may probably have been part of the same politic scheme. These acts shew a grade of depravity more devilish even than that which could approve & abet the murder of Lincoln & his chief officers. There are precedents for political assassinations, but these other iniquitous undertakings are absolutely original.

May 18. The opinion at Wash^{n} seems to be that Mr Kirby Smith does not propose to disband at present. Bad for Kirby Smith, unless he can somehow embroil us with Maximilian and Napoleon. There is talk of a cipher letter from Davis found on the person of that defunct reptile, Booth. Fiction most probably. Tho' Davis has made many & grave blunders, he is not an idiot, & is therefore unlikely to have written himself down accessory to this murder, in cipher or otherwise.

May 19. A document picked up at Richmond was produced & proven yesterday before the court that is trying the assassins, not particularly relevant to any issue in the case, but establishing J.D's connexion with & approval of the Arson plot by a full endorsement in his own chivalric handwriting — a fearfully damaging piece of evidence. What's odd enough, it shews that my old acquaintance, our runaway Prof^{r} McCulloh was in the plot, & the inventor of the doughty combustible that was to devastate Northern territory, destroy our shipping & our cities, discourage & demoralize the North, & so secure the

Independence of Secessia. This makes it quite likely that Joy & Torrey were right in supposing this ill-visaged caitiff to have had something to do with getting up the Riots of July /63, and that he was a secret agent of Secesh-dom. The disclosure takes one back to the great Columbia College controversy of 1854, when McCulloh the traitor & sneaking incendiary was elected, and our own Alumnus Wolcott Gibbs defeated, by the votes of Rev: Haight, Gouv: Ogden, Gardiner Spring, & Dr Beadle, & by the politic neutrality of Hon: Hamilton Fish. Much credit the successful candidate has done them & the College!

G.C.A. looked in a moment this ev'g with his brother Henry just returned from a twelve years residence at *Batavia*, where I suppose he has made his fortune. Asked him what was the most remarkable sight he had seen in the Eastern tropics. He said, on reflection, it was a lot of monkies on the shore at Penang, with their tails in the water, fishing for crabs. G.C.A. says his clerical brother Edward has received a letter from a Georgetown clergyman enquiring for some vacant parish farther North. He says he ca'nt stand it any longer where he is, because the Ladies of his Congregation are carrying about little card photographs representing *Booth's* head crowned with laurel. Can this be true? If so, how should such women be disposed of? I should consign them to our Penitentiaries & State Prisons, as menials, to minister to the wants of such convicts as are not of special extraordinary wickedness like their own — make them scrubbers of prison cells, bed-makers & laundresses to criminals not below average Convict depravity. Upon my word, I think the instincts of a true gentleman would make him *kick* such a woman if she crossed his path (Heaven grant G.C.A's story may be all a mistake & that there are no female monsters extant so depraved & base) with as little ceremony as he would bestow on a female swine that got in his way.

May 20. Jeff: Davis reported to have reached Fortress Monroe. It's said that the petticoats he wore when he was run down are to be sent for exhibition to the Chicago Fair. Farther details of the Yellow Fever Plot appear in the morning papers, received from Canada, where Dr Blackburn has been arrested "for breach of the neutrality laws". These details tend to shew the Plot larger than we supposed — that it aimed at infection not only by yellow fever but by small-pox — that it caused the fearful epidemic of yellow fever at Newbern — that a trunk full of very fine & costly *shirts*, carefully saturated with poison, was sent to *Lincoln* "as a present", but did not reach him, or failed to do it's work, and that this devilish scheme was concocted or approved by the squad of High-Toned Southern gentlemen domiciled in Canada for sometime past. — !!! If the Church's power of working Miracles be in abeyance, Satan clearly retains *his*, & has been using it of late with freedom wholly unprecedented. This pestilence generating project and the Rebel policy toward prisoners are certainly *Miracles* (according to Hume's definition) for they contradict or transcend the experience of mankind. And if they be miracles they can be attributed to no other than the Lord of Hell.

Illustrations occur every day of the devilish ingenuities & refinements of tyranny & cruelty suggested to Rebels by the Devil, & executed by that Potentate through their agency, during the last four years. For instance, Collins took the affidavit, to day, of a broken down Andersonville prisoner, who swears that the Rebel officer who had his squad in custody used to call on them now & then to swear allegiance to "the Confederacy" & take service in the Rebel Army. One or two would give in, but the great majority would stand fast. Then he would order their starvation rations cut off for that day. When more than usually irritated by failure to secure renegades by this process, he would have some of them tied hand & foot & laid on the ground, & then lay his Revolver *on* the ear of the recusant, & fire off it's chambers. Blood flowed from the ear, and the Chivalric Southerner — beloved by Albion — said "There: I guess you wo'nt hear any *more* words of command from any d—d Yankee Captain." Collins' patient was made deaf for life by this treatment. Shall we try to conciliate this races of beasts, and beg them to be good enough to consent to be "reconstructed"? I, for one, say NO. — South Carolina, Virginia, &c, claimed the right to "Secede", and did "Secede", and have asserted their right of Secession these four years, very bravely, with rifle and bowie knife. They are beaten & subjugated now. But they are estopped from claiming any right to resume their allegiance. They have fought us claiming to have become a Foreign Power by virtue of their Secession. Being defeated, they are a conquered race, entitled to no privileges, without right to a voice in the Government of the Country that has subdued & suppressed them. On their own theory, the region South of the Ohio & Potomac is conquered territory, with which *The United States* may deal at it's own discretion. It may probably find it convenient to promote these vanquished communities from the status of subdued Rebellious provinces to that of *States*, whenever loyal feeling shall be so developed within their borders as to make the restoration safe & prudent.

May 22. After dinner to U.L. Club, where I spent an hour turning over Vol. I. of M[r] Townsend's 50 or 60 dumpy folios filled with newspaper cuttings illustrating the History of the War. This vol: covered *Dec: 1860*. It seemed like reading the records of some remote age, & of a People wholly unlike our own. So many notions were then put forward as axioms which are now seen to have been preposterous, and so many conspicuous men were molluscous & invertebrate who were so soon thereafter transmuted into mammalia, that we have forgotten their indecision & gelatinous quiverings of but little more than four years ago.

With Jeff: Davis & suite at Fortress Monroe is the distinguished Alex: H. Stephens, pseudo Vice Pres'dt &c &c. He seems to have surrendered himself, & will doubtless be let off easy. In fact however the perceptions of Right against which he sinned were clearer than those of any other Rebel Chief.

Farther details of Davis' capture add no dignity to his transition from the status of a fugitive to that of a prisoner. It now appears that when his tent was surrounded by our pursuing Cavalry, his wife begged that it might not be invaded till the ladies had finished their toilettes & made themselves presentable. Our squad of Vandal Scum acquiesced, of course, & waited. After a while there appeared unto them M[rs] J.D. & her sister escorting an elderly lady. They requested (according to one account) that they might take their old mother out of danger from stray bullets — two circumambient cavalry forces having fortuitously concurred & got into a fight by an unhappy mistake — (according to another) that the same old lady might be allowed to bring them water for their morning ablutions from a neighbouring spring. But some inquisitive mudsill trooper spied a great beard under the good old lady's muffler & great Boots coming & going beneath her petticoats, not exactly "like little mice", like big rats rather. He "*smelt a mice*" *& a Rat*, & a little investigation revealed the astounding fact that under the Skirts of this venerable woman there was a President of a "Southern Confederacy". — Report to day that Kirby Smith has been killed by one of his Paladins in a "difficulty" growing out of some operation in Cotton. Very possibly untrue. — McMahon gave me this incident of the War last ev'g. A Col: Whipple of a N. Hampshire Reg[t] was visited by a Wandering Christian, a missioneering Evangelical Nomad, who expatiated on the blessed work that was going on in the Army. — He had baptized twenty men in the camp of that Pennsylvania Regiment, over there, yesterday. "Did you?" said this Col: W. "All Right — but I wo'nt be beat by any D— Penn: Regiment. — Adjutant! Detail *thirty* men for baptism immediately after evening parade."

May 23. Evidence on the Assassination trial has brought out an important fact. Among the captured "Archives" of Rebeldom was a letter to J.D. from one W. Alston (I think that's the gentleman's name) an officer in J.D's service, asking facilities to go North in the capacity of Confederate Assassin. This letter was not put into the fire by J.D. but formally referred, as appears by endorsement, to the "Secretary of War", who in like manner formally referred it to the A. Gen[l] "for attention", & it was found among the documents of the A.G.'s office. This letter with it's endorsements would not convict Davis at the Oyer & Terminer as accessory to Lincoln's murder, but it will damage him in public opinion & in history.

N.B. We have ascertained J.D's reasons for assuming feminine attire when he was run down by our troopers. Information on that point is generally conveyed through a preliminary conundrum. Q. Why did J.D. put on petticoats when he was about to be caught? — A. Because he was just expecting to be *Confined*!!!

May 25. Newspapers full of the grand Parade and Review at Washington preliminary to mustering out a large part of the Armies of Atlanta & Richmond. Two hundred thousand men, it's said, marched past the White House, in column twenty one miles long, during two days, amid vast crowds of spectators — realizing Max Piccolomini's glowing description, on the greatest scale. A memorable Pageant, and much more than a pageant. I hope it is not premature. I think it is not. All Secessia this side the Mississippi, when it speaks at all, declares itself conquered humbled & ruined. It asks for "reconstruction" & for charity, & promises more or less sulkily to *behave* & to try to love it's old Uncle Sam. It thinks it will begin to love him again when it has had time to get over it's fearful spanking. But there are plenty of broken insolvent vindictive hot-blooded desperadoes left there, of the Wade Hampton type, subtle intriguers & good fighters, on whose consciences a parole sits lightly. They are quiet now, but we shall hear of them before long. Local outbreaks will be attempted & may become formidable unless very promptly put down. There will be no end of plotting & treason till this generation of Southern fire-eaters & Northern dirt-eaters has passed away. More assassinations will be undertaken within the year, or I am no prophet. That crime is catching. Among the thousands of gentlemen (so-called) whom the war has reduced from wealth to poverty & to a necessity of work that makes life worthless to them — boiling inwardly with hate & spite & humiliation — trained from boyhood to consider crime & violence virtues, there will almost certainly be found two or three whom Booth's infamy will tempt to follow his example & to become Martyrs in the cause of the Devil. This strong probability may be increased should capital punishment be inflicted on Jeff: Davis. It seems clear however that no State from Virginia to Louisiana can renew the Struggle on any large scale for years. They are all shattered & paralyzed. We may hope & expect that emigration & immigration will soon so change the Southern breed that the type of Depravity heretofore known as "Chivalric" will disappear, and the inhabitants of the South will become a civilized people, disinclined to rebel & to make war from mere passion & without grievances.

Magruder & Kirby Smith still hold Texas, & stand fast. Sheridan is to take charge of their case. Their prospects are not brilliant, but they may cost us much trouble yet.

May 29. Down the river by Mary Powell this morning. Discoursed Mahan who came on board at West Point. The steamboat halted a moment in Haverstraw Bay to receive the morning Papers, & memorable news — even

PEACE

herself at last, for Smith & Magruder have surrendered — if Gen: Canby's despatch to the War Department be truthful. So here I hope & believe *Ends* — by God's great & undeserved mercy — the Chapter of this Journal I opened with the heading of "*War*" on the night of April 13 1861. We have lived a century of common life since then. Only within the last two months have I dared to hope that this fearful struggle would be settled so soon.

Of course there will be periods of anxiety before the South is in stable equilibrium. Already we hear that the State Elections (!) of Virginia held under the auspices of "Gov[r]" Pierpont pronounce "against the Union". But there are some 200.000 men quartered in & about Alexandria & Washington, & they are quite competent to keep Virginia in her place. May her newly elected legislators try to assert their State Rights *at once*, & before any of the 200.000 shall be mustered out of service!

The South will probably try to bring it's Freedmen back to Slavery by some process of apprenticeship or penal servitude the moment it's State Governments are re-established. It's effort to do so will need watching. The only sure prophylactic is "*Manhood Suffrage*" administered to every Southern State. I would prescribe this heroic remedy, fully aware that it may well make the Gulf States communities of Black men. But how can we "constitutionally" induce South Carolina & Mississippi to swallow the dose?

There is one source of discord. Then we cannot hope that this vast bleeding wound, so many hundred thousand miles square, will heal up all over without occasional aggravations during the process, & the appearance of inflamed & gangrenous spots requiring yet a little more knife & caustic. But I believe it is tending to heal by the first intention, & that our four years agony is over.

What a time it has been — say from Dec: 21 /60 when we heard that the process of National decomposition had set in with the secession of cantankerous little South Carolina

— on through disaster & depression — for four years & nearly six months — till to day, with it's tidings that the *last* Army Rebeldom has organized out of the many hundred thousand men it has seduced or coerced into fighting for its felonious flag exists no longer. As I look back now to Bull Run — Fort Donelson — the Seven Days — Antietam — Gettysburgh — Chancellorville — &c &c I wonder my thoughts have not been even more engrossed by the development of the great Tragedy, that I have been able to pay any attention to my common routine, to be interested in anything outside the tremendous Chapter that History has been taking down in short hand.

News that a party of six or seven Rebel fugitives was captured off Cape Sable. That sneak Prof: R.S. McCulloh seems to have been among them. The despatch that reports the names the prisoners gave says the names are probably fictitious. But few Rebels have made themselves so base as to be willing to assume so disgraceful an alias as McCulloh's.

May 30. Tuesday. Perspiring weather. Diligent down town. Now the war is over — as we hope — I must try, with God's help, to get myself into relations with the ordinary duties of peaceful days once more. Those duties have been sadly neglected these four anxious years. At N° 823 was Chas Bowles who discoursed me near two hours about what he did & what he saw at Washington. I disputed none of his statements, so he need not have made them with such wearying emphasis & vehemence.

Johnson seems doing his difficult work wisely & well. His two Proclamations, as to Amnesty in general & N. Carolina in particular, are judicious & not over-flavored with rose-water. Jeff: D. has been indicted for treason & is to be tried in the ordinary course of law, like any other malefactor. I fear any jury that can be impanelled in Washington will disagree. The true course would be to have him indicted for Treason committed say April 12 /61 — to indict him for another several act of Treason on the 13th, & another on the 14th, & so on — a separate indictment for each day of his official life as Head of the Rebellion. If he cannot be convicted on indictment N° 1, he should be brought to trial on N° 2. Before N° 1200 was disposed of he would probably be dead & buried. Should he be convicted

I suppose we shall be favored with diplomatic advice & remonstrance from France & England. We need none of their counsel, & are utterly indifferent as to their approval or disapproval. The last Saturday Review contains an article headed "Wilkes Booth" wh: seems to me more heinous than anything I ever saw in any periodical of the 19th Century. It's a jesuitical circumlocutory apology for political assassinations, justifying that crime by faint censure. "*War*," it says, "is merely assassination on a large scale" — which is bad for the fame of Wellington & Nelson! It quotes sundry casuists of 200 years ago who hold Princes to be rightful subjects of murder in certain cases, and it shews clearly that we have no right to set up the *Divino Jure* doctrines of Charles Second's divines (!!!) against the theories of the men who murdered Abraham Lincoln. — This paper is the special organ of English University men — of the more cultivated & scholarly aristocracy of England. — Alas for England! "Non Angli, sed Angeli" — of Darkness.

Called this aftn at the studio of W.B.G. Stone, my old Catskill friend who walked me quite off my legs eleven years ago, & of whom I had lost sight ever since. He has been in the army, and enjoyed large experience therein, especially on secret service, as disguised Inspector of Mosby's camps — a perilous duty! When I used to know him he was working only with the pencil, & three or four sketches of his have long adorned the house, sketches of Catskill landscape. He has taken up *Color* since he left the Army, & he shewed me three pictures, one of which was bad — one tolerable — & one very good. —

June 1. Thursday. Very warm. Most shops & offices closed: this being the National Day of Mourning for the President's Murder. Attended service in Trinity Ch: awhile. Kept in the back ground and shied the sermon. — By the by, there was a special meeting of T.C. Vestry yesterday aftn, at wh: I could not assist because of a previous engagement with School of Mines, & Cutler, Mus: Doc: & organist was relieved from farther duty. Cause, insubordination & overstaying leave of absence. He has been trotting some of the little chorister boys over the country on concert tours, thereby tempting Scoffers to call Trinity choir "Cutler's Minstrels". I am glad we are rid of him, though he is undeniably an efficient Kapell-meister & drill sergeant. It is to be hoped he will take all his rubbishy Services & Anthems away with him. His provisional successor is his late Assistant — Diller (?) by name. So Morgan Dix told me this aft^{n}.

After dinner to U.L. Club. Gen: Hooker expected there, to receive a Sword presented by California. Rooms crowded — gas-lights many — carbonic acid & Caloric predominant — so after a couple of hours spent investigating a volume or two of the Townsend Opus Magnum, the great Corpus of Newspaper Cuttings, I came off. The *Excerpta*, preserved in those folios, from the World, News, & Express of the summer of /63 are stupendous monuments of the Northern Treason that was trying to paralyze us by riot & arson in concert with Lee's invasion of Pennsylvania. There has seldom been a much baser exhibition of dirt-eating scoundrelism.

Trial of the assassination conspirators moves slowly. The Judge Advocate introduces much matter not strictly relevant, e.g. proof that prisoners were starved & tortured by the Rebels — & of the Blackburn Yellow Fever device &c. He is in fact trying the Confederacy & Jeff: Davis before the Country & all Christendom, rather than conducting the prosecution of Spangler Atzerodt & Co.

"Jefferson Davis *Yeoman*", as his Indictment presumes to style him, is or soon will be at Washington awaiting arraignment & trial in due course of law. He is reported to say that "the U.S. will never dare to hang him", but his past mistakes should make him hesitate about any more predictions. His prophesyings of four years ago have proved disastrous to himself & to all who put faith in him. He told his people that the North would never undertake a War against Secession — and that France & England would have to become active allies of the South or perish for want of Cotton. His people believed this flattering tale, & rebelled. Most of them regret it just now!

Southern Statesmanship is among the ancient delusions this War has blown away. Southern leaders have displayed Energy, activity, audacity — intense purpose — perseverance under discouragement, all the virtues of the Belligerent Carnivorous

Animal. No Grizzly Bear ever shewed greater ferocity or less rational forethought. Their administration of affairs has been most plucky & resolute, but without a trace of Science except in military strategic engineering work, learned at West Point years ago. It has been a series of blunders worthy to succeed their first great blunder of Rebellion. All the calculations on which that fatal move was founded, after thirty years of preparatory study & intrigue, have proved untrustworthy. Their most extreme & desperate measures have re-acted against their cause. E.g. their starving their prisoners. Any intelligent child could have told them that whatever they thereby gained in the course of Exchanges would be far more than counterbalanced by the invigoration this atrocity gave Northern War-feeling, & by the trouble it inflicted on Northern allies of Rebellion. But they saw only so many Northern soldiers starved & tortured into imbecility to be exchanged against a like number of Rebel Soldiers returned from well fed & furnished Northern depots in better physical condition than when they were captured — and they could not look beyond that grateful spectacle. Another gross blunder was their perseverance to the last in swaggering about Death before Re-Union with the hated Yankees. Had they made any thing like a shew (however fraudulent & illusory) of willingness to talk about "Re-construction" on any terms — the conservation or restoration of Slavery for instance — at any time before Lincoln's re-election, they would have enabled Northern traitors to make a fearfully damaging diversion in their favor. There would have been ruinous division here. Lincoln would have been defeated. The National Government would have passed into the hands of friends of the South. Buchanan would have come back to life in the person of that unhappy *McClellan*, bringing with him Southern Independence on easy terms, & a Continental Chaos. That men so false subtle & unscrupulous as the Rebel leaders left this most obvious stroke of policy unattempted is due — under God's blessing — to the blindness brought on them by feverish heat of wrath & arrogance. Any Ward politician of a New York corner Grocery would have been more sagacious & politic than Jeff: Davis & C°. What could Barlow & Belmont & their confederates do for the South while the South was swearing it would never listen to *any* proposals of Restoration?

June 3. Sat: — Warm. Up town rather early for a visit to Acad: of Design with Ellie, G.C.A. & Temple. Find E. radiant. She called on *Sherman* this morning with her father, at Scott's in 23^{d} St. & when she said she was going to West Point Monday (with Miss Helen Stanley, for a day or two) she was invited to join the Gen'l's party Monday morn'g. Rapture!!! G.C.A. dined here. After dinner came in Dr Duncan of Sherman's army & of somebody's Staff, an original racy person.

Bellows, Agnew & Blatchford here last night. Blatchford reports 225.000 men camped around Washington, & in special need of San: Com: supplies, signs of Scurvy being prevalent. During this process of "mustering out" it is specially difficult to get Requisitions duly honored. Hospital population on the 30th 89000 of which not much less than half is within sight of the dome of the Capitol.

There is a score or so of paroled pauper Rebel Colonels & Captains at the N.Y. Hotel, spunging on Copperhead Cranston for rooms & meals, & negotiating with their Northern friends the subsidies that give them pocket money, and one good Solid *Drunk* per diem. Certain people caress them, ask them to dinner, & give them old clothes. Mr George Deas is there, who resigned his commission in April /61. He hailed Willy Cutting the other day, in front of this Rebel Hotel. "Willy! Willy!! How are you? Do'nt you remember me? I'm Geo: Deas!" Cutting bowed, said he knew nobody of that name, & walked on. It's Deas that tells this. Good for Cutting. The world has moved since the New York Club Squabble four years ago, when he was furious against any formal Club censure of *Deas.* Deas & his colleagues — haughty hightoned superior aristocratic creatures all — consent to pocket eleemosynary five dollar greenbacks & to put on cast-off Yankee breeches without perceptible pain or struggle & without much expression of thankfulness.

June 4. Mr S.B.R. dined with us. He recovers slowly from his recent illness. He was here again this ev'g — also Dr Peters & wife, Mrs Lily Clymer, C.E.S., G.C.A., Graham & *Dr Duncan*, who kept us entertained with reminiscences of Georgia & S.C. for just four hours. He is very queer & quaint. "As to the fellows that had charge of our prisoners" says the gracious Duncan,

— "Hell is too cool for them anyhow. I'd have it heated up hotter than Nebuchadnezzar's fiery furnace was, when *he got up that Jew-bake*, and then I'd put an extension on to Eternity." He thinks S. Carolinians the loudest talkers & poorest fighters in Rebeldom — Wade Hampton a mere braggart & bully. — Description of Sherman on the march thro' S.C. looking about him at columns of Smoke rising near & far & farther, five, ten & twenty miles away — "*That's* Slocum: — *that* must be Howard — *that's* probably so & so. Boy! If you can find a deserted house anywhere around, just set it on fire, & let them know where *we* are". — Georgia Woman watching the progress of a cavalry regiment past her door — loquitur. "Why-y! Did *you-uns* come all the way down hee-ah, *Critter-back*?"

June 7th. Weather continues dull & cool. Ellie writes of supreme days at West Point, and Johny writes that he is catching turtles & dissecting them, & building a Log Cabin in the "Little Glen" at Cornwall, in a state of free perspiration. Discoursed E.C. Fisher our London San: Com: Agent at 823 this aftn, just from London. He tells me our Report on Rebel treatment of prisoners has done us vast service in England: that Anglo-Americans are mostly copperheads — peerage-worshipping snobs, & that the Archbp of York & the Bishops of Oxford & London are our friends. Glad to know that any Princes of the Church of England are on our side in this our struggle against Anarchy & Iniquity. — Dined here to day C.E.S. — G.C.A. — & his Javanese brother Henry, a merchant of Batavia, full of talk about the marvels of the tropical region in which he has spent the last ten years.

— God grant we may not incur the guilt of treating Rebels *unjustly*. We are in danger of a weak policy of pardon & conciliation. It would be unjust — wicked — wrong. A dozen of these caitiff leaders of Rebellion should be hanged. — Public talk dwells mainly on the Black-Suffrage question, & on that of the suspension or non suspension [per collum] of J. Davis. Incidental to this latter question is that of his personal complicity in the hyper-diabolical works & plottings of his Booths & Blackburns. Few doubt it. If he be convicted of Treason, it will be this, rather than his treason, that will hang him. The evidence of his guilt comes mainly from men of dubious standing, but crimes like his can seldom be proven but by spies — informers — or scoundrels more or less penitent. There is documentary proof moreover that some of these flagitious devices — unknown to Civilized War — were proposed to him, & by him officially referred to subordinates with instruction to enquire whether they were feasible. There is proof enough against Jeff: Davis & his "Confederate" pals to determine the judgment of Mankind — Englishmen excepted. They will doubtless still uphold & glorify "the gallant gentleman & Christian Statesman who was chosen to be the Leader of a Great People".

June 8. At 823 to day was an Andersonville prisoner, who said he had seen his brethren there on their hands & knees around the *latrines* of that infernal pen, grubbing among fæces for undigested beans & grains of corn wherewith to mitigate the pains of slow starvation.

June 13. Newspapers report that Society in certain regions of Georgia & Alabama has gone to chaos & disintegration — an asthenic passive dry gangrene & death. Most property there, public & private, is destroyed, the bare soil is left. That soil could support ten times it's population, but it is left untilled. Cuffee will not work because Mass'r has no ready money wherewith to pay him. Cuffee is distrustful & suspicious, & gives no credit. — "Mass'r" belongs to a First Family, was not born to work, & would rather starve than work, & he & his house seem to be starving, partly for the sake of spiting the Yankees. If Mas'r have any money put away at the North or in London, he means to leave the Country. "It is not our Country any more, you d——d yankees have conquered it, & we are aliens: Take our Country, & let us get out of it, leaving our curse behind us". Parts of Secessia may have to pass through a period of absolute anarchy & barbarism, longer or shorter, before they become Christianized & Civilized. — Per contra, Gouv: M. Wilkins read me a letter from one Turnbull, a nephew of his in Mississippi, stating the measures in progress in his district to re-establish order, & they seemed healthy & hopeful. — But very many Southern aristocrats — probably a majority of them, are utterly broken & ruined & incapable of any resolute effort to recover their lost position.

Some of these broken men will straggle Northward, to join the congenial gamblers & bullies of Northern cities — their allies of old. Therefore we may expect a reign of crime — assassination — poisoning & incendiarism. For these wretches are as full of hate, malice, & thirst for revenge, as any fiend, & absolutely unscrupulous as to the means of gratifying their vindictiveness. No extant vermin are more useless & more hateful than Southern Gentlemen of the fully developed Southern type.

June 14. *Mitchel* of the Daily News arrested for treason & sent to Fort Lafayette. Glad of it. This impudent Celtic runagate after editing a Richmond paper till the rebellion collapsed, came here, & took charge of the "News", a paper no less disloyal & perhaps more mischievous. Only this morning he published an insolent* editorial to the effect that he "was not here under the provisions of any amnesty (as reported) — nor had he received any pardon. He was much obliged to the President for his alleged clemency but he had no immediate use for the article, not being convicted of anything as yet." — Irishman & Southern Secessionist combined produce the most offensive Kakodylic Gas known to Political Chemistry. It is painful to the patriot to think that this bully and traitor will never be pilloried or flogged — not even hanged.

Bowles of Paris at 823. Agnew says Bowles is a Simoom, & that when Bowles begins talking he (Agnew) begins to pant & stifle & wants to bow down on all fours, like a Camel in the desert, & bury his nose in the carpet till the storm be overpast. I believe the decrees of Divine Providence remove Bowles from this City before the end of the present week. He contemplates a speedy return to Paris — may he stay there!

Trustees of Lincoln Home to night at 45 Grove St. — Our Superintendant, Dr Marsh, grumbles — offended by criticisms of Agnew's. Talked about resigning & is as hyperæsthetic as a grizzly *Bar* with a gumboil.

[*letter]

June 16. Friday. Hope to have Mrs Ellie home again tomorrow. Nothing extra down town. Talking of Extras, how flat & vapid the newspapers are now! I did not go to the corner of Pine &

William Sts to day to inspect the Commercial Advertiser's Bulletin Board — it's 1.30 P.M. proclamation, & I doubt whether I have omitted that pilgrimage in pursuit of knowledge, till to day, for four years & a half. — At 823 this P.M. were Agnew & I. We are running the San: Com: machine, autocratically, for Bellows is skylarking at the Chicago Fair. Our cash balance has gone down to $270.000, & I think the proceeds of the Fair will not largely increase it. So we took vigorous action, & directed M[r] Gen: Sec'y Blatchford to suppress all relief Stations in Virginia except those in & about Washington, & to dismiss everybody who can be spared. We ought to hold a general meeting of the Commission within a month, & proceed to wind up.

June 17. Proof given on the assassination Trial that "Hon:" Ben Wood, F'nandy Wud's brother, the traitorous proprietor of the Daily News, received a check for $25000.00 from the treason-fund of the Rebel refugees & plotters in Canada. I do not perceive the relevancy of this fact to the issues on trial, but it is valuable as a contribution to future histories. — M[r] S.B.R. seems not to have returned from Washington. Very unfortunate. The special Com: on Lieber was to meet to day, & the College Board meets Monday. Lieber continues to pepper me with notes & memoranda. He writes to day that he inclines to think Barnard sympathizes somewhat with this move to displace him. The unsuspicious Teuton! Barnard got it up.

Death of Judge Cha[s] H. Ruggles of Po'keepsie, aged about 75. A good man, a strong lawyer, & a patriot — tho' a Democrat.

Gen: Dix has gone to Montreal to attempt unravelling some of the Rebel intrigues there. [He was educated at the Jesuit College or School of Montreal it seems, & has not been there since he was a boy] — Conover, one of the most important witnesses produced by Government on the Assassination Trial, was sent to Canada to make farther investigations. He had stated, inter alia, that among the pseudonyms by which he was known in Rebel coteries was that of Ja[s] Watson Wallace. On arriving in Canada he resumed that *alias*, & published under it a statement that Conover's testimony was untrue, that *he* was the real J.W.W. & that Conover had been fraudulently adopting his personality. This ingenious device was meant to blind Cleary & Jake Thompson & their pals. But they smelt something, & secured J.W.W's arrest by civil process, on some pretext or other. Part of Dix's mission is to get him out of jail. Those caitiffs would cheerfully murder any man they think likely to disclose their detestable enormities.

June 19. According to Fish, Gov: Aiken of S.C. says Lieber taught pure Calhounism while a citizen of that State. I believe this statement untrue. But Lieber is to all practical intents & purposes *dismissed* with his present salary continued till next May. There is no saving him. Stanton & Seward might be stimulated to raise a breeze about it in the newspapers, but it would be useless.

To night Agnew, Blatchford & Parrish here — a San: Com: conference — We decide to draw in our tentacles — dismiss agents — close Relief Stations — curtail work & expenditure — everywhere & at once — & to be diligent in gathering & arranging material for a final Report — the Last Dying Speech & Confession of the San: Com: — Thank God the time for San: Com:'s release & disembodiment seems so near at hand at last!

June 20. This evening young Lee here, & a very agreeable Major Nichols of Sherman's staff, full of anecdotes of the great March from Atlanta to Raleigh. He confirms the story told by all Sherman's officers that the braggarts of S. Carolina were the slowest fighters, & are the most abjectly whipped Rebels, in all Rebeldom. They did nothing but whine, he says, as Sherman's Column marched over their plantations. — N.B. a rebel prisoner who called at 823 to day to ask after a little tobacco, observed to Collins that if he'd known N.Y. was such a H— of a big place he would'nt never have fit agin it.

Joe Dukes, ci-devant S. Carolinian, now N.Y. lawyer, & always opposed to Secession, tells C.E.S. of letters he receives from the South on which he prophesies a War of extermination by the White race on the Black, or else vice versâ, & more probably the latter. He holds that the two races cannot long remain in peaceful contact under their altered relations, & that a struggle must soon begin which will wipe out one or the other. It does not seem likely, but no one can form an opinion on the question without intimate knowledge of the South as it was, & as it is. Secessia has no more hope from her present population, than our S.W. frontiers have from the Comanches. They are alike incapable of civilization & progress & must be displaced to make room for a better breed. It is to be hoped the displacement may be through a peaceful process of immigration, gradually changing the stock by intermarriage. But it may be destined to come with tragical abruptness, & bring with it all the horrors of San Domingo.

I rather expect a depopulation of the South by pestilence. The vital forces of Southern men & women are lowered by a profound sense of failure defeat mortification & subjugation, especially damaging to so arrogant a race. Add to this a very general privation of the means of living, & in many regions (as reported) destitution & starvation, even unto death, & there seems abundant provocation for an Epidemic of the deadliest type.

The Political Pots of Washington are simmering ominously & are not unlikely to reach boiling heat before long. Advanced Republicans grumble over Pres'dt Andrew Johnson's reconstruction-policy, & say he is selling his party, after the manner of dirty old Tyler, 25 years ago. I do not "see it in that light," and have faith in the President's judgment & honesty. But a split in the party seems certainly coming, & Copperheads chuckle over the prospect, to my serious aggravation. Next winter will probably find Sumner Wilson & C° organized as an opposition, & "conservative" Republicans sustaining the Administration, in alliance with Northern "democrats" & malignants & restored penitent Congressmen from the Carolinas with bowie knives about their persons. Next session of Congress will be an anxious time. "Darkey-Suffrage" is a dark & troublesome question, and it must be met. That Freedmen, who have as a class, always helped the National cause to the utmost of their ability, at risk of their lives, should have political rights at least equal to those of the bitter enemies of the Country who are about to resume those rights, sullenly & under protest, & only because they are crushed coerced & subjugated, is (abstractly considered) in the highest degree just & right. But the average field hand would use political power as intelligently as would the mule he drives.

June 22. "The venerable Edmund Ruffin", who asked & obtained the privilege of firing the first gun on Sumter, has fired his last gun on himself. It was a musket the muzzle whereof was in his mouth, & it blew off the top of his head, scattering his brains — such as they were. He left a paper certifying his inability to live under Yankee government. He was 80 years old & might have waited a little, for a release in the course of nature. If his example be generally followed by Secessionist leaders, the problem of re-construction will be simplified.

Lieber has had a long interview with one of his old S.C. pupils, a son of Trenholm, Jeff: Davis' Secretary of the Treasury. The youth was an original fire-eating Secessionist, served in the Rebel Army, & is here as a paroled prisoner, trying to secure influence to get his papa out of jail. Lieber lent me a letter from him which is interesting & instructive. He professes to hold that his old theories have been practically refuted by the fortunes of War, & that the States are now "provincialized", & declares his intention henceforth to live up to the letter & spirit of the oath of Allegiance to the General Government which he took at Columbia. As to his *affections*, he says he must be allowed his year of mourning for the dead Confederacy, which seems a frank avowal of natural feeling. Lieber gave me also a memorandum of the substance of their long talk together. The young man told him that the great & only object of *his set* was Independence, not because they suffered any grievances but because they hated Northerners. When that was secured they expected to establish a strong consolidated Government, perhaps a Monarchy, without the least respect for State Rights, to abolish Slavery, & to concentrate their National energies on internal improvements. He probably represents the more cultivated & thoughtful young men of Charleston & of the Gulf States generally. He says they respect the North now, having learned it's strength of purpose & it's capacity for fight, & that he thinks there is more Rebellion in the N.Y. Hotel than in all S. Carolina. Very likely. That hotel is a nest of traitors. Half its inmates deserve hanging ten times over.

June 26. U.L.C. to night — after discourse with E. about the great problem of Education, which has so engrossed her thoughts of late. Spent an hour at Club dipping into pamphlet literature of the last four years. It's attractive reading. — I tend steadily toward the opinion that our National debt would be a thousand millions less had McClellan & Fitz-John Porter followed their instincts & gone to their own proper place, with Lee & Magruder & C° in April 1861. They seem to have been Benedict Arnolds both, only negative instead of positive. — N.B. Galveston — the last Rebel port — is held & occupied by National forces. The Customs-Collecting Genius of Columbia has opened an office there, so the Blockade of Fifty months is RAISED at last. Of which fact please take notice, dear "neutral" John Bully! Old Brougham has been making a speech about us, at some "banquet" or other. It's very good of him. His doubly Renegade Lordship hopes the voice of the best friends of the American People — the voice of those who have stood by them through evil report & good report — may reach us in this hour of victory gained by exertions & perseverance & military talent that are really — in point of fact — not altogether discreditable, you know, to mere Americans, and that the voice aforesaid may be received as a Warning to temper Justice with Mercy & to hang the Traitors. The old Humbug! He has been giving the lie these four years to all his political life before them by upholding Slavery & Oligarchy for the sake of doing his little all to destroy his dear American People. The Quarterly & Blackwood of thirty years ago estimated Harry Brougham at his true value, though I used to think otherwise.

I fully admit however that the expediency of hanging Jeff. D. for treason is an open question. His suspension per collum would be "veré dignum et justum, æquum" but *perhaps* not "salutare". He is the Representative Man of Secession & Disunion. He is now hateful to 9/10 of such Southerners as are capable of forming an opinion about him. If he be allowed to die a natural death he will be hateful to generations yet unborn, & the cause with which his name is identified — Disunion — will always be weakened by the Association. If he be hanged he will be transmuted into a Martyr, & his name will become a Word of Power — like John Brown's. — There are weighty reasons on the other side however.

June 27. Our S.C. balance is down to $270.000. & will not be very largely reinforced by proceeds of the Chicago Fair. S.C. cannot take in sail too fast. — Gibbs is interested in Lieber's case, & I think understands its pros & cons. — At U.L.

Club to night, looking into the Pamphlets of three years ago — especially at half a dozen fat volumes I had bound up & gave the Club when it's Library was first launched. Two lamentable diatribes entitled "American Bastilles" or some such thing I found particularly refreshing. They are detailed personal narratives by disloyal Marylanders bagged in Sept. /61 & detained near six months in Fortress Monroe Fort Lafayette & Fort Warren. They had mere army rations to eat — their coffee was not good — they had no liquor except what they bought & paid for & except the baskets of champagne sent them by N.Y. & Boston sympathizers — "Tadpoles" (qu: musquito larvae?) occurred in their drinking water — & worst of all they were mixed up with mere common men from N. Carolina, captured at Fort Hatteras! Their pork was intolerably fat, & their soup thin, poor fellows. Their pamphlets are well defined specimens of Slave-ownic Secesh literature, which embodies the characteristics of (1) the Northern *gent*, who tries to mask his vulgarity by Deportment & swagger & much talk about his own exalted Gentility, (2) the Swash-buckler, Alsatian, "bully-ruffian" or "Mohock" of 160 years ago, & (3) the Sharp Attorney of the present day, whose clients are found in the Tombs, & whose vocation it is to keep thieves & burglars from being consigned to Blackwell's Island by invoking Law in their behalf. — The *typical* Southerner is a Snob — a bully — a "Shyster" — & (I fear) an assassin.

June 29. The "*Daily News*", the organ of Secesh-dom in this City, making hardly a decent pretence of loyalty to Government (which the "*World*" tries to do) prints an Elaborate editorial earnestly advocating Negro Suffrage! This was of course dictated South of the Potomac, & it shews that some at least among the leaders of Secessia propose changing their base. But the move is inexplicable to me. It is possible, though improbable, that they think the change sure to be made, & are therefore hastening to make friends among the Ethiopian Voters of the Future. Perhaps they want to embarrass & bother the Administration, or to promote schism in the Republican party. Whatever may be the politic purpose they have in view, the "progress of human events" since 1860, is bewildering. Never did Human Events make such *time* before. Southern newspaper articles of three or four years ago make me feel very old. They seem mediæval relics. When I remember having read them on their first appearance, my sensations are those of the Wandering Jew refreshing his recollections of political literature under Commodus. Centuries seem to have elapsed since the Richmond papers went into spasms about the invasion of Virginia & the occupation of Alexandria, & proclaimed no quarter to any black man allowed to shoulder a musket in the National Army. GOD be praised for the prospect of a solution of our National troubles so much more speedy than we hoped or deserved, & for the progress we have made toward becoming a United People from the St Lawrence to the Rio Grande! — Though the subtle vindictive savages of the Woman-whipping Chivalry must still be watched & kept down, they no longer confront the Country with Armies & strong places. The backbone of this base brutal social system that called itself Chivalric is broken, & it lies under the feet of the Nation. Unless we make some fearful blunder we can keep it there. Let us hope that Southern-ism will be as obsolete & dead, twenty years hence, as Jacobitism.

June 30. *Herald* follows in the wake of *Daily News* & urges Negro-suffrage — because the present "Abolition Congress" will refuse to admit representatives from penitent & reconstructed Rebel States unless their Constitutions include this feature. Once admitted, these representatives will "hold the balance of power". I suppose that the next step is then to be another amendment of State Constitutions kicking Sambo out into the cold again. If this be the programme of Southern leaders, they are certainly "groggy" & fighting wild.

Dipping into "Rebellion Record". We begin now to be able to look at the Union War as a whole. Of course we shall have a better view of it as we get farther off, but from our present position, *July 4th 1863* stands out as *the* critical day that determined it's result. Gettysburgh seems to have been the turning point of the four years' struggle. I believe moreover that Lee's failure on that field saved us from an organized Copperhead rising in N.Y., headed by sneaking Horatio Seymour's underlings — traitors bolder but not baser than their chief. That the plot was matured is certain. — Meade's victory & the fall of Vicksburgh disheartened the conspirators — but the Draft Riots of July were a partial deflagration & explosion of the combustible ruffianism that had been stored away for yet worse mischief on a larger scale. Had Meade been routed at Gettysburgh, Seymour would have screwed his courage up to a coup d'etat, backed by the Mayor & Aldermen of this city & all the rest of it's Rascaldom in office & out. With Lee riding in triumph over Pennsylvania, & New York arrayed against Government, the National cause would have been nearly hopeless: — Unless indeed Mackarelville & the Mayor should have made *McClellan* (for whom the Keltic rioters cheered so heartily) Commander of their Forces. In that case the Country might have survived the shock. Thank Heaven, the day of those dogs is *over*, at least for the present.

Copperheadism is not dead, to be sure, any more than Original Sin. But it sleeps just now — or rather lies comatose & senseless, stunned by blows that have smashed it's cranium. It's only sign of life is an incoherent babbling, now & then, about the sufferings of Sambo as Freedman, — the dreadful consequences of hanging M[r] J. Davis, — the virtues of General Lee, — and the "New England fanatics who brought about the late War". — I see no issue yet, on which Copperheadism can revive & resume it's hostility to the Country. But it will revive, when Congress meets, if not sooner, and find something or other for it's venomous fangs to bite on. Scoundrels like Gunther, Gideon Tucker, Win: Chanler, Ben Wood &c cannot long remain inactive & innocuous.

July 3[d]. The Herald still clamors for Ethiopian suffrage. Very few even of the Southerners who will be allowed to vote under A.J.'s Reconstruction system will see the question in that light. The Freedman is in their eyes merely a domesticated animal that used to be docile & valuable, but which having got loose & escaped to the woods, has certainly become worthless, & is probably a mere nuisance & breed of mischievous vermin. — Perhaps they are right, but I think they are fearfully wrong. They must work out their own Destiny.

Lord Brougham takes occasion to remark in the House of Lords that "He *never* gave His approbation to the Slave-holding & Slave-mongering States of the South". Nobody cares whether he did or did not — So this Noble & learned Peer & Humbug need not have lowered himself by uttering this monstrous fiction, especially as it imposes on nobody. We care little now for the dicta of Brougham Palmerston Gladstone & C°. The last four years have de-*provincialized* us. This Country was in 1861 a dependency of England in all but political relations. If a Cockney tourist censured our Shad as too bony, our Hotels as too flashy, our oysters as too big, or the Mississippi as too muddy, we cried, & scolded, & felt dreadfully abused. But we have outgrown that childish weakness. We have learned that the American People is "some Punkins" — that the ruling Caste of England is selfish sordid & false — & that her political philosophers and soothsayers are quacks.

July 4th. I supposed the City would be far noisier than usual to day, but this has been a rather quiet Fourth. We have been living under such pressure of stimulants that we cannot become excited over a mere 4th of July or any other anniversary. Such days as April 3d, 10th, & 15th, blunt people's sensibility for some time. — N.B. Wonderful to think how many yarns about The Wilderness & Five Forks & Nashville & Sherman's great March & the fall of Richmond &c &c are being spun to night by returned soldiers in village bar-rooms or on shady farmhouse porches. How many nice country girls all over New England & all thro' the West are listening, with blue or black eyes as big as saucers, to the prodigious stories of brother Sam or cousin Billy!

July 6. Result of the Assassination Trial announced this ev'g. Payne, Herold, Atzerodt & Mrs Surratt sentenced to death — sentence approved — & Execution ordered for *tomorrow*. Dr Mudd, Arnold, & one O'Laughlen to be imprisoned for life. Spangler, who probably helped Booth to get out of Ford's theatre, & possibly knew of his design, to be imprisoned six months. The guilt of Payne & Herold is manifest. But I fear the evidence on which the other five are convicted will not bear scrutiny, & that their punishment will enable copperheads to get up a howl against Government. No Justice of the Peace in the most benighted rural district has Judicial capacity much below that of the average Military Court. "Crowner's 'quest law" is sounder than that of most Major Generals. I have read the testimony as it has been published from day to day — not very critically to be sure — but I remember nothing that establishes more than a strong suspicion that Mrs Surratt was privy to the plot — or that Dr Mudd had any connexion with it or with any of the conspirators, except that when Booth called on him with a broken leg, he did his professional duty, set the leg, & asked no questions. — I do not like the look of this. It will do us harm. Better to have erred on the other side, & spared the lives even of Herold & Payne — & that is saying much. Reaction against this will save Jeff: Davis' worthless neck. Major Nichols, who was here this ev'g, heartily endorses my estimate of Military Courts — "only more so". The most unusual promptness with which Execution follows judgment in this case, will shock public feeling. Perhaps unreasonably — but it will hurt & weaken the Administration. The philanthropes of the *Tribune* will give us interesting matter to read tomorrow. So will the Rebel sympathizers of the *World*.

July 7. Friday. Piping hot. Have just been perspiring copiously for two hours in Rev: Bellows' study, with him, Agnew, & Blatchford. We settled, among other things, the draft of a San: Com: valedictory to Branches & Aid Societies, & directed a telegram to San Francisco in substance "You need not trouble us with any more money unless you particularly wish it". A remarkable change of base!

Extr-r-ry Times this aft^n^ — (our first Extra for two months I think) — announced that Payne & Co, Mrs Surratt included, had been duly & decorously hanged. — That word *Extra* has been a word of power all thro' these four years. How many scores or hundreds of times has the suspicion of it's distant sound started me up from this very desk, at midnight or later, & sent me down stairs to unlock the front door & stand outside, in hope of way-laying a circumambient newsboy. How often have I jumped up spasmodically, saying to Ellie, "There's an Extra!" & rushed off to secure it. And what a bad article of news I often got! "Here it is Sir. Extry Herald Sir. Last Edition

Sir. Great Battle at — Sir. Total defeat of Gen. —, sir, [e.g. McClellan] & great loss of life" —

People seem better satisfied with the findings of the Military Commission than I thought they would be. The feeling seems general that the four who were capitally convicted & whose sentence is now executed, got no more than they deserved. There are a few to whom hanging a woman (Mrs Mary E. Surratt) is rather distasteful, but it troubles them little. Killing women is certainly an unpleasant office, but if a man & a woman be both guilty of a murder, the woman deserves the severer punishment. The depravity that produced the crime must be presumed greater in her case, because it had to overcome & outweigh the instincts of her womanly nature. So poor old Johannes Sprenger's Malleus Maleficarum lays down the rule that priests & women, when they once go wrong, go altogether to the Devil, become necromancers, & are the most frequent criminals of that class — because "the corruption of the best makes the worst". So English Law used to punish the woman convicted of Petty Treason more cruelly than the man.

July 8. Sat: — The fervent heat in which we have frizzled all day has been mercifully mitigated by an elastic atmosphere & a fresh breeze. Sky has been clear blue with great fleecy masses of cloud sailing under it & swiftly changing their forms. Active in Wall St. making ready for a journey to Washington next Monday. May it be our last Washington session! I look forward to two days of misery in hot & dusty R.R. cars, with a period between them of calcination by day & of stewing, with an adagio accompaniment of musquitoes, by night. Dr Marsh at 823. Stroll after dinner, & inspected newspapers at Soc^y^ Library. The *Daily News* (Rebel organ in N.Y.) screeches itself into danger of sore throat over the hanging of Payne, & the rest, by sentence of a Military Court, & wants "the People" to organize & subscribe & agitate till all members of the Court & the Judge Advocate & the Provost Marshal shall have been duly indicted for murder. The nasty *Express* whines the same tune — pianissimo, & sotto voce. The News has always done what it could to damage the National cause manfully & openly, but the Express has been for the last five years the basest meanest dirtiest periodical within my knowledge. Had they been the hundredth part as tender & scrupulous about violations of Law, when their friends of the Woman-flogging oligarchy were threatening to "secede", there would have been no Secession & no War. But they, & the "Democracy" in general, tempted our poor Southern brethren into Rebellion & ruin, by the assurance that at least half the North sympathized with their seditious purposes & would tolerate no attempt to "coerce" them. Twenty Abolitionists in Boston & a dozen in N.Y. so endangered Southern Society, they said, & exposed every Southern matron & maiden to such serious & imminent peril, that the South was quite right to secede. The "Democracy" was strong enough to prevent Abolitionists & Railsplitters from interfering with the South. It was this wretched traitorous talk of Northern newspapers that determined the course of leading Southerners by the score. S. Carolina's bombardment of *Sumter* converted most members of the Democratic Party into Citizens of the U.S. — but a few invincible misbelievers still survive, including the editorial Staff of the Express & News.

July 13. Our San: Com: session has been far shorter than I expected. Our new Gen: Sec: is, unlike either of his predecessors, a man of business. He brings forward every subject in a clear compact form, so that we can dispose of it in the minimum of time, & is a man of greater administrative ability & decision than he has seemed to me. I took him for a formal soft-spoken red-tapy Miss Nancy.

Blatchford had provided us quarters far better than have ever been secured us at Washington. "M[rs] Dull's" boarding house N° 248 F. St. is close to N° 244 — & entirely unoccupied during this summer vacation. Each of us had a most eligible bed-room (barring a few musquitoes, & a bull-rooster in the back yard [possessed of a magnificent barytone organ] who began roaring soon after midnight) & our Table was luxurious. "Goodwife Dull" was away, but represented by a couple of pleasant mannered daughters.

Only Bellows, Agnew, Binney, Stillé, & I, at this meeting. Newberry's default unaccountable. We needed his counsels, but being without them, went on according to our best judgment, & took order for winding up of our affairs, & publication of a final Report. There was no substantial disagreement in our long discussion of these two questions & especially of the former. Dr B. rather favored a slow & gradual closing up. Agnew & I preferred a more expeditious & less costly process. Binney & Stillé on the whole inclined the same way. Knapp & Dr Parrish, who were with us, would of course prefer a longer lease of power to expend a few thousands every month. — We shall probably devolve the duty of preparing our final Report — the History of the San: Com: — on Stillé — a man of leisure & culture. Drive yesterday af^tn thro' beautiful woods to the Scene of the last of our battles with Rebellion in the immediate neighbourhood of Washington, *just a year ago.* — Forts *Slocum*: *Massachusetts*: *Reno.* Burial ground — in which lie 48 National soldiers, killed in repelling that raid. Had Ewell the Rebel known how weak we were on that line, he could *probably* have marched into Washington, & could (*possibly*) have secured a triumph for Rebeldom.

July 14th. Stayed at home to night, "fixing" material for Vol. XIV of my San: Com: series — the only perfect record of our work in existence. Many of our earlier papers are out of print, & there are suppressed & privately printed papers, of which I *guess* mine are the only copies extant.

July 15th. Wall St: & 823 as usual. Putting up a lot of San: Com: documents for a certain Dr Von Haurowitz of the Russian Army who came to see me yesterday. He is sent here by his government to investigate our Hospitals &c. He seems to think the San: Com: a very big thing, — bigger than it really is, in fact — tho' Seward does write Bellows that it's "the noblest Charity of the Age".

No political news. Prof. McCulloh in durance at Washington. If he is tried for arson, convicted, & hanged, does Etiquette require me as an acquaintance & a Trustee of Col: Coll: to attend the execution? — The South is quiet & passive. But there are abundant signs that the old Plantation spirit ("Plantation Bitters"?) of truculence & lawlessness is not dead but sleeping, or rather shamming dead. It takes more than one licking to cure a bully. — The World & the News & their rapidly diminishing train of followers continue wailing over a Violated Constitution — There has been only outrage after outrage for the last four years, & the series continues. What fools they are! Of course subordination of Government to the Constitution & to Law is good — very good — among the very best things. But it's not the only good thing. To save the Country is also good. To prevent Jeff: Davis from chasing Lincoln out of Washington in /61 was an object of some public importance. Emergencies are certainly conceivable that justify a little unconstitutionality. Perhaps our recent experiences are of that class. The only people I know, that maintain their Constitution absolutely inviolate, no matter what happens, are the Chinamen. Poland did so too, with her *Liberum Veto* & her *Right of Confederation* — "Constitutional" rights too sacred for interference. They made her a nuisance to her neighbours, & too weak to prevent them from *abating* her & using her to manure their own estates. Respect for written law & constitutions may be excessive & no less deadly than hypertrophy of the heart. A Nation (or a church) that has finally crystallized into permanent definite form & become incapable of developing new organs or agencies to meet new conditions is *dead*, & will begin to decompose whenever Time brings the new conditions. A° Dmi 1861 brought us a batch of new conditions, & Abraham Lincoln met them wisely & well. He saved the country. If learned Counsel prove by word-splitting that he saved it unconstitutionally, I shall honor his memory still more reverently than I do now. A.D. 1865 the situation is wholly changed once more. The whole South is in a state of Subjugation — indignation — emancipation — ruination — & starvation. — It's a chaos of hostile elements mitigated & quieted by Bayonets — a collocation of acids & bases hardly restrained from fizzing into furious disastrous reaction at any moment. Our Constitution-framers never dreamed of this state of affairs & made no provision for it. One would think it most desirable to get the South into good order again without delay. But our Chinese conservatives protest against any step that way, unless chapter & verse of the Constitution can be cited for it. They are political Pharisees, who would let Government perish (Gov[t] being not in the hands of "our party") rather than see it saved "on the Sabbath Day".

It must be admitted, though, that the present & the late Administrations are responsible for violations of Law that can be justified by no plea of public necessity. The last of these misdemeanors is the closing of *Ford's Theatre* by order of the Secretary of War. Of course the performance of plays suited to the taste of a Washington audience, in the very building in which Abraham Lincoln — our Martyr-President — was so recently murdered, would have been unseemly & shocking. But what right has the Sec: of War to tell the owner of a place of public amusement that his Capital must be unemployed because there are sentimental objections to it's lawful employment?

Stanton has done the Country great service, & will take high place in History. But he is a born Tyrant. He likes to use official Power to crush & destroy Rebels, & Sympathizers with Rebellion, & anybody else who may happen to stand inconveniently in his way. — And I think he likes this use of his power best when it has the "game flavor" *of illegality*. Some of his acts (e.g. at West Point) have been most abominable. He is wholly "incorruptible" in the ordinary sense, but most corruptible by prejudice & passion. — If this able, unscrupulous, arbitrary man leave his office at last, & surrender the great & ill defined power he has been necessarily allowed to assume, without permanent damage to public liberty, it will prove that the People has little to fear from usurpation.

July 19. Reports from the South are of diverse quality. We have stories of sullenness, & reluctant submission to force, with mutterings about trying it again hereafter — of bitter hatred of all Northmen, especially among Secesh women — of infamous cruelties & outrages upon Freedmen — &c &c. On the other hand, Southern Orators & Editors confess the South thoroughly beaten, preach the duty & the advantage of loyalty to the re-established Government, & prophesy a comfortable increase of profit from Free Labor. On the whole the symptoms seem to me far more favorable than we had any right to hope. Universal acquiescence in failure — enthusiasm for the Star-spangled Banner — approval of Emancipation — could not be expected.

July 21. M[rs] John Sherwood has found a young M[r] Eugene Schuyler who will become historiographer of the Great Metropolitan Fair for a consideration. He came to see me this morn'g, & we arranged & agreed on certain questions touching the Report. But he was not prepared to state what would be his charge for his services as Editor, so final action was postponed. Agnew & Bellows are out of town, so I am the San: Com: at present, under a resolution passed at it's last Wash[n] session. I "meet" by myself every afternoon, & keep the minutes of my meeting with great formality.

Death is lively of late among people I knew. Bishop Potter of Penn[a] died the other day quite suddenly at San Francisco, whither he went to recruit his health — with his wife N[o] 3, a sister of Alf: Seton's.

Rebel Generals, Congressmen, officials, & leaders of every class, are flooding Wash[n] with prayers for leave to take the Oath, & be thereby whitewashed & restored to citizenship. This morn'g's Times notes the fact as significant of a great deal, & so it is. The Cause these penitent Traitors worked & fought for is simply destroyed by force, without any treaty or compromise or concession wherewith to justify their submission, or soften it's pang — doubly humiliating when they remember their savage swagger & bluster of by-gone days. The Nation rides rough-shod over State Rights & Abolishes Slavery!!! Cavaliers of 1650 — Puritans of ten years later, — Jacobites anytime after 1688 — Tories after our Revolution — Legitimists after the French Revolution — Red Republicans of our own day — have chosen death or civil disabilities or exile before allegiance to the new order against which they had struggled in vain. Our Rebels are elbowing each other as they crowd up to the office where the Oath is administered. A few special caitiffs, such as Magruder Breckinridge & Kirby Smith, have run away. One man — "the venerable E. Ruffin" has blown out his addled old brains. But these cases are exceptional. Subjugated Rebeldom is generally eager to conform itself to it's state of Subjugation. It's eagerness proves (or rather confirms the historical fact) that this Rebellion was founded on no substantial wrong or grievance, but was merely a most maleficent outbreak of provincialism — that it was inspired by no deeper feeling than wrath because N.Y. is a bigger city than

Charleston, & because Northerners turned up their noses at Slaveholders.

Poor Bidwell does'nt see things in that light however. He reminds me of Lord Dufferin's dismal valet Wilson in those delightful "Letters from High Latitudes", & is rather more doleful now than he was in Chancellorsville time, or the days when McClellan changed his base. "The rebels are entirely unsubdued" says Dismal Bidwell. — "We have given up everything to them. This Executive Clemency is going to be fatal. Just read Perry's speech in South Carolina the other day. We shall have the whole thing to do over again in a year or two. But I think on the whole, that we sha'nt make another effort to put them down — We ca'nt get the money. As it is the War Debt will never be paid. It will be repudiated. We shall have to let them go, & let the country be divided. Just think of their not celebrating the last 4th of July down South!" I asked him whether he supposed Geo: II's birthday was celebrated with much enthusiasm in the Highlands the year after Culloden. In reply he groaned, & retired, observing with a kind of doleful solemn gloomy exultation that the Southern States would certainly proceed without delay to reduce their colored people to Slavery again, that he "had no confidence" in A. Johnson — or anybody — & that the Rebellion was rather more rampant now than it was three years ago. "Was ne'er prophetic sound so full of Woe!" It's a curious style of talk for so excellent a man, but it's his settled habit. What makes it most aggravating, is it's expression of a kind of sombre joy in the prospect of affliction — like that of an undertaker prophesying an epidemic — or (more accurately) like one of the cockiest of Foxe's martyrs confidentially informing a friend that it's to be a *slow* fire, & that he's rather proud of the distinction.

But I am well aware of the rocks that lie ahead — or of some of them. The South when reconstructed will probably league itself with all the Scoundrelism & "Democracy" of the North, and clamor for Repudiation. There is danger of war with France, in honor of the "Monroe Doctrine" for wh: I care less than two pence. What is it to me whether Mexico is in chronic Revolution, or governed by an Austrian Prince sitting uneasily on French bayonets? Heaven grant the Senate & House may strictly scrutinize the qualifications of those who will ask for seats next winter as representatives of the "wayward" States! There is ground for hope that the arrogant caste which ruled the South so long is broken up & destroyed, and that this Revolution will upheave a new stratum. But if Reconstruction is to restore a gang of Wigfalls & Brookses & Masons & Wises to our National Councilboard, there to conspire with caitiffs like Ben Wood & Win: Chanler, GOD have mercy on our reconstructed Nation!

July 24. I'm as blue as Bidwell to day. He's a sensible man, & his views on all political questions are entitled to great respect. I incline to endorse them. Everything is going to the demnition bow-wows, & I'm heading the march. I shall be totally impecunious before I've paid my taxes & my summer Hotel bills. Morgan Dix notified me this morn'g that as a Trustee of the decayed & insolvent old Theological Seminary I was expected to subscribe $50. to carry it thro' the current year. — So I called & handed over a check. Congratulated the Rector on the brilliant success of his efforts as a Provisional member of the Fire Department on the roof of St Paul's during the Barnum Conflagration. N.B. is not that the first case on record of a Whale burned to death, unless possibly by some geological sub-marine-volcanic performance?

Weather dull & muggy — oppressing & depressing. My liver must be out of order. Eheu! Suppose I commit something, & get myself sent to the Dry Tortugas or Sing-Sing? "He that is low need fear no fall", so one source of worry would be dried up. And I should have no more bother with $—, $—, $—, (generally with a negative sign prefixed) or with the price of gold (which is 143!) or the extreme expensiveness of Beef.

Walked hard last night for two hours, but am none the brighter for it. — Here enters Temple's very sociable & well-bred Tortoise shell kitten — much given to purring, & the best little Puss I'm acquainted with except my little two-footed Puss now at Lebanon.

No special Southern news. Of course there are plenty of cases there of the most cantankerous carryings on, by returned Rebel Soldiers & officers. But a Parole & an Amnesty & the Oath cannot be expected to transmute ruffians & bullies into civilized Christians & gentlemen all at once.

July 27. At 823 this P.M. Agnew & I were so moved by the reports of Scurvy in the Texan army of occupation that we nullified the Resolution adopted at our last Wash^{n} session, stopping the purchase of Army supplies, & ordered a large consignment of Onions, to go South by Saturday's steamer. *We are to have 100.000 men on the Rio Grande* — & to night's papers report that L. Nap. is to send heavy reinforcements into Mexico. Another War is clearly on the cards. L. Nap. cannot afford to back out, and I think our Gov^{t} does not intend to tolerate a Franco-Austrian Emperor in Mexico. War on that issue will be popular, strange to say — except perhaps with Capitalists & Importers. I think it will be upon us within three months. It will be madness, but we must stand by Government.

July 28th. Friday. Enviable C.E.S. now listening to the surf on the rocks of Point Judith! If this weather be not grossly unconstitutional, where's the good of a Constitution? Sa-a-ay! Lieber is appointed Chief of a New Bureau at Washington which is to examine analyze & classify all the grocers' bills, state papers, dunning letters, lying manifestoes & other archives found in possession of the Rebel Government at the date of decease. A precious cinder-heap for him to sift. The order appointing him to this Literary Executorship bears date a week ago — & he lets us hear of it thro' the newspapers — which is not treating us very handsomely. Of course he cannot hold this position & his Professorship too.

Mr Gen: Sec: Blatchford at 823 this aft^{n}. (Agnew at Newport attending to old Mrs Kennedy) — We went over a good deal of ground together. Tho' he is so slow of speech, & hums & haws, before getting hold of the word he wants, till one is nearly frantic, Blatchford is a most efficient clear-headed valuable man.

July 29. Sat. In a Niagara of perspiration. O my distracted Country, how hot it is! G.C.A. returns from Richfield, supersaturated with brimstone waters & exhaling sulphuretted hydrogen like a bad egg. [It's indecently & intolerably hot to night.] — With Agnew at our Protective War-claim Agency this P.M. to meet Cha[s] Tracy, Theo: Roosevelt, & Fred: De Peyster, representing the corporators under an Act of the Legislature for establishment of a rural Hotel des Invalides. They want a slice of our (San. Com's) possible surplus. [Pestilent hot & no sign of a sea-breeze!] — Went to 823, & on the strength of conference with Agnew & a letter from Bellows & another from D[r] Harris, diminished that possible surplus by $15.000 to be expended in vegetables for our scorbutic Armies in Texas, & entered an order to that effect on our Minutes. It is clear that the troops in that region are suffering from scurvy more severely than any part of our forces at any period of the War. And it will be six weeks before the Medical Bureau becomes officially aware of the fact.

Agnew is actually going to Europe for two months — to attend an Ophthalmological Council at Heidelberg or somewhere else, & to get rid of the permanent pain in the back of the head that has haunted him for a year. So I am likely to be the Sanitary Commission for the rest of the summer. My nephew D[r] Hasket Derby went off to attend the same Conference on the 19th. — O how hot it is! Southerners, who live where it's still hotter, are to be judged leniently. This temperature makes me feel reckless lawless & desperate.

C.E.S. encountered Maunsell Field yesterday morning, exquisitely got up — even to lemon-colored kids. So he is over his spree. But it has been so bad a spree that Union Club men talked about expelling him for beastly drunkenness on their premises & for p—ing all about their elegant parlors & reading rooms.

Aug: 1. With Agnew at 823. After my cup of coffee, walked up to Central Park, & walked a mile or two in it. Pleasant ev'g. At U.L. Club afterwards, where M[r] Superintend[t] Kennedy tells me that there were killed, during the riots of /63, 1155 persons, exclusive of those who were supposed to have been smuggled to their graves. He thinks there were many deaths beside from injuries received in the course of that performance, because the number of deaths by sunstroke reported during August & the latter half of July /63 was more than double the number of deaths from that cause during all the twenty one summer months of the next preceding seven years. He supposes that many of our Keltic fellow citizens returned to their hod-carrying too soon after their heads had been broken by the locusts of his myrmidons.

Cholera reported in England. Then we shall doubtless have it here. This stinking town is ripe for it's sickle, & if it invade the South, there will be a fearful harvest. All classes at the South, black & white, are in a condition to explode into death on the first spark of pestilence. ¶ The so-called Liberals seem to have gained ground in the late Parliamentary elections. Who cares? ¶ — The Election at Richmond coolly & summarily nullified by military order, because the Union ticket (so called) was defeated. Very good. It's a step toward the only Re-construction that will last — tho' the constitutionality of the proceeding does not protrude so far as to be conspicuous. The N.Y. World notices this fact. ¶ C.E.S. returned from P[t] Judith. ¶ — We daily expect news of the Great Eastern with Atlantic Telegraph Cable N[o] 2. I expect a failure like that of 1858, or a success that will endure but for a season. I shall feel no disappointment *now*. I have ceased to love England, since /58, & wish she were thirty thousand miles off instead of three — the sordid heartless money-grubbing old Babylon! Heaven give her Pharisees all prosperity, but "I do desire we may be better strangers". ¶ — Meeting of scoundrels in Broad St. to devise ways & means for getting Jeff: Davis out of jail. About a dozen present (so Kennedy tells me), Peter Y. Cutler & M[r] Surrogate Gideon J. Tucker among them. May mangy dogs defile the tombs of their ancestors, & may Heaven prolong my life beyond this Surrogate's official term, & spare me the indignity of being admitted to Probate by so uncommonly disreputable an official! Benedict Arnold was a Hampden compared with these caitiffs & reptiles. ¶. S[t] Thomas Church sold, & it's congregation is to emigrate up town, so we shall lose an old land-mark.

Aug: 4th. Little news. Signs of peace & amity & loyalty & reconstruction do *not* multiply. Healthy granulations form slowly in the lacerated tissues of the South. Perhaps because the patient is still in a state of "shock", prostration, & collapse. Everybody being ruined, Society disorganized, the old established relations between Labor & Capital destroyed, & the greater part of the Country in a transition stage between the old regime & the new, planters cannot get laborers. They could probably get plenty of them by the exercise of a little common sense, but that article is rare, South of the Potomac. When affairs have settled down & Southerners see their way to making a little money once more, reaction will set in, & the wounds of war begin to heal rapidly. It is to be remembered that this is the only great Civil war ever undertaken without any substantial wrong or grievance, political, social, religious, or personal, to justify it. The South went to war, just as the individual Southerner has gone into a duel or a gouging match — because it felt insulted & "*riled*" by Northern prosperity, & by Northern toleration of Phillips & Sumner & Garrison who had the audacity to sniff at Slaveholders. This was all that made the Southern masses secessionize — their leaders of course had politic purposes of their own, & used this Southern feeling of soreness & taste for a fight (under favorable conditions) to carry out those purposes. But a certain large portion of Southerners, having gone to War on the strength of this feeling alone — finding themselves whipped in a fair fight, after having done their best — will regard their conqueror as the duellist with a scar from a flesh wound, or with a shattered arm, regards the man he fought on a mere point of etiquette, with no question of substantial wrong on either side. Parties to such a controversy are apt to become special friends. — But there is undoubtedly a deal of sourness & malignity still fermenting in the Carolinas & the Gulf States, in Virginia Kentucky & Tennessee — all thro' the Sunny South, in fact. Contrabands are maltreated & murdered. Northern emigrants are warned to keep away. It may be well that Southerners are thus blinded to their own interests, that they should keep their representatives from admission to Congress, & their states under military Rule a year or two longer.

Aug: 7th. To night's clear splendid sunset, with it's marked contrasts of color & sharp-cut forms of cloud, suggests hope of a N.W. wind & cool weather. To day has been very torrid. At U.L.C. to night were Mr Ruggles (just from Long Branch) Hoppin & G.W. Blunt, who never sins on the side of undue taciturnity. *Wade Hampton* publishes a cheeky letter to his fellow countrymen of S. Carolina. Tells them not to think of emigrating, though he fully admits the universal prevalence of ruin. Advises them to stay at home & do what they can toward rebuilding society, tho' the job does seem nearly hopeless, and above all to elect to office (whenever they get a chance to elect anybody) only Rebels of undoubted genuineness who have given their proofs. Politicians who did'nt fight, Unionists & lukewarm friends of Rebellion, and men who stayed at home & made money out of the War, should in his judgment be excluded from office by the Nation of S. Carolina. All which is refreshingly plain-spoken & cool.

Aug: 9. Trustees of Lincoln Home to night. No quorum, but we got thro' with business informally & subject to ratification by a future meeting. The establishment is certainly overcrowded.

Reports from the South continue to be "mixed", but on the whole not discouraging. Newspapers generally say in substance "We are thoroughly whipped. Only a lunatic would dream of farther struggle against Government. We cannot be expected to be jolly & jubilant over our defeat & suppression, but we must take things as they come & make the best of them. The best thing for us is to acquiesce in our failure, save what we can out of the general wreck, try to re-organize the ruins of Society, submit in good faith & without reservation to the National Rule imposed on us by the chances of war, & get ourselves restored to our normal place in the National System as soon as may be". Some of these newspapers devote themselves to long dreary articles, of the true Virginian type, on questions of Constitutional interpretation. I suppose there must be Virginians who read these ingenious lucubrations and like them — which is bad for Virginia. But there are wiser Editors who dwell rather on the advantages of free Immigration, the importance of encouraging it, the undeveloped resources of every Southern state, the value of skilled mechanics to the community, & the Dignity of Labor!!! The World moves indeed! Of course there are signs of gall & bitterness, breaking out sometimes into overt acts of ruffianism. But the Wonder is they are so few.

Aug. 18. Bishop Elliott of Georgia publishes a letter about the Re-union of the Church, North & South — a fine example of Southern arrogance. "Still in their ashes live their wonted fires". He admits that the Schismatic Dioceses must come back, sooner or later, now that the Rebellion (which he & his R[t] Rev. & Rev. Brethren instigated for the sake of their right to flog women, sell children, & grind the faces of the Poor) is put down. But he is uneasy lest they should seem to come back as penitents & prodigals & without recognition as a separate Ecclesiastical Body. It does not suit him that Southern Bishops should present themselves at the General Convention next Fall & claim their seats in the Upper House. He prefers that the Convention appoint a "Committee with power" to wait on the "Council" of the Secession Church, in November, & humbly beg that the Past may be forgotten & our old relations restored. He is uneasy lest somebody say something to the disadvantage of that gunpowder Prelate, Bishop Major-General Polk — "our beloved Polk" — at whose funeral this same Elliott preached a remarkably infamous Sermon. — I humbly trust the next Convention will maintain a masterly inactivity on the Southern Schism, silently admitting those Bishops who ask to be received again, & passing over the "Southern Council" & all it's works without a word of notice. Perhaps though it will have to take up one question growing out of Secession. The Rebel Bishops have consecrated one Wilmer to the Episcopate of I forget what Diocese. Their act was uncanonical & irregular, unless we admit their separation lawful. It is probably best to compromise the matter, to condone the irregularity, & mark it by an Act of Indemnity. The Convention need fear no permanent Schism now, & may therefore treat Southern Churchmen coolly but kindly. They will come back fast enough. They need Northern money to rebuild the ravaged Southern Zion, &, with all their high-sniffing insolence, they will scramble for a position from which they can beg their share of it. They look down on the mudsills of Philad[a] & N.Y. from an immeasurable height, but if the mudsill have a spare five dollar greenback in his pocket, they will go through any process of humiliation — Re-union included — for the sake of a grab at the unconstitutional paper currency of an Abolition Puritan Horde.

Aug. 21. Curious effect of War in changing the Flora of a district. Throughout Virginia, the Canada Thistle is springing up abundantly in the track of every Northern column & Cavalry raid, or in other words over all the State. It used to be nearly unknown there. But it's seeds were mingled with Northern oats & passed undigested through the bowels of myriad Northern Horses. — The appearance of our Eastern *Milkweed* in abundance along the lines of wagon travel over the great Western Plains is not so easily accounted for. Horses & cattle eat no milkweed seeds, & the only animals that specially affect it, so far as I have noticed, are certain slim longicorn Coleoptera. — *Notable fact* — A young lady on trial before a Military Commission in N. Carolina for *murder*. A colored house servant "*sassed*" the defendant's mamma for undertaking to whip her (the servant) or the servant's child, I forget which. Whereupon the gushing & hightoned young lady shot her handmaiden dead with a revolver she happened to have about her. Testimony of colored persons — ci-devant Slaves — admitted for the prosecution. O North Carolina, has it indeed come to this? Finding of the Court & sentence not yet announced. It seems the clearest case of wilful murder. But after that scandalous preposterous verdict in the *Harris* case at Wash^{n}, I do not see how the homicidal young lady can be hanged with any consistency or decency. The Harris female killed a Treasury-clerk deliberately & with premeditation because of certain ancient grievances, real or fancied. This Southern girl, educated from babyhood in Southern notions, killed a mutinous chattel in a fit of passion brought on by seeing the chattel behave as if she were a Woman with rights of her own to assert — a spectacle probably unprecedented in the experience of the murderess, & from her point of view, unnatural, criminal, & revolting.

By the by, it is worth considering what will come of the fact that Education has been suspended South of the Potomac these four years past. The one-horse Colleges & Academies of Secesh-dom shut up shop when the War broke out. Northern Institutions received no students from that region, of course. Only a very few can have been sent abroad. The boys of the ruling caste therefore who were from ten to sixteen years old in /61 have spent these four important years of their lives (& will probably pass two or three more) without opportunities of culture *in literis humanioribus.* What will they be like when they begin to take part in public life a few years hence? I predict that their lack of Culture will not seriously weaken them, and that they will help to prove our Colleges & other Education-Engines of less value than we suppose.

These Southern boys of to day, with so many years of young life spent in hardship trouble & sorrow, in an atmosphere of feverish excitement, self-sacrifice, & burning patriotism (or what they mistook for it) have been & are going through a training that favors the production of strong men. Very probably we shall begin to hear of them ten years hence.

As to the present generation of Southern gentlemen, they seem, by all accounts, so sodden with bad whiskey as to be powerless for good or Evil on any large scale.

Aug: 22. Trial of that miscreant *Wirz* begun & then suspended for some cause unknown. He is the caitiff the Rebel Government employed to "dispose of" our prisoners in their pen at Andersonville, & he did dispose of many thousand most effectively by starvation & slow torture. Somebody says he thus proved "the Pen mightier than the Sword".

Aug: 24. The London Index — Rebel "organ" — a smart reckless lying paper — writes it's own obituary, drops a tear on the dead Confederacy, & declares itself Defunct. Why have not the N.Y. World — News — Freeman's Journal & Express grace to follow it's good example? — Joe Johnston writes a short plain letter to somebody who wanted his opinion on Things in general to the effect that the South is beaten & must make the best of it, and that it is every Southern man's duty to recognize the fact & to do what he can toward restoring general prosperity, & putting himself rectus in Curiâ with the Gov^{t} of the U.S. — Like indications of the temper of Southern leaders appear every day. I distrust them, & fear that Southerners will talk in another tone as soon as their sham humility has restored them to their old places of power. They will then have a formidable force of Northern Scoundrelism to help them in mischief — Repudiation of the War-Debt, re-establishment of Slavery under new forms, or something else. But I may give them too much credit for subtlety & policy. Their hearts are false but their brains may be shallower than I suppose them to be. Their talk about submission to facts & to the fortunes of War may be sincere. Their course for the last four years has been guided by passion, not by sagacity. They neglected chance after chance of palsying the North & winning their game by diplomacy & manœuvring that any Wall St. operator could have taught them.

Aug: 30. Wednesday. Warmish. Letter from Ellie. All well at W. Point. Chas Stillé — Gibbs — Newberry — severally dissatisfied with the action of the Saratoga Conference. Stillé evidently wants to be Historiographer of the Commission, & he should be. Bellows would write a livelier History, but he lacks discretion. Parrish covets the office, but he must be content with a single department, that of the Supply system. Knapp is the only man who can do justice to the subject of Special Relief. My Report on Finance will be a very simple affair. I fear we shall make our first Report too voluminous to be readable. — Stillé & Binney hold Parrish very cheap, I regret to say.

U.L. Club to night. Geo: W. Blunt, Geo: Gibbs &c. — Report that *Olmsted* is about leaving Mariposa & the Rocky Mountains, to become Executive officer of some "Freedman's Bureau." Mariposa stock was at 50 two years ago. It is now at 10 or thereabouts. I guess Olmsted mistook his vocation when he undertook gold-digging.

Aug. 31. Blatchford at 823 this P.M. — Suggested to him the many advantages of having our San: Com: letters — reports — &c &c *bound*, & he took kindly to the suggestion. It's the only way to secure their preservation.

It is idle & false to say that the social system of the South did not oppress the Poor. It ground their faces into stupid brutality — except so far as the lawless lusts of the ruling class brought into the world mulattoes & quadroons & Octoroons & at last fair-haired blue eyed girls & boys, whose approximation to the physical type of the tyrannous Master-race did not save them from it's tyranny. Would not Bishop Elliott & Bp Wilmer think themselves "oppressed", at least a little, if an Act of the next

Congress forbade any one to teach their children to read, denied them the right to give evidence of any injury done them by anybody in the service of the U.S., & empowered every U.S. Provost Marshal to separate them from their wives & children? Would not Bp Elliott feel it rather *oppressive* if any officer of Gov[t] had authority to take his young daughter from his side, & consign her to the custody of a stranger a thousand miles away, without the power of testifying to any wrong she might suffer at his hands — ? But this is what Southern Dives has been doing to poor Stupid Southern Lazarus for years & years.

Half a century ago this wickedness was no part of Southern Xtianity. Slavery — Slaveholding — was then held to be a misfortunate & a Wrong that would slowly but certainly be remedied. Then came Whitney's fatal gift of the Cotton-Gin, & increased profits of Slave labor, & then the South discovered that Slavery was a Divine Institution, & all our Southern Bishops & Presbyters ripened into fervent advocacy of Rebellion & schism for the sake of Cotton & of their Constitutional Right to oppress grind & torture their Poor. They called the doubt or denial of this Right "Infidelity" & denounced everyone who was shaky about the Ethics of Slaveholding as if he were an Atheist. They made their system of Oppression the cornerstone of their system of Religion & of Polity.

They tried to found their practice on the curse inflicted on Cuffee's hypothetical Ancestors. But disease & death are curses inflicted on all mankind for Sin. — If we are bound to enforce the former, we are equally bound to repudiate medicine & medical treatment in our own case. — If the words "Cursed be Canaan, a servant of Servants shall he be unto his brethren" forbid our doing anything to improve the condition of Cuffee, then the words "Cursed is the ground for thy sake . . . . . . thorns also & thistles shall it bring forth to thee" prohibit scientific agriculture, & make any legislation for the extirpation of the Canada Thistle a flying in the face of Providence. For the same reason we must deny chloroform to the woman in childbed, lest she fail of her appointed suffering.

Sept: 4th. My main comfort at W.P. was that noble up-river view from the North Piazza. Looked at Ev'g Parades with Ellie. Called on Grandma Cullum (Gen[l] C.) the Superintend[t],

& spent last ev'g with Prof: Bartlett. Bartlett's highly distinguished son-in-law, Gen: Schofield [a most distinguished Lieutenant of Sherman's] seems a brick. Gave Bartlett some Magnesium wire. He had never seen it before. He thinks it may be made most useful in our Signal Service, naval & military. At Hotel, I like "Commander J.H. Strong" U.S.N. a nice intelligent man of large pattern, who has done his devoir in Mobile & Charleston Harbors. *Inter alia*, he helped smash the Rebel Ram "Tennessee" — & also Capt: Robert, who wears spectacles & looks a little like Morgan Dix, & has (unlike most Army men) Ideas outside the Army Register.

Sept: 6th. The Geneva International Conference invite us & their allied organizations throughout Europe to undertake the office of permanent public Almoners in case of calamities occurring in time of Peace, such as Epidemics, inundations, conflagrations. It would be a fine position to hold, & I believe the People would cheerfully concede it to us. But the San: Com: was called into being by a special & terrible emergency, which has at last come to an end. The Com: has done it's work fairly & honestly & with some degree of success during these four years of struggle & anxiety. To wind up it's affairs, pay it's debts, if any, and cease to exist (except nominally, as a sort of Club, meeting to dine, perhaps, once a year) now that the War is over, is it's natural & legitimate course. It can die now with decency & with a record *totus teres atque rotundus*, having finished the job it undertook to do, & having succeeded therein beyond all it's hopes. It will have a certain reputation — a certain place among the memories of the Great Anti-Slavery War — a place not very conspicuous, but respectable. It's success has been mainly due to good luck in the choice of those on whom it's work has fallen — viz: Bellows, Van Buren, Agnew, Gibbs, Newberry, & a little later, Binney & Stillé. I suppose I must include myself in their company, tho' my services to the commission have been mainly the receiving & paying out of some five millions of dollars without stealing from the Treasury. But we have all felt that we could fully trust each other. No one of us has had any private end to promote by the Commission's means & machinery. I am the San: Com: this summer, by special resolution of our last Wash^{n} meeting,

& sit every aft[n] at 823 B'way, passing bills, & appropriating little sums of $20.000. or so to the Wash[n] office, but I do not believe my unlimited control of our assets disturbs any of my colleagues. Agnew has used like authority on many expeditions to the front. Confidence so well-founded is uncommon among the administrators of a great monied trust. Should we keep up an active organization ten years longer, we should probably be obliged in the course of nature to fill vacancies & bring in new men. I fear we could not preserve the purity of our original stock, & that we could not keep the Com: up to the honorable standard of 1861 . . 5. — The only exception (& that but partial) to the rule of absolute trust & confidence in each other that has prevailed among the eight working men of the Commission has been the venerable Bellows himself — our *Murat*, brilliant, dashing, efficient, full of resource, but needing to be watched lest he get us into some scrape by hasty action & lack of judgment. He has compromised us gravely, more than once, by his thoughtlessness. "There is always a Cockroach in his rice-pudding" Agnew says, but Agnew underrates him. With all his indiscretions he has been the life of the Commission.

Sept: 7th. Handsome Phil: Lydig, who served with credit as one of Burnside's aids, married to Miss Pauline Heckscher, a pretty brunette. Clarence Cram's marriage also announced, to some young woman nobody ever heard of, from Elmira or thereabouts.

We look forward to an Epidemic of Cholera next summer at latest. It will make havoc in our scandalous Tenement Houses, & then — "by induction" — in the "brown stone fronts" of Fifth Avenue & it's tributaries. It may depopulate Secessia & simplify the process of Reconstruction.

State Convention of the wicked old pseudo-democratic party in session at Albany. I fear it will carry the state in Nov[r]. That ancient Institution is a great public misfortune.

Sept: 8. Raining hard, & I take up this journal for want of anything better, having read myself stolid, tho' it's only 7½ P.M.

The Democracy (so called) by the Resolutions of its Albany Wittenagemote impliedly excommunicates & casts out the Woods Barlows, Seymours & other Copperhead Caitiffs of the

"Peace" faction — or professes so to do. That these politic astute wire-pullers & professional observers of the public pulse think it judicious to do so, is an encouraging symptom. Their ticket points the same way. E.g. they nominate Lucius Robinson for Comptroller. It would not be easy now to draw a line between "Democrats" & Republicans, Conservatives & Radicals, unless in regard to Negro-Suffrage — & that's a question to be left to the Southern States themselves, & not a National issue. Were it National, I think the Radicals, so called, would be beat on it.

Sept. 11. Nothing new in town. Hon: Henry A. Wise publishes a letter stating that he had become an abolitionist long before the War was over. Solidified carbonic acid is not cooler than this. We shall have Lee claiming the credit of taking Richmond in April, & J. Davis producing certificates of his unqualified loyalty during the last four years, I suppose. Bully Wise is in many of his qualities a typical Southerner. Being thoroughly flogged, he avers that a flogging was the object for which he had been biting & gouging, & that his Doctor had told him that his health would be permanently improved by a few bruises & gashes. — Woe to us when these impudent Copper Captains return to their old place in Congress & begin caballing with their old pals of the "Democracy"!

Sept. 13. I devoutly hope the so-called Democrats will regain no power at the Fall Elections. But the law of political oscillation & reaction is in their favor everywhere, & the Squabble between Weed & Greeley will help them in N.Y. — We have yet to see whether their record for the last four years will be remembered against them. It probably will be. The Federalists died because they were factious in opposition to Government during the War of 1812. England never forgave the Whigs for the part they played during her Anti Napoleonic struggles. Neither party displayed a tenth part of the malignity that characterized our Democracy from 1862 to the end, & neither dared so frankly to avow it's sympathy with the Public Enemy & its wish to hinder & embarrass Government. May the People have wisdom enough to consign the men who backed J. Buchanan & G.B. McClellan to the outer darkness of a life gladdened by no office — a future without salaries — jobs — or stealings. The traitors who ruled us in the dark days of 1860 & who framed the Chicago Platform in /64, ought to be civilly dead, & excluded from return to place & power, *in sæcula sæculorum*, Amen.

Sept. 18. Prof: Mahan tells me that little Dabney H. Maury is to open a classical & mathematical School at Fredericsburgh. If all the dismounted Southern Brigadiers follow this sensible precedent, & take to peaceful & useful pursuits it will be well for the Country. — Old John Austin Stevens (always most gracious to me of late) tells me that the prospects of Southern trade are brilliant — that far more specie has been hoarded at the South than we suppose, & that S. merchants are ordering largely, & (wonderful to relate) paying off their old debts. As Pres^{dt} of the Bank of Commerce, Stevens ought to know, & what he says is colored by no S. partialities.

Sept: 20. With Bellows & Stillé last night & again this P.M. — Dr Parrish seems disposed to decline any mere subordinate function in the preparation of our final Report. No great loss.

Sept: 22^{d}. Friday. Weather warming up again. Ellie working like a dragon to get her household in order. What an efficient little *Hausfrau* she is! Lazy in Wall St. — At 823 Bellows Gibbs & Blatchford, & some business despatched. Not a house, unless furnished, can be hired in N.Y. that is suited to be a Depositary for our "Archives" & an office for condensing these into a final Report. So we shall probably *buy* premises in West 22^{d} St. near VIth Av: for about $20.000.

The Republican Convention has put up it's Platform. Nearly identical with that of the "Democrats". I greatly fear that the Democrats will carry the State in Novr. If they do not, it will be thro' the defection of the "Daily News" & it's gang — the unalloyed Traitors of the Party. The Fall Elections will give us an important observation of the orbit in which Northern opinion is moving. Straws shew which way the wind blows, so it may be worth while to note the talk of *Ned Bell.* That foolish garrulous Copperhead confesses that he has been all wrong for the last four years, tho' guided by Conscientious conviction all the time. He now finds fault with Government only because it will keep pardoning rampant Rebels who ought to be hanged.

Sept: 28th. Another shindy among our San: Com: people. Darius Forbes sends a bundle of documents from Washn with an ill-tempered truculent letter. Never mind the details. — Drilled Temple this P.M. in spelling & the multiplication table. He bungles with the former, but grasps ideas of number readily.

How thankful I should be for the half hour after dinner which I spend over a cigar coffee & the Ev'g Post while Mamma is singing & teaching her boys to sing "Shouting the battle-cry of Freedom" & the "Year of Jubilo" — & other patriotic ditties in the next room. I confess these little voices & the memories of these terrible four years last past bring tears into my eyes — tho' the melodies are not of the first class & their words generally commonplace.

We have gone through a fearful Agony & struggle for life & death. Shall we be able to hold what we have gained or shall we mix it all up in a mush of conciliation & offer it as a sacrifice to the Constitutional right of Rebels who gave up making war on the Country & the Constitution only because they found our artillery stronger than theirs?

Talk with Phil: Lydig this morning. He worships Burnside & not without reason. — U.L. Club awhile to night.

Reports of Southern feeling are still contradictory. One set of correspondents reports all the Secesh talk — Cases of cruelty to freedmen — & relics of plantation arrogance — that it can pick up, and reports nothing else. Another set sends it's newspapers only professions of loyalty, civilities to Yankees, & fair bargains between *ci-devant* Master & *ci-devant* Slave. The former writes for the Tribune, the latter for the World, & both for the Herald. Probably each furnishes about the same percentage of truth & of fiction. I incline to think that most Southerners are fast becoming reconciled to the downfall of Slavery, that many of them have long seen the economic disadvantages of the system, but have been afraid to say so. But the old spirit of braggart insolence that claimed the title of a "Master-race"

— "descendants of Cavaliers" &c — is still unbroken. Many of these people doubtless still regard the War as a *Jacquerie* in which Southern Gentlemen ought to have ridden down & dispersed the Northern mob of tradesmen & cobblers & snobs of every species, as Froissart's Knights & Princes squelched the Weavers of Ghent at Rosebecque — & would have done it had not the *Canaille* been too strong for them — And they still hold any future Legislature of Virginia or S. Carolina to be divinely endowed with Papal authority to dispense with a release from the obligation of any oath or vow of allegiance or fidelity to the National Government. The Country should deal most cautiously with these suppressed but unconverted traitors. They may yet do us far worse harm than they did at Bull Run, on the Peninsula & at Fredericsburgh & Chancellorsville. — Talk with old Judge Chambers of L[a]. Very secesh.

Sept: 30. At 823. We are selling off what surplus stores San: Com: has on hand, here & at Washington. — At U.L. Club awhile to night.

Oct. 6th. Stand'g Com: of San: Com: at Bellows' to night. B—, Stillé, Blatchford, & I. We dropped Dr Parrish. — Dr Blake whilom our Newbern Inspector is the subject of ugly charges, & brings no accounts & few vouchers to Wash[n] for an expenditure of several thousand dollars.

Oct. 13th. To night Bellows here. We were Stand'g Committee of San. Com. & this was our weekly Evening session. Bellows is just from Philad[a]. He & Bp Clark of R.I. were guests of C.J. Stillé's. Clark says the House of Bishops is all one way as to the question of receiving back into full communion the Rebel prelates & dioceses of the South. Any Clamp or Chain that connects North & South — Rebeldom & Loyalty — is useful just now. The Anglo-American Church has not been so conspicuous for zeal in the cause of Nationality & Freedom, during the last five years, as to disqualify it for service in reuniting the fractured bones of the Country. As Clark says, it's sometimes convenient that one's clothes be dirty; it enables one to undertake without annoyance or damage jobs that are necessary but very dirty indeed.

Oct. 16. General Convention tabled a Resolution offered by Binney, asking the House of Bishops to appoint a day of thanksgiving for the restoration of National Authority & for the removal of the great cause of National discord. This was done after an angry debate. I am becoming ashamed of the Church, or at least of her leaders & Chief Ministers. Their servility to Southern Slaveholding Potentates will long be remembered against them, & compared with that of English Prelates to the Stuarts, and such comparison will be much to our disadvantage. The N.Y. delegation (including Mr S.B.R.) is said to have voted right on this question.

Oct. 21. "Republican" Ratification Meeting at Cooper Institute last night was lively & hopeful. There is naturally much apathy & a full vote will not be polled, but the prospects of the pseudo-democracy — the party of Buchanan & the *Chicago Platform*, of H. Seymour, Toucey, Vallandigham & the Anti draft Riots of 1863 — are bad in this State & in New Jersey — thank God! I am no party-man, but I vote henceforth with any party that is in opposition to that Party.

Nov. 2. The "Freemans Journal" says the "Democracy" is disorganized & demoralized & in a bad way. That the party of Buchanan & of the Chicago Platform should have the impudence to survive at all is indecent. But it's chief Scoundrels will perhaps do less mischief hereafter under their own disgraced name of Democrat than in some new organization & under some political *alias*. Let them, by all means, keep their old banner flying. It reminds the people of the infamy Northern Democrats tried so honestly to achieve all through the War. They go into next week's elections with a prodigious αλαλαγμος or War-Whoop & a heavy fire of dirt & mendacity, but with little to encourage them.

Nov: 3^{d}. G.C.A. dined here. San: Com: Standing Com: meeting here to night. Bellows, Agnew, & I. Also the prolix & urbane *Harris*, who is a useful man, & of self-sacrificing public spirit, in spite of his weaknesses. The Commission has kept snubbing him most pointedly & cruelly for the last four years — (he is said to have rather forced himself on the original expedition to Wash^{n} early in /61 which resulted in the reluctant appointment of the Com: by Gov^{t}) but Harris has shewn no personal feeling — has punctually attended our Sessions & diligently performed every duty we tossed over to him. He has a morbid fondness for confidential talks with Congressmen & Government officials — an instinct for intrigue — a taste for the mysterious & the surreptitious — but never, so far as I know, for selfish ends. We have always distrusted him & once at least — a year or two ago — invited him to resign. He seems useful now in getting up the Medical & Surgical details of our forthcoming Final Report.

Nov: 4th. San: Com: has secured possession for two years of Townsend's unique "Encyclopædia of the Rebellion" — the forty odd great folio volumes of Newspaper Cuttings now on deposit at U.L. Club. They will be of great use as books of reference in the preparation of our final Record or Report. We lend him $4000.00 for two years, taking a chattel mortgage, which I drew this morning, on the Books, as security, & they are to be transferred to 21 W. 12th St.

Nov: 5. M^{r} & Mrs D. Colden Murray have returned from Europe, and are lying in the lower Bay, quarantined till Wednesday, as being possibly choleriferous. No quarantine precautions against this disease will prevail. What we need is practical Sanitary Reformation of back streets, tenement houses, & pestiferous bone-boiling establishments. Thereby, & by nothing else, can the inevitable epidemic be mitigated. The City Government will not do this, or any other good work, honestly & thoroughly, for it is rotten to the Core. The "Citizens Association" will do what it can. It is free from corruption, I believe. If it have, or can raise, sufficient means, it will doubtless take prophylactic measures, to the great benefit of the Community. Ev'g Post invites San: Com: to undertake that work. But that work is far outside the duties Gov^{t} assigned to San: Com: in 1861. When the Rebellion was squelched & Peace returned to us, San: Com: became *functus officio*. We now exist only in liquidation — for the winding up of our affairs. I sacrificed four years to the public service, because the Country, in deadly grapple with a malignant Rebellion, demanded every sacrifice of private interest from every loyal American.

Nov: 7. Tuesday. Clear winter day, with a March flavor. Voted a clean Repub[n] or Union Ticket, tho' with misgivings as to the Judiciary. Then a few minutes at 21 W. XIIth St. (poor 823 Bdway dismantled & nearly closed. The third floor is to be retained as Headquarters of the Medical Committee.) — The San: Com: is in session — probably for the last time. Bp Clark is on hand — Gibbs — Stillé — besides our N.Y. Members. Binney ca'nt come — his mother being ill & I suppose near her end — for she is an ancient lady. Dr Gould also with us. Staid only long enough to present my Treasurer's Report.

Nov. 8. Wednesday. Cold. Morn'g papers brought good news. Democrats have lost New York by 24000 majority, & marvellous to relate *New Jersey* beside. Marcus L. Ward is elected Governor, & the Unionists have both branches of the Legislature.

Spent the morn'g at San: Com: session W. 12th St. Gould read an interesting Report on certain of his statistical enquiries — among others, as to the ages of enlisted men at date of enlistment. Certain ages — 25, 30, &c — were slightly in excess, wh: he accounted for by the tendency of the uneducated man to prefer a good round number before accuracy. Bp Clark said very simply that he quite understood that tendency — in making up his own accounts he always put down *fives* — they were so much easier to add up. At half past two we went to Brady's at the invitation of that artist — & some ten of us were photographed, including Blatchford & Gould — Then I proceeded to School of Mines where I met M[r] Ruggles by appointment. It is fast getting into shape & order.

Nov: 9th. Thursday. San: Com: sat from 10 to two P.M. & again to night till half past ten, when this Session adjourned. We kept close to business, & settled many points as to expenses, the reduction of our roster, the form of our final Report — it's mode of publication &c — details that will not appear on our minutes. M[r] Sec: Blatchford keeps his official work well in hand. He is not an originator like Olmsted, but he is the most systematic & satisfactory Secretary we have had.

A vigorous campaign is to be opened against the Medical Bureau in Congress. Most of the leading volunteer Surgeons mustered out of service are organizing for a combined Assault.

Many of the best officers of the Bureau say they wish *they* were well out of the service that they might speak what they know. Lyman is a type of the former class, Cuyler of the latter. The Bureau is in lower degradation under Barnes than it was under Finley. — We shall probably do a little to help this movement, either by an open statement & appeal to Congress, or by contributing to the expenses of the movers. No application of our funds can be more proper or more useful.

Learned with consternation this morn'g that my lamentable *larmoyant* client M[me] Berthemy has left Paris for these shores — & is among us again like the Cholera. We have suffered much from the Berthemy by letter for many years, but nothing in person since /58.

R.M. Blatchford has just returned from Wash[n]. He claims to be intimate with Johnson & Government. He tells Bellows that the Admin: is relieved from grave concern by the result of the N.Y. & N.J. Elections. It was feared that those elections would shew reflux of feeling, or apathy, at the North, that would encourage Democrats to league themselves with Congressmen from "re-constructed" Rebel States, & undo all the good the War has done. — But Northern Democrats must be satisfied now that their constituents desire to see no such alliance — & that the "Democratic" party must be in a bad way when *New Jersey* elects a "Republican" Governor & Legislature. I think a large class of "waiters on Providence" will soon be ratting from the Democratic party. That party was capitally convicted of *the Chicago platform* a year ago. *This* election was a *motion for a new trial* — founded on public recantation of the damnable heresies of Chicago. But the people refuses another trial — or (to express the result in another form) grants it & the same verdict is brought in — viz: guilty of Treason — guilty of doing it's best & worst to maintain the technical rights of traitors, & of doing *nothing* toward upholding & defending the Country against Rebellion.

Nov: 10. Wirz of Andersonville memory was hanged at Wash[n] this morn'g. It was very meet right & our bounden duty to hang somebody for that deepest & most damnable crime of the late Confederacy — the politic murder of thousands of it's prisoners by slow torture, and Winder having died a natural death, Wirz was the most prominent agent in that homicide, & a proper subject for the Execution of National Justice. But I suppose his moral guilt was not of special intensity. He seems to have been merely a man without feeling or compassion, who did as he was ordered, without compunction.

Nov: 14. I fear *San: Com:* is about to enter on a period of attack & abuse. We have certain monies still on hand & everybody has his own crude notion as to what we ought to do with it. Everybody knows of some disabled soldier, or of some deceased soldier's representatives direct or collateral, who ought to have at least ten thousand dollars out of our funds. But to work our "Pension Bounty & Backpay" agencies all over the Country until the claims lodged with them are disposed of, will use up a large slice of our present assets. Another slice will be required for the publication of our Medical & Scientific Record. But it's not every philanthropist that can be expected to see the value of this latter work. — Collins, tho' the most admirable trustworthy & unselfish of mankind, is unwittingly doing great mischief, now that he has left our service (under a first-class salute of deserved complimentary resolutions) by talking of our affairs to outsiders, in his characteristic spirit of fault-finding, & telling everybody, with authority, just what money we have on hand, & how this that & the other expenditure is, in his judgment, unwise.

Nov: 17. After dinner to Stand'g Com: of San: Com: at 21 W. 12th St. — henceforth our place of meeting. So that long series of pleasant weekly evening sessions, at Van Buren's, Agnew's, Bellows', Gibbs', & on these premises, that began in /61, & were devoted to business from 8 to 10, & to a simple supper from 10 to 12 (at which the lady or ladies of the house commonly assisted) is over & done with. They were always comfortable & hopeful, even when our prospects were darkest. I think those frugal Symposia did "the State some service" — by keeping San: Com: in good heart & up to it's work.

Gen: Grant is to dine here tomorrow with his staff, & I feel quite nervous about so august a transaction.

Nov. 18th. Our Symposium did not go into operation till half past six — for the Lt Gen: & his staff were behind time, like Grouchy at Waterloo. Grant appeared at last however, with Mrs G. & with Gen: Comstock, Col: Badeau & Col: Babcock of his staff. I made it a point to have Johny, Temple, & Lewis present, & to bring them severally up to shake hands with the General. They will remember it fifty years hence, if they live so long, & tell their children of it, if they ever have any. Mrs Ellie had organized her dinner table thus

Mrs G.T.S.

Genl Grant		Senator Foster of Conn:
Mexican Gen: or Senor Romero		Mrs Morgan
Mrs Gen: Grant		Henry J. Raymond
Mr S.B. Ruggles		Col: Babcock
Gov: Morgan		Mrs Dix
Gen: Dix		Col: Badeau
Mrs Ruggles		Chas Bristed
Gen: Comstock		Mrs Foster

Egomet Ipsissimus

It was a brilliant distinguished or "nobby" assemblage, & they all seemed to have a pleasant time, as people always do at any party organized by Mistress Ellen. I must say that I think it a great honor & privilege to have received Grant here, and there is no element of snobbishness in my feeling about it. We owe the privilege to Ellie's attractions & tact. Foster took her to call on Mrs Grant, who was much delighted with her, & asked her to lend her aid & countenance to the Reception at 5th Av: Hotel Monday night. E. slipped in an invitation to dinner & it was cordially accepted. Wm B. Astor's was declined — but I am verging on Snobbery. — I had a pleasant session with Mrs Foster & Bristed. After the ladies withdrew, Bristed Comstock Mr S.B.R. Foster &c got together & screwed a certain amount of clear compact talk out of the Lt General. Dr Peters joined us, and Macdonough & Bininger, a Committee from Century Club. The Lt Gen: thinks black regiments trustworthy if they have good officers, but not otherwise. He holds Gen: Lee in high respect.

Mrs Grant is the plainest of country women, but a lady, inasmuch as she shews no trace of affectation or assumption, & frankly admits herself wholly ignorant of the social usages of N.Y.

Nov: 20. After dinner I took Ellie down to Metropolitan Hotel. She had promised Mrs Grant to stand by her during to night's august & solemn "reception" at 5th Av: Hotel, of which ceremonial that simple Western lady stood in great awe. As I could not attend in person, I left her in the General's parlor, after bidding Grant & his staff good bye. They were very polite & kind. Our little dinner of Saturday seems to be considered a most "brilliant" & "distinguished" transaction. I believe the people enjoyed themselves reasonably well, & that is all there is to say about it — except that I am gratified to have had Grant here.

Nov: 24. To N° 21 W. 12th St. *Olmsted* with us, *returned from California day before yesterday* by Nicaragua route. He has given up Mariposa. After our Com: meeting we adjourned to Delmonico's & had a very nice little supper. Olmsted had much to tell us. He looks well & is as bright as ever.

Dec: 4. Congress organized to day, very harmoniously. It's Repub^{n} majority shews no sign of the split Copperheads have been predicting. Southern members are to be kept out in the cold a little longer. And there are already steps toward most important legislation. Bills are introduced to prevent the practical restoration of Slavery by the ci-devant Slave States.

Dec. 5. Part of President's Message in Ev'g papers. It looks very well. But we miss *A.L's* plain practical sense & straightforward simplicity, & his unconventional & sometimes ungrammatical words. His state papers were more true honest & real than any that have been concocted for centuries.

In the Quadrilateral contest for the Mayoralty, *Roberts* has been gaining on Recorder *Jno T. Hoffman* of late. For the last few days, Heckerites & Guntherites have been demoralized, & going over to Hoffman or to Roberts. I voted for Roberts, not very heartily, but his three competitors were Copperheads, more or less malignant, during the War, & can therefore never receive a vote from me for any office, little or big.

At U.L. Club to night it seems that Roberts is beaten by about 1100, & H. elected. There was a good-natured crowd at the Club, chaffing one Hyatt [a "War Democrat"] for voting for J.T. Hoffman.

Dec. 7. The Presdt's Message seems to me a paper of great power. It will produce an impression abroad. This is what our *tailors* can do. Is it much inferior to the average work of hereditary statesmen — of peers who were first classmen at their University? Stanton's Report, McCulloh's, & Gen[l] Grant's, are, each in it's way, of great merit & value. M[r] S.B.R. thinks it "mean" in Stanton to have said nothing about San: Com: — but "I do'nt see it." The Sec: of War was not officially called upon to report as to the work of the Commission. Had it's operations been an hundred fold more important, they would still have been outside his official sphere. As Sec: he could know nothing of any voluntary effort by the People to supplement the work of Gov[t] & provide relief in it's frequent instances of inevitable failure. I do not love Stanton, but he is right in ignoring San: Com: when he is reporting on the work of the War Department.

Since the first Thanksgiving sermon was preached in New England, this People has seen no such Thanksgiving day. What country has ever passed thro' like peril & come out with like gain? Look at the marvellous results achieved & dangers escaped since April /61 — the miraculous uprising of the North after *Sumter*, when the Nation seemed dying of apathy & dry-rot — the beneficent disaster that saved us from a patched up shortlived reconstruction, opened our eyes to the cause of all our troubles & forced us to recognize it & abolish it, & that gave Rebellion the means of living long enough to be thoroughly killed, from it's fangs & forked tongue to the last rattle in it's tail — Sheridan's timely victories that saved us from McClellan & National suicide — the appearance of the Monitor off Fortress Monroe, when it was a question of hours whether the Army of the Peninsula should or should not be forced to surrender by the destruction of the fleet on which it depended for supplies: — These are among our more marvellous escapes.

— Look at the positive results. Peace — Armies quietly disbanded, half a million of veterans resuming their places in Civil life. — Victory & submission absolute & unqualified. (How few Wars end otherwise than in some sort of compromise!) — The amazing development of charity liberality & patriotic work all over the land (— vide Records of San: Com:) — our clearer sense of National life — the universal confession that the old heresy of State Rights has been for ever practically refuted by the logic of bayonets & rifled Parrotts — the Extinction of Slavery — the ruin of the barbaric caste of Slaveholding Chieftains that ruled us so long & so brutally. The list could be much lengthened.

These four years have reduced me to something like pauperism. But I am profoundly thankful for them nevertheless. They have given me — & my wife & my boys — a country worth living in & living for, & to be proud of. Up to April /61 it was a mean sordid money worshipping country, in my judgment at least, and I think I was not far wrong.

The Legislature of S. Carolina, meekly making haste to ratify a Constitutional Amendment abolishing Slavery, in /65, is a phenomenon which her Legislators of 1860 did not think very likely to occur in their day & generation! Indeed any one who should have predicted Dec: 7th 1860 the political *status* of to day, would have been held to be without foresight judgment & common sense, & laughed at as a madman, by North & South alike. Only a year ago, Victory seemed but a shadow in the dim distance. Thorough pacification through all the length & breadth of the land, & a frank admission by all Rebeldom of it's defeat & subjugation, were not among the contingencies talked of as belonging to our day.

Dec. 13. To night at meeting of Trustees of Lincoln Home. Evidence collected by Dr Bellows from all parts of the country shews that the demand for establishments of this class is small & grows daily smaller, & that people everywhere begin to see it's smallness. It would be hard to collect a corporal's guard of disabled *Native* soldiers willing to live on public charity, or without reliances & resources of their own. Had we a grand

Hotel des Invalides now open, it's only inmates would be Kelts & Teutons, with a few natives, who may just as well be cared for in the Alms House on Blackwell's Island, because they would be there if they had never enlisted.

Dec. 18. Gen: Barlow last ev'g discoursed much of the absence of Strategy in our battles. He holds the overthrow of the Rebellion due to the rank & file & to Regimental officers, & above all to our overwhelming superiority of resources, but not to generalship, & thinks that the nature of the Country we fought over made combinations and changes such as Frederick, Napoleon, & Marlborough conceived on the battlefield, under the inspiration of actual conflict, absolute impossibilities. He says that when Pope, Burnside, Hooker, or Grant, found himself obliged to deliver a battle, the Corps commanders were assembled & told to "go in" & do the best they could, & whether they succeeded or failed, to act on their own judgment. They gave like instructions to Generals of Division — & so downwards — & each Colonel took in his own Regiment to fight on it's own front, without concert or system. This is exaggerated, but there is some truth in it. Barlow over states the case a little — in a half affected spirit of self depreciation pardonable in a man who fought his own way from the ranks to the grade of Major General, & was left for dead on two such fields as Antietam & Gettysburgh. No doubt the Rebel practice was primitive or Homeric, no less than ours.

As to our superiority in resources, the contest would have been most unequal without it. For the Rebels had only to stand on their defence. They enjoyed moreover the special stimulus of a fight *pro aris et focis*. We had to over-run a vast wilderness, to reduce the most formidable strongholds, to open rivers protected by obstructions, batteries, torpedoes, & every device known to Science, to protect long lines of communication through a rude & hostile country — to maintain, in short, the Affirmative of the great issue. A drawn game would have been National failure — Rebel triumph. There was yet greater disparity of resources as between England & her colonies in 1776. — So with Spain agst Holland, Napoleon & his allies v. Russia. But the back-bones of the Yankee Rebel, Dutch Burgher, & Russian peasant, were stronger than that of the Secessionist.

Disaster inspired him with no new fervor of desperate resolution: Under it's pressure he passed at once, — within a period of time to be expressed in terms of hours, not even of days — from supreme altitudes of truculent brag to the profoundest abyss of submission & of acknowledged Subjugation. His alacrity of sinking was beyond historical precedent. He is trying now to get into the National Legislature, from which he scornfully withdrew five years ago, & to obtain by policy & by alliance with Northern Scoundrelism what he failed to secure by force & arms. May Congress be wise & firm! No Congress, Wittenagemote, Parliament, or Council of Notables, for the last thousand years, has had a job to do more difficult delicate & weighty than that with wh: our Congress, now sitting at Wash[n] is charged to day. If we could but trust these subjugated Rebels, & believe their professions, the problem before Congress would be simplified. But I for one distrust them. I believe that their representatives, if admitted, would at once league themselves with such disloyal Northern Scum as Wood Brooks & Chanler, & thereupon proceed to repudiate the National Debt, or to make the Confederate War debt a National burthen, to legislate Slavery into life again, or to indemnify the ex-slaveholding Oligarchs of the South for the loss of their slaves, at the National cost.

Dec. 20. *The first snow-storm of the season in full blast* since 7 P.M. to my disgust. It threatens to be heavy. Material for a weeks bad walking is deposited already. — In Congress, Thad: Stevens & Cha[s] Sumner seem inclined toward open War on the Presdt's "reconstruction" policy, as perilously lenient. They may be right. There is room for diverse opinion pro & con. But Sumner was wrong in denouncing the Pres'dt's Report or Communication on Southern affairs as "a whitewashing Message, like Pierce's on Kansas". It was certainly an indecorum, & he was rebuked for it by his own friends.

Dec: 24. Another Christmas close at hand, & a specially good one. *Et in terra Pax* — thank God. We cannot say

"No War nor battle's sound
Was heard *the world around*" — for Juarez

& Maximilian are skirmishing & cutting throats in Mexico. But there is Peace within *our* borders, & the Rebel Armaments that were so truculent last Xmas Eve are disbanded & dispersed & have disappeared like last winter's snow. Slaveholding is gone, too. The Constitutional Amendment has been duly ratified by State Legislatures, and the Oligarchs of S. Carolina reign no longer. They may still irritate Chas Sumner & H. Greeley with their efforts to maintain the tyrannous supremacy of their caste, but the Institution of Slavery is dead.

CHRONOLOGY

NOTE ON THE TEXTS

NOTES

GENERAL INDEX

REGIMENTAL INDEX

Chronology

1820 Born January 26 in New York City to George Washington Strong, a prominent lawyer, and Eliza Catherine Templeton Strong, daughter of a New York merchant. Father's first wife Angelina Lloyd had died aged twenty-nine in 1814, leaving Strong's half sisters Eloise Lloyd Strong, born 1810, and Mary Amelia Strong, born 1813.

1822 Family moves from 50 Franklin Street to 108 Greenwich Street. Brother John Wells is born December 3.

1824 Instructed by his mother, Strong is a precocious young reader. Brother dies December 14.

1826–27 Continues to be taught by mother and half sister Eloise, and by father in Latin. Gives up dreams of being the captain of a Hudson River steamboat and decides to be a soldier. Enters school and quickly becomes head of his class.

1828 Father buys piano for Strong for $280, and Strong learns to play by ear.

1829 Takes first prize in his school at age nine, with second prize going to a fifteen-year-old.

1832 During summer cholera epidemic in New York City the family lives in Wilton, Connecticut. In fall, Strong enters the Grammar School attached to Columbia College, with Professor Charles (Bull) Anthon as rector.

1834 Passes entrance exam for Columbia College. Half sister Eloise marries wealthy Boston attorney Elias Hasket Derby in September.

1835 Takes final examination for Grammar School, earning top score in classics. Makes first diary entry on October 5. Writes in 1865: "It was under the stimulus of a cup or cups of strong coffee — a Sunday evening tea-table indulgence, then recently introduced among the domestic institutions of 108 Greenwich St. I perfectly remember my cogitating intensely over the project & considering what manner of Book I should use. Vague aspirations were floating through my mind I think toward some huge folio volume like a Bank Ledger." Joins student-run Philolexian Society at Columbia College in November and becomes an enthusiastic member and contributor to the society's magazine.

1836 In October, views balloon ascension of French-born aeronaut Louis Anselm Lauriat at Castle Garden in lower Manhattan. "I went inside of the railings — I dont think I ever had an opportunity before of examining a balloon close by — . It has a very *fragile* appearance — rather a slippery concern to trust one's self in at the height of a couple of miles or so — ." Visits phrenologist Orson Squire Fowler at Clinton Hall on December 29. "He has been wrong in several instances — but on the whole he gives a true account of what I believe to be my real character — & that without any previous knowledge of me — & without any information gained by 'pumping.'"

1837 Buys camera lucida at Benjamin Pike's store on Broadway. Sails for Boston with his family on the *Narragansett*. Visits exhibition of paintings at the Boston Athenaeum. "This is the hardest City I ever was in, to find one's way through — Even with a map its next to impossible — for half the streets have no name on them." Half sister Eloise's infant son George dies of dropsy.

1838 Visits New York Society Library in March with his father, who buys him a membership share. Watches departure of the *Great Western* from New York Harbor in May. Serves as president of the Philolexian Society. Graduates Columbia with high honors in October. Two days later begins three-year clerkship at his father's law firm Wells & Strong. Writes, "I'm bent on making myself thorough in the Law — But really & truly, I don't think I've got *one* lawyerlike faculty."

1839 Hears oration by John Quincy Adams at New-York Historical Society in April. Visits Boston and Nahant. On July 27, visits Green-Wood Cemetery in Brooklyn. Spends most of August and September in Whitestone, Long Island. Views plans for the new Trinity Church in September. Elected treasurer of Columbia Alumni Association in October.

1840 Visits Erben's in April to discuss ordering a new organ for the Strong home. Leaves for Nahant with his mother in July on the *Massachusetts*. Visits Hartford and sees Gilbert

Stuart's portrait of George Washington. On December 29, receives first parts of a large organ he has ordered from Erben. Writes, "I met the whole affair — i.e. instalment No 1 — sailing majestically down Broadway — the big cart piled ten feet deep with pipes & mahogany — & cutting altogether a most terrific figure."

1841 Visits Academy of Design on May 26 and writes, "Scarce anything there but portraits — & one or two are rather pretty ones. — Generally they're terrible — there's quite a collection of infants & they all look like *fœtuses* — one would think hydrocephalus epidemic." Travels to Utica and passes examination on July 15 to be admitted to the bar. Goes to Saratoga July 29 to see Reuben Hyde Walworth, Chancellor of the State, and be made a solicitor.

1842 Visits Trinity Church, then under construction, on March 24. "They've altered the design of the tower, and I dont know but they have improved it. The side windows are to be omitted & their places supplied by niches with statues — & a profusion of ornamental carving." Attends demonstrations of mesmerism and "animal magnetism." Appears in court for first time, in Marine Court case. On October 14, views celebration marking the arrival of drinking water from the Croton Reservoir. On December 29, is daguerreotyped ("a great bore"), attends a performance of *The Christmas Bells*, a cantata by Charles E. Horn ("many passages remarkably neat and graceful"), and takes a cab to Water Street to view a large fire that broke out during the performance.

1843 Views Great Comet of 1843, thought by the Millerite sect to signal the end of the world. Elected member of the New-York Historical Society.

1844 Visits Benjamin Pike's on June 29 and buys "some electro-magnetic apparatus of his, that's reported to be sovereign for sickheadache." Passes two examinations to become a counselor-at-law, qualified to practice in the higher courts. Ascends spire of the new Trinity Church on October 23: "Its now rather over 200 ft. I believe — glorious views of the City & parts adjacent."

1845 Visits Grace Church, designed by James Renwick, Jr., on March 3: "It will certainly *look* well when completed — and the pipestems of columns that support the clerestory will tend to impress the congregation with a sense of the uncertainty of human life." Describes the Great New York City Fire of 1845, June 19–20, which starts in a whale oil and candle factory, causes a massive explosion at a warehouse storing saltpeter, and destroys 345 buildings. Becomes a named partner at his law firm.

1846 Attends Shakespeare's *Richard III* at Park Theatre, starring Charles Kean, on January 9. Visits Montauk, Long Island, writing after his return on August 17, "Very glad I've been to Montauk, — just as I'm glad to have had the measles and the whooping cough — it's gone through with, and a recurrence of the thing is'nt likely."

1847 Studies German and French. On May 25, buys a horse named Tornado for $200: "He's a pretty animal, with pleasant paces & a gentlemanly sort of deportment — but he pulls like a newly bitted mastodon, or megalosaurus — & has got to be rode with a curb whether it frets him or not." In September receives a "giantly black Newfoundland cub" from a friend and writes, "He's stretched out over many a rood of carpet by the side of my chair, & snorting & sighing at intervals like a bull buffalo." In October mourns his pet squirrel, who "expired after a tedious illness Friday night — poor little thing — he was so weak & unable to move that he could'nt have enjoyed life much." Reports on October 26 having suffered two years from "this blighting paralyzing disgraceful hideous unspeakable disease of nervous dejection & instability that has been down upon me like ten thousand tons of granite."

1848 Reports in January on experiments with chloroform: "The sensations of a week are crowded into two minutes." Proposes in March to Ellen Ruggles, daughter of Samuel B. Ruggles, a lawyer and real estate developer. The couple is married in Grace Church in May. In September reads Thackeray's *Vanity Fair*: "Not a 'work of *genius*' as some people call it, by any means — but a remarkable book — written on a new principle, & likely to have many imitators in this age — the principle being the exclusion of any sort of *idealism* in character plot or catastrophe."

1849 Wins case for wealthy merchant Moses Taylor, relieving him of a $40,000 judgment. On April 23 Ellen Ruggles Strong delivers a stillborn baby girl and nearly dies of puerperal fever. On May 10, Strong witnesses riot at Astor

Opera House; state militia opens fire on the crowd; an estimated twenty-two to thirty-one people are killed. In June, cholera breaks out in New York City. Strong and his wife move into a house built by Strong's father on Gramercy Park at 74 East 21st Street, next to his father's own newly built residence and that of Strong's aunt; the houses are connected by underground passageways.

1850 Attends séances. Describes enthusiastic mobs that greet the arrival of Jenny Lind in early September.

1851 Attends concert by Jenny Lind on May 14: "She is not pretty — nor handsome — nor exactly fine looking — but there's an air about her of dignity self-possession modesty & goodness that is extremely attractive." Son John Ruggles Strong is born October 20.

1852 On July 29 the steamboat *Henry Clay* catches fire and sinks while racing the *Armenia*, killing wife and daughter of Strong's friend Jacob Whitman Bailey.

1853 Father-in-law Samuel B. Ruggles financially ruined over a project to build warehouses on the Atlantic Docks in Brooklyn. Strong defends Ruggles against Francis Griffin's allegations of fraud and deception. Attends lecture by Thackeray in November. Visits Crystal Palace with Ellie and others in September and October. Mother dies on November 24 after a month's illness. Strong writes, "So our life saddens as it's path winds downward. At each stopping place we look back & wonder to see how bright it was — how much brighter than it can ever be again." Elected trustee of Columbia College in December, joining Clement Clarke Moore, Hamilton Fish, and other prominent New Yorkers.

1854 Advocates appointment of Wolcott Gibbs, a Unitarian, to professorship of science at Columbia. Gibbs is defeated by conservative religious faction on the board. Strong and Ruggles publish "The Duty of Columbia College to the Community," a pamphlet protesting the decision. The paddle steamer *Arctic* collides with another steamer and sinks on September 27, killing several of Strong's friends and acquaintances. Strong orders a Ross microscope, receiving it in early November.

1855 Describes enormous crowd at the funeral of Know-Nothing leader Bill Poole on March 13. Views paintings of Frederic Church at Academy of Design on March 18: "*Church*'s beautiful tropical landscapes, the result of his late visit to Ecuador, are the chief attraction." On March 22 attends performance of Carl Maria von Weber's opera *Der Freischütz* at Niblo's Garden. Father dies on June 27 at age seventy-two. Strong writes on July 10, "I do'nt yet realize it — I find myself every morning expecting to see him in his accustomed place at the desk where he worked honestly wisely & untiringly for fifty years."

1856 Son George Templeton Strong, Jr., known as Temple (later a composer and painter who lived most of his life in Europe), is born May 26. In June Strong doses a mouse with chloroform as an experiment and is saddened when the mouse dies. Experiments with hashish in August and records hallucinations. On October 9 attends a talk by Bronson Alcott, "the father I suppose of Yankeo-Platonism & hyperflutination."

1857 Reports in diary on murder of dentist Harvey Burdell in January, "strangled and riddled with stabs in his own room by some person unknown." Witnesses the death of two Irish laborers killed on July 6 when a house excavation collapses. Sets up a saltwater aquarium in September, borrowing starter fish from his friend George Anthon. Notes that "Wall St. blue with collapse" in October due to financial crisis: "Everything is limp & flaccid like a defunct Actinia."

1858 On April 10 explores the "remote regions of Southern Brooklyn" with George Anthon, "near Gowanus & the place where was of old the Penny Bridge." Describes celebrations of the completion of the Atlantic Cable in August. Witnesses fire that destroys Crystal Palace on October 5. In November, elected trustee of the Bank for Savings on Bleecker Street. Attends performances of the operas *Don Giovanni* and *The Marriage of Figaro*, and Shakespeare's *Merchant of Venice*.

1859 Hears reading of *The Tempest* by Fanny Kemble on January 14. Visits observatory of Lewis Rutherfurd and views a "miserable little loafing comet" in May. On May 7 admires Frederic Church's *The Heart of the Andes* at the Tenth Street Studio Building. Observes construction work at Central Park. Attends performances of *The Magic Flute* in November.

1860 Son Lewis Barton Strong is born May 7. In Dr. James Wynne's *Private Libraries of New York*, Strong is listed as the owner of one of the thirty-one most important collections. His library includes illuminated manuscripts and John Donne's *Poems* with notes by Samuel Taylor Coleridge.

1861 On April 18, sees Sixth Massachusetts march through Manhattan: "Immense crowd — immense cheering. My eyes filled with tears & I was half choked — in sympathy with the contagious excitement." In June, joins United States Sanitary Commission as treasurer and member of the executive committee. On June 4 meets with five formerly enslaved men at Fort Monroe in Virginia. Sees President Lincoln when he passes through New York, then meets Lincoln in October: "He seems to me clear headed & soundhearted — tho' his laugh is the laugh of a Yahoo, with a wrinkling of the nose that suggests affinity with the Tapir & other pachyderms, and his grammar is weak."

1862 Meets President Lincoln again on January 28. "He is a barbarian — Scythian — Yahoo — or Gorilla, in respect of outside polish (e.g. uses 'Humans' as English for *Homines*) but a most sensible straightforward honest old codger." February 3, notes that the Sanitary Commission has received $700,000 at its central office, plus "three or four millions worth of stores of every sort contributed at our depots."

1863 Helps found Union League Club of New York City with Sanitary Commission colleagues Henry Whitney Bellows, Frederick Law Olmsted, and Oliver Wolcott Gibbs. First official meeting held March 20. Members arm themselves to defend the clubhouse at 26 East 17th Street, facing Union Square, when Draft Riots break out on July 13: Strong and Wolcott Gibbs urge Mayor Opdyke and General John Ellis Wool to declare martial law. Strong joins Thomas Egleston in developing a School of Mines for Columbia College.

1864 Strong's "Origin, Struggles and Principles of the U.S. Sanitary Commission" is published in January issue of the *North American Review*. On August 29, pays $1,100 to "a big 'Dutch' boy" named Herman Henderman, age twenty-two, to serve in the Union army in his place. Henderman joins the Seventh New York Volunteer Infantry and survives the war.

1865 Appointed director of the Kenzua Mining Company, in which his father-in-law has invested. Helps organize the establishment of a School of Mines at Columbia. Travels to Washington, D.C., on April 18 with Henry Bellows and Louisa Schuyler to attend funeral of Lincoln.

1866 Appears before United States Supreme Court in February in the Savings Bank case. Writes on February 10, "I have seen the face of the S.C. of the U.S. & yet live — (tho' with a slight headache)." Describes destruction of the Academy of Music by fire on May 22. Contributes chapter "Financial History of the Commission" to Charles J. Stillé's *History of the United States Sanitary Commission.*

1867 On April 2 comments on purchase of Alaska, "It would seem that the Administration is buying Russian America for seven millions! What can the country gain by ownership of that desolate dreary starved region? It produces a few *furs* — steadily diminishing in quantity as the otters & seals &c are yearly persecuted toward extermination — & it produces nothing else I know of." Writes on July 15: "I am *living beyond my income*, pauperizing Johny & his little brothers. That is what's slowly killing me — & killing me by slow torture." Serves as pallbearer for Professor Charles Anthon on July 31.

1868 Hears Fanny Kemble read *Cymbeline* at Union League Club on April 28. Writes, "I am specially fond of that play, for Imogen has always seemed to me the most lovable & the very noblest of all Shakespeare's portraits of noble & lovely women." Joins Hasket Derby on a sixty-day European tour through Switzerland and to Vienna.

1869 On February 13 visits Edwin Booth's new theater on 23rd Street to see *Romeo and Juliet.* Views solar eclipse on August 7. On August 10 visits animals collected for Zoological Garden in Central Park. Founds Church Music Association, which offers public concerts of religious music. Objects to applications of three young women for admission to Columbia Law School, writing on October 9, "No woman shall degrade herself by practising law, in N.Y. especially, if I can save her."

1870 Elected president of Philharmonic Society of New York, serves until 1874. Sees statue of Lincoln in Union Square, writing on September 29, "A grim unearthly weird monstrous 'sooterkin' — suggesting a Caliban run to seed — or Bogey — or Moloch. It's Legs are as two steamboat smokestacks." On December 3, reports "Caisson of the East River Bridge severely damaged by fire yesterday. I dont believe any man now living will cross that bridge."

1871 Reads *The Descent of Man* by Charles Darwin in May, and concludes that the theory of evolution "is without a scintilla of evidence." Visits Museum of Natural History in Central Park on May 31. Visits Prospect Park in Brooklyn on July 18 and writes: "This Park beats Central P. ten to one, in trees. I'ts wealth of forest is most enviable." Reports explosion of the Staten Island ferryboat *Westfield* on July 30, killing more than 126 people.

1872 Views *The Slave Ship* by J.M.W. Turner on September 26, writing, "The heaving sea appears to me to be mere lunacy, & so does the foreground with it's preposterous fish & the iron manacles that are floating about. But the picture, *as a whole*, gave me an impression of prodigious genius — of immense power manifested without effort — such as one receives from a Beethoven symphony." Accepts his last major case on behalf of the Associated Savings Bank. Strong's law partner Elias G. Drake, Jr., announces his resignation on October 22. Two days later, Marshall Bidwell dies of apoplexy at his desk.

1873 Reports financial panic and bankruptcy of Jay Cooke & Company in September. Accepts offer from John Astor to become comptroller of Trinity Corporation. Retires from legal practice.

1874 Reports raids on grog shops by "mobs of pious women" urging temperance. Describes on May 13 the construction of new post office on Broadway: "The naked iron ribs & tendons of the New P.O. Dome begin to be covered by healthy granulations, apparently of *slate*. An anomalous iron structure, hybrid of dome & steeple, is sprouting at the S. end of the building." Reports on scandal of Henry Ward Beecher's alleged adultery with Mrs. Elizabeth Tilton. Relations are strained with teenage son Temple, who is sent upstate for the summer. In December Temple's school informs the family of his unsatisfactory progress and dismisses him.

1875 In April, major quarrel with Temple leads to rift with the family; Temple lives in rented accommodations after he is locked out of house, working as an oboist with the Metropolitan Opera. Strong writes and then erases several diary entries about the matter, and in May begins referring to Temple in diary as "XY." Diagnosed with tumor of the mesenteric gland and enlargement of the liver. On June 25, writes, "One day last week I had a woful day of headache nausea & malaise, which left me as weak as a sea-anemone at low water. Since then no improvement." Dies July 21 at his home. Buried in Trinity Churchyard on July 23.

Note on the Texts

This volume presents selections from George Templeton Strong's diary from November 1860 to December 1865. The entries transcribed and printed here focus on Strong's experience of the Civil War, both as an opinionated observer and as the treasurer of the United States Sanitary Commission.

Strong began keeping what he called his "Private Journal" at age fifteen and wrote in it regularly for the rest of his life. His complete diary, running to more than four million words, is currently in the collection of the New-York Historical Society. A substantial portion of the entire diary was published by Macmillan in 1952 in four volumes edited by Allan Nevins and Milton Halsey Thomas. The present volume overlaps to some degree with the third volume of the Macmillan edition, subtitled *The Civil War 1860–1865*. However, the selection here is larger (about 45 percent of the approximately 300,000 words in the present volume are published here for the first time) and the transcription is guided by different editorial policies.

With a few exceptions, such as corrections to names of people that might be confusing if left unemended, the text printed here reproduces Strong's diary as he wrote it, including spellings, contractions, and forms of punctuation that are now outmoded or that represent Strong's idiosyncrasies. Instead of the more standard possessive "its," for example, Strong generally uses "it's," a form that was not uncommon in the nineteenth century. His frequent abbreviations are preserved without editorial interventions to standardize or regularize their usage. Strong uses parentheses and brackets interchangeably, and this usage has been followed here. (However, dash length, which here takes the form of an em-dash preceded and followed by a space, has been standardized.) These editorial policies emphasize that Strong's diary was a form of private writing not intended for publication and not subject to the stylistic conventions of nineteenth-century American publishing.

As noted above, the selection from Strong's diary has been made with an eye to his responses to the Civil War, though it also contains other sorts of material (family matters, attendance at concerts, etc.). Omissions within a particular day's entry are indicated by a hairline rule.

Notes

In the notes below, the reference numbers denote page and line of this volume (the line count includes headings but not blank lines). No note is made for material that is sufficiently explained in context, nor are there notes for material included in standard desk-reference works such as Webster's Eleventh Collegiate, Biographical, and Geographical Dictionaries or comparable internet resources such as Merriam-Webster's online dictionary. Foreign words and phrases are translated only if not translated in the text or if words are not evident English cognates. Quotations from Shakespeare are keyed to *The Riverside Shakespeare*, edited by G. Blakemore Evans (Boston: Houghton Mifflin, 1974). Quotations from the Bible are keyed to the King James Version. For further biographical information than is contained in the Chronology, see *Strong on Music: The New York Music Scene in the Days of George Templeton Strong*, edited by Vera Brodsky Lawrence, 3 vols. (Chicago: University of Chicago Press, 1988–1999), and *The Diary of George Templeton Strong*, edited by Allan Nevins and Milton Halsey Thomas, 4 vols. (New York: Macmillan, 1952). Grateful acknowledgment is made to Martin Michalek for his assistance in translating the Greek words and phrases used by Strong.

1860

5.3 Ellie] Strong's wife Ellen Ruggles Strong (1825–1891).

5.3 her brother Jem] James Francis Ruggles (1834–1895), a graduate of Columbia College and Harvard Law School who served as secretary to New York Governor Washington Hunt, 1851–52.

5.4 Wide-awake] The Wide-Awake marching clubs, first organized by the Republicans during the 1856 campaign and revived in 1860, staged mass torchlight parades and other events in support of Lincoln's election.

5.6 "Palace Gardens"] Pleasure gardens at the corner of 14th Street and Sixth Avenue, renamed Cremorne Gardens in 1862.

5.9 Bengal lights] Blue flares or fireworks. Bengal, a region in present-day India and Bangladesh, was a source of the saltpeter used to make them.

5.11 N.Y. Hotel] The New-York Hotel at 721 Broadway was across the street from the Republican Campaign Club.

5.20 Mr R.] Strong's father-in-law Samuel B. Ruggles (1800–1881), a lawyer and real estate developer who created Gramercy Park in 1831 and later served as a Whig member of the New York Assembly, 1838–39, and as a state canal commissioner.

5.29 *Home Squadron*] The Home Squadron was organized by the U.S. Navy in the 1830s to protect coastal commerce, aid ships in distress, suppress piracy and the Atlantic slave trade, make coastal surveys, and train ships to carry out relief operations.

5.33 Fort Moultrie] Fort Moultrie was constructed in 1776 on Sullivan's Island to protect Charleston, South Carolina, from British attack.

6.6 Locofocoism] The Locofocos, named after a kind of friction match, were a faction of the Democratic Party formed in 1835. Founded in New York City in opposition to the party's influential Tammany Hall faction, they supported laissez-faire and opposed monopolies. The word came to be applied disparagingly to all Democrats.

6.17 N.Y. Express] Newspaper founded in 1836, originally a Whig publication, owned by the Democratic congressman James Brooks (1810–1873) and his brother Erastus Brooks (1815–1886).

6.23–24 "Black-Republican"] Disparaging term for abolitionist members of the Republican Party.

6.33 Life & Trust Co] The New York Life Insurance and Trust Company, founded in 1830. Strong was nominated to its board of trustees in 1856.

6.37 Trinity School Board] Trinity School was founded in 1709 as a public school to instruct the children of the poor free of charge. After city government funding ceased in 1825 it reincorporated as a private college preparatory school. Strong became a trustee in 1857.

7.4 Fusion] In the 1860 presidential election, supporters of Stephen A. Douglas (Northern Democratic), John C. Breckinridge (Southern Democratic), and John Bell (Constitutional Union) combined to run anti-Lincoln Fusion tickets in New York, New Jersey, and Rhode Island; there was also a Douglas-Breckinridge ticket in Pennsylvania and a Douglas-Bell ticket in Texas.

7.6–7 River . . . Counties] The Hudson River counties include New York, Bronx, Westchester, Rockland, Orange, Putnam, Dutchess, Ulster, Greene, Columbia, Albany, Rensselaer, Saratoga, Washington, Warren, and Essex; the western counties include Allegany, Cattaraugus, Chautauqua, Erie, Genesee, Livingston, Monroe, Niagara, Ontario, Orleans, Schuyler, Seneca, Steuben, Wayne, Wyoming, and Yates.

8.2 Palmetto Flag] A version of the Moultrie Flag that was flown over Fort Moultrie during the American Revolution, featuring a white crescent on a dark blue background. The palmetto tree was added in 1861.

8.8 Miss Puss] Kate Fearing Strong (1851–1907), daughter of Charles Edward Strong (1824–1897) and Eleanor Fearing Strong (1831–1903).

8.8 Charley] Strong's cousin Charles Edward Strong, an attorney who was a partner in Strong, Bidwell, and Strong, the law firm of his uncle George Washington Strong (1793–1855), George Templeton Strong's father. Charles E. Strong was also counsel for the Bank of Savings and Seamen's Bank. He married Eleanor Fearing in 1860.

8.10 G.C.A.] George C. Anthon (1820–1877) graduated from Columbia College in 1839 and studied law in Strong's office before moving to New Orleans and taking up teaching as a profession. He returned to New York and was appointed professor of Greek at New York University.

9.4–5 "le monstre Pitt" . . . their analogues in Paris sixty years ago] William Pitt (1759–1806), prime minister of Britain, 1783–1801 and 1804–6, was denounced as "the enemy of the human race" ("l'ennemi du genre humaine") by a decree of the French National Convention in 1793. In the anthology *Poetry of the Anti-Jacobin* (1800), a footnote to a passage in a poem imagining Pitt being guillotined reads "Le Monstre Pitt, l'ennemi du genre humain."

9.15–16 Mr[s] Sally Hampton] Strong's cousin Sarah Baxter Hampton (1833–1862), known as Sally, who in 1854 married the South Carolina planter Frank Hampton (1829–1863).

10.15 Oct. /57] The Panic of 1857, severe U.S. economic crisis linked to speculation in land and railroads, among other factors.

10.21 Laurence Williams] Union officer (1833–1879) who in 1863 would be dismissed from the army for being absent without leave, November 1862–March 1863. His younger brother Orton (1839–1863), a Confederate soldier, was captured and hanged as a spy in June 1863.

10.33 First Board . . . the Second] The First Board was the New York Stock Exchange's morning trading session, held between 10:30 A.M. and noon, and the Second Board was the afternoon session, held between 2:30 and 3:00 P.M.

11.1 Border States] Delaware, Maryland, Kentucky, and Missouri, joined by West Virginia when it was created as a state in 1863.

11.8 "Personal Liberty" laws that interfere with the Fugitive Slave Law] The Fugitive Slave Law of 1850 passed by Congress gave jurisdiction over fugitive slave cases to federal commissioners appointed by the courts, authorized federal marshals to summon all citizens to assist in enforcing the law, and established criminal penalties for harboring fugitives. In response, Ohio, Michigan, Wisconsin, and the New England states passed personal liberty laws guaranteeing various due process protections to persons accused of being escaped slaves.

12.11 Johny] John Ruggles Strong (1851–1941), the oldest son of George Templeton Strong. Awarded a law degree from Columbia in 1875, he practiced law in New York City. He married Laura Coster Stewart (1860–1906) in 1885 and later moved to Cambridge, Massachusetts.

12.16 the big Electrical Machine] An electrostatic generator, likely a source of curiosity and wonder for Strong's children and visitors. (While a college student Strong built such a device; it is not clear if he is referring to this particular machine.)

14.25 Right of Petition — & the *Giddings* business] In response to an increasing number of petitions calling for the abolition of slavery in Washington, DC, the House of Representatives adopted a rule on May 26, 1836, requiring that all petitions regarding slavery be tabled without being read or printed. After a prolonged struggle over the right to petition, the rule was revoked on December 3, 1844. Joshua R. Giddings (1795–1864) of Ohio was an antislavery Whig, and later Republican, who served in Congress from 1838 to 1859. On March 21, 1842, he introduced nine resolutions in the House regarding the *Creole*, an American brig carrying enslaved captives from Virginia to New Orleans that was seized by slave mutineers in November 1841 and taken to Nassau in the Bahamas, where British authorities freed the enslaved who had not participated in the revolt (the mutineers were released in April 1842). Drafted by the abolitionist Theodore Weld, the resolutions declared that the captives on board the *Creole* had "violated no law of the United States, incurred no legal penalty, and are justly liable to no punishment" for "resuming their natural rights of personal liberty," and that attempts to reenslave them would be "unauthorized by the Constitution" and "incompatible with our national honor." The next day the House voted 125–69 to censure Giddings. He immediately resigned his seat and was returned to the House after winning a special election, 7,469–393.

14.36–37 S.A. Douglas . . . the Missouri Compromise] In 1819 Northern opposition prevented the admission of Missouri as a slave state. The following year Congress passed legislation admitting Missouri as a slave state and Maine as a free state while excluding slavery from the remainder of the Louisiana Purchase territory north of 36° 30′ latitude. In 1854 Democratic Senator Stephen A. Douglas (1813–1861) of Illinois secured passage of the Kansas-Nebraska Act, which repealed the Missouri Compromise line and allowed the question of whether slavery would be permitted in the newly organized territories to be decided by their legislatures.

14.38 effort to force slavery on Kansas] In November 1857 a convention held at Lecompton in Kansas Territory approved a proslavery constitution, and in December it was approved in a referendum boycotted by free-state settlers, in which voters were denied the choice of rejecting the document outright. President Buchanan asked Congress in February 1858 to approve the constitution and admit Kansas as a slave state. Despite the opposition of Senator Stephen Douglas, who denounced the Lecompton constitution as a violation of the principle of popular sovereignty, the admission of Kansas was approved by the Senate, 33–25, but was rejected by the House, 120–112. Both the House and the Senate then approved a bill resubmitting the Lecompton constitution under the guise of a land-grant referendum, and on August 2, 1858, it was rejected by the voters of Kansas, 11,300–1,788.

14.40–15.1 brutal beating . . . Sumner] In his antislavery speech "The Crime Against Kansas," delivered in the Senate May 19–20, 1856, Charles Sumner (1811–1874) of Massachusetts described Senator Andrew Butler (1796–1857) of South Carolina as having chosen "the harlot, Slavery" as his "mistress." On May 22 South Carolina Congressman Preston Brooks (1819–1857), a cousin of Senator Butler, approached Sumner as he sat at his desk in the Senate chamber, accused him of libeling South Carolina and Butler, and beat him unconscious with a cane. After a measure to expel him from the House failed to win the necessary two-thirds majority, Brooks resigned his seat and was reelected by his district. Sumner did not return regularly to the Senate until December 1859.

15.2 the project to revive the slave trade] During the 1850s several prominent Southern proslavery advocates began calling for the reopening of the African slave trade. Their proposal failed to win the support of most Southerners.

15.36 Presd^t's Message] President Buchanan delivered his fourth annual message to Congress on December 3, 1860. In it he said, "The long-continued and intemperate interference of the Northern people with the question of slavery in the Southern States has at length produced its natural effects."

16.1 Old Public Functionary] Derisive nickname given to Buchanan, who referred to himself as an "Old Public Functionary" in his third annual message to Congress, December 19, 1859. ("O.P.F." on pp. 31, 35, and 38 refer to Buchanan.)

16.29 Croton Aqueduct has *busted.*] The Croton Aqueduct, constructed 1837–42, carried clean water by gravity from the Croton River in Westchester County to reservoirs in Manhattan. On December 5, two water mains broke on Fifth Avenue, draining one of the reservoirs.

17.2 Bobadils] Bobadil was a braggart soldier in *Every Man in His Humour* (1598, revised 1616) by the English writer Ben Jonson (1552–1637).

17.31 Commercial] The *New-York Commercial Advertiser*, founded by Noah Webster (1758–1843) in 1793 as the *American Minerva.*

18.12 Lancashire & Lowell] The county of Lancashire in northwest England had more than two thousand cotton mills by 1860. Lowell, Massachusetts, was a major industrial center for the production of cotton fabric.

19.9 following the example of Mr Sec^y *Cobb*] Howell Cobb (1815–1868) was a congressman from Georgia, 1843–51 and 1855–57, and its governor, 1851–53. He served as secretary of the treasury in the Buchanan administration from 1857 until his resignation on December 10, 1860, and was subsequently accused of having deliberately undermined the national finances. Cobb supported secession in 1861 and served as a Confederate general, 1862–65.

19.37 proselyte of the Gate] Jewish category for a Gentile who followed certain Jewish customs but was not required to be circumcised or comply entirely with the Torah.

20.10 C.E.S.] Charles Edward Strong (see note 8.8).

20.16 *Booth*] Edwin Booth (1833–1893), American classical and Shakespearean actor.

20.21–23 More . . . *Tenterden Steeple* . . . Bishop Latimer] Hugh Latimer (c. 1485–1555), chaplain to Henry VIII and bishop of Worcester, was an English Protestant reformer. A sermon of his preached in 1550 tells of how an elderly Kentish peasant told Thomas More (1478–1535) that the construction of a church in the town of Tenterden accounted for the formation of the Goodwin Sands, a ten-mile sandbank off the coast of Deal, about forty miles away. "Tenterden steeple was the cause of Goodwin Sands" has come to signify the attribution of illogical causes to explain events.

20.29–30 M[r] & M[rs] Philip Allen] Perhaps Philip Allen (1785–1865), Democratic governor of Rhode Island, 1851–53, and U.S. senator, 1853–59. He married Phoebe Aborn in 1815.

21.2 Free Soilers] The Free Soil Party, founded in 1848, opposed the expansion of slavery into the western territories. The party merged with the Republican Party in 1854.

21.29–30 Negro-suffrage amendment to the Constitution] Defeated 1860 New York State constitutional amendment that would have given all Black men aged twenty-one or older the right to vote, which had already been extended to Black men who owned property valued at $250 or more.

22.34 Algerine states] Although nominally under the authority of the Ottoman sultan, the regencies of Algiers, Tunis, and Tripolitania were in fact each ruled independently by a pasha or dey.

22.38–23.1 Charleston Convention] A convention on South Carolina's secession from the United States met in December 1860, first in Columbia and then in Charleston. The convention issued an Ordinance of Secession on December 20, signed by all 169 delegates, and a Declaration of Secession on December 24.

24.2 Herzogthum] German (modern spelling *Herzogtum*): duchy or dukedom.

25.6 the passage of the Pacific R.R. Bill thro' the House] In February 1860, Samuel Curtis (1805–1866), Republican U.S. congressman from Iowa, introduced a bill to construct a transcontinental railroad from Iowa to California. Despite opposition from Southern states, which wanted a southern route for the railroad, the bill passed the House but could not be reconciled with the Senate's railroad bill and failed to become law.

26.21–23 South Carolina Clerk . . . dubious person Jno B. Floyd] Godard Bailey (1825–1877), a clerk in the Department of the Interior who was married to a cousin of Secretary of War John B. Floyd (1806–1863), had given $870,000 in Indian trust fund bonds to William H. Russell (1812–1872), a heavily indebted army contractor, in return for promissory notes endorsed by Floyd. Bailey confessed his role in the scheme to President Buchanan on December 22, 1860. Floyd resigned on December 29.

1861

31.22 Φιλαδελφια] Greek: Philadelphia.

31.23 Girard House] Luxury hotel at 823–835 Chestnut Street in Philadelphia.

31.31 O.P. F.'s Fast day] In a proclamation issued in December 1860 President Buchanan had designated January 4, 1861, as a national day of fasting and prayer. President Lincoln also declared the national days of fasting and prayer that occurred on September 26, 1861 (see p. 146) and April 30, 1863.

33.3 Prof: Eliot] Probably Samuel Eliot (1821–1898), professor of history and political science at Trinity College, 1856–74, and the college's president, 1860–64.

33.14–15 M[rs]. Georgey P.] Georgiana Snelling Peters (1830–1910); "M[rs] Eleanor" refers to Eleanor Fearing Strong (see note 8.8).

33.16 Dahlgren guns] This muzzle-loading naval gun was designed by John A. Dahlgren (1809–1870), a U.S. Navy ordnance officer.

33.17 Maynard Rifles] The breech-loading Maynard carbine, invented by Edward Maynard (1813–1891), was first manufactured around 1858–59. Praised for its accuracy and reliability, it was used by both sides in the Civil War.

33.23 Lorings] Presumably the family of Edward G. Loring (1802–1890), who served from 1858 to 1877 on the Court of Claims, a federal court that heard claims against the U.S. government.

33.28 Copperhead] Any Northerner who opposed the Civil War and advocated a negotiated settlement with the South.

34.8–9 Seventh Regiment] The Seventh Regiment of the New York State Militia, located in New York City, had been organized in 1847 from earlier military groups dating back to 1806. It was known as the "Blue-Bloods" or the "Silk Stocking" regiment because many of its members belonged to the social elite.

34.14–16 Star of the West . . . *fired upon*] On January 9, 1861, South Carolina batteries opened fire on *Star of the West*, a chartered civilian steamer carrying reinforcements and supplies to Fort Sumter in Charleston Harbor. The ship withdrew without casualties, and the Fort Sumter garrison did not return fire.

35.20–21 Calm dishonorable vile submission] Shakespeare's *Romeo and Juliet*, III.i.73 ("O calm, dishonorable, vile submission!"). Also quoted at 53.6.

35.26–28 Gen[l] Dix . . . open his portfolio as Sec[y] of Treasury] John A. Dix (1798–1879), who had been a Democratic senator from New York, 1845–49, served as secretary of the treasury in the Buchanan administration, January–March 1861.

36.2 "Vestiges of Creation"] The anonymously published *Vestiges of the Natural History of Creation* (1844), a widely read proto-Darwinian account of the universe; in 1884 it was revealed to have been written by the Scottish author and publisher Robert Chambers (1802–1871).

36.11 Washington "Constitution"] Short-lived newspaper, 1859–61.

36.36 *Crittenden* has taken decided ground in the Senate] On December 18, 1860, Senator John J. Crittenden (1786–1863) of Kentucky proposed a series of constitutional amendments that would restore the Missouri Compromise line while offering new protections for slavery. His measures were referred to a special Senate committee but got no further.

37.4 *Teredo*] A genus of saltwater clams that bore into wood.

39.14 Newgate Calendar] Originally a mid-eighteenth-century monthly bulletin of executions at London's Newgate Prison. The title was soon used for chapbooks containing stories about notorious criminals.

40.22 French Theatre] The Theatre Français, at the time located at 585 Broadway.

40.22 Miss Rosalie] Mary Rosalie Rathbone Ruggles (1800–1878), Strong's mother-in-law.

40.23 "Les Canotiers de la Seine"] *The Seine Boatmen* (1858), French theatrical spectacle by Henri Thiéry (1829–1872) and Adolphe Depeuty.

40.28 Isaac of York to Front-de-Bœuf and the Grand Master] Characters in *Ivanhoe* (1819), novel by the Scottish novelist and poet Walter Scott (1771–1832).

42.2 Panhandle] The panhandle of Virginia is now the northernmost part of West Virginia.

43.11–12 Beati pacifici] Latin: Blessed are the peacemakers, from Matthew 5:9.

43.19–20 *Georgia* has seized five N.Y. vessels . . . stoppage of *arms*] On the orders of Georgia Governor Joseph E. Brown (1821–1894), five ships owned by New Yorkers were seized in the port of Savannah on February 8, 1861, in reprisal for the New York police's confiscation on January 22 of a large shipment of muskets from a vessel bound for Savannah.

44.37 Brooklyn] In January 1861 the USS *Brooklyn*, a sloop of war built in 1859, was ordered to Charleston to deliver instructions to the *Star of the West* (see note 34.14–16), though by the time the *Brooklyn* arrived the *Star of the West* had departed the area.

45.4 Buncombe] Or bunkum, a term for nonsense.

45.37 Japanese embassy] In March 1860, about eighty Japanese diplomats arrived in San Francisco before proceeding to Washington, DC, Baltimore, Philadelphia, and New York City.

46.10–11 S[t] Thomas' Church] Episcopal church at the corner of Broadway and Houston Street.

46.12 Astor House] Hotel at the corner of Broadway and Vesey Street.

48.27 Council of Notables] Unsuccessful peace conference with delegates from twenty-one states held in Washington, DC, February 4–27, 1861. It recommended a series of compromise measures that failed to win approval from Congress.

54.38 Col: Coll:] Columbia College.

58.4 Wabash] Launched in 1855 and decommissioned in 1860, the frigate USS *Wabash* was recommissioned in April 1861 and was the flagship of the Atlantic Blockading Squadron.

58.4–5 North Carolina] The USS *North Carolina*, a seventy-four-gun ship of the line, was launched in 1820. Beginning in 1839, it served as a receiving ship (a vessel that housed new naval recruits) at the New York Navy Yard.

60.11–12 Exsurgat Deus . . . ejus.] Latin version of Psalm 68.1: "Let God arise, let his enemies be scattered: let them also that hate him flee before him."

61.39 the Light Brigade at Balaklava] During the Crimean War battle of Balaklava, October 25, 1854, confusing orders sent by Lord Raglan (1788–1855), the British commander-in-chief, led the Light Brigade of British cavalry to attack down a valley to their front instead of moving onto the ridge to their right. Of the 673 men in the brigade, 109 were killed and 159 were wounded in the battle. An eyewitness account by correspondent William Howard Russell (1827–1907) inspired Alfred Tennyson (1809–1892) to write his poem "The Charge of the Light Brigade."

62.36 *CAM*] Perhaps Colonel Charles Augustus May (1818–1864), who fought in the Mexican War, served under Albert Sidney Johnson, and resigned his commission in April 1861.

67.22 Fifth Avenue Hotel] Hotel, 1859–1908, occupying the block between 23rd and 24th Streets.

68.29 Old Hundred] Hymn beginning "All people that on Earth do dwell," a version of Psalm 100 sung to a tune attributed to Louis Bourgeois (c. 1510–1560) and first published in the 1551 Geneva Psalter.

73.32–33 79th & 8th Regiments . . . Corcoran] Colonel Michael Corcoran (1827–1863) led the 69th (not 79th) New York Infantry Regiment into action at the First Battle of Bull Run. The 8th New York Infantry Regiment was recruited in New York City and mustered into service in April 1861. Commanded by Colonel Louis Blenker (1812–1863), it was known as Blenker's Rifles.

75.20–22 "Hear *THIS*, ye old men . . . your Fathers?"] Joel 1:2.

76.1 revolted Sepoys] The Indian rebellion of 1857–58 began with a series of mutinies by soldiers (sepoys) of the British East India Company.

76.32 "N.Y. Rifles"] Unit soon to be consolidated with the Shepard Rifles. In October 1861 the Scott Rifles, Union Rifles, and Shepard Rifles merged to form the 51st Infantry Regiment.

78.38 W.A. Bartlett — of "diamond wedding" notoriety] The ostentatious wedding in October 1859 of the daughter of naval officer Washington Allon Bartlett (1818–1865) to a Cuban landowner received extensive newspaper coverage, including the satirical poem "The Diamond Wedding" by Edmund Clarence Stedman (1833–1908) published in the *New-York Tribune*.

79.6 Firemen's "Zouave" regiment] The 11th New York Infantry was made up of volunteer firemen from New York City. Colonel Elmer E. Ellsworth (1837–1861), the regiment's commander, had read law in Lincoln's office in Springfield before the war.

79.9 Soaplock] A nickname for the rowdy young working-class men of the Bowery.

80.2 Do'nt Give Up the Ship Lawrence] James Lawrence (1781–1813), who commanded the frigate USS *Chesapeake* in its battle with the frigate HMS *Shannon* off Boston in 1813. The *Chesapeake* was boarded by the British, and Lawrence, mortally wounded, cried out to his men, "Don't give up the ship!" The engagement ended with the British capture of the American vessel.

81.11 Sharpe's Rifles] Beginning with a design by Christian Sharps (1810–1874) in 1848, the Sharps rifles were single-shot, large-bore (.52-caliber), breech-loading rifles known for their long-distance accuracy.

81.35 Schiller's *Max Piccolomini*] Character loyal to the Holy Roman Emperor in the *Wallenstein* trilogy, published in 1800, by the German poet and playwright Friedrich Schiller (1759–1805).

83.13 Billingsgate] Crude language, named for the Billingsgate fish market in London.

83.31 in articulo mortis] Latin: at the moment of death.

83.31–32 Dragon of Wantley in Percy's Reliques] A ballad from *Reliques of Ancient English Poetry*, published in 1765.

84.34 Hope Chapel] Originally a religious assembly hall, Hope Chapel at 720 Broadway became a theater in 1855 and was renamed Donaldson's Opera House and, the following year, the Academy of Minstrels.

86.25 Aquila G.] Aquila G. Stout (1799–1857), insurance company president.

90.8–9 *Winans* concern] Based in Baltimore, Ross Winans (1796–1877) was the inventor of the Winans steam gun.

91.10–11 *sold into Slavery*!!!] After sailing to Texas to pick up seven companies of Union troops, the *Star of the West* was captured near Matagorda Bay by Colonel Earl Van Dorn (1820–1863) and two militia units from Galveston.

91.17 street fight in St Louis] On May 10, 1861, a volunteer force of recruits made up mostly of German immigrants led by Union Captain Nathaniel Lyon (1818–1861) captured more than six hundred secessionists at Camp Jackson outside St. Louis, suspecting that they were planning to raid the federal arsenal in the city with the support of pro-Southern Governor Claiborne Fox Jackson (1806–1862). As the captured men were being led through the streets toward the arsenal, crowds threw stones at the Union troops, who then fired into the crowd, killing at least twenty-eight people and triggering days of rioting.

92.32 Tyrtæus] Tyrtæus was a Greek poet of the seventh century BCE. His war poems were said to have been composed to help Sparta win the Second Messenian War.

93.28–29 son of Judge W—'s] Lockwood De Forest Woodruff (d. 1876), son of Judge Lewis Bartholomew Woodruff (1809–1875).

94.2 "ohne Hast, ohne Rast"] German maxim "Without haste, without rest," attributed to the German writer Johann Wolfgang von Goethe (1749–1832).

94.23 Deus salvam fac Rempublicam] Latin: God save the Republic.

95.37 Troy Regiment] The 2nd New York Infantry Regiment, known as the Troy Regiment, was mustered into service in May 1861 at Camp Willard in Troy, New York.

97.19–20 "Union Defence Committee,"] Organization created in April 1861 by the New York City Common Council.

98.4 Columbia Springs] Located in Virginia near the Long Bridge.

98.5 W. & A. Rail Road] The Washington and Alexandria Rail Road, which ran from the Long Bridge to Alexandria, Virginia.

98.8 Culpepper County] Virginia's Culpeper County is southwest of Columbia Springs.

98.28 "tua res agitur cum proximus ardet Ucalegon"] A conflation of Horace's line "tua res agitur, paries cum proximus ardet" ("It concerns you when your neighbor's wall is on fire," *Epistles*, Book I, Epistle 18, l. 84) and Virgil's "proximus ardet Ucalegon" ("Ucalegon burns next," *Aeneid*, Book II, l. 311). In the *Aeneid* the prominent Trojan Ucalegon is a next-door neighbor to Anchises, Aeneas's father.

99.17 "Manasses Gap Junction"] The Manassas Gap Junction in Virginia was an important connection between the Shenandoah Valley and the Manassas Gap Railroad.

100.33 Federal Hill] Union troops commanded by General Benjamin Butler (1818–1893) occupied Baltimore's Federal Hill in May 1861 and pointed cannons at the city center across the harbor.

101.1–2 (D'Utassy . . . Garibaldi Guard] Named for the Italian revolutionary Giuseppe Garibaldi (1807–1882), the 39th New York State Volunteers was recruited in New York City and contained companies made up of Hungarian, German, Swiss, Italian, French, Spanish, and Portuguese immigrants. Colonel Frederick George D'Utassy (1827–1892) commanded the regiment until 1863, when he was cashiered and sentenced to one year at hard labor after being court-martialed for fraud and embezzlement.

101.17–18 (not Jas A's Aleck, but John C's)] James A. Hamilton (1788–1878) and John C. Hamilton (1792–1882) were sons of Alexander Hamilton.

101.19 Alexandrian movement] On May 24, 1861, U.S. forces occupied Alexandria, Virginia.

101.40 Dr Bellows] Congregational minister Henry W. Bellows (1814–1892) served as president of the United States Sanitary Commission, 1861–78.

102.13 N.Y. 9th] The 9th New York Infantry Regiment, known as Hawkins' Zouaves, was organized by Colonel Rush C. Hawkins (1831–1920) in May 1861.

102.14 ["Brooklyn Zouaves"]] The 14th New York militia regiment, also known as the 14th Brooklyn. In 1860, after seeing the United States Zouave Cadets, an Illinois militia unit commanded by Colonel Elmer E. Ellsworth, on their East Coast tour, the regiment adopted a similar French-style military uniform.

102.16 *Long Bridge*] First built in 1809 and replaced several times, the Long Bridge connects Washington, DC, to Arlington, Virginia. Ten thousand Union troops took over the bridge in May 1861.

102.20 tete du pont] Bridgehead.

102.35 Mansion House] The largest hotel in Alexandria. It was confiscated in November 1861 and converted into a five-hundred-bed military hospital for the Union.

102.35 Shooter's (or Sutler's) Hill] Shuter's Hill in Alexandria is thought to have been named after a man who lived in the area in the 1740s. Later in 1861 Fort Ellsworth was constructed on the site, which was also known as Shooter's Hill.

103.27 N.Y. 12th] The 12th New York State Militia, led by Colonel Daniel Adams Butterfield (1831–1901), was mustered into three months' service in May 1861.

104.12–13 Col: Burnside's Rhode Island Camp] Ambrose Burnside (1824–1881), then a colonel in the Rhode Island militia, raised the 1st Rhode Island Infantry Regiment and was appointed its colonel in May 1861.

104.18–19 Goddards & other Prov: millionaires] Robert Hales Ives Goddard (1837–1916) was a partner in Goddard Brothers, a successful textile manufacturing firm in Rhode Island. He enlisted as a private in the Rhode Island militia in 1861 and later served as an officer on the staff of General Ambrose Burnside. His brother William Goddard (1825–1907) also served in the 1st Rhode Island militia.

104.22–23 fieldpreaching . . . Lauderdale and Clavers] Following the restoration of episcopacy in Scotland by Charles II (1630–1685) in 1662, Presbyterian Covenanters began holding their services in the open air. John Maitland, Duke of Lauderdale (1616–1682), secretary of state for Scotland, 1660–80, and John Graham of Claverhouse (1648–1689), who commanded royal troops in Scotland from 1678 until his death at the Battle of Killiecrankie in 1689, became notorious for their persecution of Covenanters.

104.32–33 Wise of the Navy . . . Edw: Everett.] A cousin of the Virginia secessionist Henry Wise, Lieutenant Henry Wise (1819–1869) was a naval officer who also wrote popular travel books and adventure novels under the name "Harry Gringo." A Unitarian clergyman and professor of Greek at Harvard who served as president of the college, 1846–49, Everett (1794–1865) was also a congressman from Massachusetts, 1825–35, governor of Massachusetts, 1836–40, U.S. minister to Great Britain, 1841–45, secretary of state, 1852–53, a senator from Massachusetts, 1853–54, and the vice presidential candidate on the 1860 Constitutional Union ticket.

104.35 N. P. Willis] Nathaniel Parker Willis (1806–1867), a journalist, poet, and writer of short stories and travel sketches.

105.1 Gen: Mansfield] Brigadier General Joseph King Fenno Mansfield (1803–1862) commanded the Washington defenses in spring 1861. He later led a division in Virginia and a corps at Antietam, where he was fatally wounded.

105.3 *Bache* . . . Trowbridge] Alexander Dallas Bache (1806–1867) was superintendent of the U.S. Coast Survey from 1843 until his death. William P. Trowbridge (1828–1892) was assistant superintendent of the survey.

105.9 Fairfax C.H. skirmish] The Battle of Fairfax Court House, June 1, 1861, the war's first engagement on land with fatalities: one dead on each side.

105.28–29 Col: Washington who was lost on the San Francisco] On December 24, 1853, the steamship *San Francisco* was disabled amid a severe storm in the Atlantic about two hundred miles east of Charleston. Colonel John MacRae Washington (1797–1853), a former governor of New Mexico, was washed overboard and drowned.

106.7–8 *Arlington House* . . . Col: Lee] The house had been built by George Washington Parke Custis (1781–1857), grandson of Martha Custis Washington and the adopted son of George Washington. His will gave a life interest in the property to his only child, Mary Custis Lee (1807/8–1873), who had married Robert E. Lee in 1831.

106.38 Chain Bridge] Bridge over the Potomac connecting Arlington, Virginia, with Washington, DC.

107.6 Old Point Comfort] Site of Fort Monroe in Hampton, Virginia.

107.9 "Adelaide"] Built in 1854, the steamship *Adelaide* was used by the U.S. Navy as a transport ship to support the blockade of waterways under Confederate control.

107.25 North Point] North Point, site of a battle during the War of 1812, is formed by the confluence of the Back and Patapsco Rivers.

108.10 Fox Hill] Fishing village, now a neighborhood in Hampton, Virginia.

109.12 "furor Normannorum"] Latin: fury of the Northmen.

109.21–22 Eastman Johnson's "old Kentucky Home" picture.] Alternate title (echoing the title of Stephen Foster's popular 1852 song "My Old Kentucky Home") for *Negro Life at the South* (1859) by the American artist Eastman Johnson (1824–1906), the painting that made Johnson famous when it was displayed at the National Academy of Design exhibition in Washington and at the Boston Athenæum in 1859. The scene depicted is in Washington, DC, not Kentucky.

111.24–26 Billy Wilson's Regiment . . . *pariahs*] The English-born former boxer and Democratic politician William Wilson (1823–1874) led the 6th New York Infantry, also known as "Wilson's Zouaves." Its recruits had a reputation for their rowdiness and possible criminal pasts.

113.22–23 Vides, mi fili, quam parvâ sapientiâ] Latin: You see, my son, with how little wisdom [governs the world].

114.17 Dr Agnew] Cornelius Rea Agnew (1830–1888), an ophthalmologist, was surgeon general of New York state, 1859–62. A member of the executive committee of the Sanitary Commission, Agnew served as medical director of the New York Volunteer Hospital during the Civil War, treating wounded Union soldiers.

114.18 D[r] Newberry] John Strong Newberry (1822–1892), physician, professor, and secretary of the Western Department of the Sanitary Commission beginning in September 1861.

115.16 Camp Denison] Named for Ohio Governor William Dennison (1815–1882), Camp Dennison was established near Cincinnati in 1861 and served as a military recruiting, training, medical, and supply post.

115.19 Union Club] The Union Club of the City of New York was founded in 1836. From 1855 to 1903 its clubhouse was at Fifth Avenue and 21st Street.

116.10 Temple] George Templeton Strong, Jr. (1856–1948), known as Temple, studied the piano, violin, and oboe at an early age. In 1879 he studied music at the Leipzig Conservatory in Germany. He moved to Wiesbaden, Germany, in 1886 and returned to the U.S. in 1891, where he taught counterpoint and composition at the New England Conservatory in Boston. He moved to Switzerland in 1897 and worked there as a composer and professional artist for the rest of his life.

118.19 in sæcula sæculorum] Latin phrase from the Vulgate that has been translated "for ever and ever" and "world without end."

120.20 *Comet*] The Great Comet of 1861 was first visible in the Northern Hemisphere on June 29. It could be seen by the naked eye through August.

121.21 If it be lawful to pull an ox . . . Sabbath] Cf. Jesus's words in Luke 14:5: "Which of you shall have an ass or an ox fallen into a pit, and will not straightway pull him out on the sabbath day?"

123.29 *Wormley's*] James Wormley (1819–1884), a free Black citizen born in Washington, DC, managed boardinghouses on I Street. In 1869 he opened the Wormley Hotel at the corner of 15th and H Streets.

123.34 Giraud Foster] Jacob Post Giraud Foster (1827–1886), New York City lawyer and a member of the Century Association.

123.35 ὁ φιλανθρωπος)] Greek: the philanthropist. Charles Loring Brace (1826–1890) founded the Children's Aid Society in 1853 and served as its executive officer until his death.

124.8 McChesney's Regiment] The 10th New York Infantry Regiment, known as the National Zouaves, was organized in New York City by Colonel Walter V. McChesney.

124.32–33 Sawyer gun] Powerful cannon with a range of more than three miles invented by Sylvanus Sawyer (1822–1895).

125.24 Penniman's house] James Fenner Penniman (1807–1876) was a merchant and art collector.

128.25 Five Points] Slum in New York City.

135.14 Theolog: Seminary] The General Theological Seminary, founded in 1817 in New York City, is the oldest seminary of the Episcopal Church.

137.15 "Was ne'er . . . Wo"] Cf. "Were ne'er prophetic sounds so full of woe," from "The Passions: An Ode for Music" (1746) by the English poet William Collins (1721–1759).

138.38 σωτηριων πραγματων ευαγγελος] Greek: the good news of deliverance.

139.18–19 Col: Weber's *Turner* Regiment] The 20th New York Infantry Regiment, known as the United Turner Rifles, was led by Colonel Max Weber (1824–1901), a German immigrant. It was recruited from German American gymnastics clubs known as Turner societies or *Turnvereine.*

141.4 Gallinippers] Southern term for large aggressive insects, particularly mosquitoes.

141.25 "Brightwood"] At this time, Brightwood included the area north of Brightwood Park, east of Rock Creek, and south of the city border with Maryland.

141.29 Cha[s] Kingsley's sermons] Charles Kingsley (1819–1875) was a prominent Anglican clergyman, social reformer, and author.

142.24 in fieri] Latin: in the course of execution.

143.26 skirmish at Lewinsville] Brief and inconclusive engagement near Lewinsville, Virginia, on September 11, 1861.

143.38 Sir Anthony Absolute] Brusque father in *The Rivals* (1775), comedy by the Irish dramatist Richard Brinsley Sheridan (1751–1816).

144.25–26 I saw the "French Lady"] The Confederate officer Richard Thomas (1833–1875), who called himself "Zarvona," was captured on July 7, 1861, and imprisoned at Fort McHenry after he attempted to seize the steamer *Mary Washington* near Annapolis while disguised as a woman. In June Zarvona had impersonated a Frenchwoman to board the steamship *St. Nicholas,* which he and his accomplices then captured.

145.8 S.R.] Savin Rock, a seaside resort in West Haven, Connecticut. Strong had traveled to Savin Rock to visit with Ellen and their sons, who spent part of the summer there in 1861.

147.21 Knapp] Frederick Newman Knapp (1821–1889), superintendent of the Sanitary Commission's Special Relief Department, in which role he supported disabled veterans and helped soldiers return to civilian life.

150.10 John Jay] John Jay (1817–1894), a grandson of the chief justice, was a lawyer who had helped organize the New York Republican Party.

150.11 Queen Elizabeth's Homily against Rebellion] "An Homily Against Disobedience and Wilful Rebellion" (1570), written in the aftermath of a failed 1569 rebellion in support of Mary, Queen of Scots (1542–1587), against Elizabeth I (1533–1603). The sermon was not written by Elizabeth herself.

150.35 24 Union Square] The home of Samuel and Rosalie Ruggles.

151.28–29 *Tom Pinch* in Dickens' "Martin Chuzzlewit."] Virtuous character in the novel (1844) by Charles Dickens (1812–1870). Mark Tapley (mentioned at 157.17) is a cheerful, optimistic character in the novel.

154.12 D[r] Hammond U.S.A. of Baltimore] The physician and neurologist William A. Hammond (1828–1900) was chair at the University of Maryland School of Medicine at the time; he would be appointed surgeon general of the Union army in 1862.

157.19 Camp Floyd] Camp Floyd near Salt Lake City was constructed by the U.S. Army in 1858 to suppress a supposed Mormon rebellion.

157.26–27 "Where's the coward . . . land!"] From Walter Scott's *Marmion* (1808), Canto IV, stanza 30.

160.32–33 "*seculars*"] Volunteer officers.

160.36–37 "Les Noces de Jeannette" . . . "Betly"] *Les Noces de Jeannette* (Jeannette's Wedding, 1853), light opera by the French composer Victor Massé (1822–1884); *Betly* (1836), comic opera by the Italian composer Gaetano Donizetti (1797–1848).

161.13–14 Plutarchian parallels between King U.S. Log & King C.S. Stork] In Aesop's fable "The Frogs Who Desired a King," a group of frogs asks for a king from Zeus, who sends them a log, which does nothing instead of governing them. After the frogs complain, they are a sent a stork, who proceeds to eat them. The Greco-Roman historian Plutarch (46–c. 120 CE) compared historical leaders in his *Parallel Lives*; here the log would be Abraham Lincoln and the stork Jefferson Davis.

162.23–24 Were I "born to set them right"] Cf. *Hamlet*, I.v.188–89: "The time is out of joint. O cursed spite, / That ever I was born to set it right!"

163.17 "Afflavit Deus et dissipantur"] "God blew and they are scattered," Latin phrase that appeared on medals commemorating the English defeat of the Spanish Armada in 1588, which was aided by severe storms and bad weather.

164.9–10 Mason & Thomas' Classical Soirees] The seventh season of chamber music performances at Dodworth's Hall (806 Broadway, near 11th Street), presented by the composer and pianist William Mason (1829–1908) and the violinist and conductor Theodore Thomas (1835–1905).

164.19–20 Lynch has run for Sheriff as successfully as he ran with Varian's Battery] James Lynch (1821–1872), a Democrat, was elected sheriff of New York County in the election of November 5, 1861. He had served in an artillery unit that was part of the 8th New York Infantry Regiment at the First Battle of Bull Run.

164.27–38 Gen: *Frémont* is superseded . . . memorable Proclamation] General John C. Frémont (1813–1890) was removed as commander of the Department of the West on November 2, 1861. On August 30, he had ordered the emancipation of all enslaved persons in Missouri whose masters did not declare their loyalty to the Union. After Frémont clashed with President Lincoln and refused to modify the order, it was rescinded by Lincoln on September 11.

167.22 *vino gravatus*] Latin: weighed down by wine.

167.28 the famous privateer Sumter] The Confederate commerce raider *Sumter*, commanded by Raphael Semmes (1809–1877), captured eighteen merchant vessels in 1861. After arriving in Gibraltar in January 1862, the ship was blockaded by Union vessels and required extensive repairs, resulting in its abandonment.

167.37–168.1 Wilkes of the San Jacinto . . . War with England] On November 8, 1861, Captain Charles Wilkes (1798–1877) of the USS *San Jacinto* boarded the British mail packet *Trent* off Cuba and seized the Confederate envoys James M. Mason (1798–1871) and John Slidell (1793–1871). The incident caused a major diplomatic crisis that continued until the Lincoln administration decided on December 26 to release the envoys in order to avoid a possible war with Great Britain.

168.30 Pecksniff] Villain in Dickens's *Martin Chuzzlewit.*

169.20 Winthrop Chanler] John Winthrop Chanler (1826–1877), lawyer and Democratic politician who served in the New York State Assembly, 1858–59, and the U.S. House of Representatives, 1863–69.

169.24 "Adlatus"] Latin: Assistant.

173.11–12 "Wo unto you . . . you".] Cf. Jesus's words in Luke 6:26: "Woe unto you, when all men shall speak well of you! for so did their fathers to the false prophets."

176.14 "through much tribulation"] Acts 14:22.

1862

179.7 Port Royal S.C.] In 1861 the extensive cotton plantations of Port Royal, South Carolina, came under federal control, and the cultivation of these lands was managed as an experiment in free labor and supervision by formerly enslaved individuals. The enterprise was successful enough to cause the free Blacks to assume they would eventually own the land, but at the end of the Civil War the land was returned to the former slave-owning planters. "Jack Ehninger" is Strong's friend the American artist and illustrator John Whetten Ehninger (1827–1889).

180.10 "Natick cobbler"] Nickname for Henry Wilson (1812–1875), Republican U.S. senator from Massachusetts, 1855–73, and vice president of the United States, 1873–75. He had been a shoemaker in Natick as a young man.

181.16 *Vade retro Sathanas*] Latin: Get behind me, Satan: Jesus's rebuke to Satan in Matthew 16:23 and Mark 8:33.

183.27 Stillé] The historian and educator Charles Janeway Stillé (1819–1899), author of the pamphlet *How a Free People Conduct a Long War: A Chapter from English History* (1862) and a member of the Sanitary Commission.

184.5 Δημος] Greek: people.

185.39 I shall become a Timon, hostis humani generis] Timon was a legendary ancient Athenian known for his misanthropy (and later the title character of a play by Shakespeare); "hostis humani generis" means "enemy of the human race."

186.18–19 A "Proclamation to the People of Georgia" by certain very valiant rebels] "Address to the People of Georgia" (1862) by Howell Cobb (1815–1868), Robert Toombs (1810–1885), Martin J. Crawford (1820–1883), and Thomas R. R. Cobb (1823–1862).

186.33 Wycliffe] The reformist English cleric and philosopher John Wycliffe (c. 1330–1384).

187.14–15 the "*Legal Tender*" bill . . . not dare to dissent] The Legal Tender Act, authorizing the U.S. Treasury to issue paper money ("greenbacks") not secured by specie, was signed into law by President Lincoln on February 25, 1862.

189.4–5 the returns . . . Waterloo.] Napoleonic War battles with massive casualties: Leipzig, October 16–19, 1813; Eylau, February 7–8, 1807; Borodino, September 7, 1812; and Waterloo, June 18, 1815.

190.10 "Commodore Nutt"] Stage name of George Washington Morrison Nutt (1848–1881), an adolescent dwarf who, beginning in 1861, was exhibited at the American Museum, an exhibition hall with "lecture-room" theater at the corner of Broadway and Ann Street founded by American entrepreneur P. T. Barnum (1810–1891).

190.10 the "What-is-it?"] At Barnum's American Museum a Black man with an unusually small head (William H. Johnson, d. 1926, and possibly one other person), falsely claimed to have been captured in Africa, was displayed with the suggestion that he potentially represented an evolutionary "missing link" between animals and humans.

192.9–10 "Veré dignum et justum est, æquum et salutare"] From the Catholic Mass: "It is truly right and just, proper and fitting for our salvation."

193.7 Ericsson Battery] Another name for the Union ironclad *Monitor*, designed by the Swedish-born American engineer John Ericsson (1803–1889).

193.15 Eheu!] Latin: Alas.

195.6–7 The wicked flee when no man pursueth] Proverbs 28:1.

196.3 "tents d'abri"] Shelter tents.

199.36 iron clad Ganoid sea-monster] The ganoid scales on certain types of fish provide armor-like protection.

199.38 Gustave Doré] French artist Gustave Doré (1832–1883), whose many illustrations included those for an edition of Dante's *Inferno* in 1857.

201.12–13 periculosum plenum opus aleâ] Latin: a dangerous work full of risk, derived from a phrase in *Ars Poetica* (c. 13 BCE) by the Roman poet Horace.

203.9–10 Ulm & Baylen] Battle of Ulm, October 16–19, 1805, in which the French army defeated the Austrians without much fighting; Battle of Bailén, July 19–22, 1808, decisive French defeat in the Peninsular War.

203.10 Saragossa] Or Zaragoza, Spanish city that was the site of two prolonged and bloody sieges by the French, 1808–9.

203.30 "Pittsburgh Landing"] Battle also known as Shiloh, April 6–7, 1862, a Union victory.

204.3 *Gratias agimus Tibi*] Latin: We give thanks to Thee [God], Christian liturgical phrase.

205.5–6 Non cuivis hominum &c.] Beginning of a quotation from Horace, *Epistles*, Book I, Epistle 17, line 36, "Non cuivis hominum contingit adire Corinthum" ("Not everyone has the luck to go to Corinth").

206.22–23 "Pour on, I will endure."] Shakespeare, *King* Lear, III.iv.21.

206.24–25 *Bierstadt* . . . Wüst . . . Haseltine] The German-born American painter Albert Bierstadt (1830–1902); the Dutch-born American painter Ferdinand Alexander Wüst (1837–1876); the American landscape painter William Stanley Haseltine (1835–1900).

210.4 Gottschalk] The acclaimed pianist and composer Louis Moreau Gottschalk (1829–1869).

210.24 M.S.B.] Marshall Spring Bidwell (1799–1872) was a partner in the law firm of Strong's father.

212.11 "Poquossin" bay . . . not sure I have got it's chivalric name right] Strong is referring to the Poquoson River, which flows into the Chesapeake Bay.

213.24 Sebastopol] During the Crimean War the British and French besieged Sevastopol, the main Russian naval base in the Black Sea, from October 1854 until its evacuation by the Russians in September 1855.

217.2 wife of the N.Y. Times!] Juliette Raymond (née Weaver, 1822–1914) was married to Henry J. Raymond (1820–1869), a cofounder of *The New York Times* and its editor, 1851–69.

218.38 ευαγγελος] Greek: messenger of good news.

219.27 Next *15th May*] The Strongs' wedding anniversary; they were married on May 15, 1848.

221.5–6 Gen: Hunter at Port Royal proclaims a *general Emancipation*] On May 9, 1862, General David Hunter (1802–1886) issued his General Order No. 11, proclaiming all slaves in Georgia, Florida, and South Carolina free; President Lincoln rescinded the order on May 19.

221.8 seven-league boots] Magic items in folklore allowing the wearer to take strides of seven leagues (approximately twenty-one miles) at a time.

233.9–10 after the pattern of Moscow.] Most of Moscow was burned by the Russians shortly after Napoleon reached the largely abandoned capital in September 1812.

233.36 Zebras & Onagras] "Onagra" is an obsolete word for a female onager or wild ass. The *Oxford English Dictionary* records its use only in the 1860s.

233.36 a *Rarey*] John Solomon Rarey (1827–1866), celebrated American horse trainer whose methods were outlined in his book *The Modern Art of Taming Wild Horses* (1858).

234.5 "crowning mercy" of victory] See the letter of Oliver Cromwell (1599–1658) to William Lenthall, September 4, 1651, written after Cromwell's decisive victory over Royalist forces at the Battle of Worcester (1651), which effectively ended the English Civil War: "The dimensions of this mercy are above my thought. It is for aught I know a crowning mercy."

238.13 fiorituri] The Italian word *fioriture* refers to musical embellishments, often improvised.

238.14 Tannhauser & Euryanthe] Operas by the German composers Richard Wagner (1813–1883) and Carl Maria von Weber (1786–1826), which premiered in 1845 and 1823, respectively.

238.23–24 "sweeping by . . . pall".] See "Il Penseroso" ("The Serious Man") by the English poet John Milton (1608–1674), published in 1645: "let gorgeous Tragedy / In sceptr'd pall come sweeping by."

240.14 κακαγγελοι] Not an actual Greek word but a composite of the prefix "kak-" (evil) and "angeloi" (angels or messengers): thus "messengers of bad news."

244.11 *Kehama*] *The Curse of Kehama* (1810), epic poem in twelve books by the English poet Robert Southey (1774–1843).

245.31 two French Princes] Robert Philippe d'Orléans, duc de Chartres (1840–1910), grandson of the deposed French monarch Louis-Philippe, and his brother Louis-Philippe d'Orléans, comte de Paris (1838–1894), served as aides to McClellan from September 1861 to July 1862.

246.2 Heintzelman] Brigadier General Samuel P. Heintzelman (1805–1880) commanded the Third Corps of the Army of the Potomac, March–October 1862.

250.16 Prince de Joinville] François d'Orleans, prince de Joinville (1818–1900), Louis-Philippe's third son and a naval officer in the French navy.

251.34 Hamilton K.] Lieutenant Hamilton Kuhn of the 27th Pennsylvania Infantry Regiment was killed on June 30, 1862, at New Market Crossroads, Virginia.

254.36 F.F.V.] First Families of Virginia, a group of early settler families who became socially and politically powerful.

256.18 John the Waiter] John Nolan was a waiter for the Strong family.

257.15 Tippecanoe & Tyler too] Slogan for the "Log Cabin" 1840 presidential campaign of Whig candidates William Henry Harrison (1773–1841) and John Tyler (1790–1862), referring to Harrison's command of U.S. troops in a battle fought in 1811 against Shawnee fighters along the Tippecanoe River in northern Indiana.

258.9–10 "garden-sass"] "Garden sass" or "garden sauce" was a term for vegetables.

258.16 ajee] Askew.

259.38 *vis a tergo*] Latin: force from behind.

262.35 Marshal "Vorwärts" . . . *Rückwärts*] Prussian Field Marshal Gebhard Leberecht von Blücher (1742–1819) was nicknamed "Marshal Forward" for his aggressiveness. *Rückwärts* means "backwards" in German.

262.38–39 what Wendell Phillips calls him, — "a first rate *second-rate man*"] Phillips (1811–1884), a prominent abolitionist, made the remark in a speech in Abingdon, Massachusetts, August 1, 1862.

268.32 Miss Emily] Emily Anthon (1826–1903), sister of George C. Anthon.

268.32 M[rs] Reginald A.] Katherine Anthon, the wife of George C. Anthon's brother Reginald Heber Anthon (1834–1866).

269.18 Spero Meliora] Latin: I hope for better things.

274.2 Durchlauchtigkeit] German: Serene Highness.

274.6–8 Sabrina fair . . . amber-dropping hair] Cf. lines 859–863 of John Milton's masque *Comus* (1634), addressing the water nymph Sabrina: "Sabrina fair, / Listen where thou art sitting / Under the glassy, cool, translucent wave, / In twisted braids of lilies knitting / The loose train of thy amber-dropping hair."

274.28 W.L.C.] Walter Livingston Cutting (1817–1885), the brother of Robert Livingston Cutting (1812–1887), onetime president of the New York Stock Exchange.

275.1 Belmont] The financier August Belmont, Sr. (1813–1890), chairman of the Democratic National Committee, 1860–72.

275.1 James & Rat Brooks] See note 6.17.

275.15 Quam parvâ sapientiâ mundus regitur!] See note 113.22–23.

275.28–29 French's Division Hospital] The field hospital set up on the farm of Dr. Otho J. Smith, northeast of Sharpsburg, Maryland, treated Union as well as Confederate wounded at the Battle of Antietam, September 17, 1862. Brigadier General William H. French (1815–1881) commanded the Third Division of the Second Corps.

276.14 scornful dogs have to eat dirty puddings.] Jamaican proverb, meaning "you may find yourself in the same situation you criticized."

276.26 "*Baltimore Clippers*"] Founded in 1839, the *Baltimore Clipper* newspaper endorsed John Bell in the 1860 presidential election but supported President Lincoln during the war.

280.33–34 sit venia loquendi] Latin: if you permit me to say this.

284.2 Wallack's old theatre] James W. Wallack (c. 1794–1864) and his son Lester Wallack (1819–1888) managed a theater at 485 Broadway from 1852 to 1861. The Wallacks then relocated to 844 Broadway at 13th Street.

284.3 Entführung aus dem Serail] *The Abduction from the Seraglio* (1782), opera with music by the Austrian composer Wolfgang Amadeus Mozart (1756–1791).

284.30–31 Charlestown (the City of John Brown)] In autumn 1859 John Brown (1800–1859) was tried, convicted, and executed in Charles Town, Virginia (after 1863 in West Virginia).

285.18 το καλον] The Greek "to kalon" can refer to the beautiful, noble, or fine in an ideal sense, as discussed in Plato's *Symposium*.

285.24 "Sinfully dogged & snappish."] The Irish Quaker physician John Rutty (1697–1775) kept a spiritual journal, in which he often referred to himself as "dogged" or "snappish." In a letter to Sir Adam Ferguson of August 2, 1827, Sir Walter Scott says of a Highland terrier named Ourisk, "She has become what Dr. Rutty, the Quaker, records himself in his journal as having sometimes been — sinfully dogged and snappish."

285.32–33 Hackett as *Rip Van Winkle* . . . "His Last Legs".] The American actor James Henry Hackett (1800–1871), well-known for his comic and Shakespearean roles, frequently portrayed the title character of *Rip Van Winkle*, a stage adaptation (1834) of the Washington Irving story by the American-born English playwright William Bayle Bernard (1807–1875). Bernard also wrote the two-act farce *His Last Legs* (1839).

286.23 My cousins the *Bs*] The family of Sally Baxter (see note 9.15–16).

286.24–25 Thackeray's monograph] *The Book of Snobs* (1848), satirical work cataloguing various types of snobs by the English writer William Makepeace Thackeray (1811–1863).

287.4–5 "Orpheus C. Kerr papers"] Collection of pseudonymous humorous articles (1862) on politics by Robert Henry Newell (1836–1901); the pseudonym is a play on words ("office seeker").

293.22–23 "Without the shedding of blood . . . remission of sins."] Cf. Hebrews 9:22: "almost all things are by the law purged with blood; and without shedding of blood is no remission."

294.18 "hewers of wood"] From Joshua 9:27: "And Joshua made them that day hewers of wood and drawers of water for the congregation."

294.24–25 ὁμοιουσιον . . . ὁμοουσιον] Greek words meaning "of a similar substance" and "of the same substance"; these terms were central to the Arian Controversy of the early Christian Church. Athanasius (293–373), bishop of Alexandria, vehemently defended the position of the Council of Nicaea (present-day Iznik, Turkey) in 325 that God and Christ were of one substance; opponents of this doctrine were called "Arians," after Arius (256–336), an excommunicated priest who argued that Christ was subordinate to God in the Trinity.

296.16 "Expectat dum defluat amnis."] Latin: He waits for the river to flow away, from Horace, *Epistles*, about not taking action: "A peasant waits for the river to flow away, / but it flows on, and will so flow for all eternity" (Book I, Epistle 2, lines 39–43).

297.18–19 "The Earl of Chatham . . . Sir Richard Strachan" &c &c] The anonymous satirical poem continues, "And Strachan, as eager to get at 'em, / Was waiting for the Earl of Chatham." General John Pitt, 2nd Earl of Chatham (1756–1835) and Admiral Richard Strachan (1760–1828) commanded, respectively, the British army and naval forces in the disastrous Walcheren expedition in the Scheldt estuary, July–December 1809.

300.25–26 in *pendente Symposis*] Roughly, "during the symposium."

301.28 "O Abraham, O mon Roi!"] "Ô Richard, ô mon Roi!," an aria from the 1784 opera *Richard Coeur-de-Lion* by André-Ernest-Modeste Grétry (1741–1803), was adopted by Royalists during the French Revolution.

302.7 "mutato nomine"] Latin: with the name changed.

303.3 Egleston] Thomas Egleston (1832–1900), director of the mineralogical collections and laboratory of the Smithsonian Institution. In 1864 he founded the School of Mines of Columbia College.

303.10–11 Chas J. Stillé . . . has published a clever pamphlet] More than 500,000 copies of Stillé's pamphlet *How a Free People Conduct a Long War* (see note 183.27) were eventually distributed.

1863

308.2 statue of *Lt Worden*] Lieutenant John L. Worden (1818–1875) commanded the *Monitor* during its battle with the CSS *Virginia*, March 9, 1862, until he was temporarily blinded by a shell burst.

310.17 Vallandigham] Clement L. Vallandigham (1820–1871), a Democratic representative from Ohio, 1858–63, was a leader of the "Peace Democrats" opposed to emancipation and the continued prosecution of the war. He was arrested in Dayton, Ohio, in May 1863, tried for expressing "disloyal sentiments and opinions," and expelled into Confederate-held territory in Tennessee. He was nominated for governor of Ohio by the Democratic Party, made his way to Canada in June 1863, and ran unsuccessfully for the office. He returned to the U.S. in June 1864 and helped draft the peace platform adopted by the Democratic national convention.

311.26 John R. Strong & his two younger brethren] John Ruggles Strong, see note 12.11. George Templeton Strong, Jr., see note 116.10. Lewis Barton Strong (1860–1910) was the longtime controller of Trinity Parish.

313.23 *In*judicious Hooker!] A negation of the epithet "judicious Hooker" applied to the Anglican theologian Richard Hooker (1554–1600).

314.25 Benedict Arnold] Arnold (1741–1801) was a general in the Continental Army who secretly met with a British officer, Major John André (1750–1780), on September 21, 1780, to arrange for the surrender of West Point to the British. André was tried as a spy and hanged on October 2, 1780; Arnold defected to the British, and in the United States his name became a byword for treachery.

316.36–37 the Bianchi & the Neri] Whites and Blacks, opposing Guelph factions in medieval Florence.

318.23 periculosae plenum opus aleæ] Latin: a dangerous game full of gambles.

319.12 fortem in arduis rebus servare mentem] Latin: a slight misquotation of Horace, *Odes*, Book II, Ode 3, lines 1–2: "Remember to keep a clear head in difficult times."

319.26–27 *Rabelais* furnishes a case equally difficult] In *Gargantua and Pantagruel* (1532–64), author's prologue to Book 4, by the French writer François Rabelais (c. 1483–1553), adapting an ancient tale about the uncatchable Teumessian fox and the fox-catching dog Laelaps.

321.24 Sir Mungo Malagrowther] A character in Walter Scott's 1822 novel *The Fortunes of Nigel.*

321.27 "the Son of Man came Eating & drinking"] Matthew 11:19.

322.36–37 "Black-Cockade Federalists"] During the American Revolution, the black cockade was worn by American patriots. With the outbreak of the French Revolution, the black cockade was retained by the Federalist Party as a symbol of support for Great Britain, while the Democratic-Republic Party adopted a red, white, and blue cockade in support of the French.

322.37 Hartford Convention] Federalist delegates from New Hampshire, Vermont, Massachusetts, Rhode Island, and Connecticut met in Hartford from December 15, 1814, to January 5, 1815. The convention proposed the adoption of seven constitutional amendments designed to protect New England against southern and western domination of the federal government, but its recommendations failed to win support in the aftermath of the American victory at New Orleans and the signing of the peace treaty with Great Britain.

323.33 Marble] Manton Marble (1835–1917) was the editor and owner of the *New York World*, 1862–76.

324.2 Ballo in Maschera] Italian: Masked ball, a reference to *Un Ballo in Maschera* (1859), opera with music by the Italian composer Giuseppe Verdi (1813–1901).

324.8 Dundreary] Lord Dundreary, a vapid aristocrat in the popular comedy *Our American Cousin* (1858) by the English playwright Tom Taylor (1817–1880).

324.11 μιλορδος] *Milordos*, a modern Greek borrowing of the English "My Lord," with the added Greek ending *-os.*

326.26–27 the junior Lincoln] Abraham Lincoln's son Robert Todd Lincoln (1843–1926).

328.33 a lay Hildebrand] Pope Gregory VII, born Hildebrand of Sovana (c. 1015–1085), was known for his struggle to establish the primacy of papal authority.

329.25–26 descendants of the venerable *Elder John Strong*] The English-born John Strong (1610–1699) was cofounder and ordained elder of the First Church of Northampton in Massachusetts.

330.9 *Non tali auxilio nec defensoribus istis.*] Latin: The time does not require such help nor such defenders. From Virgil's *Aeneid*, Book 2, line 521.

334.23 Trent affair] See note 167.37–168.1.

335.17–18 "fools & blind"] What Jesus calls the scribes and Pharisees in Matthew 23:17 and 23:19.

336.6 *Fiat Voluntas Tua*] Latin: Thy will be done, phrase from the Lord's Prayer.

339.12 *Fidelio*] Opera (1814) by the German composer Ludwig von Beethoven (1770–1827).

339.21–22 the Freyschutz & *Sonnambula*] The operas *Der Freischütz* (The Marksman, 1821) by Carl Maria von Weber and *La Sonnambula* (The Sleepwalker, 1831) by the Italian composer Vincenzo Bellini (1801–1835).

340.5 *mirabile dictu*] Latin: wonderful to relate.

342.2–3 Cowper . . . Somers, Erskine] The English poet William Cowper (1731–1800); the English jurist John Somers (1651–1716); the English lawyer and politician Thomas Erskine (1750–1823).

343.13 Habakkuk Mucklewrath] A Covenanter preacher in Walter Scott's 1816 novel *Old Mortality.*

343.39 Bull Anthon] The classical scholar Charles Anthon (1797–1867), author of more than fifty books and for many years a professor at Columbia College.

347.9 *Fuit Anglia*] Latin: England was.

348.14–15 our Fabius Minimus] The Roman General Quintus Fabius Maximus Verrucosus (c. 280–203 BCE) was called Cunctator (the Delayer) for his cautious tactics in the war against Hannibal.

355.19 vaunted rebel gunboat "Atlanta", alias "Fingal"] Built in Glasgow in 1861 as a steam-powered merchantman, the *Fingal* was purchased as a blockade runner by a Confederate agent later that year. After failing to break out from Savannah with a load of cotton, the *Fingal* was converted to an ironclad in early 1862 and renamed *Atlanta*.

357.27 Kissingen] Mineral water from Bad Kissingen, Germany.

358.10 "comme un Diable dans un benitier"] French: like a devil in a font of holy water.

360.9 Pleasonton] General Alfred Pleasonton (1824–1897) commanded the Cavalry Corps of the Army of the Potomac during the Gettysburg campaign.

360.27–28 as Burgoyne & Cornwallis were bagged near a century ago.] During the American War of Independence, the English Generals John Burgoyne (1722–1792) and Lord Charles Cornwallis (1738–1805) surrendered their armies to the Americans at Saratoga (1777) and Yorktown (1781), respectively.

361.5 sauve qui peut] French: every man for himself (literally, "save who can").

362.10 General . . . Mack or a Du Pont.] The Austrian General Karl Mack von Leiberich (1752–1828) surrendered his army to Napoleon at Ulm (see note 203.9–10). The French General Pierre Du Pont de l'Étang (1765–1840) surrendered 17,600 soldiers after being defeated by Spanish forces in the Battle of Bailén, July 16–19, 1808.

362.14 Δημος] Greek: The people. The Latin phrase that follows can be translated "By the Grace of Satan, King of New York."

366.35 Brian Boroo Redivivus] The Irish national hero Brian Boru Reborn. Brian Boru (941–1014) was high king of Ireland, 1012–14.

367.1–2 "swinging slow with sullen roar"] Milton, "Il Penseroso," l. 76.

367.18–19 Sebastian Brant . . . *Navis Stultifera.*] The illustrated book *Das Narrenschiff* (The Ship of Fools, 1494) was a popular satirical work by the German poet Sebastian Brant (1457–1521).

367.26 ci-devant] French: formerly.

367.30–31 "so cool, so calm, so bright,"] From the opening line of "Virtue" (1633), poem by the English poet George Herbert (1593–1633).

370.14 Ατκληπιος] Asclepius, the Greek god of healing and medicine.

371.13 S[t] Bartholomew's] Referring to French Catholic violence against Huguenots in 1572 that began on St. Bartholomew's Day, August 24.

372.22 as in 1688] The Williamite War in Ireland, 1689–91, between the forces of James II (1633–1701), the Catholic British king who had been deposed in the Glorious Revolution of 1688 (and was supported by Irish Catholics), and those of the Protestant William of Orange (1650–1702), who had ascended to the British throne.

375.13–14 "Uns ist . . . Kuonheit"] The first lines of the Middle High German poem *Nibelungenlied* (c. 1200). G. H. Needler translates them as "To us in olden story / are wonders many told / Of heroes rich in glory, / of trials manifold."

375.22 Apage Satanas] Latin: Begone, Satan (see note 181.16).

376.30–31 Tyndall's Lectures on *Heat & Motion*] *Heat Considered as a Mode of Motion* (1863) by the British physicist John Tyndall (1820–1893), collecting twelve of his lectures.

376.35 Κοσμος] Greek: Cosmos.

377.22–23 Caleb Strong . . . States-Rights-man] During the War of 1812, Massachusetts Governor Caleb Strong (1745–1819), a Federalist who opposed the war, refused to order the Massachusetts militia into federal service, arguing that only the governor of a state, and not the president, had the authority to call out its militia.

381.12 coprophagous Coleoptera!] Dung beetle.

381.33 Rumor of a Corps d'Afrique] In May 1863 Major General Nathaniel P. Banks (1816–1894) had announced plans to organize a "Corps d'Afrique" of eighteen Black regiments in Louisiana. The name was later used by both Northerners and Southerners to refer to Black troops in general.

384.15–16 "Eget mauri jaculis" . . . "integer vitæ"] See Horace, *Odes*, I.xxii, lines that are quoted by Demetrius in Shakespeare's *Titus Andronicus*: "Integer vitae, scelerisque purus, / Non eget Mauri jaculis, nec arcu": "The man who is of pure life and free from sin / needs not fear the bows and arrows of the Moor."

384.22–24 Russell . . . "Diary"] *My Diary North and South* (1863) by the British journalist William Howard Russell. The book does not contain the characterization of Southerners that Strong attributes to it here.

385.6–8 Sickles . . . a *Pariah*] Daniel E. Sickles (1819–1914), a Democratic congressman from New York, 1857–61, shot and killed Philip Barton Key (1818–1859), U.S. attorney for Washington and the son of Francis Scott Key, on February 25, 1859, shortly after learning that Key was having an affair with his wife, Teresa Bagioli Sickles (1836–1867). Sickles was acquitted of murder in April 1859, becoming the first defendant to successfully use the defense of temporary insanity in an American court. He became a major general in the Union army and lost a leg at Gettysburg.

387.19 *Aliunde*] Latin: From elsewhere.

388.11 Pediculus family] Lice.

388.15 massacre just perpetrated at Lawrence] On August 21, 1863, Confederate guerrillas from Missouri led by William C. Quantrill (1837–1865) raided Lawrence, Kansas, killing 180 men.

390.15 a "miraculous draught"] Reference to miraculous catches of fish in Luke 5:1–11 and John 21:1–14.

393.36–37 Battle . . . Charles Martel] In 732 the Frankish ruler Charles Martel (c. 686–741) defeated the invading forces of the Ummayad Caliphate at the Battle of Tours.

395.38 *Col: Charles G. Halpine*] Charles G. Halpine (1829–1868), Irish-born journalist, editor, poet, and Union officer best known for publishing humorous topical articles under the name of "Miles O'Reilly," a purported private in the 47th New York Infantry.

398.4 cum grano salis] Latin: with a grain of salt.

399.27 Prof: Oken] Lorenz Oken (1779–1851), German naturalist.

400.18 "igneous fatuous"] Ignis fatuus, an illusion or false hope.

401.16 Prof: McCulloh . . . sent in his resignation] Richard Sears McCulloh (1818–1894), a professor of physics at Columbia, resigned his position at the college "to cast his lot with that of the South." The school's Board of Trustees responded by formally expelling him in October. McCulloh used his knowledge of chemistry to help develop a lethal gas for the Confederacy that was never used on the battlefield. He was captured in Florida in May 1865 and imprisoned in Washington, DC, in 1865–66.

402.38–403.1 "Saga of Burnt Njal" as translated by Mr Dasent] English translation by the British scholar George Webbe Dasent (1817–1896) of the Njáls saga, thirteenth-century Icelandic poem.

404.4 Charlotte Cushman] American Shakespearean actor (1816–1876).

408.22 *pro tanto*] Latin: to that extent.

410.16 Trovatore] Giuseppe Verdi's opera *Il Trovatore* (1853).

410.24 Wittenagemote] Council in medieval England prior to the Norman Conquest.

410.38–39 "the runagates continue in scarceness"] From Psalm 68:6 as given in the Book of Common Prayer.

411.12–13 A British squadron has just been shelling a Japanese city] The British Royal Navy bombarded Kagoshima, August 15–17, 1863, in retaliation for the killing of a British merchant.

411.30 Friar Gerund and Geo. Francis Train] Friar Gerund, hero of the satirical novel *History of the Famous Preacher Friar Gerund de Campazas, otherwise Gerund Zotes* (1758) by the Spanish Jesuit priest José Francisco de Isla (1703–1781); George Francis Train (1829–1904), American businessman and author noted for his eccentric behavior and espousal of a number of causes.

414.39 *re infecta*] Latin: with the matter unfinished.

416.4–5 the *Alexandra* case] The steamer *Alexandra*, built in Liverpool for use as a Confederate navy cruiser, was seized in April 1863 by British authorities following concerns raised by American officials. The firm building the ship was brought up on charges related to the Foreign Enlistment Act (1819), which made it illegal to build ships for a foreign power for the purpose of waging war. The verdict in the Court of Exchequer's initial trial favored the defendants; eventually the case went before the House of Lords, which also ruled in favor of the firm.

416.15–16 "Columbæ et Gallinæ sunt Aves"] Latin: Doves and chickens are birds.

417.7–8 unknown author of "the New Gospel of Peace"] The political satire *The New Gospel of Peace According to St. Benjamin* (1863) by Richard Grant White (1822–1885) was first published anonymously.

418.6 as the Clans were after 1745] The Highland clan system in Scotland was severely weakened through legislation passed in Britain after the failed Jacobite Rebellion, 1745–46, which sought to place Charles Stuart (1720–1788), grandson of the deposed James II of England and Ireland, on the British throne.

418.7 Parton's life of Butler] *General Butler in New Orleans* (1863) by the English-born author James Parton (1822–1891).

419.15 L. Napoleon] Louis-Napoléon Bonaparte (1808–1873), president of the French Second Republic, 1848–52, and, as Napoléon III, ruler of the Second French Empire, 1852–70.

423.13 J.A.S. J[r]] John Austin Stevens Jr.

1864

427.4 "*Gold-Stick* in waiting"] Bodyguard position for the English monarch created by Henry VIII, which became a ceremonial role.

427.17 *totis viribus*] Latin: with all our might.

428.38–39 Hughes . . . imbecility of his address to the Rioters last July] John Joseph Hughes (1797–1864), Roman Catholic archbishop of New York,

1850–64, was a supporter of the war and opponent of abolitionism. On July 17, 1863, the last day of the New York draft riots, Hughes spoke from the balcony of his residence to a crowd of several thousand people and appealed for the restoration of peace and order. As reported in the *New York Herald*, he began his speech by saying: "Men of New York: They call you rioters but I cannot see a rioter's face among you (applause). I call you men of New York, not gentlemen, because gentlemen is so threadbare a term that it means nothing positive (applause)."

430.15 Copake Iron Works] The Copake Iron Works in Copake Falls, New York, was established by Lemuel Pomeroy II in 1854.

431.36 "learns nothing & forgets nothing"] A remark frequently attributed to Charles Maurice de Talleyrand-Périgord (1754–1838).

434.37–38 "as of a hidden brook in the leafy month of June"] Slight misquotation from "The Rime of the Ancient Mariner" (1798) by the English poet Samuel Taylor Coleridge (1772–1834), Part V, stanza 18.

434.40 "*What-is-it*"s] See note 190.10.

435.5 Buhler's restaurant] Buhler's Restaurant at 322 Pennsylvania Avenue NW was owned by John Welcker, a German immigrant who moved from New York City to Washington in 1861.

440.1–2 *malum prohibitum . . . malum in se*] Latin: evil because it is prohibited . . . evil in itself.

440.12–14 tithes of mint & cummin . . . weightier matters.] See the admonition of Jesus in Matthew 23:23: "Woe unto you, scribes and Pharisees, hypocrites! for ye pay tithe of mint and anise and cummin, and have omitted the weightier matters of the law, judgment, mercy, and faith: these ought ye to have done, and not to leave the other undone."

440.33 "Beati pauperes"] Latin: Blessed are the poor, from the Sermon on the Mount (Matthew 5:3–12).

441.36–37 "Es ist kein Pfafflein . . . seyn."] German: There is no little priest so small that he would not like to be a little pope.

443.7–8 "Empire Works"] The Empire Works, a six-story building that housed a grain dealer, a tannery, and manufacturers of pianos, hoopskirts, shovels, watch movements, rope, twine, and other goods, was owned by Samuel Leggett.

443.37 Count Gurowski's] Adam Gurowski (1805–1866) was a Polish writer who spent his last seventeen years in the United States; he worked for the *New-York Tribune* and was a translator for the State Department.

443.38–444.2 κυνος ομματ'εχων . . . κϛαδιην δ'ελαφοιο] Greek: having the eyes of a dog . . . but the heart of a deer. See *Iliad*, I, lines 224–27, where Achilles addresses Agamemnon: "Heavy with wine, with the eyes of a dog and the heart of a deer, you never have the courage to arm with the rest of the people for battle, or go into ambush with the best of the Achaians" (tr. Richmond Lattimore).

443.38 Thersites] Greek soldier in *The Iliad* and in Shakespeare's *Troilus and Cressida* who rails bitterly at Agamemnon and Achilles.

444.22 Hall & Labagh] Thomas Hall (1791–1874) opened an organ shop in New York City around 1817. In 1846 he formed a partnership with John Labagh (1810–1892).

447.18–19 Bryant's Minstrels] Bryant's Minstrels were led by three brothers from upstate New York named O'Neill who took the stage name Bryant. They first performed in 1857.

447.30–31 Speke's book on the Nile.] *The Discovery of the Source of the Nile* (1864) by John Hanning Speke (1827–1864), explorer of East Africa who traveled with Richard Burton (1821–1890) in search of the river's source.

448.14 Puritani] *I Puritani* (The Puritans, 1835), opera by Vincenzo Bellini.

450.4–5 *Mirifica Opera Tua*] Latin: Your wonderful works.

453.17–18 any popular Anti-Anglican insult to a set of British swells . . . Forrest & Macready row of /49?] Supporters of the rival Shakespearean actors Edwin Forrest, an American, and William Charles Macready (1793–1873), an Englishman, became increasingly hostile to each other during Macready's tour of the United States in 1849, with newspaper coverage fanning the flames as a conflict of British versus Americans. On May 10, 1849, the National Guard was called in to restore order outside the Astor Place Opera House when fighting broke out during a performance of *Macbeth* starring Macready. The guardsmen fired into the rioting crowd outside the theater and killed more than twenty people, injuring around one hundred. Strong witnessed the event.

453.35–36 "black but comely"] Song of Solomon 1:5.

455.10–11 Kilpatrick's Raid . . . Poor young Col: Dahlgren] Beginning on February 28, 1864, Brigadier General H. Judson Kilpatrick (1836–1881) led 3,500 men on a raid intended to attack Richmond and free Union prisoners of war. The attack failed, and Colonel Ulric Dahlgren (1842–1864), who led a supporting detachment of 500 men, was killed in action.

455.13–14 the "Orders" found in his pocket] Richmond newspapers published documents found on Dahlgren's body outlining plans to kill Jefferson Davis and burn Richmond. Kilpatrick denied any knowledge of the alleged plot.

455.18 Tyng & Spring] Stephen Higginson Tyng (1800–1885) and Gardiner Spring (1785–1873) were Episcopal and Presbyterian clergymen, respectively.

457.4 Vehm-Gericht] The Vehmgericht or Vehmic courts were secret courts that operated in Westphalia (present-day Germany) during the late Middle Ages.

457.27 "Le Noir Faineant"] In Walter Scott's historical romance *Ivanhoe*, Richard I returns to England disguised as a knight known as "Le Noir Faineant" ("The Black Sluggard").

457.31 "the seal of Solomon"] In medieval occult traditions, a magical ring giving its bearer supernatural powers.

458.1 Townsend-Sarsaparilla-Spingler] Samuel P. Townsend (1813/14–1870), a former contractor who began making and selling sarsaparilla tonic in 1839, completed construction on a brownstone mansion in 1855. In 1859 he sold the mansion to Gorham D. Abbott (1807–1874), a Presbyterian minister and founder of the Spingler Institute for Girls, which held classes in the building.

458.7–9 Jerome's (not the Saint but the stockjobber) . . . second story] The American financier Leonard W. Jerome (1817–1891), the maternal grandfather of Winston Churchill, had stables on the lot of his mansion at 26th Street and Madison Avenue; on the second floor of the stables was a ballroom used for theatrical performances.

458.25 G.M.O.] Gouverneur Morris Ogden (1814–1884) was the treasurer of Columbia College.

468.23 G.G.G.] George Griswold Gray (1830–1875) belonged to the politically influential Griswold family, which made a fortune in the China trade and the iron and steel industry.

471.33 "cruel only to be kind"] *Hamlet*, III.iv.178.

472.25 λατρεια] Greek: worship.

473.29 "Nimium ne crede colori".] From Virgil, *Eclogues*, II, line 17: "Trust not too much to your complexion."

474.4 *en grand Seigneur*] French: in the manner of the great lord; magnanimous.

474.22–23 "The Follies of a Night,"] *The Follies of a Night: A Vaudeville Comedy in Two Acts* (1842) by the English playwright and actor James Robinson Planché (1796–1880).

474.35 "The Dead Shot"] One-act farce (1845) by the English comic actor and playwright John Baldwin Buckstone (1802–1879).

475.23 "Circumstances Alter Cases"] Comic operetta by the English-born American composer Alfred B. Sedgwick (1821–1878).

475.37 Edwd Anderson] Edward Henry Anderson (1840–1886) was the son of Henry James Anderson (1799–1875), a geologist and a professor of mathematics and astronomy, as well as the maternal grandson of Italian poet and librettist Lorenzo da Ponte (1749–1838).

477.27 "Dignum et justum est."] See note 192.9–10.

478.12–13 "Marius amid the ruins of Carthage"] The Roman general Gaius Marius (c. 157–86 BCE) was elected consul seven times. In 88 BCE the Senate chose Lucius Cornelius Sulla (138–78 BCE) to head the army, and the assembly chose Marius. Sulla quickly withdrew his troops from Rome and in a surprise move turned and marched on the city. Defeated, Marius fled Rome for Africa. The depiction of Marius in the ruins of Carthage was a subject for artists such as the American painter John Vanderlyn (1775–1852) and the French artist Léon Cogniet (1794–1880).

478.17 "The Ladies Battle"] English adaptation (1851) by Thomas William Robertson (1829–1871) of the comedy *Un Duel en Amour* by the French playwright Eugène Scribe (1791–1861).

478.26 Allen v. Schuchardt] In this case, the court found that a contract of sale made in Rhode Island through an oral agreement could be enforced in New York, where these agreements were normally not enforceable.

479.13–14 Aedibus Hieronomycis . . . Hieronomycalibus.] Strong is trying to say, in Latin, "at the house of Jerome," i.e., at Leonard Jerome's residence on 26th Street (the "Theatre San Jeronimo" referred to at 479.6). See note 458.7–9.

482.9 "a glad light green"] From the anonymous Middle English poem "The Floure and the Leafe" (c. 1470), whose authorship had been attributed to Chaucer: "Every tree well from his fellow grew, / With branches broad, laden with leaves new, / That sprangen out against the sunne sheen; / Some very red; and some a glad light green."

487.24–25 "Happy whom He finds in battle's Splendor"] Translation by the Scottish philosopher, historian, and essayist Thomas Carlyle (1795–1881) in *Sartor Resartus* (1833–34) of a line from what he calls "Faust's Death-song" in Goethe's *Faust*, part I (1808).

490.8 Our newspaper *Jominis*] Antoine-Henri Jomini (1779–1869) was a Swiss-French military officer and a largely self-taught military strategist.

490.31 "Fest der Freude,"] German: festival of joy.

493.4 Εκκλησιαζουσαι] Greek: The women of the assembly, the title of a comedy (c. 392 BCE) by Aristophanes (c. 446–c. 386 BCE).

493.21 ιδιωτης] Greek: a private citizen who does not participate in public affairs.

494.26 M[r] F.A. was his superior in physical strength] Frederick Anthon (1820–1868), brother of the classics professor Charles E. Anthon (see note 343.39), was an accomplished amateur boxer.

495.18–19 *sub judice*] Latin: under judicial consideration.

495.26 *In Te Domine Speravi*] Latin version of the opening line of Psalm 31: "In thee, O Lord, do I put my trust."

495.33–34 "the Lord God Omnipotent reigneth" . . . Handel.] The line quoted is repeated throughout the Hallelujah Chorus from the oratorio *Messiah* (1741) by the German-British composer George Frideric Handel (1685–1759).

498.34–35 *Eikon Basiliké* in view of his possible dethronement] *Eikon Basilike: The Portraicture of His Sacred Majestie in his Solitudes and Sufferings* (1649) was purportedly written by the imprisoned Charles I before his execution on January 30, 1649; it was likely ghostwritten by John Gauden (1605–1662), bishop of Exeter.

499.19 Arcades Ambo] Latin: Arcadians both; i.e., two people having the same interests, tastes, or professions, an expression derived from a line in Virgil's seventh eclogue.

502.3 Lupanar] Brothel.

505.14 Jebusites & Ammonites.] Ancient peoples in conflict with the Israelites as recorded in the Bible.

507.4–5 Sir Pandarus] I.e., a procurer of women. Pandarus, a character in Chaucer's *Troilus and Criseyde*, was a go-between for the poem's eponymous lovers.

508.5 quantum mutatus ab illâ Angliâ] Latin: how changed is England from what it once was, adapting Aeneas's words when encountering Hector's bloody ghost in a dream ("how changed is he from what he once was") in Virgil's *Aeneid*, II, line 274.

508.11 much debated *Laird rams*] On September 3, 1863, responding to protests from U.S. Minister Charles Francis Adams (1807–1886), British Foreign Secretary Lord Russell (1792–1878) ordered that two ironclad rams built for the Confederacy by the Laird shipyards near Liverpool be detained in port. Two days later Adams warned Russell that the United States would go to war with Great Britain if the rams were permitted to sail. Russell ordered the ships' seizure on October 8.

508.24 David's Island] Davids Island in Long Island Sound, named for its owner Thaddeus Davids, was leased to Simeon Leland in 1862, who subleased it to the U.S. War Department as the site of the DeCamp General Hospital.

508.31–32 οφθαλmologist] Ophthalmologist.

510.11 Sniggelfritz . . . Schweitzer Käse] "Sniggelfritz" is a variant of the German "Schnickelfritz," which can be translated "chatterbox child" or "rascal"; "Schweitzer Käse" means "Swiss cheese."

510.15 "Woman wailing for her Demon Lover"] From Samuel Taylor Coleridge's "Kubla Khan" (1797), line 16.

511.34 "thrasonicall huffe-snuffe".] Phrase used by the Elizabethan writer Thomas Nashe (1567–c. 1601), in his preface to Robert Greene's *Menaphon* (1589), to criticize the translation (1582) of the first four books of Virgil's *Aeneid* by Richard Stanyhurst (1547–1618). Thrasonical, meaning "boastful," is derived from Thraso, a braggart soldier in the Roman playwright Terence's comedy *The Eunuchs*. "Huffe snuffe" means "bombastic nonsense." See also 549.19–20.

514.6 Bςεκεκεκκεκεκεξ κοαξ κοαξ] Comic refrain of the frogs of the underworld in Aristophanes's play *The Frogs*, with added "kekekeke" syllables.

515.17–18 "The maiden . . . the Moon"] From "The Cloud" (1820), lines 45–46, by the English poet Percy Bysshe Shelley (1792–1822).

516.7 X] Peter Remsen Strong (1823–1879), George Templeton Strong's cousin. In 1862 his wife, Mary Emeline Stevens Strong (1833–1895), confessed to an affair with his brother Edward. When Mary became pregnant, she accused her husband of forcing her to have an abortion and of having an affair with the female abortionist. She then vanished with their four-year-old daughter, Allie, until the couple's divorce trial in 1865.

518.4 *enceinte*] French: pregnant.

518.12 forerunners and patents of revolution . . . Duc du Praslin] On August 18, 1847, Charles de Choiseul-Praslin, duc de Praslin (1805–1847), murdered his wife in Paris, then committed suicide while in custody. The scandal surrounding the case contributed to public discontent with the July Monarchy of Louis-Philippe, who was deposed in February 1848.

520.11 *coup de soleil*] French: sunstroke.

521.6 "equus marinus"] Latin: sea horse.

524.15 Io Triumphe!] Latin: Hail, Triumph, exclamation used in Roman victory processions.

524.24 honi soit qui mal y pense] "Shame to him who thinks evil," the motto of the Order of the Garter.

533.9 "bistoury"] A surgical knife.

533.29–30 destructive fire yesterday noon] According to the *New York Times*, "The most destructive fire that has occurred in Brooklyn for many years took place yesterday afternoon in the warehouses of Messrs. SCHENCK & RUTHERFORD, on the dock at the foot of Joralemon-street, and, although the value of property destroyed was great, it is fortunate that there was no loss of life, or, as far as ascertained, no person very seriously injured."

536.22–23 "Es *Kann* nicht seyn . . . *nicht*] German: It *can*not be, can*not* be, cannot *be*! / Do you see it *cannot*?

536.29–30 Catiline . . . Republic.] Lucius Sergius Catilina (c. 108 BCE–62 BCE), known as Catiline, plotted to overthrow the Roman Republic during the consulship of Cicero and Gaius Antonius (63 BCE). After the plot was discovered and denounced by Cicero, Catiline fled Rome. In 62 BCE, forces under Gaius Antonius engaged with Catiline's army near Pistoia, Italy, where Catiline was killed.

536.31 Balmerinos & Kilmarnocks of 1745] Arthur Elphinstone, 6th Lord Balmerino (1688–1746), and William Boyd, 4th Earl of Kilmarnock (1705–1746), took part in the Jacobite Rebellion of 1745–46. They were taken prisoner at the Battle of Culloden and executed in 1746.

536.32–33 Despards & Thistlewoods] Edward Marcus Despard (1751–1803) was tried and executed as the alleged ringleader of a plot to assassinate George III. In 1820 Arthur Thistlewood (1774–1820) was executed for treason for his involvement in the Cato Street Conspiracy, a plot to kill the members of the British cabinet.

538.15 "Dona nobis Pacem"] Latin: Grant us peace.

542.10–11 "Only those & nothing more."] Reference to the last line of the first stanza of "The Raven" (1845) by Edgar Allan Poe (1809–1849): "Only this and nothing more."

543.16–17 calm dishonorable vile submission] See note 35.20–21.

543.28 Charlotte Corday] Corday (1768–1793) assassinated the French revolutionary leader Jean-Paul Marat on July 13, 1793, and was guillotined four days later.

544.11 φευ φευ ελελευ — Ullaloo — Ochone — Ochone —] Ancient Greek lamentations akin to *ullaloo and ochone* from Irish and Scottish Gaelic.

544.11–12 Οιμοι — ω ποποι] Ancient Greek interjections of agony and anger, respectively.

548.7 "Maledicti Pacifici"] Cursed are the peacemakers, the opposite of the biblical "Blessed are the peacemakers" (see note 43.11–12).

548.17 "dark & bloody ground"] A phrase more frequently used to describe Kentucky, attributed to Cherokee Chief Dragging Canoe (Tsiyu Gansini, c. 1738–1792).

549.13 Pauper et miserrimus!] Latin: Poor and most wretched.

550.20 "Lias formation"] Jurassic fossils are found in the Lias geological formation in France.

550.28–29 "swapping horses . . . A.L.] Referring to Lincoln's use of the proverb "Don't swap horses in the middle of the stream" in his reelection campaign.

555.8 Danville Road!] The Richmond & Danville Railroad.

559.21 *Georgia* . . . British colors.] Confederate agents purchased the British steamer *Japan* in 1863 and had her outfitted at sea as a commerce raider. After capturing nine American ships, the *Georgia* was decommissioned as a warship in Liverpool on May 10, 1864, and subsequently sold to a British merchant. The ship was seized off the coast of Portugal on August 15, 1864, by the USS *Niagara* and taken to Boston, where a federal court condemned her as a lawful prize on account of her previous belligerent status.

560.1–6 Is all our travail . . . Peace?"] Shakespeare, *1 Henry VI*, V.v.102–7.

561.12–13 "Knights of the Golden Circle"] A secret society founded in the 1850s to promote the creation of a "golden circle" of slaveholding states surrounding the Gulf of Mexico and the Caribbean. During the Civil War Union authorities alleged that it was a predecessor of various Copperhead secret societies, including the Organization of American Knights and the Sons of Liberty.

561.26–28 Fuller . . . we were prosperous."] From *Mixt Contemplations in Better Times* (1660) by the English clergyman Thomas Fuller (1608–1661).

564.4 "O Peuple babillard, si tu savais agir!"] French: O babbling people, if only you knew how to act! From a pamphlet by the French revolutionary Jean-Paul Marat (see note 543.28) addressed to Jerome Pétion, the former mayor of Paris, in September 1792.

564.12–13 "I do desire we may be better strangers."] Shakespeare, *As You Like It*, III.ii.258.

565.1–2 She went *Hell-bent* . . . etcetera.] From an 1840 Whig campaign song: "Oh, have you heard how old Maine went? / She went hell-bent for Governor Kent / And Tippecanoe and Tyler, too!" Edward Kent (1802–1877) was governor of Maine, 1838–39 and 1841–42. For "Tippecanoe and Tyler, too!" see note 257.15.

568.17 Earl of Strafford & the Duke d'Alva] Thomas Wentworth, 1st Earl of Strafford (1593–1641), advisor to English King Charles I; Don Fernando Álvarez de Toledo y Pimentel, third Duke of Alba (1507–1582), governor of the Spanish Netherlands, 1567–73.

568.19 Doctor Francia, Dictator of Paraguay] José Gaspar Rodríguez de Francia (1766–1840), who ruled Paraguay from 1814 to 1840.

568.26 "An Apoplexy, catarrh, or cough o' the lungs"] See the lines spoken by the Duchess of Malfi before her executioners in Act IV.iii.220–21 of *The Duchess of Malfi* (c. 1613) by the English playwright by John Webster (c. 1580–c. 1632): "The apoplexy, catarrh, or cough o'th' lungs, / Would do as much as they do."

568.30–31 "Ab omni . . . Domine".] Latin: From all foolishness and madness, Deliver us, O Lord.

568.33–35 "the ragged Infantrie of Stewes and Brothels . . . Taverns & Dicing houses"] From John Milton's *Eikonoklastes* (1649).

569.5–6 enjoys herself at Cozzens'] Cozzens' West Point Hotel, about a mile and a half south of the United States Military Academy, was a fashionable resort on the Hudson.

569.10 the Mexican *Cortinas*] The rancher Juan Nepomuceno Cortina (1824–1894), a political and military leader in the border region between Texas and Mexico.

571.4–6 with somebody in *Beaumont & Fletcher* . . . sad?"] Old Merrythought's lines in the comedy *The Knight of the Burning Pestle* (1607), II.viii, by the English playwrights Francis Beaumont (1584–1616) and John Fletcher (1579–1625).

571.6–7 *Sydney Smith*] English clergyman, essayist, and wit (1771–1845). Smith's maxim, quoted in part here, is "Take short views, hope for the best, and trust in God."

571.9–10 Henry Nicoll] A prominent New York City attorney (1812–1879).

571.16 Burns' lines to the Devil] "Address to the Devil" (1786) by the Scottish poet Robert Burns (1759–1796). Strong goes on to quote the poem's final stanza.

572.24–25 Solvebantur Tabulæ Risu] Latin: The records will be wiped away with laughter.

573.9 *Malum Ovum*] Latin: Bad egg.

573.10–11 *cacoethes scribendi*] Latin: mania to write.

575.8–9 Noyades . . . French Revolution.] Punitive mass drownings in Nantes, November 1793–February 1794, under the supervision of Jean-Baptiste Carrier (1756–1794).

580.27 Meigs' murder by bush-whackers] Lieutenant John R. Meigs (1841–1864), the son of Quartermaster General Montgomery C. Meigs, was killed near Dayton, Virginia, on October 3, 1864, after he encountered three Confederate cavalry scouts. His death was attributed to guerrilla "bushwhacking," and more than twenty houses were burned in retaliation.

583.8 *Struldbrug*] In *Gulliver's Travels* (1726), satirical novel by the Anglo-Irish writer Jonathan Swift (1667–1745), a member of a race of immortals who are not granted eternal youth or health.

583.18 "Maryland, my Maryland"] Pro-secession song (1861) with words by James Ryder Randall (1839–1908), sung to the German folk tune "Lauriger Horatius" (the same music as "O Tannenbaum!").

583.25 She goes to Rider's] Francis Rider was the proprietor of the West Point Hotel from 1840 to 1852. In 1864 the proprietor was Stephen R. Roe.

585.10–11 "England, with all thy faults, I love thee still."] From Book II of *The Task* (1785) by William Cowper (1731–1800).

588.11–13 "Come unto . . . Sings"] Songs from *The Tempest*, I.ii.375–87, and *Cymbeline*, II.iii.20–26.

592.4 Lord Lyons] Richard Bickerton Pemell Lyons (1817–1887), Lord Lyons, was the British minister to the United States, 1858–65.

592.11–12 "venerable Edmund Ruffin" who fired the First Gun on Sumter] The Virginia planter Edmund Ruffin (1794–1865), a prominent defender of slavery and advocate of secession. Frustrated by Virginia's failure to secede in early 1861, he went to South Carolina and enlisted as a private in the Palmetto Guards. From Morris Island he fired one of the first shots on Fort Sumter on April 12, 1861. On June 17, 1865, Ruffin shot himself after writing in his diary of his "unmitigated hatred" for the "perfidious, malignant, & vile Yankee race."

594.18–19 Joannes Pfefferkorn — (vide Epist: Obsc: Virorum).] The German Jew Johannes Pfefferkorn (1469–1523) converted to Catholicism in 1505 and led a campaign that aimed to confiscate and burn Jewish books; he was satirized in the anonymously published *Epistolae Obscurorum Virorum* (Letters of Obscure Men, 1515–17).

595.13 *Claverhouse*] See note 104.22–23.

595.19 *felo de se*] Latin: literally "felon of himself," i.e., suicide.

596.39–597.1 "Submersi sunt . . . vehementibus"] They sank as lead in the mighty waters, Latin version of Exodus 15:10 describing the drowning of the Egyptian army in the Red Sea in pursuit of the Israelites.

597.35–37 *Fagin . . . Artful Dodger*] Thieves in Dickens's novel *Oliver Twist* (1838).

601.26 Gunpowder Plot] Failed 1605 plot to blow up Parliament in London and assassinate James I as part of a wider effort to bring a Catholic monarch to the English throne.

603.13 Boanerges] A name for a fiery preacher, typically translated as "sons of thunder" and applied by Jesus to his disciples James and John in Mark 3:17.

603.17 Isocrates] Athenian orator (436–338 BCE).

604.25 Quod felix faustumque sit] Latin: May this be fortunate and auspicious.

605.8 "like an angel, with bright hair"] See Clarence's description of a nightmare in Shakespeare's *Richard III*, I.iv.52–54: "Then came wand'ring by / A shadow like an angel, with bright hair / Dabbled in blood."

606.36 Libby Prison] Prison for Union officers established in a Richmond warehouse formerly used by Libby & Sons, a ship provisioning company.

611.35–38 when one Hill was convicted . . . Rebel Colonies.] The Scottish-born criminal James Aitken (1752–1777), also known as James Hill, John Boswell, and "John the Painter," spent about two years in the American colonies before returning to England in mid-1775. After meeting with American envoy Silas Deane (1737–1789) in Paris, he believed that he had American support to attack British shipyards on behalf of the colonists' cause. He carried out several acts of sabotage against English dockyard facilities, including the destruction of the rope warehouse in Portsmouth, for which he was apprehended, tried, convicted, and hanged.

612.38–39 "Corsican Brothers"] Popular stage adaptation (1852) by the Irish-born playwright and actor Dion Boucicault (1820–1890) of an 1844 story by Alexandre Dumas *père* (1802–1870).

614.36 our partners in the *German*] The German dance was a generic term for partner dances with three beats to the bar, such as the waltz.

616.36 *vice Pisciado*] Latin: in place of Pisciado (Hamilton Fish).

617.1 Dicite Io Pæan, et Io bis dicite Pæan!] Latin: "Cry 'Hurrah! Triumph!' and 'Hurrah! Triumph!' cry once more." From *The Art of Love* by the Roman poet Ovid (43 BCE–17 CE), II, line 1.

617.12–14 "out of sight" I fear . . . raved about the Spanish Fleet] See Act II, scene 2, of *The Critic* (1779), play by the Irish dramatist Richard Brinsley Sheridan (1751–1816), where Tiburnia provides a detailed description of a fleet of Spanish ships as if they were visible to her offstage, only to be told by her father, "The Spanish fleet thou *canst* not see because it is not yet in sight!"

618.2 Don Sebastian] Last seen and likely killed at the Battle of Alcazarquivir (1578) in Morocco, the Portuguese King Sebastian (1554–1578) became the subject of legends in which he had survived and would reclaim his throne.

618.36 Rosinante] Don Quixote's horse.

619.35–36 Howard & Florence Nightingale] John Howard (1726–1790), English prison reformer and philanthropist; Florence Nightingale (1820–1910), English nurse, social reformer, public-health advocate, and philanthropist.

620.39 St Albans Raiders] A band of Confederate raiders based in Canada attacked St. Albans, Vermont, on October 19, 1864, and robbed its banks. One civilian was mortally wounded during the raid.

621.4–6 in the case of the Caroline, when American sympathizers were aiding Provincial rebellion.] During the 1837 rebellion against British rule in Upper Canada (Ontario), the American steamer *Caroline* supplied arms and other material support to the rebels across the Niagara River. On December 29, 1837, it was boarded by a Canadian militia under the command of British officers, torched, and sent over the falls.

621.39 go & sin no more.] The command of Jesus at the end of the story of the woman caught in adultery: "Neither do I condemn thee: go, and sin no more" (John 8:11).

622.17 Zaüberflötte] *Die Zauberflöte* (The Magic Flute, 1791), opera with music by Wolfgang Amadeus Mozart libretto by the German poet, actor, and opera impresario Emanuel Schikaneder (1751–1812).

623.36–37 Orientis partibus] Latin: From the Eastern parts.

626.11 Kingsley's queer fanciful "Water Babies" story] Charles Kingsley's *The Water-Babies: A Fairy Tale for a Land Baby* (1862–63), published as a magazine serial and then as a book.

627.13–14 "Senator" Foote ("Hangman Foote") . . . ratted.] Henry S. Foote (1804–1880) was a Democratic U.S. senator from Mississippi, 1847–52, its governor, 1852–54, and a representative in the Confederate Congress, 1862–65. Late in 1864 Foote attempted to flee ("ratted") the Confederacy for Washington, DC, but was apprehended en route on January 10, 1865 (see 638.37–40), and was returned to Richmond, where he was censured by the Confederate Congress. Soon afterwards he reached the North on a second attempt. He had been nicknamed "Hangman" after threatening to hang anti-slavery New Hampshire Senator John P. Hale (1806–1873) if Hale were ever to visit Mississippi.

628.15 the Black Prince] Edward the Black Prince (1330–1376), prince of Wales, knight and duke of Cornwall, was renowned for his military prowess and chivalry during the Hundred Years' War.

632.27–28 et in secula seculorum — Libera nos Domine.] Latin: and forever and ever — Deliver us, Lord, common phrases in Christian liturgy.

1865

637.22 *Berg-werke*] German: mines.

637.28 "the runagates continue in scarceness"] See note 410.38–39.

639.40 *Nunc Dimittis*] Luke 2:29, from the Vulgate: "Now lettest thou depart," and the name of a canticle sung or recited in Anglican and Episcopal services.

640.16 "A voice of weeping heard & loud lament"] From John Milton's poem "Hymn on the Morning of Christ's Nativity" (1629), stanza 24.

641.21 *Solon Shingle*] Main character played by the actor John E. Owens (1823–1886) in *The People's Lawyer* (1856), comedy by Joseph Jones (1811–1877).

642.19 Slave-ocracy? (Δουλοκρατεια?)] Strong repeats the word in Greek in letters.

644.3–6 "Before the curing . . . shew evil."] Shakespeare, *King John*, III. iv.111–15.

644.38 Van Amburgh Menagerie] Isaac A. Van Amburgh (1811–1865) was a dealer and trainer of wild animals who operated a traveling menagerie.

645.14 Apollyon] In Revelation 9:11, the angel of the bottomless pit, Abaddon in Hebrew, Apollyon in Greek.

646.23–26 Supreme Court of the U.S. just been admitting a colored person . . . dust that was Roger B. Taney] Roger B. Taney (1777–1864) was chief justice of the Supreme Court, 1836–64, and the author of the majority opinion in the *Dred Scott v. Sanford* (1857) case, in which he wrote that Blacks had "no rights which the white man was bound to respect."

646.29–30 Brooks' chivalric bludgeon] See note 14.40–15.1.

650.4 "*Duke Gwin*"] William McKendree Gwin (1805–1885), who had been a proslavery Democratic senator from California, 1850–61, sought French support for his plans to colonize Sonora in northern Mexico with American settlers largely drawn from the Confederate states. Based on rumors that he would be ennobled in France if his colonization project was realized, American newspapers referred to him as "Duke Gwin."

650.28–29 If M[rs] Dombey could have been induced to "make an effort" . . . survived.] See chapter 18 of Charles Dickens's novel *Dombey and Son* (1848), in which Mrs. Chick, the aunt of the recently deceased six-year-old Paul Dombey, Jr., cast blame for his death on the boy's mother, who had died shortly after giving birth to him: "Nothing shall ever persuade me [. . .] but that if that effort had been made by poor dear Fanny, the poor dear darling child would at least have had a stronger constitution."

651.14 Beall] The Confederate operative John Yates Beall (1835–1865) was involved in several acts of sabotage, piracy, and espionage against the Union, including the seizure of two steamers on Lake Erie in September 1864 and a failed attempt to derail a train with Confederate prisoners in western New York in December 1864. Arrested on December 16, he was sentenced to death by a military commission. Despite a petition to President Lincoln signed by nearly one hundred members of Congress asking for commutation of the sentence or a deferral of the execution, Beall was hanged on Governors Island on February 24, 1865.

663.35–36 "vere dignum . . . et salutare."] See note 192.9–10.

666.11 the new 7–30 loan] In 1861, to help finance the war, the government began issuing Treasury notes with an annual interest rate of 7.3 percent, payable semiannually in gold. They were known as seven-thirties.

666.32–33 "Was ne'er prophetic sound so full of woe".] See note 137.15.

667.15–16 Scornful dog never ate a dirtier pudding.] See note 276.14.

667.30–31 Jerusalem when Titus was battering her towers] In 70 CE Jerusalem was besieged by the Roman army commanded by Titus (39–81 CE), son of the Roman Emperor Vespasian and later emperor, and the Second Temple was destroyed.

669.32 Quicunque vult decipi, decipiatur] Latin: Whoever wants to be deceived, so let them be deceived.

670.32–34 "sae rantingly, sae dauntingly . . . the gallows tree"] From "McPherson's Farewell" by Robert Burns (1759–1796).

671.29 "Druid"] Henry M. Flint (1829–1868), who used the pen name Druid, had been arrested by military authorities in January on a charge of disloyalty.

677.6 "feu d'enfer"] French: fire of hell.

679.23–24 Old Hundred . . . Doxology] The Doxology is a liturgical hymn beginning "Praise God from whom all blessings flow," with words written c. 1674 by Thomas Ken (1637–1711), sung to "Old Hundred" (see note 68.29).

680.14–18 Miss Abby Stevens . . . a sister of Mrs P.R.S. of J.A.S. Jr & of Mrs L.H.] Abigail Austin Stevens married General Robert Brown Potter (1829–1887) in September 1865. She was the sister of Mary Emeline Stevens, the estranged wife of Peter Remsen Strong (see note 516.7); John Austin Stevens, Jr. (1827–1910); and Lucretia Ledyard Heckscher (née Stevens, 1830–1907). Potter received his third wound of the war in the final assault on Petersburg, Virginia, in April 1865.

682.25 my leanness, my leanness!] Isaiah 24:16.

682.34 Brown Brothers] Potter's brother Howard (b. 1826) was a banker for the firm of Brown Brothers.

684.10 "Year of Jubilo"] Popular song (1862) also known as "Kingdom Coming" by Henry Clay Work (1832–1884); "Linkum" at 684.11 is a dialect rendering of "Lincoln."

686.13–14 Gloria in Excelsis DEO . . . *bonæ voluntatis*] Cf. Luke 2:14 in the Latin Vulgate: "Gloria in altissimis Deo, et in terra pax hominibus bonæ voluntatis." In the King James Version the verse is translated "Glory to God in the highest, and on earth peace, good will toward men."

687.19–20 Φαντασματα θεια, και σκιαι των οντων] Greek: divine reflections, and shadows of the things that are, an allusion to the Allegory of the Cave in Plato's *Republic*, VII.

692.17–18 by-word yet, like Punica fides.] The ancient Romans used the phrase "Punica fides" or "Carthaginian trustworthiness" ironically to denote treachery.

695.6–7 *Let the Dead bury their Dead. Follow thou Me.*] See Jesus's words in Matthew 8:22 and Luke 9:60.

695.25 *Princess Charlotte's* death] Princess Charlotte of Wales (1796–1817), only child of George, prince of Wales (later George IV), died at twenty-one after giving birth to a stillborn son in 1817 and was greatly mourned across Great Britain.

696.27–28 hewing (Southern) Agag in pieces before the Lord] 1 Samuel 15:33: "And Samuel hewed Agag in pieces before the Lord in Gilgal." Agag, king of the Amalekites, was spared by Saul from a decree of death, then cut to pieces by Samuel.

698.3 Blanco White's great sonnet] "Night and Death" (1828) by the Spanish-born English poet and journalist Joseph Blanco White (1775–1841).

700.19–23 "My Uncle Silas" . . . "Charles Auchester"] *Uncle Silas* (1864), Gothic novel by the Irish writer Joseph Sheridan Le Fanu (1814–1873); *Charles Auchester* (1853) by Elizabeth Sara Sheppard (1830–1862) was based on the life of Felix Mendelssohn and features fictionalized versions of other celebrated musicians.

701.16 Maw-worm & Chadband type.] Mawworm is a character in *The Hypocrite* (1768), play by the Irish playwright Isaac Bickerstaffe (1733–1812). Chadband, a similar character in Charles Dickens's novel *Bleak House* (1852–53), is a greedy and hypocritical preacher.

702.30 Delaroche] The French history painter Paul Delaroche (1797–1856).

706.25 *Folter-Haus*] German: torture house.

707.1 King of Dahomey . . . slavery] The kingdom of Dahomey, located in present-day Benin, sold captives to agents of the Atlantic slave trade in exchange for rifles, gunpowder, fabrics, cowrie shells, tobacco, pipes, and alcohol.

708.6–7 Lt Greble's father, of Big Bethel memory] Edwin Greble (1806–1883) was the father of Lieutenant John T. Greble (1834–1861), killed on June 10, 1861, at the Battle of Big Bethel in Great Bethel, Virginia, between Hampton and Yorktown. Greble's death was well-known because it was the first battle death of a regular U.S. Army officer in the Civil War.

708.16 Blackwood] Influential Edinburgh conservative literary journal and review, 1817–1980.

708.25 Booth & Herold] Lincoln's assassin John Wilkes Booth (1838–1865) and his coconspirator David Herold (1842–1865) were pursued by Union soldiers through Maryland and Virginia in the days following the assassination on April 14, 1865. Discovered in a tobacco barn on the Garrett farm near Port Royal in the early morning hours of April 26, Herold surrendered after the barn was set on fire; Booth was shot and died of his wounds two hours later.

709.27–28 The news of April 3^{d}] The fall of Richmond.

713.1 1688 to a "Forty five"] From the Glorious Revolution of 1688–89, in which James II was deposed and William III and his wife, Mary II, acceded to the English throne, to the Jacobite Rebellion, 1745–46, which failed to replace George II as monarch with James II's grandson Charles Edward Stuart.

716.15–16 the Hotel burning plot of last Nov[r]] A team of Confederate operatives set fire to several hotel rooms in New York City on November 25, 1864, but failed to cause widespread destruction. Most of the arsonists escaped to Canada, but one Confederate officer, Robert Cobb Kennedy (1835–1865), was captured, tried by a military commission, and hanged.

716.39 *ad salices*] Latin: to the willows.

717.1 Fleet Camilla scoured the plain] See "An Essay on Criticism" (1711), poem by the English poet Alexander Pope (1688–1744): "Not so when swift Camilla scours the plain / Flies o'er th' unbending corn, and skims along the main."

717.13–14 Lincoln's entry into Washington . . . long Cloak"] Lincoln traveled in disguise to Washington, DC, for his first inauguration due to concerns about a possible assassination plot.

717.16–17 like Charles Second . . . Sir John Falstaff] Charles II claimed that he dressed like a peasant (not like a woman) to avoid recognition in the weeks after his defeat by Parliamentary forces at the Battle of Worcester in 1651; Charles Stuart disguised himself as an Irish maid after his defeat at the Battle of Culloden in 1746; William Maxwell, 5th earl of Nithsdale (1676–1744), was sentenced to death in 1716 for his involvement in a Jacobite uprising but escaped the Tower of London by wearing women's clothes and makeup; Falstaff impersonates a "fat woman of Brentford" in an attempt to elude his mistress's husband in Shakespeare's comedy *The Merry Wives of Windsor*, IV.ii.

718.14 Æstivall] Derived from Latin *aestivus*, "pertaining to summer."

719.21–22 Mr Punch's frank self-condemning Palinode.] "Abraham Lincoln: Foully Assassinated, April 14, 1865," an anonymous poem praising and mourning Lincoln published in the London periodical *Punch*, May 6, 1865.

720.23 Maximilian] The Habsburg Archduke Ferdinand Maximilian, 1832–1867, was installed by the French in Mexico in 1864.

722.11–12 *Miracles* (according to Hume's definition) for they contradict or transcend the experience of mankind.] In *An Enquiry Concerning Human Understanding*, the Scottish philosopher David Hume (1711–1776) defines a miracle as "a transgression of a law of nature by a particular volition of the Deity, or by the interposition of some invisible agent."

725.3–4 Max Piccolomini's glowing description] See note 81.35.

725.12–13 Wade Hampton type] A wealthy plantation owner and politician, Wade Hampton III (1818–1902) had risen to the rank of lieutenant general in the Confederate army. He later served as governor of South Carolina, 1877–79, and as U.S. senator, 1879–91.

728.16–17 "Non Angli, sed Angeli"] Latin: Not Angles but angels. According to Bede's *Ecclesiastical History of England*, Gregory the Great (c. 540–604) inquired about some British children who were slaves in Rome. He was told, "They are Angles" (*sunt Angli*), to which he replied, "They are not Angles but angels" (*non Angli sed angeli*), and added that they would become Christians. Later as pope he sent missionaries to the British Isles.

732.2 Nebuchadnezzar's fiery furnace] In Daniel 3, the devout Jewish men Shadrach, Meshach, and Abednego were saved by divine intervention from the "fiery furnace" into which they were thrown under the orders of the Babylonian King Nebuchadnezzar.

739.10 Old Brougham] Henry Peter Brougham, 1st Baron Brougham and Vaux (1778–1868), English lawyer, man of letters, and politician who served as lord chancellor, 1830–34.

741.4 the Wandering Jew] According to a legend that spread in Europe during the Middle Ages, a man who mocked the condemned Jesus was forced to wander until the Second Coming.

741.5 Commodus] Second-century CE Roman emperor (r. 177–192 CE).

744.3–4 "Crowner's 'quest law"] Coroner's inquest law, as referred to by one of the two gravediggers by Ophelia's grave in *Hamlet*, V.i.22.

745.14 So poor old Johannes Sprenger's Malleus Maleficarum] *Hammer of Witchcraft* (1487), a book on witchcraft in Latin by Heinrich Kramer (c. 1430–1505), with later editions attributing authorship to Johannes Sprenger (c. 1436–1495).

748.15–16 Poland . . . *Liberum Veto*] During the seventeenth and eighteenth centuries, the right of any member of the Polish parliament to veto legislation.

751.5 "Letters from High Latitudes"] The travel book *Letters from High Latitudes: Account of a Voyage in the Schooner Yacht "Foam" to Iceland, Jan Mayen and Spitzbergen in 1856* (1857) by Lord Dufferin (1826–1902).

751.29 Foxe's martyrs] *Actes and Monuments* (1563), commonly known as *The Book of Martyrs*, is a history of Christian martyrdom by the English scholar John Foxe (1516/1517–1587), with particular focus on English Protestants from the fourteenth to mid-sixteenth centuries.

752.19–20 Barnum Conflagration] On July 13, 1865, Barnum's American Museum at the corner of Broadway and Ann Street caught fire. The tank in which two whales were kept was broken open in the hope that the water would extinguish the fire. A wax figure of Jefferson Davis dressed in a petticoat was thrown from a window.

755.19 failure like that of 1858] The first transatlantic telegraph cable began operating in mid-August 1858, but the quality of its transmissions rapidly deteriorated and it failed completely after three weeks in service.

755.24 "I do desire we may be better strangers."] See note 564.12–13.

758.3–4 "Still in their ashes live their wonted fires"] from "Elegy Written in a Country Churchyard" (1751) by the English poet Thomas Gray (1716–1771).

758.17–18 gunpowder Prelate, Bishop Major-General Polk] Lieutenant General Leonidas Polk (1806–1864), an Episcopal bishop, was killed by an artillery projectile at Pine Mountain, Georgia, on June 14, 1864, while commanding the Third Corps of the Army of Tennessee.

759.22 *Harris* case] In a highly publicized case, Mary Harris (b. c. 1845) fatally shot Adoniram Burroughs in a Treasury Building hallway in Washington, DC, on January 30, 1865. Burroughs had brought Harris from Iowa to Chicago in 1863, then moved to Washington to work as a clerk in the Treasury Department. After reading a newspaper announcement of his engagement to another woman, Harris traveled to Washington and killed him. In July the Supreme Court of the District of Columbia, acting as a criminal court, found her not guilty by reason of temporary insanity, ascribed to Harris's experience of menstrual pain.

760.1 *in literis humanioribus*] Latin: in the humanities.

760.30 rectus in Curiâ] Latin: right in court.

761.10 Saratoga Conference] On August 29, 1865, *The New York Times* reported that the Executive Committee of the Sanitary Commission had met at Congress Hall in Saratoga Springs to agree on a plan for clearing up its business and writing a history of its work.

762.9–10 Dives . . . Lazarus] Jesus tells a parable in Luke 16:19–31 about the beggar Lazarus and an unnamed rich man, often called Dives ("rich man" in Latin).

762.24–25 curse . . . hypothetical Ancestors.] The biblical Ham was one of Noah's sons. Because Ham had seen the drunken and naked Noah asleep in his tent, Ham's son Canaan was cursed to be "a servant of servants . . . to his brethren." Ham has often been regarded as a Black man because African peoples were listed among his descendants in Genesis 10:6–20 or because, according to a view first put forth in the fifteenth century, the descendants of Canaan were Black while those of his uncles Shem and Japheth (Noah's other sons) were white.

762.40 Gen[l] C.] George Washington Cullum (1809–1892) served as a general in the Union army and as the sixteenth superintendent of the U.S. Military Academy.

763.6 Commander J.H. Strong] James Hooker Strong (1814–1882) commanded the ships *Mohawk*, *Flag*, and *Monongahela* in the Civil War. During the Battle of Mobile Bay, his ship was the first to ram the Confederate ironclad *Tennessee*.

763.25 *totus teres atque rotundus*] Latin: entire in itself, smooth and round. From Horace, *Satires*, II.vii, line 86.

768.5–6 Froissart's Knights & Princes . . . Rosebecque] The French won a victory during the Hundred Years' War over the Flemish at Roosebeke (or Rosebecque), November 27, 1382, a battle recounted in the *Chronicles* of the medieval historian Jean Froissart (c. 1337–c. 1405).

769.29 αλαλαγμος] Ancient Greek war cry.

770.35 *functus officio*] Latin: having fulfilled one's duty.

771.24 Brady's] The studio of American photographer Mathew Brady (1822–1896).

774.22 Egomet Ipsissimus] An emphatic form in Latin of "I myself," used for comic effect.

778.32 *pro aris et focis*] Latin: for altars and hearths.

779.36–37 No War nor battle's sound . . . *around*] From Milton's "Hymn on the Morning of Christ's Nativity."

779.37 Juarez] Benito Juárez (1806–1872), president of Mexico, 1858–72; he led the republican forces that defeated Emperor Maximilian.

General Index

Regimental Index

This book is set in 10 point ITC Galliard, a face designed for digital composition by Matthew Carter and based on the sixteenth-century face Granjon. The paper is acid-free lightweight opaque that will not turn yellow or brittle with age. The binding is sewn, which allows the book to open easily and lie flat. The binding board is covered in Brillianta, a woven rayon cloth made by Van Heek–Scholco Textielfabrieken, Holland.

Composition by Dianna Logan, Clearmont, MO.

Printing by Sheridan, Grand Rapids, MI.

Binding by Dekker Bookbinding, Wyoming, MI.

Designed by Bruce Campbell.

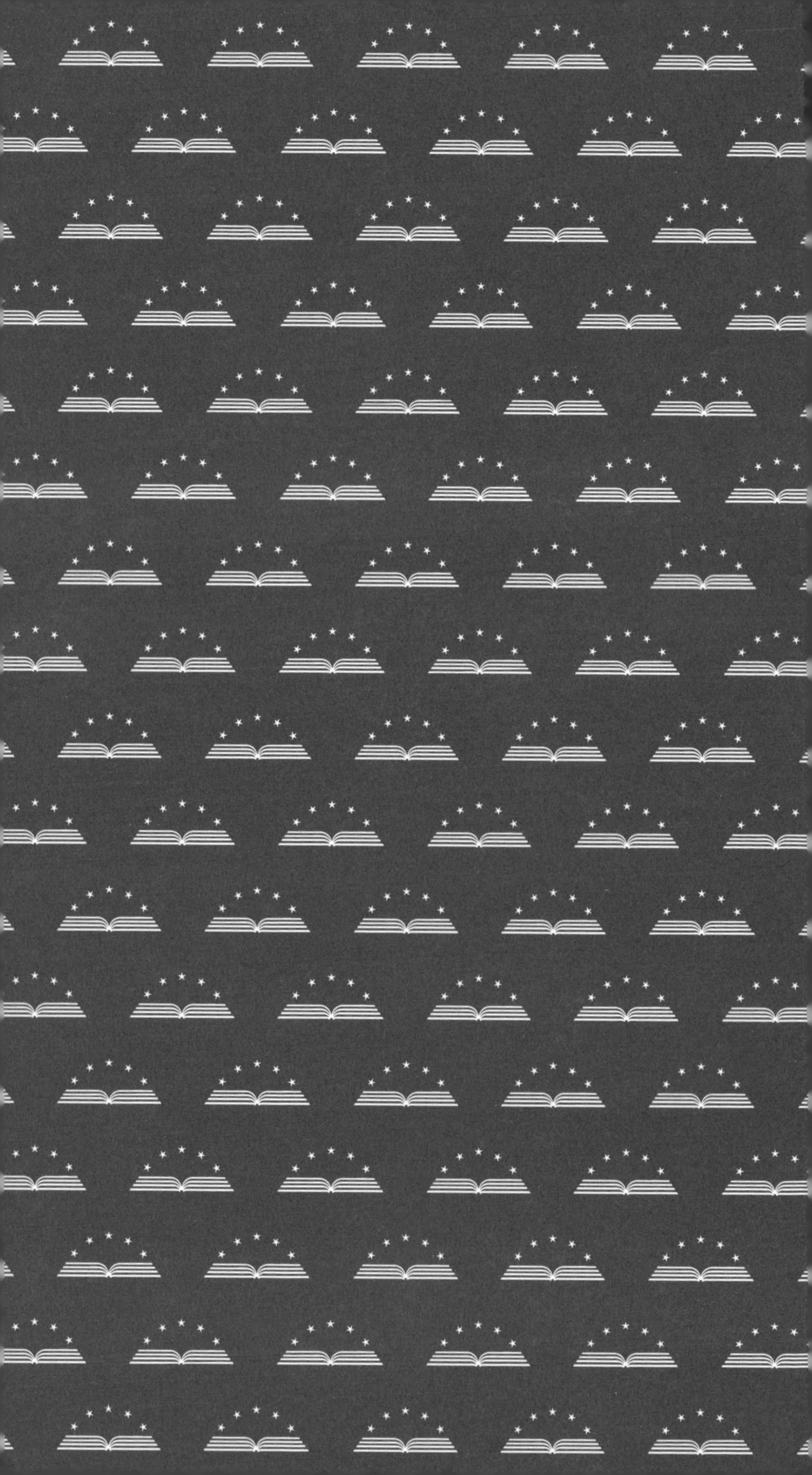